March 22-26, 2014
Dublin, Ireland

I0047547

**Association for
Computing Machinery**

Advancing Computing as a Science & Profession

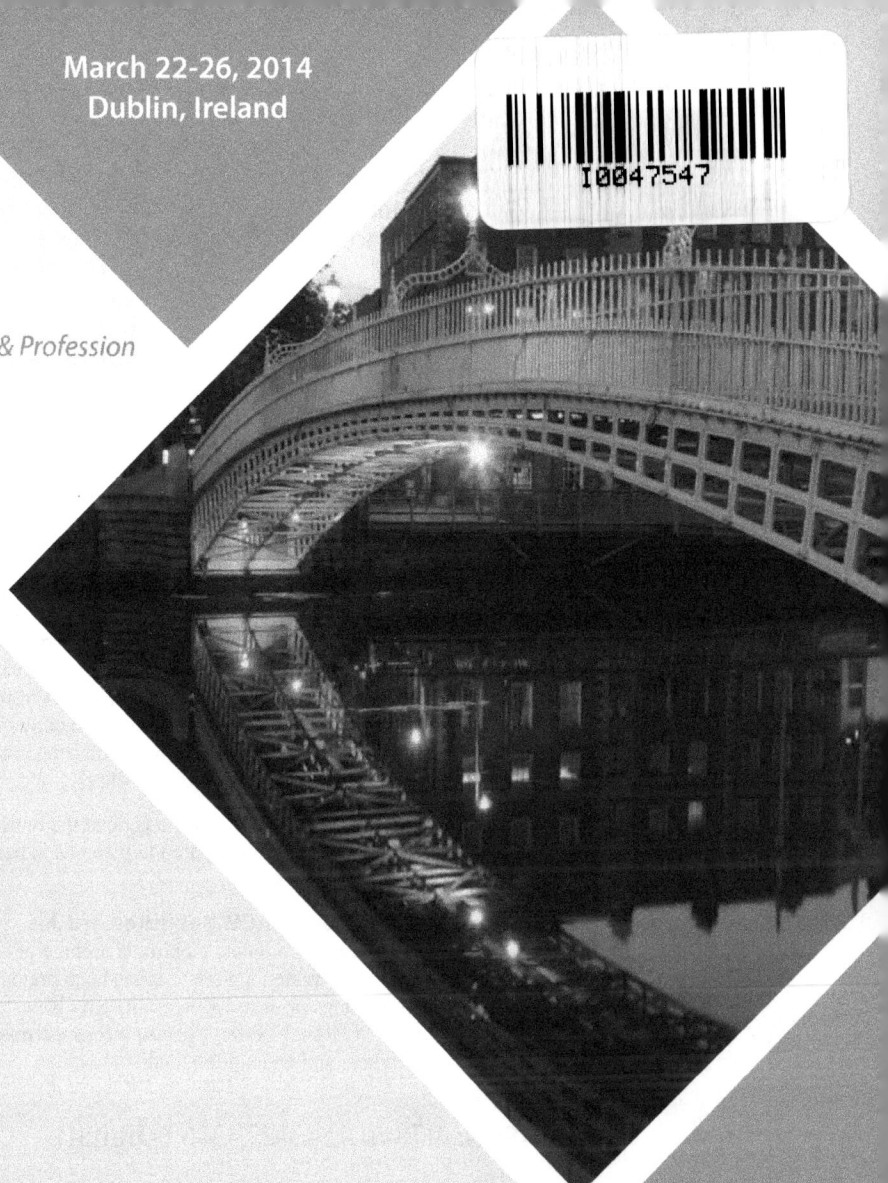

ICPE'14

Proceedings of the 5th ACM/SPEC International Conference on

Performance Engineering

Sponsored by:

ACM SIGMETRICS, ACM SIGSOFT, and SPEC Research

Supported by:

Lero, Cisco, and Intel

Association for
Computing Machinery

Advancing Computing as a Science & Profession

The Association for Computing Machinery
2 Penn Plaza, Suite 701
New York, New York 10121-0701

Notice to Past Authors of ACM-Published Articles
ACM intends to create a complete electronic archive of all articles and/or other material previously published by ACM. If you have written a work that has been previously published by ACM in any journal or conference proceedings prior to 1978, or any SIG Newsletter at any time, and you do NOT want this work to appear in the ACM Digital Library, please inform permissions@acm.org, stating the title of the work, the author(s), and where and when published.

ISBN: 978-1-4503-2733-6 (Digital)

ISBN: 978-1-4503-3105-0 (Print)

Additional copies may be ordered prepaid from:

ACM Order Department
PO Box 30777
New York, NY 10087-0777, USA

Phone: 1-800-342-6626 (USA and Canada)
+1-212-626-0500 (Global)
Fax: +1-212-944-1318
E-mail: acmhelp@acm.org
Hours of Operation: 8:30 am – 4:30 pm ET

Printed in the USA

General Chairs' Welcome

It is with great pleasure we welcome you to ICPE 2014. ICPE is an annual meeting that provides a forum for the integration of theory and practice in the field of performance engineering. It brings together researchers and industry practitioners to share ideas, discuss challenges, and present results of both work-in-progress and state-of-the-art research on performance engineering of software and systems. This year is the 5th ICPE, which grew out of the ACM Workshop on Software Performance (WOSP since 1998) and the SPEC International Performance Engineering Workshop (SIPEW since 2008).

Firstly many thanks go to the Program Co-Chairs, Walter Binder and José Merseguer for the enormous efforts they have put in, attracting an excellent Technical Program Committee and continuing the high quality of ICPE papers with an exciting research track. The Industrial Chair, Raghunath Nambiar, has done an outstanding job in selecting a strong set of industry research papers with his program committee. The Organizing Committee has been invaluable in running a smooth process and in particular we acknowledge the efforts of Anja Bog, for her dedicated job as Finance Chair; the Tutorial Chair, Alexandru Iosup, for his thoughtful efforts in assembling the tutorial program; Samuel Kounev and Meikel Poess, the conference Award Chairs, for proposing and running the award process; Kirk W. Cameron and Anthony Ventresque, the Poster and Demo Chairs, for their efforts in selecting and putting together the poster and demo exhibit; Kevin Casey, for all the activity involved in putting together the proceedings as the Publication Chair; our Publicity Chairs, Danilo Ansaloni and Bob Cramblitt, for broad and timely advertisements of the conference across many publicity channels; Nicola Stokes, who successfully managed the job of Registration Chair; Cathy Sandifer, the Webmaster, for her continuous help and quick responses to our demands; and Patrick McDonagh, for handling the multitude of local arrangements.

In particular ICPE would not exist without the support and efforts of André Bondi and Samuel Kounev. Their assistance – from the preparation in 2012 of the bid to host ICPE in Dublin, right up to the conference start – was critical to making ICPE 2014 a success.

Following on from the inclusion of workshops last year, there are two co-located with the main conference in 2014: HotTopiCS which was also held with ICPE 2013, and new this year to ICPE is the 3rd workshop on Large Scale Testing. These workshops help broaden the ICPE community and furthermore inspire new research directions.

Our sincere thanks go to the corporate supporters, who at the time of writing include SPEC, LERO, Cisco and Intel, who through their generous financial contributions have made this conference possible. We are also thankful to SPEC and ACM, through its SIGSOFT and SIGMETRICS special interest groups, for continuing support of the ICPE conference.

We were delighted to be able to attract three excellent keynote speakers, Toyotaro Suzumura, Petr Tůma and Xiaoyun Zhu, who we are sure the conference attendees will enjoy.

On behalf of the organizing committee, we welcome you to Dublin and hope you will enjoy the conference and your stay here.

Klaus-Dieter Lange
Hewlett-Packard, USA
ICPE 2014 General Co-Chair

John Murphy
University College Dublin, Ireland
ICPE 2014 General Co-Chair

Program Chairs' Welcome

Dear members of the ICPE community,

We are delighted to bring an outstanding technical program to the *2014 International Conference on Performance Engineering - ICPE'14* in Dublin. The Research track of the conference attracted 56 submissions. Thanks to the diligent efforts of the members of the Program Committee, each paper received a minimum of three reviews. After extensive deliberation, the Program Committee decided to accept 14 submissions as regular papers and two as short papers.

The Industry and Experience track focuses on the application of research results to industrial performance engineering problems and addresses in particular innovative implementations, the novel application of performance-related technologies and the reporting of insightful performance results. This track received 22 submissions of which 7 were selected for presentation at the conference.

The papers accepted to the Research track and to the Industry and Experience track cover several topics such as software, including evaluation-based papers as well as different concerns of Java performance. Distributed system performance is also an important aspect, which in this edition addresses SOA, middleware and Web issues. Papers devoted to performance aspects of self-adaptive systems and power consumption are also relevant. Reports of experience complete the program.

As in previous editions, the Vision/Work-in-Progress track is a feature of ICPE that allows researchers to present and discuss ideas that they are still working on or that they are planning to work on in the near future. It is a great forum for learning about the direction of research in the area. This year we received 19 submissions to this track and we accommodated 6 short presentations in the conference program. The topics covered by this track are similar to those in the Research track, which suggests that they are likely to be featured again in subsequent editions of ICPE.

We would like to thank the members of the Program Committee for the many hours that they spent reviewing papers and participating actively in the discussions and the authors for their diligence in preparing their manuscripts and camera-ready papers. Thanks also go to the authors of those papers that were not selected for presentation at the conference. We would like to encourage them to use the feedback received through the reviewing process and continue their work on performance engineering. Finally, we would like to thank the General Chairs as well as the Program Chairs of ICPE'13 for their valuable assistance in the organization of the conference program.

In summary, there were 97 submissions in total across the three tracks, of which 29 were selected for presentation. We are now looking forward to several days of great presentations and stimulating discussions at ICPE'14 in Dublin. It has been a privilege and a pleasure for us to be involved.

Walter Binder
ICPE'14 Program Co-Chair
University of Lugano, Switzerland

José Merseguer
ICPE'14 Program Co-Chair
Universidad de Zaragoza, Spain

Raghunath Nambiar
ICPE'14 Industrial Chair
Cisco, USA

Table of Contents

Session: Keynote Address II

Session: Best Industrial Paper Candidates

Session: Distributed Systems Performance I

Session: Distributed Systems Performance II

Session: Posters

Session: Reports of Experience and Test

Session: Keynote Address III

Session: Work in Progress and Vision Papers I

Session: Work in Progress and Vision Papers II

Author Index

ICPE 2014 Conference Organization

General Chairs: Klaus-Dieter Lange *(Hewlett-Packard Company, USA)*
John Murphy *(University College Dublin, Ireland)*

Program Chairs: Walter Binder *(University of Lugano, Switzerland)*
José Merseguer *(Universidad de Zaragoza, Spain)*

Industrial Chair: Raghunath Nambiar *(Cisco, USA)*

Tutorial Chair: Alexandru Iosup *(TU Delft, Netherlands)*

Demos and Posters Chairs: Kirk W. Cameron *(Virginia Tech, USA)*
Anthony Ventresque *(University College Dublin, Ireland)*

Publication Chair: Kevin Casey *(Dublin City University, Ireland)*

Finance Chair: Anja Bog *(SAP, USA)*

Publicity Chairs: Danilo Ansaloni *(University of Lugano, Switzerland)*
Bob Cramblitt *(Cramblitt & Company, USA)*

Registration Chair: Nicola Stokes *(University College Dublin, Ireland)*

Award Chairs: Samuel Kounev *(Karlsruhe Institute of Technology, Germany)*
Meikel Poess *(Oracle, USA)*

Local Organization Chair: Patrick McDonagh *(Dublin City University, Ireland)*

Web Chair: Cathy Sandifer *(SPEC, USA)*

Steering Committee: Andre B. Bondi *(Siemens Corporation, NJ, USA)*
Samuel Kounev *(Karlsruhe Institute of Technology, Germany)*
Meikel Poess *(Oracle Corporation, CA, USA)*
J. Nelson Amaral *(University of Alberta, Canada)*
Vittorio Cortellessa *(University of L'Aquilla, Italy)*
Klaus-Dieter Lange *(Hewlett-Packard Company, USA)*
Raffaela Mirandola *(Politecnico di Milano, Italy)*
Jerry Rolia *(HP Labs, UK)*
Kai Sachs *(SAP AG, Germany)*
Bran Selic *(ObjecTime Limited, Canada)*
Peter Tuma *(Charles University, Czech Republic)*
Murray Woodside *(Carleton University, Canada)*

ICPE 2014 Sponsors & Supporters

Sponsors:

ACM SIGMETRICS
special interest group on performance evaluation

SIG SOFT
SPECIAL INTEREST GROUP ON SOFTWARE ENGINEERING

spec Research

Gold Corporate Support:

lero THE IRISH SOFTWARE ENGINEERING RESEARCH CENTRE

Silver Corporate Support:

CISCO

Bronze Corporate Support:

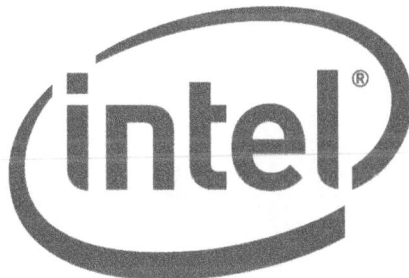

intel®

Extreme Big Data Processing in Large-Scale Graph Analytics and Billion-Scale Social Simulation

Toyotaro Suzumura
IBM Research
Tokyo, Japan
suzumurat@gmail.com

ABSTRACT
This paper introduces some of the example applications handling extremely big data with supercomputers such as large-scale network analysis, X10-based large-scale graph analytics library, Graph500 benchmark, and billion-scale social simulation.

Categories and Subject Descriptors
C.4 [**Performance of Systems**]: C.5.1 [**Computer System Implementation**]; D.2.11 [**Software Architectures**]; E.1 [**Data Structures**]

Keywords: Distributed computing, graph algorithms, social simulation, X10

1. Large-Scale Graph Analysis
Recently, social network services such as Twitter, Facebook, MySpace, LinkedIn have been remarkably growing. Haewoon performed the analysis of the Twitter network on June 2009 and showed the degree of separation in Twitter network. However, the number of users on 2009 is about 41.7 million, the graph scale is not very large compared to continuously growing current graph. Our study in [1] shows the transition of the number of users on Twitter from June 2006 to September 2012. The number of users on September 2012 attains 469.9 million and the number of relationships attains 28.7 billion. This data collection is obtained by our series of crawling for 3 months conducted in late 2012. Therefore, it is considered that with increasing users, the graph characteristics has changed greatly and we analyzed for the current large graph. The motivation of our work [1] is to understand how such characteristics is changed and evolving from the results in 2009. We used HyperANF API as an analysis tool to compute approximate degree of separation and diameter in a sampling based fashion. To obtain the precise result as much as possible, the tool requires more memory. Our computation was performed on a 64-core machine with 512 GB memory that is one of the TSUBAME 2.0 super computer located Tokyo Institute of Technology.

In order to obtain the degree of separation and diameter with HyperANF from the crawled Twitter network, a list of preprocessing are required. In this preprocessing and the resulting

ICPE'14, March 22–26, 2014, Dublin, Ireland.
ACM 978-1-4503-2733-6/14/03.
http://dx.doi.org/10.1145/2568088.2576096

output consumes around 20 TB approximately. Currently Hadoop and Web Graph APIs are used for the preprocessing.

1. Prepare user id lists containing serial number from zero to renumber

2. Create edge lists from follower-friend data and renumber with the user id lists.

3. Convert the renumbered edge lists to adjacency lists formatted Ascii Graph.

4. Finally, Convert the adjacency lists to compressed data with BV compression API .

Note that the adjacency lists and the compressed data size are 263GB and 73GB, respectively. We conduct a Twitter network analysis in terms growth by region, scale-free, reciprocity, degree of separation and diameter using Twitter user data with 469.9 million users and 28.7 billion relationships. We report that the value of degree of separation is 4.59 in current Twitter network through our experiments. Some of the hints such as storage requirements, tools, workflow towards exascale computing in this domain can be obtained by this kind of analysis.

2. ScaleGraph: X10-Based Large-Scale Graph Analytic Library
Graphs will be a prominent computational workload in Exascale era as demonstrated in our work [8][9][13][14]. Large graph analysis is a dilemma faced by programmers in various domains such as scientific applications, biology, national security, business analytics described in previous section. We have developed ScaleGraph [2] which is an open-source X10 library available from [3] for massive graph analytics targeting large scale graph analysis scenarios. The differentiating features of ScaleGraph is as follows:

(1) High Productive HPC Graph Analysis : ScaleGraph library has been developed to reduce complexity and increase programmer productivity involved in use of HPC systems for large graph analysis. We provide an object oriented interface for users of ScaleGraph while preserving scalability in large scale distributed environments.

(2) Comprehensive PGAS Library for Large Graph Analysis : Our library is designed from ground up with aiming complex network analysis community.

(3) Scalability Analysis in Distributed Environment : We demonstrated scalability of our library in distributed environments such as TSUBAE 2.0. We are currently expanding a set of graph analytics and also doing the same web mining analysis as the work in previous section.

3. Graph500 Benchmark
As an alternative to Linpack, Graph500 [4] was recently developed. We conducted a thorough study of the algorithms of

1

the reference implementations and their performance in an earlier paper [5]. Based on that work, we implemented a scalable and high-performance implementation of an optimized Graph500 benchmark for large distributed environments [6][7]. In contrast to the computation-intensive benchmark used by TOP500, Graph500 is a data-intensive benchmark. It does breadth-first searches in undirected large graphs generated by a scalable data generator based on a Kronecker graph. There are six problem classes: toy, mini, small, medium, large, and huge. Each problem solves a different size graph defined by a Scale parameter, which is the base 2 logarithm of the number of vertices. For example, the level Scale 26 for toy means 226 and corresponds to 1010 bytes occupying 17 GB of memory. The six Scale values are 26, 29, 32, 36, 39, and 42 for the six classes. The largest problem, huge (Scale 42), needs to handle around 1.1 PB of memory. As of this writing, Scale 38 is the largest that has been solved by a top-ranked supercomputer. Our work [6] proposed an optimized method based on 2D partitioning and other methods such as communication compression and vertex sorting. Our optimized implementation can handle BFS (Breadth First Search) of a large graph with Scale 35 with 462.25 GE/s while using 1366 nodes and 16,392 CPU cores. This competition is greatly challenging since new scalable algorithms have been proposed rapidly. We have been continuously enhancing the scalable algorithm and implementation on various supercomputers.

4. Billion-Scale Social Simulation

We introduce billion-scale social simulation [10][11][12] in this section. Towards the contribution to the human society, global economy, ecology, the analysis of human brain characteristics and our daily life, the research in multi-agent simulation is entering into the era of simulating billion-scale agents. Although prior arts tackle distributed agent simulation platform to achieve this goal, it is not sufficient to simulation billion-scale agent behaviors. Based on this observation, we report the first effort for building such an infrastructure platform that handles billion-scale agent simulation platform. In our previous work, we introduce X10-based agent simulation platform for such a purpose and presents its application to traffic simulation. We were able to handle only at maximum 10 millions of agents, but the performance was not scalable due to various reasons such as work load imbalance, global synchronization. Our work in [12] present the work of purely implementing the whole simulation stack including both the simulation runtime and the application layer such as traffic simulation [11] by the use of the state-of-the-art PGAS language. By implementing the system in such a manner and evaluating the system in highly distributed systems, it is observed that the system can be close to handle billion-scale agents in near real-time. The first experimental result is that the performance scalability is greatly achieved by simulating 1 millions of agents on 1536 CPU cores and 256 nodes. By compiling fully X10-based agent simulation system into C++ and MPI, it only takes 77 seconds for 600 simulation steps which is nearly 10 times faster than real-time. Moreover, by using the entire whole country-wide network of India as the agents' underlying infrastructure, we successfully simulated 1 billion agents with 400 nodes in TSUBAME 2.0. This is the first attempt to deal with such a gigantic number of agents and we believe that this infrastructure would be the basis of large-scale agent simulation in various fields.

5. REFERENCES

[1] Masaru Watanabe and Toyotaro Suzumura, "How Social Network is Evolving ? A Preliminary Study on Billion-scale Twitter Network", LSNA 2013 Workshop in conjunction with WWW 2013

[2] Miyuru Dayarathna, Charuwat Houngkaew, Toyotaro Suzumura, "Scalable Performance of ScaleGraph for Large Scale Graph Analysis", HiPC 2012 (IEEE International Conference on High Performance Computing)

[3] ScaleGraph Library: http://www.scalegraph.org/

[4] Graph500 : http://www.graph500.org/.

[5] Toyotaro Suzumura, Koji Ueno, Hitoshi Sato, Katsuki Fujisawa and Satoshi Matsuoka, "Performance Evaluation of Graph500 on Large-Scale Distributed Environment", IEEE IISWC 2011

[6] Koji Ueno and Toyotaro Suzumura "Highly Scalable Graph Search for the Graph500 Benchmark", the 21st International ACM Symposium on High-Performance Parallel and Distributed Computing (HPDC), 2012/06, Delft, Netherland.

[7] Koji Ueno and Toyotaro Suzumura, "Parallel Distributed Breadth First Search on GPU", HiPC 2013 (IEEE International Conference on High Performance Computing), India, 2013/12

[8] Charuwat Houngkaew and Toyotaro Suzumura, "X10-Based Distributed and Parallel Betweenness Centrality and Its Application to Social Analytics", HiPC 2013 (IEEE International Conference on High Performance Computing), India, 2013/12

[9] Koichi Shirahata, Hitoshi Sato, Toyotaro Suzumura and Satoshi Matsuoka, "A Scalable Implementation of a MapReduce-based Graph Processing Algorithm for Largescale Heterogeneous Supercomputers", 13th IEEE/ACM International Symposium on Cluster, Cloud and Grid Computing (CCGrid), Delft, Netherlands, 2013/5

[10] Toyotaro Suzumura and Hiroki Kanezashi, "Highly Scalable X10-based Agent Simulation Platform and its Application to Large-scale Traffic Simulation", 2012 IEEE/ACM 16th International Symposium on Distributed Simulation and Real Time Application

[11] Takayuki Osogami, Takashi Imamichi, Hideyuki Mizuta, Toyotaro Suzumura, and Tsuyoshi Ide, "Toward simulating entire cities with behavioral models of traffic," *IBM Journal of Research and Development*, **57**(5): Paper 6, 2013

[12] Toyotaro Suzumura and Hiroki Kanezashi, "A Holistic Architecture for Super Real-Time Multiagent Simulation Platform", Winter Simulation Conference 2013, 2013/12, Washington D.C., US

[13] Miyuru Dararathna and Toyotaro Suzumura, "XGDBench: A Benchmarking Platform for Graph Stores in Exascale Clouds", IEEE CloudCom 2012 conference, Taipei, Taiwan, 2012/12

[14] Bao Nguyen and Toyotaro Suzumura, "Towards Highly Scalable Pregel-based Graph Processing Platform with X10", The 2nd International Workshop on Large Scale Network Analysis (LSNA 2013) In conjunction with WWW 2013, 2013/05, Rio de janeiro, Brazil.

Uncertainties in the Modeling of Self-adaptive Systems: a Taxonomy and an Example of Availability Evaluation

Diego Perez-Palacin
Politecnico di Milano
Dipartimento di Elettronica, Informazione
e Bioingegneria
Milano, Italy
diego.perez@polimi.it

Raffaela Mirandola
Politecnico di Milano
Dipartimento di Elettronica, Informazione
e Bioingegneria
Milano, Italy
raffaela.mirandola@polimi.it

ABSTRACT

The complexity of modern software systems has grown enormously in the past years with users always demanding for new features and better quality of service. Besides, software is often embedded in dynamic contexts, where requirements, environment assumptions, and usage profiles continuously change. As an answer to this need, it has been proposed the usage of self-adaptive systems. Self-adaptation endows a system with the capability to accommodate its execution to different contexts in order to achieve continuous satisfaction of requirements. Often, self-adaptation process also makes use of runtime model evaluations to decide the changes in the system. However, even at runtime, context information that can be managed by the system is not complete or accurate; i.e, it is still subject to some uncertainties. This work motivates the need for the consideration of the concept of uncertainty in the model-based evaluation as a primary actor, classifies the avowed uncertainties of self-adaptive systems, and illustrates examples of how different types of uncertainties are present in the modeling of system characteristics for availability requirement satisfaction.

Categories and Subject Descriptors

D.2.4 [**Software Engineering**]: [Software/Program Verification]; I.6.4 [**Computing Methodologies**]: Simulation and Modeling

Keywords

Uncertainty; Self-adaptive software; Models;

1. INTRODUCTION

Today software is increasingly permeating (safety-)critical areas of daily life, from bank accounting to homeland security, from transport applications to power plant management and health care systems. Currently, there is also a huge increment in the demand of software applications that offer services to their users through mobile devices, which require minimum effort to install, configure and run. In these domains, non-functional properties like performance

and availability of software are highly relevant, either to avoid damaging effects that can range from loss of trust on essential services to loss of human life in the critical system domain, or the loss of business and competitiveness in the marketplace for the mobile devices domain. Therefore, software should continuously meet its non-functional requirements.

To allow building software that executes with the appropriate quality, model-based evaluation methods at design time [3, 9] have been proposed as a viable solution. However, design-time analysis cannot always provide accurate results because the information of the environment where the application will be deployed may not be completely known when applications are initially architected; and even worse, such execution environment may change continuously during application lifetime. For example, when developing an application that can be potentially deployed over several platforms with different characteristics, software engineers have only a partial and incomplete knowledge of the external environment in which the application will be deployed. Consider, for example, a mobile device whose availability and reliability is very affected by the environment temperature. With the increase of the temperature, the CPU failure rate grows while the battery life decreases due to the effect of turning on fans, which consume battery. It is evident that if an instance of the application is deployed on this device, its reliability and availability properties will be strictly subject to the environmental temperature. Device constraints and temperature at which it will operate are in most cases uncertain at design time, which entails an uncertainty in the model that is used to evaluate system properties. This is further exacerbated in software that is embedded in dynamic contexts, where requirements, environment assumptions, and usage profiles continuously change. Since these changes in the context happen in a way that is hard to predict when systems are initially built, the outcome of the model analysis at design-time are in these cases subject to even higher uncertainty because assumptions upon which they rely on are not true.

To study these kind of uncertainties new methods emerged during the 1990s. The field of natural science has been a particularly active arena for methodological advancement, see for example [29, 4], and mathematical methods for quantifying uncertainties (e.g., interval analysis, fuzzy methods, probability theory and bayesian analysis [22]) have been developed in this context, starting from [18]. In the computer science field the topic of uncertainty has recently drawn the attention and some discussions and techniques have been presented in [17, 35, 10, 20, 19, 25, 32].

To deal with the lack of complete information and knowledge at design-time, in recent years, industry and academia have increasingly addressed the adaptation concern, particularly with the introduction of autonomic and self-adaptive systems. Self-adaptation endows a system with the capability to adapt itself to the environment where it executes. This capability relieves engineers from taking some decisions at design time. These decisions are delayed until runtime and made autonomously by the system, when more information is available, then dealing with the lack of knowledge about the environment at design time. Moreover, self-adaptive systems can perform successive adaptations when environment changes. In this manner, there is a possibility for the system to continuously achieve its functional and non-functional requirements even in dynamic contexts. The structure of the application may change at runtime; for example in terms of its running components and interconnections in order to improve its behavior, correct flaws, or reduce its energy needs.

Self-adaptation process entails several activities [24], some of them requiring planning, analysis and decisions. These activities can be achieved using formal models as suggested in [6] and with a seamless integration of design time and runtime verification. However, even if these models are useful and often the only possible artifact to reason about adaptations, their definition and usage raise some challenges because some uncertainties still remain present at runtime. One of the challenges is that knowledge of the environment is not complete or accurate even at runtime, which entails that the information in the models that are used to govern the adaptation process is subject to uncertainties.

In the literature, there have been proposed methods to deal with some kind of uncertainties that exist in self-adaptive systems. However, even though the works in the literature on modeling uncertainties in computing systems provide a useful approach for concrete types of uncertainty, we have not found a definition or taxonomy for uncertainty in models that can act as a pillar for building research work over it. These definitions for uncertainties in computing models can draw the big-picture that locates each piece of research in the field in its corresponding place; and therefore it will help researches to relate, connect and compare works, merge results and find similar works, ease the learning from these similar works, and push forward the research on uncertainties management. At present, in computing, the most used definitions of uncertainty simply distinguish between natural variability of physical processes (i.e., aleatory or stochastic uncertainty) and the uncertainties in knowledge of these processes (i.e., "epistemic" or state-of-knowledge uncertainty) [10, 20, 19, 25, 32, 14, 17]. Among the works in research fields that hold more maturity than computer science on the study of uncertainties, it is shown that *uncertainties in models can be seen from other perspectives different from epistemic and aleatory*. Learning from them, we have found that some of these different perspectives also exist in the modeling of computing systems; but there is not yet a general enough taxonomy for uncertainties in models in the computing field. A contribution of this paper is, exploiting the work of [33], to give a taxonomy for classifying different types of uncertainties that are present in software models. We then analyze, with respect to self-adaptive systems, the sources of uncertainties and the main approaches existing in the literature to handle them. As a second contribution, we use a concrete example of a self-adaptive system (concretely a system that can analyze its availability and adapt to increase it) with the objective of showing the existence of uncertainties in its managed models systems and how these uncertainties can be managed.

The remainder of the paper is organized as follows. Section 2 describes the existing works on uncertainty in the computer science field. Section 3 discusses the definition of uncertainty and presents a taxonomy describing different dimensions along which uncertainties can be classified. Existing sources of uncertainty and methods to deal with them in the context of self-adaptive systems are pre-

sented in Section 4, while examples of their usage are illustrated in Sections 5, 6 and 7. Section 8 concludes the work.

2. RELATED WORKS

In the computer science field the topic of uncertainty has recently drawn the attention and some discussions and techniques have been presented.

For example, works in [11, 14, 12, 13] admit that uncertainties cannot be eliminated in software systems and they propose techniques to manage the existent uncertainty. Specifically, [11, 14, 13] propose techniques to decide the suitable software architecture knowing the presence of uncertainty. They aim at minimizing the impact of uncertainty on architectural decisions. To achieve this goal, they guide how to rank, compare and choose an architectural configuration that maximizes the likelihood of satisfying the system's quality preferences. In [12], authors provide a list of sources of uncertainties that may exist in self-adaptive software systems. They also extend their method to compare the utility of an architecture by including how this utility is expected to vary over time within given constraints. Authors in [34] deal with requirements specification of self-adaptive systems and present a requirement definition language that captures the existing uncertainties. Works in [17, 7] present lists of sources of uncertainties. In particular, [17] explains the changes that uncertainties should entail in the development of software systems and it presents an enumeration of current research challenges to deal with these uncertainty. In [7] three sources of uncertainty specific for self-adaptive systems are identified namely, uncertainty in the identification of a problem in the system, uncertainty in the selection of strategy to adapt the system and solve the problem, and uncertainty in the identification the success or failure of the strategy. Authors integrate the management of these three uncertainties within the Rainbow approach.

A different set of works proposes specific techniques to deal with parameter uncertainties. Works in [15, 20, 10, 35] cope with prediction of reliability and availability of computer systems in presence of uncertainties. They share the usage of Markovian chains as mathematical model for representing software systems and present formal methods that address the challenge of uncertainties in the parameters of these mathematical models. In [10] the authors describe a Monte Carlo based approach and calculate the number of samples of uncertain parameter values necessary to produce availability results within a confidence interval. In [19, 20] authors use the method of moments for evaluating component-based software reliability under uncertainties. They deal with the presence of uncertainties in both the components estimated reliability and in the operational profile of software. Work in [15] estimates confidence levels of parameters of the software operational profile.

Model-based performance and reliability evaluation of software architectures in presence of uncertainties are tackled in [32, 26, 25]. Their methods are applied at software design time and aim at finding software designs or software component compositions that meet the non-functional requirements. They consider uncertainties in the values of the parameters of their models and propose to model this uncertainty through probability distribution functions. They extract samples of the parameter values and perform Monte-Carlo based simulations.

3. MODEL UNCERTAINTY: TAXONOMY

Several definition of uncertainties can be found in different areas of the scientific literature ranging from the absence of knowledge, to the inadequacy of information or the deficiency of the modeling process [33, 16]. Nevertheless, in computing area, the most used definitions of uncertainty simply distinguish between natural variability of physical processes (i.e., aleatory or stochastic uncertainty) and the uncertainties in knowledge of these processes (i.e., "epistemic" or state-of-knowledge uncertainty), see for example [26, 10].

Among the work of research fields that hold more maturity than computer science on the study of uncertainties, it is shown that *uncertainties* in models can be seen from other perspectives different from epistemic and aleatory. Learning from them, we have found that some of these different perspectives also exist in the modeling of computing systems; but there is not yet a general enough taxonomy for uncertainties in models in the computing field.

For proposing such a taxonomy for uncertainties in computer systems models, we base on a general definition of *uncertainty* in modeling given in [33] as: "*any deviation from the unachievable ideal of completely deterministic knowledge of the relevant system*". Such deviations can lead to an overall "lack of confidence" in the obtained results based on a judgment that they might be "incomplete, blurred, inaccurate, unreliable, inconclusive, or potentially false" [29].

We present our classification based on the same three categories or dimensions as proposed in [33]. According to these three dimensions, uncertainties are classified regarding: their location, level and nature. In the following paragraphs we explain the meaning of each dimension.

Location.

The *location* of uncertainty refers to the place where the uncertainty manifests itself within the model. An uncertainty can be located in the following parts of a model:

- *Context* uncertainty is an identification of the boundaries of the model; that is uncertainty about the information to be modeled. This uncertainty concerns the completeness of the model with respect to the real world. It refers to the kind of information that should be included in the model and the kind of information that should be abstracted away from it. In Figure 1(a), elements within the dotted line represent a model that includes in its context elements *Service*, *Hardware* and *MicroHardware*, but it does not allow to represent *CommunicationNode* elements. If *CommunicationNodes* have a strong influence in system behavior, these models will hold a strong uncertainty. In turn, continuous line in Figure 1(a) encloses an example where elements *Service*, *Hardware* and *CommunicationNode* are in the context of the model, while elements *MicroHardware* are not.

- *Model structural* uncertainty concerns the form of the model itself. This uncertainty refers to how accurately the structure of the model represents the subset of the real world that has to be modeled. Following the example in Figure 1, let us assume that in the real system, due to fault-tolerance in the connections, two additional nodes exist allowing the communication between *Service* B and C. Since the model admits the representation of *CommunicationNode*, the replication of nodes could be represented (e.g., by adding the two *CommunicationNode* in dotted lines in Figure 1(b)). The model in continuous line keeps some uncertainty since its structure could represent better the real word.

- *Input parameters* uncertainty is often identified as parameter uncertainty and it is associated with the actual value of variables given as input to the model and with the methods used to calibrate the model parameters.

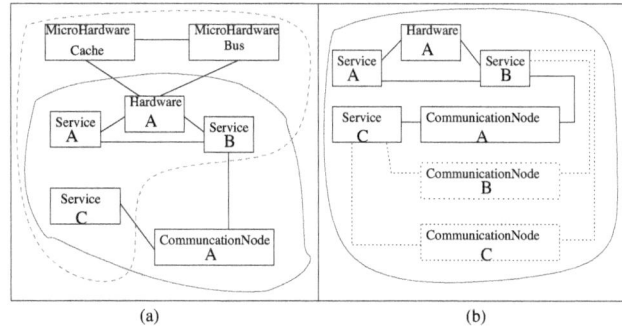

Figure 1: Example of location of uncertainties

The list of possible locations of uncertainties proposed in the literature is large. The rationale we have followed in the above selection is that we filtered out the locations that could hardly exist the models themselves. For example, we have not considered the uncertainties that are located in the solution algorithms of the models; e.g., uncertainty about the correct implementation of the algorithm that analyzes the model and produces the expected performance results of the system.

Doing an analogy to Model-Driven Engineering metamodeling levels, *context* uncertainties are related to the decisions at the meta-model definition (i.e., which kind of information can be included in the model), *structural* uncertainties are related to decisions at the model definition using the meta-model (i.e., the elements that exist in the model and their relations), and *input parameter* uncertainties are related to the values of the attributes of the model objects.

Level.

The *level* of uncertainty is where the uncertainty manifests itself along the spectrum between deterministic knowledge and total ignorance. Usual characterizations of uncertainty levels propose different values in a scale of how much knowledge lacks to achieve the knowledge necessary for studying the system deterministically.

We believe that a classification that differentiated between several amounts of lack of knowledge in a very tailored manner could misguide future research. Hereafter, to avoid classifications that could hamper the progress in the field of uncertainties management by proposing premature biased uncertainty levels, we prefer to classify the level of uncertainty following the more general ranking of *orders of ignorance* proposed in [1]. The five proposed levels of ignorance (here for uncertainty) are:

- 0th order of uncertainty. Lack of uncertainty, i.e., knowledge.

- 1st order of uncertainty. Lack of knowledge. The subject lacks knowledge about something but she is aware of such lack (i.e., *known uncertainty*).

- 2nd order of uncertainty. Lack of knowledge and lack of awareness. The subject does not know that she does not know.

- 3rd order of uncertainty. Lack of process to find out the lack of awareness. The subject does not have any way to move from not knowing that she does not know to, at least, be aware of the existence of the uncertainty.

- 4th order of uncertainty. Meta uncertainty. Uncertainty about orders of uncertainty.

5

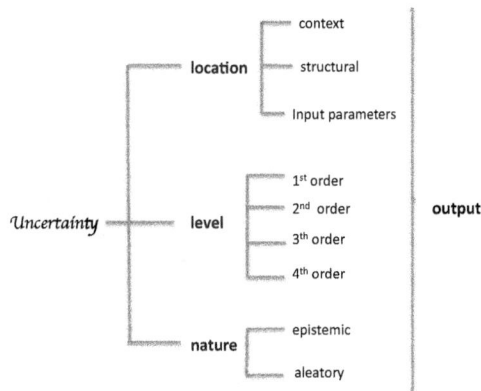

Figure 2: Uncertainty taxonomy

Following this classification, software engineers should build self-adaptive applications having in mind that uncertainties of third and fourth order in their application models should be avoided. The second order of uncertainty, instead, may be unavoidable in some cases (see for example the source of uncertainty called *problem-state identification* in [7]). What is more important for the system is that an uncertainty remains in this level in a transitory manner; i.e., eventually the uncertainty will be recognized and then it will decrease its level to the first. Once the uncertainty is in the first order, it could be used some of the known methods proposed to deal with it. The reduction from the second order to the first one may be assisted, for instance, by providing self-adaptive software both with self-evaluating mechanisms and with monitoring capabilities. In that case, if the results of model-based evaluation do not match with the real monitored characteristics, then the existence of an uncertainty in its models can be recognized (then moving the level of this uncertainty to the first order). Even in presence of these characteristics, uncertainties of second level can be present. Consider, for example, the case in which performing the model-based self-evaluation is time consuming and then it is performed only periodically. In this situation, the system may not continuously be aware of its lack of knowledge, but the uncertainty will be eventually recognized and then it will belong to the second order only for a time-bounded period.

Nature.

The *nature* of uncertainty refers to whether the uncertainty is due to the imperfection of the acquired knowledge or is due to the inherent variability of the phenomena being described. Our taxonomy uses the classical distinction between:

- *Epistemic* uncertainty due to the lack of enough data to build reliable knowledge, imperfection of the acquired data or imperfection in the process of building the knowledge from the data.

- *Aleatory* uncertainty due to inherent variability of the some parts under consideration or randomness of events.

The presented three-dimension classification is sketched in Figure 2. The aggregated effect of the different uncertainties on the results of the model analysis is the so-called model *output*. The analysis outcome will have an uncertainty that derives from the uncertainties in the information represented in model and how they are handled during analysis. Up to now, there exist methods to manage the presence of uncertainties in the model analysis, but

there do not exist methods to completely eliminate them. Therefore, the *output* uncertainty cannot be avoided. Using methods that consider the uncertainties, it is expected that the outcome of an analysis that considers the presence of uncertainties to be closer to the real values of the running system than the outcome of an analysis that do not consider their presence; though this fact cannot even be completely ensured.

4. MODEL UNCERTAINTY AND SELF-ADAPTIVE SYSTEMS

When an application is initially architected, the available information for engineers regarding some important concepts - such as the environment where the application will execute, the usage profile of the application or its requirements - is partial and incomplete. This is reinforced by the facts that all these concepts are prone to change during the application lifetime, and it is impossible to foresee every type of change, the moment in which it will occur and the value to which they will change. Therefore, models that are used to evaluate the application properties at design time hold some uncertainties.

Self-adaptive systems are an effective solution to deal with some aspects of the lack of information and actual knowledge that exist when the application is not running yet (e.g, at design time). By building a self-adaptive system, some of the decisions that should be otherwise made by engineers at design time can be delayed, and they can be made by the system itself at runtime when more information about changing concepts is available. Self-adaptive systems usually keep a model of their "world of interest", and make use of it to plan their adaptations and when to adapt. However, even at runtime, information is not complete or accurate. Therefore, information in the models used to govern the self-adaptation is subject to uncertainty [12].

Research works [17, 12] have reported concrete sources of uncertainties in software systems. Work in [8] also lists sources of uncertainty. Since the concern of [8] is a model-based software reliability evaluation, their presented sources are concentrated on the uncertainties on software architectural models. We have gathered different sources of uncertainty in software systems presented in the literature and we have investigated how these uncertainties can affect the trustworthiness of the information in the models managed by self-adaptive software. Once the effect of each source of information in the model is recognized, we can find a relation between each source of uncertainty and a type of model uncertainty according to the taxonomy presented in Section 3. We present this relation in the next subsection.

To avoid incorrect decisions about system self-adaptations, the software should know that its model contains uncertainties and apply some methods to handle them during the model analysis phase. We discuss in Subsection 4.2 methods for handling model uncertainties presented in the literature.

4.1 Sources of uncertainty

In this subsection we propose a classification of the sources of uncertainties that we have found in the literature regarding the effect they entail in the model managed by the self-adaptive system. We classify them according to the taxonomy presented in Section 3. This will make easier the comparison of the similarities and differences of the effect of different sources of uncertainties. Having them classified according to a taxonomy (instead of using simple lists) will help the selection of general approaches that can deal with a group of uncertainties concurrently, rather than a particular approach at a time for each uncertainty. This relation is shown in

Table 1. Each source of uncertainty is classified according to its *location* and *nature* dimensions of the taxonomy. The *level* dimension of the taxonomy is not shown in the table since each source of uncertainty can be of any level depending on the implemented capabilities in the system that should deal with the uncertainty.

Source of Uncertainty	Classification	
	Location	Nature
Simplifying assumptions [12]	Structural/context	Epistemic
Model drift [12]	Structural	Epistemic
Noise in sensing [12]	Input parameter	Epistemic/ Aleatory
Future parameters value [12]	Input parameter	Epistemic
Human in the loop [12, 17]	Context	Epistemic/ Aleatory
Objectives [12]	Input parameter / context	Epistemic
Decentralization [12]	Context/structural	Epistemic
Execution context/ [12] Mobility [17]	context/ structural/ input parameters	Epistemic
Cyber-phisical system [12] [17]	Context/Structural Input parameter	Epistemic
Automatic learning [17]	Structural Input parameter	Epistemic Aleatory
Rapid evolution [17]	Structural Input parameter	Epistemic
Granularity of models [8]	Context/Structural	Epistemic
Different sources of information [8]	Input parameter	Epistemic/ Aleatory

Table 1: Sources of uncertainty

Due to space reasons, we do not provide a description of each source of uncertainty here. Readers are referred to works referenced in Table 1 for further details regarding the meaning of each source of uncertainty. Nevertheless, for the sake of understandability of the process that was followed for the classification of the sources of uncertainty, we describe in the following some of them as examples. We have selected: *simplifying assumptions*, which is an uncertainty very general in modeling and easily understandable, *future parameter value* and *automatic learning* that are uncertainties more restricted to the domain of self-adaptive systems.

Simplifying assumptions: the model is an abstraction of the reality and some details whose significance is supposed to be minimal are ignored. This uncertainty can be located, for example, in the structure (i.e., *structural* location) of the model if the model language has enough modeling power to represent the lacking concepts but they have been deliberately excluded from the model. It can also be located in the boundaries (i.e., *context* location) of the model if it was decided to exclude some information within the set of type of concerns considered in the model. To illustrate the difference, let us refer again to the examples in Figure 1. If it is possible to model the characteristics of every existing *CommunicationNode* (e.g., routers) between *Services* but it was decided not to represent the replication of *CommunicationNode* between two *Services* (elements in dotted lines in Figure 1(b)), then the results of the model evaluation will be uncertain due to "simplifying assumptions" in the model *structure*. If properties of hardware micro-components such as cache memory or the bus between CPU-memory have an influence in the system properties but the language to create the model does not allow modeling the characteristics of

micro-components (continuous line in Figure 1(a)), then the results of the model evaluation will be uncertain due to "simplifying assumptions" in the model *context*. This source is related to a deliberate hiding of information in the model (i.e., *epistemic*) rather than to the random nature of the lacking elements.

Future parameter value: uncertainty in the future world where the system will execute creates uncertainties in the correct actions to take at present. For example, if the self-adaptive application is not in the optimal configuration for its current execution environment, model analysis may produce an advice to change its configuration. However, if the environment conditions are close to a change and the current configuration is the optimal for the future environment, the best behavior may be to resign itself to executing for a short period in the sub-optimal configuration without requiring any adaptation, instead of performing two adaptations in a short time interval. As future changes can involve changes in the model structure or parameters, this source of uncertainty may have *structural* or *input parameter* location. Since this source of uncertainty concerns the future of the environment it shows an *aleatory* nature.

Automatic learning: adaptive applications that include an automatic machine-learning phase usually use statistical processes to create their knowledge about their execution context and most-useful behavior. This machine-learning process can lead to applications with uncertain behavior. The location of this uncertainty may be in the model *structure* or *input parameters* depending on how general are the concepts for which the application has been provided with machine-leaning capabilities. Regarding the nature of the uncertainty, it may depend on the point of view. From the point of view of the application and its models of the world, as long as the origin of this uncertainty is that the machine had to learn using imperfect and limited data, the nature of this uncertainty is *epistemic*. From the point of view of the user, since the information may have passed through a statistical process during its learning to create the models, it produces some randomness in the model information and analysis results, and consequently it can be seen as an *aleatory* uncertainty.

4.2 Methods to manage uncertainty

While research in uncertainty analysis advances, the set of different sources of uncertainties becomes larger. Hopefully, there will be no need of a completely different and particular approach for handling each type of uncertainty in the system. Indeed, it would be much better if more general approaches for managing uncertainties could be reused for different sources of software uncertainties; for example, two uncertainties that at first sight may look very different can be managed using a similar approach.

In order to have a possibility to manage model uncertainties, the first step is to create an application that is eventually able to identify the existence of such uncertainties; i.e., the *level* of uncertainty should be at most in the 2nd order. Once the uncertainty is in the second order, its reduction to the first order one may be assisted, for instance, by providing self-adaptive software both with self-evaluating mechanisms and with monitoring capabilities. Other techniques that have been proposed in the literature that allow the software to realize the existence of uncertainties are the *multiple conceptual model* [28], which proposes the analysis of several models of the same system to realize the existence of uncertainties if their results differ from each other; and *expert elicitation* [28], which manually sets the uncertainty to belong to the 1st order. As previously mentioned, even in presence of methods to reduce the level of uncertainty to the 1st, uncertainties of second level can be temporarily present because the system does not apply these methods are continuously but only periodically.

Once the placement of the uncertainty level on the first order has been achieved, the scientific literature has proposed several methods for handling it. In the following we list the methods we have found for managing uncertainties. In order to make easier its utilization on the appropriate uncertainties, we classify them regarding the type of uncertainty for which they were initially conceived. Table 2 shows such classification. Some of these methods were not proposed in computer science but derived from other research areas. We do not argue against the possible usefulness of the methods across other types of uncertainty; further research is necessary to completely understand whether they can be used.

Since some methods for managing uncertainties were created through continuous refinements or extensions of other general analysis methods, references in Table 2 do not show the origin of the method but a work in which they are applied or their suitability is discussed. Due to space limitations, we do not provide a description of each method. We refer readers again to works referenced in the table for further details regarding the usage of each method. We selected here two of them, which are powerful techniques but not frequently used in computer science or performance evaluation field: *model averaging* and *model discrepancy*.

Model averaging: This approach proposes the generation of several models of the same system. Different modeling languages and model domains can be used. These models are competing and they are all plausible. Each model is assigned with a probability of being the "true" model; i.e., a measure of model adequacy. Every model is analyzed and the outcome of the analysis is calculated as the weighted mean -according to the measure of model adequacy- of the outputs of the models. A self-adaptive system should be provided with a set of methods, one for each type of model, for creating, updating and analyzing the model.

Model discrepancy: This approach assumes that the utilized model is not the "true" model of the system. Instead, it tries to unveil the discrepancy between the model output and the "true" target value. Once the discrepancy is known, it is created a "discrepancy term". For creating the outcome of the analysis, both the model analysis output and the discrepancy term value are considered. Ideally, the discrepancy term is equal to the difference between the output of the model running at its best (i.e., where the input values of the model are all equal to the real values) and the real results (the true target quantity). Calling X the input of the model, $f(X)$ its output and Z the real values; then, the discrepancy term δ_x ideally satisfies $Z = f(X) + \delta_x$. Using statistical techniques and a subset of inputs $X_1, X_2...$ and outputs $Z_1, Z_2, ..$, the discrepancy term δ_X can be estimated parametrically to be used in subsequent analysis.

5. APPLICATION EXAMPLE

In this section we exemplify some of the model uncertainties classified in Section 3. We base our examples in the field of self-adaptive service-oriented systems availability evaluation.

Consider a software application whose functionality is the viewing of video in streaming (real-time events, films, etc.). To meet its mission, it requires services that are offered by third-party service providers over the Internet; e.g., streaming video servers. As there may be multiple providers for each required service, to increase the application's quality, it will be engineered with self-adaptive capabilities in terms of dynamic *service provider selection*; e.g., if it is using a service provider and it becomes unavailable, the application will be able to autonomously bind another different provider. Let us assume that there are N third party-providers, named sp_n such that $n \in [1..N]$. Figure 3 represents a system of this kind. In this example, the software application resides in a mobile device and can connect to the internet using several access media and proto-

cols. Let us assume that there are M access media, named am_m such that $m \in [1..M]$. The application can adapt its behavior for availability reasons (the kind of network that it is using and the third-party server that is requested to execute the service). If the user starts watching a stream and it disrupts, he will be dissatisfied with the application.

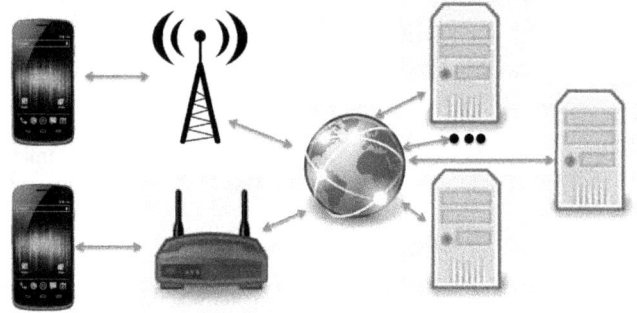

Figure 3: System base case example

To perform the model-based evaluation of the application's availability, the application itself needs the availability models of the world where it executes. In the following sections, we present a modeling study of this application from different perspectives and we highlight the existence of different types of uncertainty among the ones identified in Section 3 in the availability models, and a manner to handle each type of uncertainty. We divide the presentation according to *Location* dimension in the sections below and we concentrate on the dimensions *input parameter* and *model-structure* for the sake of space. Although it is a modeling study, to make realistic examples, we use real data. In particular, due to lack of accessibility to the logs of real deployment of this system, we use the availability logs published in [2, 5, 21, 27, 30] regarding the availability of internet servers. In the examples below we will use data from these logs and we select each time the log containing the more representative data to illustrate the uncertainty we are dealing with.

6. INPUT-PARAMETER UNCERTAINTIES

Nature: aleatory.

To generate the availability model, when the user wants to watch a stream, the application monitors the responsiveness of each element it needs; i.e., the lack of deadlock in the application, the responsiveness of internet access points (via mobile phone antenna or WiFi router) and third-party servers. Using this information, it can fill a block diagram model for availability. Figure 4 represents an instance of this model, where the field `status` of each block is filled with the information monitored.

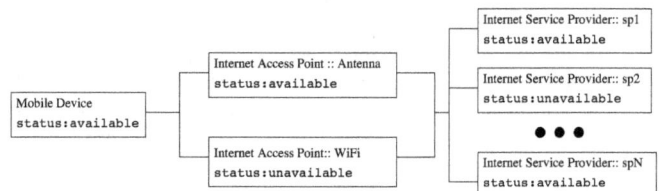

Figure 4: Block diagram model for availability analysis

Location	Nature	Method
Input parameter	Epistemic/ Aleatory	Reliability bound [35], Confidence intervals [35], Probability distributions [35], Fuzzy methods, Range of values, mean and variance, Sensitivity analysis,Sensitivity to information sources [8]
Structural	Epistemic/ Aleatory	Increasing parameter uncertainty to account for structural uncertainty [28]
Context/ Structural	Epistemic	Sensitivity to model granularity [8]
	Epistemic/ Aleatory	Structural uncertainty term [28], Model averaging [23], Model discrepancy [31], Framework for the establishment of plausible models in [28]

Table 2: Methods to manage uncertainty

In this case, since there is a path from the beginning of the diagram until its end that passes through blocks whose `status=available`, the analysis results will inform about the availability of the system, the application will bind an unavailable service provider and it will inform that the stream can be watched.

Problem:

In this case, the application is not aware that there is *uncertainty in the future state* of service providers and access points during the stream viewing. In consequence, the availability analyses ignores that the state of service providers and access points can change in the near future. Thus, the user will be dissatisfied if the system becomes unavailable because he had been informed that the access to the stream was granted.

Since the sample space size in the availability modeling of an element is two (either `status=unavailable` or `status=available`), the outcome of a study that ignores the aleatory nature of availability parameters of required elements is obviously insufficient for informing the user about system availability.

Taming uncertainty:

The availability analysis should consider that some servers may become unavailable, others may become available, mobile phone coverage may be lost or a wifi access point may be gained. In this manner, the application is aware that the state of the required elements during the streaming is not deterministically known; which moves it to the first level of uncertainty and enables the uncertainty management.

This type of uncertainty is a well-studied case in the literature (e.g., the exponential distribution is broadly used to model the time-to-fail of elements, while the accessibility of an element at a certain moment is usually modeled as a Bernoulli trial within a Bernoulli process) and well covered in availability evaluation research field [35, 10, 20]. The random nature of the availability parameter value of an artifact when its execution is required is usually captured by *probability distributions*.

Once the existence of this uncertainty is recognized, instead of representing in the availability model the status of an element as either `available` or `unavailable`, we model the aleatory uncertainty of each element using a Bernoulli distribution with parameter p: each third-party provider sp_n, accessing media am_m and application app has a parameter $p_{element}$ denoting a probability value, where $element \in \{sp_1..., sp_N\} \cup \{am_1, ...am_N\} \cup \{app\}$.

The application needs now a source of information to obtain the $p_{element}$ values. As a straightforward method, the application can record the availability information of each element periodically and create logs with the historical data of elements availability.

Using the data in the selected availability logs, $p_{element}$ values are calculated as the proportion of time that the element is accessible divided by the amount of time covered in the logs. Let us consider, for example, the availability log file `web-sites.avt` in [2]. Specifically, we focus on the availability information of the

7th server in the log for our provider sp_1, which corresponds to the information monitored during 209 days about the availability of mail.yahoo.com, and we obtain that the server was reachable 99.29% of time; therefore we set $p_{sp_1} = 0.9929$. Following a similar procedure, we derived the parameter values of the availability model in Figure 5. The probabilities have been computed using as availability log the file `web-sites.avt` in [2] and servers in lines 2,3,4,5,7,8 corresponding to servers: asia.cnn.com, canberra.yourguide.com.au, digital.library.upenn.edu, games.yahoo.com, mail.yahoo.com and msdn.microsoft.com, respectively.

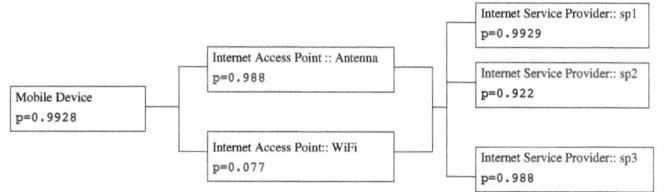

Figure 5: Block diagram model with probabilities for availability analysis

Using standard techniques of availability analysis of series/parallel blocks:

$$SystemAv = appAv \cdot amAv \cdot spAv = 0.98177$$

where $appAv = p_{app} = 0.9928$, $amAv = 1 - \prod_{m=1}^{M}(1 - p_{am_m}) = 0.9889$ and $spAv = 1 - \prod_{n=1}^{N}(1 - p_{sp_n}) = 0.999993$.

Therefore the system knows that, in this configuration, it has a probability of 0.98177 for being available and can allow the user to make an informed decision whether to use the application in this moment or not.

Note that in this example, the modeling of the availability uncertainty through a probability may seem evident. However, this kind of uncertainty is not always modeled when the main outcome of the study is not the availability evaluation but, for instance, performance evaluation. In these cases, the randomness in the availability of components or service providers is not represented and they are represented as "always available".

Nature:epistemic.

In the application example, the p_{sp_n} value characterizing a provider has been calculated as the proportion of time that the provider was available with respect to its lifetime. All data in the provider log has then been used to calculate p_{sp_n} with the underlying assumption that the log contains data regarding the steady-state behavior of uptimes and downtimes.

Problem:

The application in our example collects availability data from entities that run and are engineered independently of the rest of the system. As the application cannot acquire more information about the third-party service providers, these data may be biased.

The real steady-state availability behavior of the service provider, indeed, may be different from the one deduced from the log. For example, consider the case in which some bugs that caused unavailability periods are detected and corrected, in this case the real availability will be higher with respect to the predicted one. On the contrary, if it happens that after the deployment is finished, the service is no longer the protégé and the engineering team and sysadmins change their priorities to other projects, in this case the real availability can decrease.

This uncertainty does not stem from a random nature of changing elements in the service provider but it is due to a lack of knowledge about how to interpret the data that are collected during the monitoring and which data will be used to give value to model parameters. Therefore, this is an epistemic uncertainty in the model parameters.

Taming uncertainty:

This kind of uncertainty has been tackled in the literature conducting sensitivity studies [20], using confidence intervals or distribution functions for the value of parameter p_n [25, 32, 11].

Hereafter, instead of showing what it does mean dealing with this uncertainty considering a first order level, we illustrate how to tackle the second order level. In other words, we illustrate the change from a situation where the application does not know that the availably log does not contain enough information to a situation where the application knows that the information in the log does not represent the service provider's current behavior.

Let us focus the study on one service provider, sp_n. We use as availability log for sp_n the availability data in the 13th line in `web-sites.avt`[1]. The usual availability probability calculation based on the proportion of time the system was available regarding the total amount of time would give us:

$$p_{sp_n} = \frac{17,924,686 \, seconds}{18,135,257 \, seconds} = 0.98838$$

To recognize whether the information in the trace represents the steady-state availability behavior of the provider or not, we split up the trace in two halves where each half covers the same amount of time. Then we compare the availability obtained considering the whole trace and the ones related to the two halves. If the log contains the steady-state information, the availability calculated in the three cases above should be similar.

Let us start with the information in the second half of the log. In this case we obtain:

$$p_{sp_n} = \frac{9,061,128.5 \, seconds}{9,067,628.5 \, seconds} = 0.99928$$

Therefore, in terms of availability, using only the data in the second half of the log we obtain a probability of downtime of the provider that is $\frac{1-0.98838}{1-0.99928} \simeq 16$ times lower than the one obtained using the complete log.

To strengthen the study, we calculate the availability of other parts of the logs representing the most recent information. For example, if we calculate the availability using the last quarter of the log trace, we obtain

---

[1]The monitored website corresponding to the 13th line is vlib.org, and the trace covered almost 210 days

$$p_{sp_n} = \frac{4,532,654.25}{4,533,814.25} = 0.99974$$

representing a system whose downtime seems $\frac{1-0.98838}{1-0.99974} \simeq 45$ times less probable with respect to the information derived analyzing all data in the trace. Besides, we calculate the mean length of each time interval when the system is available and the mean length of each time interval when the system is unavailable. Figure 6 shows this information. Figure 6 (a) shows the mean time interval length that the service is continuously available when using the complete log (x-axis is 100%), the last half of time (x-axis is 50%) and the last quarter of time (x-axis is 25%). In turn, Figure 6 (b) shows the mean time interval length that the service is continuously unavailable (i.e., repair time) for the same log partitions. These figures show that the availability of the service is evolving positively.

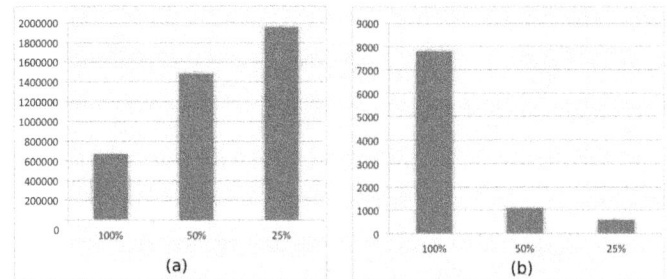

Figure 6: Mean length of time intervals where the service in the 13th line in `web-sites.avt` is continuously: (a) available, (b) unavailable

Observing the differences in the calculated availability depending on the considered data in the log, we can suppose that the log does not show steady state availability information (in the beginning the system is much more unavailable than in the end). Thus, the calculation of the availability probability using the proportion of time that the system has been available since the first moment of existence is not accurate because there is a epistemic uncertainty in the model input parameters [2].

Using this procedure, the existence of the uncertainty can be realized. At this point, an approach among the ones presented in the literature, for instance in [10, 15, 8], can be used.

7. MODEL STRUCTURAL UNCERTAINTIES

Nature: aleatory.

The model in Figure 5 calculates the probability of finding available a service provider as the proportion of time that the provider was available regarding the whole time monitored. A service provider is represented as an element of *Internet Service Provider::spN* in the model structure, and the availability model contains an *Internet Service Provider::spN* element for every service provider that have been registered in the log.

Problem:

Let us now consider the same system and model from a different perspective. As a system that operates in the open-world and uses third-party service providers, new service providers that offer

---

[2]The calculation of the threshold values for which it is assumed that the average system availability is either similar or different to the recent system availability is out of the scope of this example.

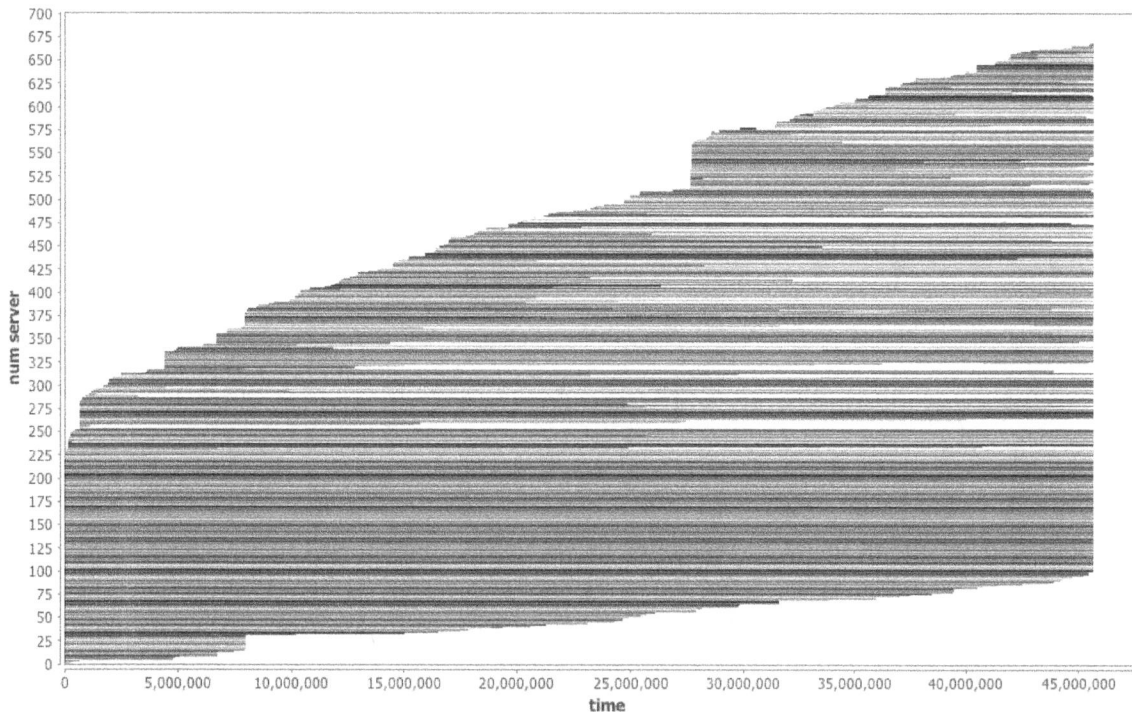

Figure 7: Birth and Death times of servers in PlanetLab ordered chronologically

the same service may appear and existing providers may disappear from the world. Therefore, the number of existing service providers at a given moment may vary over time. The appeareance of a service provider may be represented in the log by a timestamp denoting the time in which it was available by the first time. However, disappearance of servers is not represented in the log. As a consequence, the availability model is not completely accurate because it may consider providers with a calculated availability that do no longer exist.

As a concrete example, let us consider the information in file `pl-app.avt` in [30] as availability log of service providers. This file contains information regarding the availability of 669 servers of PlanetLab platform. Therefore, service provider availability log shows the availability sessions of 669 service providers. Figure 7 shows, for each provider, the first time and the last time its service was available. So, each line in the figure represents the lifetime of a provider. We can see that the first session of availability of some providers was in a point of time days away from the starting of the application (situation in which we could say that these providers did not exist in the beginning but they appeared in the world later). In the same way, we can see that some service providers passed through periods of availability and unavailability until a certain point in time in which they started to be continuously unavailable (situation in which we could say that they had disappeared from the world). This figure shows that 669 different providers have appeared in the world at some point but the average number of existing providers is 384.8.

To illustrate an example of uncertainty in availability modeling, let us consider the value *numServer*=51 in Figure 7 [3]. This provider was available since the first time the application was executed and

the last time that this provider was available was 24,895,542 seconds after the application was firstly executed. The current timestamp is 45,573,054. Between the starting point at 0 and 45,573,054, the server was found available for 21,659,147 seconds, which gives it a calculated availability probability $p_{sp_{310}} = 0.4753$. However, since the provider has not been available during the last 45,573,054 - 24,895,542 = 20,677,512 seconds (239 days), it is hardly believable that the provider is just temporarily unavailable. The reasonable option is to consider that the provider does not longer exists, and therefore its representing block *Internet Service Provider::sp51* in the block diagram should be removed from the model structure.

The appearance and disappearance of providers happen many times and cannot be anticipated deterministically because they depend on the decision of third-parties and these are random events from the point of view of the application. From a modeling point of view, since each existing server is represented as an element in the structure of the model, and this element can be present or not, this is an uncertainty of aleatory nature located in the model structure.

Taming uncertainty:

To deal with this uncertainty, assuming that its existence has been recognized and so it belongs to the first order level, several techniques can be applied. In the following we illustrate the application of the model averaging technique.

Let us assume that, from previous experiences, engineers know that observing a continuous unavailability of a provider during the last week would likely mean that this provider disappeared. Following this assumption may entail both pessimistic prediction errors (e.g., providers that suffered a serious downtime of more than one week but they will be available again, the so called false positives), and optimistic ones (e.g., providers that have left the world only a couple of days ago would still be considered as currently existing, the so called false negatives).

---

[3]This line corresponds to line 310 in file `pl-app.avt` in [30], with `ip=152.3.136.1`

Following the model averaging technique, we create three different availability models. The input data we use in this experiment are the first 14 lines in file `pl-app.avt` in [30]; thus we consider that in the world up to 14 different providers have appeared at some point in time. Figure 8 depicts the birth and death moments of each of these providers.

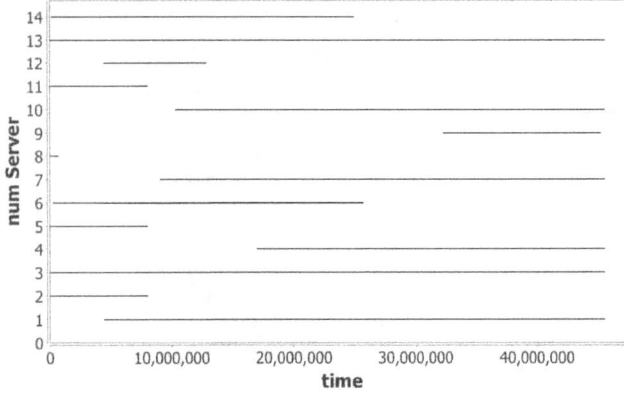

Figure 8: Birth and Death times of PlanetLab servers in the 14 first lines in `pl-app.avt`

The *first availability model, M1* is generated by considering only the providers that have not been continuously unavailable during the last week. That is, since in the used traces the current time is the 45,573,054th second, we take into account servers whose last monitored availability was after the $45,573,054 - secondsInOneWeek = 44,968,254$-th second. This gives us an availability model that includes N=7 service providers in its structure. The calculated availability of service providers ($spAv$) using the standard techniques of availability analysis of parallel blocks gives us an availability of

$$spAv = 1 - \prod_{n=1}^{N=7}(1 - p_{sp_n}) = 0.9999982.$$

The *second availability model, M2* is intended to mitigate the uncertainty inaccuracies due to too pessimistic assumption. This is done by using the calculated availability of every provider since the first time it appeared in the world until the current time. The availability of the system is calculated as if none of the providers had never left the world. This gives us an $spAv = 1 - \prod_{n=1}^{N=14}(1 - p_{sp_n}) = 0.9999996214$. Note that although $spAv$ value in this case can seem similar to the previous one, this availability value represents a system almost five times more available than the previous one.

The *third availability model, M3* considers as existing providers only those that are currently available at the 45,573,054-th second. Among the 14 providers, 6 of them are currently available. Therefore the structure of the availability model for the service providers has 6 blocks. We calculate the p_{sp} of each of these T service providers and we use these probabilities to calculate $spAv = 1 - \prod_{n=1}^{N=6}(1 - p_{sp_n}) = 0.99999617$. Note that this availability value represents a system around half time less available than the one obtained with $M1$.

None of the three availability models exactly represents the real situation regarding the number of providers that currently exist in the world as this is an aleatory uncertainty. The first one makes a prediction regarding the moment in which a provider can be assumed as disappeared, the second one makes an over-estimation of existing providers and the third one makes a sub-estimation.

M1	M2	M3	Mave
0.9999982	0.9999996214	0.99999617	0.9999981

Table 3: Availability of service providers $spAv$

Model averaging techniques propose to manage this uncertainty by weighting the availability results of each model in order to produce a new result. In our example, we assume to be quite confident about the one-week existence assumption and we provide a weight of 0.7 to $M1$, 0.15 to $M2$ that over estimates the existence of providers and 0.15 to the model $M3$ that under-estimates it. This gives us a service provider averaged availability of $spAv = 0.7 \cdot 0.9999982 + 0.15 \cdot 0.9999996214 + 0.15 \cdot 0.99999617$, so

$$spAv = 0.9999981$$

Table 3 summarizes the results obtained with the different models.

Nature:epistemic.

The application in our example communicates with service providers through Internet Access Points. In Figure 3 and in the block diagram in Figure 4, two Internet Access Points, a WiFi point and an Antenna working in parallel are represented. This model assumes that the communication across Internet between the application and service providers is a single-hop process transmitted by an Internet Access Point.

Problem:

In the actual system, the communication between the service provider and the application is not a single-hop process routed in isolation by the Internet access point of the application. There are other elements that can fail in the communication, for example, the Internet Access Point of providers, DNS servers or Internet traffic routers in between. We concentrate this example on the Access Point of providers.

When the service is monitored as not available, the reason can stem from an unavailability of its Internet Access Point rather than from the unavailability of the service itself. Monitoring the availability of Internet Access Point of providers is not as trivial as controlling the unresponsiveness of the service, although tools as `traceroute` can identify failures in communication elements. If the access point fails, services may be available but they cannot be reached. Although it is easily noticeable that the lack of the Internet Access Points in the availability block diagram creates an inaccuracy in the model, it is also reasonable to justify that the annotated availability in the service provider block already covers every possible unavailability in the communication elements. Nevertheless, by avoiding the modeling of the Internet Access Points of the service provider, we are also falling into a modeling inaccuracy regarding the independency of the availability of service providers among each other. Next paragraph exemplifies this case.

Nowadays, many companies and service providers over the internet are moving their computing infrastructure to the cloud, let us assume that this is the case of the service providers in our example. In this case, two or more providers can rely on the same cloud provider and belong to the same *availability zone*. Therefore, they share the same Internet Access Point, i.e., the owned by the cloud provider. In our availability model, by using the common formula $spAv = 1 - \prod^{N}(1 - p_{sp_n})$ it was implicitly assumed that each service provider was unavailable independently of others, but in reality there are single motives that can make them be useless at the same time.

The nature of this uncertainty is epistemic because it is due to a lack of knowledge of how the communication between the application and service providers proceeds. It is located in the model structure because the Internet Access Points of service providers are not considered as blocks in our model, even if it would be possible since the type *Internet Access Point* already exists in our availability block diagram.

Taming uncertainty:

The uncertainty related to the lack of knowledge on the model structure is difficult to be identified at the beginning of the execution. It is most likely that the application becomes aware of the uncertainty during its lifetime, when more data about services availability is acquired. Therefore, this uncertainty will start belonging to the second order, and eventually will become of first order. For this reason, we believe it is more convenient to illustrate afresh the taming of the uncertainty of second level, suggesting then more classical methods to deal with it when it is at the first level.

A reasonably easy manner to realize the existence of uncertainty in the modeling of providers reachability is to check the likelihood of concurrent unavailability of services. The application should first recognize that providers are not behaving independently, although at this point it could not be clear which are the actual dependencies. If it is possible to identify the Internet Access Point of providers as the source of dependency, then the uncertainty will be of first order. The system will know that the structure of its model is not completely correct because there are dependencies in the availability behavior of providers but it lacks complete information to include them in the model.

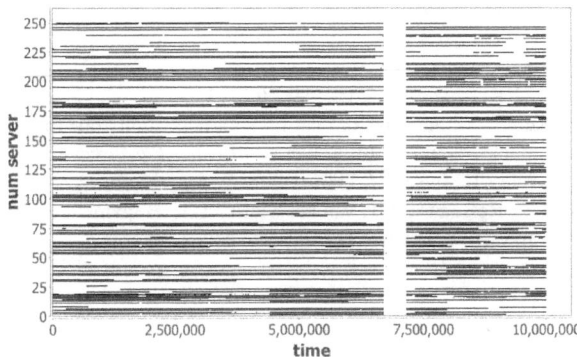

Figure 9: Availability intervals of 250 first servers in `pl-app.avt`

Figure 9 shows the availability intervals of the first 250 servers in file `pl-app.avt` in [30] during the first ten million seconds. Let us assume that this is the availability behavior of $N = 250$ services of our example system. Each y-axis value represents the availability behavior of a service. Horizontal lines are depicted during the periods when the service sp_n was available. It can be seen that availability of the services is not independent because around second 7,000,000 none of the services was reachable (there is a lack of horizontal lines in that period). This fact also happens around seconds 1,769,200 and 5,847,200, although the concurrent unavailability happens during short periods and the Figure does not show it so obviously. Figure 10 shows it more clearly as it depicts the number of services available at each moment between the initial time and the 10,000,000th second. We can see also in this figure that at some times the number of available services decreases abruptly even if it does not reach the zero value (e.g., around 8,675,000th

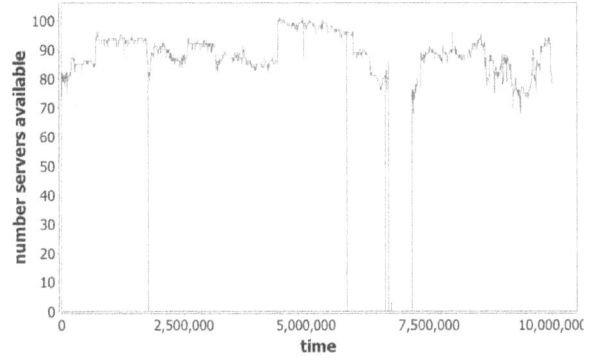

Figure 10: Number of servers available among the 250 first servers in `pl-app.avt` during the firsts 10,000,000 seconds

second). This fact reinforces the argument that some event happens in the system that affects the availability of a subset of services concurrently. These abrupt changes in the number of available servers allow the application to suspect that service availability is not independent and that the analysis of its availability block diagram produces too optimistic results, ergo the level of ignorance changes from the second to the first level, and methods described in Section 4.2 can then be applied.

8. CONCLUSION AND FUTURE WORK

In this paper we have discussed how different types of uncertainties can affect the definition and evaluation of software models. In particular, exploiting works existing in the literature and belonging to the field of natural science, we have proposed here a definition of uncertainty that can be used in computer science research, together with a taxonomy of different types of modeling uncertainties, that considers their location, nature and level, with respect to quality evaluation. Focusing on self-adaptive software systems, we have then analyzed possible sources of uncertainties together with existing methods to reduce their impact in the model evaluation step. We have also shown, using a concrete example together with a set of realistic data logs, what it does mean taking into account the different types of uncertainties and their input on the final availability prediction/evaluation using state-of-the art methods.

This research can be extended along several directions. We intend to explore how to generalize methods that have been proven useful for taming a very concrete uncertainty to allow them to tame more uncertainties of the same type. Furthermore, we plan to explore possible dependencies among the different uncertainties and their relationships and impact on different quality attributes. Finally, we intend to analyze the different uncertainties in the context of real-world application scenarios, to assess possible correlation and identify best practice procedures.

Acknowledgments

The work has been partially supported by the FP7 European project Seaclouds. The authors are grateful to Vincenzo Grassi for insightful discussions on this research.

9. REFERENCES

[1] P. G. Armour. The five orders of ignorance. *Commun. ACM*, 43(10):17–20, Oct. 2000.

[2] M. Bakkaloglu, J. J. Wylie, C. Wang, and G. R. Ganger. On correlated failures in survivable storage systems. Technical Report CMU-CS-02-129, Carnegie Mellon University, 2002.

[3] S. Balsamo, A. D. Marco, P. Inverardi, and M. Simeoni. Model-based performance prediction in software development: A survey. *IEEE Trans. Software Engineering*, 30(5):295–310, 2004.

[4] B. Beck and G. van Straten. *Uncertainty and forecasting of water quality*. Springer-Verlag, 1983.

[5] W. J. Bolosky, J. R. Douceur, D. Ely, and M. Theimer. Feasibility of a serverless distributed file system deployed on an existing set of desktop PCs. In *Proc. SIGMETRICS*, 2000.

[6] R. Calinescu, C. Ghezzi, M. Z. Kwiatkowska, and R. Mirandola. Self-adaptive software needs quantitative verification at runtime. *Commun. ACM*, 55(9):69–77, 2012.

[7] S.-W. Cheng and D. Garlan. Handling uncertainty in autonomic systems. In *Proc. of the Int. Workshop on Living with Uncertainties (IWLU'07)*, Atlanta, GA, USA, 2007.

[8] L. Cheung, L. Golubchik, N. Medvidovic, and G. Sukhatme. Identifying and addressing uncertainty in architecture-level software reliability modeling. In *Int. Parallel and Distributed Processing Symposium. IPDPS 2007*, pages 1–6, 2007.

[9] V. Cortellessa, A. D. Marco, and P. Inverardi. *Model-Based Software Performance Analysis*. Springer, 2011.

[10] A. Devaraj, K. Mishra, and K. S. Trivedi. Uncertainty propagation in analytic availability models. In *Proc. of the Symposium on Reliable Distributed Systems*, SRDS '10, pages 121–130, Washington, DC, USA, 2010. IEEE Computer Society.

[11] N. Esfahani, E. Kouroshfar, and S. Malek. Taming uncertainty in self-adaptive software. In *Proc. of ESEC/FSE '11*, pages 234–244, New York, NY, USA, 2011. ACM.

[12] N. Esfahani and S. Malek. Uncertainty in self-adaptive software systems. In *Software Engineering for Self-Adaptive Systems II*, volume 7475 of *LNCS*, pages 214–238. Springer Berlin Heidelberg, 2013.

[13] N. Esfahani, S. Malek, and K. Razavi. Guidearch: guiding the exploration of architectural solution space under uncertainty. In *Proc. of the International Conference on Software Engineering*, ICSE '13, pages 43–52, Piscataway, NJ, USA, 2013. IEEE Press.

[14] N. Esfahani, K. Razavi, and S. Malek. Dealing with uncertainty in early software architecture. In *Proc. International Symposium on the Foundations of Software Engineering*, FSE '12, pages 21:1–21:4, New York, NY, USA, 2012. ACM.

[15] L. Fiondella and S. Gokhale. Software reliability with architectural uncertainties. In *Int. Parallel and Distributed Processing Symposium, IPDPS 2008*, pages 1–5, 2008.

[16] S. Funtowicz and J. Ravetz. *Uncertainty and Quality in Science for Policy*. Springer, 1990.

[17] D. Garlan. Software engineering in an uncertain world. In *Future of Software Engineering Research workshop*, FoSER '10, pages 125–128, New York, NY, USA, 2010. ACM.

[18] C. F. Gauss, C. H. Davis, and M. of America Project. *Theory of the motion of the heavenly bodies moving about the sun in conic sections*. Boston,Little, Brown and company, 1809. http://www.biodiversitylibrary.org/bibliography/19023.

[19] K. Goseva-Popstojanova and S. Kamavaram. Assessing uncertainty in reliability of component-based software systems. In *Proc. of the 14th International Symposium on Software Reliability Engineering*, ISSRE '03, pages 307–, Washington, DC, USA, 2003. IEEE Computer Society.

[20] K. Goseva-Popstojanova and S. Kamavaram. Software reliability estimation under certainty: generalization of the method of moments. In *Proc. of International Symposium on High Assurance Systems Engineering*, pages 209–218, 2004.

[21] S. Guha, N. Daswani, and R. Jain. An Experimental Study of the Skype Peer-to-Peer VoIP System. In *Proc. of the International Workshop on Peer-to-Peer Systems (IPTPS '06)*, Santa Barbara, CA, 2006.

[22] J. C. Helton, J. D. Johnson, W. Oberkampf, and C. J. Sallaberry. Representation of analysis results involving aleatory and epistemic uncertainty. *Int. J. General Systems*, (6):605–646, 2010.

[23] J. B. Kadane and N. A. Lazar. Methods and criteria for model selection. *Journal of the American Statistical Association*, 99(465):279–290, 2004.

[24] J. Kephart and D. Chess. The vision of autonomic computing. *Computer*, 36(1):41–50, 2003.

[25] I. Meedeniya, A. Aleti, and L. Grunske. Architecture-driven reliability optimization with uncertain model parameters. *J. of Systems and Software*, 85(10):2340–2355, Oct. 2012.

[26] I. Meedeniya, I. Moser, A. Aleti, and L. Grunske. Architecture-based reliability evaluation under uncertainty. In *Proc. of the international conference on Quality of Software Architectures*, QoSA'11, pages 85–94, New York, NY, USA, 2011. ACM.

[27] J. Pang, J. Hendricks, A. Akella, B. Maggs, R. D. Prisco, and S. Seshan. Availability, usage, and deployment characteristics of the domain name system. In *Proc. IMC*, 2004.

[28] J. C. Refsgaard, J. P. van der Sluijs, J. Brown, and P. van der Keur. A framework for dealing with uncertainty due to model structure error. *Advances in Water Resources*, 29(11):1586 – 1597, 2006.

[29] J. C. Refsgaard, J. P. van der Sluijs, A. L. Højberg, and P. A. Vanrolleghem. Uncertainty in the environmental modelling process - a framework and guidance. *Environ. Model. Softw.*, 22(11):1543–1556, Nov. 2007.

[30] J. Stribling. Planetlab all pairs ping. http://infospect.planet-lab.org/pings.

[31] M. Strong, J. E. Oakley, and J. Chilcott. Managing structural uncertainty in health economic decision models: a discrepancy approach. *Journal of the Royal Statistical Society: Series C (Applied Statistics)*, 61(1):25–45, 2012.

[32] C. Trubiani, I. Meedeniya, V. Cortellessa, A. Aleti, and L. Grunske. Model-based performance analysis of software architectures under uncertainty. In *Proc. of the international conference on Quality of Software Architectures*, QoSA '13, pages 69–78, New York, NY, USA, 2013. ACM.

[33] W. Walker, P. HarremoŚs, J. Romans, J. van der Sluus, M. van Asselt, P. Janssen, and M. Krauss. Defining uncertainty. a conceptual basis for uncertainty management in model-based decision support. *Integrated Assessment*, 4(1):5–17, 2003.

[34] J. Whittle, P. Sawyer, N. Bencomo, B. H. C. Cheng, and J.-M. Bruel. Relax: A language to address uncertainty in self-adaptive systems requirement. *Requir. Eng.*, 15(2):177–196, June 2010.

[35] L. Yin, M. Smith, and K. Trivedi. Uncertainty analysis in reliability modeling. In *Proc. of Reliability and Maintainability Symposium, 2001*, pages 229–234, 2001.

On The Limits of Modeling Generational Garbage Collector Performance

Peter Libič*   Lubomír Bulej†   Vojtěch Horký*   Petr Tůma*

*Department of Distributed and Dependable Systems
Faculty of Mathematics and Physics, Charles University, Czech Republic
{libic,horky,tuma}@d3s.mff.cuni.cz

†Faculty of Informatics, University of Lugano, Switzerland
lubomir.bulej@usi.ch

ABSTRACT

Garbage collection is an element of many contemporary software platforms whose performance is determined by complex interactions and is therefore difficult to quantify and model. We investigate the difference between the behavior of a real garbage collector implementation and a simplified model on a selection of workloads, focusing on the accuracy achievable with particular input information (sizes, references, lifetimes). Our work highlights the limits of performance modeling of garbage collection and points out issues of existing evaluation tools that may lead to incorrect experimental conclusions.

Categories and Subject Descriptors

D.4.8 [**Performance**]: Measurements; D.4.2 [**Storage Management**]: Garbage collection

General Terms

Performance

Keywords

performance modeling; garbage collector; java

1. INTRODUCTION

A garbage collector (GC) is an essential part of modern runtime platforms. Whether used in mature virtual machine environments such as Oracle Java Virtual Machine (JVM), and Microsoft Common Language Infrastructure (CLI), in functional languages such as Lisp, and Haskell [15], or in dynamic languages such as Ruby, and JavaScript, the GC plays a major role in the overall system performance.

There are many ways to implement a GC—the design space comprises different algorithms and parameter configurations [10], but there is no single GC that works best for all applications. Some garbage-collected environments provide multiple GC implementations—either to enable workload-specific tuning (Oracle HotSpot JVM), or to facilitate experimental variability for development and evaluation of GC algorithms (Jikes RVM).

The choice of a GC and its configuration can have significant impact on application performance [6], but due to complex interactions between the GC and the application workload, there are no exact guidelines (or algorithm) telling a developer what GC to choose and how to configure it. Instead, developers are given recommendations for trial-and-error tuning [11, 17, 16].

While many developers embraced the GC-based platforms due to increased productivity brought about by automatic memory management, the influence of a GC on application performance is significantly less well understood. Indeed, even in the performance engineering community, the GC overhead is often modeled as a constant factor to be calibrated with other model parameters [5, 25]. However, the accuracy of such models is at best difficult to ascertain, because anomalous GC overhead under certain workloads can account for tens of percents of execution time [12].

Assuming the perspective of an application developer with knowledge of GC principles—but very limited influence on particular GC internals—our goal is to determine whether the developer can get a reasonably intuitive understanding of GC performance, which would allow to relate GC behavior to application-level performance and vice versa. Mismatches between the observed and expected application-level performance would indicate situations where special attention is needed, especially if predictable performance is desired.

To this end, we investigate the performance behavior of a real GC implementation compared to a simplified model implemented as a GC simulator. In particular, we evaluate the model accuracy on a variety of workloads and perform sensitivity analysis with respect to the input describing the application workload. Our contribution is as follows:

- We define simplified models of a one-generation and a two-generation GC, and evaluate their GC prediction accuracy on a variety of workloads, showing surprisingly good results for some of them.

- We analyze how the prediction accuracy depends on the information present in the input data, and discuss the

ICPE'14, March 22–26, 2014, Dublin, Ireland.
Copyright 2014 ACM 978-1-4503-2733-6/14/03 ...$15.00.
http://dx.doi.org/10.1145/2568088.2568097.

results in light of the complex interactions that govern the behavior of contemporary garbage collectors.

- We highlight the limits of GC performance modeling, pointing out issues that hinder experimental evaluation and that may lead to incorrect conclusions with existing tools.

The paper is structured as follows: we complement the introduction with a short overview of related work in Sect. 2. In Sect. 3, we present the general approach applied to modeling one-generation GC in Sect. 4 and two-generation GC in Sect. 5. We analyze model sensitivity to reduced and inaccurate input in Sections 6 and 7, respectively, and conclude the paper in Sect. 8.

2. RELATED WORK

The primary source of information on GC performance is the GC research community—a GC design necessarily needs to make many low-level design decisions related e.g. to barriers, data structures, or traversal algorithms [9, 2, 22, 4, 7], and the overhead of every proposed GC algorithm is carefully evaluated. Despite the insights provided by the research on GC design, it is difficult for both developers and performance engineers to relate the knowledge of GC internals to application-level performance. To gain information on observable performance, benchmarks from established benchmark suites such as SPECjbb, SPECjvm, or DaCapo are typically used. Of these three, the SPECjbb and SPECjvm suites are intended for general JVM performance evaluation, while the DaCapo suite is designed to exercise the GC [6].

A significantly smaller body of work can be found in the area of GC modeling. Since object lifetimes play a major role in GC behavior, an efficient algorithm for collecting the lifetime data has been developed [13] and implemented [20]—yet attempts at modeling garbage collector performance are rare. The performance engineering community typically models GC overhead as a constant factor [5, 25], while more specific models can be mostly found in the domain of GC parameter optimization. Vengerov [23] derived an analytical model for the throughput of the generational GC in the HotSpot JVM, which allows optimizing the sizes reserved for the young and old object generations. White et al. [24] used a control-theoretic approach (a PID controller) to adapt the heap size in response to measured GC overhead.

3. GENERAL APPROACH

In general, our approach is based on comparing the behavior of a GC model to the behavior of a real GC implementation. We consider both a simple one-generation GC and a more common two-generation GC. For each GC type, we define a simplified model based on the principles inherent to that particular type. Compared to a real GC implementation, the model omits technical details (such as what the barriers look like or how the GC manages used and free memory) that an application developer would be unlikely to care about or unable to control.

We use the frequency of garbage collection cycles as the metric to evaluate the model accuracy on. We investigate the reasons for mismatches between the modeled and observed behavior—from the application developer perspective, these mismatches indicate situations where the GC behavior cannot be explained based on the intuitive understanding of the basic principles of GC operation. Knowing what the underlying cause for the mismatch is allows the developer to either look for a GC that behaves more predictably, or adapt the application code to avoid triggering the behavior.

To analyze the sensitivity of the model to the input describing the application workload, we compare the behavior of the real and simulated GC with different inputs, ranging from complete traces (containing object lifetimes, object sizes, and reference updates) to minimal input in form of probability tables (capturing object lifetime and size distributions). In contrast to the existing work, we measure object lifetime in total object allocations, instead of method invocations [20], or total bytes allocated [13].

At this stage, we do not attempt to model GC overhead in terms of execution time, because that is virtually impossible without getting the fundamental metrics right and thus being able to tell when a collection occurs. Our initial experiments suggest that the duration of individual collections is often in an approximately linear relationship with the number of objects surviving the collection, but we defer detailed investigation to future work.

4. ONE-GENERATION COLLECTOR

To validate the feasibility of our approach, we first consider a one-generation GC and build a simplified model with the following assumptions: (a) objects have headers and observe address alignment rules, (b) objects are allocated sequentially in a single heap space, (c) garbage collection is triggered when the heap runs out of free space, (d) all unreachable objects on the heap are reclaimed in a single GC run, and (e) there is no significant fragmentation on the heap.

To determine when (in terms of virtual time represented as object allocation count) a garbage collection occurs, we reason about the operation of a lifetime trace-based simulator. A lifetime trace contains a chronological record of all object allocations in an application, along with size and lifetime (number of allocations until an object becomes unreachable) of each object. Using this trace, the simulator allocates objects as directed, and when the combined size of allocated objects reaches the heap size, a garbage collection is triggered. The simulator then discards all unreachable objects (whose lifetime has expired) from the simulated heap. We model this behavior using the following equation:

$$HS = \left(\sum_{j=n_{i-1}+1}^{n_i} SIZE\,[j] \right) + \left(\sum_{\substack{j \in \{1 \ldots n_{i-1}\} \\ DEATH[j] \geq n_{i-1}}} SIZE\,[j] \right) \quad (1)$$

HS is the size of the modeled heap. In real VMs, this corresponds to setting both the minimal and maximal heap size to this value.[1]

n_i is the virtual time of i-th garbage collection. Since the virtual time is measured in object allocations, we know that i-th GC occurred after allocating n_i objects.

SIZE[j] is the size of j-th allocated object in bytes.

DEATH[j] is the virtual time of j-th object's death (object became unreachable). This happens after allocating

---

[1]Using the -Xmx and -Xms (or similar) parameters.

16

object number $DEATH[j]$ and before allocating object number $DEATH[j] + 1$. Given the lifetime trace, $DEATH[j] = j + LIFETIME[j]$.

The first term of Eq. 1 thus represents the amount of memory occupied by objects allocated between collections $(i-1)$ and i, while the second term represents the amount of memory occupied by objects surviving the previous $(i-1)$ collections. The whole equation must be understood as an approximation—it is unlikely that the allocated object sizes would exactly add up to the given heap size. However, this particular relaxation simplifies reasoning and makes the equation less complex.

For a given application and heap size, the n_i series is the only unknown in Eq. 1. The values of n_i can be computed with the knowledge of object sizes and lifetimes contained in a lifetime trace, but it requires collecting and processing huge amounts of data.

To make the formula more practical, we replace the exact object sizes and lifetimes by averages, which are easier to obtain. The average object size can be measured by observing the individual allocations. The average object lifetime can be determined indirectly, exploiting the fact that it is necessarily equal to the average number of live objects on the heap, which can be calculated from samples of the number of live objects after each garbage collection. Given the average object size OS and the average lifetime LT, we can simplify Eq. 1 into:

$$n_i - n_{i-1} = \frac{HS}{OS} - LT \qquad (2)$$

The equation then captures an intuitive observation that the average number of objects allocated between consecutive collections (left side) must correspond to the average amount of garbage collected per collection (right side).

4.1 Model Evaluation

Although Eq. 2 is fairly simple, the potential loss of accuracy introduced by averaging is difficult to estimate analytically. We have therefore validated Eq. 2 experimentally for the DaCapo 2006.10 benchmark suite [8] running on the Jikes RVM 3.1.0 with the BaseBaseSemiSpace configuration [3].

For each benchmark, the results in Table 1 list the range of evaluated heap sizes, the average lifetimes, the average object sizes, and the ratio of the measured to the predicted collection intervals (i.e. the number of allocations between collections). A ratio of 1.0 means exact prediction, values greater than 1.0 mean Eq. 2 predicts fewer allocations between collections and vice versa.

Given the extreme simplicity of Eq. 2, we consider the results promising—while not usable for accurate performance prediction, they suffice for better-vs-worse analysis and similar uses. We now proceed with a similar investigation for a common two-generation collector.

5. TWO-GENERATION COLLECTOR

Compared to the one-generation GC discussed earlier, the behavior of a two-generation GC is considerably more complex. We make the following assumptions to build our simplified model: (a) objects have headers and observe address alignment rules, (b) sizes reserved for generations are fixed, (d) the young generation uses copying GC, its memory consists of one eden space and two survivor spaces, (e) the old generation uses mark-and-sweep GC, its memory consists of one old space, (b) GC stops the mutator, (f) minor collection

(young generation only) is triggered by full eden space, (g) full collection (both generations) is triggered by close-to-full old space, (h) objects are tenured (promoted from the young to the old generation) after surviving certain number (tenuring threshold) of minor collections, or when a minor collection fills the survivor space, or on a full collection, (i) references pointing from the old to the young generation are in root reference set of minor collections, (j) order of reference traversal is arbitrary, and (k) there is no significant fragmentation on the heap.

Re (b). While generation sizing is usually adaptive, we assume the adaptation to eventually reach a stable state—it is generally recognized that the generation sizes may need to be fixed for optimal performance [16].

Re (d) (e). The choice of a particular type of GC for the young and old generations in our model is not essential—from the modeling perspective, we are mainly interested in the number of memory spaces (and their respective size limits) a particular design uses. We therefore chose to mimic a widely used configuration.

Re (g). The close-to-full condition is modeled by reserving a space in the old generation corresponding to the average size of objects that were promoted during few recent minor collections. The old generation is considered full when the amount of available space drops below this reserve.

Re (j). Order of reference traversal may become important in connection with the tenuring rules. We do not address this aspect due to space constraints.

The above assumptions are a close match for the Serial and Parallel collector configuration found in the HotSpot JVM, and in general fit the GC configuration recommended for maximum throughput in the Oracle HotSpot JVM versions starting with 1.4.

Even after abstracting from the implementation details, the behavior of a two-generation GC remains too complex to hope for useful analogues of Equations 1 and 2—these would turn out to be either overly complex or overly simplified. We therefore proceed by evaluating the model using a simulator.

5.1 Two-Generation GC Simulator

To evaluate the accuracy of our simplified two-generation GC model, we again test the ability of the model to predict the frequency and type (minor or full) of garbage collection cycles. To this end, we have implemented a simulator that takes an application trace, heap configuration, and tenuring threshold as its input and produces a record of all garbage collections triggered during the simulation, including their type and sizes of heap spaces before and after the collection.

The application trace is a more detailed variant of the lifetime trace used for the one-generation GC. Besides object sizes and lifetimes, it also contains records for all reference updates, both in fields and array elements. The heap configuration defines the sizes of the eden and survivor spaces in the young generation, and the size of the old space in the old generation.

During operation, the simulator replays actions from the application trace and keeps track of all objects in all heap spaces, as well as all references that point to objects in the young generation (because such references can make some unreachable objects in the young generation survive minor collections). When a garbage collection is triggered, the simulator performs the appropriate collection and outputs a corresponding collection record.

Table 1: Collection intervals measured / predicted by Eq. 2.

Benchmark	-Xmx, -Xms		LT		OS		Measured / Predicted
antlr	64 −	192 MB	251 293.41 −	266 981.03	65.08 −	65.18	0.88 − 0.95
bloat	128 −	384 MB	459 737.93 −	510 697.55	44.14 −	44.41	0.95 − 1.01
fop	64 −	192 MB	424 407.13 −	483 685.75	48.87 −	49.39	0.94 − 0.96
hsqldb	512 −	1 536 MB	4 182 741.2 −	5 580 740	46.75 −	48.14	0.75 − 0.77
jython	128 −	384 MB	506 214.03 −	506 559.54	69.50 −	69.52	0.79 − 1.00
luindex	64 −	192 MB	239 975.48 −	272 593.07	39.78 −	39.80	0.97 − 1.08
lusearch	128 −	384 MB	281 455.74 −	283 635.68	109.88 −	110.47	1.55 − 1.70
pmd	128 −	384 MB	385 953.04 −	386 825.17	31.35 −	31.36	0.89 − 1.07

5.2 Obtaining Application Traces

There are two basic approaches to obtaining the object lifetime information. The first relies on periodically forcing garbage collection to discover unreachable objects. It is easy to implement but fairly slow and the result accuracy depends on the period between the forced collections. The second approach—based on the Merlin algorithm [13]—is both faster and more accurate, but also more complex and difficult to implement on widely used JVMs.

Because Elephant Tracks [20] (probably the sole currently working implementation of the Merlin algorithm) was not available at the time, and now uses a time metric different from ours, we have developed a tracing tool using DiSL [14] and a custom JVMTI [18] agent. We use the brute force approach to obtain object lifetimes, and always report the granularity (period of forced garbage collections expressed in object allocation units) at which they were collected.

To track object allocations, we instrument the NEW, NEWARRAY, ANEWARRAY, and MULTIANEWARRAY bytecode instructions to report allocation events to the agent, which also receives the VMObjectAlloc events from the JVM. The agent tracks the virtual time (object allocation count) and collects information on object sizes and allocation times. After a specified number of allocations, the agent forces a garbage collection and collects the lifetime information for unreachable objects reported by the JVM via the ObjectFree callback. To track reference updates, we instrument the PUTFIELD and AASTORE bytecode instructions to report reference update events to the agent, which records the new reference and the target it is written to.

5.3 Model Evaluation

To evaluate the accuracy of the model implemented by the GC simulator, we again compare the frequency of young generation and old generation GC cycles reported by the simulator to that observed on a real GC implementation. We perform all experiments on the OpenJDK 1.6.0-22 JVM[2], with heap spaces fixed to predefined sizes and adaptive heap space sizing disabled.[3] This also results in fixing the tenuring threshold at the default value of seven.

We collect the application traces for selected workloads from the DaCapo 9.12-bach benchmark suite [8]—here, we

report specifically on the batik, fop, xalan and tomcat workloads. Given that these are fixed-duration benchmarks, the evaluation metric can be simplified to the number of garbage collection cycles.

Because all the workloads have relatively modest memory footprints, we iterate over each workload 100 times.[4] To provide an alternative scaling method, we implemented a modified benchmark harness that executes multiple copies of the same workload in parallel and uses multiple class loaders and separate data directories to isolate the executing workload instances. Using this harness, we run the workloads in 8 threads, iterating over each workload 10 times in each thread. Due to various technical issues, this scaling method works reliably only with the fop workload, which we refer to as multifop.

Limiting the spectrum of the benchmark workloads was motivated by different factors for each workload. The eclipse, tradebeans and tradesoap workloads use class loading in a manner that is not compatible with the code instrumentation required by our experiments. The avrora, lusearch and luindex workloads do not exhibit interesting behavior with respect to garbage collection frequencies. The h2 and jython workloads generate an excessively large trace that our infrastructure was not able to accommodate.

We should point out that despite omitting some workloads, the range of experiments we perform is still extreme—a single set of traces from the selected workloads is close to quarter of a terabyte in size. Just collecting such a set takes over a month of parallel execution time on a 2.33 GHz eight-core machine, and the time to simulate the considered heap size configurations for a single workload—a single line in some of the plots presented later—is measured in days.

We first report the results obtained when providing the simulator with a complete application trace, which includes object lifetimes, sizes, and reference updates.

For the baseline evaluation, the application traces were collected with the following granularities: 10000 allocations for batik and fop, 2000 allocations for multifop and tomcat, and 1000 allocations for xalan. These choices help maintain variability between the experiments while balancing accuracy and overhead.

For the heap size configuration, we use a combination of 8 young generation sizes and 6 old generation sizes, yielding 48 heap size configurations for each benchmark. The range of young generation sizes is the same for all benchmarks: 16, 24, 32, 48, 64, 96, 128, and 192 MB. The size of each of the two survivor spaces is always 1/8 of the young generation

---

[2]OpenJDK Runtime Environment IcedTea 6 1.10.3 Gentoo Build 1.6.0-22-b22 and OpenJDK 64-Bit Server VM Build 20.0-b11 Mixed Mode

[3]Using the -XX:ParallelGCThreads=1 -XX:-UsePSAdaptiveSurvivorSizePolicy -XX:NewSize -XX:MaxNewSize -Xmx -Xms JVM options.

[4]Using the DaCapo -no-pre-iteration-gc -n100 options.

size, leaving the remaining 6/8 for the eden space. The range of old generation sizes is given in the following table—the benchmarks differ in memory requirements, we therefore choose the ranges so that the smallest size in the range is always close to the bare minimum required to execute the benchmark.

Due to space limitations, we plot results from this and the following two sections together in Figures 1–12. The legend to the plot labels is in Table 2, the first four labels are relevant to this section. While this arrangement makes it difficult to discern individual results, it fits the goal of illustrating the differences between results of various experimental configurations in the limited space of the paper.

Benchmark	Old generation sizes (MB)					
batik	128	160	192	256	384	512
fop	64	128	192	256	384	512
multifop	256	288	320	384	512	1024
tomcat	48	64	96	128	192	256
xalan	160	192	256	384	512	768

Table 2: Plot legend labels

Legend label	Configuration
JVM: JIT	JVM in default mode with JIT enabled
JVM: no JIT	JVM in interpreted mode (-Xint option)
JVM: DiSL	JVM with instrumented code
Default	Simulator with complete input
P(survived)	Simulator with lifetime trace and probability of object being marked and because of that surviving
P(marked)	Simulator with lifetime trace and probability of object being marked
LT&SZ only	Simulator with lifetime trace and object sizes only
Generated 1	Simulator with generated lifetime trace, seed 1
Generated 2	Simulator with generated lifetime trace, seed 2

The plots in Fig. 1 and in Fig. 2 show the young generation GC counts for the fop and multifop workloads, respectively. The results obtained from the GC model simulator with full application trace as an input are labeled *Default*, while the results observed on a real GC are labeled *JVM: JIT*. We omit plots for other workloads to save space, because all result variants are very similar to fop, and in general show good accuracy with the exception of the multifop workload.

The minor collection counts for the simulated and the real GC should approximately equal the total size of all allocated objects divided by the eden size. The large difference between the simulated and the observed collection counts therefore indicates that the total sizes of objects observed during the trace collection and during the actual JVM execution differ. The reason for the difference rests with the escape analysis performed by the JIT. It is used to introduce stack allocation for objects that only exist in the scope of one method. Because our instrumentation calls a native method with a newly allocated object as a parameter, it makes all object escape and thus effectively disables the stack allocation.

Until we can include this optimization in the GC model, we can disable it by running the benchmarks with the tracing instrumentation inserted (even when no agent is using it). In the plots, the results of this configuration are labeled

JVM: DiSL. The minor collection counts from the simulator then become very similar to the counts observed in the instrumented JVM. As a sanity check, we also execute the benchmarks in interpreted mode, with results labeled *JVM: no JIT* in the plots. We should point out that this particular issue is likely to impact all tools that rely on instrumentation to collect traces, even when those tools claim to be precise, such as Elephant Tracks [20].

The plots in Figures 3, 5, 7, 9 and 11 show the full GC counts for the batik, fop, tomcat, xalan, and multifop workloads, respectively. The results from the GC model simulator obtained using complete application trace are labeled *Default*, while the results from a real GC observed in three JVM runs—default, instrumented, and interpreted—are labeled *JVM: JIT*, *JVM: DiSL*, and *JVM: no JIT*, respectively. Depending on the workload and heap configuration, the prediction accuracy varies from very high (fop in smaller heap) to very low (tomcat in smaller heap). The plots alone contribute to our goal of illustrating how far a simplified model explains a real GC implementation. We analyze some reasons in more detail in the following sections.

6. IMPACT OF REDUCED INPUT

In this section we complement the baseline evaluation with experiments that focus on finding the limits and trends in model accuracy depending on the available input data. Complete application trace—lifetimes, object sizes and reference updates—are huge, easily into gigabytes for workloads that only take a few minutes to execute. Collecting such traces is neither always possible nor always practical, and simulation with complete input data is also computationally expensive—merely reading the input data usually takes longer than executing the workloads. It is therefore important to understand what accuracy can be expected when some of the input data is aggregated or approximated, which is an approach any practical models would have to follow.

In Sect. 6.1, we approximate the reference updates information in the input data with a single probability value, leaving only the lifetimes and object sizes. In Sect. 6.2, we experiment with ignoring the reference updates altogether. And finally, in Sect. 6.3, we also replace object lifetimes and sizes with probability distributions.

6.1 Lifetime Trace with Mark Probabilities

This is the experiment where we start to shrink the model input data. We start with the reference update trace, which usually makes up more than 80 % of the input size. Our goal is to discard this data but still model the fact that some unreachable objects in the young generation survive minor collections due to references from the old generation.

Our approach is to replace the reference update trace with one of two stochastic approximations. We compute the probability that an object is reachable from the old generation—marked for short—during a minor garbage collection, either for all objects (denoted *P(marked)*) or for objects whose lifetime has expired (denoted *P(survived)*). For illustration, we show the probabilities for fop in Fig. 13 and for tomcat in Fig. 14. Both probabilities are relatively stable for a given young generation size across all our benchmarks, we therefore evaluate our model with one value of *P(marked)* and one value of *P(survived)* for each young generation size.

We calculate the average probabilities for each heap configuration using our simulator—we were hoping to approximate

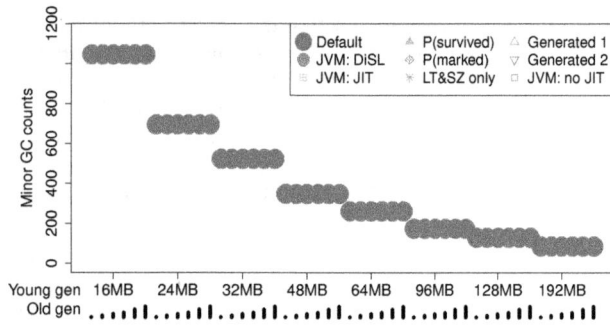

Figure 1: Young GC counts: fop

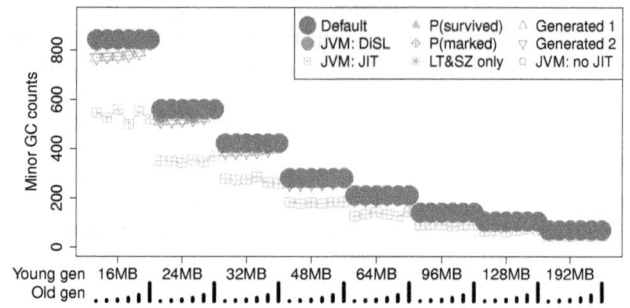

Figure 2: Young GC counts: multifop

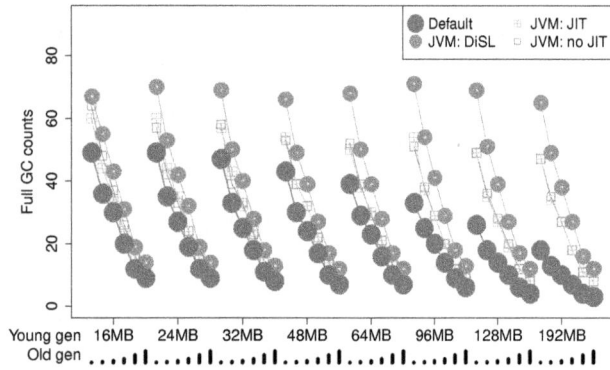

Figure 3: Full GC counts – JVM: batik

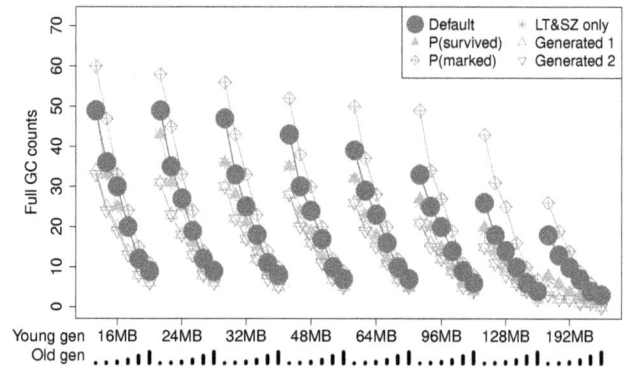

Figure 4: Full GC counts – simulators: batik

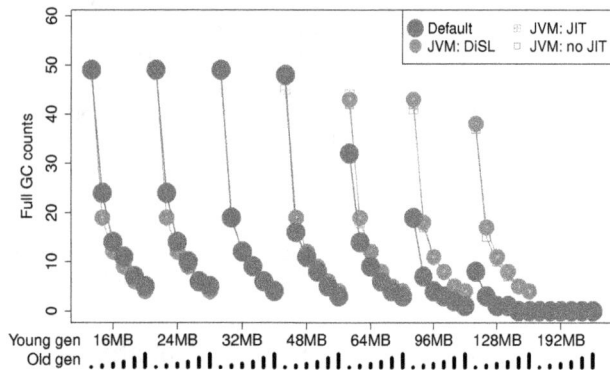

Figure 5: Full GC counts – JVM: fop

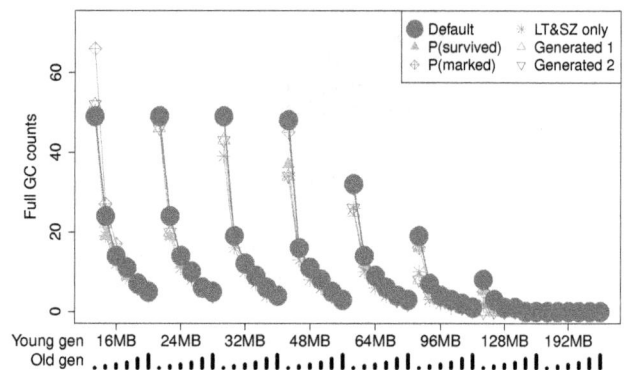

Figure 6: Full GC counts – simulators: fop

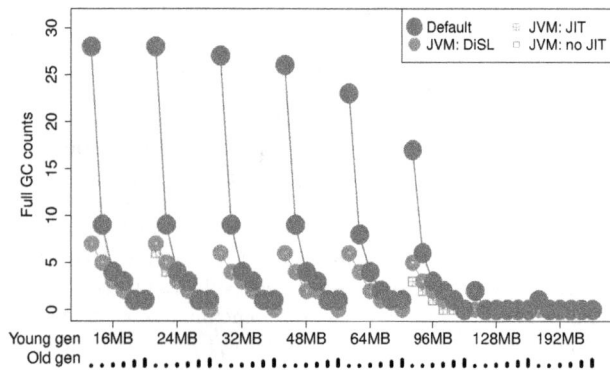

Figure 7: Full GC counts – JVM: tomcat

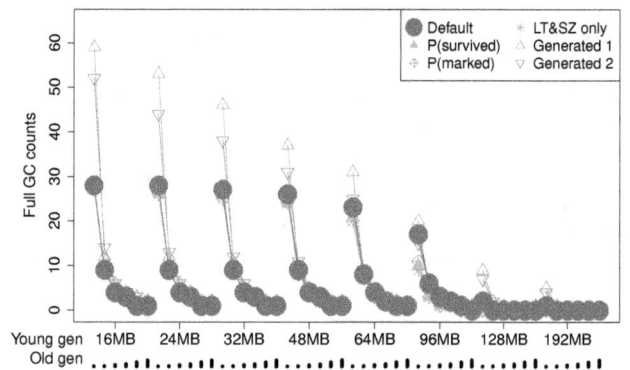

Figure 8: Full GC counts – simulators: tomcat

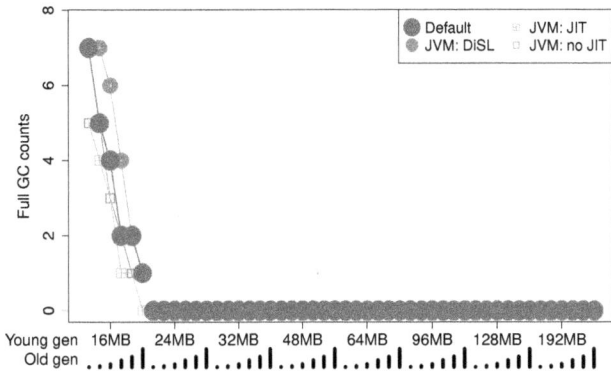

Figure 9: Full GC counts – JVM: xalan

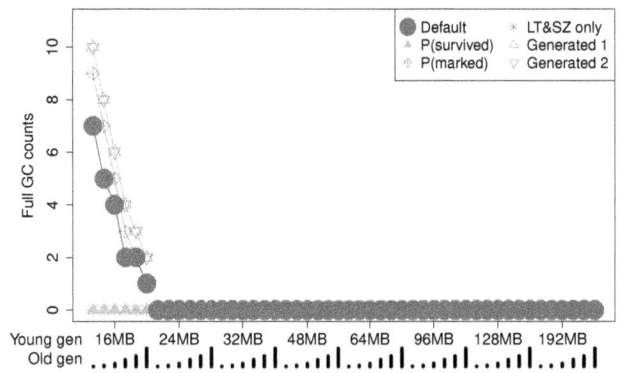

Figure 10: Full GC counts – simulators: xalan

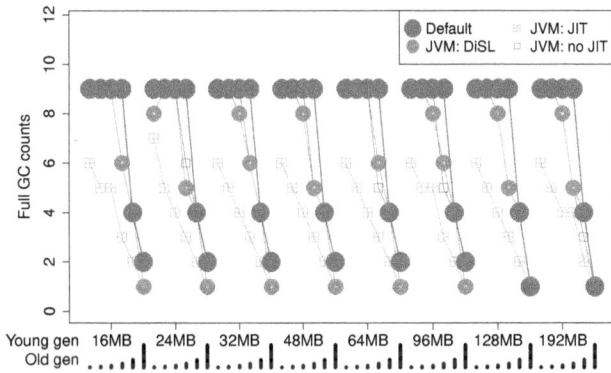

Figure 11: Full GC counts – JVM: multifop

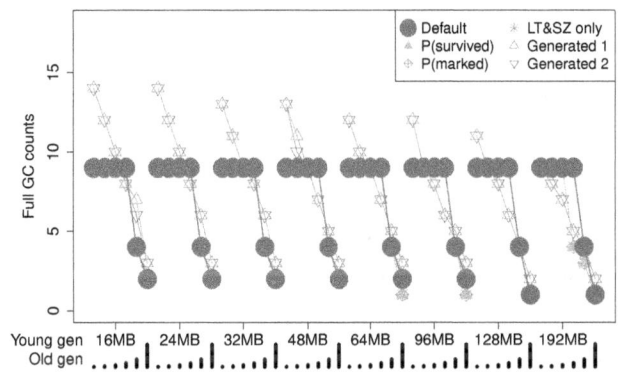

Figure 12: Full GC counts – simulators: multifop

the probabilities from some benchmark or configuration characteristic, but we have not found a way to do so.

When using the *P(marked)* probability, the simulator randomly marks all objects in the young generation every minor collection, with probability *P(marked)*. When using the *P(survived)* probability, the simulator randomly marks only those objects whose lifetime has expired, with probability *P(survived)*. In both cases, the marked objects survive the minor collection regardless of their actual lifetime.

The results from the experiments described in this section are in Figures 4, 6, 8, 10 and 12. The results labeled *Default* are from simulations with complete input, the results labeled *P(marked)* and *P(survived)* are from simulations that respectively use one of the two probabilities.

6.2 Lifetime Trace Only

In this set of experiments, we completely avoid reference updates and use only lifetime and size of objects. This means that no unreachable objects survive the simulated collection—both minor and full collections are complete. The number of minor collections should not change, the number of full collections can be smaller than in the previous experiments—this is confirmed in Figures 4, 6, 8, 10 and 12, where the results from this experiment are labeled *LT&SZ only*.

6.3 Lifetime and Size Distributions

The last set of experiments uses the smallest input, replacing the entire trace with a table that tells the probability of records with particular lifetime and object size appearing in the trace. The table consists of buckets that correspond to lifetime ranges, each bucket lists unique object sizes and counts for objects with that lifetime. In addition to the table, which characterizes lifetimes and object sizes, we use the *P(survived)* probability from Sect. 6.1.

The lifetime ranges are used to keep the table reasonably small, however, we have to be careful to avoid losing too much information. Accuracy is essential for objects with small lifetimes, where fluctuations influence the tenuring decision, and for objects with large lifetimes, where fluctuations influence average old generation occupancy. In contrast, knowing medium lifetimes accurately is of smaller importance. We use tables of 200 buckets, with eight lifetime ranges for the smallest lifetimes and five lifetime ranges for the largest lifetimes growing and shrinking in logarithmic steps, the ranges of the remaining buckets are of equal size.

The buckets keep exact sizes and counts. Our benchmarks use only about 500 to 1200 different object sizes, which makes keeping exact sizes possible. For workloads that generate objects of many different sizes (for example arrays with varying sizes), we would modify the algorithm to create size buckets as well.

To avoid potentially error-prone modifications, we keep our simulator as is and run it on synthetic traces that conform to the description in the table—that is, we first compute the tables that characterize our benchmarks and then simulate GC on traces generated from these tables. The procedure of generating such traces is described next.

21

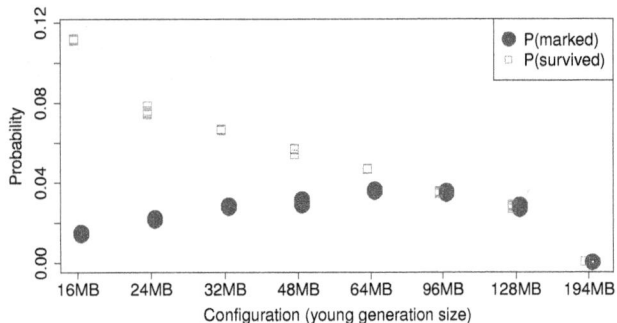

Figure 13: Mark probabilities: fop

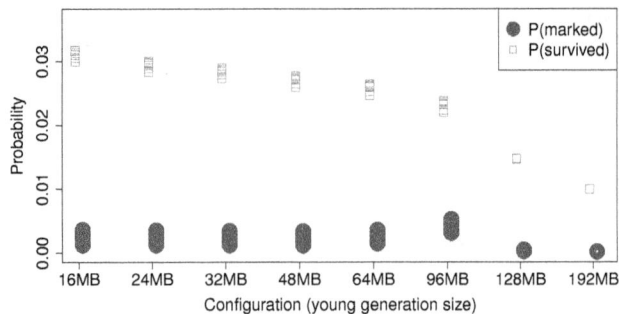

Figure 14: Mark probabilities: tomcat

Trace Generator Description.

The procedure of generating a trace from the table of lifetimes and sizes is complicated by the fact that individual lifetimes are not independent random variables—in particular, when there are only N allocation events left to generate in the trace, the biggest lifetime the allocated object can have is also N.

Our trace generation algorithm addresses the problem as follows. At any moment, we know the number of allocation events still to be generated (denoted N), the bucket whose lifetime range includes N (here called the oldest bucket), and the number of objects to be generated from the oldest bucket (denoted I). For the oldest bucket, we prepare I random lifetimes in the corresponding lifetime range, sorted by value. When N is greater than the oldest prepared lifetime, we pick a random bucket and a random size from that bucket and emit a corresponding allocation event into the generated trace. When N reaches the oldest prepared lifetime in the oldest bucket, we pick a random size from that bucket and emit an allocation event with the oldest prepared lifetime and the chosen size. After emitting an event, we decrement N (this may designate new bucket as the oldest bucket), decrement the count of objects of the used size in the used bucket, and remove the prepared lifetime from the oldest bucket if applicable.

The random bucket choice uses a discrete probability distribution, the probability of picking a bucket corresponds to the share of objects to be generated from the bucket. The random lifetimes are picked from a uniform distribution with minimum and maximum corresponding to the lifetime range of the bucket. For practical reasons, we do not prepare the random lifetimes for the buckets with shortest lifetimes.

We present results of two simulations for each benchmark. The input was created using the trace generation algorithm with two different random number generator seeds. The results are displayed in Figures 4, 6, 8, 10 and 12. We use the legend labels *Generated 1* and *Generated 2* for the data.

6.4 Accuracy Metric

Besides the visual evaluation using the plots in Figures 5–12, we also provide a numeric accuracy metric. Among typical model evaluation metrics are the ratio of the model results to the measured values, or the proportion of successful predictions (i.e. results within tolerance) to all predictions.

In our case, such metrics would allow reporting arbitrarily good accuracy by including more configurations where no collections happen—as in the xalan workload. We therefore use a metric based on the relative area difference in the

plots, which eliminates the effect of configurations with no collections. We denote this metric as inaccuracy, calculated as follows:

$$Inaccuracy = \frac{AREA_{differences}}{AREA_{baseline}} \qquad (3)$$

The $AREA_{differences}$ is the area between the two lines of plots we compare and $AREA_{baseline}$ is the area under the plot depicting the baseline—the two areas, which can overlap, are shown on the following illustration.

For the scale, we use collection count on the vertical axis and equidistant units on the horizontal axis. For the full collections, the results are shown in Table 3. We use the instrumented JVM runs as the baseline. The smaller the value is, the better the accuracy—zero means perfect fit.

The table shows that although the results across benchmarks fluctuate, the overall tendency is a gradual decrease in accuracy as the inputs are reduced. As an anomaly, the accuracy with the reduced input based on *P(marked)* appears better than the accuracy with full input. This is due to the fact that using *P(marked)* leads to overestimating the number of objects surviving young collections, and because the model with full input tends to predict fewer collections, this overestimation turns out to be helpful.

Table 3: Inaccuracy for full collections

Simulator	batik	fop	multifop	tomcat	xalan
Default	0.46	0.28	0.14	1.31	0.26
P(marked)	0.30	0.35	0.13	1.09	0.13
P(survived)	0.57	0.30	0.13	1.10	1.00
LT&SZ only	0.57	0.38	0.13	1.08	1.00
Generated 1	0.66	0.36	0.23	2.39	0.17
Generated 2	0.67	0.36	0.22	2.26	0.17

Overall: *Default* 0.41, *P(marked)* 0.32,
P(survived) 0.48, *LT&SZ only* 0.50, *Generated* 0.60

6.5 Results Discussion

From the results presented on the GC count plots (Figures 1–12), we can tell that the simulation gives accurate counts of minor collections, but the accuracy of the full collection counts is limited. This is mostly an expected result, because our simplified model does not capture all the behavior of the JVM collector implementation and because the input trace is not precise—we illustrate the sensitivity to inputs in Sect. 7.

The good accuracy in predicting minor collections is related to the simplicity of the triggering condition. The matching results confirm that the total size of the objects in the trace is roughly the same as in the real application run. We have observed only one exception (especially visible in the multifop workload), which we attribute to the use of escape analysis for stack allocation. We have separated the effect in evaluation by using the instrumented JVM runs as the baseline.

Another optimization that could affect the accuracy is the usage of Thread-Local Allocation Buffers (TLAB)—small memory buffers the threads allocate from to minimize locking. Among our workloads, xalan, tomcat and multifop use more mutator threads, but the results show no anomalies, we therefore conclude that TLAB use does not affect the minor collection count considerably.

Restricting the input data sets cannot impact the predicted minor collection count except for the randomly generated traces. In the other experiments, the total size of objects in the traces does not change and therefore the minor collection counts must remain the same as well. For the generated traces, some differences may occur in principle, but our results show they are small—the total inaccuracy in predicting minor collections in the two simulations with generated traces is 0.069 and 0.072, almost the same as in the simulations with measured traces (0.068 across all traces).

When it comes to the full collection counts, we can summarize the results as follows: good accuracy for multifop and xalan, often but not always good accuracy for fop, poor accuracy for batik and tomcat workloads. This summary is for the JVM runs with instrumentation enabled, which isolates the escape analysis issue.

One reason for the poor accuracy cases rests with the trace collection method, as analyzed in [13]. For a particular tracing granularity, the collected lifetimes increase on average by half the granularity value. This increase is reflected in larger live heap sizes and should therefore cause more collections. This is not what we observe, however—when inaccurate, the simulator tends to predict fewer full collections. This suggests our trace collection method is not the (sole) cause of the result inaccuracy.

As an important observation, we note that the full GC counts are fractions of 100 ($100/X - 1$ for various X, i.e. 99, 49, 32, 24) for a surprisingly large number of heap configurations. Given that we use 100 iterations in the DaCapo workloads, this is unlikely to be a coincidence. We illustrate the effect in detail in Fig. 15, where we show the full collection counts for fop across more heap configurations—the old generation sizes are 44, 48, 52, 56, 60, 64, 72, 80, 88, 96, 112, 128, 160, 192, 224, 256, 320 and 384 MB. The data points would normally roughly follow the $1/x$ hyperbolic shape, as is the case for the 128 MB young generation size, but the results show clusters at 49, 32 and 24 collections (emphasized by dotted lines in the plot) for the other three young generation sizes.

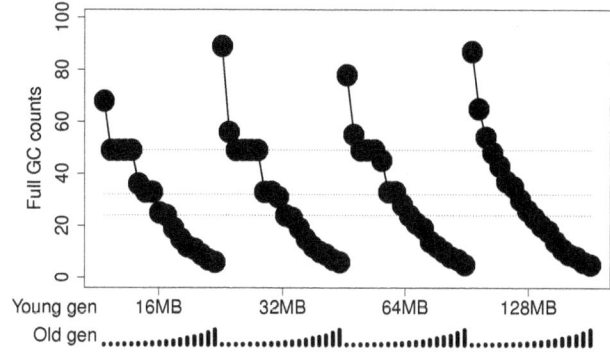

Figure 15: Dense configurations: fop

To explain this phenomenon, we look into how the live size of the workloads changes in time. Using the allocation count as the time unit, we plot the live heap sizes calculated from the traces of the batik, fop, multifop and tomcat workloads. Figures 16 and 18 show the first four iterations out of 100 for fop and batik, Fig. 17 the first four out of 10 for multifop, and Fig. 19 the first nine out of 100 for tomcat. The sawtooth shape suggests all four workloads release most of the objects allocated in each iteration. Additionally, the gradual rise between iterations in tomcat resembles a memory leak.

The sawtooth shape is due to the way the DaCapo harness implements iterations. Most of the objects allocated in an iteration become garbage at the iteration end. This makes the minimum memory requirements of the workload (minimum heap size where the workload still executes) close to the minimum memory requirements of a single iteration. Each new iteration will allocate new objects and unless the heap size exceeds the minimum requirements at least twice, GC will be triggered. This GC will release objects from the past iterations (which since became garbage), providing enough memory for this iteration but not the next one, and the entire cycle will repeat. As a result, the number of collections will match the number of iterations for any heap size between the minimum requirements and twice the minimum requirements. Along the same lines, the number of collections will be half the number of iterations if two but not three iterations fit the heap size, and so on. This explains the clusters in Fig. 15.

The sawtooth shape not only makes the workload less sensitive to heap size changes, it also makes the GC more difficult to predict. Clearly, a GC cycle triggered just before the end of an iteration will free much less memory than a GC cycle triggered just after the end of an iteration, even though the two can be just a few allocations apart. The impact on GC count can be large because the former situation will require another GC sooner rather than later, and there is no guarantee the new GC will be more successful. As an example of this effect, the batik workload (configuration with 16 MB young and 128 MB old generation) triggers full garbage collections with the live sizes of 60 MB in the instrumented JVM and 40 MB in the default simulator. This is a major factor for the prediction accuracy results we observe.

Our analysis is further supported by the difference in results between the default simulator and the simulation with generated traces—the traces generated from the tables do not exhibit the sawtooth shape of the live heap size, making the clusters disappear. This is very visible on the results for the

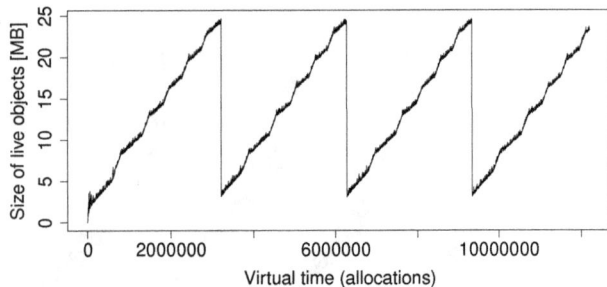

Figure 16: Partial live size trace: fop

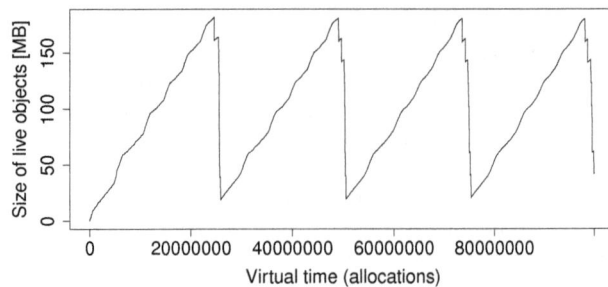

Figure 17: Partial live size trace: multifop

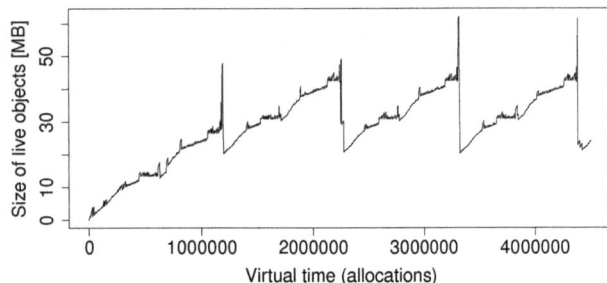

Figure 18: Partial live size trace: batik

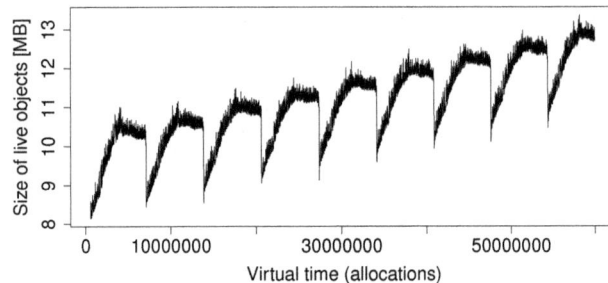

Figure 19: Partial live size trace: tomcat

multifop workload (Fig. 12), where horizontal clusters evident when simulating real traces change into gradual slopes with the generated traces.

Finally, the gradual rise in the live heap size between iterations in tomcat also complicates predictions. As the heap becomes more and more occupied, the GC frequency increases and any loss of accuracy is magnified.

7. IMPACT OF INACCURATE INPUT

Collecting inputs for the GC model simulator is non-trivial and not always guaranteed to provide fully accurate information—this is most pronounced in the case of object lifetimes, where the collection granularity directly influences lifetime accuracy (see Sect. 5.2). Technically, the inaccuracy due to data collection process results in different values for object sizes and lifetimes in the input data—we can as well modify the input data ourselves to determine how certain changes in the workload, e.g. systematically allocating more objects or enlarging object sizes, influence the GC behavior.

We therefore perform sensitivity analysis to determine how certain changes in object lifetimes and sizes impact the model results. For object lifetimes, we consider changes due to an additive constant, a multiplicative factor, a random error, and limits on the minimum and maximum lifetimes. For object sizes, we consider changes due to an additive constant, a multiplicative factor, and a random error. Due to space limitations, we only report results for changes due to a multiplicative factor, and a random error.

7.1 Sensitivity to Lifetime Changes

Multiplying object lifetimes by a constant factor models two hypothetical situations. In the first, a process collecting lifetime information systematically ignores certain allocations, perhaps because it could not instrument all paths in the JVM that allocate objects. In the other, we may be interested in

what happens if a certain workload started to systematically allocate more objects with short lifetimes. In both cases, if either the missing or additional allocations were spread evenly throughout the workload, it would correspond to scaling all object lifetimes.

Figure 20 shows how the number of full collections changes when all lifetimes are scaled using a constant factor, i.e. $l' = l \times k$ for chosen values of k. For $k < 1$, the object lifetimes are shortened, and the resulting trace may contain reference updates on objects whose lifetime has already expired—we remove such invalid reference updates from the trace. We only investigate the impact on the number of full collections, because minor collections are lifetime insensitive.

The results illustrate how lifetime scaling interacts with the young generation size. For a young generation that is small relative to the workload requirements (16 MB), the effect of scaling the lifetimes down is subdued—most objects still live long enough to be promoted and cause full collections. For a young generation that is large relative to the workload requirements (64 MB), it is the effect of scaling the lifetime up that is subdued—most objects that die young before scaling also die young afterwards.

Adding a random error to object lifetimes models the effect of collecting lifetimes with a particular collection granularity, which necessarily impacts our experiments (c.f. Sect. 5.2). To include both frequent small deviations and occassional large ones, we model the error as a random variable with a shifted exponential distribution, the observations of which are added the object lifetimes, i.e. $l' = l + Exp(1/\mu) - \mu$ for chosen values of μ. We adjust the possibly negative lifetimes so that the modification preserves the average lifetime.

The results for selected values of μ are shown in Fig. 21. The observed effects are again related to the young generation size—the average object size in fop is 95 B, a young generation of 16 MB can accommodate about 155000 such objects, an object therefore has to live at least around million allocations

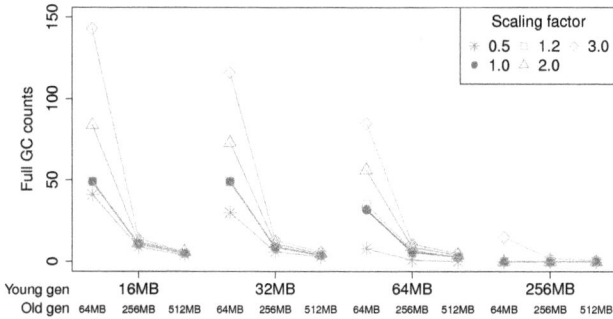

Figure 20: Lifetime scaling: fop

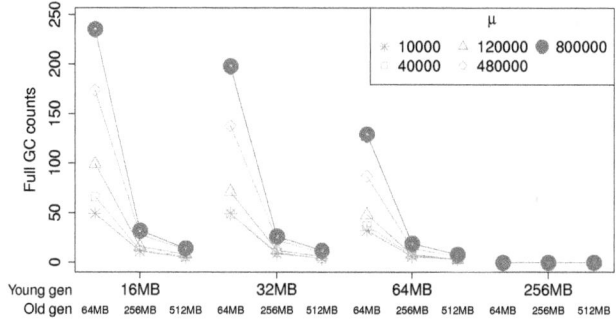

Figure 21: Lifetime randomization: fop

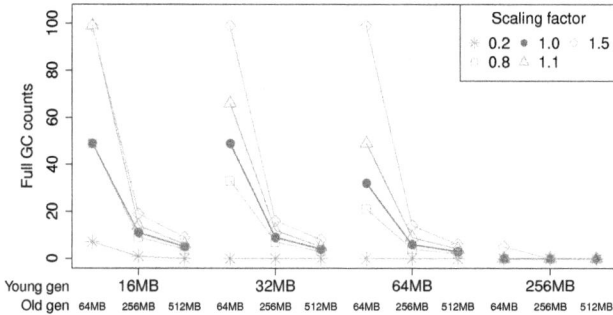

Figure 22: Size scaling: fop

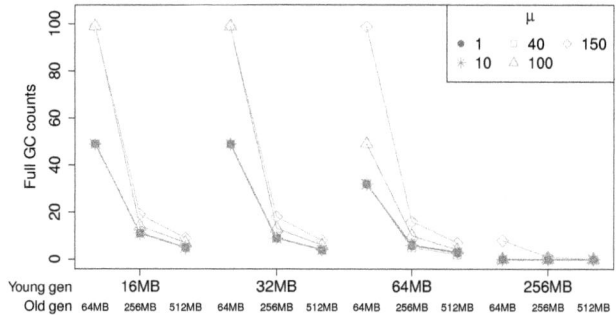

Figure 23: Size randomization: fop

to be tenured. With larger young generations, the numbers grow further, making it less likely that the positive random errors get enough objects tenured to impact the number of full collections. The negative random errors in our experiment are bounded by μ and therefore even less significant than the positive ones.

7.2 Sensitivity to Object Size Changes

Multiplying objects sizes by a constant factors models a situation where we change the size of a fundamental data type that is used by most objects, e.g. by introducing compressed references [1] to reduce memory overhead on 64-bit systems.

Figure 22 shows how the number of full collections changes when all object sizes are scaled using a constant factor, that is, $s' = s \times k$ for chosen values of k. The results again highlight the clustering effect discussed in Sect. 6.5—for the young generation size of 16 MB, deflating all objects by 20 % has no effect, and inflating all objects by 10 % has the same effect as inflating by 50 %.

Adding a random error to object sizes again models the inaccuracies we may encounter when collecting application traces, e.g. a systematic measurement error due to object size alignment rules. Again, we model the error as a random variable with a shifted exponential distribution, the observations of which are added the object sizes, that is, $s' = s + Exp(1/\mu) - \mu$ for chosen values of μ.

The results for selected values of μ are shown in Fig. 23. They again confirm the clustering effect and show that it is not sensitive to small changes in object size.

8. CONCLUSION

Motivated by the need to understand garbage collection behavior from the application developer perspective, and

some motivating results from one-generation GC, our work uses extensive experiments to compare the behavior of a real GC implementation with the behavior of a simplified model, such as the developer may form based on commonly available information [19, 21].

Given an almost-complete information about workload behavior in the form of application traces with object sizes, lifetimes, and reference updates, we show that the model can fairly accurately predict frequency of minor garbage collections in a two-generation GC.

The model retains a relatively stable prediction quality across workloads and inputs ranging from full application traces to probabilistic distributions of object sizes and lifetimes. However, predicting the frequency of full collections for the very same two-generation GC turns out to be a very different story—even with full application trace used as the simulator input, the prediction quality is mediocre, ranging from 14 % inaccuracy to 131 % inaccuracy in our examples.

We illustrate how the prediction quality gradually deteriorates as the inputs of the model are reduced. The overall tendency is a gradual decrease, from 41 % inaccuracy to 60 % inaccuracy in our metric. Looking at the individual workloads, the inaccuracy could be much worse, exceeding 200 % in case of tomcat.

The prediction quality ultimately depends on the ability of the GC model to accurately evaluate the GC triggering conditions. In the case of the full collections, this seems to be particularly difficult, because small changes in the input or in the interactions among detailed features can significantly impact the observed behavior. In our experiments, we have seen how reducing object size by 20 % did not impact full collection count at all, or how increasing object size by 10 %

doubled the full collection count, but further increase by 40 % did not have an impact anymore.

This is unfortunate from the developer perspective, who would naturally expect a reasonable reaction to workload changes. While we explain the causes for such behavior when analyzing the results, we were only able to do that with detailed insight, which goes beyond the basic principles our GC model is built with. Therefore, besides illustrating the complex character of interactions that govern the behavior of contemporary garbage collectors, our work also explains why—rather than getting definite instructions on garbage collector configuration—application developers are instead given recommendations for trial-and-error tuning.

Our experiments are also related to the available knowledge about sensitivity to workload parameters. Earlier work [13] points out that exact knowledge of object lifetimes is important for accurate simulation of several garbage collector metrics including ratio of live to allocated objects or number of reference updates that cross generation boundaries. We illustrate the sensitivity to lifetime changes and object size changes on the simplified model.

Finally, our experiments draw attention to drawbacks of the existing garbage collector evaluation methods. One concerns the process of collecting the workload traces—we highlight how program instrumentation interferes with the escape analysis, effectively disabling a class of stack allocation optimizations. This makes it possible to better qualify the behavior of tools that use instrumentation to collect the workload traces, such as Elephant Tracks [20]. While such tools may collect an accurate trace of the allocation operations in the application, this is not necessarily an accurate trace of the operations that manipulate the heap.

The final issue concerns the behavior of the workload scaling method in the DaCapo benchmark suite [8]. The repetition of isolated workload instances creates memory usage profiles that regularly make most objects unreachable, leading to possibly anomalous situations where changes in the heap size have no impact on the garbage collection frequency.

To complement our submission, complete tools and results are available on-line at http://d3s.mff.cuni.cz/papers/gc-modeling-icpe.

Acknowledgements

This work was partially supported by the Czech Science Foundation project GACR P202/10/J042, the EU project ASCENS 257414, the Swiss National Science Foundation project CRSII2_136225, and the Charles University institutional funding.

9. REFERENCES

[1] A. Adl-Tabatabai et al. Improving 64-bit Java IPF performance by compressing heap references. In *CGO*, 2004.

[2] T. A. Anderson. Optimizations in a private nursery-based garbage collector. In *ISMM*, 2010.

[3] B. Alpern et al. The jalapeño virtual machine. *IBM Syst. J.*, 39(1), Jan. 2000.

[4] K. Barabash and E. Petrank. Tracing garbage collection on highly parallel platforms. In *ISMM*, 2010.

[5] S. Becker, H. Koziolek, and R. Reussner. The Palladio component model for model-driven performance prediction. *J. Syst. Softw.*, 82(1), 2009.

[6] S. M. Blackburn, P. Cheng, and K. S. McKinley. Myths and realities: the performance impact of garbage collection. *Perform. Eval. Rev.*, 32(1), 2004.

[7] S. M. Blackburn and K. S. McKinley. Immix: a mark-region garbage collector with space efficiency, fast collection, and mutator performance. In *PLDI*, 2008.

[8] S. M. Blackburn et al. The DaCapo benchmarks: Java benchmarking development and analysis. *SIGPLAN Not.*, 41(10), 2006.

[9] D. Detlefs, C. Flood, S. Heller, and T. Printezis. Garbage-first garbage collection. In *ISMM*, 2004.

[10] R. Jones, A. Hosking, and E. Moss. *The Garbage Collection Handbook: The Art of Automatic Memory Management*. Chapman & Hall/CRC, 1st edition, 2011.

[11] S. Joshi and V. Liaskovitis. *Java Garbage Collection Characteristics and Tuning Guidelines for Apache Hadoop TeraSort Workload*, 2010.

[12] P. Libič, P. Tůma, and L. Bulej. Issues in performance modeling of applications with garbage collection. In *QUASOSS*, 2009.

[13] M. Hertz et al. Generating object lifetime traces with merlin. *ACM Trans. Program. Lang. Syst.*, 28(3), May 2006.

[14] L. Marek, Y. Zheng, D. Ansaloni, W. Binder, Z. Qi, and P. Tuma. DiSL: an extensible language for efficient and comprehensive dynamic program analysis. In *DSAL*, 2012.

[15] S. Marlow, T. Harris, R. P. James, and S. Peyton Jones. Parallel generational-copying garbage collection with a block-structured heap. In *ISMM*, 2008.

[16] Oracle. *Java SE 6 HotSpot Virtual Machine Garbage Collection Tuning*. http://www.oracle.com/technetwork/java/javase/gc-tuning-6-140523.html.

[17] Oracle. *Tuning Garbage Collection with the 5.0 Java Virtual Machine*, 2003. http://www.oracle.com/technetwork/java/gc-tuning-5-138395.html.

[18] Oracle. *JavaTM Virtual Machine Tool Interface*, 2011. http://docs.oracle.com/javase/6/docs/technotes/guides/jvmti/.

[19] T. Printezis. *Garbage Collection in the Java HotSpot Virtual Machine*, 2004. http://www.devx.com/Java/Article/21977.

[20] N. P. Ricci, S. Z. Guyer, and J. E. B. Moss. Elephant tracks: portable production of complete and precise gc traces. In *ISMM*, 2013.

[21] Sun Microsystems, Inc. Memory management in the Java HotSpot virtual machine. http://www.oracle.com/technetwork/java/javase/memorymanagement-whitepaper-150215.pdf, 2006.

[22] K. Ueno, A. Ohori, and T. Otomo. An efficient non-moving garbage collector for functional languages. In *ICFP*, 2011.

[23] D. Vengerov. Modeling, analysis and throughput optimization of a generational garbage collector. In *ISMM*, 2009.

[24] D. R. White, J. Singer, J. M. Aitken, and R. E. Jones. Control theory for principled heap sizing. In *ISMM*, 2013.

[25] J. Xu, A. Oufimtsev, M. Woodside, and L. Murphy. Performance modeling and prediction of enterprise JavaBeans with layered queuing network templates. *SIGSOFT Softw. Eng. Notes*, 31(2), 2006.

Speeding Up Processing Data From Millions of Smart Meters

Jiang Zheng, Zhao Li, Aldo Dagnino
ABB Inc., US Corporate Research
940 Main Campus Drive, Raleigh, NC, USA
{jiang.zheng, zhao.li, aldo.dagnino}@us.abb.com

ABSTRACT

As an important element of the Smart Grid, Advanced Metering Infrastructure (AMI) systems have been implemented and deployed throughout the world in the past several years. An AMI system connects millions of end devices (e.g., smart meters and sensors in the residential level) with utility control centers via an efficient two-way communication infrastructure. AMI systems are able to exchange substantial meter data and control information between utilities and end devices in real-time or near real-time. The major challenge our research was to scale ABB's Meter Data Management System (MDMS) to manage data that originates from millions of smart meters. We designed a lightweight architecture capable of collect ever-increasing large amount of meter data from various metering systems, clean, analyze, and aggregate the meter data to support various smart grid applications. To meet critical high performance requirements, various concurrency processing techniques were implemented and integrated in our prototype. Our experiments showed that on average the implemented data file parser took about 42 minutes to complete parsing, cleaning, and aggregating 5.184 billion meter reads on a single machine with the hardware configuration of 12-core CPU, 32G RAM, and SSD Hard Drives. The throughput is about 7.38 billion meter reads (206.7GB data) per hour (i.e., 1811TB/year). In addition, well-designed publish/subscribe and communication infrastructures ensure the scalability and flexibility of the system.

Categories and Subject Descriptors

D.1.3 [**Programming Techniques**]: Concurrent Programming – *Parallel programming;* F.1.2 [**Computation by Abstract Devices**]: Modes of Computation – *Parallelism and concurrency;* H.3.4 [**Information Storage and Retrieval**]: System and Software – *Performance evaluation (efficiency and effectiveness).*

General Terms

Algorithms, Measurement, Performance, Design, Experimentation, Verification.

Keywords

Architecture, Concurrency, Parallelism.

1. INTRODUCTION

A "Smart Grid" generally refers to a modern electric utility grid that uses computer-based information and communication technology to collect and manage information in an automated fashion [22]. Smart Grid technologies are able to significantly improve the quality of the production and distribution of electricity, especially in efficiency and economics. Stimulated by the concept of Smart Grid, Advanced Metering Infrastructure (AMI) systems have been widely deployed in the world in the past several years. An AMI system usually consists of smart meters, two-way communications networks, and data management systems. Unlike traditional home energy monitors, smart electrical meters not only record consumption of electric energy in intervals of 15 minutes or even every minute, but also communicate information back to the utility for monitoring and billing purposes. Additionally, unlike legacy utility communication systems, such as Supervisory Control and Data Acquisition (SCADA), an AMI system offers an efficient two-way communication infrastructure, connecting millions of end devices (e.g., smart meters and sensors in the residential level) with utility control centers, and exchanging substantial meter data and control information between them in real-time or near real-time. AMI systems break through the traditional fences of substations and transformers, pushing forward the boundaries of grid visibility to the residential territory [20].

A Meter Data Management System (MDMS) is responsible for collecting meter data that originates from large amount of smart meters, storing and transforming meter data into information that may be used by utility applications, such as Demand Response (DR) billing, Customer Information Systems (CIS), Outage Management Systems (OMS), Distribution State Estimation (DSE), and Voltage Var Optimization (VVO). These utility applications can now access and analyze interval meter measurements via AMI to provide more sophisticated functionality. For example, DR billing systems can offer better analytic results and a more flexible pricing infrastructure based on Time-of-Use (TOU). As a key component for managing large amount of meter data and unleashing the potentials of AMI, an MDMS not only simplifies IT integration of AMI, but also facilitates the distribution of the meter data across the utility enterprise by framing the volumes of interval data retrieved from the field into manageable and understandable information packets.

In the past few years, enhancements and benefits brought by AMI and MDMS to the utility customer information system have been widely witnessed and accepted and in return have attracted more efforts to build larger scale applications on top of AMI. Based on estimations from IDC Energy Insights, the North American market in MDMS will grow up to $869.1 million (USD) in 2013, in which a smaller utility will spend up to $250,000 on MDMS solutions while large utilities will potentially sign contracts ranging from $2 million to $4 million [8].

As one of the primary vendors with a good reputation in the power grid management market, ABB has produced power grid management products that are widely accepted by major utilities in the US [21]. However, ABB's existing MDMS products were not designed to manage meter data generated by millions of smart meters. The desired MDMS is required to collect ever-increasing large amount of meter data from various metering systems (e.g., AMI and advanced meter read (AMR)), clean, analyze and aggregate the meter data to support its customer information system in the short term, and a plethora of smart grid systems and applications in the long run. The input to the desired MDMS is the interval meter data measurements collected from 3~5 million residential smart meters every 15 minutes or even every minute in the future. The collected measurements are not only energy consumption but also engineering measurements (e.g., current and voltage) and/or power quality events (e.g., outage information).

We designed a lightweight architecture to fulfill the non-functional requirements, especially in the aspects of performance and scalability, of such a system. In order to meet critical high performance requirements, various concurrency processing techniques, such as Task Parallel Library (TPL) [18] and in-memory lock-free data structures, were implemented and/or integrated in our prototype (henceforth called the *System*). Our experiments demonstrated that on average the data parser for data files was able to complete parsing, cleaning, and aggregating 5.184 billion meter reads in 42 minutes 8 seconds on a single machine with the hardware configuration of 12-core CPU, 32G RAM, and SSD Hard Drives. The throughput is about 7.38 billion meter reads (206.7GB data) per hour (i.e., 1811TB/year).

In addition, well-designed publish/subscribe that provides a flexible interface to easily integrate with other systems and applications, as well as the communication infrastructure ensure the high scalability and flexibility of the system.

The rest of this **industrial paper** is organized as follows. Section 2 introduces the background and related work. Section 3 presents research challenges and constraints, as well as critical architectural requirements. Section 4 describes the design and implementation in detail. Section 5 shows the performance evaluation results. Section 6 provides further discussion. Section 7 presents conclusions and future work of this study.

2. BACKGROUND AND RELATED WORK

In this section, background information and related work of Meter Data Management Systems (MDMS), and Data Extract, Transform, and Load (ETL) are described in Section 2.1 and Section 2.2, respectively.

2.1 Meter Data Management Systems

As a centralized storage facility, a MDMS collects meter data from various metering systems, processes them, and provides the processed meter information to various utility applications (e.g., outage management, workforce management, and customer billing system). In addition, beyond collecting data from metering systems, most MDMS can also send signals back to smart meters and control them.

At the time of this study, based on the Pike Pulse Report in 2011 [14], Oracle, eMeter, and Itron were ranking the top three of MDMS vendors in the North American Market. Oracle attained the highest overall score due to its broad MDMS product line, massive scale, geographic presence, technical innovations, and integration of MDM with other Oracle products. At the time of this study, according to [23], the announced test results demonstrated that a system, consisting of Oracle Smart Meter Gateway, Oracle utilities meter data management system, and Oracle utilities customer care and billing system, can process more than 1 billion records and generate 500,000 customer bills within an eight hour nightly window. The tests were conducted against real business scenarios, in which the meter measurements are generated by 10 million smart meters in every 15 minutes [23]. In 2011, Siemens Energy announced the acquisition of eMeter and integrated its meter data management software into Siemens smart grid product line [6] [26]. Thereby, the new product, called EnergyIP, having both the meter data management the smart grid applications, appeared on the market. Siemens announced its MDMS centralized architecture that can manage up to 50 million smart meters [6]. Itron also has a strong metering system product line, which ranges from smart meters, AMI communication infrastructures, AMI high-end meter data collectors, and meter data management, but relatively weak in developing smart grid applications based on top of its MDMS [12][27]. As far as we had known when we were conducting this study, none of the above work dealt with meter read data in one minute interval. Also our experiments demonstrated that our design and prototype was able to meet the high performance requirements in processing big data files, meanwhile maintaining a relatively small footprint.

2.2 Data Extract, Transform, and Load

In the area of data processing, Extract, transform, and load (ETL) refers to a process of (1) extracts data from outside sources, (2) transforms the data to fit operational needs, and (3) loads the data into data storage such as database or data warehouse. ETL may be parallelized to obtain higher performance.

Agarwal et al. proposed an approach of parallel processing of ETL jobs involving XML documents. Their approach parallelizes ETL jobs by performing a shallow parsing of XML documents in parallel on one or more processors. [1] The method needs to generate intermediate XML documents, while our method will not have any intermediate XML documents. Also the producer and consumer are in same processor in their method, while the producer and multiple consumers will run in different threads/processors in our method.

Candea et al. provided a method of high-throughput ETL of program events for subsequent analysis. An event tap associated with a server was utilized to transform a server event into a tuple. They used the event tap to reduce the computational burden on the database and at the same time keep the server event data in the database relatively fresh. [3] [3]Our major challenge in ETL was to process files or file stream that contains bulk data.

Chen et al. proposed an ETL method for data cleaning in electric company based on genetic neural network to handle missing values. The method was able to improve the accuracy of missing data prediction by the global search ability of genetic algorithm and the nonlinear mapping ability of neural network. [4] We focused on the throughput of the ETL process for huge and ever increased meter data.

3. ARCHITECTURAL REQUIREMENTS

In this section, we will introduce general challenges and constraints, as well as critical architectural requirements, in this research.

3.1 General Challenges and Constraints

The foremost challenge was to effectively managing a large amount of data with minimal machine footprint. An MDMS that claimed to manage millions of meters usually has a large machine footprint. For example, Oracle demonstrated a MDMS system consisting of 32 servers to manage data from 10 million meters [23]. However, the high costs of building and maintaining a large cluster may prevent the MDMS from being widely deployed. Additionally, following long-term technical strategy of adopting the Microsoft technology stack for future products, Microsoft .NET and C# technologies were required to prototype the architecture design.

3.2 Critical Architectural Requirements

Although we needed to consider many quality attributes in the process of architecture design (e.g., scalability and flexibility), performance, especially throughput, was the most critical quality attribute type.

According to the functional requirements, the meter measurements are imported either from a bulk data file (*Data File Scenario*) or from an interval-based data stream (*AMI Data Stream Scenario*). Section 3.2.1 and 3.2.2 describes these two scenarios in detail, respectively.

3.2.1 Data File Scenario

The typical Data File Scenario is to import the previous day's meter reads from a bulk data file, and process the meter data load accumulated in 24 hours in only one hour.

Depending on the load style, the file scenario can be classified into the following two cases: the *Regular Case* and the *Extreme Case*. In the *Regular Case*, the regular intervals of meter loads are 15 minutes, i.e., 96 times per day. Each meter load contain three "channels" which means three data reads (i.e., records) with the values of energy consumption, current, and voltage, respectively. So there are 288 regular reads per day for each meter. In addition, for each day, three hours of Demand Response (DR) reads with only the energy consumption value are also collected. However, DR reads are collected in only one-minute intervals (i.e., 180 data reads per day). In total 468 data reads are collected per day for each meter. So in the *Regular Case*, 1.404 billion data reads are contained in a bulk data file for 3 million meters. The *Extreme Case* further extends the DR reads from three hours to 24 hours per day, i.e., 1440 DR data reads per day.

Based on the requirements, all the meter data shall be imported, cleaned, and aggregated in one hour. To clarify our analysis, we define the concept of throughput as the number of processed meter reads per hour. Based on this definition, the throughput in the Extreme Case is 5,184 billion meter reads per hour, which is far higher than that of the major competitors (e.g., the throughput of Siemens's system was 200 million meter reads per hour and the

throughput of Oracle's MDMS was about 40 million meter reads per hour) at the time of this study.

The formal performance – throughput requirement for the Extreme Case of the File Scenario is as follows:

PERF_1 - The Extreme Case of the File Scenario

Requirement Statement:

The System shall load bulk data file in CSV format that contains up to 5.184 billion meter reads (i.e., data from up to 3,000,000 meters per day), store raw data, fill missing data, aggregate data, and export aggregated data to the CIS system in 1 hour. The maximum file size is 145.152 GB under Assumption (1). The maximum throughput is to process 5.184 billion meter reads per hour (i.e., 145.152 GB data per hour under Assumption (1)).

Calculation:

*- 96 fifteen-minute reads per day * 3 channels for 288 regular reads/meter, plus 24 hours * 60 minutes for 1,440 Demand Response reads/meter. (288 + 1440) * 3 million meters for 5.184 billion meter reads per day.*

*- 5.184 billion meter reads * 28 bytes / meter reads = 145.152 GB data.*

Assumption:

(1) Data size (in CSV format) for each meter read is 28 bytes.

(2) Multiple day's file can be processed separately by multiple servers in the System in one hour.

3.2.2 AMI Data Stream Scenarios

Unlike importing data from bulk data file, a typical AMI Data Stream Scenario is to import data stream from AMI, in which meter loads are evenly distributed in a day. Also, each meter read from AMI contains more bytes because AMI meter data is in XML format instead of CSV format.

The formal performance – throughput requirements for the Regular Case and the Extreme Case of the Stream Scenario are as follows:

PERF_2 – The Regular Case of Stream Scenario

Requirement Statement:

During the non-peak times of Demand Response (i.e., for regular reads), the System shall receive data from up to 5,000,000 meters from AMI in 15 minutes interval (i.e., up to 1.44 billion meter reads per day), store raw data, fill missing data, aggregate data, and export aggregated data to the ROMO system. The maximum throughput is to process 15 million meter reads per 15 minutes (i.e., 1.5 GB data per 15 minutes).

PERF_3 – The Extreme Case of Stream Scenario

Requirement Statement:

During the peak times of Demand Response, the System shall receive, store, and manage data that originates from up to 5,000,000 meters in 1 minute interval in addition to the regular reads described in the PERF_2 requirement, i.e., up to 8.64 billion meter reads per day. The maximum throughput is to process 20 million meter reads per 1 minute (i.e., 2 GB data per 1 minute).

Calculation:

*96 fifteen-minute reads per day * 3 channels for 288 reads/meter, plus 24 hours * 60 minutes for 1,440 Demand Response reads/meter. (288 + 1440) * 5 million meters for 8.64 billion meter reads per day. (5 million "regular" meter reads per 1 minute * 3 channels + 5 million Demand Response meter reads per 1 minute * 1 channel) for 20 million meter reads per 1 minute.*

Assumption:

(1) The demand response reads are in addition to the "regular" reads during the peak times.

(2) The data stream is in XML format in CIM model [6].

(3) Data size for each meter read is 100 bytes.

Table 1 shows a summary of the performance – throughput requirements for all the cases of both the Data File Scenario and the AMI Data Stream Scenario. Among these cases, the **Extreme Case** of the **Data File Scenario** has the largest processing throughput (5.184 billion reads per hour) and data throughput (145.152 GB data per hour).

4. DESIGN AND IMPLEMENTATION

In this section, we will highlight key techniques that contribute to the high performance and scalability of the *System*.

4.1 Overall Architecture

Figure 1 shows the component diagram for the *System*. At the high level, the components of the *System* can be classified into the following four parts: the meter data input layer in the left part of the figure, the meter data storage and the message coordinator in the middle part of the figure, and the application connectors in the right part of the figure.

Meter Data Input Layer

The meter data input layer consists of three modules: the protocol translation module, the stream parser module and the file parser module. The protocol translation module supports different AMI communication protocols and information models used by AMI, translating the input data into a standard information model (e.g., IEC61968-9) and sending it to the stream parser for processing.

The stream parser construes, cleans, and aggregates the meter data received from the protocol translation module. The file parser construes, cleans, and aggregates the meter data received from the bulk file in CSV format that contains one-day meter measurements. The parsers have two types of output: cleaned raw data and aggregated data. The former will be stored into the data repository, and the latter will be stored and also sent to Smart Grid applications (e.g., CIS). Section 4.2 describes the file parser in detail.

Meter Data Storage

The meter data storage is used to store both aggregated data and cleaned raw data. It consists of two parts: a relational database (RDBMS) and flat files. The former is used to store the aggregated data, and the latter are used to store the raw data. Section 4.3 describes the hybrid flat file / RDMBS storage mechanism.

Message Coordinator

The message coordinator is a publish/subscribe infrastructure, coordinating the behaviors of components in the *System*. As connected through the publish/subscribe infrastructure, the

components of the *System* are loosely coupled: by sending a message to the Message Coordinator, one component can coordinate its behavior with other components that subscribed to the sent message. Traditional applications of publish/subscribe infrastructures extend across the entire enterprise, whereas the use of publish/subscribe here is limited to the confines of the *System*. There is no need to deploy a heavy-duty middleware function to fulfill this function.

Table 1. Summary of Throughput Requirements

	Data File Scenario		AMI Data Stream Scenario	
	Extreme Case	Regular Case	Regular DR	Extreme DR
Data Format	CSV	CSV	XML	XML
# of meters	3M	3M	5M	5M
# of channels	3 for regular reads, 1 for DR reads	3 for regular reads, 1 for DR reads	3	3 for regular reads, 1 for DR reads
# of regular reads / day for each meter	288	288	288	288
# of DR reads / day for each meter	1440	180	0	1440
# of reads / day	5.184 billion	1.404 billion	1.44 billion	8.64 billion
Max processing throughput	**5.184 billion reads / hour**	1.404 billion reads / hour	15 million reads / 15 mins	20 million reads / 1 min
Data size for each read / command	28 bytes	28 bytes	100 bytes	100 bytes
Max data throughput	**145.152 GB / hour**	39.312 GB / hour	1.5 GB / 15 mins (6 GB / hour)	2 GB / 1 min (120 GB / hour)

As components in the *System* are loosely coupled and connected through messages, adding a new component to the *System* becomes easy: register messages sent by the new components to the message coordinator, identify the subscribers who are interested in these messages and link the subscribers with the newly added component by subscribing to the messages sent by the newly added component. In addition, each component only focuses on one specific function (e.g., the file parser only process the large data file), which makes the whole system easy to maintain. Section 4.5 provides detailed information in how the Message Coordinator works.

Application Connectors

Application Connectors are responsible for sending meter information tailored to certain Smart Grid applications. A connector tailors information from a standard meter information model to diversified information models and conforms to the communication protocols used by different Smart Grid applications.

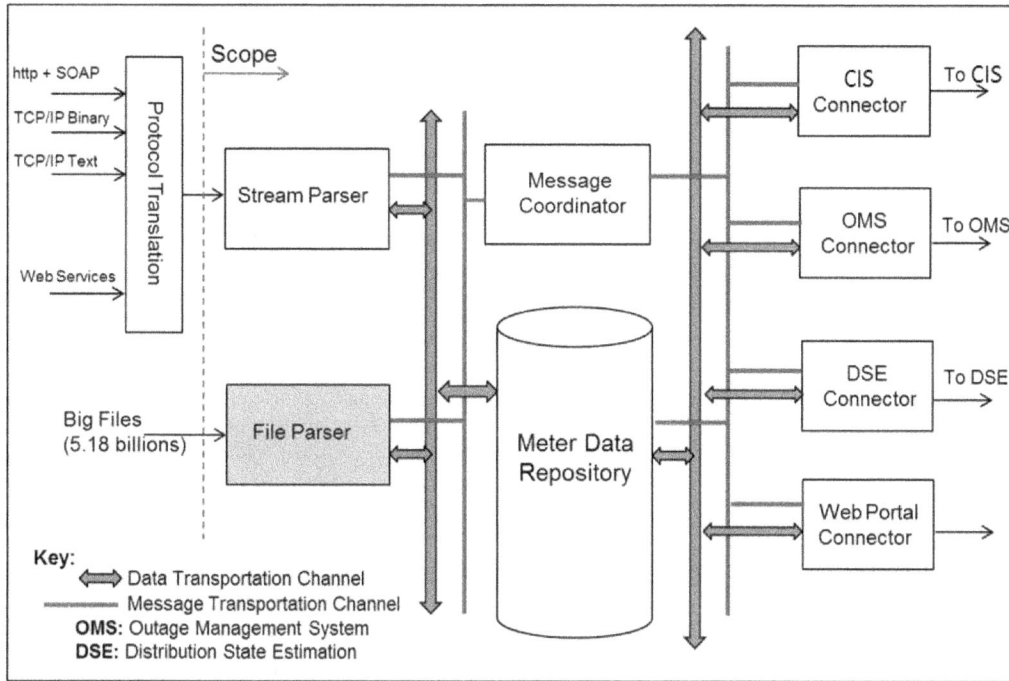

Figure 1. Overall Architecture

4.2 Meter Data Parser

The meter data parser works with large amount of meter data in the following steps.

Step 1: Large amount of mostly structured raw data is generated by various sensors, end devices, automatic data generation infrastructures, and/or other data sources. The raw data may be imported as files in different predefined formats, such as Comma-Separated Values (CSV), Extensible Markup Language (XML), or other user-defined formats. Partial of the dataset may be missing or duplicated, and there may be mistakes in the generated raw data.

Step 2: Before loading the raw data from the field, the data parser creates and initializes well-designed large-scale data structures in memory in order to stage and organize input data, and preserve aggregated datasets before storing them into databases or files. These data structures are thread-safe so that they can be accessed by multiple threads concurrently without any concurrency defects. The data parser also loads necessary metadata, such as configuration data for aggregation and summary of historical data, from databases or other data storage mechanisms. Different metadata may be loaded depending on different accumulative aggregation/analysis algorithms to be conducted in memory after loading the raw data.

Step 3: After the initialization described in Step 2, the data parser concurrently loads the raw data files or collects the raw data stream from the data sources in the stream fashion. Each thread works on one file. For each line or block of raw data, the data parser parses the raw data depending on the predefined data formats, eliminates useless text such as commas, spaces, and XML tags, and converts useful data from plain text to corresponding data types.

Step 4: Various algorithms of validation, estimation, and editing (VEE), such as foreign key validation, individual numeric data

validation, duplication validation, and missing data estimation, are applied to the converted raw data in order to clean up the input data. During the scanning of the raw data, many statistical and aggregation algorithms can also be executed to accumulatively analyze and aggregate the cleaned staging data. In-memory configuration information and historical aggregation data that has been loaded in Step 2 can help to perform aggregation for broader time periods. Large-scale thread-safe data structures constructed and maintained in memory are suitable for efficiently accepting and organizing both cleaned staging data and aggregated data. These data structures also help to remove a large amount of redundant or duplicated information in input data.

The technique of layered key/value pairs is used to implement the in-memory input data dictionary. In this data structure, the value of each key/value pair is a set of key/value pairs, except for the last layer. Figure 2 illustrates an example of the layered key/value pairs (two layers) that is used as the input data dictionary for one day meter reads generated from 3 million meters.

Assuming that each meter read contain four fields: 1) meter ID, 2) timestamp, 3) read type, and 4) read value of either energy or current or voltage, depending on the read type. The set of key/value pairs in the first layer is implemented by thread-safe Concurrent Dictionary [16] in order to avoid data racing. There are 3 million entries in the first layer thread-safe dictionary. For each entry of the first layer key/value pairs, the key is a unique meter ID, and the value is a Sorted List [17]. Sorted Lists cost smaller size of memory comparing to other types of key/value pairs, because a Sorted List stores data in linear arrays but Dictionaries store data in tree structures. For each entry of the Sorted List, the key is a concatenated string. The string is one of the possible combinations of the hour and the minute in a day and the meter read type. The value of each entry of the Sorted List is a float variable that stores the read value of this meter read. During the initialization step, the float variable is set to a special value such as -1, indicating this specific meter read has not been received. When receiving a piece of meter read, the layered key/value pairs allows the data parser to find the corresponding position in the large-scale data structures for this piece of meter read using an O(1) operation. Then the float variable is changed to the read value in this piece of meter read, indicating this specific meter read has been received. With the help of the data dictionary, the data parser is able to organize and sort the whole raw datasets with an O(n) operation while loading them. Duplicated meter reads can be easily detected as well. After this step, the data parser converts input raw data into cleaned staging data and aggregated data and stores all the data in the large scale thread-safe data structures in memory.

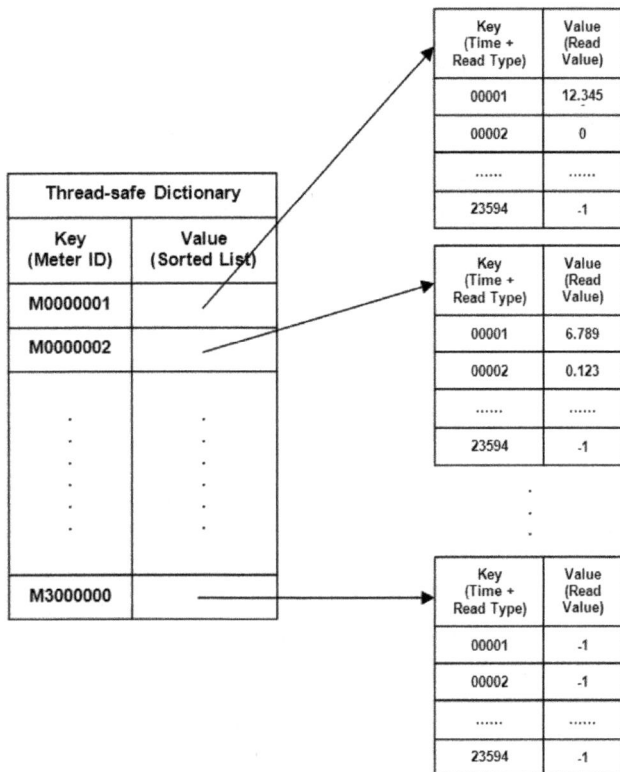

Figure 2. In-memory Data Dictionary Using Layered Key/Value Pairs

Step 5: The well-organized cleaned staging data and aggregated data in memory can be conveniently traversed and stored into relational database management systems and/or flat files on hard drives for future usage.

A key advantage of the design is the ability to receive and process data at a very high throughput. Section 5.2 shows the detailed results of performance evaluation.

4.3 Hybrid Flat-file / RDBMS Storage

The traditional RDBMS stores not only the data set but also related meta-data that are used to accelerate data retrieval. When the size of managed data set is small, the cost and performance overhead caused by the meta-data can be effectively covered because of its performance gain. For instance, the purpose of index is to define a short-cut path to access data. Because of the index, the performance of data retrieval can be significantly improved.

However, the cost and overhead of building, managing and utilizing meta-data are significantly increased when the data size is getting large. Our experiments demonstrated that inserting 1.5 billion meter reads, each of which carries the information on energy consumption and its related timestamp, into a table in an Oracle database, took more than ten hours. By contrast, creating and storing the same amount of data into flat files took less than 10 minutes on the same hardware configuration because of no such meta-data related overhead.

The performance of querying a large relational table deteriorates with the data set getting large. Based on our experiments, a query that conducts the sum operation against a data set with 1.19 million meter reads in Oracle 11g spent more than four hours. While the same operation fulfilled by flat files and streaming took less than six minutes. These experiments demonstrated that the traditional relational database management system becomes inefficiency when the data set is getting large. On the contrary, the flat file technologies become efficient under the same situation.

Nowadays, the size of raw data collected from millions of end devices at a certain time interval (e.g., every 15 minutes or even shorter) is huge and ever increased. In the Extreme Case of the Data File Scenario, the daily data collected from three millions smart meters maximally contains 5.184 billion reads (about 145GB), which already surpasses the size of data that a traditional database application can handle in its life cycle.

Figure 3 illustrates the infrastructure of the newly designed data storage solution, which is suitable for managing a large amount and ever-increasing data. Unlike traditional database technologies, the storage of the database is split into two parts: the relational DB and flat files. The relational DB is used to store aggregated data, which is in small volume, while the flat files are used to store the raw data, which is in huge volume.

The data parser collects meter measurements from data stream and/or data files. After cleaning and aggregation, the data are classified into two parts: the aggregated data and the cleaned raw measurements. The aggregated data, such as the maximal daily or monthly energy usage, are eventually stored to the relational database and the cleaned raw measurements are saved to the flat files. The query engine is used to analyze and redirect the income queries to either the relational DB or the flat files. Generally, the aggregated data stored in the relational DB can answer most queries. For those queries that cannot be handled by relational DB, such as queries on data in long time span have to be extracted from flat files, will be processed by streaming the flat files.

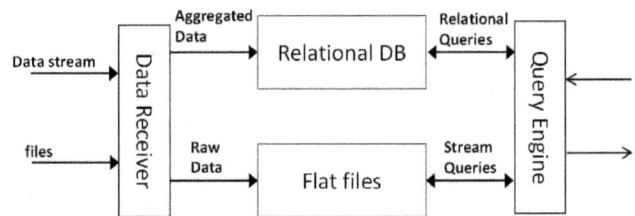

Figure 3. Hybrid Flat-file / RDBMS Storage Infrastructure

The performance of querying large data files eventually overpasses the performance of querying a large relational table when the size of the data set large enough to reach a certain point. In our experiments, conducting an aggregation operation against a large relational table with 0.8 billion reads took 30 minutes (i.e.,

1.6 billion reads per hour). Conducting the same aggregation operation by streaming a large file containing 4.8 billion reads spent only 6 minutes (i.e., 48 billion reads per hour).

4.4 Communication Infrastructure

In the *System*, the scenario of transporting data through a communication infrastructure occurs in several places (e.g., transporting the collected meter data from the protocol translation module to the stream parser module and transporting the aggregated meter measurements from the CIS adapter to the CIS system). We abstracted a common communication infrastructure, which can be applied to each individual transportation scenario in the *System*.

The Communication Infrastructure is composed of nodes and bindings. A node has a unified address describing where a message should be sent and logic defining what the message should look like and how the message is sent. A binding is a communication channel decorated by a set of binding elements, which "stack" one on top of the other to create the communication infrastructure. The binding elements can be transportation protocols (e.g., HTTP and TCP/IP), encoding approaches (e.g., text or binary) and other advanced features (e.g., security). Decoupling the node and binding make it easy to combine a node with different bindings. For example, originally a node sends messages through a HTTP binding. As a node is decoupled with a binding, it only needs to construct a new TCP/IP binding and link the node with the newly created binding. In this way, a message can be sent through the TCP/IP communication channel. The permutations and combinations of the binding elements can construct diversified communication channels in reality.

Figure 4 illustrates the queue-based communication infrastructure. Instead of sending a message directly to a receiver, a sender sends a message over a queue to a receiver. The transportation processes that send messages from a sender to a queue and from a queue to a receiver are transaction-based. Therefore, during the transportation, if an error happens, the transportation processes would be rolled back. This makes the communication more stable and therefore, enhances the availability of the *System*. The queue-based communication greatly improves the communication efficiency by saving the communication bandwidth from the sender to the queue.

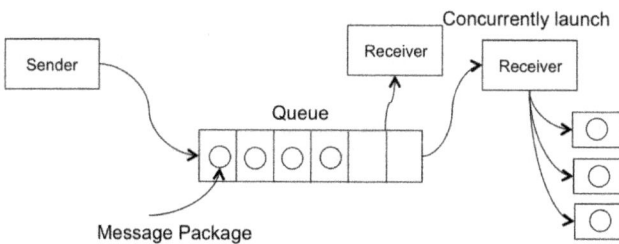

Figure 4. Queue-based Communication

Concurrently processing the received messages is another primary way to improve the throughput of the communication channel. Concretely, on receiving a package, the receiver quickly launches a new thread to process (parsing, cleaning and aggregating) the message, meanwhile the receiver itself starts receiving the next package.

The Windows Communication Foundation (WCF) in .NET 4.5 was used to implement the designed communication infrastructure. Nodes and bindings are available in WCF.

Generally a node has a unified address, visible by other nodes from different locations/machines. In the WCF library, various communication channels and their decorations have been implemented. A developer only needs to configure the features of the communication channel, such as communication protocol (e.g., HTTP and TCP/IP) and security facilities, through a configuration file, rather than develop them from scratch.

Two scenarios were primarily implemented in the prototype: queue-based (MSMQ) communication and HTTP-based communication. The former is suitable when both sender and receiver are in the .NET platform, primarily implementing a communication channel with high performance and high availability. The latter emphasizes the interoperability of the communication channel: through HTTP + SOAP, components in the *System* can communicate with the component implemented by technologies other than windows and .NET (such as Linux and Java). In this case, interoperability is the major focus.

4.5 Message Coordinator

From the architectural aspect, it is important for the *System* to extend its capability to interface with the potential systems and applications, which may use different communication protocols and information models. In addition, low cost maintainability is a highly desired feature too.

A message-based publish/subscribe infrastructure, called Message Coordinator, was designed to address the above two requirements. In the publish/subscribe infrastructure, all components are connected through messages. Modifying one component will not influence other components. In addition, each component can have its own special functionalities. The above loosely coupled relationship between components increases the *System*'s maintainability and extensibility. Additionally, unlike the "formal" publish/subscribe architecture, which is across the entire enterprise and supported by a heavy commercial middleware, the proposed publish/subscribe architecture is a lightweight structure that is limited to the *System*, potentially connecting only tens of components.

The publish/subscribe infrastructure is composed of three types of components, as shown in Figure 5: a publisher, a message coordinator and a subscriber. The publisher publishes message to the message coordinator. The message coordinator maintains the relationship between the publisher and subscribers. When a new message arrives, the message coordinator identifies the subscribers of the incoming message and broadcasts the message to them. A subscriber registers itself to the message coordinator for certain messages during the initialization. After registration, the subscriber will receive the registered messages once they are published.

For example, the file parser and the stream parser of the *System* are message publishers, while the CIS connector is a message subscriber. The file parser will send out a message to the message coordinator once it finishes processing bulk data files. On receiving this message, the message coordinator will forward the message to subscribers. By parsing the message, the CIS connector knows that the data has been cleaned up and aggregated. Based on this message, it will pick up the data from the public area (either database or shared memory) and send it to CIS.

It is easy to add a new component to the message-based infrastructure. For example, assume that we want to integrate the *System* with a system that fulfills Demand Response (DR) functionality. A new subscriber, called the DR connector, is developed using Java technologies, which packs the DR information received from the file parser and sends it to the DR system; to connect to the message coordinator, the new message is defined for the DR connector. During the whole process, only the message coordinator and the DR connector are involved. The rest of the system is not affected.

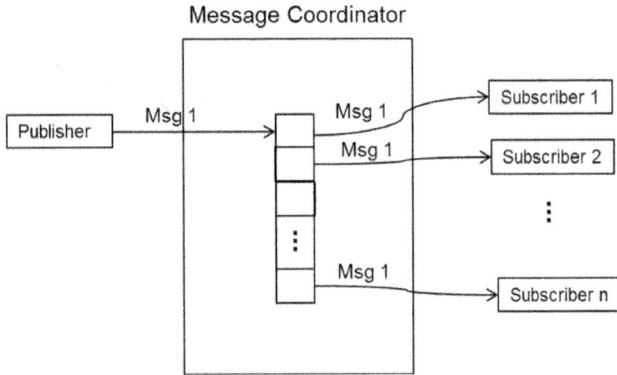

Figure 5. Message Coordinator

The publish/subscribe infrastructure may be considered as the control center of the *System*, which coordinates the status of the components in the *System* through messages. In our prototype, to make the *System* more scalable and extensible, the publish/subscribe infrastructure was hosted in Internet Information Service (IIS) and the HTTP communication protocol was used to transport messages. In such a configuration, the components located in different machines can communicate with the logic of the publish/subscribe infrastructure hosted in the IIS. As a major advantage, hosting the service in IIS automatically utilizes the functions of IIS, such as listening for incoming message and automatically waking up the publish/subscribe logic when the message arrives, greatly reducing the development efforts.

5. PERFORMANCE EVALUATION

In this section, we will present results of performance evaluation of the *System*.

5.1 Testing Environment

Two computer systems were configured for the evaluation. We highlighted our thoughts on selecting hardware components of the testing systems as follows:

- High performance CPU for intensive computation

- High throughput disk for frequent disk I/O

- Four-channel high speed memory for high performance memory operations (e.g., parsing and cleaning meter data in memory)

- Large capacity of memory for pre-storage VEE tasks

Additionally, Visual studio 2012 was selected for fully utilizing advanced data structures (e.g., the lock-free concurrent dictionary), the user-friendly multithreading API, and the latest version of the WCF implementation. Table 2 summarizes the configuration of the testing system.

Table 2. Testing System Configuration

Resource	Specification
CPU	Intel Core i7-3930K @ 3.20GHz, 6 cores with Hyper threads (12 logical cores), 15 M L3
Memory	32GB DDR3 (1600MHz) Four-Channel
Hard Disk	SSD (from Samsung and OCZ)
Network	1Gb/s
OS	Windows 7 Enterprise 64
Dev. Tool	Microsoft Visual Studio 2012 Ultimate

5.2 Data File Parser

To prototype the meter data parser described in Section 4.2, Solid-State Disk (SSD) hard drives [7] were used due to the tremendous disk I/O throughput. The new Task Parallel Library (TPL) [18] in .NET 4.5 was selected to address the high throughput requirement because TPL has easy understanding multi-thread APIs, through which launching multi tasks becomes simple and straightforward.

The input of our experiments is 12 bulk files in CSV format with meter read data including meter ID, Timestamp, read type, and read value. The size of each read (i.e., line) is within 24~29 bytes. Parsing a CSV string into memory variables was the most time-consuming task in the file parser. In comparison with several CSV parsers in state of the art, a fast CSV parser [15] was selected, which was claimed to be the fastest CSV parser in the .NET platform at the time of this study and free for use. Regarding the VEE rules, without loss of generality, a comprehensive survey was conducted against the VEE rules used by primary MDMS products in the current market, based on which we selected and implemented seven popular VEE rules as follows:

(1) *Device ID Validation*: To validate if data is received from a valid meter,

(2) *Timestamp Validation*: To validate if meter reads have valid timestamps,

(3) *Interval Validation*: To validate if meter reads have valid intervals,

(4) *Individual Numeric Data Validation*: To validate if the energy consumption value in each read is within a proper range,

(5) *Summary Numeric Data Validation*: To validate if the total energy consumption value for each meter is within a proper range,

(6) *Duplication Validation*: To validate if the received data has duplicated reads, and

(7) *Missing Data Estimation*: To estimate missing mete read data.

Additionally, the data processing includes a billing aggregation based on Time-of-Use (TOU). The TOU-based billing aggregation calculates the bill charges for each meter for a day according to the pre-defined TOU configuration. The implemented TOU configuration includes the following impact factors: (1) Daylight Saving Time; (2) Season; and (3) Peak

Hours. The input of this data analytics is the 15-minute interval data of consumption for each meter.

Table 3 shows the performance of the Data File Parser based on different input workloads. We conducted experiments five times for each workload. For a testing workload with 0.1404 billion meter reads from 0.3 million meters, it took about 11 seconds to complete the initialization step, i.e., creating and initializing large-scale thread-safe data structures in memory. Then it spent around 71 seconds on completing the whole data processing, including concurrently loading data files, reading and parsing lines, converting text to proper data types for analysis, 7 VEEs, and the TOU-based billing aggregation. For the workload of the *Regular Case*, the initialization time and processing time was 3 minutes 37 seconds and 12 minutes 19 seconds on average, respectively. With regard to the *Extreme Case*, on average it spent 9 minutes 28 seconds on completing the initialization followed by 42 minutes 8 seconds on finishing up the data processing. As a normalization, the experiments demonstrated that in the *Extreme Case* the data parser for data files has a throughput about 7.38 billion meter reads (206.7GB data) per hour (i.e., 1811 TB/year) for parsing, cleaning, and aggregating meter reads data on a single machine with the system configuration shown in Table 2. Unfortunately we did not conduct more experiments to show the linear scalability more clearly due to budget limitations.

Table 4 lists the data processing time for each of the 12 threads for all these experiments. All threads completed their work at almost the same time in the testing case and *Regular Case*. In the *Extreme Case*, the differences between the fastest thread and the slowest thread in these five runs ranged from 31 seconds to 48 seconds. Comparing to more than 40 minutes' data processing time, we still consider that the performance of the data file parser is stable.

Table 3. Performance of Data File Parser

Workload (billion meter reads)	Avg. Initialization Time (min:sec)	Avg. Processing Time (min:sec)	Avg. Processing Throughput (million reads per sec)
0.1404	0:11	1:11	1.9775
1.404	3:37	12:19	1.8999
5.184	9:28	42:08	2.0506

The data parser appropriately allocates the load among various computer resources, such as CPU power, RAM, and hard drives, to achieve best performance (specifically, responsiveness and throughput). The data parser is able to utilize all CPU cores (90+% overall CPU usage) to load the raw data files (or collect the raw data stream) and perform data cleaning and analysis.

5.3 Communication Infrastructure

The permutations and combinations of features of the communication channel generate a variety of communication scenarios (HTTP with no security, HTTP with security and TCP/IP with security). Enumerating and evaluating all of these scenarios is beyond the budget of this study. Therefore, we chose the queue-based communication scenario as shown in Figure 4, which is a relatively complex and highly stable communication approach.

Table 4. Performance of Each Thread for Each Test

Workload	Test	Completion Time for Each Thread (minute:second)
0.1404 billion meter reads	1.1	1:11, 1:11, 1:11, 1:11, 1:11, 1:11, 1:11, 1:11, 1:12, 1:12, 1:12, **1:12**
	1.2	1:10, 1:10, 1:10, 1:10, 1:10, 1:10, 1:10, 1:11, 1:11, 1:11, 1:11, **1:11**
	1.3	1:10, 1:10, 1:10, 1:10, 1:11, 1:11, 1:11, 1:11, 1:11, 1:11, 1:11, **1:11**
	1.4	1:10, 1:10, 1:10, 1:10, 1:10, 1:10, 1:10, 1:10, 1:10, 1:10, 1:11, **1:11**
	1.5	1:10, 1:10, 1:10, 1:10, 1:10, 1:10, 1:11, 1:11, 1:11, 1:11, 1:11, **1:11**
1.404 billion meter reads	2.1	12:03, 12:08, 12:10, 12:11, 12:11, 12:12, 12:12, 12:14, 12:15, 12:15, 12:15, **12:16**
	2.2	12:06, 12:09, 12:09, 12:09, 12:09, 12:10, 12:10, 12:10, 12:12, 12:13, 12:14, **12:16**
	2.3	12:05, 12:10, 12:14, 12:16, 12:16, 12:17, 12:17, 12:18, 12:19, 12:19, 12:19, **12:21**
	2.4	12:11, 12:12, 12:15, 12:15, 12:16, 12:16, 12:16, 12:17, 12:17, 12:18, 12:19, **12:23**
	2.5	12:05, 12:07, 12:09, 12:12, 12:12, 12:13, 12:14, 12:14, 12:15, 12:15, 12:17, **12:18**
5.184 billion meter reads	3.1	41:25, 41:30, 41:30, 41:31, 41:36, 41:42, 41:42, 41:45, 41:45, 41:50, 41:58, **41:59**
	3.2	41:21, 41:26, 41:31, 41:31, 41:31, 41:37, 41:40, 41:41, 41:44, 41:47, 41:50, **42:08**
	3.3	41:25, 41:26, 41:29, 41:35, 41:37, 41:40, 41:42, 41:42, 41:48, 41:51, 42:01, **42:13**
	3.4	41:23, 41:33, 41:40, 41:44, 41:44, 41:48, 41:49, 41:51, 41:56, 41:58, 41:59, **42:03**
	3.5	41:48, 41:53, 41:55, 41:56, 41:57, 41:58, 41:59, 42:08, 42:11, 42:13, 42:13, **42:19**

The queue-based communication architecture is composed of a sender, a receiver and a queue. In the prototype, both sender and receiver were .NET console applications. The queue used the MSMQ 4.0 service, the queue service in the .NET platform. To make the communication more stable, the queue was decorated with the transaction feature. In other words, the communication between .NET consoles (e.g., sender and receiver) and queue was transaction based: if a transaction fails, the delivery would be rolled back.

The sender packed each meter measurement into an XML string. The example of the XML formatted meter measurement was as follows:

```
<Meter>
  <MeterID>abcd1234</MeterID>
  <Timestamp>10:15 4/15/2012</Timestamp>
  <Energy>10.3</Energy>
  <Category>1</Category>
</Meter>
```

A package, the basic unit of the transportation, consisted of 250 of the above XML formatted meter measurements. Transporting 3 million meters data required 12,000 packages, and transporting 5 million meters data required 20,000 packages. The receiver was integrated with VEE functionalities used in the Data File Scenario. The receiver concurrently launched a new thread to conduct VEE and aggregation algorithms on receiving a package.

Table 5 illustrates the performance of the queue-based transportation. On average it took about 1 minute and 40 seconds to transport 3 million meters data between two computers and conduct VEE and aggregation, and about 3 minutes and 12 seconds to transport and process 5 million meters data.

Table 5. Performance of Queue-based Transportation

Workload (records)	Number of Packages	Average Transportation Time (minute:second)
3 million	12,000	1:40
5 million	20,000	3:12

Based on the performance requirements, during the regular meter read phase, 5 million meters measurements arrive in every 15 minutes. Since the queue-based transportation took less than 4 minutes, the requirement of receiving the meter data stream from 5 million meter measurements can be met. Regarding delivering the aggregated meter measurements for 3 million meters data generated in the Data File Scenario to CIS, with the consideration of the transportation time, the total time spent was about 50 minutes on parsing, cleaning, and aggregating, and 1 minute and 40 seconds on transportation, which met the one hour requirement.

In the Regular Case, where the meter data includes regular meter reads and DR reads, the total data that needs to be transferred was $(15 + 1) \times 3 = 48$ million meter reads (15 is the DR reads from 3 million meter in 1 minute). Considering the transfer and cleaning of the 3 million meters data took 1:40, transporting the 48 million meter reads spent about 26.6 minutes beyond the 15 minutes scope. Two alternative solutions for this situation: one is to increase the transportation speed using 10Gb/s network card, which is ten times faster than the current network in theory. The other one is to keep the current setup and increase the size of the queue. In the Regular Case, the three hours DR reads can be temporarily put into the queue and processed after the peak hour.

In the Extreme Case, as the DR reads come in every minute, the queue solution wouldn't work. We had to construct several 10Gb-based communication channels to transport data from one machine to the other. The messaging based architecture allows us to perform such transportation.

6. OTHER QUALITY ATTRIBUTES

Regarding scalability, the *System* is able to be scaled up and scaled out to meet the performance requirements in the future. Scaling up refers to enhancing hardware for the existing machine, while scaling out means extending the *System* across machines. Since the Message Coordinator is deployed in the IIS, and HTTP is used as the primary communication protocol, it is easy to build a system across multiple machines.

With regard to maintainability, the message-based system is composed of loosely coupled modules. When changing the functionality of a module, the source code changes will be restricted only within the module itself, or within the modules that are directly connected to the initially changed module in the modules call graph to adapt the updated messages or newly defined messages.

In terms of reliability, as the components in the architecture are loosely decoupled, it is easy to build "hot" backup for important components. In addition, the queue-based communication can effectively handle the network failures and therefore increase the reliability of the whole M3 system.

Additionally, two aspects of security, authentication and authorization of the local machines or a domain, were implemented by the .NET infrastructure. The communication security is implemented by the WCF.

7. CONCLUSIONS AND FUTURE WORK

AMI systems are an important element of the Smart Grid as they offer an efficient bidirectional communication infrastructure. AMI systems connect millions of end devices with utility control centers and exchange substantial meter data and control information between them in real-time or near real-time. As deployment of AMI systems become more ubiquitous, the amount of smart meters and data handled by these systems continues to grow exponentially. Therefore, it is imperative to design a system capable of collecting, cleaning, analyzing, aggregating and manipulating this data to support smart grid applications and semi-automated decision making.

This paper discusses the development of a lightweight architecture that is able to manage data that originates from millions of smart meters to enhance the capabilities of the Smart Grid. We implemented the prototype system using various concurrency processing techniques, including new Task Parallel Library and latest Windows Communication Foundation, fast CSV parser, in-memory lock-free data structure, layered key/value pairs, hybrid flat-file/RDBMS storage, and SSD, to satisfy critical high performance requirements. Our experiments demonstrated that in the *Extreme Case* the throughput of the data parser for data files is about 7.38 billion meter reads (206.7GB data) per hour (i.e., 1811TB/year) for parsing, cleaning, and aggregating meter reads data on a single machine with the hardware configuration of 12-core CPU, 32G RAM, and SSD Hard Drives. In addition, well-designed publish/subscribe and communication infrastructures ensure the scalability and flexibility of the system.

It is important that the implementation of an AMI system requires incorporating important quality attributes in the system such as maintainability, reliability, and security, besides high performance and scalability. In our future work, we will continue to enhance the architecture to address other quality attributes, and balance the tradeoffs of architectural design.

Another discussion was that, Hadoop [2] might not be very suitable for implementing the *System* mainly because that there is a high risk of not meeting throughput requirements when Hadoop processes small amount of data with a small cluster. Executing Hadoop on a limited amount of data on a small number of nodes may not demonstrate particularly high performance as the overhead involved in starting Hadoop programs is relatively high. Other parallel/distributed programming paradigms may perform much better on two, four, or perhaps a dozen machines. [9][10][28] Hadoop is built to process "web-scale" data on the order of terabytes or petabytes. It is not recommended to use Hadoop if the data and computation fit on one machine. Hadoop requires large footprint to demonstrate its power in processing really huge data. In the Extreme Case, the performance (throughput) goal was to complete processing 5.184 billion meter reads in one hour. Our experiments proved that one computer was enough to process this amount of data. Our design and prototype provide a lightweight way to conduct validation, estimation and editing as well as some analytics in memory for relatively large amount of data. However, it would be more convincing if we have hands-on performance and scalability measurements to compare the Hadoop implementation with our existing implementation. It would be more useful to explore and understand the expected boundaries and scope limitations of the alternate solutions. We will establish Hadoop clusters, write MapReduce programs, and conduct more experiments on Hadoop in the future.

8. ACKNOWLEDGMENTS

We would like to thank our software development teams for their assistance in understanding the requirements of the *System*. We are also very thankful of Marisa Zindler, Kevin Burandt, and Samantha Hines for their expert knowledge.

9. REFERENCES

[1] Agarwal, M. K., Bhide, M. A., Kotwal, S., Mittapalli, S. K., and Padmanabhan, S. March 2011. Parallel Processing of ETL Jobs Involving Extensible Markup Language Documents. U.S. Patent, Pub. No.: US 2011/072319 A1.

[2] Apache. Hadoop. http://hadoop.apache.org/. Retrieved November 2013.

[3] Candea, G., Argyros, A., and Bawa, M. July 2008. High-throughput Extract-Transform-Load (ETL) of Program Events for Subsequent Analysis. World Intellectual Property, Pub. No.: WO 2008/079510 A2.

[4] Chen, X. and Zhang, X. October 2010. Extract-Transform-Load of Data Cleaning Method in Electric Company. In Proceedings of the International Conference on Artificial Intelligence and Computational Intelligence 2010. 345-349.

[5] Dean J. and Ghemawat, S. December 2004. MapReduce: Simplified Data Processing on Large Clusters. In Proceedings of the Sixth Symposium on Operating System Design and Implementation. OSDI'04.

[6] Edwards, C. A., Johnson, L. M., King, C. S., Prasad, N., Wambaugh, J. O., and Lofgren, T. D. March 2008. Message-Bus-Based Advanced Meter Information System with Applications for Cleaning, Estimating, and Validating Meter Data. United States Patent, Pub. No.: US 2008/0074284 A1.

[7] Ekker, N., Coughlin, T., and Handy, J. January 2009. Solid State Storage 101: An introduction to Solid State Storage. Technical Report. Solid State Storage Initiative (SNIA).

[8] Geschickter, C. August 2010. The Emergence of Meter Data Management (MDM): A Smart Grid Information Strategy Report. Technical Report. GTM Research.

[9] Glover, A. Java development 2.0: Big data analysis with Hadoop MapReduce. http://www.ibm.com/developerworks/java/library/j-javadev2-15/index.html. Retrieved Nov. 2013.

[10] Google. Introduction to Parallel Programming and MapReduce. http://code.google.com/edu/parallel/mapreduce-tutorial.html. Retrieved November 2013.

[11] IEC. 2009. IEC61968-9, Application integration at electric utilities – System interfaces for distribution management – Part 9: Interfaces for meter reading and control.

[12] Itron, "Itron Enterprise Edition™ Meter Data Management", https://www.itron.com/na/productsAndServices/Pages/Itron Enterprise Edition Meter Data Management.aspx. 2011.

[13] Li, Z., Wang, Z., Tournier, J., Peterson, W., Li, W., and Wang, Y. October 2010. A Unified Solution for Advanced Metering Infrastructure Integration with a Distribution Management System. In Proceedings of the First IEEE International Conference on Smart Grid Communications. SmartGridComm'10. 566 - 571.

[14] Lockhart, B. and Gohn, B. 2011. Pike Pulse Report: Meter Data Management - Assessment of Strategy and Execution for 11 Leading MDM Vendors. Tech. Report. Pike Research.

[15] Lorion, S. November 2011. The Fast CSV Reader. http://www.codeproject.com/Articles/9258/A-Fast-CSV-Reader.

[16] Microsoft. ConcurrentDictionary <TKey, TValue> Class. http://msdn.microsoft.com/en-us/library/dd287191(v=vs.110).aspx. Retrieved November 2013.

[17] Microsoft. SortedList<TKey, TValue> Class. http://msdn.microsoft.com/en-us/library/ms132319(v=vs.110).aspx. Retrieved November 2013.

[18] Microsoft. Task Parallel Library (TPL). http://msdn.microsoft.com/en-us/library/dd460717.aspx. Retrieved November 2013.

[19] Mohagheghi, S., Stoupis, J., Wang, Z., Li, Z., and Kazemzadeh, H. October 2010. Demand Response Architecture: Integration into the Distribution Management System. In Proceedings of the First IEEE International Conference on Smart Grid Communications. SmartGridComm'10. 501-506.

[20] National Energy Technology Laboratory. February 2008. Advanced Metering Infrastructure. Technical Report. U.S. Department of Energy.

[21] Network Manager. Retrieved November 2013. ABB Inc. http://www.abb.com/industries/us/9AAC30300663.aspx

[22] Office of Electricity Delivery and Energy Reliability. February 2008. The Smart Grid: An Introduction. Technical Report. U.S. Department of Energy.

[23] Oracle. Meter-To-Cash Performance Using Oracle Utilities Applications on Oracle Exadata and Oracle Exalogic. January 2012. Technical Report.

[24] Ramachandran, V., Hubbard, D., and Skog, J. October 2005. Method and System for Validation, Estimation and Editing of Daily Meter Read Data. United States Patent, Pub. No.: US 2005/234837 A1.

[25] Rustagi, A. September 2008. Parallel Processing for ETL Processes. U.S. Patent, Pub. No.: US 2008/222634 A1.

[26] Siemens/eMeter, "Siemens to Acquire eMeter to Enhance Smart Grid Offering", http://www.emeter.com/company/news/2011-press-releases/siemens-to-acquire-emeter-to-enhance-smart-grid-offering/. December 2011.

[27] Sonderegger, R. May 2010. System and Method of High Volume Import, Validation and Estimation of Meter Data. United States Patent, Pub. No.: US 2010/0117856 A1.

[28] Yahoo Developer Network. Hadoop Tutorial. http://developer.yahoo.com/hadoop/tutorial/module1.html. Retrieved November 2013.

Automated Analysis of Performance and Energy Consumption for Cloud Applications

Feifei Chen, John Grundy, Jean-Guy Schneider, Yun Yang and Qiang He
School of Software and Electrical Engineering
Faculty of Science, Engineering and Technology
Swinburne University of Technology
Melbourne, Australia 3122
{feifeichen,jgrundy,jschneider,yyang,qhe}@swin.edu.au

ABSTRACT

In cloud environments, IT solutions are delivered to users via shared infrastructure. One consequence of this model is that large cloud data centres consume large amounts of energy and produce significant carbon footprints. A key objective of cloud providers is thus to develop resource provisioning and management solutions at minimum energy consumption while still guaranteeing Service Level Agreements (SLAs). However, a thorough understanding of both system performance and energy consumption patterns in complex cloud systems is imperative to achieve a balance of energy efficiency and acceptable performance. In this paper, we present StressCloud, a performance and energy consumption analysis tool for cloud systems. StressCloud can automatically generate load tests and profile system performance and energy consumption data. Using StressCloud, we have conducted extensive experiments to profile and analyse system performance and energy consumption with different types and mixes of runtime tasks. We collected fine-grained energy consumption and performance data with different resource allocation strategies, system configurations and workloads. The experimental results show the correlation coefficients of energy consumption, system resource allocation strategies and workload, as well as the performance of the cloud applications. Our results can be used to guide the design and deployment of cloud applications to balance energy and performance requirements.

Categories and Subject Descriptors

C.4 [**Computer System Organization**]: Performance of Systems; K.4.1 [**Public Policy Issues**]: Use/abuse of power; [**Software Engineering**] D.2: Tools; B.8.2 [**Performance Analysis and Design Aids**]

General Terms

Measurement, Performance, Experimentation

Keywords

Cloud computing; green cloud; energy consumption; performance analysis; automation.

1. INTRODUCTION

Cloud Computing is a new and promising computing paradigm which delivers computing infrastructure as a utility [1]. It provides rented services for computation, application software, and data storage via the Internet. Key advantages for consumers include flexible scaling on demand to their computing and data storage needs without the traditional large upfront investment and continuing maintenance costs of computing infrastructure. Over the last few years many large-scale data centres have been built to meet the massive growth in demand for high performance cloud data and computational services.

As cloud computing becomes more widespread, increasing data storage and computation needs significantly raise the energy consumption of large cloud infrastructures. Most modern data centres are considered as mega data centres [2, 3] because they house over tens of thousands of servers that consume tens of mega-watts of energy per hour at peak times. High energy consumption directly contributes to data centres' operational costs, especially as the energy unit cost continues to rise significantly. Power consumption currently contributes up to 42% of a data centre's monthly expenses [4]. In addition, the huge amount of power consumption of data centers potentially accelerates global climate change. According to a *New York Times* study, data centres use about 30 billion watts of electricity per hour worldwide, equivalent to the output of about 30 nuclear power plants [5]. Therefore, for both financial and environmental reasons, energy consumption has become a critical concern in designing modern cloud-based systems.

Many efforts have been made to improve energy efficiency in cloud environments. Some simple techniques provide basic energy management for servers in cloud environments, including turning on and off servers, putting them to sleep or using Dynamic Voltage/Frequency Scaling (DVFS) [6] to adjust servers' power states. DVFS adjusts the CPU power, and as a result the performance level, according to the workload. However the scope of DVFS optimisation is limited to CPUs. Another approach for improving energy efficiency is to adopt virtualisation techniques to get better resource isolation and reduce infrastructure energy consumption through resource consolidation and live migration [7]. Using virtualisation techniques, several energy-aware resource allocation policies and scheduling algorithms have been proposed to optimise the total energy consumption in cloud environments [8]. However, the system performance and energy consumption of cloud systems vary greatly with different system configurations and allocation strategies, as well as the workload and the types of running tasks in cloud environments[9].

One of the important requirements for a cloud system is to provide reliable Quality of Service (QoS). Ideally, the performance of a cloud system must not be jeopardised by the energy consumption minimisation. Therefore, a thorough understanding of the performance and energy consumption patterns in complex cloud systems is imperative. We need to learn how energy consumption and cloud system performance are affected by different workloads and system configurations, including cloud application structuring and deployment. In our earlier work, we proposed an energy consumption model for calculating the energy consumption of specific types of tasks in cloud systems [10]. In our model, runtime cloud tasks are divided into three types: computation-intensive, data-intensive and communication-intensive. We conducted experiments to collect fine-grained system performance and energy consumption data with varying system configurations and workloads based on individual types of tasks [11]. However, profiling and analysing system performance and energy consumption in cloud systems is time consuming. Extensive experiments with different parameters, metrics and workloads need to be conducted. Manual generation of load test plans, change of system configurations and application of load tests are very tedious and error-prone. In addition, most of existing cloud system performance and energy profiling approaches limit the types of tasks running in the profiling process to only discrete individual types [11, 12]. In real cloud environments, users send mixes of computation-intensive, data-intensive and communication-intensive tasks to cloud systems simultaneously. The way different types of runtime tasks are composed and deployed will impact the performance and energy consumption of the cloud application [3]. Therefore, it is essential to investigate how different task and resource allocation strategies impact performance and energy consumption.

In order to address these issues, we have developed StressCloud, a performance and energy consumption profiling and analysis tool for cloud systems. StressCloud can effectively and accurately collect the performance and energy consumption data of cloud systems. We adopt stochastic form charts [13] to model realistic cloud user behaviour load. A stochastic form chart is extended from the basic form chart model which is a technology-independent bipartite state diagram used to simulate user behaviour of submit/response systems. From these stochastic from charts we automatically generate load tests and profile the performance and energy consumption data of a cloud system under test. Using StressCloud, we have conducted extensive experiments to empirically analyse the performance and energy consumption of cloud systems. Our experimental results demonstrate the relationship between the performance and energy consumption of cloud systems with different resource allocation strategies and workloads. Our analytical results can be used as guidelines for resource provisioning and task scheduling in cloud systems to maximise performance and minimize energy usage.

Section 2 briefly summarises the state-of-the-art of energy-saving policies, performance and energy consumption profiling and analysis approaches. Section 3 describes the architecture of StressCloud and the profiling framework of performance and energy consumption. The performance and energy consumption profiling setup and methods are described in Section 4. Section 5 presents a range of profiling results and detailed analysis. The observations derived from the experiments are discussed in Section 6. Finally, we summarise our key findings and discuss directions for future research in Section 7.

2. RELATED WORK

Energy-saving policies of cloud systems have been an active research topic in the past few years. VirtualPower [14] is proposed to exploit power management decisions of guest VMs on virtual power states. The virtual power states of guest VMs are considered as preconditions to run local and global energy management policies across the computation. Verma et al. [15] use the characteristics of VMs, such as cache footprint and the set of applications running on the VMs, to drive power-aware placement of VMs. Liu et al. [16] describe a new cloud infrastructure which can dynamically consolidate Virtual Machines (VMs) based on CPU utilisation of servers to identify idle physical servers. Idle physical servers can be turned off to save energy. However these energy saving policies do not take into consideration the workload in cloud systems and hence are very coarse-grained.

Research efforts have also focused on profiling and analysing the energy consumption of cloud systems. Most existing profiling efforts have been conducted using energy benchmarks or closely monitoring the energy profiles of individual system components at runtime, such as CPU, cache, hard disk and memory. Chen et al. [17] develop a linear power model that presents the behaviour and power consumption of individual hardware components of a single physical server. A framework is proposed by Stoess et al. [18] for energy optimisation and the development of energy-aware operation systems based on the availability of energy models for each hardware component. Joulemeter, a power meter for VMs [19], makes use of software components to monitor the resource usage of VMs and then converts the resource usage into energy consumption based on the power model of each individual hardware component. Although some of the profiling and analysis are conducted based on specific applications in cloud systems, the evaluation only includes an individual type of cloud applications. For instance, Lefèvre and Orgerie [20] evaluate the energy efficiency of cloud systems on a multicore platform. However, they focus only on CPU cores and conduct their evaluation of the energy consumption during migration of VMs only with computation-intensive cloud applications.

Some existing research has attempted to leverage the relationship between the performance and energy consumption of cloud systems. Grace et al. [12] investigate the energy efficiency of data centres by running benchmark applications on cloud servers. However, they focus on a black box to benchmark performance and energy consumption of cloud systems without looking into the parameters of the application. Yong and Albert analyse energy efficient utilisation of resources in cloud computing systems [3]. Their results assume that energy consumption scales linearly with the processor without considering the impact of associated RAMs. In fact, cloud resources include not only physical processors but also various RAMs. They conclude that the energy consumption can be reduced when two or more tasks are consolidated rather than solely assigned to one resource. However, they do not consider the performance aspect of such tasks. In our previous research [11], we profile and analyse the performance and energy consumption of cloud systems based on individual types of tasks.

The experimental results show that system configurations and task workload highly impact the performance and energy consumption in cloud systems. However, the types of tasks running in the profiling process are limited to only discrete individual types.

3. STRESSCLOUD

To address the abovementioned issues, we have developed StressCloud, a new tool for profiling the performance and energy consumption of cloud systems. We also conducted extensive and comprehensive experiments to using StressCloud. Our experimental results demonstrate the impact of system resource allocation strategies on system performance and energy consumption; the impact of realistic workloads with mixed types of tasks on system performance and energy consumption; and the relationship between performance and energy consumption.

Based on the high-level workload model and cloud system architecture model specified by the user, StressCloud can automatically deploy load test services to a cloud system and generate load tests. It can also profile the performance and energy consumption of the cloud system automatically. For proposed cloud systems or what-if analysis of proposed re-engineering changes, we allow the user to generate model cloud application services composed of data, compute and communication tasks to load test. In this section, we briefly describe the profiling process, system architecture and user interface of StressCloud.

Figure 1 shows how StressCloud is used to perform load tests to profile the performance and energy consumption of a cloud application. As depicted in Figure 1, the performance engineer first defines the cloud application workload model (1). These are a set of tasks modelling the target cloud application behaviour. Based on the major type of resource consumed by a task, we categorise runtime tasks into three types: computation-intensive, data-intensive and communication-intensive. In real applications, cloud application services are made up of composite tasks that may consume multiple types of cloud resources, including CPU, RAM, data storage and network devices. Thus, we introduce a "composite task" in our workload model to represent such composites. This workload model is then modified by the performance engineer with transition probabilities and properties between different types of tasks to form a workload model. A series of cloud services have been developed in order to model the target cloud application. These services take the user requests to perform tasks defined in the workload model and give corresponding responses. In addition, StressCloud can also stress a real deployed cloud application. Alternatively, instead of specifying a workload model, the performance engineer specifies what deployed cloud services to invoke (1). In this case, the engineer must specify valid requests and data to send to the real deployed application.

For each task, a *stochastic form chart* is created to specify the detailed user requests and required responses from the cloud system. This is a probabilistic model of user and service request behaviour that enables us to model a variety of usage scenarios on cloud application services, whether initiated by users or by other calling services [13]. The performance engineer needs to elaborate the form chart model with suitable probabilities on all transition links between services in the application.

A cloud system architecture model is then defined by the performance engineer to specify the elements in the target cloud system, Figure 1 (2). Our cloud architecture model includes all available resources in the target cloud system and their detailed

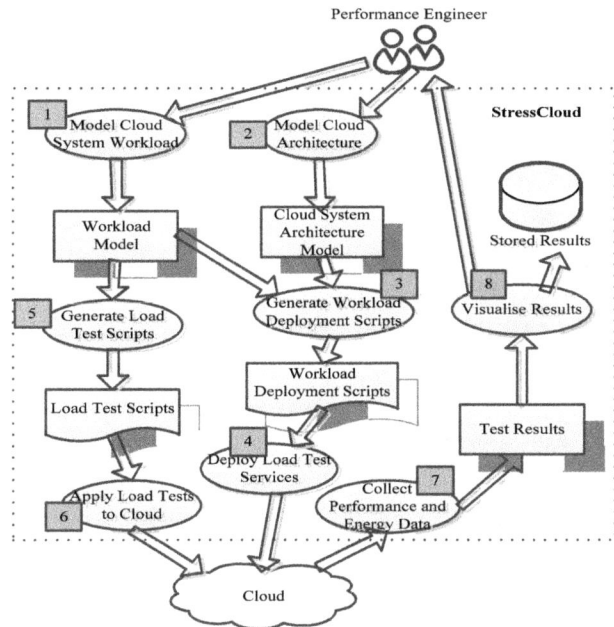

Figure 1. StressCloud Performance and Energy Consumption Data Profiling Process.

configurations. After mapping the tasks defined in the user workload model to corresponding resources in the cloud system architecture model, workload deployment scripts are generated (3). Based on the deployment scripts, load test services are uploaded and deployed to the VMs in the target cloud system (4). These cloud loading services were developed based on our previous research that incorporates CPU, RAM and data-intensive tasks, and support service to service communication-intensive tasks. Load test scripts are then automatically generated based on the workload model (5).

Next, the load tests specified are performed automatically on the target deployed cloud model or application based on the load test scripts (6). The performance and energy consumption information of the target cloud system are collected (7) and visualised (8). The visualised system performance and energy consumption data are updated at a user-specified rate, defaulting to 20 seconds. The test results are stored for future reference and for comparison to new tests run with differing tasks, loads and deployment models.

Figure 2 shows an example of StressCloud in use modelling an exemplar problem - JPetStore[1]. Figure 2 (a) shows a composite model of part of the JPetStore representing data, compute and communication tasks, composed together to form a definition of this cloud application service. For instance, the *"Signin"* task is a composite task of one communication task and one data task. The transition probabilities between different types of tasks have been specified to model the chance of users sending a particular task to the cloud application. A *Client* component represents a client-side start-up component for load test scripts generation, as all testing plans need an entry point. The *Quit* component is also manually added to the generated model to describe the real client behaviour. Figure 2(b) shows an example stochastic form chart model describing one usage scenario of *"GetProductDetail"* task, which is a communication task. The rectangle *"GET"* represents the

---

[1] http://java.sun.com/developer/releases/petstore/

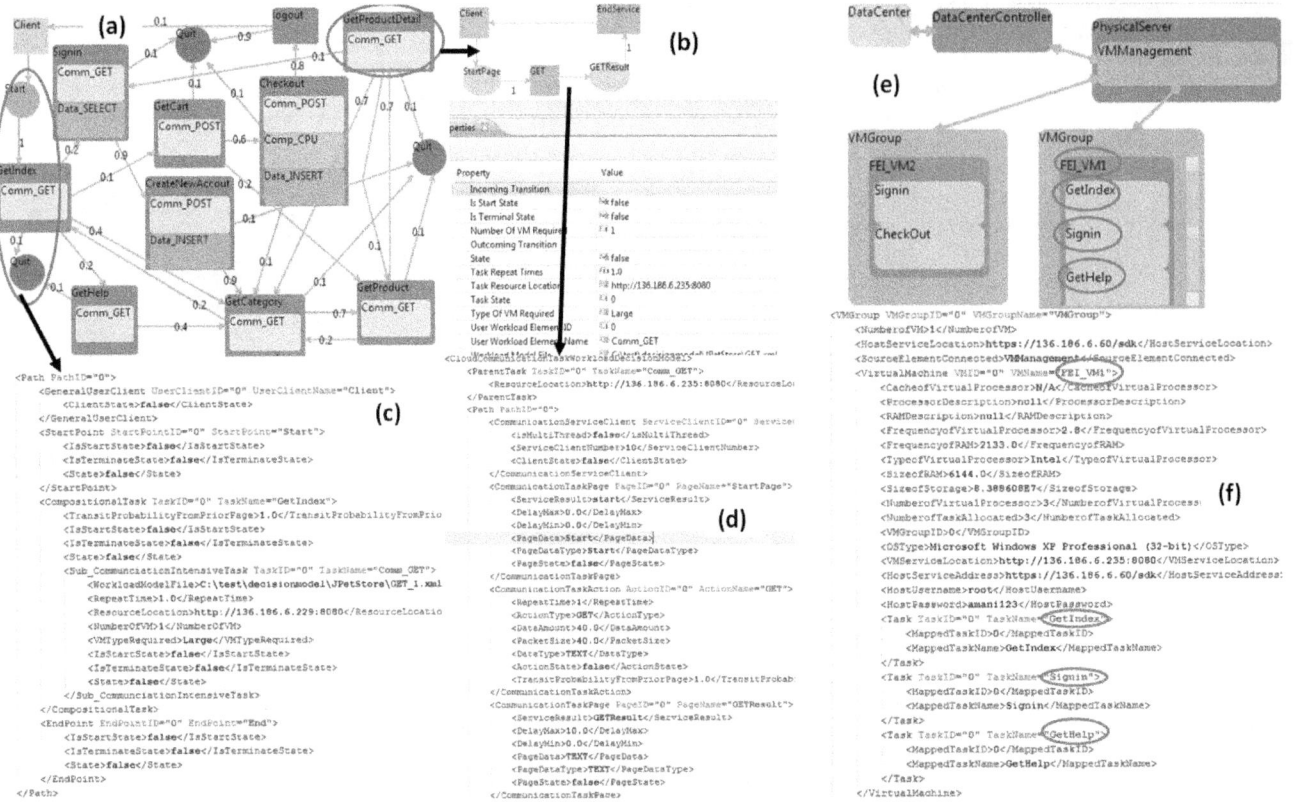

Figure 2. JPetStore Workload Model (a)(b) and Load Test Scripts (c)(d); Cloud Architecture (e) and Deployment Script (f).

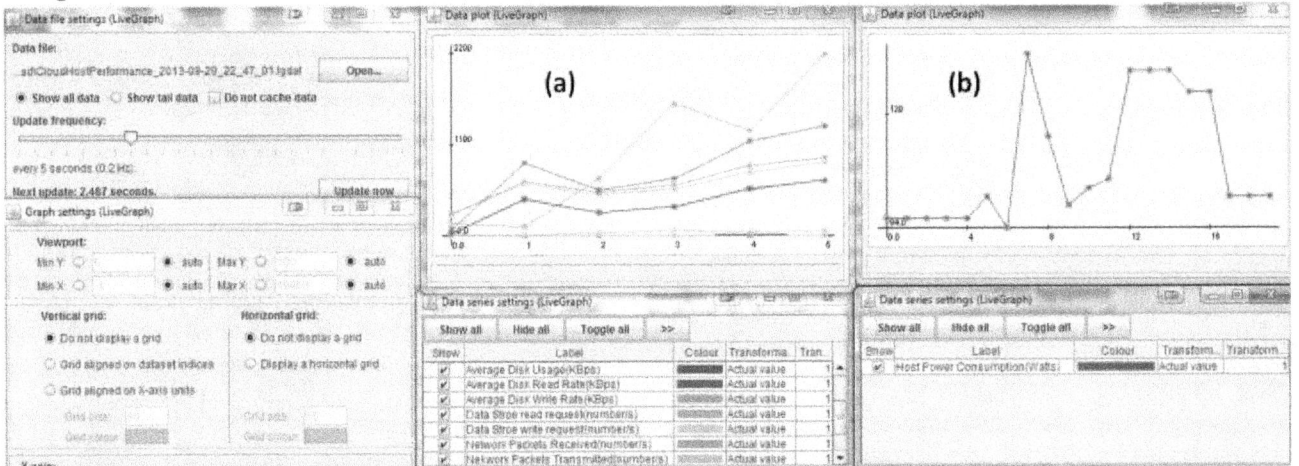

Figure 3. Visualised (a) Performance and (b) Energy Data.

detailed user requests and the oval "*GETResult*" represents required responses. Figure 2(c) and Figure 2(d) show part of loading scripts generated from a combination of the task models, load models and deployment models for our example cloud application.

Figure 2(e) shows an architecture diagram describing a deployment specification scenario for the cloud application. This shows the cloud environment contains one cloud server. Two VMs have been created on the server and they belong to different VM groups. Tasks "*GetIndex*", "*Signin*" and "*GetHelp*" in the workload model have been deployed on VM named "*FEI_VM1*". Figure 2(f) shows an example script generated from the deployment specification model.

Figure 3(a) shows an example of visualisations of various aspects of cloud system performance, including disk, network and CPU usage, for a running cloud application. The performance engineer can choose and customise the appearance of a range of system KPIs. Figure 3(b) shows the energy consumption of the profiled cloud system.

4. EXPERIMENTAL SETUP

Our new sets of experiments of performance and energy consumption profiling and analysis were performed to replicate and then extend our previous research results [10, 11]. We aimed to collect system performance and energy consumption data for the analysis of the correlation coefficients of system performance, energy consumption, workloads and resource allocation strategies. The analytical results can be adopted as guidelines for the development of energy efficient cloud resource provisioning and task consolidation strategies.

We profiled the performance and energy consumption of a cloud system by creating heterogeneous VMs in the cloud system and running composite tasks with various workloads and resource allocation strategies. This section describes our experimental setup.

Table 1. Specifications of HP Z400

Basic Specification		Notes
Number of Cores	4	
Number of Threads	2	Intel Hyper-Threading Technology
CPU Frequency	2.8GHz	Fixed CPU Frequency
Memory	8GB	Memory Speed 1333 MHz
Hard Drive	1TB 7200 RTM SATA	
Network Interface	Intel e1000 Gb	

4.1 Test-bed

Our experiments were conducted in SwinCloud, a private cloud that provides a common computational infrastructure to researchers at Swinburne University of Technology. SwinCloud was experimented in the Energy Research Lab (ERL) at Swinburne University of Technology. By using the extensive and sensitive power monitoring facilities provided by the lab, we could precisely monitor the power consumption of the SwinCloud servers. The power consumption measurement was realised and managed using PowerNode, a power usage profiling equipment developed by GreenWave Reality[2]. It supports measurement of both immediate and average power consumption. Collected power data were reported to the GreenWave Gateway, which is used to create a mesh-based Home Area Network (HAN). StressCloud retrieves power consumption from the GreenWave Gateway once every second to guarantee the accuracy of the power consumption data.

Table 2. Type of VM

Virtual Machine	Number of Cores	RAM	Hard Disk
Small	1	2GB	80GB
Medium	2	4GB	80GB
Large	3	6GB	80GB
XLarge	4	8GB	80GB

The energy consumption of a cloud system includes the energy consumed by the constituent servers and the scheduling overhead across the servers. We focused on the energy consumption of individual servers as it is the predominant part [21]. In addition, the cross-server scheduling and communicational overhead of one cloud system can be significantly different from another, depending on the scheduling mechanism adopted by the cloud systems and the distribution of the constituent servers. In this research, we focused on the system performance and energy consumption of tasks running on a single discrete server. The

energy consumption incurred by cross-server scheduling and computational overhead is part of our future work.

The server deployed in SwinCloud is a HP Z400. Table 1 lists the specifications of HP Z400. The Virtual Machine Manager (VMM) used is VMware ESX 4.1 and the operating systems running on the VMs are Windows XP Professional. In the experiments, all VMs were assigned with 2GB, 4GB, 6GB or 8GB RAM. The number of virtual CPUs (vCPUs) of each VM varied from 1 to 4 in steps of 1. The number of vCPUs equalled to the number of physical cores assigned to the VM. The configuration scales of the VMs are shown in Table 2.

Figure 4 shows the system performance and energy consumption profiling framework used in our experiments. A PowerNode monitor was connected to the cloud server. StressCloud was installed on a client PC. All workloads were modelled and generated using StressCloud and sent to the cloud server. A series of web services for load tests were deployed on the VMs. These are configured by the generated StressCloud scripts from the cloud application workload models. The system performance and power consumption data were collected by StressCloud for analysis.

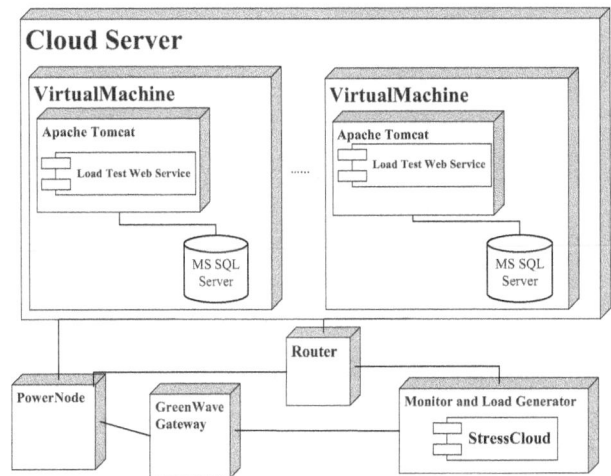

Figure 4. Performance and Energy Data Profiling Framework

4.2 Profiling Method

The define energy consumption for a task as the difference of average power consumption between the server with and without workload multiplied by the execution time of the task. We firstly retrieved the average power consumption measured by PowerNode with no workload in the cloud system as our idle state benchmark. Then, we used StressCloud to retrieve the real-time power consumption measured by PowerNode during the load tests every second. After that, we calculated the average power consumption and then multiplied the average power consumption by the average execution time of a single task to obtain the total energy consumption of the task.

Based on our previous research results [11], system performance and energy consumption are highly influenced by the workload and system configuration. As such, we took the cloud system workloads and system configurations as inputs of our experiments, and set energy consumption and system performance as the outputs. We selected the throughput of the system as one of the key performance indicators (KPI). This is because throughput is

---

[2] http://www.greenwavereality.com/

often the key performance parameter monitored in cloud systems and it has the advantage of reflecting resource usage accurately [22]. The other KPI selected is the response time as it is a major performance QoS requirement in cloud environments [23]. For computation-intensive tasks, the throughput is defined as the total number of user interactions requested and completed successfully per hour. For data-intensive tasks and communication-intensive tasks, the throughput is defined as the total number of user interactions requested and completed successfully per second. The response time is defined as the interval from the initiation of a request to the receipt of the corresponding response. We also selected and profiled other KPIs, such as CPU usage, memory usage etc.

4.3 Test Case Design

The basic types of cloud workload tasks modelled in our experiments were computation-intensive, data-intensive and communication-intensive, depending on the major resource consumed by the task. We designed and conducted five series of experiments. The first three series of experiments focused on individual types of tasks. We aimed to further investigate the impact of workload and resource allocation strategies on system performance and energy consumption of single type of tasks, as well as validate the correctness and effectiveness of StressCloud. We were able to compare these results to our previous results obtained by hand-developed workload models and loading scripts.

The last two series of experiments focused on the mixed type of tasks, examining energy and performance for tasks with e.g. a 75% compute and 25% data intensive mix of workload. The objective of the last two series of tests was to model the workloads of real cloud applications and investigate the system performance and energy consumption with different resource allocation strategies e.g. what happens when split data and compute load over different VMs vs same VM? Only one aspect was changed in each test set to try and isolate the impact factors of system performance and energy consumption. The detailed five experimental designs are described as follows.

1. Computation-intensive tasks: The major cloud resources consumed by computation-intensive tasks are CPU cores and RAM. We can further divide the computation-intensive tasks into CPU-intensive tasks and memory-intensive tasks. We deployed a web service in StressCloud which calculates a Fibonacci sequence as a representative CPU-intensive task. Each invocation of this web service was a CPU-intensive task. As the largest number of the Fibonacci sequence determined the duration of each calculation, we mapped this number to the workload of each CPU-intensive task – defined as LN. We deployed another web service in StressCloud to process big file using memory. The web service consumes as much memory as possible based on the size of memory allocated to it. Each invocation of this web service was a memory-intensive task. The size of processed file determined the workload of the memory-intensive task. We first ran CPU-intensive tasks to calculate Fibonacci sequence and increased the LN of the tasks gradually with fixed resources allocated in test suite I described in Section 5.1.1. Then, we keep resources allocated to the tasks and LN constant. In test suite II described in Section 5.1.1, we keep the number the tasks and total resource allocated constant while changing the resource allocation strategy. Another major resource consumed by a computation-intensive task is the RAM. We also measured the energy consumption and system performance by running memory-intensive tasks in test set I described in Section 5.1.2. We firstly

fixed the resources allocated to the memory-intensive tasks and increased the file size of each task. Then we increased the resources allocated to the tasks while keeping the workload of each task constant.

2. Data-intensive tasks: A data-intensive task in a cloud environment is usually I/O bound and needs to process large volumes of data. It devotes most of its processing time to the movement and manipulation of data in databases or files. In order to investigate the system performance and energy consumption of this type of task, we deployed a web service in StressCloud which could query and manipulate data records on a rational database as representative of data-intensive tasks. In test suite I described in Section 5.2, we profiled the system performance and energy consumption of different operation types (query, add, update, delete and combinations) and data size to investigate the impact of different types of database operations on the energy consumption and system performance. The database operations included "insert", "delete", "select" and "update", i.e., the most common ones. In test suite II presented in Section 5.2, we mixed all four types of database operations and kept the ratio of each type of operation constant while changing the data size of each operation, the total number of the requests and the resource allocation strategies.

3. Communication-intensive tasks: A communication-intensive task in a cloud application usually generates a huge amount of network transactions between cloud user devices and cloud systems. We have identified that the number of user requests and the data size of each request can highly impact the system performance and energy consumption [11]. In addition, the resource allocation strategies also impact the energy consumption of communication-intensive tasks [24]. Therefore, we profiled and analysed the system performance and energy consumption of communication-intensive tasks with different task workloads and resource allocation strategies. We deployed a web service in StressCloud that took client requests of varying frequency and with varying payload size and generated responses of varying size. In test suite I described in Section 5.3, we firstly fixed the resource allocation while increasing the number of user requests and the packet size of each requests. We then fixed the packet size of each request while changing the number of user request per second and resource allocation in test suite II described in Section 5.3.

4. Mixed Computation-intensive and Data-intensive tasks: Increasing computation and data processing power allow more and more scientific and business applications to be deployed in cloud environments. A scientific task is usually a mix of both computation-intensive and data-intensive tasks [25]. As a rapidly increasing number of scientific tasks have been moved to the cloud, it is important to investigate the system performance and energy consumption of cloud systems with such types of mixed task types. We modelled the client load of some representative scientific applications with mixed computation-intensive and data-intensive tasks using StressCloud. We then analysed the system performance and energy consumption of the target cloud system with different workload models and resource allocation strategies in test suites I and II described in Section 5.4.

5. Mixed Computation-intensive, Data-intensive and Communication-intensive tasks: As most cloud applications require a Web server to handle user requests and a database server to process the database queries in response to the user requests. Similarly, service-oriented architectures have multiple distributed compute and data services with significant inter-service communication. Therefore, a cloud application typically has workload tasks composed of a mixture of communication-intensive tasks, data-intensive tasks and computation-intensive tasks. Different services have different mixes of these workload task types. We aimed to investigate the impact of the application workloads and the allocated resources on the system performance and energy consumption of the cloud system. We selected JPetStore as the cloud application to test in our experiment as it has been widely used as a representative Web application that produces a transactional workload. We modelled the workload of JPetStore using StressCloud based on the client load model introduced by Cai [26]. We profiled and analysed the system performance and energy consumption with different client load models and different resource allocation and deployment strategies in test suites *I* and *II* presented in Section 5.5.

5. EXPERIMENTAL RESULTS

We conducted five major sets of tests to analyse the system performance and energy consumption incurred by different types of cloud tasks in order to analyse the impact of workload and resource allocation strategy on system performance and energy consumption. We took system workloads and system configurations as inputs. The energy consumption of each task, the system throughput and the response time were the outputs of our experiments. In order to reduce measurement error, each set of tests was repeated ten times. We evaluated the correctness of StressCloud by comparing the test results of computation-intensive tasks and communication-intensive tasks conducted by StressCloud to our manually obtained previous test results presented in [11]. We analysed the correlation coefficients of energy consumption, system resource allocation strategies and workload, as well as system performance in cloud systems. The results can be used as guidelines to improve overall energy efficiency of cloud systems.

5.1 Computation-Intensive Workloads

A computation-intensive task can be further categorised into CPU-intensive and memory-intensive based on the major resources it consumes. A CPU-intensive task in cloud systems requires a number of isolated processes to perform the computation. A memory-intensive task consumes large amount of memory to store and manipulate data during task execution.

We deployed a web service in StressCloud that calculates Fibonacci sequences as CPU-intensive task. We mapped the largest number of the Fibonacci sequence to the workload of each CPU-intensive task – defined as LN (See Section 4.3). We deployed another web service in StressCloud to process big file using memory. The web service consumes as much memory as possible based on the size of memory allocated to it. Each invocation of this web service was a memory-intensive task. The size of processed file determined the workload of the memory-intensive task.

5.1.1 CPU-Intensive Workload
Test Suite *I*: Keeping the number of tasks constant, while gradually increasing the CPU cores allocated to the task, and the workload of the task.

The total number of tasks was set to 10. This set of tests was initially run on a Small VM (see Table 2 for specification details). We then gradually increased the number of CPU cores configured on the VM in the test. The results of performance and energy

consumption are presented in Figure 5 (a) and Figure 5(b). In order to validate the correctness of StressCloud, we compared the results obtained manually, shown in Figure 5(c) and Figure 5(d). We draw the same conclusions from both sets of experimental results. We observed increasing energy consumption per task caused by increasing the LN of the Fibonacci sequence as showed in Figure 5 (a). Moreover, the energy consumption of each task decreased dramatically as the number of CPU cores allocated to the task increased. This is because the execution time of a task will decrease as more CPU cores are allocated to the task. However, the increase in average energy usage rate caused by an extra core is not as much as the execution time of the task. Therefore, the energy consumption decreases accordingly. In addition, we observed a slight turning point of the energy consumption when the number of CPU cores allocated to the task reaches three. For instance, when we set the largest number of the Fibonacci sequence *LN* to 54, the energy consumption with a Large VM increased 3.6% compared to energy consumption with an XLarge VM. This shows that the overhead of scheduling an extra core can cancel out the task running time saved and will also cause more energy consumption. The system throughput is shown in Figure 5(b). As expected, the more resources allocated to the task the better the system throughput obtained. This result shows that, for CPU-intensive tasks, the system throughput rises with the number of allocated cores and the increase of system throughput is nonlinear.

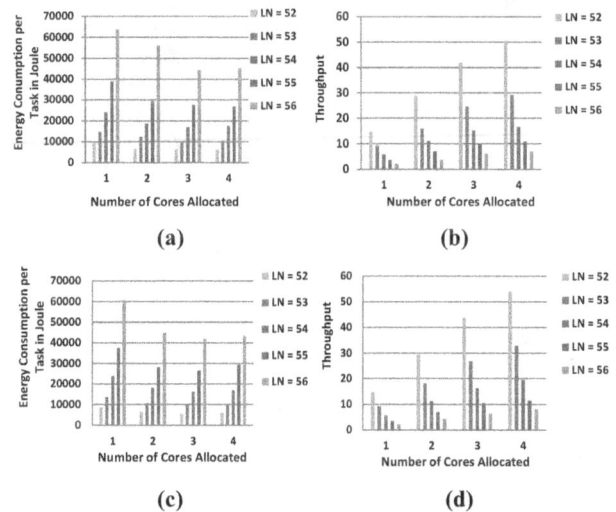

Figure 5. Energy Consumption (a) and Throughput (b) obtained by StressCloud; Energy Consumption (c) and Throughput (d) obtained manually.

Test Suite *II*: Keeping the number of tasks and resource allocated to the tasks constant, while changing the resource allocation strategy. The total number of tasks was set to 16. This set of tests was run on one XLarge VM, two Large VMs and four Small VMs respectively. All workloads were evenly distributed on all the VMs. The results of performance and energy consumption are presented in Figure 6(a) and Figure 6(b). The energy consumption per task and throughput were at the same level under different resource allocation strategies. However, the energy consumption and throughput increased slightly when we changed the resource allocation from one XLarge VM to four Small VMs. For instance, when we set the largest number of the Fibonacci sequence *LN* to 46, the energy consumption increased 1.1% and throughput increased 1.1% with four Small VMs compared to energy consumption and throughput with an XLarge VM. As the more VMs configured, the more scheduling overhead was introduced. Therefore, energy consumption was higher. On the other hand, more VMs configured make all the running tasks take full advantage of other resources such as memory. Thus, throughput was improved.

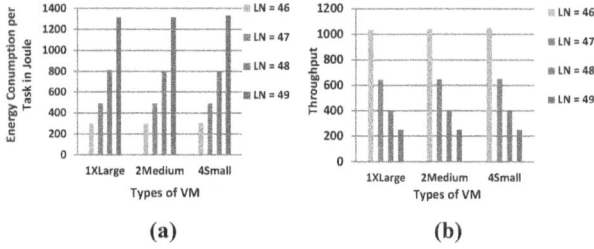

(a)   (b)

Figure 6. Energy Consumption (a) and Throughput (b).

5.1.2 *Memory-Intensive Workload*
Test suite *I*: Keeping the number of tasks constant, while gradually increasing the size of RAM allocated to the task, and the workload of the task.

The total number of tasks was set to 10. This set of tests was initially run on a Small VM. We then gradually increased the size of RAM configured on the VM in the test. With each RAM configuration, the size of file processed was set to 10G, 15G, 20G and 25G respectively. The server power consumption and average memory usage are presented in Figure 7(a) and Figure 7(b). When we increased total memory allocated to the tasks from 2GB to 8GB, the average memory usage of the server increased accordingly as showed in Figure 7 (b). However, the power consumption of the server remained at the same level as displayed in Figure 7(a). Task memory usage has only slight impacted on total power consumption. Other research on the power consumption of memory reports that the power consumption of memory remains constant regardless of the workloads. However, power consumption of memory is proportional to the number of memory chips [27]. In addition, the execution time of a task will increase when we increase the size of file processed by the task. Therefore, the energy consumption of each task will increase and the system throughput will decrease, as presented in Figure 7(c) and Figure 7(d).

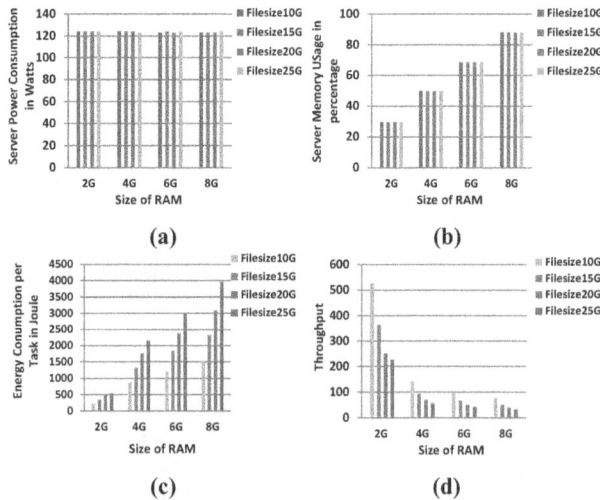

(a)   (b)

(c)   (d)

Figure 7. Server Power Consumption (a) and Memory Usage (b); Task Energy Consumption (c) and Throughput (d).

5.2 Data-Intensive Workloads
A data-intensive task in cloud environment usually involves processing and manipulating large amounts of data to and from storage. We deployed a web service in StressCloud that can query and manipulate data records in a rational database to process data-intensive tasks. We selected mixes of database operations, "insert", "update", "delete" and "select". Each invocation of this web service was a data-intensive task. The size of data processed by the database operations determined the workload of the data-intensive task.

Test suite *I*: Keeping the number of tasks constant, while gradually increasing the workload of each task. The total number of tasks was set to 1000 and user request rate was set to 10 per second. This set of test was run on an XLarge VM. SQL server 2005 was installed to process all the database requests. The result of energy consumption is presented in Figure 8(a). System throughput and response time are presented in Figure 8(b) and Figure 8(c) respectively. As illustrated in Figure 8(a), energy consumption of "insert" and "update" operations increased dramatically when we increased the record size of each request. However, the energy consumption of "delete" and "select" operations only had a slight increase. The "insert" and "update" operations both require reading and writing large amount of data on the disk compared to "select" and "delete" operations, which results in more power consumption of the server. In addition, the response time of "insert" and "update" operations were much longer than "delete" and "select" operations. Therefore, task execution time of "insert" and "update" operations increased, which caused high energy consumption and low throughput as displayed in Figure 8(b).

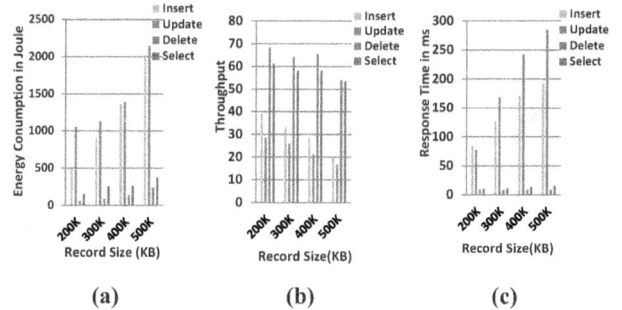

(a)   (b)   (c)

Figure 8. Energy Consumption (a), Throughput (b) and Response Time (c).

Test suite *II*: Keeping the ratio of each type of operation and total number of tasks constant while changing record size of database requests and user request number per second. A research on relational database workload characterisation reports that the ratio of "select", "delete", "update" and "insert" in database workload are 75.86%, 4.69%, 7.75% and 11.69% respectively [28]. We adopted the abovementioned ratio of each database operation in our tests. The total number of tasks was set to 1000. We gradually increased the user request rate from 10 to 40. In this set of tests, the record size of each database request was set to 400KB and 500KB respectively. This set of tests was run on an XLarge VM. SQL server 2005 was installed with default configurations to process all the database requests. The system performance and energy consumption are presented in Figure 9. As displayed in Figure 9(b), the throughput decreased slightly while increasing the record size from 400KB to 500KB. This is because response time increased as the record size increased as displayed in Figure 9(c). Therefore, the task execution time increased and throughput decreased accordingly. As presented in Figure 9(a), the energy consumption of all the tasks increased dramatically as record size increased. Total amount of data read and write on hard disk increased as the record size increased, which resulted in longer task execution time. In addition, the bigger record size introduced more data reading/writing scheduling overhead and the power consumption of the server increased. Therefore, the energy consumption increased. As presented in Figure 9(a) and Figure 9(b), the energy consumption decreased and throughput increased when we increased the number of user requests per second. However, there was a turning point when the number of user requests per second reached 30. For instance, when we set the record size to 500KB and user requests per second to 40, the energy consumption increased 7.8% and the throughput decreased 3.2%. This is because task consolidation will increase the resource utilisation which will reduce the total execution time. However, when the user requests reach 40 per second, the overhead of scheduling and synchronising user requests can cancel out the task running time saved and will cause more energy consumption.

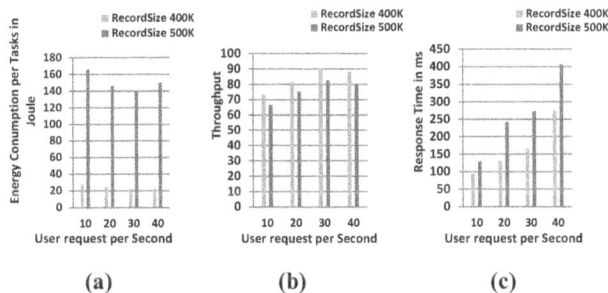

Figure 9. Energy Consumption (a), Throughput (b) and Response Time (c).

5.3 Communication-Intensive Workloads

A communication-intensive task in cloud environments usually generates a huge amount of network transactions between cloud user devices and cloud systems. Therefore, we deployed a web service in StressCloud that handled user requests and generated responses upon the receipt of user requests.

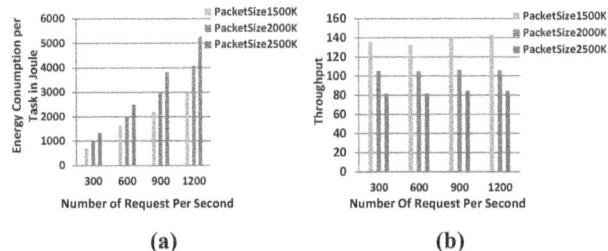

Figure 10. Energy Consumption (a) and Throughput (b).

Test suite I: Keep the resource allocation strategy constant while increasing the number of user requests and the packet size of each request. This set of test was running on a Small VM. We increased the user requests per second from 300 to 1200 in steps of 300. The packet size of each user request was increased from 1500KB to 2500KB in steps of 500. The results of energy consumption and throughput are presented in Figure 10. As presented in Figure 10(a), there was an increase in the energy consumption of the task when we increased the packet size. For instance, when we set the user requests per second to 300, the energy increased 36.7% when we increase the packet size from 1500KB to 2500KB. Furthermore, the throughput decreased as

the packet size increased. Bigger packet size usually leads to more transmission time over the network and more processing time in the cloud environment. Accordingly, throughput decreases and energy consumption increases for the communication-intensive task.

Test suite II: Keep the packet size of each request constant while changing the number of user request per second and resource allocation strategy. The packet size in this test set was set to 2500KB. The results of energy consumption and throughput are presented in Figure 11. When we increased the VM allocated to the task from Small to XLarge, the energy consumption decreased while system throughput increased in general. Intuitively, the more resources used the greater the energy consumption. However in this case, the smaller the instance the higher the disk accesses due to the thrashing of the cache, which leads to increase in energy consumption. Noticeably, when the size of the VM changed from Large to XLarge, the system throughput decreased and the system energy consumption increased in general. When we set the type of VM to XLarge, the total capacity of the VM reached the full capacity of the physical server. The resources left for VM management were less, which led to longer processing time of each user request. Therefore, deploying the task on a Large VM is the most energy efficient.

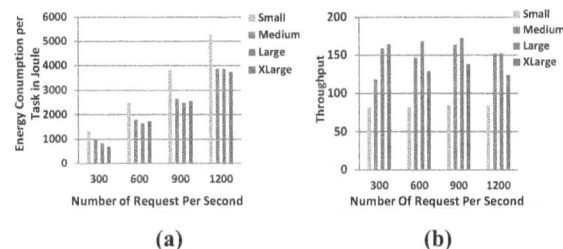

Figure 11. Energy Consumption (a) and Throughput (b).

5.4 Mixed Computation- and Data-Intensive Workloads

Increasing computation and data processing power allow more and more scientific and business applications to be deployed in cloud environments. A scientific application is both computation-intensive and data-intensive, where computed and retrieved data sets from the cloud data centre are often gigabytes or even terabytes. We modelled the client load of a small scale scientific application with 50% computation-intensive tasks and 50% data-intensive tasks. Firstly, a computation-intensive task and a data-intensive task are executed sequentially. Then the process is repeated until all data have been processed.

Test suite I: Keep the resource allocation strategy and total amount of data processed constant, while changing the size of each data set. The scientific application was deployed on an XLarge VM in this set of test. We set the total amount of data processed to 2GB. We increased the data set size of the data-intensive task from 1000KB to 8000KB. The computation-intensive task scale *LN* was increased from 36 to 39. The results of energy consumption and system throughput are presented in Figure 12. From Figure 12(a), we can see that the application energy consumption decreased when we increased the size of the data set in a linear manner. As the size of the data set increased, less overhead information needed to be processed and stored, which led to shorter execution time of the same workload. Therefore, system throughput increased, shown in Figure 12(b).

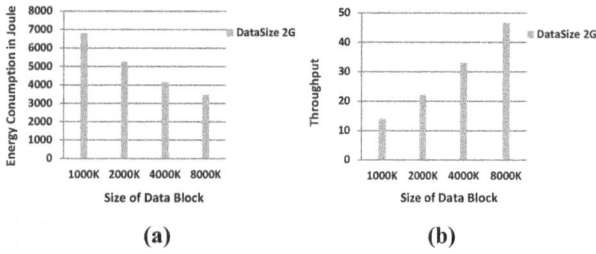

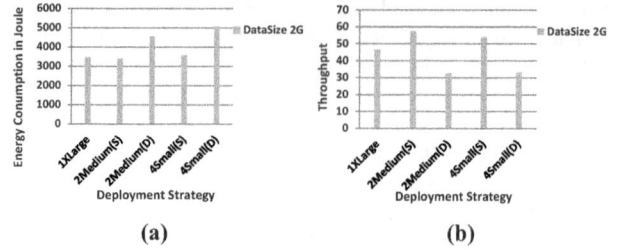

Figure 12. Energy Consumption (a) and Throughput (b).

Figure 13. Energy Consumption (a) and Throughput (b).

Test suite *II*: Keep the total amount of data processed and size of each data set constant, while changing the resource allocation strategy. In this set of test, the data set size of the data-intensive task was set to 8000KB and the task scale *LN* of computation-intensive task was set to 39. Firstly, we deployed the scientific application on one XLarge. Then, we deployed the scientific application on two Medium VMs and four Small VMs respectively with computation-intensive task and data-intensive task deployed on the same VM. We named the deployment strategies "2Medium(S)" and "4Small(S)" respectively. The workload was evenly distributed on all the VMs. Finally, we deployed the scientific application to two Medium VMs and four Small VMs respectively with computation-intensive task and data-intensive task on different VMs. We named the deployment strategies "2Medium(D)" and "4Small(D)" respectively. The workload was also evenly distributed on all the VMs. The results of application energy consumption and system throughput are presented in Figure 13. As displayed in Figure 13(a), the energy consumption of the application varied with different deployment strategies. When we deployed the application on the VMs with the same scale, the energy consumption increased when we changed the deployment strategy of the computation-intensive task and data-intensive task from the same VM to different VMs. In contrary, the system throughput increased as displayed in Figure 13(b). For instance, when we change the deployment strategy from "2Medium(S)" to "2Medium(D)", the energy consumption increased 33.5% while throughput decreased 40.3%. This is because deploying the computation-intensive task and data-intensive task on different VMs will introduce more communication overhead between VMs, which will result in more processing time. In addition, when we increase the number of VMs, the energy consumption increased and system throughput decreased no matter how the two kinds of tasks were deployed (on the same VM or different VMs). For instance, when we change the deployment strategy from "2Medium(S)" to "4Small(S)", the energy consumption increased 4.5% and throughput decreased 5.8%. This is because more VMs will introduce extra operation system scheduling overhead, which will cause longer service requests processing time of the cloud application. The more VMs are allocated to the cloud application, the more concurrent processes are created to process the service requests of the cloud application. However, the extra service requests processing time introduced by the extra VM operation system scheduling overhead cannot be cancelled out by the new created concurrent processes. The overall application execution time will be longer. Therefore, energy consumption will increase and throughput will decrease accordingly. In summary, deploying the scientific application on two Medium VMs with all kinds of cloud services on the same VM is the most energy efficient while achieving the best system performance.

5.5 Mixed Computation-, Data- and Communication-Intensive Workloads

Most cloud applications have workload tasks composed of a mix of communication-intensive tasks, data-intensive tasks and computation-intensive tasks. Different services have different mixes of these workload task types. JPetStore was selected as the cloud application to test in our experiment as it has been widely used as a representative Web application that produces a transactional workload. We modelled the workload of JPetStore using StressCloud based on the client load model introduced by Cai [26] and shown in Section 3.

Test suite *I*: Keep the resource allocation strategy constant while changing workload. This cloud application was deployed on a Large VM in this set of test. The initial number of users was set to 10. We increased the concurrent requests number of each user from 50 to 200 in steps of 50. The results of energy consumption and system throughput are presented in Figure 14. As the number of concurrent requests increased, the energy consumption increased as displayed in Figure 14(a). The throughput decreased accordingly as shown in Figure 14(b). Intuitively, more user requests will introduce more scheduling and synchronising overhead in the cloud application, which will result in increase of the processing time of each user request.

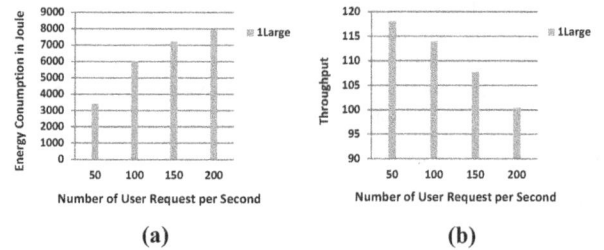

Figure 14. Energy Consumption (a) and Throughput (b).

Test suite *II*: Keep the workload constant while changing the resource allocation strategy. The initial number of users was set to 10 and the concurrent user requests of each user were set to 100 in this set of tests. We firstly deployed the cloud application on one Large VM. Then we deployed the cloud application on three Small VMs with computation-intensive tasks, data-intensive tasks and communication-intensive tasks on different VMs respectively, named "3Small(D)". Finally, we deployed the cloud application on three Small VMs with workload evenly distributed on all three VMs, named "3Small(S)". The energy consumption and system throughput are presented in Figure 15. Although the total resources such as CPU and RAM allocated were the same, the energy consumption decreased when deploying the cloud application on multiple VMs compared to deploying the cloud application on single VM as shown in Figure 15(a). The system throughput increased accordingly as displayed in Figure 15(b). When deploying the cloud application on multiple VMs, the service requests of the cloud application were processed in more concurrent processes, which reduced the execution time of the cloud application. In addition, we observed that the energy consumption with deployment strategy "3Small(S)" increased 0.8% compared to "3Small(D)". The system throughput of "3Small(S)" decreased 2.1% compared to "3Small(D)". This is because in the client workload we have modelled in this test, the majority of all the tasks are communication-intensive. Deploying all communication-intensive tasks on one single VM greatly reduces the overhead of concurrent processes between different VMs. In summary, deploying this cloud application on three Small VMs and separating different types of cloud services on different VM is most energy efficient while achieving the best system performance.

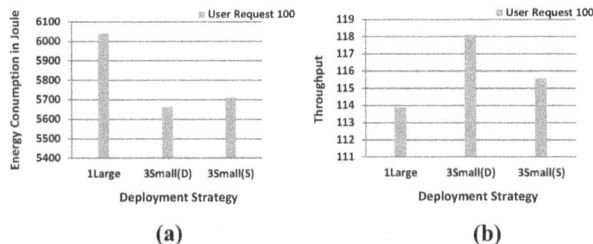

Figure 15. Energy Consumption (a) and Throughput (b).

6. DISCUSSION

Based on our experimental results to date, we have derived a set of guidelines which can be adopted to achieve energy efficient cloud application deployment. Note that performance engineers can use StressCloud to model an application workload and its cloud platform deployment model in a wide variety of ways. They can then generate and run extensive tests and obtain energy and performance data for these specific application models. They can thus make specific judgements for each application and deployment about their best configuration for energy efficiency and performance.

From our results above we see that the organisation of cloud application workload does indeed highly impact energy consumption and system performance. As seen in Section 5.4, when we scaled up each data set processed by the scientific application and kept the total amount of data processed constant, the system performance increased while energy consumption decreased. For some cloud applications, their workload is either known or can be empirically determined and is relatively constant. However, due to the dynamic nature of many cloud applications and the demand of different hosting platforms, the workload of different cloud applications can drastically change over time. The need to find out the workload patterns for different cloud applications, in order to schedule them for optimal performance and energy consumption, has emerged.

The type of cloud application workload impacts energy consumption and system performance. For instance, as discussed in Section 5.1.1, the energy consumption of CPU-intensive task increased dramatically when CPU usage increases. However, as presented in Section 5.1.2, the energy consumption of memory-intensive remained at the same level regardless of the memory usage. The elasticity in the pay-as-you-go cloud business model requires allocating cloud resources to different cloud applications adaptively according to on-demand user requirements. However, it is very challenging as resource under-provisioning will unavoidably jeopardise system performance and cause SLA violations, while resource over-provisioning will result in resource idleness and energy waste. Thus, it is important to accurately predict the resources needed by the cloud application.

For a specific cloud application, the resource allocation strategy can greatly affect the energy consumption and system performance. For instance, deploying the scientific application on two Medium VMs with computation-intensive tasks and data-intensive tasks isolated on two different VMs is the most energy efficient. On the contrary, when we deploy the JPetStore to three Small VMs with all tasks evenly distributed on all the VMs is the most energy efficient. As discussed, both of the abovementioned resource allocation strategies result in the reducing communication and scheduling overhead inside the deployed cloud application. Therefore, it is important to avoid communication overhead within the cloud application when deciding deployment options.

7. SUMMARY AND FUTURE WORK

Understanding performance and energy consumption dynamics is important for the design and deployment of cloud applications to balance energy and performance requirements. In this paper, we presented StressCloud, a new tool for profiling the performance and energy consumption of cloud systems. Using StressCloud, we conducted extensive experiments to profile and analyse system performance and energy consumption with different types and mixes of runtime tasks in a controlled, representative cloud system. We profiled the performance and energy consumption of cloud application models under various task workloads and resource allocation strategies. The correlation of system performance and energy consumption was analysed based on our experimental results. These results provide guidelines for developing resource provisioning and management solutions at minimum energy consumption while still guaranteeing Service Level Agreements (SLAs).

Currently, we are running further experiments including large scale composite workloads on heterogeneous cloud servers. We compare the results of performance and energy consumption with different resource allocation strategies. We analyse overhead of cross-server scheduling and communication overhead of a cloud system. In addition, an energy cost rate and an "energy dirtiness rate" will be adopted to factor in the costs – monetary and environmental - of cloud energy generated by different resources. The energy cost will be investigated in order to achieve the best energy, cost and performance balance in cloud systems.

ACKNOWLEDGMENTS
We thank Professor Ryszard Kowalczyk for providing the facilities of Swinburne Energy Research Lab. This research is partly supported by the Australian Research Council under Discovery Project DP110101340.

REFERENCES
[1] Armbrust, M., Fox, A., Griffith, R., Joseph, A. D., Katz, R. H., et al. *Above the clouds: a Berkeley view of cloud computing.* Technical Report UCB/EECS-2009-28, UC Berkeley Reliable Adaptive Distributed Systems Laboratory, USA, 2009.

[2] Greenberg, A., Hamilton, J., Maltz, D. A. and Patel, P. The cost of a cloud: research problems in data center networks. *ACM SIGCOMM Computer Communication Review*, 39(1):68-73, 2009.

[3] Lee, Y. C. and Zomaya, A. Y. Energy efficient utilization of resources in cloud computing systems. *The Journal of Supercomputing*, 60(2):268-280, 2012.

[4] Hamilto, J. Cooperative expendable micro-slice servers (CEMS): low cost, low power servers for internet-scale services. In *Proceedings of the 4th Biennial Conference on Innovative Data Systems Research(CIDR2009)*, pages 1-8, Asilomar, California, USA, 2009.

[5] Babcock, C. *NY Times data center indictment misses the big picture.* InformationWeek Cloud, New York, USA, 2012.

[6] Shang, L., Peh, L.-S. and Jha, N. K. Dynamic voltage scaling with links for power optimization of interconnection networks. In *Proceedings of the 9th International Symposium on High-Performance Computer Architecture(HPCA2003)*, pages 91-102, Anaheim, California, USA, 2003.

[7] Clark, C., Fraser, K., Hand, S., Hansen, J. G., Jul, E., et al. Live migration of virtual machines. In *Proceedings of the 2nd Symposium on Networked Systems Design and Implementation(NSDI2005)*, pages 273-286, Boston, Massachusetts, USA, 2005.

[8] Raghavendra, R., Ranganathan, P., Talwar, V., Wang, Z. and Zhu, X. No "power" struggles: coordinated multi-level power management for the data center. In *Proceedings of the 13th International Conference on Architectural Support for Programming Languages and Operating Systems(ASPLOS2008)*, pages 48-59, Seattle, WA, USA, 2008.

[9] Zhang, Z. and Fu, S. Characterizing power and energy usage in cloud computing systems. In *Proceedings of the 3rd IEEE International Conference on Cloud Computing Technology and Science(CloudCom2011)*, pages 146-153, Athens, Greece, 2011.

[10] Chen, F., Schneider, J.-G., Yang, Y., Grundy, J. and He, Q. An energy consumption model and analysis tool for Cloud computing environments. In *Proceedings of the 1st International Workshop on Green and Sustainable Software(GREENS2012)*, pages 45-50, Zurich, Switzerland, 2012.

[11] Chen, F., Grundy, J., Yang, Y., Schneider, J.-G. and He, Q. Experimental Analysis of Task-based Energy Consumption in Cloud Computing Systems. In *Proceedings of the 4th ACM/SPEC International Conference on Performance Engineering(ICPE2013)*, pages 295-306, Prague, Czech Republic, 2013.

[12] Metri, G., Srinivasaraghavan, S., Shi, W. and Brockmeyer, M. Experimental Analysis of Application Specific Energy Efficiency of Data Centers with Heterogeneous Servers. In *Proceedings of the IEEE 5th International Conference on Cloud Computing*, pages 786-793, Honolulu, Hawaii, USA, 2012.

[13] Draheim, D., Grundy, J., Hosking, J., Lutteroth, C. and Weber, G. Realistic Load Testing of Web Applications. In *Proceedings of the 10th European Conference on Software Maintenance and Reengineering (CSMR'06)*, pages 70-81, Bari, Italy, 2006.

[14] Nathuji, R. and Schwan, K. VirtualPower: coordinated power management in virtualized enterprise systems. In *Proceedings of the 21st ACM Symposium on Operating Systems Principles(SOSP2007)*, pages 265-278, Stevenson, Washington, USA, 2007.

[15] Verma, A., Ahuja, P. and Neogi, A. Power-aware dynamic placement of hpc applications. In *Proceedings of the 22nd Annual International Conference on Supercomputing(ICS2008)*, pages 175-184, Island of Kos, Greece, 2008.

[16] Liu, L., Wang, H., Liu, X., Jin, X., He, W., et al. GreenCloud: A New Architecture for Green Data Center. In *Proceedings of the 6th International Conference Industry Session on Autonomic Computing and Communications Iindustry Session (ICAC-INDST '09)*, pages 29-38, Barcelona, Spain, 2009.

[17] Chen, Q., Grosso, P., van der Veldt, K., de Laat, C., Hofman, R., et al. Profiling energy consumption of VMs for green cloud computing. In *Proceedings of the 9th IEEE International Conference on Dependable, Autonomic and Secure Computing(DASC2011)*, pages 768-775, Sydney, Australia, 2011.

[18] Stoess, J., Lang, C. and Bellosa, F. Energy management for hypervisor-based virtual machines. In *Proceedings of the 2007 USENIX Annual Technical Conference(USENIX2007)*, pages 1-14, Santa Clara, CA, USA, 2007.

[19] Kansal, A., Zhao, F., Kothari, N. and Bhattacharya, A. A. Virtual machine power metering and provisioning. In *Proceedings of the 1st ACM Symposium on Cloud Computing(SoCC2010)*, pages 39-50, Indianapolis, Indiana, USA, 2010.

[20] Lefèvre, L. and Orgerie, A.-C. Designing and evaluating an energy efficient Cloud. *Journal of Supercomputing*, 51(3):352-373, 2010.

[21] Zhang, Q., Cheng, L. and Boutaba, R. Cloud computing: state-of-the-art and research challenges. *Journal of Internet Services and Applications*, 1(1):7-18, 2010.

[22] Koller, R., Verma, A. and Neogi, A. WattApp: An Application Aware Power Meter for Shared Data Centers. In *Proceedings of the 7th International Conference on Autonomic Computing(ICAC2010)*, pages 31-40, Reston, VA, USA, 2010.

[23] Wang, Q., Kanemasa, Y., Li, J., Jayasinghe, D., Kawaba, M., et al. Response Time Reliability in Cloud Environments: An Empirical Study of n-Tier Applications at High Resource Utilization. In *Proceedings of the 31st Symposium on Reliable Distributed Systems*, pages 378-383, Irvine, CA, USA, 2012.

[24] Dargie, W., Strunk, A. and Schill, A. Energy-aware service execution. In *Proceedings of the IEEE 36th Conference on Local Computer Networks(LCN)*, pages 1064-1071, Bonn, Germany, 2011.

[25] Yuan, D., Yang, Y., Liu, X., Li, W., Cui, L., et al. A Highly Practical Approach toward Achieving Minimum Data Sets Storage Cost in the Cloud. *IEEE Transactions on Parallel and Distributed Systems (TPDS)*, 24(6):1234-1244, 2013.

[26] Cai, Y., Grundy, J. and Hosking, J. Synthesizing Client Load Models for Performance Engineering via Web Crawling. In *Proceedings of the 22rd IEEE/ACM International Conference on Automated Sofeware Engineering(ASE)*, pages 353-362, Atlanta, Georgia, USA, 2007.

[27] Peter, K., Bergman, K., Borkar, S., Campbell, D., Carlson, W., et al. *ExaScale Computing Study:Technology Challenges in Achieving Exascale Systems.* FA8650-07-C-7724, 2008.

[28] Yu, P. S., Chen, M.-S., Heiss, H.-U. and Lee, S. On Workload Characterization of Relational Database Environments. *IEEE Transactions on Software Engineering*, 18(4):347-355, 1992.

An Experimental Methodology to Evaluate Energy Efficiency and Performance in an Enterprise Virtualized Environment

Jesus Omana Iglesias
School of Computer Science and Informatics
University College Dublin
Dublin, Ireland
10289844@ucdconnet.ie

Philip Perry
School of Computer Science and Informatics
University College Dublin
Dublin, Ireland
philip.perry@ucd.ie

Liam Murphy
School of Computer Science and Informatics
University College Dublin
Dublin, Ireland
liam.murphy@ucd.ie

Teodora Sandra Buda
School of Computer Science and Informatics
University College Dublin
Dublin, Ireland
teodora.buda@ucdconnect.ie

James Thorburn
IBM
Software Group
Toronto, Canada
jthorbur@ca.ibm.com

ABSTRACT

Computing servers generally have a narrow dynamic power range. For instance, even completely idle servers consume between 50% and 70% of their peak power. Since the usage rate of the server has the main influence on its power consumption, energy-efficiency is achieved whenever the utilization of the servers that are powered on reaches its peak. For this purpose, enterprises generally adopt the following technique: consolidate as many workloads as possible via virtualization in a minimum amount of servers (i.e. maximize utilization) and power down the ones that remain idle (i.e. reduce power consumption). However, such approach can severely impact servers' performance and reliability.

In this paper, we propose a methodology to determine the ideal values for power consumption and utilization for a server without performance degradation. We accomplish this through a series of experiments using two typical types of workloads commonly found in enterprises: TPC-H and SPECpower_ssj2008 benchmarks. We use the first to measure the amount of queries responded successfully per hour for different numbers of users (i.e. *Throughput@Size*) in the VM. Moreover, we use the latter to measure the power consumption and number of operations successfully handled by a VM at different target loads. We conducted experiments varying the utilization level and number of users for different VMs and the results show that it is possible to reach the maximum value of power consumption for a server, without experiencing performance degradations when running individual, or mixing workloads.

Categories and Subject Descriptors

C.4 [**Performance of Systems**]: Measurement techniques; D.2.8 [**Software Engineering**]: Metrics—*performance measures*

1. INTRODUCTION

Nowadays large investments have been made to build data centers (i.e. purpose-built facilities composed of thousands of servers, providing storage and computing service within and across organizational boundaries). In our previous work, we show that one of the main contributors to the overall cost of running a server is the energy-related cost [23]. Nevertheless, it is often the case that enterprises have idle servers operating at very low levels of utilization, whilst consuming between 50 and 70% of their peak power [10]. Moreover, data collected from more than $5,000$ production servers over a six-month period showed that servers operate only at 10-50% of their full capacity most of the time, leading to expenses on over-provisioning, and thus extra Total Cost of Acquisition (TCA) [9]. With the increase of energy costs, the research community has been trying to solve the energy efficiency problem from two different perspectives: (i) creating servers that consume energy proportional to their utilization level, and (ii) maximizing the utilization of the minimum number of servers. In this work, we solely address the impact of the second perspective.

In order to maximize utilization, enterprises generally consolidate workloads via virtualization. Virtualization is a technique that enables applications to share the same physical server by creating multiple virtual machines in such a manner that each application can assume the ownership of the virtual machine (VM) [14]. One of the benefits of virtualization is the potentially more efficient utilization of the server's hardware resources. This can be accomplished when VMs with complementary workload patterns achieve the maximum utilization level that a server can handle, or when the workloads in each VM have complementary resource usage patterns. Furthermore, our work is focused on virtualized environments that run the type of workloads that are typically used in enterprises. We define in detail the performance degradation for a VM depending on the type of workload in section 4.3.

However, high levels of utilization tend to be associated to a higher performance degradation. For instance, it is expected that an application with average utilization approaching 100% is likely to have difficulty meeting its performance requirements (i.e. throughput and latency service-level-agreements). Due to this fact, enterprises will not risk the performance of their VMs in order to maximize the utilization of their servers, thus leading to low levels of utilization. Furthermore, to the best of our knowledge this is the first attempt of analyzing empirically whether it is possible to reach a balance between performance and energy efficiency for typical enterprise workloads. Moreover, previous work [13, 21], assume that when VMs with complementary resource usage patterns reach the maximum utilization level, there will be no performance degradation. However, through our experiments, we show conclusive results that this hypothesis is not always true. In addition, previous work did not study whether the state of a VM influences the performance degradation. For instance, we show that idle VMs do not affect performance regardless of how intensively the active VMs are used. We present this in detail in section 4.4.

The main goal of this paper is to present a methodology for achieving energy-efficiency in a server with no performance degradation per VM. For this purpose, we experimentally investigate the relationship between performance degradation and energy-efficiency for two typical workloads used in enterprises: SPECpower_ssj2008 [4] and TPC-H [8] benchmarks. We use SPECpower_ssj2008 for exploring the number of operations successfully handled by a VM and the power consumption associated at several levels of utilization. We further refer to SPECpower_ssj2008 as SPECpower in the remainder of this paper. We use TPC-H for evaluating the response time for business-oriented ad-hoc queries and concurrent data modifications. In particular, we use the metric *Throughput@Size* from TPC-H which measures the amount of queries that can be executed per hour for different amounts of users.

We explore different scenarios in which a server increases its utilization and dependability and especially how that relates to performance degradation. In order to vary the scenarios we introduced the concept of states of a VM (e.g, idle, constant) to aids the detection of performance degradations. We experimentally studied the relationship between throughput (i.e, queries per hour or number of operations) and performance degradation. Furthermore, we also investigated the relationship between the type of workload (i.e., TPC-H or SPECpower) and performance degradation. Finally, we examined the consequences in performance and energy-efficiency of mixing these two types of workloads. It is important to mention that this experimental methodology can be adapted to a concrete implementation, and provide an automated technique to find a balance between power consumption and performance.

This paper is structured as follows: Section 2 presents the two benchmarks used in this work, namely SPECpower and TPC-H. Section 3 presents a set of relevant questions that need to be addressed in order to find a balance between energy-efficiency and performance. In section 4 we address these questions with the use of a set of scenarios. Section 5 provides an overview of the related work. Finally, section 6 concludes the paper and presents future work.

2. BACKGROUND

In this section, we present the main features of the two benchmarks used in this work, namely, an overview of their design and functionality in order to facilitate the understanding of the questions addressed in this work and their results.

2.1 Overview of SPECpower benchmark

The SPECpower benchmark was designed to produce consistent and repeatable performance and power measurements. The purpose of the benchmark is to imitate a server-side Java transaction processing application. SPECpower strains the CPU, caches, and memory hierarchy, as well as the implementations of the Java virtual machine (JVM), just-in-time (JIT) compiler, and garbage collection. The benchmark is based on the SPECjbb2005 benchmark [4]. It has strict rules for compliance in case the user wants to upload the results into their website. For example, it is necessary to use two systems, namely a system under test (SUT) and a system for control and collection (CCS) [5]. However, due to the amount of experiments that we needed to perform we set the SUT and CCS in the same VM. Furthermore, we first perform the experiments using a laptop as a CCS and did not find any significant difference in the results.

SPECpower executes different types of transactions such as: new order, payment, order status, delivery, stock level, and customer report. The input for each transaction is randomly generated and it modifies in-memory data structures such as warehouses and customers. Transactions are grouped together in batches for scheduling purposes. The delay between batches is calculated to achieve the desired throughput for each target load. In essence, SPECpower runs the workload at different load-levels and reports the power and performance at each load-level [6].

The benchmark starts with a calibration phase, which determines the maximum throughput. The calibrated throughput is set as the throughput target for 100% load-level. The throughput target for the rest of the load-levels is calculated as a percentage of the throughput target for 100% load-level. For example, if the calibrated throughput is 200,000 server-side Java operations per second (i.e. ssj_ops), the 50% target load would have a target throughput of 100,000 ssj_ops. With 10 warehouses, each warehouse needs to sustain a throughput of 10,000 ssj_ops, since there are 2,000 transactions per batch, each warehouse will execute an average of 5 batches per second. Thus, the mean delay between batches is 200 ms. The downside of this feature is that in some cases the benchmark may have an error between the target and the actual load, which may be easily mistaken as performance degradation. For instance, in figure 4(a) there is a $\pm$ 1% of error margin due to the way the ssj_ops are batched.

The benchmark supports a set of configurable parameters. For example, the maximum target throughput can be manually configured, as well as the sequence of load-levels, the time of each load, the number of calibrations, etc. The reader can refer to [7] for more information on which parameters are configurable. The flexibility, coupled with the consistency and repeatability of SPECpower, allow us to investigate a balance between energy-efficiency and performance for enterprise-class server workloads.

2.2 Overview of TPC-H benchmark

The TPC-H benchmark is a decision support benchmark comprising a suite of business oriented ad-hoc queries and data modifications [8]. The term decision support implies that managers and executives would need to retrieve data from the database in order to draw a pattern of the company financial results and facilitate their decision making process. TPC-H creates the data for a relational database comprised of eight tables that stores typical product supply information. The benchmark also involves ad-hoc workload that aims to produce unpredictable queries [17].

The workload of the benchmark consists of 22 queries and 2 update procedures, all representing frequent decision making questions. Furthermore, the 22 queries have a high-level of complexity and give answers to real-world business questions. The queries include a rich scope of operators and selectivity constraints, access a large percentage of the populated data and tables and generate intensive disk and CPU activity on the part of the database server. The update procedures are called refresh functions (RFs) [8]. The refreshing functions are not included in the benchmark and they were created by us following the TPC-H guidelines. For instance, RF_1 adds new sales information to the database, the insertion takes place in the two most populated tables and represents 0.1% of the initial population of these two tables. Moreover, RF_2 removes old sales information from the database.

We use DBGEN, which is a data generator provided in the TPC-H package to create the data to be inserted and deleted by the refreshing functions.

Setting the Environment for TPC-H.

In order to perform any test with TPC-H it is necessary to: (i) create the database with the exact schema proposed by the Transaction Performance Council (TPC); (ii) add the constraints; (iii) generate the raw data files using the DBGEN tool; (iv) load the data into the database tables; (v) generate the workload queries to be executed using the TPC-H query generation tool (QGEN); and (vi) develop and install the necessary stored procedures, i.e, RF_1 and RF_2. After all these steps are finished, we are able to run the workload and measure the execution times.

Throughput Test.

The purpose of the throughput test is to measure the ability of the system to process the most queries in the least amount of time [17, 8]. In other words, this test is used to demonstrate the performance of the system against a multi-user workload. Each user is represented by a stream (S), which runs 21 queries in a random order. The stream executes queries in a serial manner but the streams themselves are executed in parallel. We did not consider one of the queries because its execution time was too long (i.e. more than 1 hour). The throughput test must be executed in parallel with a single refresh stream session [8].

The *Throughput@Size* metric is defined as:

$$Throughput@Size = \frac{n \times 21}{T_s} \times 3600 \times SF$$

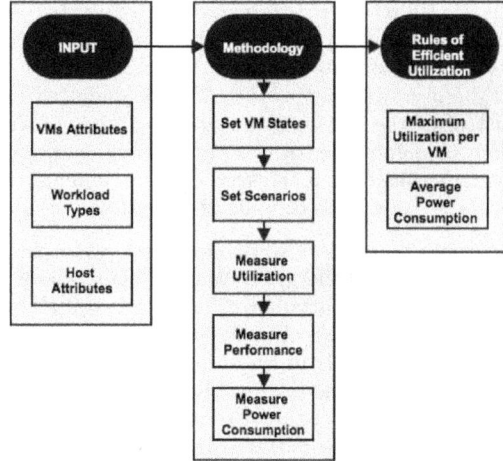

Figure 1: Overview of the proposed experimental methodology

Where n, is the total amount of users on the test. T_s is the time (in seconds) passed until all the streams executed their 21 queries. SF is the size of the database in GB. For this work $SF = 1$.

3. BALANCING ENERGY-EFFICIENCY AND PERFORMANCE

The main objective of this experimental methodology is to study the feasibility of running a server at high levels of utilization without performance degradation. In particular, we investigate the maximum value for energy consumption without any performance degradation in order to maximize the utilization of the server and reach energy-efficiency. Moreover, we study the effects of other scenarios (e.g. idle VMs) on both performance and energy consumption.

The diagram in Figure 1 presents an overview of the inputs, the methodology and finally the expected outputs. The inputs of our experimental methodology are a set of VM attributes (e.g. Number of VMs, Number of VCPU, RAM and Disk), workload types (e.g. SPECpower or TPC-H) and the characteristics of the host (e.g. CPU Cores, RAM, and Disk). After receiving the inputs, our methodology measures the performance, levels of utilization and power consumption in several scenarios using predefined VM states. The output is a set of rules of thumbs that will explicitly define the maximum level of utilization per VM in order to not experience performance degradation, together with the power consumption achieved at such levels of utilization.

3.1 Proposed Study

In this subsection, we categorize this analysis under three important relationships between performance and energy-efficiency:

1. Relationship between power consumption and performance, when there are idle VMs in a server and while varying the levels of utilization of the other VMs. We analyze this relationship on the grounds that generally users are not willing to wait the time required for a VM to boot up and demand having their VM always ready to receive workload (section 3.3).

2. Relationship between throughput, performance degradation, and energy-efficiency when reaching maximum levels of utilization. We study this relationship in order to discover whether performance degradation occurs just after the server attains certain levels of utilization, or on the contrary, VMs can have performance degradations even if the server is not running at particularly high levels of utilization (section 3.4).

3. Relationship between workload mixes, performance degradation and energy-efficiency when reaching maximum levels of utilization. This relationship explores one of the main benefits of virtualization, namely to have different VMs in the same server running workloads that consume different hardware resources (e.g, CPU, RAM, Disk) in order to maximize the utilization of the server. Thus, in this analysis we use benchmarks that simulate real applications that are typically used in enterprises, instead of considering benchmarks that use a single resource. It is important to mention that in the majority of the real-case scenarios, workloads consume more than one type of hardware resource at the same time (section 3.5).

Each of these relationships explores a set of questions that will be answered through the testing of a set of inquiries (INQ). Moreover, it is necessary to evaluate each benchmark separately since their performance metrics are different from each other. Before presenting the inquiries in detail, we first introduce the concept of VM states.

3.2 VM States

We define the state of a VM v as a pattern of utilization aimed to discover performance degradation symptoms. We denote by $U(v)$ the utilization levels of v during a single run and we define it as: $U(v) = \langle u_1, u_2, \ldots, u_n \rangle$, where u_i represents the level of utilization of v at step i, $u_i \in \{0, 10, 20, \ldots, 100\} \wedge i \in [1, n]$. Below we present the VM states considered in function of their utilization pattern:

- **Idle**: The VM runs at 0% of utilization at all steps: $\forall i \in [1, n], u_i = 0$.

- **Constant**: The VM runs SPECpower at a constant percentage of utilization at all steps: $\forall i \in [1, n], u_i = ct$, where $ct \in \{10, 20, \ldots 100\}$.

- **Active**: The VM runs SPECpower at different percentages of utilization during a single run and respects the following condition: $\forall i \in [1, n], u_i \in \{10, 20, \ldots 100\} \wedge |u_{i+1} - u_i| \leq 10$.

- **N Users**: VM running the *Throughput@Size* test with N users, where $N \in [2, 7]$.

3.3 Presence of Idle VMs

In this subsection we present two inquiries that intend to explain the effects, if any, of idle VMs on performance and power consumption. Moreover, the *baseline* for the TPC-H performance degradation was established after averaging the results from six identical experiments in which there were no *Idle* VMs.

INQ 1. *Is there an increment in the power consumption of the server due to the presence of Idle VMs? If so, is it constant regardless of the percentage of utilization in the Active VM?*

We plan to validate this relationships by running VMs at different target loads in the case of SPECpower and with different number of users in the case of TPC-H.

Regarding SPECpower we answer this inquiry by comparing the average power consumption of running one and two *Active* VMs from 10% to 100% of its maximum target load against running the same experiment but with one and two additional *Idle* VMs for the case that there is one *Active* VM, and with one *Idle* VM in the case that there are two *Active* VMs. We decided to use *Active* VMs because this will allow us to perform measurements in a very progressive and controlled environment.

With respect to TPC-H, we analyze the effects of simultaneously running VMs with different amount of users, we stress the server by running a minimum of four users (between two VMs) and a maximum of 21 users (between three VMs). We investigate if varying the amount of users when having one or two *Idle* VMs, besides the ones running in an *N Users* state, will have any repercussion in power consumption.

INQ 2. *Is there a performance degradation due to Idle VMs in a server? If so, is it constant regardless of the percentage of utilization in the Active VM?*

In order to solve this question we calculated the performance values while running the same set of experiments from INQ 1 and compared them against the *baseline*. The state of the VMs as well as the number of users for solving this question is identical as the one described in INQ 1.

3.4 Finding the maximum number of operations

We intend to empirically find the maximum number of operations that a server can handle and to test if the VMs will not experience performance degradation as long as this maximum number of operations is not reached. Below we present three inquiries that explain the effects in performance and energy-efficiency whenever the sum of utilization of the VMs gets closer to the maximum number of operations that a server can handle.

INQ 3. *Is it possible to find the maximum number of operations that a server can perform regardless of the number of VMs hosted in that server without performance degradation?*

The main goal of this inquiry is to establish a rule of thumb for maximum levels of utilization without performance degradation for both benchmarks (i.e. SPECpower and TPC-H).

In the case of SPECpower we first set two *Active* VMs with targets of utilization between 60 and 100%. Afterwards, when having three *Active* VMs we set the targets between 40 and 70%. This range of values was selected after noticing in INQ 2 that it is likely to find performance degradation between those levels of utilization.

INQ 4. *Does the state of the VM influence the maximum number of operations until the performance degrades?*

The purpose of this investigation is to observe whether depending on the state of the VM, that particular VM will experience performance degradation faster than when the server reaches its maximum levels of utilization. In the case that this is true the rule of thumb will be modified accordingly. For SPECpower, we first set a VM to a high (between

80 and 100% of utilization) *Constant* state, and then we set another VM to an *Active* state, and study if the VM that is running at a high *Constant* state experiences degradation in performance faster than the other. In another scenario, we set two VMs at a relatively low *Active* state (between 10 and 60%) and a third VM in an *Constant* state, to corroborate if the performance degradation is due to high levels of utilization or to constant levels of utilization.

INQ 5. *Is there a relationship between the results of INQ 3, INQ 4 and energy-efficiency?*

This inquiry aims to discover whether the average power consumption values from the maximum levels of utilization presented in the previous inquiries are equal to the maximum power consumption of the server. In particular, we want to explore whether it is possible to achieve the maximum energy-efficiency with no performance degradation.

3.5 Mixing different types of workloads

Following we present a set of experiments in which we combine SPECpower and TPC-H at different VM states and with different amounts of users in order to corroborate the effects of mixing different types of workload in the same server. As we already mentioned in the introduction of this work, one of the benefits of virtualization is that we could potentially allocate workloads that use different hardware resources in order to maximize the utilization of the server. It is not often the case, especially for enterprises, to find workloads that use only one particular hardware resource. More often is the case that a type of workload uses more than one hardware resource at the same time, however using more intensively one of the resources. For instance, TPC-H heavily uses CPU and Disk. However, Disk is used more intensively than CPU. SPECpower, as we already explained in section 2, it uses mostly CPU.

We primarily want to evaluate if the maximum number of operations found in the previous inquiries is the same when we substitute an *Idle* VM by a VM running TPC-H and to determine if we achieve better energy-efficiency levels when combining different types of workloads.

INQ 6. *Is it possible to combine different types of workload on the same server in a way that they do not interfere with each other and that there is no performance degradation?*

The main goal of this question is to show the effects on performance when running complementary workloads (i.e. they utilize different hardware resources). We performed several experiments with different number of users (in the case of TPC-H) and different levels of utilization for *Constant* states (in the case of SPECpower) in order to analyze the effect of workload mixes. For this inquiry, we set the experiments for SPECpower to have the same length in duration as TPC-H depending on the number of users. For instance, as $T_2 < T_7$ SPECpower will run for less time when evaluating TPC-H with two users than with seven users. We are mostly interested in finding whether the rule of thumb applies in this scenario.

INQ 7. *Is there a relationship between the results of INQ 6 and energy-efficiency?*

This inquiry presents the increment in the average power consumption values when running different types of workloads simultaneously. We have performed experiments both with two VMs and three VMs that combine the two different types of workload.

4. EVALUATION

In this section, we present the results of the inquiries defined in section 3. Furthermore, we first introduce the environment used for the experiments, along with the experimental setup.

4.1 Environment

We present below a description of the hypervisor, the characteristics of the server under test (SUT), and the characteristics of the VMs.

In order to measure the balance between energy-efficiency and performance it is necessary to establish a reliable virtualized environment. The hardware attributes of the SUT: the CPU processor is an Intel Core i7-2600 CPU at 3.40GHz. The processor has a total of 4 cores and 8 logical cores when hyper-threading is ON, as in our experiments. The SUT has 16GB of memory, a Hard Disk of 500GB, and runs a Linux Kernel version 3.2.0-4-amd64. We employ a HAMEG HM8115-2 power meter [2] for our power measurements.

When running the experiments it is necessary to emphasize that the commands were sent via ssh, meaning that no graphical interface was used in order to avoid unnecessary usage of hardware resources. Moreover, we monitored the server and VM's utilization with collectd [1].

4.1.1 KVM/QEMU

KVM (Kernel Virtual Machine)[3] is a Linux kernel module that allows a user space program to utilize the hardware virtualization features of various processors (e.g. Intel VT or AMD-V). QEMU is a generic and open source machine emulator and virtualizer [3]. KVM uses QEMU for I/O hardware emulation. KVM lets a program like QEMU safely execute guest code directly on the host CPU. This is only possible when the target architecture is supported by the host CPU; (currently is limited to x86-on-x86 virtualization only).

The main responsibilities of the KVM/QEMU package are:

- Set up the VM and I/O devices.

- Execute the operating system guest code via KVM kernel module.

- I/O emulation and live migration. Note that we enabled paravirtualized devices (i.e., virtio) to improve the I/O performance.

4.1.2 Virtual Machine Attributes

Three identical VMs were created and configured. The VM attributes are: CPU - 2 virtual CPUs ($VCPUs$) (out of a theoretical maximum of 8); RAM - 4GB; Disk - 20 GB. All the virtual machines have the same OS, namely, Ubuntu 12.04.2 LTS.

In order to run the benchmarks we installed the following software: MySQL 5.5.32 for the TPC-H benchmark (i.e., each VM has its own database), and Java 1.7.0_25 open-JDK for the SPECpower benchmark. Finally, we created a database of 1GB in each of the VMs.

4.2 Experimental Setup

Next we describe the criteria used for our evaluation.

- A fixed target load was defined from averaging the results of 10 SPECpower calibrations.

- The SUT began in an idle state prior to the launch of each experiment and was allowed to return to this idle state for at least 20 minutes between runs. This allows the machine to 'cool down' and return to its idle energy consumption levels.

- An *Active* run consisted of at least seven possible target loads. Target loads do not necessarily have to be unique from each other.

- In the majority of the cases in which we used SPECpower, each target load was given 4 minutes, excluding pre and post measurements. We also established a delay of 10 seconds between loads.

- We collected utilization data from the hardware resources and the power meter every 2 seconds.

- In all our results, we report the average power consumption and hardware resource's utilization values over six runs.

- Before each experiments we force the kernel to drop clean caches, dentries and inodes from memory.

4.3 Metrics

For the purpose of this work, we define performance degradation, based on each workload as follows:

Definition 1 (Performance degradation for SPECpower).

$$PD_S = \frac{ssj\_ops - no\_ops}{ssj\_ops}$$

where ssj_ops represents the number of operations targeted, and no_ops the number of operations actually performed.

Definition 2 (Performance degradation for TPC-H).

$$PD_T = \frac{baseline - Throughput@Size}{baseline}$$

where the baseline represents the average between six Throughput@Size in a single VM with all the other VMs powered off and Throughput@Size represents the result achieved in the new scenario.

Finally, as we plan to determine the energy-efficiency level for a server, we measure the power consumption in Watts and we calculate the average power consumption per number of users (in the case of TPC-H) or per target of utilization (in the case of SPECpower).

4.4 Results

Below we present the results corresponding to the inquiries introduced in section 3.

4.4.1 Effects of having idle VMs

INQ 1: Figure 2 shows the variations in power consumption between a VM running as a single *Active* VM in a server, and an *Active* VM running with one or two VMs in an *Idle* state when using the SPECpower benchmark.

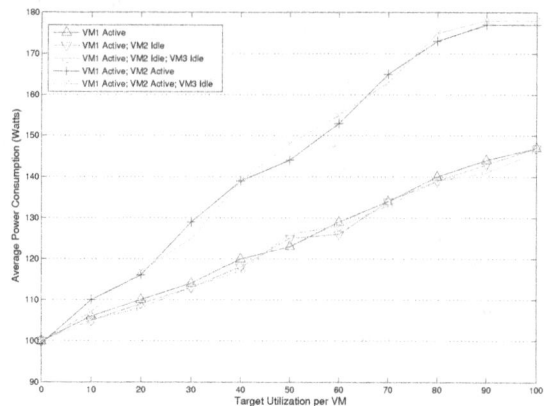

Figure 2: Average power consumption for different VM states (SPECpower)

The figure also presents the relation between two VMs in *Active* state and two *Active* VMs running with a third *Idle* VM. The reader can notice that the difference in the average power consumption at every level of utilization is almost negligible. Thus, the differences between having or not having *Idle* VMs with regards to the average power consumption is 3 Watts maximum, and -1 Watt minimum. In terms of percentage the difference is never more than 1.81%.

In the case of TPC-H, we notice that increasing the amount of users will not increase the average power consumption (see figure 3). However, Table 1 shows that the execution time for two users is significantly lower than for seven users, thus, the total amount of energy consumed by two users is lower than the amount of energy consumed by seven users. Figure 3 also presents the relation between two VMs in *N Users* state and two *N Users* VMs running with a third *Idle* VM. We notice how the average power consumption between the first scenario and the second is of no more than 25 Watts. Here we can also refer to Table 1 and observe that the average execution time for two VMs with two users is much lower than the average execution time for two VMs with seven users, namely, the total average consumption is higher for the former.

Number of Users	2	3	4	5	6	7
T_s one VM	650	980	1329	1766	2004	2386
T_s two VMs	720	1020	1705	1990	2521	2900

Table 1: Execution Time For *Throughput@Size* with different amount of users

It is important to mention that even though in the figures we present the averages, the maximum value over the six runs was not more that 2% higher than such averages, and the minimum value was just 1% lower than the averages presented. In fact, we discovered that the maximum standard deviation for the graphs presented in this paper is 1.8. Furthermore, in the majority of the cases the standard deviation was always below 0.5.

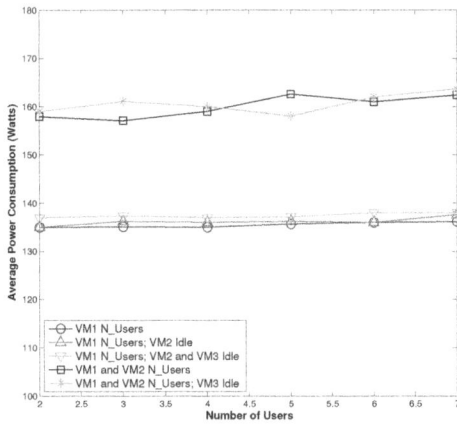

Figure 3: Average power consumption for different number of users (TPC-H)

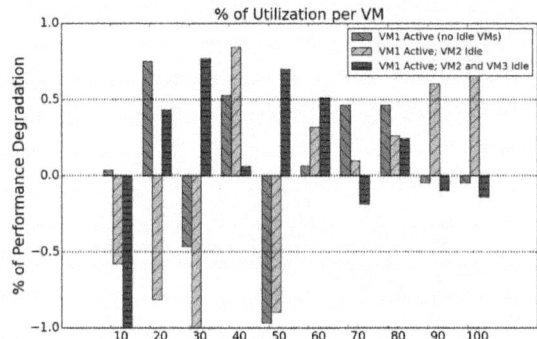

(a) 1 Active VM

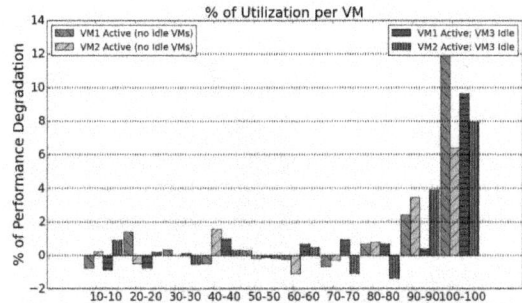

(b) 2 Active VMs

Figure 4: Performance degradation with *Idle* VMs running SPECpower

INQ 2: In order to solve this question we calculated the performance values (i.e. PD_T and PD_S) while running the experiments for the previous inquiry.

The values for PD_S are presented in figure 4. In figure 4(a) the reader can notice that the performance degradations are almost identical between the experiments in which there were no *Idle* VMs and the ones in which there were one or two *Idle* VMs. Furthermore, it is important to mention that during our experiments we sometimes noticed a PD_S of $\sim \pm 1.5\%$. The reasons for this degradation are that we use two warehouses per VM and we set the maximum number of operations to $107,500$. We assume that these conditions together with the policy that SPECpower follows to dispatch its batches of ssj_ops (refer to section 2.1) are the causes of this acceptable performance degradation.

Figure 4(b) shows that the performance degradation is reached at the same time for both scenarios (i.e. when there was an *Idle* VM and when there was no *Idle* VM). For instance, there is performance degradation when both VMs are running at 90% of utilization. Based on the observe results, we deduce that having *Idle* VMs will neither generate more performance degradation nor will it make either one of the VMs experience performance degradation at lower levels of utilization than when not having *Idle* VMs.

In the case of PD_T, the results are presented in Figure 5. In figure 5(a) we can observe that the difference in performance between the baseline and when having one or two *Idle* VMs is never higher than 1%. Thus, since the best *Throughput@Size* value for any amount of user is of 251.16 queries per hour, this represents a worst case scenario of approximately performing 2 queries less per hour when there are *Idle* VMs. Figure 5(b) presents the results when having two VMs with *N Users*. We can notice that there is a fluctuation in the performance degradation per VM. However, if we sum the degradation for each VM, we find that regardless of the number of users, the results remain almost identical. This concludes that even when the VMs are close to their peak capacity, the effects of *Idle* VMs remains the same, namely a maximum difference between having or not having *Idle* VMs of 1%.

Similar to the previous inquiry, the minimum and maximum values over the six runs are very close to the average presented.

4.4.2 Effects of increasing the total number of operations

INQ 3: Figure 6 shows the maximum levels of utilization for two and three VMs. In the figure the reader can recognize that we gradually increased the levels of utilization in each *Active* VM, maintaining each VM almost at the same level of utilization, while measuring the effects of each increment on performance. Figure 6(a) presents for two *Active* VMs the maximum number of operations until we find a performance degradation, which is when both VMs are running at 80% of utilization. This represents 172,000 ssj_ops. Furthermore, we performed another set of experiments in order to find the maximum number of operations when having three *Active* VMs. Figure 6(b), presents results for three VMs, the result shows that the maximum utilization levels without performance degradation is achieved when the three VMs summed 160% of utilization. This represents exactly 172,000 ssj_ops, which is the same amount that we found when running two VMs. We conclude that in the case of SPECpower, we can precisely find the maximum number of operations that can be performed without experiencing performance degradation regardless of the number of VMs.

In the case of TPC-H, we have previously found in *INQ 2* that there is performance degradation even in a simple scenario of three VMs running queries for two users (see figure

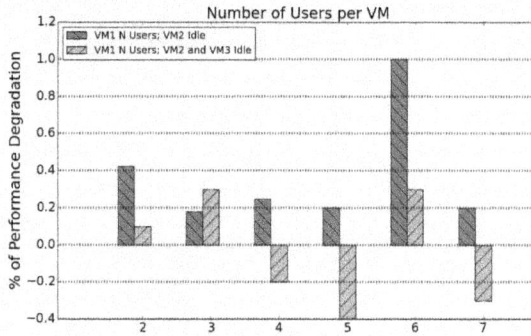

(a) TPC-H VM1 N Users

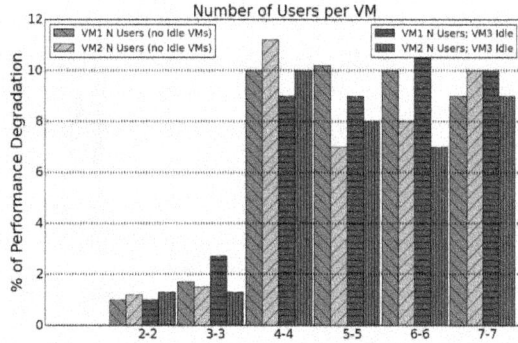

(b) TPC-H VM1 and VM2 with N Users

Figure 5: Performance degradation with *Idle* VMs running TPC-H

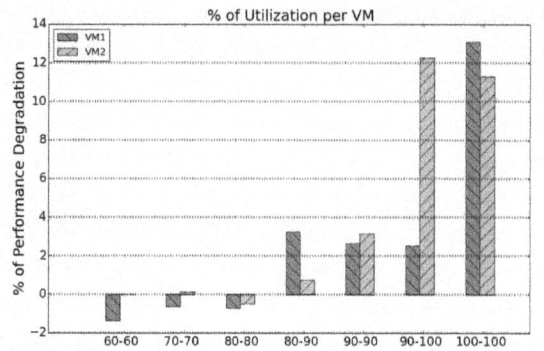

(a) Determining the maximum levels of utilization with two *Active* VMs

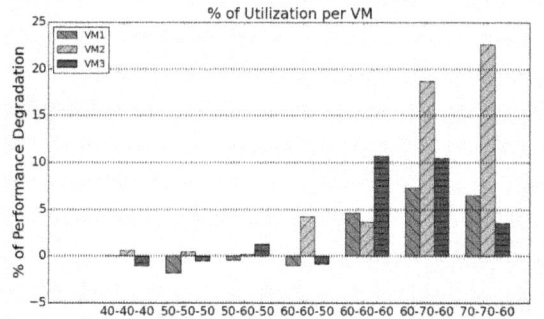

(b) Determining the maximum levels of utilization with three *Active* VMs

Figure 6: Determining the maximum levels of utilization before experiencing performance degradation

5(b)). Thus, this inquiry is not applicable to TPC-H, since we observed that it is not possible to not encounter at least a small percentage degradation when running multiple queries for decision support systems. Furthermore, examining the values from the monitoring tool we discovered that the reason is that this type of complex queries fully utilize the VM's available resources (mostly CPU and Disk). Thus, even for a small amount of users the resource utilization is near the maximum capacity, and consequently, increasing the number of users will simply increase the time required to finish the query execution.

Finally, as with the previous inquiry, the minimum and maximum values over the six runs are very close to the average presented.

We can now partially define the following rule of thumb for no performance degradations in the case of SPECpower:

Rule of Thumb 1. *(preliminary) There are no performance degradations for a virtualized server s in an enterprise environment, when using only SPECpower, when:* $\sum_{i=1}^{m} u_i \leq 160\%$, *where u_i represents the level of utilization of VM v_i in s and m represents the number of VMs in s.*

INQ 4: Contrary to what we expected, results show that for the studied environment there is no guarantee of not experiencing performance degradation even if the maximum number of operations is not reached. Figure 7, portraits the performance degradation when one VM is running at high

Constant levels of utilization. In the figure we can observe that if one of the VMs is demanding most of the available resources (i.e. 100%) then a degradation in performance will occur faster for that particular VM. We performed the same experiments with two VMs in an *Active* state and one VM in a *Constant* state and we found a very similar behavior than with two VMs (see figure 8). Therefore, we determined that if a VM is running at more than 80% of its peak utilization levels, it is likely that the VM will experience performance degradation before the server reaches its maximum capacity.

We can now update and conclude our rule of thumb for no performance degradations in the case of SPECpower:

Rule of Thumb 1. *(final) There are no performance degradations for a virtualized server s in an enterprise environment, when using only SPECpower, when:*

$\forall i \in [1, m] \ u_i \leq 80\% \wedge \sum_{i=1}^{m} u_i \leq 160\%$, *where u_i represents the level of utilization of VM v_i in s and m represents the number of VMs in s.*

We present the average over six runs, but as with the previous inquiries, the minimum and maximum values over the six runs are very close to the average presented.

INQ 5: We analyze how the results from Figure 6 (i.e. SPECpower) relate to power consumption and ultimately to energy efficiency. As it can be seen, in figure 9 we marked with a dashed line the last step before the performance

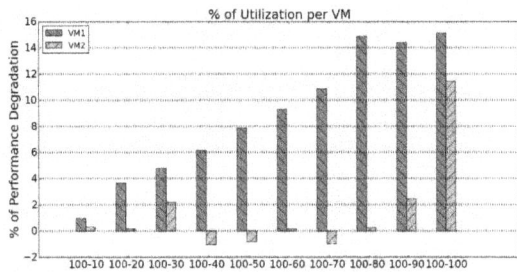

(a) VM1 at *Constant* 100%; VM2 *Active*

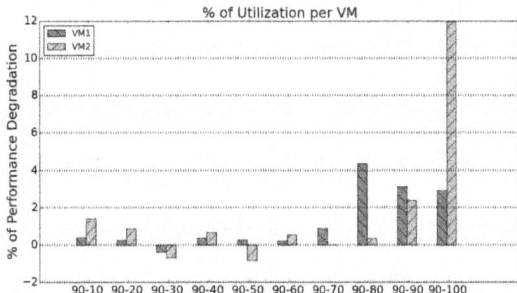

(b) VM1 at *Constant* 90%; VM2 *Active*

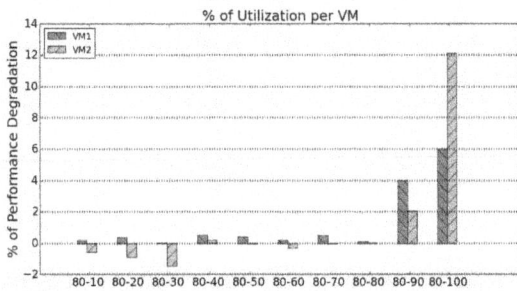

(c) VM1 at *Constant* 80%; VM2 *Active*

Figure 7: Performance degradation when one VM is running at high *Constant* levels of utilization

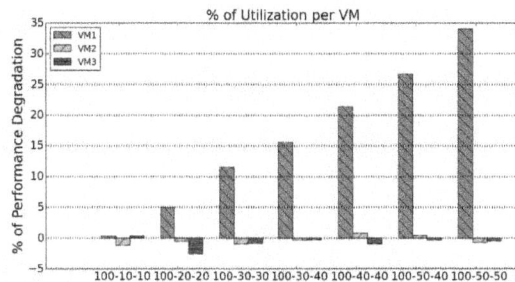

(a) VM1 at *Constant* 100%; VM2 and VM3 *Active*

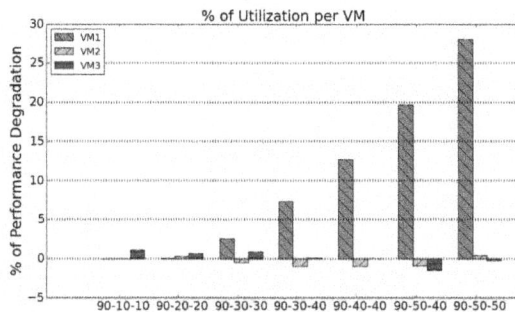

(b) VM1 at *Constant* 90%; VM2 and VM3 *Active*

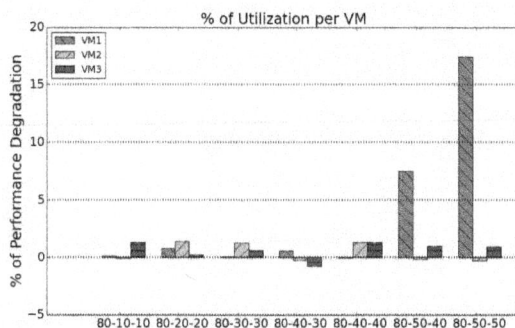

(c) VM1 at *Constant* 80%; VM2 and VM3 *Active*

Figure 8: Performance degradation when one VM is running at high *Constant* levels of utilization

degradation occurs. The reader can notice that the maximum average power consumption is 180 Watts and that it is possible to reach an average power consumption of 178 Watts, when there are two *Active* VMs, and 179 Watts when there are three *Active* VMs, before experiencing any type of performance degradation. In conclusion, it is possible to arrive near peak power consumption without experiencing any type of performance degradation.

Furthermore, figure 10 presents the average power consumption when running one VM at high *Constant* state (refer to figure 8). We marked with a dashed line the moment in which at least one of the VMs start experiencing performance degradation. We used a blue line in the case that one of the VMs was running at *Constant* 100% of utilization, a red line for the case in which one VM was running at a *Constant* 90% of utilization, and a black line in the case that one of the VMs was running at *Constant* 80%). We can observe that in the first two scenarios, the sever is using on average 160 and 165 Watts when experiencing performance degradation, on the contrary to figure 9 or when a VM is

running at a *Constant* 80%, where the server reached at least 176 Watts of average power consumption before experiencing any performance degradation.

As with the previous inquiry, the minimum and maximum values over the six runs are very close to the average presented.

4.4.3 *Effects on performance and power consumption when mixing different types of workloads*

INQ 6: In Table 2, we present the values for the different permutations in the levels of utilization for SPECpower and in the number of users for TPC-H. Evaluating this table we can conclude that in the case of SPECpower there is no performance degradation for the VM running at less than 100% of utilization. However, when the VM is running at 100% of utilization, we observe a performance degradation of approximately 11% in the case of SPECpower and

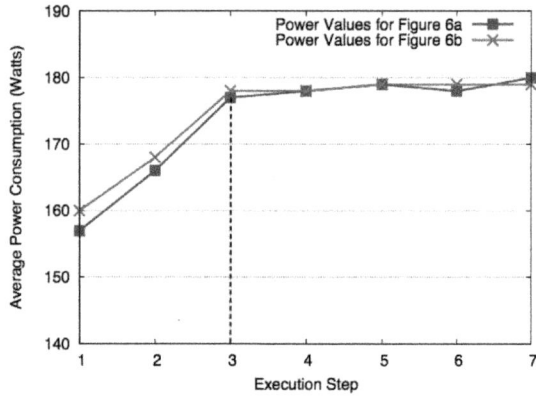

Figure 9: **Average power consumption for utilization levels of Figure 6**

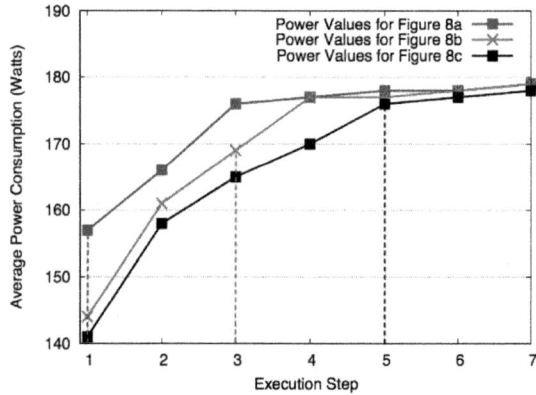

Figure 10: **Average power consumption when there is a VM running at a high _Constant_ state**

% of Target Load	PD_S (%)	Number of Users	PD_T (%)	Average Watts
10	0.13	3	0.23	∼149
10	0.27	7	0.24	∼151
80	0.3	3	0.41	∼169
80	0.51	7	0.37	∼172
90	**1.22**	**3**	**0.51**	**∼175**
90	**0.51**	**7**	**0.62**	**∼174**
100	10.7	3	12.43	∼178
100	11.4	7	13.27	∼179
50	0.37	5	0.4	∼162

Table 2: **Mixing workloads for two VMs**

% of Target Load	PD_S (%)	% of Target Load	PD_S (%)	Num of Users	PD_T (%)	AVG Watts
100	7.3	10	0	3	12.2	∼177
90	3.6	10	0	3	6.7	∼177
80	1.9	20	0	3	3.7	∼176
80	**0**	**10**	**0**	**3**	**0.87**	**∼ 176**
80	**0**	**10**	**0**	**7**	**1.2**	**∼ 176**
70	0	20	0	7	0.33	∼176
60	0	30	0	7	0.32	∼176
50	0	40	0	7	0.41	∼176

Table 3: **Mixing workloads for three VMs**

between 12 and 13% in the case of TPC-H, depending on the number of users. In the case of TPC-H we found very small performance degradation in almost every case except when the SPECpower was running at 100% of utilization. We observe that the number of users has little or no impact in performance degradation in the case of two VMs with two different types of workloads. In this scenario, the performance degradation are smaller, as generally the VMs are complementary in using mainly different resources (TPC-H-Disk, SPECpower- CPU).

We can now partially formulate our rule of thumb in the case of mixed of workloads:

Rule of Thumb 2. _(preliminary) There are no performance degradations for a virtualized server s in an enterprise environment, when mixing SPECpower and TPC-H, regardless of the number of users when:_ $\forall i \in [1, m], v_i$ _running SPECpower,_ $u_i \leq 90\%$, _where_ u_i _represents the level of utilization of VM_ v_i _in s and m represents the number of VMs running SPECpower in s._

Table 3 shows the effects of mixed workloads using three VMs: two running SPECpower and one running TPC-H. The table shows that in general if there is a degradation in performance in one of the VMs running SPECpower, then there will also be a degradation in the VM running TPC-H.

We noticed that if the sum of utilization for two VMs with SPECpower is not higher than 90% then there will be no performance degradation regardless of the number of users on the VM running TPC-H. We identified that the threshold in utilization level for each VM running SPECpower is 80%(i.e. lower than 90% as in the previous scenario). Based on the results from these two tables, we observe that mixing different types of workloads brings some benefits, such as running TPC-H without encountering performance degradation. This situation does not occur in an environment running only TPC-H (see _INQ 3_). We observe that in addition to running TPC-H, we can perform 56.25% of the maximum total SPECpower utilization level with no performance degradation in the server (i.e. from 160% to 90%). The reason for this decrement is the fact that both workloads are CPU intensive.

We can now finalize the formulation of our rule of thumb in the case of mixed of workloads:

Rule of Thumb 2. _(final) There are no performance degradations for a virtualized server s in an enterprise environment, when mixing SPECpower and TPC-H, regardless of the number of users when:_ $\forall i \in [1, m], v_i$ _running SPECpower,_ $u_i \leq \mathbf{80\%} \wedge \sum_{i=1}^{m} u_i \leq \mathbf{90\%}$, _where_ u_i _represents the level of utilization of VM_ v_i _in s and m represents the number of VMs running SPECpower in s._

As with the previous inquiries, the minimum and maximum values over the six runs are very close to the average presented.

INQ 7: We analyzed how the results from Tables 2 and 3 relate to power consumption and ultimately to energy efficiency. The reader can observe that in both cases (i.e. when mixing workloads for two and three VMs) the average values for power consumption are very close to the peak value (i.e. between 174 and 176 Watts). The main reasons for the high values in power consumption are: (i) the server reaches very high levels of CPU utilization, and (ii) multiple hardware resources utilized at the same time (i.e. TPC-H uses mainly Disk and CPU, and SPECpower uses mainly CPU).

Finally, as with the previous inquiries, the minimum and maximum values over the six runs are very close to the average presented.

5. RELATED WORK

In this paper we perform a thorough analysis between performance and energy efficiency in a virtualized environment using two enterprise benchmarks (i.e. SPECpower_ssj2008 and TPC-H).

Reviewing the literature we found several techniques for improving one of these two variables. For instance, a general view for improving energy-consumption is to use server consolidation. However, the impact of consolidating several VMs in the same server is not properly studied. Examples of such approaches are: Srikantaiah, et al in [27] discuss consolidating applications or tasks on a lower number of physical machines. However, they do not consider the impact of a virtualized environment. Moreover, there is also a vast literature available about the use of virtual machine placement for server consolidation ([19, 22, 26]). However, such approaches tend to place VMs based on their average resource utilizations, disregarding the effects of peaks utilization in one of the VMs or if such consolidation makes the server reaches energy-efficiency levels.

Other researchers go further and present their approaches to address the problem of achieving energy efficiency and its impact in performance. In this regard, Kephart et al. [18] proposed a coordination strategy based on utility functions for managing power and performance using two separate managers. However, the applications studied are very simple, as they consume just one resource, making them unlikely to be used in a typical enterprise. Furthermore, Gao et al. [15] propose a model for predicting the performance and energy consumption of a server. However, they simplify the power consumption measurements to a linear progression between the 'base' utilization and the maximum CPU utilization, omitting the increments in power consumption by using other hardware resources. Moreover, their work is focus on dynamically resizing the size of the VMs depending on their levels of utilization in order to consolidate them in the minimum amount of servers. Leite et al. [20] developed a coordinated technique for controlling end-to-end performance and minimizing power consumption using Dynamic Voltage Scaling (DVS) in a three-tier web application environment. Moreover, Brihi et al. [11] studied the effect in performance of varying power states in modern computing servers. However, such techniques do not properly address the problem of energy-efficiency, which can only be solved by increasing the utilization of the computing server to its maximum capacity. Furthermore, Rong et al [16] developed an analytical model for investigating energy-performance for parallel workloads. They investigate how to identify an optimal system configuration for running a given parallel workload. The difference is that our work is focused on enterprise type of application running in a virtualized environment.

There have been a number of recent efforts to understand the relationship between performance and power consumption in a virtualized environment. For instance, Smith et al [25] propose a technique for assigning tasks to compute nodes with the aim of balancing the trade-off between energy consumption and the application's performance. However, they use benchmarks that perform very simple tasks (e.g. compress files in memory or read and write a 1024MB test file to and from the hard disk). In addition, they do not study if it is possible to reach energy-efficiency without performance degradation, but rather they aim to spread the workloads in order to consume just the 'base' power consumption. Moreover, Chen et al [12] propose to characterize and profile the energy consumption for different type of tasks and study how the throughput for different type of workloads relates to power consumption. However, our work differs in the sense that we present a measure for performance degradation and how such performance is associated to power consumption and utilization. Finally, with regards to the benchmarks used in this work, Poess et al [24] studied the trends in performance and power consumption for the TPC-H benchmark and Subramaniam et al [28] utilized SPECpower to investigate the feasibility of achieving energy-proportional operations. To our best knowledge, this is the first comprehensive analysis in which there is a set of scenarios that could be found in any enterprise environment. Moreover, we answer a set of inquiries that aim to clarify some limitations of virtualized environments and to discover if performance and energy-efficiency can be achieved simultaneously.

6. CONCLUSION AND FUTURE WORK

The main contribution of this work is a methodology for detecting performance degradations for two typical workloads, namely SPECpower and TPC-H, in an enterprise environment. In order to achieve this, we introduced the concept of VM states based on their utilization levels. The methodology identifies the performance degradations based on predefined scenarios that combine VM states. The scenarios we used include up to three virtual machines, however, the methodology can be adapted for multiple machines by using the same patterns of VM states. Moreover, we evaluate how performance degradation is related to power consumption in a virtualized environment with the objective of reaching energy efficiency. The methodology has been verified on a specific type of server and yielded two rules of thumb to enable the optimum trade off point to be found. It is expected that the methodology could be used to similar effects on other types of servers.

We demonstrated that it is possible to achieve energy-efficiency without any performance degradation in the scenarios studied. Furthermore, we identified the maximum level of utilization with no performance degradation both for a server and a VM and defined accordingly a rule of thumb. Through our analysis we concluded that a server does not experience performance degradation as long as any of the virtual machines in the server under study does not reach high levels of utilization and the servers' utilization doesn't reach its peak capacity. Moreover, we investigated the case of a decision support system. In this case, the system performs complicated queries that require hardware resources for a significant amount of time. Due to this fact, the VMs are constantly required to be at high levels of utilization, leading to performance degradation for the VMs running that type of workload. Finally, we investigated the case of mixed workloads and defined a rule of thumb such that the server reaches high levels of utilization and none of the VMs experience performance degradation.

As future work, we plan to create an automated model that performs the analysis provided in this paper. The model will take as input the workload type, and a server power model, to subsequently investigate the feasibility of achieving energy-efficiency without performance degradation in the particular server. If energy-efficiency is reachable, the model will output the conditions for balancing performance and energy-consumption (e.g. maximum utilization level).

7. ACKNOWLEDGMENTS

We thank Anthony Ventresque and Ulrich Dangel for their valuable support and feedback. This work was supported by the Science Foundation Ireland under grant 10/CE/I1855 to Lero - the Irish Software Engineering Research Center (www.lero.ie), and by Enterprise Ireland Innovation Partnership in cooperation with IBM and University College Dublin under grant IP/2010/0061.

8. REFERENCES

[1] collectd - the system statistics collection daemon. https://collectd.org.
[2] HAMEG HM8115-2 power meter. http://www.hameg.com/O.147.0.html.
[3] KVM - Kernel Based Virtual Machine. www.linux-kvm.org.
[4] SPECpower_ssj2008. http://www.spec.org/power_ssj2008/.
[5] SPECpower_ssj2008 - Design Document CCS. http://www.spec.org/power/docs/SPECpower_ssj2008-Design_ccs.pdf.
[6] SPECpower_ssj2008 - Design Document SSJ Workload. http://www.spec.org/power/docs/SPECpower_ssj2008-Design_ssj.pdf.
[7] SPECpower_ssj2008 - Run and Reporting Rulest. http://www.spec.org/power/docs/SPECpower_ssj2008-Run_Reporting_Rules.html.
[8] TPC-H. http://www.tpc.org/tpch/.
[9] L. A. Barroso and U. Hölzle. The case for energy-proportional computing. *Computer*, 40(12):33–37, 2007.
[10] A. Beloglazov and R. Buyya. Adaptive threshold-based approach for energy-efficient consolidation of virtual machines in cloud data centers. In *8th International Workshop on Middleware for Grids, Clouds and e-Science (MGC)*, pages 4:1–4:6, 2010.
[11] A. Brihi and W. Dargie. Dynamic voltage and frequency scaling in multimedia servers. In *27th IEEE International Conference on Advanced Information Networking and Applications (AINA)*, pages 374–380, 2013.
[12] F. Chen, J. Grundy, Y. Yang, J.-G. Schneider, and Q. He. Experimental analysis of task-based energy consumption in cloud computing systems. In *Proceedings of the 4th ACM/SPEC International Conference on Performance Engineering*, ICPE '13, pages 295–306. ACM, 2013.
[13] G. Dasgupta, A. Sharma, A. Verma, A. Neogi, and R. Kothari. Workload management for power efficiency in virtualized data centers. *Communications of the ACM*, 54(7):131–141, 2011.
[14] U. Drepper. The cost of virtualization. *Queue*, 6(1):28–35, Jan. 2008.
[15] Y. Gao, Z. Qi, Z. Wu, R. Wang, L. Liu, J. Xu, and H. Guan. A power and performance management framework for virtualized server clusters. In *2011 IEEE/ACM International Conference on Green Computing and Communications (GREENCOM)*, pages 170–175, 2011.

[16] R. Ge, X. Feng, and K. Cameron. Modeling and evaluating energy-performance efficiency of parallel processing on multicore based power aware systems. In *Parallel Distributed Processing, 2009. IPDPS 2009. IEEE International Symposium on*, pages 1–8, 2009.
[17] A. G. Janopoulou. Ad-hoc decision-supports. Master's thesis, National Technical University of Athens, 2010.
[18] J. O. Kephart, H. Chan, R. Das, D. W. Levine, G. Tesauro, F. Rawson, and C. Lefurgy. Coordinating multiple autonomic managers to achieve specified power-performance tradeoffs. In *4th International Conference on Autonomic Computing (ICAC)*, pages 24–, 2007.
[19] K. Le, R. Bianchini, J. Zhang, Y. Jaluria, J. Meng, and T. D. Nguyen. Reducing electricity cost through virtual machine placement in high performance computing clouds. In *2011 International Conference for High Performance Computing, Networking, Storage and Analysis (SC)*, pages 22:1–22:12, 2011.
[20] J. C. Leite, D. M. Kusic, D. Mossé, and L. Bertini. Stochastic approximation control of power and tardiness in a three-tier web-hosting cluster. In *7th international conference on Autonomic computing (ICAC)*, pages 41–50, 2010.
[21] X. Meng, C. Isci, J. Kephart, L. Zhang, E. Bouillet, and D. Pendarakis. Efficient resource provisioning in compute clouds via vm multiplexing. In *7th international conference on Autonomic computing (ICAC)*, pages 11–20, 2010.
[22] K. Mills, J. Filliben, and C. Dabrowski. Comparing vm-placement algorithms for on-demand clouds. In *3rd IEEE International Conference on Cloud Computing Technology and Science (CloudCom)*, pages 91–98, 2011.
[23] J. Omana Iglesias, P. Perry, N. Stokes, J. Thorburn, and L. Murphy. A cost-capacity analysis for assessing the efficiency of heterogeneous computing assets in an enterprise cloud. In *6th IEEE/ACM International Conference on Utility and Cloud Computing (UCC)*, page to appear.
[24] M. Poess and R. Othayoth Nambiar. A power consumption analysis of decision support systems. In *Proceedings of the first joint WOSP/SIPEW international conference on Performance engineering*, WOSP/SIPEW '10, pages 147–152. ACM, 2010.
[25] J. W. Smith and I. Sommerville. Understanding tradeoffs between power usage and performance in a virtualized environment. In *6th International Conference on Cloud Computing (CLOUD)*, pages 725–731, 2013.
[26] B. Speitkamp and M. Bichler. A mathematical programming approach for server consolidation problems in virtualized data centers. *IEEE Transactions on Services Computing*, 3(4):266–278, Oct. 2010.
[27] S. Srikantaiah, A. Kansal, and F. Zhao. Energy aware consolidation for cloud computing. In *2008 conference on Power aware computing and systems (HotPower)*, pages 10–10, 2008.
[28] B. Subramaniam and W.-c. Feng. Towards energy-proportional computing for enterprise-class server workloads. In *Proceedings of the 4th ACM/SPEC International Conference on Performance Engineering*, ICPE '13, pages 15–26. ACM, 2013.

Efficient Optimization of Software Performance Models via Parameter-Space Pruning

Mirco Tribastone
Electronics and Computer Science
University of Southampton, United Kingdom
m.tribastone@soton.ac.uk

ABSTRACT

When performance characteristics are taken into account in a software design, models can be used to identify optimal configurations of the system's parameters. Unfortunately, for realistic scenarios, the cost of the optimization is typically high, leading to computational difficulties in the exploration of large parameter spaces. This paper proposes an approach to provably exact parameter-space pruning for a class of models of large-scale software systems analyzed with *fluid techniques*, efficient and scalable deterministic approximations of massively parallel stochastic models. We present a result of monotonicity of fluid solutions with respect to the model parameters, and employ it in the context of optimization programs with evolutionary algorithms by discarding candidate configurations *a priori*, i.e., without ever solving them, whenever they are proven to give lower fitness than other configurations. An extensive numerical validation shows that this approach yields an average twofold runtime speed-up compared to a baseline optimization algorithm that does not exploit monotonicity. Furthermore, we find that the optimal configuration is within a few percent from the *true* one obtained by stochastic simulation, whose solution is however orders of magnitude more expensive.

Categories and Subject Descriptors

I.6.5 [**Simulation and Modeling**]: Model Development— *Modeling methodologies*; D.2.8 [**Software Engineering**]: Metrics—*Performance measures*

Keywords

Software performance engineering; capacity planning; fluid approximations; queueing networks; monotone systems

1. INTRODUCTION

The evaluation of nonfunctional properties of software systems can be assisted by models. This is especially useful in early stages of the development process, when executable

artifacts are not available but the designer wishes to obtain estimates about the behavior of the system in order to make more informed decisions about the architecture and the implementation [15]. Motivated by the ever increasing popularity of service-level agreements that concerns aspects such as performance, reliability, and availability, much research has gone into the integration of model-based software performance engineering practices with traditional development processes [9]. In this context, it is possible to identify at least three main challenges:

i) Developing mechanisms to shield the software engineer from the technical details of the underlying mathematical machinery used for the analysis.

ii) Guaranteeing that the model is a faithful representation of the real system throughout all the stages of the development process.

iii) Providing accurate and efficient evaluation techniques that scale well with increasing system sizes.

Challenge i) seems to be relatively well understood, owing to the large body of research concerned with enriching software models with suitable annotations for nonfunctional properties, the most notable case being the SPT/MARTE profiles for the UML [27]. In this paper, we assume that ii) has been also tackled—for instance by using techniques that continuously learn the model parameters as done in [35]—and study iii), with emphasis on models for software *performance*.

In a typical scenario, a performance model can be used for *capacity planning*, i.e., for estimating the amount of resources to be allocated in order to satisfy some required quality of service, or, more in generally, for *what-if analysis*, i.e., evaluating the impact of certain changes on the overall system's behavior. This introduces two orthogonal issues about the scalability of such analyses.

The first issue is related to the effectiveness with which a given instance is evaluated. Most models of software performance are based on Markov chains, which are however prone to the infamous problem of state-space explosion for increasing populations of system components. To tackle this problem, many approaches are available that consider exact aggregations (e.g., [19]) or approximate analysis (e.g., [16]) in order to reduce the computational cost. In this paper we make use of *fluid techniques* for the analysis. These are based on ordinary differential equations (ODEs) as deterministic approximations to the average path of a continuous-time Markov chain (CTMC) that models a *population process*. In such CTMC, the state descriptor gives the populations of entities that are in a particular *local state*. For instance, in stochastic Petri nets the state lists the number of tokens in each place of the net (e.g., [4]). In queueing networks, the state may give the number of clients at each station (e.g., [5, 13]). In stochastic process algebra, each element of the state descriptor gives the copies of the components that exhibit a distinct sequential behavior [33]. In all cases, the crucial advantage of fluid techniques is that the size of the ODE system is independent from the actual population sizes, but is only dependent on the size of the state descriptor.

A fluid model is computationally much more advantageous than its stochastic CTMC counterpart, especially for large populations. However, as with CTMC analysis, the solution is generally not available in a closed form and thus it must be evaluated numerically. This implies that the results of a model with a given parameter configuration cannot be reused for solving the same model with a different one. Therefore, when fluid models are used for parameter-space explorations *each point* must be evaluated anew. This is, in essence, our second scalability issue: *The analysis is in general not scalable with the size of the parameter space.*

This paper presents a result of foundational nature that serves as the basis for tackling this very issue. Our purpose is to exploit a property of *monotonicity* of certain performance indices with respect to the model parameters. Given two vectors of parameters $\vec{v}_1$ and $\vec{v}_2$, we study under which conditions it is possible to prove that, for some partial order "$\leq$", $\vec{v}_1 \leq \vec{v}_2$ implies that $\phi(\vec{v}_1) \leq \phi(\vec{v}_2)$, where $\phi(\cdot)$ is the evaluation of the performance index for a given parametrization. This result can be readily applied. For example, when exploring the parameter space for minimizing ϕ, if $\vec{v}_1 \leq \vec{v}_2$ holds, $\phi(\vec{v}_2)$ needs not be computed because it yields a provably larger index. Importantly, checking for the inequality $\vec{v}_1 \leq \vec{v}_2$ comes at a negligible cost because it only compares model parameters, whereas the evaluation of ϕ requires solving the model, which, as discussed, may become expensive.

We study monotonicity for fluid models of closed queueing networks with arbitrary topologies, where stations serve with a generalized processor sharing (GPS) discipline. The reason for this choice is that GPS has been successfully proposed to model the dynamics of complex software systems in shared data centers and virtualized environments [14, 5, 6]. Thus, our approach is already usable for applications of practical interest. In addition, as will be discussed in more detail in Section 7, the fluid dynamics of GPS queueing networks are structurally close to those of, e.g., stochastic process algebra, stochastic Petri nets, and layered queueing networks. Thus, the approach can be easily generalizable to those techniques as well. The main theoretical contribution of this paper is to prove that the solution of the fluid model is monotone with respect to the client populations.

Armed with this result, we use it to improve the efficiency of the exploration of large parameter spaces for optimization purposes. We consider the problem of finding the best tradeoff between performance (i.e., throughput) and cost for a two-class GPS queueing network which is representative of a canonical three-layered software architecture. Similarly to [6], the network consists of a service station for each layer, and a *delay* station that models the user workload. The objective is to find the best workload mix using a genetic algorithm (GA). This represents one of the possible constraint optimization techniques, which was chosen because of its popularity in model-based software performance en-

gineering (e.g., [20, 2]). Our approach, however, can also be used in conjunction with other search strategies such as hill-climbing and simulated annealing, where frequent comparisons are made between points in the parameter space.

We show the effectiveness of our a-priori parameter-space pruning by comparing the runtimes of a baseline GA where monotonicity is not exploited against that of a tuned version where genomes with provably worse fitness are immediately discarded. The numerical results show an average twofold speed-up. Furthermore, a comparison against the *true* optimal configurations returned by evaluating GA with stochastic simulation shows excellent accuracy across a wide range of operating conditions for our example network.

Paper outline. We review related work in Section 2. In an effort to make the paper self-contained, Section 3 gives a concise account of the fluid technique used in this paper and its relation with the CTMC that it approximates. Section 4 defines the fluid model of a closed queueing network with GPS service. Section 5 defines the optimization problem and introduces the notion of monotone ODE systems. It then proves that our fluid GPS model does enjoy monotonicity, and shows how to apply this result to the optimization. Section 6 presents the numerical results for our case study of a three-layered software system. Finally, Section 7 ends with a discussion on the methodology presented in this paper and outlines lines of future work.

2. RELATED WORK

There has been a considerable amount of research concerned with the application of optimization techniques to models of software systems. Whilst we refer to [3] for an exhaustive and up-to-date survey, in this section we focus on approaches that are most closely related to the techniques presented in this paper. In particular, we consider the literature that deals with the optimization of the parameters of a model to trade-off between performance and cost. Much effort has been devoted to the studying optimal selection of components in service-based systems. In [12] this is studied by means of linear optimization. While the resulting problem can be efficiently analyzed, the underlying model is based on the crucial assumption of the absence queueing delays, which is instead the main focus of this paper. Similar assumptions hold in frameworks that deal with optimal service compositions, e.g., [34, 7].

The approach taken in [11] uses instead Markov chains and probabilistic logics for formal specification of the quality of service. Although it is possible to account for queueing effects, the resulting problem would suffer from the curse of dimensionality with increasing numbers of components.

More scalability for the analysis is offered by layered queueing networks, solved by means of approximate mean value analysis [16]. These models are featured in Litoiu *et al.*, who consider optimization for deployment in service-oriented systems, in [23], studying the optimization of the concurrency levels in a distributed system, and in [22], for cloud environments. A similar analytic model is presented in [26], which uses Menascé's two-layered extended queueing network for an optimization algorithm for service-oriented architectures. While the use of extended queues is computationally advantageous with respect to other stochastic models for the evaluation of a point in the parameter space, no results are provided regarding a-priori pruning of entire regions with provably lower cost, as is done in this paper.

Further reduction of the computational cost of the analysis is achievable by considering simpler mathematical models. Marzolla and Mirandola identify a class of BPEL workflows for web-service compositions that can be modeled as a single-class queueing network, for which they propose rapid evaluation based on bounds on steady-state performance for bottleneck identification [25]; however, an explicit optimization problem is not formulated. In [10] a performance model is presented for load balancing in service oriented architectures based on an open queueing network with $M/M/1$ stations. While this allows for closed-form expressions of the response time, the approach cannot be generalized to other situations, in particular, when multiple classes of services are to be considered. Instead, a multi-class queueing network for a similar brokering scenario is presented in [8], where the solution is based on operational analysis. However, unlike our approach, the model cannot be generalized to arbitrary topologies.

In conclusion to this section, our use of fluid techniques offers a compromise between cost and model expressiveness, since such techniques are able to incorporate queueing effects due to contention in a scalable manner. In addition, for the objective functions herein proposed, a-priori pruning of the parameter space may be obtained, thereby further reducing the computational burden of the solution of optimization problems. From a theoretical viewpoint, the paper makes a contribution to monotonicity properties of performance models. Although these have been long understood in the stochastic setting under certain conditions (see, e.g., [29]), and assumed to hold in other cases (e.g., [23]), here they are proven for fluid multi-class models.

3. PRELIMINARIES

The purpose of this section is to provide the necessary background to fluid techniques. This will be assisted by a trivial small example of a pure-delay two-station queueing network, which will only be used to build intuition and to illustrate all the notions introduced. The general model presented in Section 4, instead, will feature multiple classes of clients, arbitrary topology, and contention for the processing capacity of the servers.

Before proceeding, we fix some notation. As usual, $\mathbb{N}$ is the set of natural numbers, including 0; $\mathbb{Z}$ is the set of integers whereas $\mathbb{R}$ denotes the set of real numbers. Scalars are lowercase Roman letters, vectors have an arrow over the symbol, whereas matrices are uppercase Roman letters. When written in matrix notation, a system of ODEs is denoted by $\frac{d}{dt}\vec{x}(t) = G(\vec{x}(t))$; alternatively, to ease layout, when it is written in components the explicit dependence on t is dropped (all our ODE systems are autonomous) and Newton's *dot* notation is used instead, therefore we write $\dot{x}_i = G_i(x_1, \ldots, x_n)$, where $x_1, \ldots, x_n$ are scalars.

We begin by formally defining a *population model*.

DEFINITION 1. *A population model is defined by the following elements:*

- *A vector of n variables, denoted by $\vec{x} = (x_i)_{1 \le i \le n}$;*

- *A set of m interaction functions $f_j : \mathbb{R}^n \to \mathbb{R}$ and associated jump vectors $\vec{l}_j \in \mathbb{Z}^n$, for all $1 \le j \le m$;*

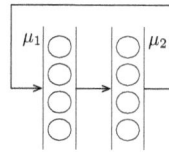

Figure 1: A pure-delay two-station queueing network.

- *An initial condition $\vec{x}_0 \in \mathbb{N}^n$.*

Intuitively, $\vec{x}$ represents the system's state whereas f_j describe the system dynamics, i.e., $f_j(\vec{x})$ describe the rate at which the state changes due to the j-th function, which may be interpreted as a force or interaction acting on the system. The impact of the interaction on each state variable is given by the jump vector. A negative (resp., positive) entry indicates a decrease (resp., increase) of the corresponding variable. Finally, $\vec{x}_0$ gives the initial state of the system. Requiring a vector of natural numbers gives the intuition behind the kinds of models considered in this paper, which are population-based, i.e., each state variable describes the evolution of a population of individuals of the same type, as discussed. The non-negativity of $\vec{x}_0$ therefore amounts to enforcing meaningfulness from a physical viewpoint.

EXAMPLE 1 (PURE-DELAY NETWORK). *Figure 1 shows a simple tandem two-delay queueing network where a single class of clients visits two stations in sequence, with rates μ_1 and μ_2, where $\mu_1, \mu_2 > 0$. The model consists of the state vector $\vec{x} = (x_1, x_2)$, denoting the number of clients at each station (the queue length), by the interaction functions f_1 and f_2, and by the jump vectors $\vec{l}_1$ and $\vec{l}_2$ defined as*

$$f_1(x_1, x_2) = \mu_1 x_1, \qquad \vec{l}_1 = (-1, +1),$$
$$f_2(x_1, x_2) = \mu_2 x_2, \qquad \vec{l}_2 = (-1, +1).$$

The functions give the total rate of service at both stations, which simply grows linearly with the queue length. The jumps indicate that each transition moves one client from one queue to another, cyclically. The model is completed by letting $\vec{x}_0 = (N_1, N_2)$ be the initial population of clients.

A model of this kind can be used to describe a continuous-time Markov chain (CTMC), which is typically called a *Markov population process* to stress the fact that the state descriptor denotes counts of individuals.

DEFINITION 2 (POPULATION PROCESS). *For a population model we define a CTMC $\{X(t), t \in \mathbb{R}\}$, with state space S and transition rates denoted by $q(\vec{r}, \vec{s})$, for all $\vec{r}, \vec{s} \in S$ and $\vec{r} \ne \vec{s}$, as follows.*

1. *Let $X(0) = \vec{x}_0$ and $\vec{x}_0 \subset S$.*

2. *Then S is defined to be the smallest set such that if $\vec{x} \in S$ and $f_j(\vec{x}) > 0$ then $\vec{x} + \vec{l}_j \in S$ and*

$$q(\vec{x}, \vec{x} + \vec{l}_j) = \sum_{j'=1, \vec{l}_{j'}=\vec{l}_j}^{m} f_{j'}(\vec{x}), \qquad 1 \le j \le m.$$

In our example, we have that $\vec{x}_0 = (N_1, N_2) \in S$; thus $\vec{x}' = (N_1 - 1, N_2 + 1) \in S$ with $q(\vec{x}_0, \vec{x}') = \mu_1 N_1$ and

$\vec{x}'' = (N_1 + 1, N_2 - 1) \in S$ with $q(\vec{x}_0, \vec{x}'') = \mu_2 N_2$, and so on. While in this simple case the cardinality of S is equal to $N_1 + N_2$, in general it is known to depend on the norm of $\vec{x}_0$ exponentially at worst—this is an instance of the *state-space explosion* problem. To tackle this, one can consider the following deterministic approximation, the *fluid approximation* (or fluid model).

DEFINITION 3 (FLUID APPROXIMATION). *The fluid approximation of a population model is an initial value problem with the following ODE system*

$$\frac{d}{dt}\vec{x}(t) = G(\vec{x}(t)), \qquad G(\vec{x}) = \sum_{j=1}^{n} \vec{l}_j f_j(\vec{x}),$$

and with initial condition $\vec{x}(0) = \vec{x}_0$.

In components, the fluid approximation of our example is

$$\frac{d}{dt}x_1(t) = -\mu_1 x_1(t) + \mu_2 x_2(t),$$
$$\frac{d}{dt}x_2(t) = +\mu_1 x_1(t) - \mu_2 x_2(t),$$

with $x_1(0) = N_1$ and $x_2(0) = N_2$. This shows the scalability of the fluid approximation: The ODE system size is independent from the actual populations (which only affect the initial conditions), and is only dependent on the length of the state descriptor (which in turn only depends on the network topology). In the remainder, we consider systems for which the fluid approximation enjoys existence and uniqueness of the ODE solution over some time interval $[0, T]$. All the examples herein proposed satisfy this property.

The ODE system can be interpreted as an estimate of the average CTMC behavior because, by a suitable approximation, it can be shown that (e.g., [28])

$$\frac{d}{dt}\mathbb{E}[X(t)] \approx G(\mathbb{E}[X(t)]),$$

where $\mathbb{E}[\cdot]$ denotes the expectation operator. For a class of models, the relationship is mathematically stronger in that the solution to the ODE is shown to be the asymptotic behavior of a suitable sequence of the associated population processes [21]. For the purposes of the present paper, however, we need not be concerned with the distinction between these two interpretations. Here it suffices to say that in general, the larger the population sizes (hence, the larger the CTMCs) the more accurate the approximation, with average errors of only a few percent (e.g., [31, 32, 33]).

In the example, every initial condition will give rise to ODE solutions that are nonnegative. This is what one would expect from any model where populations are physically relevant entities. We now provide a sufficient condition for non-negativity of the ODE solution that can be checked by inspection of the vector field of the fluid approximation.

LEMMA 1 (NONNEGATIVE FLUID APPROXIMATION). *For a population model, suppose that $G_i(x) \geq 0$ for every $1 \leq i \leq n$ and for every x such that $x_i = 0$ and $x_{i' \neq i} \geq 0$. Then it holds that*

$$x_i(t) \geq 0,$$

for every i and any $t > 0$ where the solution is defined.

PROOF. Suppose toward a contradiction that there exists at least an i and a time $t > 0$ such that $x_i(t) < 0$. By continuity, together with the non negativity of the initial conditions, this would imply the existence of a time $t_1^i \in (0, t)$ such that $x_i(t_1^i) = 0$, $x_i(t) \geq 0$ for $t < t_1^i$ and $\dot{x}_i(t_1^i) < 0$. Let $t_m \triangleq \min_i t_1^i$, then $x_m(t_m) = 0$, $\dot{x}_m(t_m) < 0$ and $x_i(t) \geq 0$ for any i and $t \leq t_m$, which contradicts the assumption $G_m(x) \geq 0$ for any x with $x_m = 0$ and $x_{i \neq m} \geq 0$. $\square$

4. GENERAL MODEL

We now consider a population model of a closed queueing network with $M + 1$ stations, labelled by $0, 1, \dots, M$, and K classes, labelled by $1, \dots, K$. Without loss of generality, we shall assume that only station 0 is a delay station, where clients do not contend for service. (An extension with an arbitrary number of delay stations is straightforward.) This is used to model the residence of clients outside the system before successive arrivals. Let $\mu_k > 0$ be the service rate for the k-th class at the delay station. The remaining M stations, instead, all serve with GPS discipline with total capacity D_i, $1 \leq i \leq M$. Let $w_i^k > 0$ be the *weight* (or priority) for class k, i.e., how much of the total capacity is proportionally assigned to each class requiring service at station i; let $\lambda_i^k > 0$ be the service rate, respectively, for class k at station $i > 0$. The routing of clients across the network is described, as usual, by K matrices, denoted by $P^k = (p_{ij}^k)_{1 \leq i,j \leq M}$ such that $p_{ij}^k \geq 0$ and $\sum_j p_{ij}^k = 1$ for all i. This implies that every client never leaves the system. The state variables describe the queue length at station i for each class k, and are denoted by x_i^k, with $0 \leq i \leq M$ and $1 \leq k \leq K$. The interaction functions are defined as follows:

$$f_0^k(\vec{x}) = p_{0j}^k \mu_k x_0^k, \qquad \vec{l}_0^k = -\mathbb{1}_{x_0^k} + \mathbb{1}_{x_j^k},$$
$$f_i^k(\vec{x}) = p_{ij}^k \frac{\lambda_i^k w_i^k x_i^k D_i}{\sum_{l=1}^{K} w_i^l x_i^l}, \qquad \vec{l}_i^k = -\mathbb{1}_{x_i^k} + \mathbb{1}_{x_j^k}, \qquad (1)$$

for all $1 \leq k \leq K$ and $1 \leq i \leq M$, $0 \leq j \leq M$, where $\mathbb{1}_{x_i^k}$ represents the vector of length $\|\vec{x}\|$ of all zeros except at the position for variable x_i^k, where it is equal to 1.

The fluid approximation for a GPS queueing network is given by

$$\dot{x}_0^k = -(1 - p_{00}^k)\mu_k x_0^k + \sum_{j=1}^{M} p_{j0}^k \frac{\lambda_j^k w_j^k x_j^k D_j}{\sum_{l=1}^{K} w_j^l x_j^l},$$
$$\dot{x}_i^k = -\frac{\lambda_i^k w_i^k x_i^k D_i}{\sum_{l=1}^{K} w_i^l x_i^l} + p_{0i}^k \mu_k x_0^k + \sum_{j=1}^{M} p_{ji}^k \frac{\lambda_j^k w_j^k x_j^k D_j}{\sum_{l=1}^{K} w_j^l x_j^l}, \qquad (2)$$

for all $1 \leq k \leq K$ and $1 \leq i \leq M$.

EXAMPLE 2. *Let us consider a model with $K = 2$ classes and, similarly to Example 1, a tandem queueing network, i.e., $M = 1$, $p_{01}^k = p_{10}^k = 1$ for $k = 1, 2$. In this case, the* *fluid approximation is given by:*

$$\dot{x}_0^1 = +\frac{\lambda_1^1 w_1^1 x_1^1 D_1}{w_1^1 x_1^1 + w_1^2 x_1^2} - \mu_1 x_0^1,$$

$$\dot{x}_1^1 = -\frac{\lambda_1^1 w_1^1 x_1^1 D_1}{w_1^1 x_1^1 + w_1^2 x_1^2} + \mu_1 x_0^1,$$

$$\dot{x}_0^2 = +\frac{\lambda_1^2 w_1^2 x_1^2 D_1}{w_1^1 x_1^1 + w_1^2 x_1^2} - \mu_2 x_0^2,$$

$$\dot{x}_1^2 = -\frac{\lambda_1^2 w_1^2 x_1^2 D_1}{w_1^1 x_1^1 + w_1^2 x_1^2} + \mu_2 x_0^2.$$

With this representation, it is evident that the assumption on closed workloads translates into a conservation-of-mass property given by the fact that

$$\frac{d}{dt}x_0^1(t) + \frac{d}{dt}x_1^1(t) = 0$$

and, similarly,

$$\frac{d}{dt}x_0^2(t) + \frac{d}{dt}x_1^2(t) = 0.$$

This implies that

$$x_0^1(t) + x_1^1(t) = x_0^1(0) + x_1^1(0)$$

and

$$x_0^2(t) + x_1^2(t) = x_0^2(0) + x_1^2(0),$$

for all t for which the solution of the fluid approximation is defined. In other words, the population of clients of each class is constant with time, and is equal to the total initial population. In general, the following proposition holds, by inspection of (2).

PROPOSITION 1. *Any GPS queuing network model satisfies the following properties:*

i) *The fluid approximation is nonnegative.*

ii) *Let $N^k > 0$ denote the initial population of class k-clients at time $t = 0$, i.e., $N^k = \sum_{i=0}^M x_i^k(0)$. Then it holds that*

$$x_j^k(t) = N^k - \sum_{\substack{i=0 \\ i \neq j}}^{M} x_i^k(t), \qquad \textit{for all } t. \tag{3}$$

5. OPTIMIZATION

This section presents the main result of this paper. The aim is to show that, when the parameters of a fluid model are to be optimized, then it is possible to prune certain regions of the parameter space which yield a provably higher cost. This can be done a priori, without ever analyzing the model in those regions. We show the applicability of this result to an optimization problem solved with GA, which is formulated in Section 5.1. Then, Section 5.2 discusses the result of monotonicity, which is the fundamental property that is exploited in our parameter-pruning approach. Finally, the implications on the optimization problem are discussed in Section 5.3.

5.1 Problem Formulation

We study the GPS model (1) with an optimization case study that aims at maximizing throughput and minimizing some operating cost. Whilst we focus on this problem in the remainder of this paper, let us remark that other scenarios are also possible. For instance, an analogous situation—by virtue of the duality between system throughput and response time by means of Little's law [24]— may consider response-time minimization and some revenue maximization.

Following [32], throughput may be estimated as a *reward measure* over the ODE solution. As an estimate of steady-state throughput, in particular, we consider a sufficiently large time point T where the solution is numerically close to equilibrium; this can be done by verifying that the norm of the ODE derivative at time T is less than a threshold.

The per-class throughput at equilibrium is given by

$$\mu_k(1 - p_{00}^k)x_0^k(T),$$

which is the total rate at which clients move from station 0 to some other station $i \neq 0$ (since this is a delay station, its throughput is proportional to the number of clients). Operating costs, instead, are assumed to be a function of the number of users (see [1] for a real case), denoted by $C(N^1, \ldots, N^K)$. This leads to the the following objective function to be minimized:

$$\phi(\vec{x}) = -\sum_{k=1}^K \mu_k(1 - p_{00}^k)x_0^k(T) + C(N^1, \ldots, N^K) \tag{4}$$

subject to the constraints

$$0 < N^k \leq U^k, \qquad \text{for all } 1 \leq k \leq K. \tag{5}$$

Therefore, this optimization program has client populations as the decision variables, with upper bounds given by constants U^k. This set-up may correspond to a practical situation where the modeler has no choice with respect to the server capacity (for instance, when a third-party server farm or cloud environment are used) and when the client demands are known. Under these conditions, the modeler may be interested in finding the workload mix, given by the per-class client populations, that optimizes the system's behavior.

5.2 Monotone Systems

At the basis of this technique is the notion of *monotone* ODE systems, which is briefly overviewed in this subsection in order to make the paper self-contained. The reader may find a detailed treatment in [30] and references therein.

First, we define O to be an orthant of $\mathbb{R}^n$, i.e., $O = \{\vec{x} \in \mathbb{R}^n : (-1)^{e_i}x_i \geq 0\}$, for $e_i \in \{0, 1\}$. For any $\vec{x}, \vec{y} \in \mathbb{R}^n$, we write $\vec{x} \leq_O \vec{y}$ if and only if $\vec{y} - \vec{x} \in O$. Now, let us consider an autonomous ODE system $\frac{d}{dt}\vec{x}(t) = G(\vec{x}(t))$ defined in $\mathbb{R} \times X$, with $X \subseteq \mathbb{R}^n$ an open and convex set and G a differentiable function in X. We call such a system *monotone* if, for any two initial conditions $\vec{x}(0) \leq_O \vec{y}(0)$, it holds that the corresponding solutions, denoted by $\vec{x}(t)$ and $\vec{y}(t)$, preserve the ordering, i.e., $\vec{x}(t) \leq_O \vec{y}(t)$, for all t for which both solutions are defined. We will be concerned with the case where O is the positive orthant of $\mathbb{R}^n$, i.e., $e_i = 0$ for all $1 \leq i \leq n$. Thus $\vec{x}(0) \leq_O \vec{y}(0)$ means $x_i(0) \leq y_i(0)$ for all $1 \leq i \leq n$. In the remainder of this paper, a comparison between two vector shall always be intended in this sense.

The following result characterizes monotonicity with respect to the Jacobian of G, denoted by $DG(\vec{x})$.

PROPOSITION 2 (SEE LEMMA 2.1 IN [30]). *Let G be a function defined on an open and convex set of $\mathbb{R}^n$ where it*

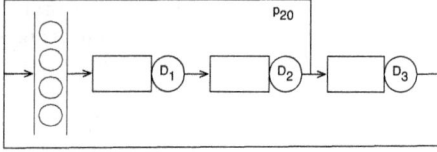

Figure 2: Queueing network model for the numerical validation of Section 6.

is differentiable. The ODE system $\frac{d}{dt}\vec{x} = G(\vec{x}(t))$ is said to be monotone *in the orthant O if and only if the matrix $PDG(\vec{x})P$ has nonnegative off-diagonal elements for every $\vec{x} \in X$, where $P = diag((-1)^{e_1}, \ldots, (-1)^{e_n})$.*

We are now ready to state the crucial proposition of this paper.

PROPOSITION 3 (MONOTONE GPS NETWORK). *Let the vector field of (2) be defined in the open and convex set such that $x_i^k > 0$ for all $1 \leq k \leq K$ and $0 \leq i \leq M$. Then, it holds that the ODE system (2) is monotone in the positive orthant.*

PROOF. See Appendix. □

5.3 Parameter-Space Pruning

Let $\vec{x}(0)$ and $\vec{y}(0)$ be two initial conditions for the fluid approximation (2) in the feasible region determined by constraints (5), with $\vec{x}(0) \leq \vec{y}(0)$. Let $\vec{x}(t)$ and $\vec{y}(t)$ represent the respective ODE solutions. Finally, let $N_x^k = \sum_{i=0}^{M} x_i^k(0)$, i.e., the total number of class-k clients in the system with initial conditions $\vec{x}(0)$. (N_y^k is defined analogously.) The above proposition yields that if $\vec{x}(0) \leq \vec{y}(0)$ then $\vec{x}(t) \leq \vec{y}(t)$ for all t.

We now exploit this fact to reduce the computational cost of the optimization program presented in Section 5.1. Let us consider the objective function (4) and write

$$\phi(\vec{x}) - \phi(\vec{y}) = C(N_x^1, \ldots, N_x^K) - C(N_y^1, \ldots, N_y^K)$$
$$+ (1 - p_{00}^k) \sum_{k=1}^{K} \mu_k y_0^k(T) - \mu_k x_0^k(T).$$

Now, the second line of the equation is nonnegative because the system is monotone. Thus, whenever the first summation is nonnegative, it holds that $\phi(\vec{x}) \geq \phi(\vec{y})$. Crucially, the sign of the first summation *can be established a-priori*, i.e., without having to solve the ODE systems, because all its terms are known parameters, i.e., the initial populations and the given cost function.

To further clarify this relation, let us consider the special case which involves setting $C \equiv 0$; this corresponds to a situation where there is no cost associated with the client populations. By inspection of the first line of the above equation, it is clear that $\phi(\vec{x}) \leq \phi(\vec{y})$: The maximum throughput is attained at the point of the feasible region with the largest populations, consistently with intuition. Hence, no computational cost for the optimization is required whatsoever.

6. NUMERICAL EXAMPLES

The purpose of this section is to study the computational advantages obtained by exploiting the results presented in the previous section. To this aim, we consider an optimization scenario based on a model of a three-tier software system modeled as a queueing network with three distinct GPS service centers (e.g., front-end, business logic, and a database-managent system) and a delay station, as illustrated in Fig. 2. In addition to being a reasonable high-level performance model of a complex distributed software system (for instance, it can be seen as a closed-workload variant of the model in [6]), the network is simple enough to keep stochastic simulation feasible, as this will be used as a baseline to assess the quality of the approximation introduced by the fluid approximation. On the other hand, the model is complicated enough to be exercised, with appropriate choice of parameters, under different operating conditions (e.g., performance bottlenecks at different stations).

The problem is solved by genetic algorithm with two approaches: a *black-box* approach (BB), which finds an optimal configuration *without* adopting parameter-space pruning; and a *grey-box* approach (GB) which does do parameter-space pruning in the following manner: Given a parameter vector $\vec{y}(0)$, of the initial populations of clients, if there exists another parameter vector $\vec{x}(0)$ with provably superior cost, then an *infinite fitness value* is assigned to it.

To show soundness of the approach, we compared the distance between the minima returned by both methods. As an index of effectiveness, we compared the runtimes of BB and GB. Finally, in order to show the overall accuracy of optimization via fluid techniques, we compared the estimated optima against those obtained by optimization via stochastic simulation of the associated CTMC, which is taken to represent the *true* behavior of the system. With this (expensive) study, we assess the *absolute quality* of fluid optimum, and we numerically evaluate the computational advantages gained by fluid analysis.

Parametrization. All tests were performed using Matlab 7.9.0, with the genetic algorithm implementation available in the *Genetic Algorithm and Direct Search* toolbox. In order to remove degrees of freedom in the set-up, unless otherwise stated the genetic algorithm was used with its default settings for both BB and GB. We considered a population of 30 individuals at each generation, and a maximum number of 20 generations.

For the evaluation of the fitness function (4) via fluid analysis we employed Matlab's `ode15s` routine by setting an absolute tolerance of 10^{-4} and a relative tolerance of 10^{-5}; all other parameters for the ODE solver were set as the default ones. The use of this solver was preferred in order to deal with potentially stiff problems, due to the randomness in the parametrization of the model, ensuring more robustness across the whole parameter space. This comes at the cost of longer execution times by `ode15s` in non-stiff models, which could be more efficiently solved by other methods, such as the well known Runge-Kutta scheme as implemented in `ode45`. However, the relative difference between these two methods is negligible compared to the difference between ODE analysis and stochastic simulation. We fixed $T = 5000.0$ for the evaluation of (4) and successfully verified that in all cases the derivatives at time T were less than 10^{-6} in norm, to ensure numerical convergence to an equilibrium.

For the evaluation of the fitness function via stochastic analysis we used Monte Carlo simulation based on Gillespie's direct method [18], which was preferred over the nu-

p_{20}^k	$\phi_{\min}^{\text{SIM}}$	*FError*		*SError*			*Runtimes*		*Confidence intervals*	
		BB	GB	BB	GB	GB	BB (speed-up)	Sim (speed-up)	GB	BB
0.85	-1.63	0.63%	0.58%	2.50%	1.65%	28.43 s	63.35 s (2.23)	37961 s (1335)	4.28%	2.97%
0.86	-2.12	0.03%	0.09%	1.18%	1.97%	28.87 s	64.52 s (2.23)	41244 s (1428)	4.97%	4.78%
0.87	-2.68	0.60%	0.51%	2.02%	1.63%	28.97 s	65.10 s (2.24)	45324 s (1564)	4.09%	4.34%
0.88	-3.28	0.75%	0.79%	2.56%	0.71%	28.46 s	63.30 s (2.22)	53240 s (1871)	4.77%	4.40%
0.89	-4.00	1.74%	1.81%	2.27%	2.04%	29.12 s	65.28 s (2.24)	53867 s (1849)	4.26%	4.20%
0.90	-5.00	0.38%	0.37%	1.62%	0.94%	31.47 s	66.05 s (2.09)	70762 s (2248)	4.60%	4.50%
0.91	-6.07	0.30%	0.27%	1.59%	1.07%	30.13 s	65.32 s (2.17)	76590 s (2541)	4.79%	4.23%
0.92	-7.42	0.80%	0.79%	1.24%	1.90%	31.21 s	65.13 s (2.09)	95300 s (3053)	4.76%	4.93%
0.93	-9.29	0.24%	0.26%	0.70%	1.00%	32.44 s	65.40 s (2.01)	125410 s (3865)	4.96%	4.96%

Table 1: **Comparison between fluid optimization using a black-box approach (BB) and our approach (grey-box, GB) with parameter-space pruning.**

merical CTMC solution because of the large state space sizes involved. The method of batch means was employed; the simulation was stopped when the largest confidence interval across all means at 95% confidence level was within 5%, with a maximum 8 batches of simulation, where the first was discarded for transient removal. Each batch was of length 5000.0; this choice was motivated by the fact that, as discussed, at that time interval all ODE solutions estimated numerical convergence to the equilibrium.

In all cases, we kept fixed the following parameters of the queueing network: $D_1 = 30.0$, $D_2 = 20.0$, $D_3 = 10.0$, $\mu_1 = \mu_2 = 1.5$, $\lambda_1^1 = \lambda_1^2 = \lambda_2^1 = \lambda_2^2 = 1.0$, $\lambda_3^1 = \lambda_3^2 = 0.1$, and $w_i^1 = 2.0$, $w_i^2 = 1.0$, for $i = 1, 2, 3$ (thus corresponding to a situation of two classes of clients with the same demands but different priorities/shares). The routing matrices were kept equal for both classes:

$$P^k = \begin{pmatrix} 0 & 1 & 0 & 0 \\ 0 & 0 & 1 & 0 \\ p_{20}^k & 0 & 0 & 1 - p_{20}^k \\ 1 & 0 & 0 & 0 \end{pmatrix}, \qquad k = 1, 2,$$

where we experimented with different values of p_{20}^k in order to test our approach for different operating conditions, since increasing p_{20}^k leads to less frequent visits to station 3 (which has the lowest capacity in the network). The initial conditions were set in such a way that the clients were evenly distributed across all stations.

The set-up of the optimization program was as follows. The constraints U^k were set to 2000, for $k = 1, 2$. The cost function was chosen in the form

$$C(N^1, N^2) = \alpha + \frac{(N^1 + N^2 - \beta)^\gamma}{\delta},$$

where α is interpreted as a fixed cost, β is a break-even total client population, γ gives the shape of the dependence of the cost from the client populations, and δ is a normalization factor that makes $C(N^1, N^2)$ comparable to the throughput, in order to exercise the model under conditions where changes in the parameters do affect cost sensibly. Notice that this normalization can always be done without loss of generality of this approach—for example, it could be interpreted as a change of monetary unit. In these experiments we set $\alpha = 5.0$, $\beta = 1000.0$, $\gamma = 2$, and $\delta = 2E05$.

Data analysis. The numerical tests were executed on machines equipped with an 8-way Opteron 2.6 GHz dual-core

with 32 GB RAM. For each value of p_{20}^k, chosen between 0.85 and 0.93 at 0.01 steps, we ran three independent replicas. All the measurement reported in the following are the averages computed across these replicas.

As an index of effectiveness, we define the notion of percentage relative error of the optimization program as follows. Let $\phi_{\min}^{\text{BB}}$ (resp., $\phi_{\min}^{\text{BB}}$) be the minimum fitness value returned by the GA with the black-box (resp., grey-box) approach using fluid analysis; similarly, let $\phi_{\min}^{\text{SIM}}$ be the *true* minimum as returned by GA where each individual is analyzed through stochastic simulation. Then, the errors for BB and GB, denoted as *FError*, are defined as

$$\begin{aligned} \text{FError}_{\text{BB}} &= \frac{|\phi_{\min}^{\text{BB}} - \phi_{\min}^{\text{SIM}}|}{\phi_{\min}^{\text{SIM}}} \times 100, \\ \text{FError}_{\text{GB}} &= \frac{|\phi_{\min}^{\text{GB}} - \phi_{\min}^{\text{SIM}}|}{\phi_{\min}^{\text{SIM}}} \times 100. \end{aligned} \tag{6}$$

This notion alone, however, is not sufficient to fully understand the behavior of the approximation. The reason is that the evaluation of $\phi_{\min}^{\text{BB}}$ and $\phi_{\min}^{\text{GB}}$, in general, incurs two kinds of error which are due to the approximations of the stochastic process via the fluid model and of the stochastic reward (in this case, throughput) with its fluid counterpart. Thus, for instance, a relatively large FError may in fact still yield excellent accuracy when the individual with the minimum fitness obtained by fluid approximation is evaluated using stochastic simulation; that is, when one computes the true fitness of the best individual returned by the fluid GA. Using similar arguments, a small FError may turn out to be associated with a fittest individual which is away from the true optimum. In order to understand the nature of the optimal solutions returned by both BB and GB, we define the notion of *SError* as the error between $\phi_{\min}^{\text{SIM}}$ and the cost function evaluated by simulation for the fittest individual of BB and GB, which is denoted by $\phi^{\text{SIM}}(N_{\text{BB}}^1, N_{\text{BB}}^2)$ and $\phi^{\text{SIM}}(N_{\text{GB}}^1, N_{\text{GB}}^2)$, respectively:

$$\begin{aligned} \text{SError}_{\text{BB}} &= \frac{|\phi^{\text{SIM}}(N_{\text{BB}}^1, N_{\text{BB}}^2) - \phi_{\min}^{\text{SIM}}|}{\phi_{\min}^{\text{SIM}}} \times 100, \\ \text{SError}_{\text{GB}} &= \frac{|\phi^{\text{SIM}}(N_{\text{GB}}^1, N_{\text{GB}}^2) - \phi_{\min}^{\text{SIM}}|}{\phi_{\min}^{\text{SIM}}} \times 100. \end{aligned} \tag{7}$$

The computational advantage provided by our GB method is measured in terms of speed-up with respect to BB. Since both methods were applied to the same total number of individuals, the speed-up is only due to the fact that in GB some individuals may be discarded a-priori because they yield provably worse fitness. As a general indication of the performance of fluid optimization, we also measured the speed-up with respect to stochastic simulation.

Results. The results of our experimental campaign are collectively reported in Table 1. Column labelled with $\phi_{\min}^{\text{SIM}}$ gives the minimum value of the fitness function returned by running the GA with stochastic simulation, to demonstrate that the chosen values of p_{20}^k do exercise the network under different steady-state conditions. Indeed, the fitness function is not explicitly dependent on p_{20}^k, hence the changes must be attributed to the different workload mixes that optimize the system's behaviour. Columns labelled with *FError* and *SError* show the accuracy indices as defined in (6) and (7), respectively. The runtime results are given as the average wall-clock execution time (in seconds) of the overall optimization program when using GB, BB, and simulation; for convenience, the speed-ups with respect to GB are also reported between brackets. Overall, the analyses required a total of 237 hours of computation time, of which 99.9% was devoted to the stochastic simulations. While the cost ODE analysis did not vary significantly across all tests, a significant increase of the simulation runtimes can be noticed as a function of p_{20}^k. This is due to the fact that the optimal configurations for larger p_{20}^k lead to increasingly saturated networks, which are notoriously more difficult to simulate. Using selected configurations that yield near-saturation conditions for $p_{20} > 0.93$, we estimated that the simulation runtimes to achieve confidence intervals within 5% would have been at least 32 times longer than for the case $p_{20} = 0.85$. This made the analysis of such models unfeasible under our given computational constraints, since the whole optimization problem might be aborted as a result of the expiration of the total time limit for a single job (i.e., 48 h) in the computer cluster where the experiments were conducted.

An analysis of the confidence intervals across all tests showed that, using the stopping criteria mentioned above, 82% of the simulations returned confidence intervals within the desired 5% level. Instead, for the other 18% of simulations (which were stopped because the maximum number of 8 batches had been reached), the median confidence interval was 6%. However, a manual analysis of the models with the highest confidence intervals showed that those were related to genomes with a significantly poor fitness. Indeed, in a typical case this was due to the exploration of regions of the parameter space with very low populations (recall that the constraints have a lower bound of 1) where the system dynamics are slower due to less frequent service requests. Instead, the average optimal workload mixes across all values of p_{20}^k were 159 and 189 class-1 and class-2 clients, respectively. For the same reason of computational feasibility as discussed above (time expiration), we could not adjust the stopping criteria for simulation in order to decrease the proportion of results with confidence intervals greater than 5%. However, to improve the precision of the optimal configuration returned by stochastic simulation, we ran longer simulations for $\phi^{\text{SIM}}(N_{\text{GB}}^1, N_{\text{GB}}^2)$ and $\phi^{\text{SIM}}(N_{\text{BB}}^1, N_{\text{BB}}^2)$ by doubling the batch length to 10000.0 time units. The last columns show the confidence intervals for the simulations under these modified stopping criteria.

Overall, this validation demonstrates that provable a-priori pruning of the parameter space can significantly reduce the

cost of the exploration (by at least a factor of 2 across all the experiments), whilst returning estimates that differ less than 2% from those returned by the baseline GA implementation. We also confirm the suitability of fluid models for optimization purposes: The estimated optima are in all cases at most 3% away from the real optima computed by simulation. However the computational cost of simulation is excessively high, even for a small network with relatively few clients, and consistently separated from ODE-based optimization by three orders of magnitude.

7. CONCLUSION

Summary of findings. Many analysis techniques are available that can efficiently evaluate a model of software performance. However, in general, from the solution of a model with a given parametrization it is not possible to infer the behavior of the same model with a different parametrization. This paper has provided a contribution in this direction in the context of software performance models with fluid techniques. We have shown a general result of monotonicity whereby fluid solutions preserve the ordering of their parameters. As an application, here we discussed a case study of minimization via genetic algorithms, whereby some genomes can be shown to yield a provably superior fitness value a priori, i.e., without evaluating the fitness function, by virtue of monotonicity. Suitably equipping the genetic algorithm to exploit this property has shown a speed-up factor of over 2 on average with respect to a baseline version of the algorithm that does not implement a-priori pruning. Furthermore, the fluid approximation consistently yielded excellent accuracy with respect to the *true* optimal configurations returned by evaluating the fitness function with simulation.

Although we focused on optimization via evolutionary algorithms in this paper, we wish to stress that monotonicity can be exploited in a much broader context, i.e., whenever the modeler wishes to analyze different configurations, and use the evaluation of one configuration in order to infer the behavioral trend of others.

Scope of validity and generalization. There are two main issues that may hinder a wider applicability of this technique. The first one is that monotonicity does not hold for every parameter of the model under consideration. For instance, it was not possible to prove it for the server capacities D_i. Let us notice that Proposition 2 gives a sufficient condition, therefore, in principle, it could be established via other routes also for D_i. This will be the subject of future work. Nevertheless, we argue that the scope of applicability made available in this paper is rather significant, as it covers monotonicity with respect to initial populations (i.e., the system's concurrency levels) which can be directly related to throughput—hence response time—as discussed in Section 5.

The second limitation might be the focus on queueing networks with GPS service discipline. Keeping in mind that these models can already be used in virtualized and cloud environments, as discussed in Section 1, here we also wish to stress that an analogous result of monotonicity may be proven for other models of software performance, using the same arguments presented in this paper. For example, the GPS interaction functions (2) are surprisingly similar to those used for the stochastic process algebra PEPA [33]. Indeed, in a typical situation, PEPA-like interaction functions can be written in the form

$$f_i(\vec{x}) = \mu_i \frac{x_i}{\sum_{i' \in I} x_{i'}} \min \left\{ \sum_{i' \in I} x_{i'}, x_j \right\}, \qquad (8)$$

where I is an index set such that $i \in I$ and $j \notin I$. Now, depending on the behavior of the minimum function, the ODE can be rewritten in terms of piece-wise differentiable functions. The case where $\min \left\{ \sum_{i' \in I} x_{i'}, x_j \right\} = \sum_{i' \in I} x_{i'}$ becomes trivial because the function reduces to a delay-type interaction $\mu_i x_i$. Instead, the case $\min \left\{ \sum_{i' \in I} x_{i'}, x_j \right\} = x_j$ can be handled in the same way as the GPS service case. Since (8) is essentially used in the PEPA encoding of layered queueing networks [31] and of stochastic Petri nets [17], monotonicity can be extended to the fluid approximations of these two other modeling techniques. A precise formalization of this extension is however beyond the scope of this paper and will be presented in future reports.

Acknowledgement

This work is supported by the EU project QUANTICOL, 600708, and by the DFG SPP-1593 project DAPS. The author wishes to thank Max Tschaikowski for discussions, and LRZ Munich for helpful support for the computing facilities.

8. REFERENCES

[1] The biggest cost of Facebook's growth. http://www.technologyreview.com/news/427941/the-biggest-cost-of-facebooks-growth/.

[2] A. Aleti, S. Björnander, L. Grunske, and I. Meedeniya. ArcheOpterix: An extendable tool for architecture optimization of AADL models. In *MOMPES*, pages 61–71, 2009.

[3] A. Aleti, B. Buhnova, L. Grunske, A. Koziolek, and I. Meedeniya. Software architecture optimization methods: A systematic literature review. *IEEE Trans. Softw. Eng.*, 39(5):658–683, 2013.

[4] H. Alla and R. David. Continuous and Hybrid Petri Nets. *Journal of Circuits, Systems, and Computers*, 8(1):159–188, 1998.

[5] J. Anselmi and I. Verloop. Energy-aware capacity scaling in virtualized environments with performance guarantees. *Perf. Eval.*, 68(11):1207–1221, 2011.

[6] D. Ardagna, B. Panicucci, M. Trubian, and L. Zhang. Energy-aware autonomic resource allocation in multitier virtualized environments. *IEEE Trans. Serv. Comput.*, 5(1):2–19, Jan. 2012.

[7] D. Ardagna and B. Pernici. Adaptive service composition in flexible processes. *IEEE Trans. Softw. Eng.*, 33(6):369–384, june 2007.

[8] E. Badidi, L. Esmahi, and M. A. Serhani. A queuing model for service selection of multi-classes QoS-aware web services. In *ECOWS*, pages 204–213, 2005.

[9] S. Balsamo, A. Di Marco, P. Inverardi, and M. Simeoni. Model-based performance prediction in software development: A survey. *IEEE Trans. Softw. Eng.*, 30(5):295–310, 2004.

[10] B. Boone, S. V. Hoecke, G. V. Seghbroeck, N. Joncheere, V. Jonckers, F. D. Turck, C. Develder, and B. Dhoedt. SALSA: QoS-aware load balancing for

autonomous service brokering. *Journal of Systems and Software*, 83(3):446–456, 2010.

[11] R. Calinescu, L. Grunske, M. Kwiatkowska, R. Mirandola, and G. Tamburrelli. Dynamic QoS management and optimization in service-based systems. *IEEE Trans. Softw. Eng.*, 37(3):387–409, 2011.

[12] V. Cardellini, E. Casalicchio, V. Grassi, F. Lo Presti, and R. Mirandola. QoS-driven runtime adaptation of service oriented architectures. In *ESEC/FSE*, pages 131–140. ACM, 2009.

[13] G. Casale and M. Tribastone. Fluid analysis of queueing in two-stage random environments. In *QEST*, pages 21–30, Aachen, Germany, September 2011. IEEE Computer Society Press.

[14] A. Chandra, W. Gong, and P. Shenoy. Dynamic resource allocation for shared data centers using online measurements. *SIGMETRICS Perform. Eval. Rev.*, 31(1):300–301, June 2003.

[15] V. Cortellessa, A. Di Marco, and P. Inverardi. *Model-Based Software Performance Analysis*. Springer, 2011.

[16] G. Franks, T. Al-Omari, M. Woodside, O. Das, and S. Derisavi. Enhanced modeling and solution of layered queueing networks. *IEEE Trans. Softw. Eng.*, 35(2):148–161, 2009.

[17] V. Galpin. Continuous approximation of PEPA models and Petri nets. *International Journal of Computer Aided Engineering and Technology*, 2:324–339, 2010.

[18] D. Gillespie. Exact stochastic simulation of coupled chemical reactions. *Journal of Physical Chemistry*, 81(25):2340–2361, December 1977.

[19] S. Gilmore, J. Hillston, and M. Ribaudo. An efficient algorithm for aggregating PEPA models. *IEEE Trans. Softw. Eng.*, 27(5):449–464, 2001.

[20] A. Koziolek, H. Koziolek, and R. Reussner. Peropteryx: automated application of tactics in multi-objective software architecture optimization. In *QoSA/ISARCS*, pages 33–42, 2011.

[21] T. G. Kurtz. Solutions of ordinary differential equations as limits of pure Markov processes. *J. Appl. Prob.*, 7(1):49–58, April 1970.

[22] J. Li, J. Chinneck, M. Woodside, M. Litoiu, and G. Iszlai. Performance model driven QoS guarantees and optimization in clouds. In *Proceedings of the Workshop on Software Engineering Challenges of Cloud Computing*, pages 15–22, 2009.

[23] M. Litoiu, J. Rolia, and G. Serazzi. Designing process replication and activation: A quantitative approach. *IEEE Trans. Softw. Eng.*, 26(12):1168–1178, 2000.

[24] J. Little. A Proof of the Queuing Formula: $L = \lambda W$. *Operations Research*, 9(3):383–387, 1961.

[25] M. Marzolla and R. Mirandola. Performance prediction of web service workflows. In *Software Architectures, Components, and Applications*, volume 4880 of *Lecture Notes in Computer Science*, pages 127–144. Springer, 2007.

[26] D. Menasce and V. Dubey. Utility-based QoS brokering in service oriented architectures. In *IEEE International Conference on Web Services*, pages 422–430, 2007.

[27] Object Management Group. *UML Profile for Modeling and Analysis of Real-Time and Embedded Systems (MARTE). Beta 1.* OMG, 2007. OMG document number ptc/07-08-04.

[28] P. Pollett, A. Dooley, and J. Ross. Modelling population processes with random initial conditions. *Mathematical Biosciences*, 223(2):142–150, 2010.

[29] J. G. Shanthikumar and D. D. Yao. Stochastic monotonicity in general queueing networks. *Journal of Applied Probability*, 26(2):413–417, 1989.

[30] H. L. Smith. Systems of Ordinary Differential Equations Which Generate an Order Preserving Flow. A Survey of Results. *SIAM Review*, 30(1):87–113, 1988.

[31] M. Tribastone. A fluid model for layered queueing networks. *IEEE Trans. Softw. Eng.*, 39(6):744–756, 2013.

[32] M. Tribastone, J. Ding, S. Gilmore, and J. Hillston. Fluid rewards for a stochastic process algebra. *IEEE Trans. Softw. Eng.*, 38:861–874, 2012.

[33] M. Tribastone, S. Gilmore, and J. Hillston. Scalable differential analysis of process algebra models. *IEEE Trans. Softw. Eng.*, 38(1):205–219, 2012.

[34] L. Zeng, B. Benatallah, A. Ngu, M. Dumas, J. Kalagnanam, and H. Chang. QoS-aware middleware for web services composition. *IEEE Trans. Softw. Eng.*, 30(5):311–327, 2004.

[35] T. Zheng, C. M. Woodside, and M. Litoiu. Performance model estimation and tracking using optimal filters. *IEEE Trans. Software Eng.*, 34(3):391–406, 2008.

APPENDIX

Here we give the proof of Proposition 3.

PROOF. First, let us consider the ODE system

$$\dot{x}_0^k = -(1 - p_{00}^k)\mu_k x_0^k + \sum_{j=1}^{M} p_{j0}^k \frac{\lambda_j^k w_j^k x_j^k D_j}{\sum_{l=1}^{K} w_j^l \left(N^l - \sum_{j' \neq j} x_{j'}^l \right)},$$

$$\dot{x}_i^k = -\frac{\lambda_i^k w_i^k x_i^k D_i}{\sum_{l=1}^{K} w_i^l x_i^l} + p_{0i}^k \mu_k x_0^k + \qquad (9)$$

$$+ \sum_{j=1}^{M} p_{ji}^k \frac{\lambda_j^k w_j^k x_j^k D_j}{\sum_{l=1}^{K} w_j^l \left(N^l - \sum_{j' \neq j} x_{j'}^l \right)},$$

$$\dot{N}^k = 0,$$

for all $1 \leq k \leq K$ and $1 \leq i \leq I$. This ODE system arises from (2) by replacing each x_j^l with $N^l - \sum_{j' \neq j} x_{j'}^l$, and by adding *slack* variables N^k as trivial ODEs that yield a constant solution with respect to time t. Due to the property *ii)* of conservation of mass, each solution to the original ODE system (2) is also a solution to (9), whenever the initial conditions $N^k(0)$ for the slack variables are set as

$$N^k(0) = \sum_{i=0}^{M} x_i^k(0).$$

Thus, monotonicity may be equivalently proven on the modified ODE system (9). Its Jacobian $DG(\vec{x})$ can be written as

$$\begin{pmatrix} \frac{\partial g_0^1}{\partial x_0^1} & \cdots & \frac{\partial g_0^1}{\partial x_M^1} & \cdots & \frac{\partial g_0^1}{\partial x_M^K} & \frac{\partial g_0^1}{\partial N^1} & \cdots & \frac{\partial g_0^1}{\partial N^K} \\ \vdots & \ddots & & & \vdots & \vdots & \ddots & \vdots \\ \frac{\partial g_M^K}{\partial x_0^1} & \cdots & & & \frac{\partial g_M^K}{\partial x_M^K} & \frac{\partial g_M^K}{\partial N^1} & \cdots & \frac{\partial g_M^K}{\partial N^K} \\ \hline \frac{\partial N^1}{\partial x_0^1} & \cdots & & & \frac{\partial N^1}{\partial x_K^M} & \frac{\partial N^1}{\partial N^1} & \cdots & \frac{\partial N^1}{\partial N^K} \\ \vdots & \ddots & & & \vdots & \vdots & \ddots & \vdots \\ \frac{\partial N^K}{\partial x_0^1} & \cdots & & & \frac{\partial N^K}{\partial x_K^M} & \frac{\partial N^K}{\partial N^1} & \cdots & \frac{\partial N^K}{\partial N^K} \end{pmatrix}$$

where g_i^k denotes the component of the vector field for the variable x_i^k, for all $0 \leq i \leq M$ and $1 \leq k \leq K$. With this block structure, it is possible to show monotonicity of the system by using Proposition 2 and Remark 1 in [30], whereby a sufficient condition is that: i) the off-diagonal elements of the top-left and bottom-right blocks be non-negative; and ii) the elements of the top-right and bottom-left blocks be non-positive.

In order to show this, we proceed by case distinction, recalling that the GPS queueing network fluid model is non-negative, all rates λ_i^k, weights w_i^k, and server capacities D_i are positive reals, and that the routing probabilities p_{ij}^k are nonnegative reals. First, we observe that the bottom blocks of the Jacobian are all trivially zero, thus we focus on the top blocks only.

For the top-left block:

i) Case $\frac{\partial g_0^k}{\partial x_i^k}$, with $i \neq 0$:

$$\frac{\partial g_0^k}{\partial x_i^k} = \frac{\partial}{\partial x_i^k} \left\{ \sum_{j=1}^{M} p_{j0}^k \frac{\lambda_j^k w_j^k x_j^k D_j}{\sum_{l=1}^{K} w_j^l \left(N^l - \sum_{j' \neq j} x_{j'}^l \right)} \right\}$$

$$= \frac{\partial}{\partial x_i^k} \left\{ \sum_{j \neq i} p_{j0}^k \frac{\lambda_j^k w_j^k x_j^k D_j}{\sum_{l=1}^{K} w_j^l \left(N^l - \sum_{j' \neq j} x_{j'}^l \right)} + \right.$$

$$\left. + p_{i0}^k \frac{\lambda_i^k w_i^k x_i^k D_i}{\sum_{l=1}^{K} w_i^l \left(N^l - \sum_{j' \neq i} x_{j'}^l \right)} \right\}$$

$$= -\sum_{j \neq i} p_{j0}^k \lambda_j^k w_j^k x_j^k D_j \frac{\partial}{\partial x_i^k} \left\{ \sum_{l=1}^{K} w_j^l \left(N^l - \sum_{j' \neq j} x_{j'}^l \right) \right\}$$

$$+ p_{i0}^k \frac{\lambda_i^k w_i^k D_i}{\sum_{l=1}^{K} w_i^l \left(N^l - \sum_{j' \neq i} x_{j'}^l \right)}$$

$$= \sum_{j \neq i} p_{j0}^k \lambda_j^k w_j^k x_j^k D_j w_i^l +$$

$$+ p_{i0}^k \frac{\lambda_i^k w_i^k D_i}{\sum_{l=1}^{K} w_i^l \left(N^l - \sum_{j' \neq i} x_{j'}^l \right)} \geq 0.$$

ii) Case $\dfrac{\partial g_0^k}{\partial x_0^{\hat{l}}}$, with $\hat{l} \neq k$:

$$\frac{\partial g_0^k}{\partial x_0^{\hat{l}}} = \sum_{j=1}^{M} p_{j0}^k \frac{\partial}{\partial x_0^{\hat{l}}} \left\{ \frac{\lambda_j^k w_j^k x_j^k D_j}{\sum_{l=1}^{K} w_j^l \left(N^l - \sum_{j' \neq j} x_{j'}^l \right)} \right\}$$

$$= -\sum_{j=1}^{M} p_{j0}^k \lambda_j^k w_j^k x_j^k D_j \frac{\partial}{\partial x_0^{\hat{l}}} \left\{ \sum_{l=1}^{K} w_j^l \left(N^l - \sum_{j' \neq j} x_{j'}^l \right) \right\}$$

$$= \sum_{j=1}^{M} p_{j0}^k \lambda_j^k w_j^k x_j^k D_j w_j^{\hat{l}} \geq 0.$$

iii) Case $\dfrac{\partial g_0^k}{\partial x_i^{\hat{l}}}$, with $i > 0$ and $\hat{l} \neq k$: similarly to ii),

$$\frac{\partial g_0^k}{\partial x_i^{\hat{l}}} = -\sum_{j=1}^{M} p_{j0}^k \lambda_j^k w_j^k x_j^k D_j \frac{\partial}{\partial x_i^{\hat{l}}} \left\{ \sum_{l=1}^{K} w_j^l \left(N^l - \sum_{j' \neq j} x_{j'}^l \right) \right\}$$

$$= \sum_{j=1}^{M} p_{j0}^k \lambda_j^k w_j^k x_j^k D_j w_j^{\hat{l}} \geq 0.$$

iv) Case $\dfrac{\partial g_i^k}{\partial x_0^k}$, with $i \neq 0$:

$$\frac{\partial g_i^k}{\partial x_0^k} = -\sum_{j=1}^{M} p_{ji}^k \lambda_j^k w_j^k x_j^k D_j \frac{\partial}{\partial x_0^k} \left\{ \sum_{l=1}^{K} w_j^l \left(N^l - \sum_{j' \neq j} x_{j'}^l \right) \right\}$$

$$+ p_{0i}^k \mu_k$$

$$= \sum_{j=1}^{M} p_{ji}^k \lambda_j^k w_j^k x_j^k D_j w_j^k + p_{0i}^k \mu_k \geq 0.$$

v) Case $\dfrac{\partial g_i^k}{\partial x_0^{\hat{l}}}$, with $\hat{l} \neq k$: similarly to ii),

$$\frac{\partial g_i^k}{\partial x_0^{\hat{l}}} = \sum_{j=1}^{M} p_{ji}^k \lambda_j^k w_j^k x_j^k D_j w_j^{\hat{l}} \geq 0$$

vi) Case $\dfrac{\partial g_i^k}{\partial x_{\hat{j}}^k}$, with $\hat{j} \neq i$, and $i, \hat{j} > 0$: similarly to i),

$$\frac{\partial g_i^k}{\partial x_{\hat{j}}^k} = \frac{\partial}{\partial x_{\hat{j}}^k} \left\{ \sum_{j=1}^{M} p_{ji}^k \frac{\lambda_j^k w_j^k x_j^k D_j}{\sum_{l=1}^{K} w_j^l \left(N^l - \sum_{j' \neq j} x_{j'}^l \right)} \right\}$$

$$= \frac{\partial}{\partial x_{\hat{j}}^k} \left\{ \sum_{j \neq \hat{j}} p_{ji}^k \frac{\lambda_j^k w_j^k x_j^k D_j}{\sum_{l=1}^{K} w_j^l \left(N^l - \sum_{j' \neq j} x_{j'}^l \right)} + \right.$$

$$\left. + p_{\hat{j}i}^k \frac{\lambda_{\hat{j}}^k w_{\hat{j}}^k x_{\hat{j}}^k D_{\hat{j}}}{\sum_{l=1}^{K} w_{\hat{j}}^l \left(N^l - \sum_{j' \neq \hat{j}} x_{j'}^l \right)} \right\}$$

$$= \sum_{j \neq \hat{j}} p_{ji}^k \lambda_j^k w_j^k x_j^k D_j w_{\hat{j}}^k +$$

$$+ p_{\hat{j}i}^k \frac{\lambda_{\hat{j}}^k w_{\hat{j}}^k D_{\hat{j}}}{\sum_{l=1}^{K} w_{\hat{j}}^l \left(N^l - \sum_{j' \neq \hat{j}} x_{j'}^l \right)} \geq 0.$$

vii) Case $\dfrac{\partial g_i^k}{\partial x_{\hat{j}}^{\hat{l}}}$, with $i, \hat{j} > 0$ and $k \neq \hat{l}$:

$$\frac{\partial g_i^k}{\partial x_{\hat{j}}^{\hat{l}}} = \sum_{j \neq \hat{j}} p_{ji}^k \lambda_j^k w_j^k x_j^k D_j w_j^{\hat{l}} \geq 0.$$

For the top-right block:

i) Case $\dfrac{\partial g_i^k}{\partial N^{\hat{l}}}$, with $0 \leq \hat{l} \leq K$, $0 \leq i \leq M$:

$$\frac{\partial g_i^k}{\partial N^{\hat{l}}} = -\sum_{j=1}^{M} p_{ji}^k \lambda_j^k w_j^k x_j^k D_j w_j^{\hat{l}} \leq 0.$$

$\square$

Exploring Synergies between Bottleneck Analysis and Performance Antipatterns

Catia Trubiani, Antinisca Di Marco,
Vittorio Cortellessa
University of L'Aquila, Italy
{catia.trubiani, antinisca.dimarco,
vittorio.cortellessa}@univaq.it

Nariman Mani, Dorina Petriu
Carleton University, Ottawa, Canada
{nmani, petriu}@sce.carleton.ca

ABSTRACT

The problem of interpreting the results of performance analysis is quite critical, mostly because the analysis results (i.e. mean values, variances, and probability distributions) are hard to transform into feedback for software engineers that allows to remove performance problems. Approaches aimed at identifying and removing the causes of poor performance in software systems commonly fall in two categories: (i) bottleneck analysis, aimed at identifying overloaded software components and/or hardware resources that affect the whole system performance, and (ii) performance antipatterns, aimed at detecting and removing common design mistakes that notably induce performance degradation. In this paper, we look for possible synergies between these two categories of approaches in order to empower the performance investigation capabilities. In particular, we aim at showing that the approach combination allows to provide software engineers with broader sets of alternative solutions leading to better performance results. We have explored this research direction in the context of Layered Queueing Network models, and we have considered a case study in the e-commerce domain. After comparing the results achievable with each approach separately, we quantitatively show the benefits of merging bottleneck analysis and performance antipatterns.

Categories and Subject Descriptors

C.4 [**Performance of Systems**]: Modeling techniques, Performance Attributes; D.2.8 [**Software Engineering**]: Metrics—*performance measures*

General Terms

Performance, Design.

Keywords

Software Performance; Model-based Performance Analysis; Bottleneck Analysis; Performance Antipatterns; Software Performance Feedback.

ICPE'14, March 22–26, 2014, Dublin, Ireland.
Copyright 2014 ACM 978-1-4503-2733-6/14/03 ...$15.00.
http://dx.doi.org/10.1145/2568088.2568092.

1. INTRODUCTION

In the software development domain there is a very high interest in the early validation of performance requirements because this ability avoids late and expensive fixes to consolidated software artifacts.

Model-based approaches, pioneered under the name of Software Performance Engineering (SPE) by Smith [24, 26, 23], aim at producing performance models early in the development cycle and using quantitative results from model solutions to refactor the architecture and design [17] with the purpose of meeting performance requirements [27].

Advanced Model-Driven Engineering (MDE) techniques have successfully been used in the last few years to introduce automation in software performance modeling and analysis [5, 13, 7]. Nevertheless, the problem of interpreting the performance analysis results is still quite critical. A large gap exists between the representation of performance analysis results and the feedback expected by software architects. For instance, the results contain numbers (e.g., mean response time, throughput, utilization, variance, etc.), whereas the feedback should include architectural suggestions, i.e., design alternatives, useful to overcome performance problems (e.g., split a software component in two components and re-deploy one of them).

Figure 1 shows the process we propose for merging bottleneck analysis and performance antipatterns in a round-trip SPE process. Ovals in the figure represent operational steps whereas square boxes represent input/output data. Vertical lines divide the process in three different phases: in the *modeling* phase, a (annotated[1]) software model is built; in the *performance analysis* phase, a performance model is obtained through model transformation, and such model is solved to obtain the performance results of interest; in the *refactoring* phase, the performance results are interpreted and, if necessary, feedback is generated as refactoring actions on the original software model.

Approaches aimed at identifying and removing the causes of poor performance in software systems commonly fall in two categories: (i) *bottleneck analysis* that allows to identify cases when the performance of a software system are limited by a number of overloaded software components and/or hardware resources [11]; (ii) *performance antipatterns* that document common mistakes made during software development, as well as their solutions [25, 8].

---

[1] Annotations are aimed at specifying system parameters such as workload, service demands and hardware characteristics.

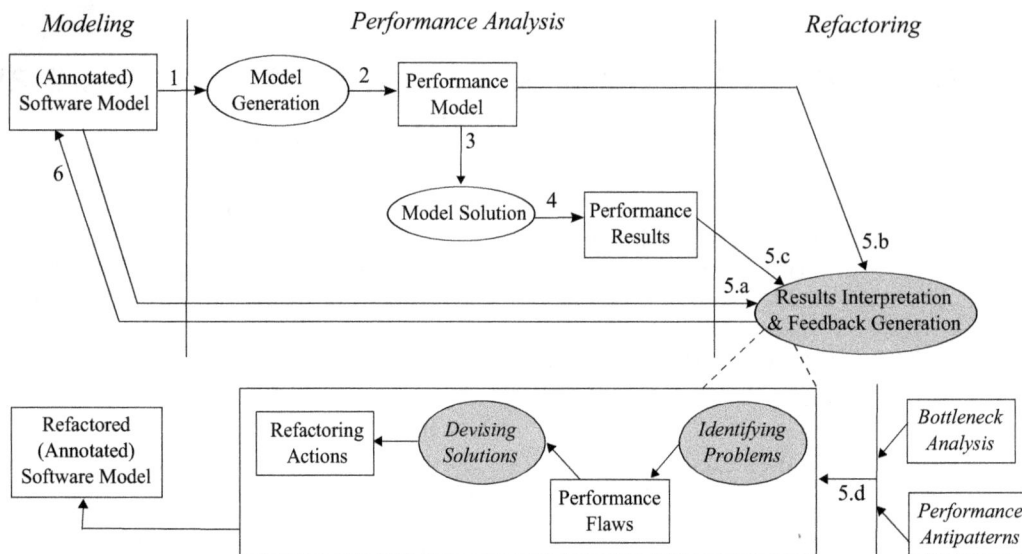

Figure 1: Exploiting bottleneck analysis and performance antipatterns in the round-trip SPE process.

In Figure 1 the (annotated) software model (label 5.a), the performance model (label 5.b), and the performance results (label 5.c) are all inputs to the *results interpretation & feedback generation* step that searches problems in the model. This step has been expanded in the bottommost part of the figure, where a fourth input has been added, that is the two analysis techniques (label 5.d) we consider in our approach, i.e. *bottleneck analysis* and/or *performance antipatterns*. In general, the performance analysis results have to be interpreted in order to identify, if any, performance problems. Once *performance flaws* have been identified (with a certain accuracy) somewhere in the software model, it is necessary to devise solutions in terms of *refactoring actions* that have to be applied to remove those flaws. A performance flaw originates from a set of unfulfilled requirement(s), such as "the estimated average response time of a service is higher than the required one". If all the requirements are satisfied then the feedback obviously suggests no changes. Both considered approaches follow the same general process but they relay on different instruments.

The goal of this paper is to look for possible synergies between performance antipatterns and bottleneck analysis, in order to strengthen the feedback process by providing to designers a sufficiently large set of alternatives for improving the system performance.

The remainder of the paper is organized as follows. Section 2 presents related work; Section 3 describes our approach; Section 4 shows the approach at work on a case study from the e-commerce domain; Section 5 reports the lessons learned from the experimentation as well as the open issues raised by the approach; and finally Section 6 concludes the paper and provides directions for future research.

2. RELATED WORK

The work presented in this paper is related to two main research areas and builds upon our previous results in these areas: (i) bottleneck analysis, and (ii) performance antipatterns.

Bottleneck analysis. In [29] an approach has been presented for automated software performance diagnosis, which identifies performance flaws before the software system implementation. It defines a set of *rules* for detecting patterns of interaction between resources. The software architectural models are translated into a performance model, i.e. Layered Queueing Networks (LQNs) [21], [28] and then analyzed. The approach limits the detection to bottlenecks and long execution paths identified and removed at the level of the LQN performance model. The overall approach was applied only to LQN models, so its portability to other notations is yet to be proven.

In [14] we studied the impact of SOA design patterns on the performance analysis of Service Oriented Architectures (SOA), and in [15] we described a technique for automatically refactoring a SOA design model by applying a SOA design pattern and then propagating the incremental changes to its LQN performance model.

Performance antipatterns. Enterprise technologies and EJB performance antipatterns are analyzed in [20]: antipatterns are represented as sets of rules loaded into an engine. A rule-based performance diagnosis tool, named Performance Antipattern Detection (PAD), is presented. However, it deals with Component-Based Enterprise Systems, targeting only Enterprise Java Bean (EJB) applications, hence its scope is restricted to such domain, and performance problems can neither be detected in other technology contexts nor in the early development stages.

In [4] we have introduced an approach based on a role-modelling language that allows the refactoring of software models through removing performance antipatterns, and in [3] we used model-driven techniques, i.e. model differencing [6], to automatically refactor software models by applying performance antipatterns.

In the general context of software model optimization methods, which aim to automate the search for an optimal design with respect to a (set of) quality attribute(s), a considerable amount of work has been based on strategy techniques aimed at exploring different degrees of freedom (e.g., allocation, sw/hw replication and/or selection, etc.) that influence the system quality [2].

In the area of software design quality improvement, several search-based refactoring techniques have been proposed. In [22], a search-based approach for refactoring the class structure of a software system is proposed, but it is limited to a restricted set of refactorings. In [12], search-based techniques are used to automatically discover useful refactorings aimed at improving the quality of software systems. Authors use the concept of Pareto optimality to search-based refactoring, hence multiple fitness functions lead to provide different Pareto optimal refactorings. In [19], multiple weighted metrics are combined into a single fitness function that is based on well-known measures of coupling between program components. All these search-based approaches share the same limitation, i.e., the search space may be huge, so the search process may be time-consuming. In the performance domain, Koziolek et al. in [16] used meta-heuristic search techniques for improving performance, reliability, and costs of component-based software systems. In particular, evolutionary algorithms search the architectural design space for optimal trade-offs by means of Pareto curves.

To summarize, this is the first paper, to the best of our knowledge, that combines two different and well-consolidated analysis techniques for producing feedback to designers on how to improve the system performance.

3. SYNERGY ANALYSIS PROCESS

In this section we present the process we follow to explore the synergies between the Bottleneck Analysis (BA) [11] and the Performance Antipatterns (PA)[8].

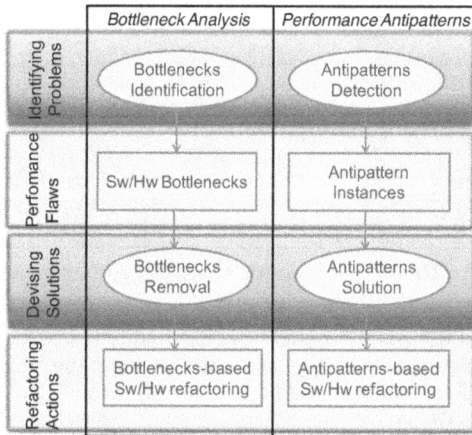

Figure 2: Customizing the refactoring phase.

Figure 2 specializes the general *Results Interpretation & Feedback Generation* process of Figure 1 in case either the BA or the PA are used to interpret the performance analysis results and to generate feedback on the software model. We recall that feedback is aimed at improving the software system performance in order to reach the goal of fulfilling the performance requirements.

The **BA** aims to identify and remove the system bottleneck. More specifically, by system bottlenecks we understand one (or a small number) of software or hardware resources that are highly utilized and will be the first to saturate, throttling the system performance. The system bottleneck indicates an imbalance in the use of resources, which needs to be resolved in order to fully utilize all the resources in the system. Hence in the BA, problem identification corresponds to *Bottlenecks Identification* which determines the *Sw/Hw bottleneck* present in the system by looking at the performance utilization of software components and hardware platforms. The devising solution step corresponds to *Bottleneck Removal* that returns the list of *Bottlenecks-based Sw/Hw refactoring* actions to be applied to the initial system model in order to improve the performance. Examples of such refactoring actions are setting the multi-threading configuration for software components and the multi-processor configuration for hardware platforms, or re-allocating the work among the system resources [29].

The **PA**, instead, aims to detect and remove performance antipatterns introduced in the software system during the design. A performance antipattern [25] identifies a problem, i.e. a bad design practice that negatively affects the software performance, and a solution, i.e. a set of refactoring actions that should be applied to remove it. Hence in the PA, problems identification corresponds to *Antipatterns Detection* step that, looking at the software models and the performance indices, identifies a list of *Antipattern Instances*. The *Antipatterns Solution* step suggests a set of *Antipatterns-based Sw/Hw refactoring* actions to obtain a new software system with improved performance. In PA, refactoring actions span from redesign software components in terms of internal behavior or their external communication, set multi-treading configuration for software components, to redeployment strategies. Note that the solution of one or more antipatterns does not a priori guarantee performance improvements, because the entire process is based on heuristic evaluations [9]. However, an antipattern-based refactoring action is basically a correctness-preserving transformation that aims at improving the quality of the software.

In this paper, we introduce an analysis process to explore possible synergies between PA and BA. Such process includes the following options:

1. Execute BA and PA separately. We compare their output results in terms of what are the refactoring actions the two techniques propose and the performance improvements we get by applying such actions. In this way it is possible to provide evidence of the relative strengths and weaknesses of the two methods.

2. Execute BA and PA alternatively. We merge the two techniques: (i) if BA is executed first, the system bottleneck will be alleviated, reaching a system configuration where there is no obvious imbalance in the usage of resources; however it is possible that the performance requirements are still not fulfilled, hence PA may be useful to further improve the output of BA; (ii) if PA is executed first, there are no bad design practices in the software system, however it may happen that it still includes sw/hw bottlenecks that throttle the system performance, hence BA may be useful to further improve the output of PA.

3. Reduce the PA solution space by means of BA. We use the output of BA *bottleneck identification* step to reduce the PA solution space by pruning the graph of design alternatives (i.e., solve the antipatterns that involve bottlenecks exclusively) thus to quickly converge towards a refactored software model that, even if it is not the optimal one, shows better performance and possibly satisfies the stated requirements.

The goal of our synergy analysis process is to strengthen the *Results Interpretation & Feedback Generation* step (see Figure 1) by increasing the performance improvement capabilities. In particular, the combination of BA and PA offers a powerful support to software engineers, since it provides a broader sets of design alternatives that may include specific solutions leading to better performance results.

4. CASE STUDY

The proposed approach is illustrated by means of a case study from the e-commerce domain, which has been modeled using UML [1]. Figure 3 shows the Use Case Diagram of the E-Commerce System (ECS). It is a web-based system that manages business data related to books and movies: *guest* users can browse catalogues and, at the same time, *customer* users can make selections of items that need to be purchased.

Software model annotations have been defined to support the performance analysis. Figure 3 uses MARTE [18] annotations to specify the system workload. In particular: (i) a closed workload has been defined for the *BrowseCatalog* service, for which the number of users is set to 98 with an average thinking time of 3 seconds; (ii) a closed workload has been defined for the *MakePurchase* service, with a population of 2 users with an average thinking time of 5 seconds.

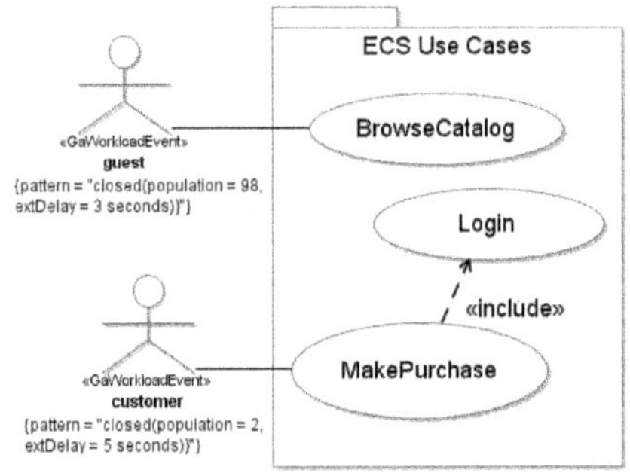

Figure 3: ECS- Use Case Diagram.

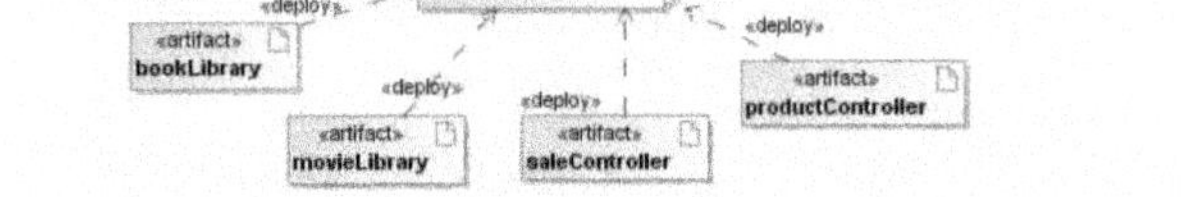

Figure 5: ECS- Deployment Diagram.

The UML Component Diagram shown in Figure 4 describes the software components and their dependencies. *guestApp* and *customerApp* components are connected to the *webServer* component that forwards users' requests to the *dispatcher* component. This latter component forwards the requests related to the *browseCatalog* service towards the *libraryController* whereas requests related to the *makePurchase* service are handled by the *saleController* component.

bookLibrary and *movieLibrary* components manage books and movies, respectively, by invoking the *catalogEngine* component that retrieves information from the *dbProducts* component. The purchases are in charge of the *productController* that communicates with *dbCustomers* and *dbProducts* to retrieve the information to successfully accomplish the purchase. The UML Deployment Diagram depicted in Figure 5 shows the deployment of software artifacts onto hardware devices (i.e., *webServerNode*, *dispatcherNode*, *libraryNode*, and *DatabaseNode*) communicating through a Local Area Network (LAN).

Note that we consider as starting ECS configuration for the analysis (called *base case* in the rest of the paper) the ECS case with single-threaded hardware and multi-threaded software (30 threads for the *WebServer* software component, and 20 threads for all the other software components, except the *dispatcher*). This configuration comes from the BA evaluation of ECS and it represents a necessary premise to the following analysis since it provides an appropriate concurrency level thus to avoid undesirable situations of software bottleneck, where all hardware resources are under-utilized. We considered that a more realistic operating point of the system would allow for full utilization of at least one hardware resource. Please refer to Section 4.1 for more details on the BA evaluation.

The performance requirements imposed on the *BrowseCatalog* and *MakePurchase* services are: (ii) the average response time of the *BrowseCatalog* service must not exceed 4 seconds. (ii) the average response time of the *MakePurchase* service must not exceed 8 seconds. Both requirements need to be fulfilled under the closed workloads defined for the *guest* and *customer* users, respectively.

The performance analysis has been conducted by transforming the software model into a Layered Queueing Network (LQN) model [28], shown in Figure 6, and solving it with the LQN Solver tool [10].

Requirement	Required Value	Predicted Value
RT(*BrowseCatalog*)	4 sec	7.73 sec
RT(*MakePurchase*)	8 sec	91.99 sec

Table 1: Response time of the ECS software model.

Table 1 reports the response times of the ECS base case model. First column reports the required index, second column the required value, and third column the predicted value (obtained from the LQN analysis). As it can be noticed, both services have response times exceeding the required ones, hence a deep analysis must be conducted to identify performance flaws and to devise solutions improving such indices. In the following we first apply the bottleneck (see Section 4.1) and the performance antipatterns (see Section 4.2) analysis techniques, then we combine these techniques in Section 4.3 to explore their synergies.

4.1 Bottleneck Analysis

The performance analysis results of the ECS system for the default configuration of single-threaded software components and hardware platforms shows a strong case of software bottleneck under the defined closed workload. An undesirable effect of software bottleneck is that none of the hardware resources gets to be utilized at full capacity, thus wasting costly system resources. Software bottleneck can be resolved by increasing the number of threads of the sw components, which raises the concurrency level in the software

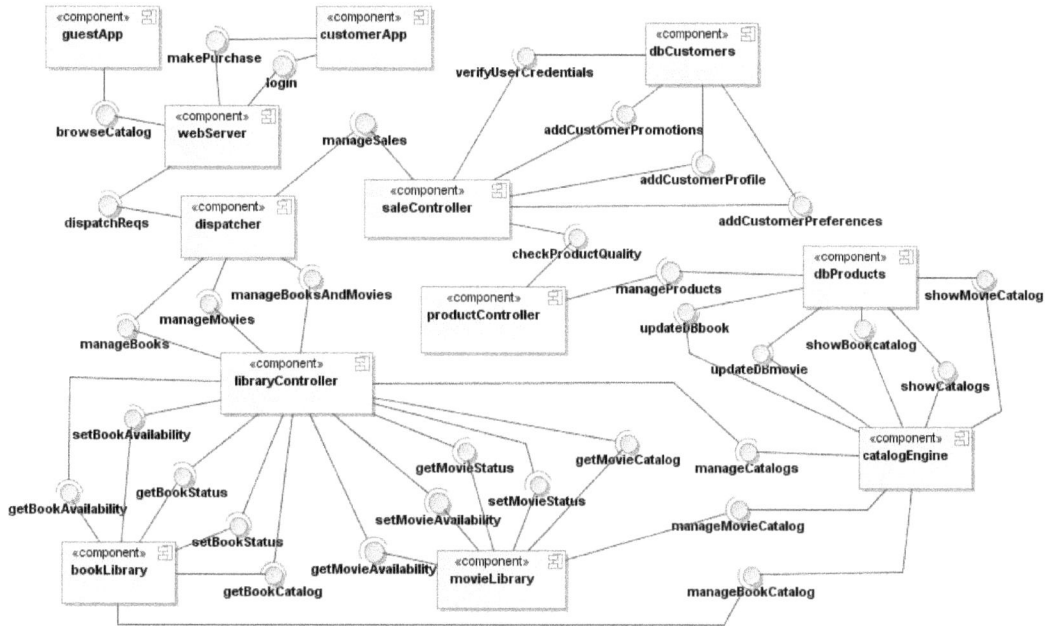

Figure 4: ECS- Component Diagram.

and pushes more workload to the hardware. A first set of experiments showed that a system configuration of 30-thread instances for the *webServer* component and 20-thread the remaining software components (with the exception of the *dispatcher*, which is single-threaded) moves the system bottleneck from software to hardware. The response time for the two classes of users (with 98 and 2 users, respectively) are 7.73 sec for *browseCatalog* and 91.98 sec for *makePurchase*. Since multi-threading the software to avoid wasting the hardware resources is often used in practice, we consider the ECS configuration with multi-threaded software components (with 30 and 20 threads, as described above) running on single-instance hardware processors as the base case for applying the BA and PA analysis.

The next BA experiments aim to remove the hardware bottleneck from the base case. LQN results show that the *libraryNode* and *databaseNode* hardware platforms are both saturated (i.e., with utilizations of 0.98 and 0.92 respectively).

A commonly adopted solution for removing this type of hardware bottleneck is to increase the number of instances for the saturated processors. Therefore, we repeat the experiment by increasing the instances of those processors from 1 to 4 and observe their utilization. Figure 7 reports the utilization of the processors under study, which decreases when the number of processor instances increases. Such refactoring actions imply faster response time for both services as shown in Figure 8. Figure 7 reports the utilization of *libraryNode* and *databaseNode* processors, which is decreasing when the number of processor instances increases. Such refactoring actions have as effect a faster response time for both services as shown in Figure 8. In particular, for the case of 4 processor instances, the response times of the two classes has improved from 7.73 to 3.76 sec. for *BrowseCatolog* service, and from 91.99 to 30.37 sec. for *MakePurchase* service. Actually, the hardware bottleneck has been removed already with 3 processor instances, but since 4-core processors are very common, we select 4 as the suggested solution.

4.2 Performance Antipatterns

Table 2 reports the output of the antipatterns detection [8]: six instances of different antipatterns have been found, i.e., Circuitous Treasure Hunt (CTH), Concurrent Processing Systems (CPS), Blob, Extensive Processing (EP), Empty Semi Trucks (EST). For example, the CTH antipattern occurs since the *saleController* component needs to invoke the *dbCustomers* database component several times before providing the user *Login* service.

Antipattern	Problem
CTH	The *saleController* component needs to invoke the *dbCustomers* database component several times before providing the user *Login* service.
CPS_x	The *databaseNode* hardware platform is much more utilized than *dispatcherNode*.
$BLOB$	The *libraryController* component performs most of the work and an excessive number of messages are exchanged with *bookLibrary* and *movieLibrary* components.
EP	The *catalogEngine* component requires extensive processing to *manageCatalogs* in comparison to *manageBookCatalog* and *manageMovieCatalog* separately.
EST	The *saleController* component needs to invoke the *productController* component several times before providing the *checkProductQuality* service.
CPS_y	The *libraryNode* hardware platform is much more utilized than *dispatcherNode*.

Table 2: ECS - detection of antipatterns.

Table 3 reports the refactoring actions we applied to solve the detected performance antipatterns. For example, the CTH antipattern is solved by refactoring the communication between *saleController* and *dbCustomers* thus to avoid an excessive number of messages.

Note that the detected antipatterns affect different software model entities hence their solution can be incrementally combined without incurring in conflicting and divergent refactorings.

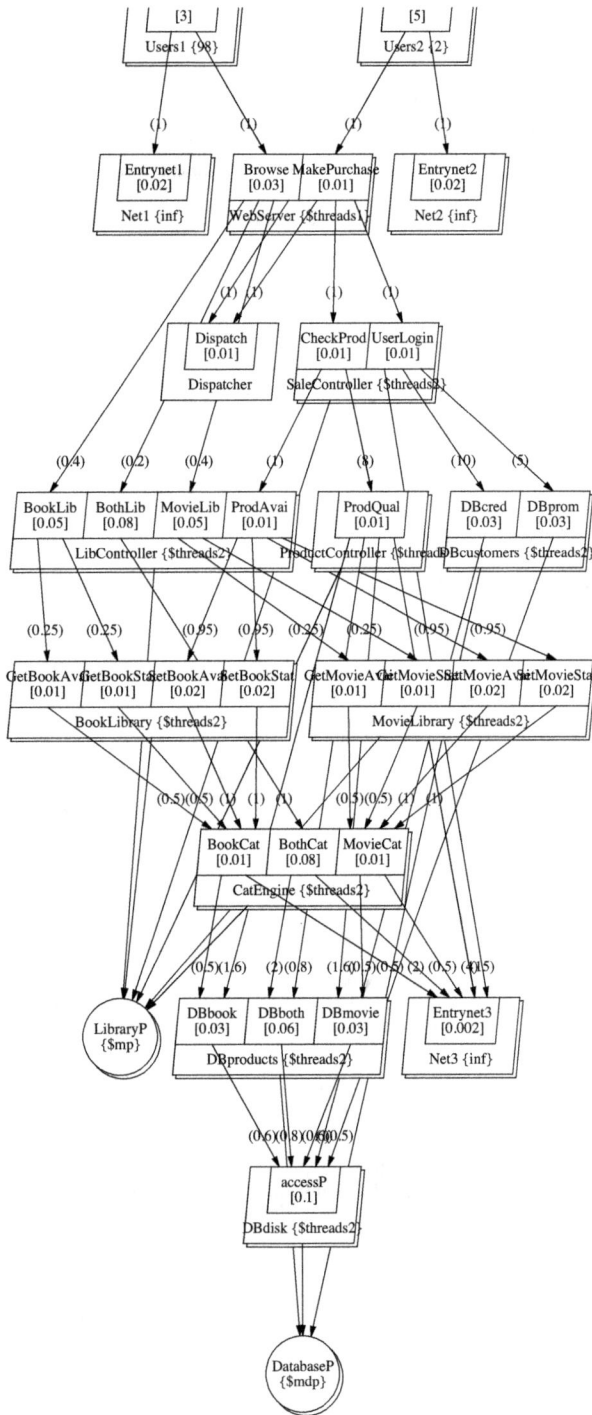

Figure 6: ECS- performance model.

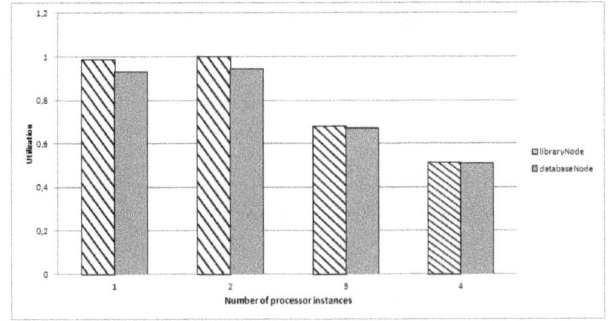

Figure 7: ECS- Utilization of hardware platforms while increasing the number of processor instances.

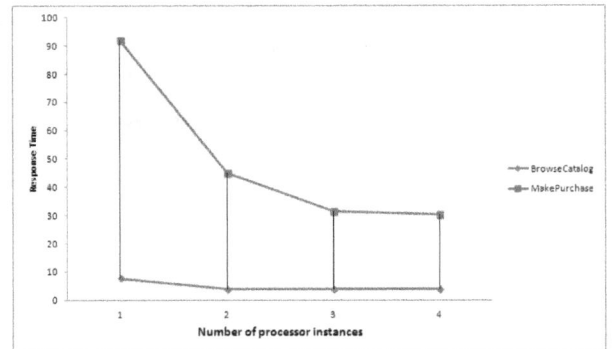

Figure 8: ECS- Response time of software services while increasing the number of processor instances.

Several iterations can be conducted to find the software model that best fits the performance requirements, since several antipatterns have been detected in the software model. At each iteration, the refactoring actions suggested by one antipattern produce a new software system design that replaces the analyzed one. Then, the detection and solution approach can be iteratively applied to all newly generated candidates to further improve the system.

Figure 9 reports the output of the antipatterns-based approach [9]. It is a graph where each node represents a design alternative and each arc is labeled with the name of the antipattern that has been applied to refactor the software model (see more details in Table 3). The ECS base case is labeled *0* and represents the root of the graph. The remaining nodes are labeled by means of digits representing the removed antipatterns, following the antipattern-to-digit mapping indicated by the legend in the bottom of Figure 9. For example, the node labeled *2.3.5* represents the ECS system where CPS_x (i.e., 2), $BLOB$ (i.e., 3) and EST (i.e., 5) antipatterns have been solved. We recall that the solution order of antipatterns is invariant since the detected antipatterns affect different software model entities, hence the node *2.3.5* is equivalent to all nodes represented by other permutations of the three digits (e.g., node *2.5.3*) that we intentionally hide in Figure 9.

Each node reports the response time of *BrowseCatalog* and *MakePurchase* services that for sake of figure readability we name *rBC* and *rMP*, respectively. Note that the solution of one or more antipatterns does not guarantee performance improvements in advance: the entire process is based on

80

Antipattern	Solution
CTH	The communication between *saleController* and *dbCustomers* has been refactored to avoid an excessive number of messages.
CPS_x	The *dbCustomers* component has been deployed from *databaseNode* to *dispatcherNode* in order to optimize the usage of available hardware resources.
BLOB	The communication between *libraryController* and *bookLibrary movieLibrary* components has been refactored by delegating some work to these latter components.
EP	The extensive processing has been delegated to a mirrored component of *catalogEngine*, called *catalogEngineMirror*, whereas the processing of *manageBookCatalog* and *manageMovieCatalog* components is still handled by the *catalogEngine*.
EST	The communication between *saleController* and *productController* has been refactored to avoid an excessive number of messages.
CPS_y	The *saleController* component has been deployed from *libraryNode* to *dispatcherNode* in order to optimize the usage of available hardware resources.

Table 3: ECS - solution of antipatterns.

heuristics evaluations. For example, if we compare the node labeled *1.2* with the node labeled *1.2.3* we can notice that this latter node improves the first index (i.e. the response time of the *BrowseCatalog* service varies from 7.75 to 6.54 seconds) but it makes worse the other index (i.e. the response time of the *MakePurchase* service varies from 68.39 to 80.63 seconds).

To compare different design alternatives and to identify the best one, we weight them using the metrics:

$$rBC * p_1 + rMP * p_2 \qquad (1)$$

where p_1 and p_2 represents the priority of rBC and rMP requirements respectively.

In our case study they are equally weighted to 0.5, and the best design alternative corresponds to the lowest weight that is achieved with the node labeled *1.2.3.5.6* where RT(Browse-Catalog)= 6.4 sec and RT(MakePurchase)= 19.58 sec.

The node labeled *1.2.3.5.6* corresponds to a design alternative where *CTH* (i.e., 1), CPS_x (i.e., 2), *BLOB* (i.e., 3), *EST* (i.e., 5), and CPS_y (i.e., 6) antipatterns have been solved. PA gives as output a refactored software model that includes the following refactoring actions:

1. the communication between *saleController* and *dbCustomers* has been refactored by avoiding an excessive exchange of messages and moving the computation from *saleController* to *dbCustomers*. In particular, the *Login* service was performed by invoking 10+5 times the *dbCustomers* component. In the refactoring the computation is moved to the *dbCustomers* component, hence the *Login* service is performed by invoking the *dbCustomers* once to check users credentials (whose demand increases from 0.03 to 0.09) and once to verify customer promotions (whose demand increases from 0.03 to 0.06);

2. the *dbCustomers* component has been redeployed from *databaseNode* to *dispatcherNode*;

3. the communication between *libraryController* and *bookLibrary movieLibrary* components has been refactored. In particular, the *BrowseCatalog* service was performed by concentrating the business logic in the *libraryController* and invoking the *get* and *set* operations only of *bookLibrary* and *movieLibrary*. In the refactoring these latter components have been redesigned and the

computation is moved from *libraryController* (whose demand decreases from 0.05 to 0.02) to *bookLibrary* and *movieLibrary* (whose demands increase from 0.03 to 0.045);

4. the communication between *saleController* and *productController* has been refactored, as shown in Figure 10. In particular, the *checkProductQuality* service was performed by invoking 8 times the *productController* component. In the refactoring the computation is moved to this latter component, hence the service is performed by invoking once such component to check the quality of products (whose demand increases from 0.01 to 0.03);

5. the *saleController* component has been redeployed from *libraryNode* to *dispatcherNode*.

All these refactoring actions have been applied on the ECS initial system. Figure 11 reports the LQN performance model corresponding to the refactored software model, where all the performance parameters (i.e., tasks and processors information as well as the frequency of calling entries) have been visualized.

4.3 Identifying synergies between BA and PA

In this Section, we first analyze the results of BA and PA executed separately on ECS in order to point out the strengthens and weakness of both techniques (see Section 4.3.1). Then, being guided by the ECS experimentation, we discuss the synergies between BA and PA, that try to overcome the identified limits. In particular, we envisage two types of synergies: (i) *combination of the two techniques*, i.e., one technique is executed on the results obtained by the other one (see Section 4.3.2); (ii) *pruning the PA graph via BA*, i.e., the results of BA are used to reduce the PA solution space to quickly converge to a design alternative with better performance (see Section 4.3.3).

4.3.1 Execute BA and PA separately

BA provides a software model candidate that greatly improves the response time of the *BrowseCatalog* service (from 7.73 sec to 3.76 sec satisfying the corresponding requirement) but it does not fully benefit the response time of the *MakePurchase* service (from 91.99 sec to 30.37 sec). PA provides a software model candidate that slightly improves the response time of the *BrowseCatalog* service (from 7.73 sec to 6.4 sec) but it provides more benefit for the response time of the *MakePurchase* service (from 91.99 sec to 19.58 sec).

BA gives as output a refactored software model where the instances of *libraryNode* and *databaseNode* have been increased from 1 to 4. Such refactoring action suggests to potentiate two processors whose cost is affordable today.

PA gives as output a refactored software model where two main refactoring actions have been performed: (i) redeployment of software components, in fact the *dbCustomers* component has been redeployed from *databaseNode* to *dispatcherNode*, and the *saleController* component has been redeployed from *libraryNode* to *dispatcherNode*; (ii) software components and communication redesign to reduce communication latency between *saleController* and *dbCustomers*, between *libraryController* and *bookLibrary* and *movieLibrary*, between *saleController* and *productController*. While the cost of the first type of refactoring is quite low, the second one could be very expensive since it involves human work. Of course, the amount of these expenses depend on

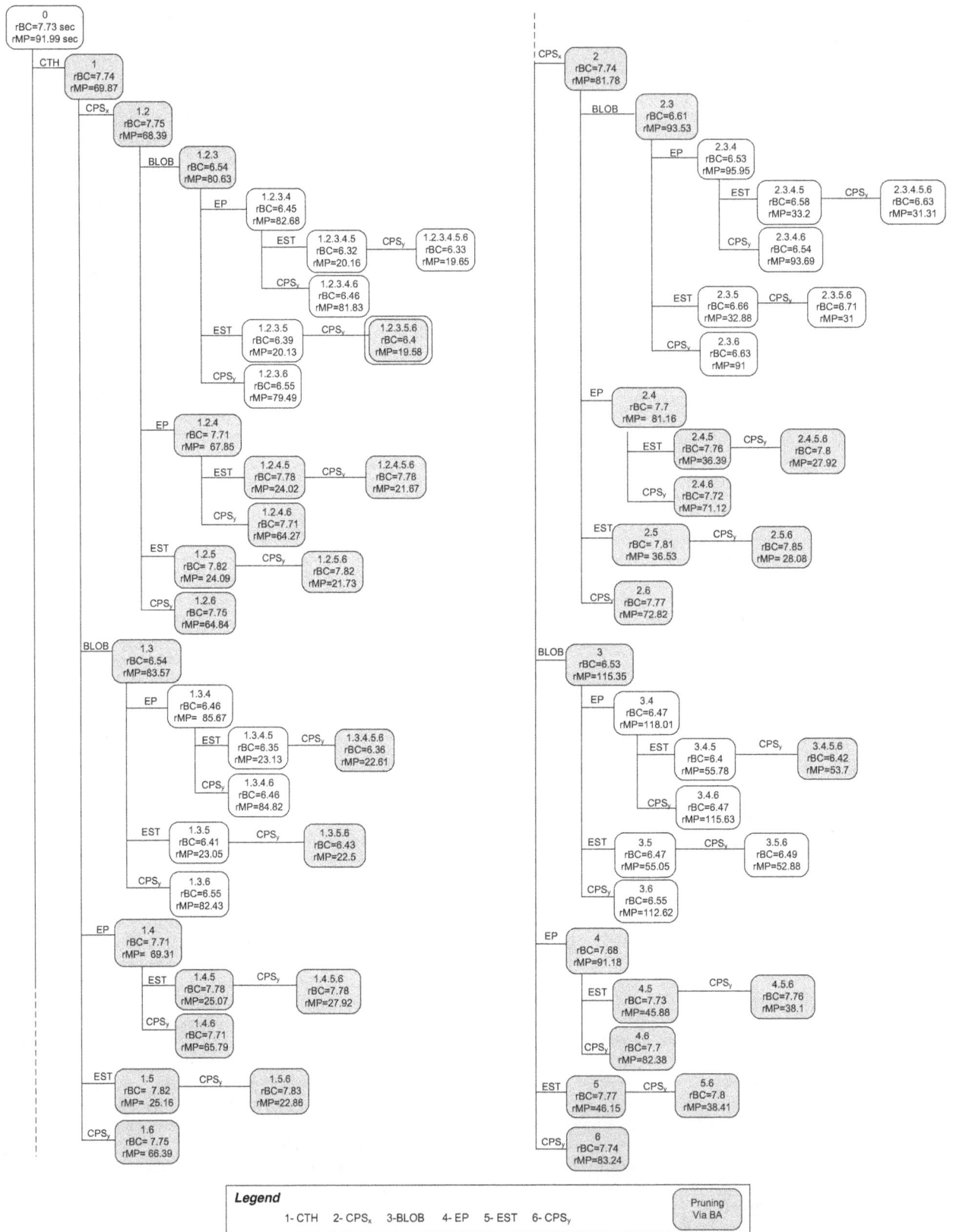

Figure 9: ECS - reduce the PA solution space by means of BA.

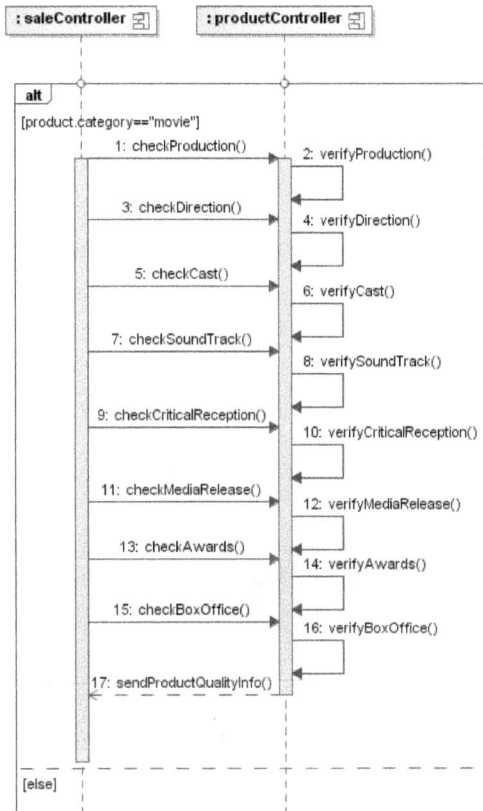

(a) An excerpt of ECS software model.

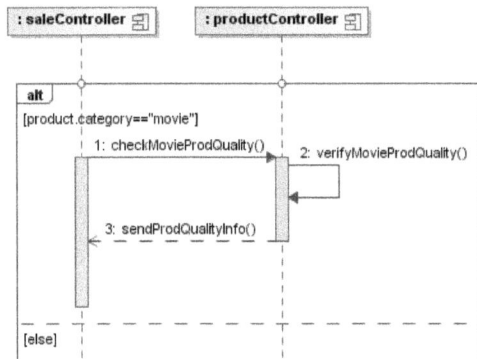

(b) An excerpt of ECS refactored software model.

Figure 10: ECS- solving the *EST* performance antipattern.

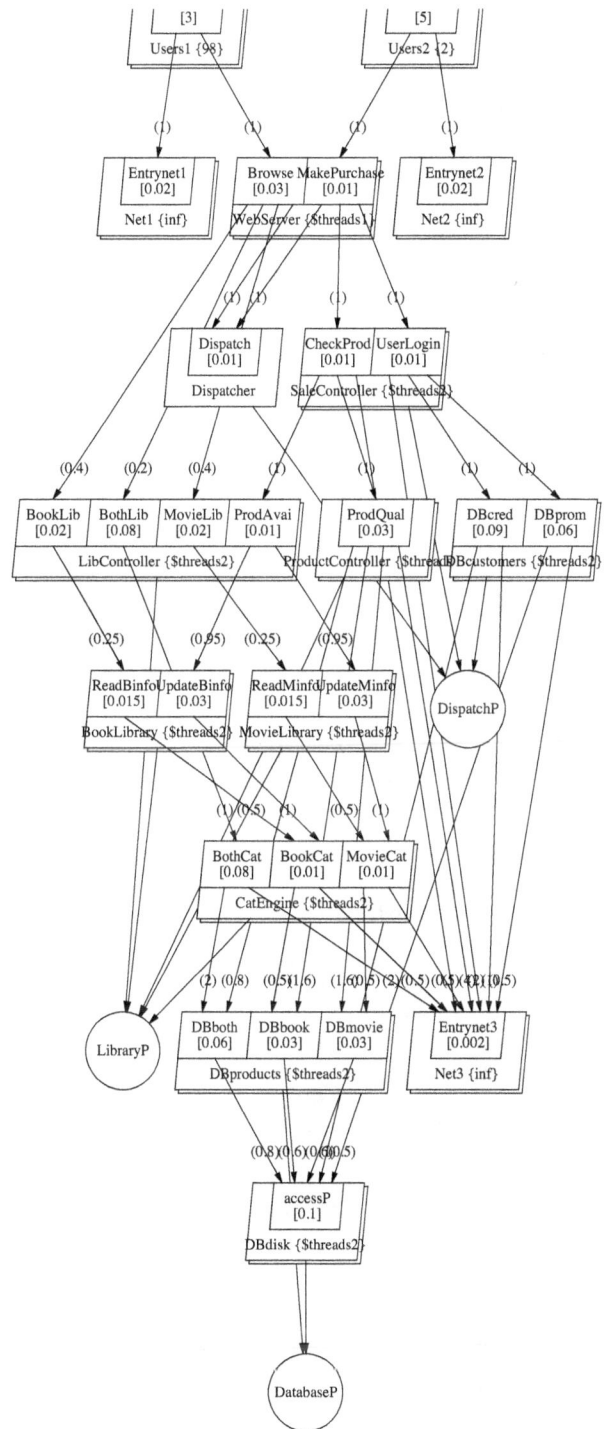

Figure 11: ECS - refactored performance model.

the complexity of the software system, on the complexity of the changes and on impact of them on the whole system.

To compare the goodness of the PA and BA suggested design alternatives, we weight the design alternatives by using the metrics (1) introduced in Section 4.2, where p_1 and p_2 are equally set to 0.5. Thus, the ECS base case is weighted 49.86, whereas the ECS after BA is weighted 17.06 and ECS after PA is weighted 12.99. The benefit of these techniques w.r.t. performance improvements is estimated by comparing the percentage of improvement achieved in this weighted sum, hence BA brings a benefit of 65.77% whereas PA brings a benefit of 73.95%. Even if BA allows to satisfy one requirement, it performs slightly worse while considering the combination of both requirements. However, the refactoring actions suggested by BA are less expensive than the ones supported by PA, since the latter requires the redesign of several software components that may involve expensive human re-work.

As final consideration, both techniques in isolation fail to suggest an alternative satisfying the performance requirements.

4.3.2 Execute BA and PA alternatively

Figure 12 reports the results of executing BA and PA alternatively. In the figure, nodes represent design alternatives with the corresponding response time of both services, while arcs are labeled by the re-factoring actions executed to obtain the reaching nodes. The root of the graph is the ECS base case.

If we first execute BA and then PA (the left-hand path) we get a software model candidate that greatly improves the response time of the *BrowseCatalog* service (from 7.73 sec to 3.83 sec) but it does not fully benefit the response time of the *MakePurchase* service (from 91.99 sec to 24.88 sec). The suggested design alternative is the one described in Section 4.1 where only CPS_y antipattern has been detected and solved, redeploying the *saleController* component from *libraryNode* to *dispatcherNode*.

On the contrary, if we first execute PA and then BA (the right-hand path of Figure 12) we get a software model candidate that greatly improves the response time of the *BrowseCatalog* service (from 7.73 sec to 3.33 sec) and the response time of the *MakePurchase* service (from 91.99 sec to 6.56 sec), and that, indeed, fulfills both performance requirements (as indicated by the shaded box of Figure 12). The suggested design alternative is the one described in Section 4.2 where *libraryNode* and *databaseNode* are 4-core processors each.

Similarly to the estimation done to compare BA and PA separately, ECS after "BA+PA" is weighted with 14.35, and ECS after "PA+BA" is weighted with 4.94. The benefit of executing these techniques alternatively is estimated by comparing the percentage of improvement achieved in this weighted sum, hence *BA+PA* brings a benefit of 71.21% whereas *PA+BA* brings a benefit of 90.08% with respect to the initial ECS weighted with 49.86.

4.3.3 Reduce the PA solution space by means of BA

Another way to exploit the synergy between BA and PA is to reduce the PA solution space by means of BA, i.e., by pruning the graph of design alternatives using the knowledge coming from BA. The goal is to quickly get a "good enough" design alternative without building the whole graph of de-

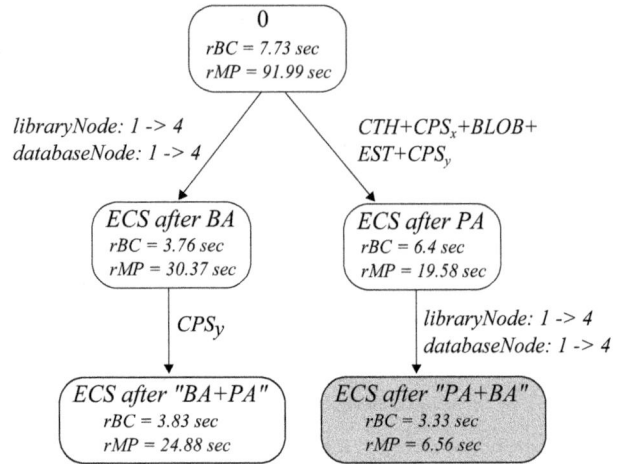

Figure 12: ECS- performance indices while executing BA and PA alternatively.

sign alternatives. Of course, the strategy is an heuristics that might not bring to the best design alternative PA can identify, but towards an alternative that, even if it is not the optimal one, shows better performance and possibly satisfies the stated performance requirements.

The pruning strategy we device suggests to keep all the nodes (of the alternative designs graph) obtained by removing antipatterns instances on hardware bottlenecks, and to discard all the others. In particular, we here consider hardware bottlenecks all the devices showing an utilization higher than 0.8.

In Figure 9 the result of the pruning strategy on the ECS case study is shown by indicating with the grey nodes the design alternatives we keep. The devised strategy allows to prune 24 nodes over 63 design alternatives the PA process builds for the ECS system (see Section 4.2 for more details), reaching the 38.1% percentage of pruning. Note that in our case study the BA heuristics allows to reach the optimal PA alternative, however this is not guaranteed in general and we intend to investigate this issue in the near future.

5. DISCUSSION

In this Section we discuss the lessons learned from the experimentation as well as the open issues raised by the approach.

Limitations of bottleneck analysis. BA is a technique that mitigates the bottleneck and balances the usage of resources. Once this goal is reached, BA cannot further help to improve performance, then PA should be used to get more insights on how to further improve the system performance. In order to better understand the ECS base case characteristics, we conducted a performance analysis without contention. The analysis reports that the lower bound for the response times of the *BrowseCatalog* and *MakePurchase* services are 3.20 sec and 12.70 sec, respectively. Again, the response time of *MakePurchase* service is far from the performance requirement (i.e. 8 sec), thus demonstrating that even in case of the best option (i.e., no contention), the system fails to satisfy the requirements. In order to improve it further, we need to change the design, e.g., by introducing some concurrency in the execution path of *MakePurchase* requests. This cannot be done with BA, whereas PA provides

84

more insights on possible refactoring actions that conduct to a better design. By detecting and removing the performance antipatterns we are able to redesign the system and, in our case study, we experience the best performance when merging the two analysis techniques. Indeed, only exploiting together BA and PA we reach an ECS design that satisfies both response time requirements.

Limitations of performance antipatterns. Our formalization of performance antipatterns [8] is based on a set of thresholds that, if not properly set, may hide bad design. Hence, the threshold tuning is a difficult task that may affect the accuracy of antipattern detection. Moreover, in this paper context the experimentation demonstrates that, if we firstly execute the bottleneck analysis and the relative refactoring actions, several performance antipatterns are hidden, as happened in ECS when PA is executed after BA (see Section 4.3.2) and only CPS_y has been detected and solved. In fact, while the bottleneck analysis is aimed at keeping the utilization of hardware devices and software tasks under certain thresholds, high utilization values are fundamental to detect many performance antipatterns [8]. If we apply PA detection on the system configuration provided by BA (i.e., the one discussed in Section 3), then most of the antipatterns are not identified, due to their limited sw/hw utilization.

Complexity vs Effectiveness. Performance antipatterns are very complex to detect because they are founded on different characteristics of a software system, spanning from static to behavioral to deployment, and they additionally include values of performance indices. However, this complexity subsumes a wide variety of refactoring actions to express, thus making this approach very powerful in the identification of performance flaws and system refactoring. Hence, the complexity is rewarded by expressiveness. As opposed, bottleneck analysis is a well-assessed technique widely supported by a solid theory and sophisticated tools. Hence, the detection of bottlenecks in performance models is not such a complex task in general. The cost to pay to this reduced complexity, as outlined above, is the limitation in expressiveness of repairing actions. BA is particularly powerful in case of good system design when the performance problems come from unbalanced load or under-estimated resources. On the contrary, it cannot help in case the performance flaw originates from software system development. PA, instead, should be applied when performance problems come from design choices and software system re-design is necessary. In fact, it gives insight on what happens in the software model and suggests solutions for modifying it. Our experimentation demonstrates that there are cases where an unsatisfied requirement cannot be overcome by only adding hardware resources, since there is a problem in software design. In these cases, there is a point beyond which if we add more hw/sw resources we do not gain better performance, or even the performance worsen. For example, the ECS base case with 4 processor instances has no more bottlenecks, but the response time for *MakePurchase* is far from satisfying the requirement. Summing up, it is preferable to execute BA first and, in case of specific constraints on the resources or in case of unsatisfactory requirements, to proceed with PA, while taking into account that BA can hide key performance antipatterns as happened in our experimentation.

Cost/Effort issues. PA costs derive to performance antipattern detection and solution complexity, that is the counterpart of their expressiveness and wide impact on the whole

system design. BA costs are instead more related to the skills and experience of performance analysts. In our case, we had to solve about 13 LQN models, while continuously changing/tuning model parameters, before removing software/hardware bottlenecks. Hence, we think that quantifying the effort required to apply BA, PA, or their combination is very difficult since both techniques have several limitations and (complexity, cost) issues cannot be avoided. Such estimation has to take into account some factors, that we intend to further investigate, such as: (i) the degree of automation, (ii) the design/performance skills required to achieve the design alternatives, (ii) the scalability in terms of number of analysed performance models together with their complexity and performance gain.

BA and PA synergies. The experimentations on ECS show that several synergies can be exploited to improve performance or to reduce the size of PA solution space. One synergy consists in alternating PA and BA. The combined usage of both techniques permits to make a step ahead, and in particular the order PA before BA is the only strategy that, on the ECS case study, conducts to a system design that satisfies both performance requirements (see Section 4.3.2). This result cannot be reached either executing separately the two analysis techniques or BA before PA, and it is justified by the fact that ECS base case suffers of bad design that throttles its performance. A second synergy has allowed us to define a heuristics based on BA that prunes the PA design alternatives graph. In this case, the BA output suggests, time by time, which antipattern instances have to be resolved and which ones can be discarded. For example, in ECS this heuristics has permitted to prune 38.1% of candidates (i.e., 39 LQN models have been solved over the 63 generated ones by PA), thus reaching the best design alternative of the whole graph by considerably reducing the costs of the PA detection and solution steps. The reduction of the PA solution space allows to speed-up the performance analysis. However, the duration of executing the performance solvers in the BA and PA may significantly vary on the basis of other application-dependent parameters (e.g., number of software and/or hardware resources) that indirectly affect the two analysis techniques.

6. CONCLUSION

This paper explores the synergies between Bottleneck Analysis and Performance Antipatterns techniques in the round-trip Software Performance Engineering (SPE) process. In order to identify strengths and weaknesses of both techniques, they have been separately applied to a software system in the e-commerce domain, and two types of synergies have been envisaged and experimented. The combination of these two techniques seems very promising, in fact we found that executing first the performance antipatterns and then the bottleneck analysis allowed to identify design alternatives satisfying all the performance requirements.

As future work, we intend to apply our approach to other case studies, possibly coming from real world systems. This wider experimentation will allow us to deeply investigate the effectiveness of BA heuristics that reduce the PA solution space, thus studying the scalability of our approach.

7. ACKNOWLEDGMENTS

This work was partially supported by the European Office of Aerospace Research and Development (EOARD), Grant

Cooperative Agreement (Award no. FA8655-11-1-3055), and the Natural Sciences and Engineering Research Council of Canada (NSERC) through its Discovery Grant program.

8. REFERENCES

[1] UML 2.0 Superstructure Specification, OMG document formal/05-07-04, 2005.

[2] A. Aleti, B. Buhnova, L. Grunske, A. Koziolek, and I. Meedeniya. Software architecture optimization methods: A systematic literature review. *IEEE Trans. Software Eng.*, 39(5):658–683, 2013.

[3] D. Arcelli, V. Cortellessa, and D. Di Ruscio. Applying model differences to automate performance-driven refactoring of software models. In *European Workshop on Computer Performance Engineering (EPEW)*, pages 312–324, 2013.

[4] D. Arcelli, V. Cortellessa, and C. Trubiani. Antipattern-based model refactoring for software performance improvement. In *International ACM SIGSOFT conference on Quality of Software Architectures (QoSA)*, pages 33–42, 2012.

[5] S. Balsamo, A. Di Marco, P. Inverardi, and M. Simeoni. Model-based performance prediction in software development: A survey. *IEEE Trans. Software Eng.*, 30(5):295–310, 2004.

[6] A. Cicchetti, D. Di Ruscio, and A. Pierantonio. A metamodel independent approach to difference representation. *Journal of Object Technology*, 6(9):165–185, 2007.

[7] V. Cortellessa, A. Di Marco, and P. Inverardi. *Model-Based Software Performance Analysis*. Springer, 2011.

[8] V. Cortellessa, A. Di Marco, and C. Trubiani. An approach for modeling and detecting software performance antipatterns based on first-order logics. *Journal of Software and Systems Modeling*, 2012. DOI: 10.1007/s10270-012-0246-z.

[9] V. Cortellessa, A. Di Marco, and C. Trubiani. Software performance antipatterns: Modeling and analysis. In *Formal Methods for Model-Driven Engineering (SFM)*, pages 290–335, 2012.

[10] G. Franks, P. Maly, M. Woodside, D. C. Petriu, A. Hubbard, and M. Mroz. Layered Queueing Network Solver and Simulator, 2013. [online]http://www.sce.carleton.ca/rads/lqns/LQNS-UserMan-jan13.pdf.

[11] G. Franks, D. C. Petriu, C. M. Woodside, J. Xu, and P. Tregunno. Layered bottlenecks and their mitigation. In *International Conference on the Quantitative Evaluation of Systems (QEST)*, pages 103–114, 2006.

[12] M. Harman and L. Tratt. Pareto optimal search based refactoring at the design level. In *Conference on Genetic and evolutionary computation (GECCO)*, pages 1106–1113, 2007.

[13] H. Koziolek. Performance evaluation of component-based software systems: A survey. *Perform. Eval.*, 67(8):634–658, 2010.

[14] N. Mani, D. C. Petriu, and C. M. Woodside. Studying the impact of design patterns on the performance analysis of service oriented architecture. In *EUROMICRO Conference on Software Engineering and Advanced Applications*, pages 12–19, 2011.

[15] N. Mani, D. C. Petriu, and C. M. Woodside. Propagation of incremental changes to performance model due to soa design pattern application. In *ACM/SPEC International Conference on Performance Engineering (ICPE)*, pages 89–100, 2013.

[16] A. Martens, H. Koziolek, S. Becker, and R. Reussner. Automatically improve software architecture models for performance, reliability, and cost using evolutionary algorithms. In *WOSP/SIPEW International Conference on Performance Engineering*, pages 105–116, 2010.

[17] T. Mens and T. Tourwé. A survey of software refactoring. *IEEE Trans. Software Eng.*, 30(2):126–139, 2004.

[18] Object Management Group (OMG). UML Profile for MARTE, 2009. OMG Document formal/08-06-09.

[19] M. O'Keeffe and M. í Cinnéide. Search-based refactoring for software maintenance. *J. Syst. Softw.*, 81(4):502–516, Apr. 2008.

[20] T. Parsons and J. Murphy. Detecting Performance Antipatterns in Component Based Enterprise Systems. *Journal of Object Technology*, 7(3):55–91, 2008.

[21] D. C. Petriu and H. Shen. Applying the UML Performance Profile: Graph Grammar-Based Derivation of LQN Models from UML Specifications. In *Computer Performance Evaluation / TOOLS*, pages 159–177, 2002.

[22] O. Seng, J. Stammel, and D. Burkhart. Search-based determination of refactorings for improving the class structure of object-oriented systems. In *Conference on Genetic and evolutionary computation (GECCO)*, pages 1909–1916, 2006.

[23] C. U. Smith. Introduction to software performance engineering: Origins and outstanding problems. In *Formal Methods for Performance Evaluation, International School on Formal Methods for the Design of Computer, Communication, and Software Systems (SFM)*, pages 395–428, 2007.

[24] C. U. Smith and C. V. Millsap. Software performance engineering for oracle applications: Measurements and models. In *International Computer Measurement Group (CMG) Conference*, pages 331–342, 2008.

[25] C. U. Smith and L. G. Williams. More new software antipatterns: Even more ways to shoot yourself in the foot. In *International Computer Measurement Group (CMG) Conference*, pages 717–725, 2003.

[26] L. G. Williams and C. U. Smith. Software performance engineering: A tutorial introduction. In *International Computer Measurement Group (CMG) Conference*, pages 387–398, 2007.

[27] C. M. Woodside, G. Franks, and D. C. Petriu. The Future of Software Performance Engineering. In *International Workshop on the Future of Software Engineering (FOSE)*, pages 171–187, 2007.

[28] M. Woodside, D. C. Petriu, J. Merseguer, D. B. Petriu, and M. Alhaj. Transformation challenges: from software models to performance models. *Journal of Software and Systems Modeling*, 2013. accepted.

[29] J. Xu. Rule-based automatic software performance diagnosis and improvement. *Perform. Eval.*, 67(8):585–611, 2010.

Adaptive Model Learning for Continual Verification of Non-Functional Properties

Radu Calinescu
Department of Computer
Science
University of York, UK
radu.calinescu@york.ac.uk

Yasmin Rafiq
Department of Computer
Science
University of York, UK
yr534@york.ac.uk

Kenneth Johnson
Department of Computer
Science
University of York, UK
kenneth.johnson@york.ac.uk

Mehmet Emin Bakır
Department of Computer
Science
University of York, UK
meb524@york.ac.uk

ABSTRACT

A growing number of business and safety-critical services are delivered by computer systems designed to reconfigure in response to changes in workloads, requirements and internal state. In recent work, we showed how a formal technique called continual verification can be used to ensure that such systems continue to satisfy their reliability and performance requirements as they evolve, and we presented the challenges associated with the new technique. In this paper, we address important instances of two of these challenges, namely the maintenance of up-to-date reliability models and the adoption of continual verification in engineering practice. To address the first challenge, we introduce a new method for learning the parameters of the reliability models from observations of the system behaviour. This method is capable of adapting to variations in the frequency of the available system observations, yielding faster and more accurate learning than existing solutions. To tackle the second challenge, we present a new software engineering tool that enables developers to use our adaptive learning and continual verification in the area of service-based systems, without a formal verification background and with minimal effort.

Categories and Subject Descriptors

D.2.4 [**Software Engineering**]: Software/program verification—*model checking; reliability; statistical methods*

Keywords

on-line model learning, runtime quantitative verification, discrete-time Markov models, service-based systems

ICPE'14, March 22–26, 2014, Dublin, Ireland.
Copyright 2014 ACM 978-1-4503-2733-6/14/03 $15.00
http://dx.doi.org/10.1145/2568088.2568094.

1. INTRODUCTION

Rarely a day passes without new announcements of yet more applications being "moved to the cloud" or "running on the Internet-of-Things" in the name of increased flexibility, richer functionality, or cost and energy savings. Nevertheless, few of these announcements mention the dependability and performance implications of such long-reaching decisions. As the applications involved increasingly include services such as UK Government ICT procurement[1], New York Stock Exchange market data analysis[2] and US Department of Defence solutions[3], this raises serious concerns.

In recent work, we advocated the continual formal verification of the non-functional properties (NFPs) of such *evolving critical systems* [2, 3], and devised theoretical and practical tools supporting the approach [4, 6, 7, 21]. These tools employ established or new, lower-overhead model checking techniques to assess whether the quality-of-service (QoS) requirements of a system continue to be satisfied as the system evolves. The approach has been used successfully in applications including QoS management and optimisation of service-based systems [4, 6], and reliability NFP analysis for cloud computing infrastructure [7, 21].

As part of the aforementioned work, we identified the key research challenges that need to be addressed in order to extend the applicability of continual verification, and to support its adoption in QoS engineering practice [3]. In this paper, we propose solutions that tackle important instances of two of these challenges. The first challenge is the maintenance of an up-to-date QoS model of an evolving critical system. The new on-line model learning method presented in the paper addresses this challenge for discrete-time Markov chains (DTMCs), such as those used for the continual verification of the reliability NFPs of evolving critical systems (e.g., [4, 8, 12]). The second challenge that we tackle is the adoption of continual verification in QoS engineering practice. We introduce a new software engineering tool that uses our model learning method, and contributes to enabling practitioners to exploit continual NFP verification with lim-

---

[1] http://gcloud.civilservice.gov.uk
[2] http://www.nyse.com/press/1306838249812.html
[3] http://aws.amazon.com/federal/

ited effort and without formal verification expertise. The main contributions of the paper are:

1. A parameterised on-line learning method that infers the state transition probabilities of a DTMC model of a system from observations of the system behaviour, and adjusts its parameters dynamically depending on the frequency of these observations. This *adaptive learning* leads to a faster and more accurate inference of the transition probabilities than that provided by existing methods.

2. Rigorous theoretical results linking the parameters chosen dynamically by our learning method to the expected error in the accuracy of the learnt state transition probabilities. This allows the configuration of the adaptive learning method so that it yields results within an acceptable expected error range.

3. A software-as-a-service (SaaS) development tool that automatically generates web service proxies which use our adaptive learning method to support continual reliability NFP verification in service-based systems. The new tool is freely available as an Amazon Machine Image (AMI) that service-based system developers can use with no installation or configuration effort.

4. The integration of the SaaS tool with our existing COntinual VErification (COVE) framework from [6]. The integrated toolset supports the end-to-end development of reconfigurable service-based systems that take advantage of the results introduced in this paper with minimal practitioner effort and formal verification expertise.

The paper is organised as follows. Section 2 introduces concepts and notation used throughout the rest of the paper. Section 3 presents our adaptive model learning method, and several experiments used to evaluate and compare its effectiveness with that of related approaches. Next, Section 4 describes our software-as-a-service engineering tool that allows developers of service-based systems to take advantage of the new learning technique. A case study from the telehealth application domain is used to demonstrate the effectiveness of this tool in Section 5, and related work is discussed in Section 6. Section 7 concludes the paper with a brief summary and an overview of future work directions.

2. BACKGROUND

2.1 Quantitative Verification of Discrete-Time Markov Chains

DEFINITION 1. *A cost-annotated discrete-time Markov chain (DTMC) is a tuple*

$$M = (S, s_0, P, L, c),\qquad(1)$$

where:

- *S is a finite set of states;*
- *$s_0 \in S$ is the initial state;*
- *P is an $|S| \times |S|$ transition probability matrix;*
- *$L: S \to 2^{AP}$ is a labelling function which assigns a set of atomic propositions from AP to each state in S;*
- *$c: S \to \mathbb{R}_+$ is a costing function that associates a cost $c(s) \geq 0$ with each state $s \in S$.*

For any states $s_i, s_j \in S$, the element p_{ij} from P represents

the probability of transitioning to state s_j from state s_i, and $\sum_{s_j \in S} p_{ij} = 1$.

Quantitative or *probabilistic* model checkers (e.g., PRISM [24], MRMC [22] and Ymer [31]) operate on Markovian models expressed in a high-level, state-based language. Given a DTMC description in this language, the low-level representation (1) is derived automatically. Our work uses the probabilistic model checker PRISM [24], which supports the analysis of DTMC properties specified in a cost/reward-augmented version of probabilistic computational tree logic (PCTL) [20], whose syntax is defined below.

DEFINITION 2. *Let AP be a set of atomic propositions and $a \in AP$, $p \in [0,1]$, $k \in \mathbb{N}$, $r \in \mathbb{R}$ and $\bowtie \in \{\geq, >, <, \leq\}$. Then a state-formula Φ and a path formula Ψ in PCTL are defined by the following grammar:*

$$\Phi ::= true \,|\, a \,|\, \Phi \wedge \Phi \,|\, \neg\Phi \,|\, P_{\bowtie p}(\Psi) \\ \Psi ::= X\Phi \,|\, \Phi\, U\, \Phi \,|\, \Phi\, U^{\leq k}\Phi \qquad(2)$$

and the cost/reward augmented PCTL state formulae are defined by the grammar:

$$\Phi ::= R_{\bowtie r}[I^{=k}] \,|\, R_{\bowtie r}[C^{\leq k}] \,|\, R_{\bowtie r}[F\Phi]. \qquad(3)$$

PCTL distinguishes between state and path formulae. The state formulae include the standard logical operators $\wedge$ and $\neg$, which also allow a formulation of other usual logical operators (disjunction ($\vee$), implication ($\Rightarrow$), etc.) and *false*. The main extension of the state formulae, compared to non-probabilistic logics, is the replacement of the traditional path quantifiers $\exists$ and $\forall$ with a probabilistic operator $\mathcal{P}$. This operator defines upper or lower bounds on the probability of the system evolution. As an example, the formula $\mathcal{P}_{\geq p}(\Psi)$ is true at a given state if the probability of the future evolution of the system satisfying Ψ is at least p. The path formulae that can be used with the probabilistic path operator are:

- the "next" formula $X\Phi$, which holds if Φ is true in the next state of a path;
- the time bounded "until" formula $\Phi_1 U^{\leq k}\Phi_2$, which requires that Φ_1 holds continuously up to some time step $x < k$ and Φ_2 becomes true at time step $x + 1$;
- unbounded "until" formula $\Phi_1 U\Phi_2$, whose semantics is identical with that of the bounded "until", but the time-step bound is set to infinity $t = \infty$.

Finally, the cost/reward operator R can be used to analyse the expected cost at timestep k ($R_{\bowtie r}[I^{=k}]$), the expected cumulative cost up to time step k ($R_{\bowtie r}[C^{\leq k}]$), and the expected cumulative cost to reach a future state that satisfies a property Φ ($R_{\bowtie r}[F\Phi]$).

The semantics of the PCTL is defined with a satisfaction relation $\models$ over the states S and possible paths $Path^M(s)$ that are possible in a state $s \in S$ of a model M with the structure from (1). Further details about the formal semantics of PCTL are available from [11, 20].

2.2 On-line Learning of DTMC Transition Probabilities

The DTMC modelling and analysis formalism from the previous section is traditionally used for the offline verification of non-functional system properties. To extend its applicability to continual verification, the DTMC model it relies upon must be updated permanently, so that it is maintained in sync with the changing behaviour of the continually verified system. Typically, this model updating involves monitoring the evolving system, and using the observations obtained in this way to learn about any changes in the DTMC transition probabilities P from (1).

A basic Bayesian on-line learning method that can be used for this purpose was proposed in [12], and extended by our work-in-progress results from [5]. This section summarises the extended on-line learning method from [5], which is used as a basis for the adaptive learning method proposed in this paper and described in detail in Section 3.

The algorithm we introduced in [5] learns the transition probabilities p_{ij} of a DTMC model M with the form in (1), starting from a priori estimates p_{ij}^0 and the observations of the last $k \geq 1$ system transitions from state s_i to states $s_j \in S$. Assuming that the l-th observation of a transition from state s_i, $1 \leq l \leq k$, is a transition to state $s_{j_l} \in S$, we define

$$x_{ij}^l = \begin{cases} 1 & \text{if } j_l = j, \\ 0 & \text{otherwise} \end{cases}, \qquad (4)$$

and we calculate the estimate probability of a state transition from s_i to s_j after the k-th observation as

$$p_{ij}^k = \frac{c_i^0}{c_i^0 + k} p_{ij}^0 + \frac{k}{c_i^0 + k} \frac{\sum_{l=1}^k w_i^l x_{ij}^l}{\sum_{l=1}^k w_i^l}, \qquad (5)$$

where $c_i^0 > 0$ is a smoothing parameter that quantifies the confidence in the accuracy of p_{ij}^0, and $w_i^l \in (0, 1]$ is a weight that reflects the age of the l-th observation. We showed in [5] that an effective choice of weights is

$$w_i^l = \alpha_i^{-(t_k - t_l)}, \qquad (6)$$

where t_l, $1 \leq l \leq k$, represents the timestamps of the l-th observation, and $\alpha_i \geq 1$ is an ageing parameter. As we showed in [5], the learning algorithm (5)–(6) has two key advantages over other learning techniques. First, the weights w_i^l decrease the impact of old observations on the estimates p_{ij}^k, significantly speeding up the detection of sudden changes in actual transition probabilities (e.g., due to failures of system components), in particular when such changes occur after long periods of relatively constant behaviour. Second, reorganising the terms in (5) allows p_{ij}^k to be calculated from p_{ij}^{k-1} in O(1) time and using O(1) memory, a key advantage for an on-line learning algorithm.

3. ADAPTIVE DTMC MODEL LEARNING

Our experiments from [5] show that the effectiveness of the transition-probability learning algorithm (5)–(6) depends on the choice of the parameters c_i^0 and α_i, and that no combination of values for these parameters is suitable for all scenarios. To address this limitation, we extend the learning algorithm with the ability to select suitable parameters c_i^0 and α_i at runtime. The dynamic selection of these parameters adapts the learning algorithm to the frequency of the observations, and is based on the following theoretical results.

PROPOSITION 1. Let x_1, x_2, ..., x_k be an independent trials process with expected value $E(x_l) = \mu$ and variance $V(x_l) = \sigma^2$, for $l = 1, 2, \ldots, k$. Let $w_1, w_2, \ldots, w_k > 0$ be a set of weights, and $A_k = \frac{\sum_{l=1}^k w_l x_l}{\sum_{l=1}^k w_l}$ be the weighted average of x_1, x_2 ..., x_k. Then

$$E(A_k) = \mu \quad \text{and} \quad V(A_k) = \frac{\sum_{l=1}^k (w_l)^2}{\left(\sum_{l=1}^k w_l\right)^2} \sigma^2. \qquad (7)$$

Proof: The expected value $E(A_k)$ can be calculated as

$$E\left(\frac{\sum_{l=1}^k w_l x_l}{\sum_{l=1}^k w_l}\right) = \frac{E\left(\sum_{l=1}^k w_l x_l\right)}{\sum_{l=1}^k w_l} =$$
(since $\sum_{l=1}^k w_l$ is a constant [19, Theorem 6.2])
$$= \frac{\sum_{l=1}^k E(w_l x_l)}{\sum_{l=1}^k w_l} =$$
(since $w_1 x_1, w_2 x_2, \ldots, w_k x_k$ are random variables with finite expected values [19, Theorem 6.2])
$$= \frac{\sum_{l=1}^k w_l E(x_l)}{\sum_{l=1}^k w_l} = \frac{\sum_{l=1}^k w_l \mu}{\sum_{l=1}^k w_l} = \mu$$
(since w_l is a constant [19, Theorem 6.2]).

In a similar way, the variance $V(A_k)$ is given by

$$V\left(\frac{\sum_{l=1}^k w_l x_l}{\sum_{l=1}^k w_l}\right) = \frac{V\left(\sum_{l=1}^k w_l x_l\right)}{\left(\sum_{l=1}^k w_l\right)^2} =$$
(since $\sum_{l=1}^k w_l$ is a constant [19, Theorem 6.7])
$$= \frac{\sum_{l=1}^k V(w_l x_l)}{\left(\sum_{l=1}^k w_l\right)^2} =$$
(since $w_1 x_1, w_2 x_2, \ldots, w_k x_k$ are independent random variables [19, Theorem 6.8])
$$= \frac{\sum_{l=1}^k (w_l)^2 V(x_l)}{\left(\sum_{l=1}^k w_l\right)^2} = \frac{\sum_{l=1}^k (w_l)^2 \sigma^2}{\left(\sum_{l=1}^k w_l\right)^2} = \frac{\sum_{l=1}^k (w_l)^2}{\left(\sum_{l=1}^k w_l\right)^2} \sigma^2$$
(since w_l is a constant [19, Theorem 6.7]). $\square$

COROLLARY 1. Consider again the independent trials process x_1, x_2, ..., x_k from Proposition 1, and let $\epsilon > 0$. Then

$$P\left(\left|\frac{\sum_{l=1}^k w_l x_l}{\sum_{l=1}^k w_l} - \mu\right| \geq \epsilon\right) \leq \frac{\sum_{l=1}^k (w_l)^2}{\left(\sum_{l=1}^k w_l\right)^2 \epsilon^2} \sigma^2. \qquad (8)$$

Proof: The result is a direct application of Chebyshev's Inequality (e.g., [19, Theorem 8.1]) to the discrete random variable A_k with the expected value and variance from (7). $\square$

PROPOSITION 2. Consider the transition-probability learning algorithm (5)–(6), and let $\epsilon > 0$. Then

$$P\left(\left|\frac{\sum_{l=1}^k w_i^l x_{ij}^l}{\sum_{l=1}^k w_i^l} - p_{ij}\right| \geq \epsilon\right) \leq \frac{\sum_{l=1}^k (w_l)^2}{4\left(\sum_{l=1}^k w_l\right)^2 \epsilon^2}, \qquad (9)$$

where p_{ij} represents the actual transition probability between states s_i and s_j of the model M from (1).

Proof: Since the actual transition probability between states s_i and s_j is p_{ij}, $x_{ij}^l \in \{0, 1\}$, $1 \leq l \leq k$, are discrete random variables with (a) distribution function $P(1) = p_{ij}$ and $P(0) = 1 - p_{ij}$; (b) expected value $\mu = E(x_{ij}^l) = 1 \times p_{ij} + 0 \times (1 - p_{ij}) = p_{ij}$; and (c) variance $\sigma^2 = V(x_{ij}^l) = E\left(\left(x_{ij}^l\right)^2\right) - \left(E(x_{ij}^l)\right)^2 = \left(1^2 \times p_{ij} + 0^2 \times (1 - p_{ij})\right) - (p_{ij})^2 = p_{ij} - (p_{ij})^2$. The inequality (9) is now easy to obtain by replacing these μ and σ^2 values in (8), and noting that $\sigma^2 = p_{ij} - (p_{ij})^2 \leq \frac{1}{4}$ for all possible values of p_{ij}. $\square$

89

Dynamic selection of learning algorithm parameters.

To take advantage of the result from Proposition 2, we consider a time interval during which the mean distance between successive observations is $\bar{t} > 0$. Accordingly, $w_i^l = \alpha_i^{-(t_k - t_l)} \approx \alpha_i^{-(k-l)\bar{t}}$ and, after straightforward algebraic manipulations,

$$\frac{\sum_{l=1}^k (w_l)^2}{\left(\sum_{l=1}^k w_l\right)^2} \approx \frac{\sum_{l=1}^k \alpha_i^{-2(k-l)\bar{t}}}{\left(\sum_{l=1}^k \alpha_i^{-(k-l)\bar{t}}\right)^2} = \frac{(\alpha_i^{k\bar{t}}+1)(\alpha_i^{\bar{t}}-1)}{(\alpha_i^{k\bar{t}}-1)(\alpha_i^{\bar{t}}+1)} \approx \frac{\alpha_i^{\bar{t}}-1}{\alpha_i^{\bar{t}}+1},$$

if $\alpha^{k\bar{t}} \gg 1$. Replacing this result in (9) we obtain:

$$P\left(\left|\frac{\sum_{l=1}^k w_i^l x_{ij}^l}{\sum_{l=1}^k w_i^l} - p_{ij}\right| \geq \epsilon\right) \leq \frac{1}{4\epsilon^2} \frac{\alpha_i^{\bar{t}}-1}{\alpha_i^{\bar{t}}+1}, \quad \text{if } \alpha_i^{k\bar{t}} \gg 1. \tag{10}$$

Our adaptive transition-probability learning algorithm uses the result in (10) to adjust the smoothing parameter c_i^0 and the ageing parameter α_i from (5)–(6) dynamically, based on the mean distance between recent observations $\bar{t}$ as follows:

1. Given a small ϵ, we select α_i such that the probability from (10) is below a small value p_{max}, i.e.,

$$\frac{1}{4\epsilon^2} \frac{\alpha_i^{\bar{t}}-1}{\alpha_i^{\bar{t}}+1} \leq p_{max} \Rightarrow \alpha_i \leq \left(\frac{1+4\epsilon^2 p_{max}}{1-4\epsilon^2 p_{max}}\right)^{\frac{1}{\bar{t}}}. \tag{11}$$

2. Having selected the α_i, c_i^0 is chosen such that $\alpha_i^{c_i^0 \bar{t}} \gg 1$. Since the first term of (5) dominates the calculation of p_{ij}^k until the number of observations k is larger than c_i^0, this ensures that the k observations play a major role in the p_{ij}^k estimate only once $\alpha_i^{k\bar{t}} \gg 1$ as well. In practice, we use $\alpha_i^{c_i^0 \bar{t}} = 10$, or

$$c_i^0 = \frac{1}{\bar{t}\log_{10}\alpha}. \tag{12}$$

Complexity Analysis.

Our adaptive learning method requires the calculation of the ageing parameter α_i from (11), smoothing parameter c_i^0 from (12), weights w_i^l from (6) and probability estimates p_{ij}^k from (5) after each observation. As we showed in [5], algebraic manipulation can be used to rearrange 5)–(6) so that the last two calculations can be performed in O(1) time and using constant, O(1) space. Calculating the mean distance $\bar{t}$ between recent observations—used to compute α_i in (11)—requires the algorithm to store the timestamps of all observations within a sliding time window of fixed duration. The number of such timestamps is proportional to the frequency f of observations, so the space complexity of this calculation is O(f). The actual calculation of $\bar{t}$, however, can be carried out in O(1) time using a running sum, and computing α_i and c_i^0 also takes constant time. Accordingly, the overall space complexity of the adaptive learning algorithm is O(f), and its time complexity is O(1).

Evaluation.

To evaluate the effectiveness of the adaptive learning method, we carried out a broad range of experiments in which we compared its results with those produced by existing learning methods. The existing methods selected for this comparison were the basic Bayesian learning method from [12], and the fixed-parameter, ageing-enabled learning method from

Table 1: Learning methods compared in the evaluation experiments

Method	Description
Method 1	basic Bayesian learning from [12], obtained by setting $w_i^l = 1$ in (5) for all $1 \leq l \leq k$, and using the smoothing parameter $c_i^0 = 500$.
Method 2	fixed-parameter, ageing-enabled learning algorithm from [5], obtained by setting $c_i^0 = 500$ and $\alpha = 1.001$ in (5)–(6).
Method 3	fixed-parameter, ageing-enabled learning algorithm from [5], obtained by setting $c_i^0 = 500$ and $\alpha = 1.01$ in (5)–(6).
Method 4	our new adaptive learning algorithm with smoothing parameter c_0 and ageing parameter α given by (11)–(12) for $p_{max} = \epsilon = 0.05$.

our previous work in [5]. The concrete methods compared in these experiments and their parameters are summarised in Table 1.

Figures 1–2 depict the experimental results of two typical scenarios in which we assessed the effectivenes of the adaptive learning method. The two scenarios involved learning the probability p of tossing heads with a biased coin from observations of coin tosses, when p changes over time between a "normal" value of $p = 0.96$ and a lower value. The aim of these scenarios was to simulate a degradation in the reliability with which a system component completed a given task within a predefined amount of time, and to test the ability of the four learning methods to identify this degradation. The two scenarios considered different types of reliability degradation—a longer (i.e., 8000-second) and more significant (i.e., down to $p = 0.87$) one in Scenario 1, and a shorter (1200-second) and less significant (down to $p = 0.9$) one in Scenario 2. Finally, learning each type of reliability degradation was attempted for two different observation frequencies. Thus, observation "inter-arrival" time was exponentially distributed, with a mean of 100ms (or a mean frequency of $10s^{-1}$) during the first half of the experiments, and a mean of 500ms (i.e., a mean frequency of $2s^{-1}$) during the second half of the experiments. A qualitative analysis of the experimental results in Figures 1–2 shows that the adaptive learning algorithm (Method 4) outperforms the existing learning algorithms (Methods 1–3) as follows:

- At the beginning of the experiment, the p^k estimate probability for the adaptive algorithm approaches p faster than for the basic algorithm in Method 1 and the two combinations of fixed-parameter ageing-enabled algorithms in Methods 2–3.

- During the "high frequency" half of the experiments, the adaptive algorithm is as good at detecting the decrease in the value of p as the "high α" algorithm in Method 3 (but with a p^k estimate that oscillates less around the actual p), and far better than the "low α" algorithm in Method 2 and the basic algorithm in Method 1;

- During the "low frequency" half of the experiments, the adaptive algorithm produces estimates that are as accurate and as smooth as the "low α" algorithm (Method 2), and much smoother than the "high α" algorithm (Method 3).

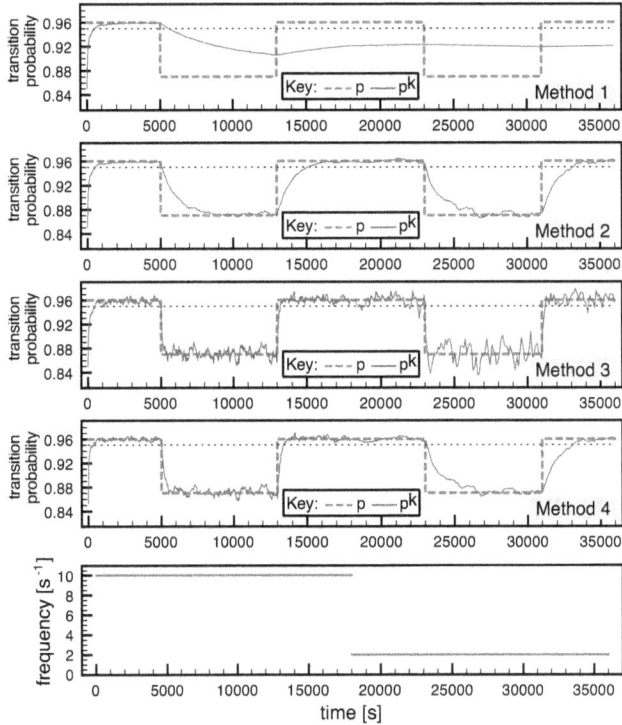

Figure 1: Experimental results—scenario 1

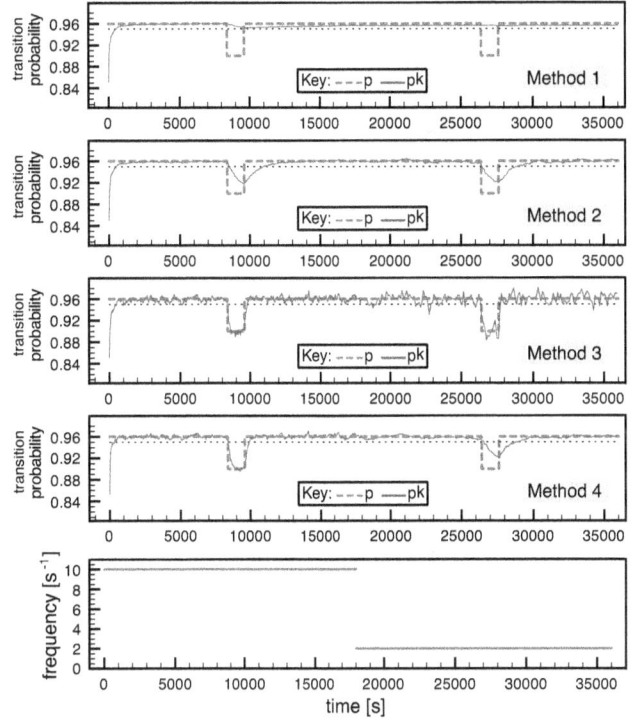

Figure 2: Experimental results—scenario 2

Although some of the estimates produced by the "high alpha" algorithm in Method 3 during the decrease in the value of p in the second half of the experiment are closer to p than the estimates produced by the adaptive algorithm, this is achieved at the expense of significant oscillation. Such oscillation is likely to trigger false alarms in a real-world scenario. If this is not a problem, then the adaptive algorithm can be configured to provide similar estimates by adjusting its confidence interval through increasing ϵ and/or p_{max}.

For a quantitative evaluation of the effectiveness of our adaptive learning method, consider a situation in which an alarm is triggered if the estimate probability p^k (representing the reliability of a system component, as explained above) drops below a threshold value $p^{required} = 0.95$. This threshold value is shown as a dotted line in all graphs in Figures 1–2. Assuming that the learning methods are used to detect such violations of a reliability threshold, we measured the following three non-functional properties of the learnt p^k values from Scenarios 1 and 2:

- The time t_{down} elapsed between the drop in the value of p and the moment when the estimate p^k becomes smaller than $p^{required}$.

- The time t_{up} elapsed between the moment when p regains its "normal" value (i.e., $p = 0.96$) after a period of degraded reliability, and the moment when the estimate p^k becomes at least $p^{required}$.

- The number of false positives n_+, i.e., instances when p^k drops below $p^{required}$ although p has its normal value.

Table 2 shows the value of these properties, separately for the periods of high-frequency and low-frequency observations from the experiments. These results indicate that Method 1 is suited for identifying only the first change in

Table 2: Quantitative analysis of the experiments in Scenarios 1–2

Scenario & Method (Sx_My)	high-frequency observations			low-frequency observations		
	t_{down} [s]	t_{up} [s]	n_+	t_{down} [s]	t_{up} [s]	n_+
S1_M1	570	—	0	—	—	—
S1_M2	95	2110	0	76	2149	0
S1_M3	6	217	54	33	239	38
S1_M4	26	405	0	128	2100	0
S2_M1	150	—	0	—	—	—
S2_M2	162	1350	0	46	1156	0
S2_M3	2	195	65	0	113	134
S2_M4	13	303	0	131	1120	0

the probability p, whereas the other methods yield p^k probability estimates that follow the changes in p with more or less accuracy. The adaptive learning algorithm (Method 4) detects the changes in the value of p faster than Method 2 in the high-frequency observation area, and, like this method, produces no false positives. In the low-frequency observation area, the two methods are comparable, while Method 3 achieves slightly lower t_{down} and t_{up} but has the significant disadvantage of generating tens of false positives. As mentioned before, if these false positives are deemed acceptable, then Method 4 can achieve similar results by choosing larger p_{max} and ϵ values than those in Table 1.

The last set of experiments described in the paper was carried out for the scenario illustrated in Figure 3. In this scenario, we assume that p represents the probability that a system will perform an operation or task over another (or over remaining idle), and we suppose that p varies over a 10-hour time period (e.g., between 8am and 6pm during a working day) as shown by the thick dashed line. Our experiments assessed to what extend the estimate probability p^k provided by each of the four learning remained with the interval $[p - \epsilon, p + \epsilon]$ while the observation frequency was

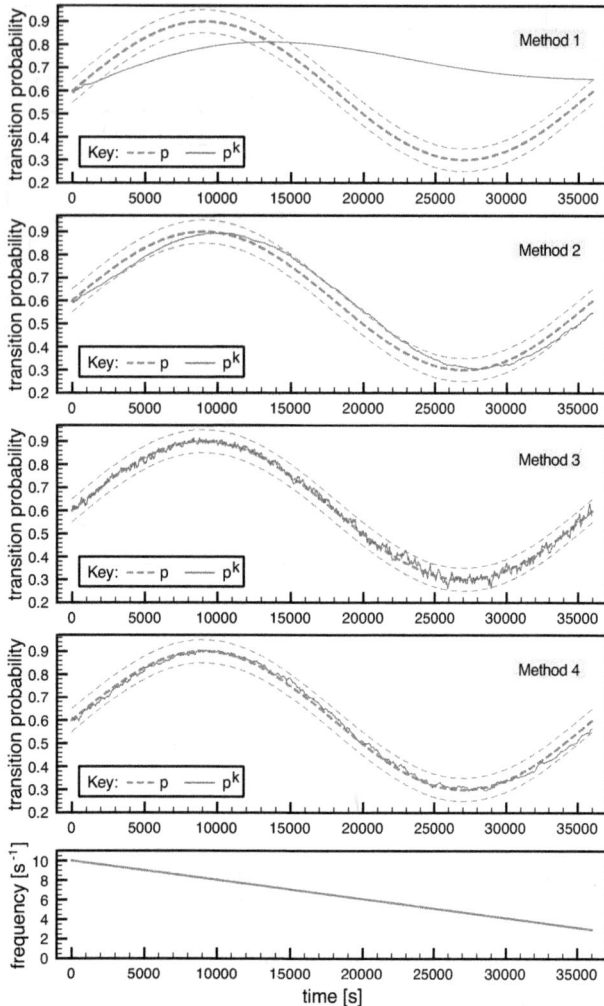

Figure 3: Experimental results—scenario 3

Table 3: Cumulated times when the estimate probability p^k is outside the interval $[p - \epsilon, p + \epsilon]$, averaged over 100 36,000-second experiments

METHOD	$t_{outside}$ [s]
Method 1	31390.64
Method 2	4791.11
Method 3	60.91
Method 4	15.17

decreased linearly from 10s^{-1} to 2s^{-1}. The value $\epsilon = 0.05$ was chosen, in order to match the value of ϵ used by the adaptive learning algorithm (cf. Table 1). The typical experimental results in Figure 3 show that Method 1 cannot handle this degreee of variability, while Method 2 yields p^k estimates within the desired interval around p most of the time. In contrast, Methods 3–4 produce estimates that remain within this interval throughout the 10-hour simulated time period. The main difference between these two methods is that Method 4 (the adaptive learning algorithm) achieves this objective with much less oscillation around the actual value p.

In order to measure the accuracy of the estimates quantitatively, we performed 100 experiments simular to those from Figure 3, for each of the four learning methods. For each experiment, we measured the cumulated time $t_{outside}$ during which the estimate probability p^k resided outside the interval $[p - \epsilon, p + \epsilon]$. Table 3 reports these times, averaged over the 100 experiments carried out for each learning method, confirming that the adaptive learning methods outperforms the other three methods according to this criterion.

4. IMPLEMENTATION

To ease the adoption of the theoretical results from Section 3 in quality-of-service engineering practice, we imple-

mented a software engineering tool and reusable middleware that allow practitioners to exploit our adaptive learning method in the development of self-adaptive service-based systems (SBSs) with the architecture from Fig. 4. This architecture comprises $n \geq 1$ operations performed by remote third-party services, and our new software engineering tool generates automatically the n *intelligent proxies* used to interface the SBS workflow with sets of remote service such that the i-th SBS operation can be carried out by $m_i \geq 1$ functionally equivalent services.

The role of the intelligent proxies is to ensure that each execution of an SBS operation is carried out through the invocation of a concrete service selected such that the non-functional requirements of the system are satisfied. Whenever an instance of the i-th proxy is created, it is initialised with a sequence of "promised" service-level agreements $sla_{ij} = (p_{ij}^0, c_{ij}), 1 \leq j \leq m_i$, where $p_{ij}^0 \in [0, 1]$ and $c_{i,j} > 0$ represent the provider-supplied probability of success and the cost for an invocation of service s_i^j, respectively. The n proxies are also responsible for announcing each service invocation and its outcome to a *model updater*, which we implemented as reusable middleware, and we integrated with our COntinual VErification (COVE) framework from [6]. The model updater uses the adaptive learning algorithm from Section 3 to adjust the transition probabilities of an initial DTMC model of the SBS workflow in line with these proxy notifications.

Finally, the up-to-date DTMC model maintained by the model updater is used by an existing COVE *autonomic manager*, which performs continual non-functional property verification to select the service combination used by the n proxies so that it satisfies the SBS requirements with minimal cost at all times. Accordingly, the proxies, model updater and autonomic manager with its quantitative verification engine implement a monitor-analyse-plan-execute (MAPE) autonomic computing loop [23].

The new software engineering tool is implemented as a Java web application, generates each intelligent proxy as a Java ARchive (JAR) component, and is freely available:

- Pre-installed as a web application on the public Amazon Machine Image with AMI ID `ami-db7020b2` and AMI Name `WB-IPGenTool-2013` from the `us-east-1` Amazon EC2 region (Figure 5). Starting an Amazon EC2 (`http://aws.amazon.com/ec2/`) virtual machine that uses this AMI has the significant advantage that multiple developers can then instantly access and use the tool from a web browser running on their local machines, with no installation or configuration effort.

- As an open-source application for deployment on a local development machine, at `http://www-users.cs.york.ac.uk/~raduc/COVE`.

The model updater and the components of the COVE framework it was integrated with are implemented as an open-source Java library, which is also freely available from `http://www-users.cs.york.ac.uk/~raduc/COVE`.

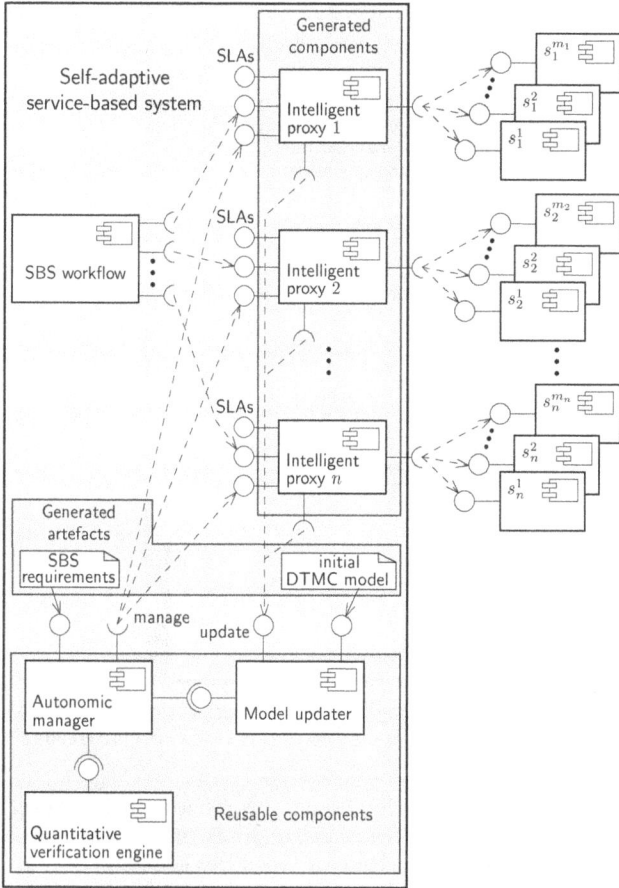

Figure 4: Self-adaptive service-based system that uses continual non-functional property verification, originally proposed in [4] and extended in [3].

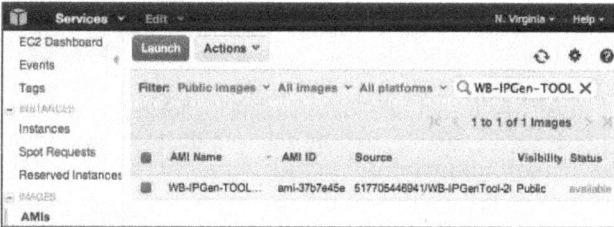

Figure 5: Public Amazon Machine Image pre-installed with the intelligent proxy generator tool

SBS Development Process.

The development of a self-adaptive SBS using the new proxy generator and middleware comprises three stages:

1. The developer selects $m_i \geq 1$ functionally equivalent services that implement the i-th SBS operation, $1 \leq i \leq n$, and uses the new proxy generator to synthesise the i-th intelligent proxy as a Java package, starting from the m_i web service WSDL definitions. The m_i services may be associated with different levels of reliability and different costs. In addition, our proxy generator can accommodate differences in the parameter and return types of the m_i web methods that implement the SBS operation, by allowing the developer to

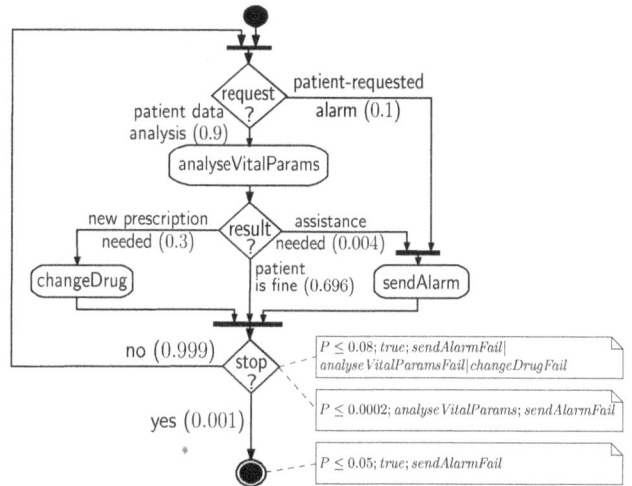

Figure 7: UML activity diagram of a telehealth SBS. Estimate *a priori* probabilities are associated with the edges that originate in a decision node, and comments specifying the SBS requirements are associated with relevant nodes.

specify conversions between these parameters and return types and those of the SBS operation. This is a key advantage of our proxy generator, since in practice it is difficult to find equivalent services whose methods also have identical signatures (Figure 6).

2. The developer uses existing COVE tools [6] to generate the initial DTMC model used to set up the model updater and to formalise the SBS requirements in PCTL, starting from an annotated SBS activity diagram in the XMI format generated by the Eclipse-based Papyrus graphical editing tool for UML 2 (http://www.eclipse.org/papyrus/). The process is presented in detail in [6].

3. The developer integrates the n intelligent proxies with the code that implements the SBS workflow, in a similar manner to using standard web service proxies. Additionally, an instance of the model updater and an instance of the COVE autonomic manager from [6] are created and initialised with the initial DTMC model and the array of PCTL requirements from the previous stage, respectively.

5. CASE STUDY

We used the adaptive model learning method from Section 3 and the tools and development process described in Section 4 to implement a self-adaptive version of a telehealth service-based system taken from [3, 4, 12]. In this SBS, the vital parameters of a patient are periodically measured by a wearable device and analysed by third-party medical services. The result of the analysis may trigger the invocation of an alarm service (that determines, for instance, the dispatch of an ambulance), may lead to the invocation of a pharmacy service to deliver new medication to the patient, or may confirm that the patient is fine. In addition, the patient can initiate an alarm by using a panic button on the wearable device. The workflow of the telehealth SBS is

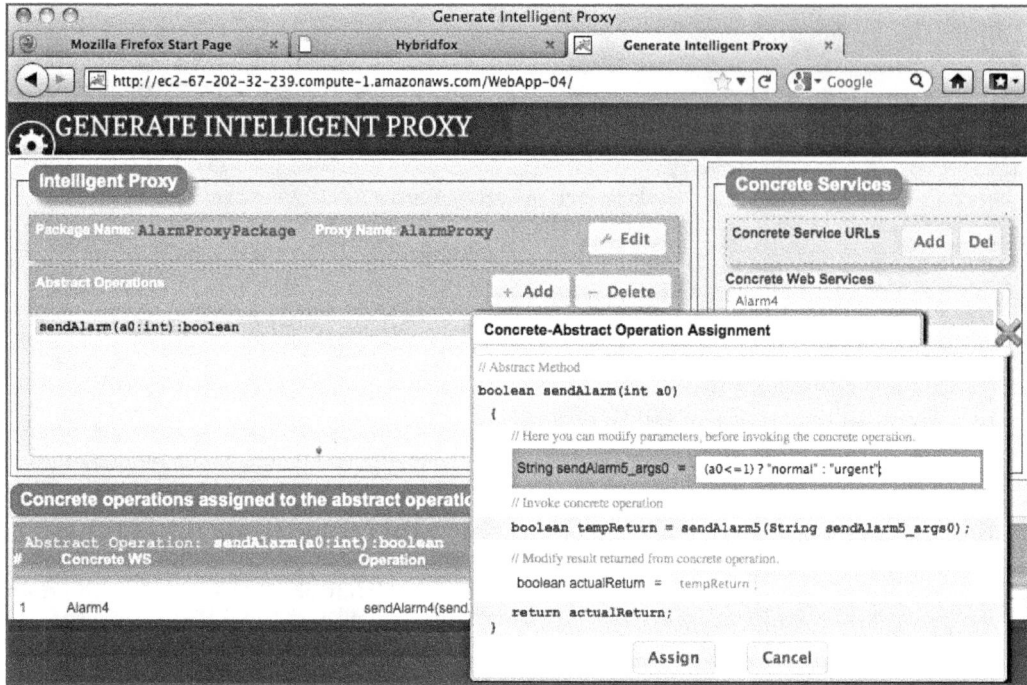

Figure 6: Instance of the intelligent proxy generator, running as a web application on an Amazon virtual machine, and used from a web browser. Parameter/return type conversions are supported between "abstract" SBS operations and "concrete" services.

Table 4: Service prior success probabilities and costs

service	prior success probability $(p_{i,j}^0)$	cost $(c_{i,j})$
sendAlarm$_1$	0.968	0.02
sendAlarm$_2$	0.968	0.01
changeDrug$_1$	0.96	0.3
changeDrug$_2$	0.95	0.1
analyseVitalParams$_1$	0.965	5.0
analyseVitalParams$_2$	0.95	4.0
analyseVitalParams$_3$	0.96	3.0

shown in Fig. 7, and the three non-functional requirements used in the case study are:

R_1: The probability that one execution of the workflow ends in a service failure is at most $p_{R_1} = 0.08$.

R_2: The probability that an alarm failure occurs within $N = 10$ executions of the workflow is at most $p_{R_2} = 0.05$.

R_3: The probability that an invocation of the analysis service is followed by an alarm failure is at most $p_{R_3} = 0.0002$.

The self-adaptive version of the telehealth SBS used $m_1 = 2$ sendAlarm services, $m_2 = 2$ changeDrug services, and $m_3 = 3$ analyseVitalParams services. These seven services were simulated using real Java web services deployed on Amazon EC2 "small instance" virtual machines. Individual configuration files were used to specify the variation of the actual probability of successful invocation for each web service, $p_{i,j}$, $1 \leq i \leq 3$, $1 \leq j \leq m_i$, over the duration of each experiment. The *a priori* success probabilities $p_{i,j}^0$ and the costs $c_{i,j}$ for an invocation of each of these services are shown in Table 4. A Java implementation of the telehealth

SBS workflow from Fig. 7 was integrated with intelligent proxies for its three operations, and was run on a standard 2.66 GHz Intel Core 2 Duo Macbook Pro computer.

Fig. 8 shows a typical experiment in which the self-adaptive SBS selects the service combinations for its telehealth workflow dynamically, over a 1.5-hour wall-clock time period. Low-cost combinations of services are preferred when their combined probabilities of successful completion satisfy all SBS relibility requirements, and are discarded in favour of higher-cost service combinations when their joint reliability violates one or more of these SBS requirements. These decisions are taken based on the estimate probabilities of success p_{ij}^k calculated by our adaptive learning algorithm (initialised with $\epsilon = p_{max} = 0.05$), and on the continual verification of the updated SBS model:

- At the beginning of the experiment, the lowest-cost service combination is selected, as the high *a priori* success probabilities $p_{i,j}^0$ of all services make all service combinations seem suitable. This is the expected behaviour, since a service whose provider-specified SLA does not satisfy the SBS requirements should not be included in the system.

- When the SBS learns that analysisVitalParams$_3$ is underperforming in the area labelled 'A' in the diagram, it starts using the higher-cost analysisVitalParams$_2$ service.

- While a higher-cost service is used for an SBS operation, the adaptive learning algorithm "rebuilds trust" in the temporarily discarded lower cost service (area labelled 'B' in the diagram). This is due to the fact that the observations of frequent failures from area 'A' are associated with weights that decrease over time, so the estimate $p_{3,3}^k$ slowly approaches the prior value

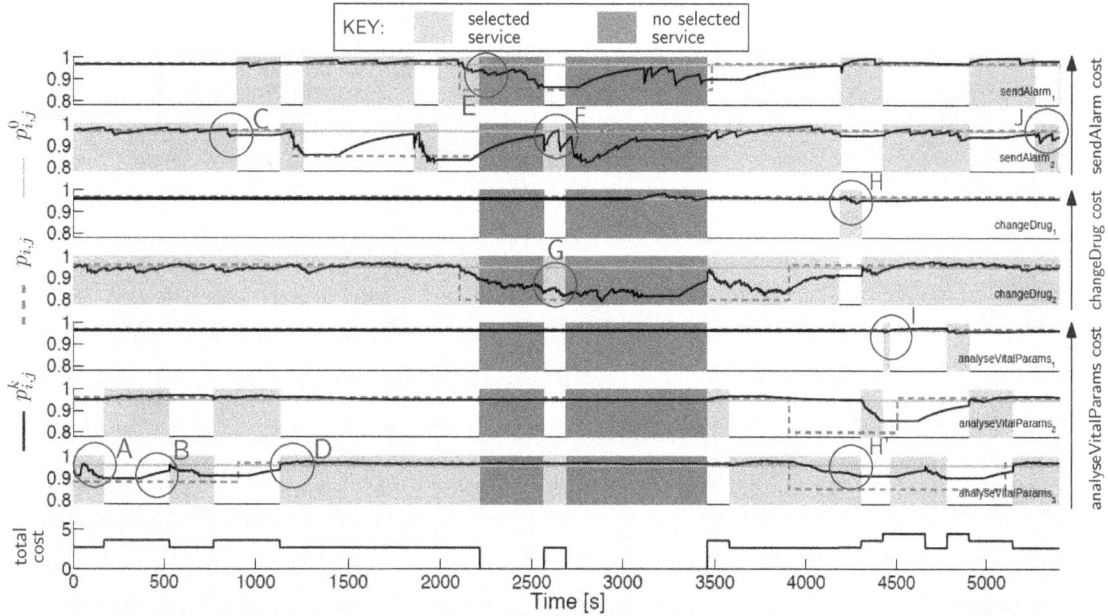

Figure 8: Automated service selection for the telehealth service-based system; the circular areas labelled 'A', 'B', etc. are analysed in Section 5

$p_{3,3}^0$. The learning algorithm was configured to assume that a service returned to its prior success probability when the autonomic manager resumes using it, which explains why $p_{3,3}^k$ grows suddenly to $p_{3,3}^0$ when the analysisVitalParams$_3$ is selected again in area B.

- In area C, a slight variation in the estimate success probability of the sendAlarm$_2$ service triggers a potentially unnecessary transition to the more expensive service sendAlarm$_1$. Choosing strict intervals of confidence (i.e., smaller ϵ and/or p_{max} parameters) for the adaptive learning could reduce such "false positives", although eliminating them altogether is not possible (cf. Proposition 2).

- In area D, the SBS resumes using analysisVitalParams$_3$, which has now recovered.

- In area E, the system learns that even the high-cost alarm service sendAlarm$_2$ is unreliable, to the extent that the SBS requirements are no longer satisfied. Under the configuration used in the experiment, no service was selected in this scenario, and an error message was generated instead to alert the system operator.

- In area F, the system retries to use the alarm service that experienced a low success rate first, and learns that this services has not yet recovered.

- Area G shows that some services have little impact on the overall SBS compliance with its requirements: given that only requirement R_1 depends on a successful completion of the changeDrug SBS operation (and only marginally), a decrease in the reliability of changeDrug$_2$ does not determine the SBS to abandon this service.

- Nevertheless, the SBS does switch to the more expensive changeDrug$_1$ service in area H–H', at a moment when changeDrug$_2$ is actually more reliable than it was

in area G. The decision is motivated by the decrease in the reliability of dataAnalysis$_3$, which the system compensates for by choosing a slightly more expensive drug service (the cost difference between changeDrug$_2$ and changeDrug$_1$ is only 0.2) instead of switching to a significantly more expensive analysis service (ceasing to use analyseVitalParams$_3$ would have amounted to a cost increase of at least 1.0 for this operation).

- The strategy adopted in area H–H' is unsuccessful, so the most expensive analysis service is eventually selected in area I.

- Finally, in area J all services have recovered and operated close to their advertised SLAs, so the self-adaptive SBS returns to using the lowest-cost service combination for the telehealth service-based system.

A key capability of our adaptive learning method is its ability to learn not only changes in the reliability of individual services, but also changes in the rates with which the SBS operations are performed. To evaluate this functionality, we considered the effect of changes in the probability $p_{request\_sendAlarm}$ that a request handled by the telehealth SBS is a patient-initiated alarm. A temporary increase in this probability may be caused, for instance, by a flu outbreak. Fig. 9 depicts the analysis of requirement R_1 from our case study, for a range of service combinations and for $p_{request\_sendAlarm}$ values between 0.05 and 0.15. This analysis shows that even a small change in the probability of alarm requests is sufficient to render unacceptable a service combination that was previously compliant with requirement R_1. This confirms the importance of updating the SBS model in line with any fluctuations in the probabilities with which the SBS operations are executed.

Scalability.

To evaluate the scalability and generality of our approach, we carried out a number of experiments that assessed the ap-

$$p_2 = p_3 = 0.94$$

A service combination with $(p_1, p_2, p_3) = (0.875, 0.94, 0.94)$ complies with requirement R_1 if $p_{request\_sendAlarm} = 0.05$, but violates R_1 if $p_{request\_sendAlarm} \geq 0.075$.

(a)

(b)

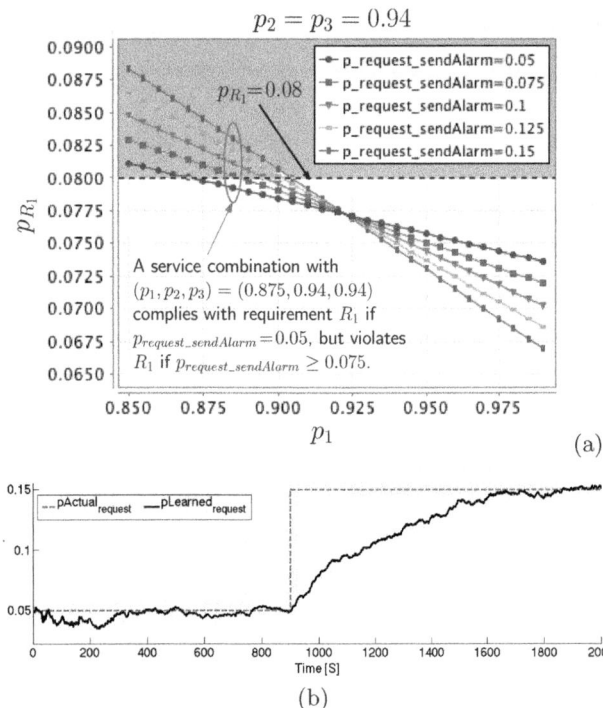

Figure 9: (a) The effect of changes in the probability of alarm requests; and (b) learning this probability

Figure 10: Scalability results for 2–5 "concrete" services per SBS operation

plicability and overheads of executing the runtime adaptive learning and model analysis in multiple scenarios. We selected the following workflows used by a number of projects in this area:

1. the healthcare case study described in this paper, and previously used in [4, 3, 12];

2. the e-commerce workflow obtained from [15];

3. the travel assistant workflow derived from the statechart representation presented in [32].

These workflows comprise invocations to three, four and five abstract operations, respectively.

For each of the workflows we devised a parameterised DTMC and defined four PCTL requirements, including one PCTL property to determine the expected cost of a single invocation of the workflow. The size of the models ranged between 11 and 17 states. As we envisage that practical self-adaptive service-based systems will rarely use more than two or three concrete services for each abstract operation, we then ran experiments that considered between two and six concrete services for each of the abstract operations. Due to space constraints, we could not include the DTMC models and properties for the e-commerce and travel-assistant workflows in this paper. However, these DTMC models and properties, and detailed descriptions of each of these experiments are available at http://www-users.cs.york.ac.uk/~raduc/COVE.

Each experiment measured the time taken to initialise the system and select the optimal concrete service configuration in the worst-case scenario whereby all combinations of concrete services satisfied the SBS requirements. Note that this is the worst-case scenarios because the autonomic

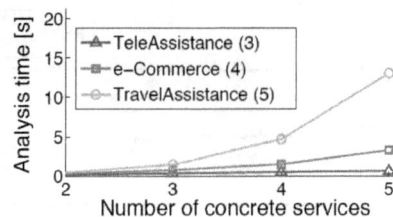

manager stops verifying the suitability of a service combination as soon as it learns that the combination violates one of the requirements. Fig. 10 summarises the results of our experiments, averaged over multiple runs. According to these results, up to three services per SBS operation can be analysed within two seconds for each of the considered workflows, which confirms the feasibility of the approach for typical SBSs of practical importance from the domains explored in our experiments. Increase the number of services to four services leads to verification times of up to $5s$, which is likely to be acceptable for many practical applications. This is particularly true when large numbers of false positives and false negatives in the associated learning process need to be avoided, so longer time is already needed to identify the changes on which the autonomic manager must act.

The growth in analysis time shown in Fig. 10 makes the current implementation of the approach suitable for systems comprising small to medium numbers of operations, and using between two and four services per SBS operation. While the second constraint is, in our opinion, not significant, the former implies that SBSs comprising large numbers of operations cannot yet benefit from this approach. However, recent work by several research groups and ourselves has led to significant advances in the use of incremental and compositional techniques to reduce quantitative verification times, often by multiple orders of magnitude [7, 14, 21, 25]. We envisage that integrating these techniques into the approach will significantly enhance its ability to support the development and operation of much larger service-based systems.

6. RELATED WORK

Significant research has focused on monitoring the performance and reliability properties of technical systems, and on modelling and analysing these properties formally. The spread of evolving critical systems [2] led to a growing need for combining techniques from the two research areas in a runtime context, in order to achieve a continual verification of the non-functional properties of these systems [3].

The projects addressing the challenges of continual verification have so far focused primarily on reducing the overheads of runtime analysis of formal models [7, 13, 14, 16, 21], with relatively little effort dedicated to ensuring that the analysed formal models are updated in line with the changes in the analysed system. The work presented in [12] proposes the on-line learning algorithm referred to as "Method 1" in the evaluation part from Section 3, where we show that our adaptive learning is better suited for all scenarios in which the learnt DTMC transition probabilities undergo multiple changes over time. The approach introduced in [34, 35] uses Kalman filter estimators to update the parameters of queueing-network performance models. Our results complement this approach, as they target DTMC reliability models. Finally, our new adaptive learning approach is a significant improvement over the on-line learning approach from our previous work in [5]. This was shown in the evaluation part from Section 3, where representative instances of the learning approach from [5] (labelled "Method 2" and "Method 3") were compared to the new adaptive learning.

The management and optimisation of SBS non-functional properties through dynamic service selection has been the focus of significant research over the past decade. The solutions proposed by this research include approaches that use intelligent control loops (e.g., [1, 9, 28]) and approaches that emulate the cooperative behaviour of biological systems (e.g., [17, 29]). The approach supported by our new intelligent proxy generator and middleware belongs to the first category, so the rest of this section focuses on comparing our work with results from this area, and in particular with solutions that employ formal models that can represent SBSs accurately and in a realistic way. The approaches proposed in [18, 28, 27, 30] use UML activity diagrams or directed acyclic graphs to synthesise simple performance models based on queuing networks [28, 27] or, like our approach, Markovian reliability models [18, 30]. These models are then used to establish the quality-of-service (QoS) properties of the analysed SBS systems. However, unlike these approaches, our solution also uses an adaptive learning technique to update the initial model based on observations of the system behaviour. The QoS-driven selection of services in self-adaptive service-based systems is addressed in [1, 9, 10, 33]. All these approaches lack adaptive learning capabilities, and propose theoretical solutions that are hard to replicate in practical SBSs. In addition, approaches such as [1, 9, 26, 33] involve the optimisation of the service selection on a per request basis. These approaches require perfect knowledge of the QoS capabilities of the available services, which renders them ineffective in the scenarios targeted by our work, where the characteristics of services need to be learnt from observations of their behaviour.

The work presented in this paper also differs from our previous results in [4], as it introduces an adaptive learning method that is underpinned by new theoretical results and used to estimate not only changes in the reliability of individual services, but also variations in the probabilities with which the operations of an evolving system are invoked. Furthermore, we describe a new proxy generation tool and model updater that are missing from our previous work.

7. CONCLUSION

We introduced a new on-line learning method for maintaining discrete-time Markov reliability models of evolving critical systems in sync with the systems they represent. Unlike existing approaches to updating such models, our new method adapts its parameters dynamically, to suit the frequency of the observations it relies upon and the developer-specified confidence intervals for its estimates. This adaptation is based on a rigorous theoretical foundation, also introduced in the paper, and we showed that our model learning method outperforms existing approaches in a range of scenarios of practical relevance.

Our adaptive model learning method is a key component for the continual verification of the non-functional properties of evolving systems. To make the new method available to practitioners interested in continual verification, we implemented a software engineering tool and middleware that en-

able its adoption by developers of self-adaptive service-based systems. This development tool is pre-installed on a publicly available Amazon EC2 machine image, so developers can use the tool without having to first install and configure it and the third-party libraries it uses. The effectiveness of the tool and its integration with our existing continual verification framework from [6] was demonstrated in a case study from the telehealth application domain, and the scalability of the approach was evaluated for three service-based systems used by projects in this area. The results of this evaluation indicate that the approach is applicable to SBS workflows of practical significance. Extending the applicability of the approach to large service-based systems requires its integration with recently emerged incremental and compositional verification techniques [7, 14, 21, 25]. Achieving this integration represents an area of ongoing work for our project. The main target of this work is the incremental verification technique we proposed in [21], which we deem particularly suitable for our purpose due to its ability to produce system-level verification results by re-analysing only the parts of the system that were affected by a change.

Another area of ongoing work for our project is the extension of the adaptive model learning method with the ability to handle models supporting the analysis of different categories of non-functional requirements (e.g., performance and energy related), along the lines of our previous work in [4].

Acknowledgment

This work was partly supported by the UK Engineering and Physical Sciences Research Council grant EP/H042644/1.

8. REFERENCES

[1] D. Ardagna and B. Pernici. Adaptive service composition in flexible processes. *IEEE Trans. Softw. Eng.*, 33(6):369–384, 2007.

[2] R. Calinescu. Emerging techniques for the engineering of self-adaptive high-integrity software. In J. Camara et al., editors, *Assurances for Self-Adaptive Systems*, volume 7740 of *LNCS*, pages 297–310. Springer, 2013.

[3] R. Calinescu, C. Ghezzi, M. Kwiatkowska, and R. Mirandola. Self-adaptive software needs quantitative verification at runtime. *Communications of the ACM*, 55(9):69–77, September 2012.

[4] R. Calinescu, L. Grunske, M. Kwiatkowska, R. Mirandola, and G. Tamburrelli. Dynamic QoS management and optimization in service-based systems. *IEEE Trans. Softw. Eng.*, 37:387–409, 2011.

[5] R. Calinescu, K. Johnson, and Y. Rafiq. Using observation ageing to improve Markovian model learning in QoS engineering. In *2nd ACM/SPEC Intl. Conf. on Performance Engineering*, pages 505–510, 2011.

[6] R. Calinescu, K. Johnson, and Y. Rafiq. Developing self-verifying service-based systems. In *28th Intl. IEEE/ACM Conference on Automated software Engineering*, 2013. To appear.

[7] R. Calinescu, S. Kikuchi, and K. Johnson. Compositional reverification of probabilistic safety properties for large-scale complex IT systems. In *Large-Scale Complex IT Systems*, volume 7539 of *LNCS*, pages 303–329. Springer, 2012.

[8] R. Calinescu and M. Z. Kwiatkowska. Using quantitative analysis to implement autonomic IT systems. In *Proceedings of the 31st International Conference on Software Engineering, ICSE 2009*, pages 100–110. IEEE Computer Society, 2009.

[9] G. Canfora, M. D. Penta, R. Esposito, and M. L. Villani. A framework for QoS-aware binding and re-binding of composite web services. *Journal of Systems and Software*, 81(10):1754–1769, 2008.

[10] V. Cardellini, E. Casalicchio, V. Grassi, and F. L. Presti. Scalable service selection for web service composition supporting differentiated qos classes. Technical Report Technical Report RR-07.59, Dip. di Informatica, Sistemi e Produzione, Universita di Roma Tor Vergata, 2007.

[11] F. Ciesinski and M. Größer. On probabilistic computation tree logic. In C. Baier et al., editors, *Validation of Stochastic Systems - A Guide to Current Research*, volume 2925 of *LNCS*, pages 147–188. Springer, 2004.

[12] I. Epifani, C. Ghezzi, R. Mirandola, and G. Tamburrelli. Model evolution by run-time adaptation. In *Proc. 31st Intl. Conf. Software Engineering (ICSE'09)*, pages 111–121, 2009.

[13] A. Filieri and C. Ghezzi. Further steps towards efficient runtime verification: Handling probabilistic cost models. In *Software Engineering: Rigorous and Agile Approaches (FormSERA), 2012 Formal Methods in*, pages 2–8, 2012.

[14] A. Filieri, C. Ghezzi, and G. Tamburrelli. Run-time efficient probabilistic model checking. In *Proc. 33rd International Conference on Software Engineering*, pages 341–350. IEEE Computer Society, 2011.

[15] A. Filieri, C. Ghezzi, and G. Tamburrelli. A formal approach to adaptive software: continuous assurance of non-functional requirements. *Formal Aspects of Computing*, 24(2):163–186, 2012.

[16] V. Forejt, M. Kwiatkowska, D. Parker, H. Qu, and M. Ujma. Incremental runtime verification of probabilistic systems. In S. Qadeer and S. Tasiran, editors, *Runtime Verification*, volume 7687 of *Lecture Notes in Computer Science*, pages 314–319. Springer Berlin Heidelberg, 2013.

[17] R. Frei, G. D. M. Serugendo, and J. Barata. Designing self-organization for evolvable assembly systems. In *Second IEEE Intern. Conf. on Self-Adaptive and Self-Organizing Systems, SASO 2008*, pages 97–106, 2008.

[18] S. Gallotti, C. Ghezzi, R. Mirandola, and G. Tamburrelli. Quality prediction of service compositions through probabilistic model checking. In S. Becker, F. Plasil, and R. Reussner, editors, *Proc. 4th International Conference on the Quality of Software-Architectures, QoSA 2008*, volume 5281 of *LNCS*, pages 119–134. Springer, 2008.

[19] C. M. Grinstead and J. L. Snell. *Introduction to Probability*. American Mathematical Society, 1997.

[20] H. Hansson and B. Jonsson. A logic for reasoning about time and reliability. *Formal Aspects of Computing*, 6(5):512–535, 1994.

[21] K. Johnson, R. Calinescu, and S. Kikuchi. An incremental verification framework for component-based software systems. In *Proc. 16th Intl. ACM Sigsoft Symposium on Component-Based Software Engineering*, pages 33–42, 2013.

[22] J.-P. Katoen, M. Khattri, and I. S. Zapreev. A Markov reward model checker. In *Quantitative Evaluation of Systems*, pages 243–244, Los Alamitos, 2005. IEEE Computer Society.

[23] J. O. Kephart and D. M. Chess. The vision of autonomic computing. *IEEE Computer Journal*, 36(1):41–50, January 2003.

[24] M. Kwiatkowska, G. Norman, and D. Parker. PRISM 4.0: Verification of probabilistic real-time systems. In *CAV'11*, volume 6806 of *LNCS*, pages 585–591. Springer, 2011.

[25] M. Kwiatkowska, G. Norman, D. Parker, and H. Qu. Assume-guarantee verification for probabilistic systems. In *TACAS'10*, pages 23–37. Springer, 2010.

[26] Q. Liang, X. Wu, and H. C. Lau. Optimizing service systems based on application-level QoS. *IEEE Trans. Service Computing*, 2:108–121, 2009.

[27] M. Marzolla and R. Mirandola. Performance prediction of web service workflows. In *International Conference on Quality of Software Architectures, QoSA 2007*, volume 4880 of *LNCS*, pages 127–144. Springer, 2007.

[28] D. Menascé, H. Ruan, and H. Gomaa. QoS management in service-oriented architectures. *Perform. Eval.*, 64(7):646–663, 2007.

[29] F. Saffre, R. Tateson, J. Halloy, M. Shackleton, and J.-L. Deneubourg. Aggregation dynamics in overlay networks and their implications for self-organized distributed applications. *The Computer Journal*, 2008.

[30] N. Sato and K. S. Trivedi. Stochastic modeling of composite web services for closed-form analysis of their performance and reliability bottlenecks. In *ICSOC*, volume 4749 of *LNCS*, pages 107–118. Springer, 2007.

[31] H. L. S. Younes. Ymer: A statistical model checker. In K. Etessami et al., editors, *Computer Aided Verification*, volume 3576 of *LNCS*, pages 429–433. Springer, 2005.

[32] L. Zeng, B. Benatallah, A. H.H. Ngu, M. Dumas, J. Kalagnanam, and H. Chang. Qos-aware middleware for web services composition. *IEEE Trans. Softw. Eng.*, 30(5):311–327, May 2004.

[33] L. Zeng, B. Benatallah, A. H. H. Ngu, M. Dumas, J. Kalagnanam, and H. Chang. QoS-aware middleware for web services composition. *IEEE Trans. Software Eng*, 30(5):311–327, 2004.

[34] T. Zheng, M. Woodside, and M. Litoiu. Performance model estimation and tracking using optimal filters. *IEEE Transactions on Software Engineering*, 34(3):391–406, 2008.

[35] T. Zheng, J. Yang, M. Woodside, M. Litoiu, and G. Iszlai. Tracking time-varying parameters in software systems with extended Kalman filters. In *Proceedings of the 2005 conference of the Centre for Advanced Studies on Collaborative research*, CASCON '05, pages 334–345. IBM Press, 2005.

Performance Queries for Architecture-Level Performance Models[*]

Fabian Gorsler
Karlsruhe Institute of
Technology (KIT)
Am Fasanengarten 5
76131 Karlsruhe, Germany
gorsler@ira.uka.de

Fabian Brosig
Karlsruhe Institute of
Technology (KIT)
Am Fasanengarten 5
76131 Karlsruhe, Germany
brosig@kit.edu

Samuel Kounev
Karlsruhe Institute of
Technology (KIT)
Am Fasanengarten 5
76131 Karlsruhe, Germany
kounev@kit.edu

ABSTRACT

Over the past few decades, many performance modeling formalisms and prediction techniques for software architectures have been developed in the performance engineering community. However, using a performance model to predict the performance of a software system normally requires extensive experience with the respective modeling formalism and involves a number of complex and time consuming manual steps. In this paper, we propose a generic declarative interface to performance prediction techniques to simplify and automate the process of using architecture-level software performance models for performance analysis. The proposed Descartes Query Language (DQL) is a language to express the demanded performance metrics for prediction as well as the goals and constraints in the specific prediction scenario. It reduces the manual effort and the learning curve when working with performance models by a unified interface independent of the employed modeling formalism. We evaluate the applicability and benefits of the proposed approach in the context of several representative case studies.

Categories and Subject Descriptors

D.2.8 [**Software Engineering**]: Metrics—*performance measures*; D.3.2 [**Programming Languages**]: Language Classifications—*specialized application languages*

General Terms

Performance, Languages

Keywords

Software Performance Engineering, Performance Prediction, Automation, Query Language, Domain-specific Language

[*]This work was funded by the German Research Foundation (DFG) under grant No. KO 34456-1.

1. INTRODUCTION

Performance and availability are crucial for today's software systems [22, 33]. Modern IT solutions introduce additional abstraction layers such as virtualization layers and need to sustain increasing workloads. The increasing complexity makes providing adequate performance a challenging task. Analyzing the performance characteristics of a software system during all phases of its lifecycle helps to avoid performance problems.

The performance of a software system can normally be analyzed through performance prediction techniques based on performance modeling formalisms. These techniques and formalisms differ in their expressiveness, prediction capabilities, computing effort and modeling effort. We distinguish between two major families of performance models. *Predictive performance models* such as Queueing Networks (QNs), Queueing Petri Nets (QPNs) or Layered Queueing Networks (LQNs) focus on capturing the temporal system behavior. They are used on a high level of abstraction and can be solved analytically or by simulation techniques [22, 17, 21]. *Architecture-level performance models* describe the software architecture, the deployment and are annotated with performance-relevant aspects of the software system. Prominent examples are the UML SPT profile [23] and its successor the UML MARTE profile [24], CSM [38], PCM [2] and KLAPER [10]. To predict performance metrics, automated model-to-model transformations into predictive performance models are normally employed.

During the performance prediction process, users execute or trigger the following tasks as shown in Fig. 1. When a performance analysis is triggered, the architecture-level performance model is transformed into a suitable predictive performance model. The resulting model is then solved by analytical or simulation means to derive performance metrics. Finally, the user extracts the metrics of interest. However, the presented process has several shortcomings arising from a lack of automation and required manual efforts: While the transformation and model solving steps are typically automated, their configuration has to be done manually and is dependent on the tooling and the performance model formalism. Furthermore, depending on the output of the model solving step, the extraction of the performance metrics of interest is a manual step and requires performance modeling expertise of the user.

In this paper, we propose a generic declarative interface for performance prediction techniques to simplify and automate the process of using architecture-level software per-

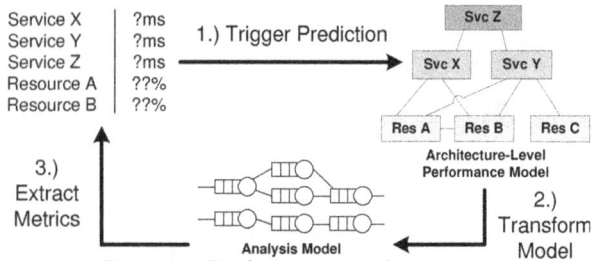

Figure 1: Performance prediction process

formance models for performance analysis. The interface allows the formulation of performance queries. A performance query specifies which performance metrics should be predicted under which scenario-specific constraints. Furthermore, performance queries may involve parameter variations for different performance model parameters such as request arrival rates or thread pool sizes.

The unified interface that is independent of the employed modeling formalism reduces the manual effort and learning curve when working with performance models. We provide our approach as an extensible architecture with an implementation that is capable to integrate third-party extensions supporting specific performance modeling formalisms and prediction techniques. To demonstrate the applicability and benefits of our approach, we present representative case studies showing how to integrate different established performance prediction techniques. Other tool developers can leverage our approach by offering an interface for their performance modeling formalism and prediction technique.

In summary, the contributions of this paper are: (i) the Descartes Query Language (DQL), a novel query language to specify performance queries with optional parameter variations, (ii) an architecture and implementation that unifies the prediction process by using DQL as declarative interface, and (iii) a detailed evaluation of the applicability and benefits of our approach in the context of several representative case studies.

The remainder of the paper is organized as follows: First, a requirements specification based on usage scenarios and user stories is presented in Sec. 2. Then we describe the DQL approach in Sec. 3. We show syntax diagrams of DQL and explain its different features. In Sec. 4, we present the architecture and implementation of our corresponding toolchain. Sec. 5 provides an overview of related work. In Sec. 6, we evaluate the applicability and benefits of the proposed approach in the context of several representative case studies. Sec. 7 concludes the paper and provides an outlook on future work.

2. REQUIREMENTS

We investigate common usage scenarios in performance engineering to derive user stories as requirements for our language for performance queries. The presented usage scenarios are based on examples from literature [3, 29, 34]. They vary in the user type and the user role. Furthermore, we distinguish whether the performance queries are issued in an *online* or *offline* context, i.e., if the system is at runtime during operation or if the system is in the development or deployment phase.

2.1 Usage Scenarios

Design Time. At software design time, a software architect tries to find a suitable assembly of components to build a software system. Using an architecture-level performance model of the system, the software architect can simulate different assemblies and configurations to predict the performance behavior. The predictions are not constrained to complete within strict time bounds, but should allow qualitative comparisons of design alternatives with high accuracy. Furthermore, the software architect may want to optimize compositions or configuration parameter settings. For that purpose, an automated design and parameter space exploration covering defined Degrees of Freedom (DoFs) is helpful [19, 14]. DoFs specify how entities in a performance model can be varied and thus span the space of valid configurations and parameter settings. Depending on the size of the configuration space and the space exploration strategy, the time-to-result of a single performance prediction gains in importance. Otherwise, the exploration might take too long to be feasible.

Deployment Time. At deployment time, a software deployer tries to size the resource environment so that the system on the one hand satisfies performance objectives and on the other hand does not waste resources. Using a performance model, this system sizing and capacity planning step can be facilitated. Expensive performance tests can be avoided, because different load situations can be simulated on different resource settings.

System Run-Time. A proactive online performance and resource management aims at adapting system configuration and resource allocations dynamically. Overload situations should be anticipated and suitable reconfigurations should be triggered *before* Service Level Agreements (SLAs) are violated. Performance predictions need to be conducted to answer questions such as: What performance would a new service or application deployed on the infrastructure exhibit and how much resources should be allocated to it? How should the workloads of the new service/application and existing services be partitioned among the available resources so that performance requirements are satisfied and resources are utilized efficiently? What would be the performance impact of adding a new component or upgrading an existing component as services and applications evolve? If an application experiences a load spike or a change of its workload profile, how would this affect the system performance? Which parts of the system architecture would require additional resources? What would be the effect of migrating a service or an application component from one physical server to another? However, there is a trade-off between prediction accuracy and time-to-result. There are situations where the prediction results need to be available very fast to adapt the system *before* SLAs are violated. An accurate fine-grained performance prediction comes at the cost of a higher prediction overhead and longer prediction durations. Coarse-grained performance predictions allow speeding up the prediction process. This trade-off should be configurable when conducting performance predictions.

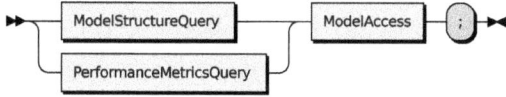

Figure 2: Descartes Query Language (DQL)

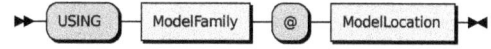

Figure 3: Model Access

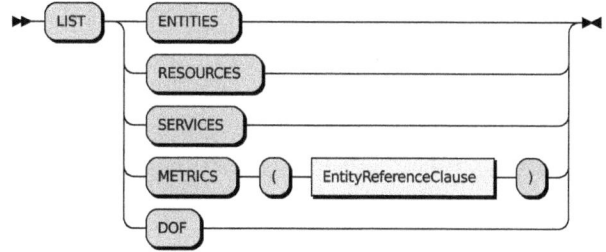

Figure 4: Model Structure Query

2.2 User Stories

We formulate the following user stories as requirements for the query language.

○ As a user, I want to issue queries independent of the underlying performance modeling formalism.

○ As a user, I want to list the modeled services of a selected performance model instance.

○ As a user, I want to list the modeled resources of a selected performance model instance.

○ As a user, I want to list the variable parameters of a selected performance model instance.

○ As a user, I want to list supported performance metrics for selected services and resources.

○ As a user, I want to conduct a prediction of selected performance metrics of selected services and resources.

○ As a user, I want to aggregate retrieved performance metrics by statistical means.

○ As a user, I want to control the performance prediction by specifying a trade-off between prediction speed and accuracy.

○ As a user, I want to conduct a sensitivity analysis for selected parameters in defined parameter spaces.

○ As a user, I want to query revisions of model instances.

We emphasize that the query language needs to be independent of a specific performance modeling formalism. Predictable performance metrics may vary from model instance to model instance and model solver to model solver, so the query mechanism needs to include means to evaluate the underlying model and list queryable performance metrics to the user. For each performance modeling formalism, the query language requires a *Connector* to bridge the mentioned gaps. Furthermore, queries should be user-friendly to write, i.c., there should be a text editor with syntax highlighting and auto-completion features.

3. QUERY LANGUAGE

In this section, we present the concepts of the performance query language. We use syntax diagrams to describe the most relevant parts of the language grammar. Details can be found in [9]. Fig. 2 shows the uppermost grammar rule. In general, there are two query classes: (i) A *ModelStructureQuery* is used to analyze the structure of performance models. It can provide information about available services and resources, performance metrics as well as model variation points. (ii) A *PerformanceMetricsQuery* is used to trigger actual performance predictions. Both query classes are followed by a *ModelAccess* part that refers to a performance model instance.

3.1 Model Access

The query language is independent of a specific performance modeling formalism. Thus, to issue a query on a performance model instance, both the location of the model instance as well as a *DQL Connector* need to be specified. A

DQL Connector is specific for a performance modeling formalism and bridges the gap between performance model and DQL. Fig. 3 shows the model access initiated by keyword USING. The nonterminal *ModelFamily* refers to an identifier that serves as reference to a DQL Connector. The DQL Connector has to be registered in a central DQL Connector registry (see Section 4). The *ModelLocation* is a reference to a model instance location.

3.2 Model Structure Query

The user can request information about which services or resources are modeled, and for which model entities the referred model instance can provide which performance metrics. In DQL notation, a model entity is either a resource or a service. Fig. 4 shows a *ModelStructureQuery* initiated by keyword LIST. Using terminals ENTITIES, RESOURCES, SERVICES the user can query for respective entities, resources or services. The result is a list of entity identifiers that are unique for the referred model instance. Listing 1 illustrates a simple query example.

Besides querying for services and resources, the user can also query for available performance metrics. We denote a performance metric as *available* if the performance metric can be derived from the performance model instance. For example, for a Central Processing Unit (CPU) resource of an application server, the average utilization is typically available. Since the available performance metrics may differ from entity to entity, the user has to specify for which entity the available performance metrics should be listed. For that purpose, the user has to provide an *EntityReference-Clause*. A *EntityReferenceClause* is a comma-separated list of *EntityReferences* whose syntax is illustrated in Fig. 5.

An entity reference thus starts with a keyword identifying the entity type (RESOURCE or SERVICE) followed by an entity identifier and an optional *AliasClause*. Listing 2 shows a corresponding query example. In the example, the user queries for available metrics of a resource with identifier 'AppServer-CPU1' and a service with identifier 'newOrder'. For the re-

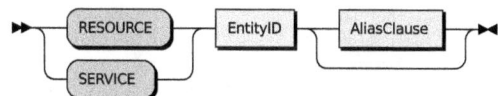

Figure 5: Entity Reference

```
LIST ENTITIES
USING connector@location;
```

Listing 1: List all Modeled Entities

```
LIST METRICS
 (RESOURCE 'AppServerCPU1' AS r,
  SERVICE 'newOrder' AS s)
USING connector@location;
```

Listing 2: List available Performance Metrics

source and the service the user sets alias r respectively alias s.

Furthermore, DQL allows querying for model variation points, also denoted as Degrees of Freedom (DoFs). The query result then is a list of DoF identifiers. The way how model variation points are modeled is independent from DQL, it depends on the DQL Connector. We provide an example of DoF queries in Section 3.3.2.

3.3   Performance Metrics Query

A *PerformanceMetricsQuery* is used to trigger performance predictions. Fig. 6 shows the syntax. First, we explain the parts of the query that are obligatory to write basic queries. For optional extensions such as query constraints, evaluations of DoFs and model revisions, we refer to Subsections 3.3.1, 3.3.2 and 3.3.3.

A user can specify the performance metrics of interest with wildcard '*' (all available performance metrics) or via the nonterminal *MetricReferenceClause*. *MetricReference-Clause* is a comma-separated list of *MetricReferences* that is shown in Fig. 7. A *MetricReference* either refers to a single metric or to an aggregated metric. A single metric is described by an *EntityIdOrAlias* followed by a dot and a *MetricId* or wildcard. Listing 3 shows a corresponding example where the utilization of an application server CPU and the average response time of a service is requested.

A specification of an aggregated metric consists of two parts. The first part (nonterminal *AggregateFunction*) selects an aggregate function. The set of supported aggregate functions is based on the descriptive statistics part of Apache Commons Math[1] and provides common statistical means, e.g. arithmetic and geometric mean, percentiles, sum and variance. The second part describes the list of performance metrics that should be aggregated. A wildcard ('*') can be used to iterate over all entities where a specific performance metric is available. An exemplary use of an aggregated met-

---

[1] http://commons.apache.org/proper/commons-math/

```
SELECT r.utilization, s.avgResponseTime
FOR RESOURCE 'AppServerCPU1' AS r,
    SERVICE 'newOrder' AS s
USING connector@location;
```

Listing 3: Trigger Basic Performance Prediction

```
SELECT MEAN(r1.utilization, r2.utilization)
FOR RESOURCE 'AppServer1' AS r1,
    RESOURCE 'AppServer2' AS r2
USING connector@location;
```

Listing 4: Query with Aggregated Metric

Figure 8: Constraint Clause

ric is shown in Listing 4, where the mean value of two application server utilization rates is computed. Note that the computation of the aggregate is provided by the DQL Query Execution Engine (QEE) (see Section 4) and *not* part of a DQL Connector. The DQL Connector only needs to support querying single metrics.

3.3.1   Constraints

In online performance and resource management scenarios, controlling performance predictions by specifying a trade-off between prediction accuracy and time-to-result can be important to act in time [16]. DQL allows the specification of such constrained performance queries. The syntax of the corresponding *ConstraintClause* is shown in Fig. 8. The *ConstraintID*s are DQL Connector specific and are intended to control the behavior of the underlying model solving process. For instance, a DQL Connector might support a constraint named 'FastResponse' to trigger fast analytical mean-value solvers or a constraint named 'Detailed' to trigger a full-blown simulation that may take a significant amount of time but is able to simulate, e.g., fine-grained OS-specific scheduling behavior [11]. Listing 5 shows a corresponding example.

3.3.2   Degrees of Freedom (DoF)

To evaluate DoFs, DQL provides several optional language constructs. Fig. 9 shows the syntax diagram of nonterminal *DoFClause*. A *DoFClause* refers to DoFs (nonterminal *DoFReferenceClause*) and an optional exploration strategy.

A *DoFReferenceClause* is a comma-separated list of nonterminal *DoFReference* that is shown in Fig. 10. It starts with a DoF identifier (with an optional alias) and is followed by *DoFVariationClause* that provides optional parameter settings (see Fig. 12). In its current version, DQL supports lists of parameter values of type Integer or Double as well as interval definitions of type Integer. Listing 6 shows an example with two DoFs. On the one hand, we vary the inter-arrival time of the open workload (values 0.1, 0.2, 0.3), on the other hand we vary the size of the database connec-

```
SELECT r.utilization, s.avgResponseTime
CONSTRAINED AS 'FastResponse'
FOR RESOURCE 'AppServerCPU1' AS r,
    SERVICE 'newOrder' AS s
USING connector@location;
```

Listing 5: Constrained Query

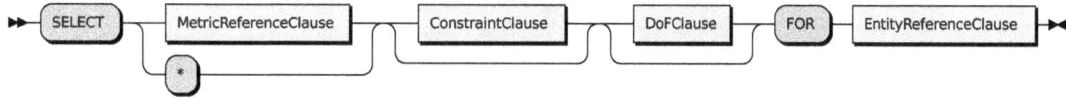

Figure 6: Performance Metrics Query

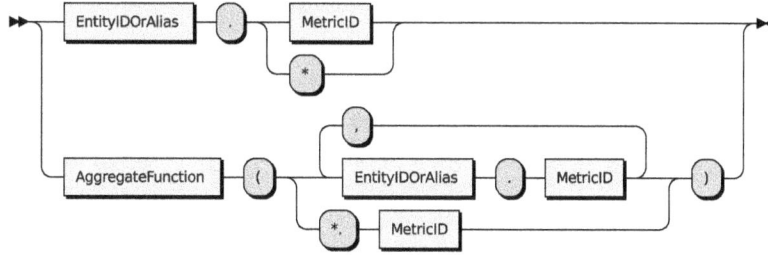

Figure 7: Metric Reference

Figure 10: DoF Reference

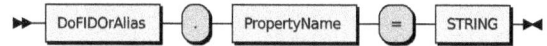

Figure 12: DoF Configuration Property

```
SELECT r.utilization, s.avgResponseTime
EVALUATE DOF
  VARYING
    'DoF_OpenWorkload_InterarrivalTime'
      AS dof1 <0.1, 0.2, 0.3>,
    'DoF_JDBCConnectionPool_Size'
      AS dof2 <10..30 BY 5>
FOR RESOURCE 'AppServerCPU1' AS r,
    SERVICE 'newOrder' AS s
USING connector@location;
```

Listing 6: DoF Query

```
SELECT s.avgResponseTime
EVALUATE DOF
  VARYING 'DoF_AppServerVM_Migration' AS dof1
  GUIDED BY 'MyExplorationStrategy'
  [dof1.targets =
    'PhysicalMachineA,PhysicalMachineB']
FOR SERVICE 'newOrder' AS s
USING connector@location;
```

Listing 7: DoF Query with Exploration Strategy

tion pool from 10 to 30 in steps of 5. Without an explicitly defined exploration strategy, the default exploration strategy is considered to be a full exploration. In the example, this means that $3 \times 5 = 15$ performance predictions are triggered. The query result set is then a list of 15 prediction results. Each prediction result contains the prediction for performance metrics r.utilization and s.avgResponseTime.

Using the optional *ExplorationStrategyID*, together with user-defined configuration properties (see Fig. 12), it is possible to trigger an alternative exploration strategy provided that the DQL Connector supports it. This is necessary for, e.g., DoFs representing migrations of Virtual Machines (VMs) from a physical host machine to another physical host machine. In these cases, it is the DQL Connector that

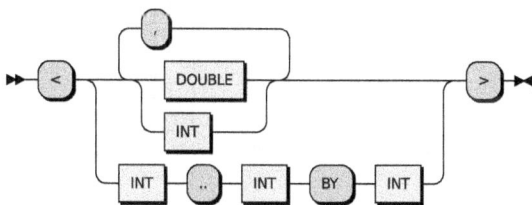

Figure 11: DoF Variation Clause

needs to provide means to iterate the configuration space. An integration of complex exploration strategies, e.g., multi-attribute Quality of Service (QoS) optimization techniques to derive Pareto-optimal solutions [18], is thus supported. Listing 7 shows a query example with an explicit exploration strategy. The query has one DoF, namely the physical machine where the appserver VM is assigned to. The configuration space, a set of two physical machines, is described as String as value of property targets. Note that the semantics of the configuration properties are specific for the DoF and the exploration strategy, i.e., the properties are not interpreted by DQL.

3.3.3 Temporal Dimension

As additional feature for Performance Metrics Queries, DQL offers facilities to access different revisions of a performance model. The assumption is that the model instances are annotated with a revision number and/or timestamp, i.e., that there is a chronological order.

In particular if the performance models are used in online scenarios, queries that allow the user to ask about performance metrics in the past, the development of performance metrics over time, or (together with a workload forecasting mechanism [12]) the development of performance metrics in the next time, are desirable. In online scenarios, performance model instances are typically part of a *performance*

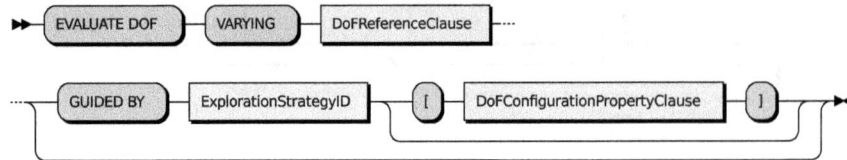

Figure 9: DoF Clause

```
SELECT r.utilization, s.avgResponseTime
FOR RESOURCE 'AppServerCPU1' AS r,
     SERVICE 'newOrder' AS s
USING connector@location
OBSERVE
   BETWEEN '2013-10-09 08:00:00'
   AND '2013-10-10 08:00:00'
   SAMPLED BY 1h;
```

Listing 8: Performance Metrics Over Time

```
SELECT r.utilization
FOR RESOURCE 'AppServerCPU1' AS r
USING connector@location
OBSERVE
   NEXT 2h SAMPLED BY 10M;
```

Listing 9: Anticipated Resource Utilization

data repository that integrates revisions of calibrated model instances and performance monitoring data [16].

DQL allows to express the temporal dimension in different ways: (i) with a time frame defined by a start and end, and (ii) with a time frame starting or ending with the current time and a time delta. Alternative (i) is used in the example in Listing 8. Resource utilization and service response time are queried for a specific time frame of one day. The results are sampled groups of one hour, possibly read from historical monitoring data, thus leading to a set of 24 result sets. The example shown in Listing 9 uses alternative (ii). The query requests the application server CPU utilization for the next two hours, sampled in twelve groups of ten minutes length each. This query triggers performance predictions, provided that a workload forecast for the next two hours is available.

4. TECHNICAL REALIZATION

Based on our query language as described in the previous sections, we provide an implementation of DQL based on an extensible software architecture. The DQL environment is built up on the OSGi Framework, Eclipse Modeling Framework (EMF) and Xtext[2]. In the following we present our realization of the DQL environment, describe internal data structures, outline control flows and give an outline for contributions of custom DQL Connectors.

4.1 Architecture and Components

The architecture of the DQL approach is shown in Fig. 13. It is realized in Java and based on the OSGi Framework [26,

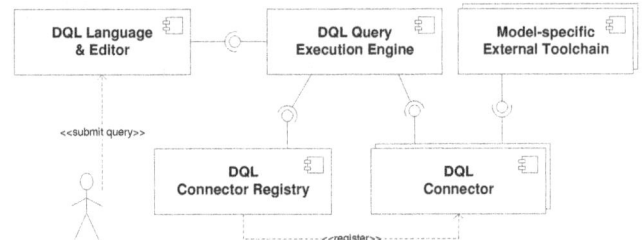

Figure 13: DQL System Architecture

27]. The current implementation is based on plain OSGi operations and runs on Eclipse Equinox[3]. Each component is encapsulated in a dedicated OSGi Bundle and activated on demand. For the interaction among Bundles, the *OSGi Service Layer* is utilized, which results in an event-driven interaction of components triggered by incoming queries.

The first component, *DQL Language & Editor*, provides the interface to users and offers an Application Programming Interface (API). The component is based on Xtext. Xtext is a framework to develop Domain-specific Languages (DSLs) and offers facilities to generate software artifacts such as text editor and parser based on a grammar specification. The component provides a DQL query parser and represents statements in an EMF model of the abstract syntax tree. For convenience, an Eclipse-based editor is also part of DQL. The Xtext-generated editor is customized, e.g., code assistance to obtain identifiers of model entities or available performance metrics. Furthermore, users can issue queries and visualize query results.

The second component, *DQL Query Execution Engine (QEE)*, provides the main execution logic in the DQL system architecture. Here, all tasks take place that are independent of a specific performance modeling formalism and prediction technique. The DQL QEE transforms queries into the internal abstraction for queries, the *Mapping Meta-Model*, which will be introduced in Sec. 4.2. The DQL QEE then selects an adequate DQL Connector to access the requested model instance, to execute the query, and to provide the results to the user. The DQL QEE also calculates aggregate functions if requested and performs the necessary pre- and post-processing steps.

The third component, a *DQL Connector*, provides functionality that is dependent on a specific performance modeling formalism and prediction technique. This includes accessing performance models, triggering the prediction process and providing additional information, e.g., about the model structure and available performance metrics. To integrate different approaches for performance prediction in a DQL environment, multiple DQL Connectors can be deployed to the OSGi run-time. As each DQL Connector

---

[2]http://www.eclipse.org/Xtext/

[3]http://www.eclipse.org/equinox/

comes with a unique identifier that needs to be referenced in a DQL query together with a model location, the DQL QEE can select a suitable DQL Connector to execute the query. To find a suitable DQL Connector, the *DQL Connector Registry* is used. The latter uses the *OSGi Declarative Service* interface to build and maintain an index of available DQL Connectors and their support for query classes.

Our proposed architecture allows to integrate various different performance modeling approaches and prediction techniques. Extensions of the DQL environment are primarily possible by contributing additional DQL Connectors. DQL Connector implementations can be partially, which allows to implement approaches that are not capable of all features of DQL.

4.2 Mapping Meta-Model

The Mapping Meta-Model is an abstraction layer to encapsulate different performance modeling formalisms, prediction approaches and requests resulting from DQL queries. An instance of the Mapping Meta-Model is used to (i) send a DQL query request from DQL QEE to a DQL Connector, to (ii) send the query result back from the DQL Connector to DQL QEE, and (iii) to present the query result to the user.

Fig. 14 shows the Mapping Meta-Model. EntityMapping is the top-level type and stores references to different parts of an architecture-level performance model or a related performance modeling formalism. Resource and Service reference elements of a performance model instance by an identifier. Both are derived from Entity which represents any kind of a performance-relevant model entity with an absolute identifier. Probe is attached to type Entity and either requests the prediction of a specific performance metric or, if the query has been processed, represents the value of the requested metric in an instance of a derived type of type Result, e.g., type DecimalResult. Thus, in case a Mapping Meta-Model instance contains instances of Probe, it is a request to be processed by a DQL Connector, otherwise it represents a result of a query. The type DoF represents the usage of a DoF in a query, or, if the query has been processed, represents a specific parameter setting of a DoF during a performance prediction. The type Aggregate is inserted in the post-processing step of DQL QEE and represents an aggregate computed on top of returned performance metric values. An example for the usage of the Mapping Meta-Model follows in the next section, detailed usage scenarios and exemplary instances are shown in [9, p. 52 ff.].

4.3 Query Execution

This section describes the sequence of query processing steps of Performance Metrics Queries. The process shown here focuses on the interaction to trigger a performance prediction and to return performance metrics to a user. Fig. 15 shows an overview of the execution sequence that consists of phases that are independent of a modeling formalism and phases that are modeling formalism specific, involving both the DQL QEE and a DQL Connector.

In the first phase, processing takes place at the DQL QEE. The steps are independent of a performance modeling formalism. They involve the look-up of a DQL Connector and its invocation, operations to parse the query, preparation of the request and the setting of configuration options for the DQL Connector. The relevant parts of the query are

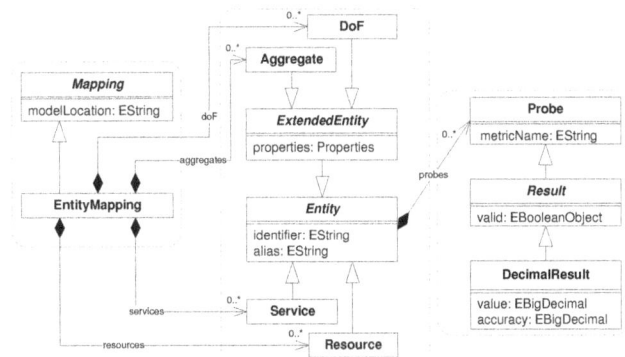

Figure 14: Mapping Meta-Model

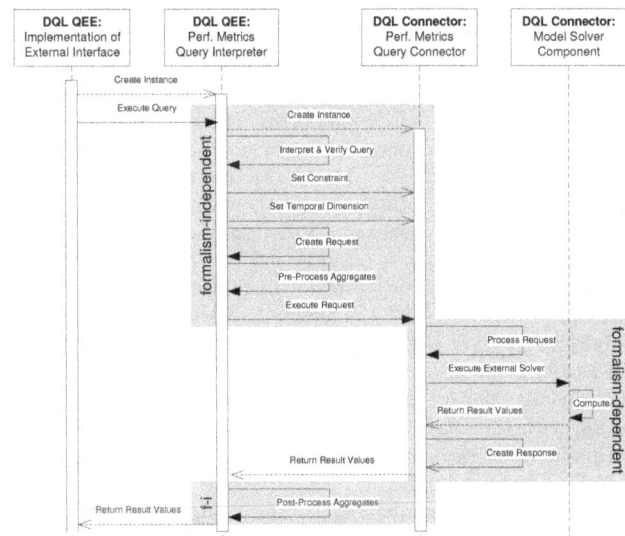

Figure 15: Execution of a Performance Metrics Query

transformed into an instance of the Mapping Meta-Model. When the necessary preparation of the request is done, the request is submitted for execution to the chosen DQL Connector. Here, steps are specific to a performance modeling formalism and prediction technique. The implementation of the DQL Connector is not constrained to specific tools but may use any kind of external service to obtain the result. When the result is available, it is represented as an instance of the Mapping Meta-Model and returned to the DQL QEE. In the third phase, post-processing operations take place. Here, the instance of the Mapping Meta-Model can be altered before it is sent back to the user as result set. This is the case if, e.g., aggregate functions are involved.

4.4 Developing DQL Connectors

To contribute a new DQL Connector, a developer has to accomplish three major tasks: (i) Create a new OSGi Bundle providing a `ConnectorProvider` as OSGi Service to the run-time, (ii) provide implementations for the relevant query classes and (iii) deploy the OSGi Bundle to the DQL environment.

For (i), the Bundle needs to be created and meta information needs to be added using the OSGi Component definition. The meta information is used to identify a DQL Connector and to register it with the DQL environment.

In (ii) the effort to implement the query classes depends on various factors and the underlying performance modeling formalism and prediction technique. `ConnectorProvider` is a factory class to create instances of classes implementing interfaces for each supported query class. For each query class a specialized interface exists, e.g. `ModelStructureQueryConnector` or `PerformanceMetricsQueryConnector`. Using this approach, in later revisions additional query classes can be added to DQL, while the compatibility with existing implementations is ensured. Within an interface, developers are free to implement only those methods for requests that should be handled by the resulting DQL Connector. For each method that requests the computation of a query, there is a corresponding method that asks for the support of the request. The DQL QEE checks for support of query requests before their invocation and in case of an unsupported method, it throws an exception. Thus, users are not required to implement each method.

To support basic queries, a DQL Connector needs to map the concepts of `Resource`, `Service` and `Probe` of the Mapping Meta-Model to representations in the performance modeling formalism that should be connected to DQL. As an entry point, we provide a DQL Connector skeleton that can be used to implement a custom DQL Connector. The skeleton contains all relevant meta-data and examples for the interaction with the DQL QEE.

Finally, after the implementation is done, in (iii) the OSGi Bundle has to be added to the run-time and queries can then be executed. As the DQL architecture is compliant to the OSGi Lifecycle Layer, a Bundle can be deployed and removed on demand.

5. RELATED WORK

DQL is related to existing work in the performance engineering domain and the model-driven engineering domain.

Intermediate Performance Models. We analyzed existing approaches in Software Performance Engineering (SPE) to reduce the efforts to transform performance models, to trigger predictions and to extract performance metrics [30]. The approaches focus on intermediate modeling techniques. The intermediate performance modeling techniques aim to generalize the transformation process from architecture-level performance models to predictive performance models utilizing an intermediate step. The approaches cope with the problem of having n input formats and m output formats (*N-to-M problem*) by providing an intermediate meta-model. The idea is that existing transformations from the intermediate meta-model to predictive performance models can be reused only by providing a transformation from an architecture-level performance model to the intermediate representation. Thus, the intermediate meta-model represents a generic performance abstraction for architecture-level performance models. Prominent examples are PMIF [32, 31], Core Scenario Model (CSM) [38] and Kernel LAnguage for PErformance and Reliability analysis (KLAPER) [10].

However, these approaches are focused on offline settings with predefined transformations, do not expose a unifying API and provide no means for a fine-granular result specification that can be used for tailored transformations as we propose with DQL.

Modeling of Degrees-of-Freedom. The analysis of DoFs in SPE is a challenging task that is common in performance prediction scenarios. In [19], DoFs are formalized for multi-objective optimization problems. Another approach is the Adaptation Points Meta-Model presented in [14]. It is mainly used to annotate model instances of system resource environments with DoFs that represent system configuration and resource allocation options. The approach also provides a language to express reconfiguration strategies [15]. Other methods for the exploration of the configuration space include, e.g., adaptive sensitivity analyses [37].

DQL is designed to integrate existing DoF modeling and corresponding exploration strategies. The mentioned approaches can thus be re-used with DQL.

Modeling Performance Metrics. As one approach for the modeling of metrics, the Objects Management Group (OMG) introduced the Structured Metrics Metamodel (SMM) as part of their Architecture Driven Modernization (ADM) roadmap [25]. Using SMM, any kind of structured metric can be modeled, measured and represented. As an example for the implementation of SMM, Measurement Architecture for Model-Based Analysis (MAMBA) [7, 6] supports a wide-range of SMM features. One notable addition of MAMBA is MAMBA Query Language (MQL) as interface to access the metrics. MQL has a Structured Query Language (SQL)-like textual syntax and supports aggregates on measurements.

However, the generic SMM and MAMBA approaches come with a significant overhead to model metric values because they are not focused on performance but aim at general analyses. They do not provide the necessary means to trigger performance predictions, but are an option for internal operations in DQL.

Domain-specific Languages. The structure of DQL is significantly influenced by the structure of SQL. SQL is a prominent example for a DSL as a query language. It allows hiding the actual data access and calculation from the user [4] and can thus be considered as role model.

6. EVALUATION

We evaluate the applicability and benefits of the proposed approach in the context of several representative case studies. We show how to query different established performance prediction techniques such as PCM [2], KLAPER [10] or QP-Nss, and how to query performance data repositories such as VMware vSphere. The results of our evaluation are presented in the following.

6.1 DQL Connector for PCM

Palladio Component Model (PCM) is a modeling language for component-oriented software systems and their deployment on resource landscapes. It is used to predict the performance of systems already at design time. The approach addresses the needs of users during design, development and maintenance phases of software systems and [29, 2]. PCM is ranked as a mature approach for performance modeling with sophisticated prediction techniques and comprehensive tool support [20]. PCM has been used successfully to model several different classes of component-oriented software systems [13, 28]. The Palladio Bench[4] is an Eclipse-based set of tools for modeling instances of PCM and to execute simulations of these models. With the Palladio Bench, users can develop model instances using editors with an Unified Modeling Language (UML)-based graphical syntax.

In our evaluation we demonstrate how to use PCM with DQL. The case study shows how DQL queries can be used to trigger complex performance predictions.

For the development of a DQL Connector for PCM, we analyze the meta-model of PCM and evaluate how to map PCM entities to the DQL Mapping Meta-Model. In the *Usage Model* of PCM, workload-specific modeling aspects are modeled by domain experts to represent usage scenarios of the modeled software system [29, p. 159 ff.]. We identify the types UsageScenario and EntryLevelSystemCall as relevant entities in the PCM Usage Model to be mapped to the type Service in the Mapping Meta-Model. In addition, PCM provides a *Repository Model* to model and store software components with their behavioral descriptions [29, p. 108 ff., p. 134 ff.]. Here, the type ExternalCallAction is relevant and mapped to the Service type of the Mapping Meta-Model. ExternalCallAction represents the call of a service provided by another component. Finally, in the *Resource Environment Model* of PCM the types ProcessingResourceSpecification and CommunicationLinkResourceSpecification can be mapped to the Mapping Meta-Model type Resource. The first type represents active resources of a hardware server, the latter type represents the network link of a hardware server.

In the DQL Connector implementation, we use the operations of the EMF API and Object Constraint Language (OCL) queries to access PCM instances and to obtain all necessary information for *Model Structure Queries*. For *Performance Metrics Queries*, we use the PCM Experiment Automation API to trigger performance predictions and the *SensorFramework*, which is part of the Palladio Bench, to obtain performance metrics. For the mapped type Resource, the *demanded time* and *utilization* are available as performance metrics, and for the mapped type Service, the metric *response time* is available. Furthermore, there are mappings for specific types of PCM to the type DoF.

```
SELECT AppServer_CPU.utilization,
  DBServer_CPU.utilization,
  DBServer_HDD.utilization
EVALUATE DOF
  VARYING '_TyV-MFBwEd6ActLj8Gdl_A'
          AS ClosedWorkloadPopulation <100, 200>
       '_Q8jwMEg9Ed2v5eXKEbOQ9g'
          AS ActionReplication <2, 8>
FOR RESOURCE '_5uTBUBpmEdyxqpPYxT_m3w@CPU'
    AS AppServer_CPU,
  RESOURCE '_tVi40Dq_EeCCbpF63PfiyA@CPU'
    AS DBServer_CPU,
  RESOURCE '_tVi40Dq_EeCCbpF63PfiyA@HDD'
    AS DBServer_HDD
USING pcm@'mediastore.properties';
```

Listing 10: Complex DoF Query in the Palladio Bench

The DQL Connector implementation is evaluated in a case study using the MediaStore example[5] [9]. First, we analyze the model structure of the example to obtain the necessary identifiers of the model entities in the MediaStore to trigger a performance prediction. Listing 10 is a DoF Query applied to the MediaStore example. Fig. 16 shows the DQL Workbench consisting of a query editor with the DoF Query in the upper half and a view to visualize results in the lower half. The query editor provides syntax highlighting as well as auto-completion features. The visualization is a tabular representation of the Mapping Meta-Model instance returned from the DQL API call. The query contains the request to vary two DoFs with two different DoF settings each. The first DoF references the workload intensity setting for the simulation using a closed workload, the second DoF modifies the behavior of a component by replicating an internal action. The query leads to a total of four PCM simulations and four independent result sets. For each simulation run, the result set contains the utilization rates of the *AppServer_CPU*, *DBServer_CPU* and *DBServer_HDD* together with the DoF setting for the simulation. All entities in the query, i.e. Resources and DoFs, are directly referenced from the MediaStore and the performance metrics are extracted from the SensorFramework after the simulation runs complete. As a complete PCM instance consists of several sub-models, they are referenced in a properties file as the model loction in the USING expression.

6.2 DQL Connector for KLAPER

KLAPER aims to generalize the transformation process from architecture-level performance models to predictive performance models through an intermediate step [10]. The approach copes with the problem of having n input formats and m output formats (N-to-M problem) by providing an intermediate meta-model. The idea is that existing transformations from the intermediate meta-model to predictive performance models can be reused only by providing a transformation from an architecture-level performance model to the intermediate representation. An implementation of the KLAPER approach is available as KlaperSuite [5].

Since the KLAPER intermediate meta-model represents a generic performance abstraction for architecture-level performance models and already provides support for several

---

[4] http://www.palladio-simulator.com/tools/

[5] http://sdqweb.ipd.kit.edu/wiki/PCM_3.3/Example_Workspace

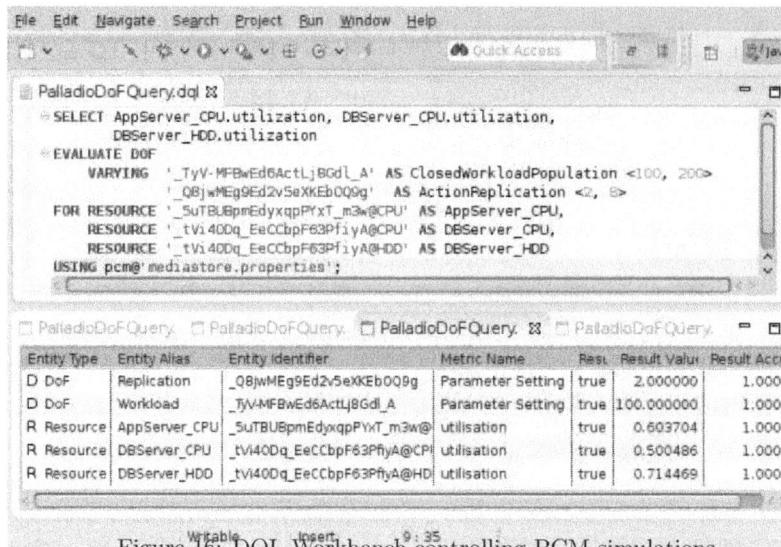

Figure 16: DQL Workbench controlling PCM simulations

modeling formalisms, it lends itself as a target model for a DQL Connector to evaluate the applicability of the DQL modeling abstractions.

We analyze the KLAPER meta-model and evaluate how to map its entities to the DQL Mapping Meta-Model. The KLAPER Meta-Model consists of different parts: (i) resources and their interaction, (ii) services and their dependencies, and (iii) the behavioral specification of services [10]. The behavior is specified in steps, which have properties to describe resource demands and performance and reliability characteristics. The Mapping Meta-Model captures only structural properties of performance models. The KLAPER types Resource and Service can be directly mapped to the Mapping Meta-Model types Resource and Service. Most of the behavioral types can be omitted in this mapping, but ActualParam and Workload can be used as DoF in the Mapping Meta-Model to express model variation points. Due to the nature of KLAPER as intermediate modeling language, the available performance metrics for Resource and Service depend on the used analysis model.

In summary, the mapping shows similarities of the structural abstractions used in KLAPER and the DQL Mapping Meta-Model. Furthermore, the KlaperSuite approach would benefit from an API to automate prediction processes and a mechanism to visualize results of performance predictions [5]. These points make KLAPER a valuable choice for a future DQL Connector implementation.

6.3 DQL Connector for VMware vSphere

VMware vSphere is a popular management product for VMware virtualization environments [36, 8]. vSphere offers several proprietary tools and an API that is being exposed through a web service [35]. We utilize vSphere as a performance data repository to obtain performance data from running vSphere environments.

We experienced several shortcomings of the vSphere API. The extraction of performance data needs a significant amount of repetitive source code, even for single data requests. The API and the underlying data model have a generic struc-

ture, which is hard to access in a simple way. To solve these shortcomings, we propose a DQL Connector implementation for vSphere. With vSphere, we evaluate the applicability of DQL to performance data repositories.

vSphere's underlying data center model organizes the data center resources in a deep hierarchy. The model covers the range from data center infrastructure down to resources of VMs like virtual Central Processing Units (vCPUs) and memory. In addition to live monitoring data, vSphere maintains historical performance data that can be accessed by corresponding API calls. The vSphere resource data structures can be mapped to the Resource type of the DQL Mapping Meta-Model. The Mapping Meta-Model does not provide means to represent the hierarchy represented in vSphere, but each vSphere resource layer can be mapped to an instance of Resource. There are no vSphere model elements that are mapped to the Service type of the Mapping Meta-Model.

With a DQL Connector for vSphere, the monitoring data access is simplified. The feature to query historical data as presented in Sec. 3.3.3 eases the access of historical data. Listing 11 is an example of an issued DQL query. The example retrieves information about the CPU and network utilization of a physical server and the mean vCPU utilization of two VMs deployed on this host. The utilization is obtained from a twelve hour time frame, in samples of one hour.

6.4 DQL Connector for Queueing Petri Nets

To show the general applicability of DQL and especially the DQL Mapping Meta-Model, we use the QPN formalism as target for an evaluation together with SimQPN as tool for simulating QPNs [1, 17]. Our goal is to show that even predictive performance models can be mapped to the Mapping Meta-Model and an integration with a DQL Connector is possible. Fig. 17 shows an example of a QPN model representing parts of the SPECjAppserver2004 benchmark application. There is an application server WLS accessing a database server DBS to serve customer requests. We refer

108

```
SELECT host.cpuUtilization, host.netUtilization
       MEAN(vm1.cpuUtilization,
            vm2.cpuUtilization)
FOR RESOURCE 'hostId' AS host,
    RESOURCE 'vm1Id' AS vm1,
    RESOURCE 'vm2Id' AS vm2
USING vsp@location
OBSERVE
    BETWEEN '2013-09-18 09:00:00' AND +12h
    SAMPLED BY 1h;
```

Listing 11: Example of a Basic Query for VMware vSphere

```
SELECT wls.utilization, order.serviceTime,
       dbs.utilization, dbsIo.utilization,
       dbsProc.population
FOR RESOURCE 'wlsCpuId' AS wls,
    RESOURCE 'dbsCpuId' AS dbs,
    RESOURCE 'dbsPoolId' AS dbsProc,
    RESOURCE 'dbsIo' as dbsIo,
    SERVICE 'newOrder' AS order
USING connector@location;
```

Listing 12: Example of a Basic Query for SimQPN

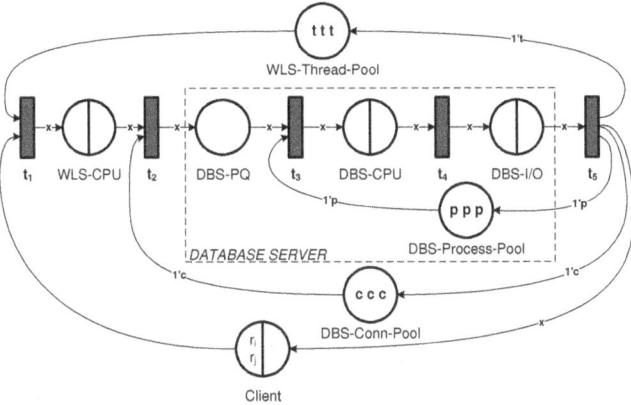

Figure 17: Part of SPECjAppserver2001 based on [17]

to [17] for the formal description of the referenced QPN and focus on the description of the mapping to DQL.

The example consists of the *queueing places* WLS-CPU, DBS-CPU and DBS-I/O. Each of these nodes consist of a queue, a scheduling strategy and a departure process. Queues are used to store *tokens* that are selected by a scheduling strategy to enter the departure process. The departure process depends on the token *color*, the token color's assigned processing time, and the number of available *servers*. We consider a queueing place in QPNs as an active resource to process requests and thus map it to the Resource type of the Mapping Meta-Model. The node Client is a special kind of queueing place and is used to model the clients in the system representing a *closed workload*. The processing time at this node is considered to be the *think time* required by clients to issue new requests. Client can also be mapped as active resource. The next family of model elements are *ordinary places*, i.e. WLS-Thread-Pool, DBS-PQ, DBS-Process-Pool and DB-Conn-Pool. These resources can be considered passive resources. These elements model shared resources within the network and are populated with a specified amount of tokens, i.e., the size of a thread pool. Client requests can only traverse the *transitions* t_i if the connected resources contain tokens. Otherwise the transitions do not *fire* and requests have to wait. Passive resources are mapped to the type Resource.

To model the workload imposed to the system, the Client queueing place is used. For a workload mix, different workload classes are specified as tokens of different colors. For each workload class $r_i, i \in \mathbb{N}$ a predefined amount of tokens is populated within the Client queue and, as different workload classes impose different processing steps, at each queueing

place the processing demand is parameterized accordingly. In DQL notation, $r_i, r_j, i \neq j$ represent two different instances of Service in the Mapping Meta-Model and i, j are considered as absolute identifiers of a Service instance.

After the type mapping of model entities is established, we describe how we obtain the available performance metrics. The mapping of available performance metrics is based on SimQPN [17]. For the different workload classes r_i, the *mean service time* is available. For the queueing places and ordinary places, the *token population*, *utilization*, *throughput* and *residence time* are available.

Listing 12 is an example to trigger a performance prediction for the QPN shown in Fig. 17. Here, the query is used to analyze the WLS-CPU and the service time of requests from the workload class *newOrder*. To determine if the *Database Server* is a bottleneck in this model, the utilization rates of DBS-CPU and DBS-IO are requested. Additionally, the population of DBS-Process-Pool is requested. In this scenario, either the resources of the Database Server are saturated or it is the process pool that is too small and thus a bottleneck. Furthermore, using DoFs the population of client can be varied to capture the behavior for different load levels.

7.   CONCLUSIONS & FUTURE WORK

We presented the Descartes Query Language (DQL), a novel query language to specify performance queries. It unifies the interfaces of available performance modeling formalisms and their prediction techniques to provide a common Application Programming Interface (API). DQL is independent of the employed modeling formalisms, hides low-level details of performance prediction techniques and thus reduces the manual effort and the learning curve when working with performance models. DQL allows expressing simple performance queries, that specify which performance metrics should be predicted under which scenario-specific constraints, and also allows complex queries that trigger an automated exploration of the configuration space of a performance model for a sensitivity analysis.

We implemented our approach using an extensible architecture. Support for specific performance modeling formalisms and prediction techniques can be easily integrated by adding new *DQL Connectors*. To demonstrate the applicability and benefits of our approach, we presented representative case studies for DQL showing how to query different established performance prediction techniques such as PCM [2], KLAPER [10] or Queueing Petri Nets (QPNs), and how to query performance data repositories such as VMware vSphere.

As part of our future work, we plan to integrate further DQL Connectors and to provide additional query classes. Additional query classes in DQL are intended to address problems like the automated detection of bottlenecks. These classes are intended as a step towards *goal-oriented queries* that can be used to express optimization problems. Furthermore, we encourage researchers and tool providers to contribute their own DQL Connectors to ease the usage of their prediction techniques.

8. REFERENCES

[1] F. Bause. Queueing Petri Nets - A formalism for the combined qualitative and quantitative analysis of systems. 1993.

[2] S. Becker, H. Koziolek, and R. Reussner. The Palladio component model for model-driven performance prediction. *Journal of Systems and Software*, 2009.

[3] F. Brosig, N. Huber, and S. Kounev. The Descartes Meta-Model. Technical report, Karlsruhe Institute of Technology (KIT), Karlsruhe, 2012.

[4] D. D. Chamberlin and R. F. Boyce. SEQUEL. In *FIDET '76*, New York, New York, USA, 1976. ACM Press.

[5] A. Ciancone, M. L. Drago, A. Filieri, V. Grassi, H. Koziolek, and R. Mirandola. The KlaperSuite framework for model-driven reliability analysis of component-based systems. *Software & Systems Modeling*, 2013.

[6] S. Frey, R. Jung, B. Kiel, and W. Hasselbring. MAMBA: Model-Based Software Analysis Utilizing OMG's SMM. 2012.

[7] S. Frey, A. van Hoorn, R. Jung, W. Hasselbring, and B. Kiel. MAMBA: A measurement architecture for model-based analysis. 2011.

[8] Gartner Inc. Magic Quadrant for x86 Server Virtualization Infrastructure, 2013.

[9] F. Gorsler. Online Performance Queries for Architecture-Level Performance Models. Master's thesis, Karlsruhe Institute of Technology (KIT), 2013.

[10] V. Grassi, R. Mirandola, E. Randazzo, and A. Sabetta. KLAPER: An Intermediate Language for Model-Driven Predictive Analysis of Performance and Reliability. Lecture Notes in Computer Science. Springer Berlin / Heidelberg, 2008.

[11] J. Happe, H. Groenda, M. Hauck, and R. H. Reussner. A Prediction Model for Software Performance in Symmetric Multiprocessing Environments. QEST '10, pages 59–68. IEEE Computer Society, 2010.

[12] N. R. Herbst, N. Huber, S. Kounev, and E. Amrehn. Self-Adaptive Workload Classification and Forecasting for Proactive Resource Provisioning. In *ICPE 2013*, New York, NY, USA, April 2013. ACM.

[13] N. Huber, S. Becker, C. Rathfelder, J. Schweflinghaus, and R. H. Reussner. Performance modeling in industry. In *ICSE '10*, New York, New York, USA, 2010. ACM Press.

[14] N. Huber, F. Brosig, and S. Kounev. Modeling dynamic virtualized resource landscapes. In *QoSA '12*, New York, New York, USA, 2012. ACM Press.

[15] N. Huber, A. van Hoorn, A. Koziolek, F. Brosig, and S. Kounev. Modeling Run-Time Adaptation at the System Architecture Level in Dynamic Service-Oriented Environments. *Service Oriented Computing and Applications Journal (SOCA)*, 2013.

[16] S. Kounev, F. Brosig, N. Huber, and R. Reussner. Towards Self-Aware Performance and Resource Management in Modern Service-Oriented Systems. In *SCC '10*. IEEE, 2010.

[17] S. Kounev and A. Buchmann. SimQPN - A tool and methodology for analyzing queueing Petri net models by means of simulation. *Performance Evaluation*, 2006.

[18] A. Koziolek, D. Ardagna, and R. Mirandola. Hybrid multi-attribute QoS optimization in component based software systems. *Journal of Systems and Software*, 86(10), 2013.

[19] A. Koziolek and R. Reussner. Towards a generic quality optimisation framework for component-based system models. *CBSE '11*, 2011.

[20] H. Koziolek. Performance evaluation of component-based software systems: A survey. *Performance Evaluation*, 2010.

[21] J. Li, J. Chinneck, M. Woodside, M. Litoiu, and G. Iszlai. Performance model driven QoS guarantees and optimization in clouds. In *ICSE '09*. IEEE, 2009.

[22] D. A. Menasce, L. W. Dowdy, and V. A. F. Almeida. *Performance by Design: Computer Capacity Planning By Example*. Prentice Hall PTR, Upper Saddle River, NJ, USA, 2004.

[23] Object Management Group. UML Profile for Schedulability, Performance, and Time Specification 1.1. 2005.

[24] Object Management Group. Meta Object Facility (MOF) 2.0 Query/View/Transformation, 2011.

[25] Object Management Group. Structured Metrics Metamodel 1.0, 2012.

[26] OSGi Alliance. OSGi Service Platform Core Specification - Release 4, Version 4.3. 2011.

[27] OSGi Alliance. OSGi Service Platform Service Compendium - Release 4, Version 4.3. 2012.

[28] C. Rathfelder, S. Becker, K. Krogmann, and R. Reussner. Workload-aware System Monitoring Using Performance Predictions Applied to a Large-scale E-Mail System. In *WICSA/ECSA '12*. IEEE, 2012.

[29] R. Reussner, S. Becker, E. Burger, J. Happe, M. Hauck, A. Koziolek, H. Koziolek, K. Krogmann, and M. Kuperberg. The Palladio Component Model. Technical report, Karlsruhe Institute of Technology (KIT), Karlsruhe, 2011.

[30] C. Smith and C. Lladó. Model Interoperability for Performance Engineering: Survey of Milestones and Evolution. Lecture Notes in Computer Science. Springer Berlin Heidelberg, 2011.

[31] C. U. Smith, C. M. Llado, and R. Puigjaner. Model Interchange Format Specifications for Experiments, Output and Results. *The Computer Journal*, 2010.

[32] C. U. Smith, C. M. Lladó, and R. Puigjaner. Performance Model Interchange Format (PMIF 2): A comprehensive approach to Queueing Network Model interoperability. *Performance Evaluation*, 2010.

[33] C. U. Smith and L. G. Williams. *Performance Solutions - A Practical Guide to Creating Responsive, Scalable Software*. Addison-Wesley, 2002.

[34] E. Thereska, D. Narayanan, and G. Ganger. Towards Self-Predicting Systems: What If You Could Ask "What-If"? In *DEXA '05*. IEEE, 2005.

[35] VMware Inc. VMware vSphere Web Services SDK, 2012.

[36] VMware Inc. vSphere Monitoring and Performance, 2013.

[37] D. Westermann, J. Happe, R. Krebs, and R. Farahbod. Automated inference of goal-oriented performance prediction functions. In *ASE 2012*, ASE 2012, New York, New York, USA, 2012. ACM Press.

[38] M. Woodside, D. C. Petriu, D. B. Petriu, H. Shen, T. Israr, and J. Merseguer. Performance by unified model analysis (PUMA). In *WOSP '05*, New York, New York, USA, 2005. ACM Press.

The Taming of the Shrew: Increasing Performance by Automatic Parameter Tuning for Java Garbage Collectors

Philipp Lengauer
Christian Doppler Laboratory MEVSS
Johannes Kepler University Linz, Austria
philipp.lengauer@jku.at

Hanspeter Mössenböck
Institute for System Software
Johannes Kepler University Linz, Austria
hanspeter.moessenboeck@jku.at

ABSTRACT

Garbage collection, if not tuned properly, can considerably impact application performance. Unfortunately, configuring a garbage collector is a tedious task as only few guidelines exist and tuning is often done by trial and error. We present what is, to our knowledge, the first published work on automatically tuning Java garbage collectors in a black-box manner considering *all* available parameters. We propose the use of iterated local search methods to automatically compute application-specific garbage collector configurations. Our experiments show that automatic tuning can reduce garbage collection time by up to 77% for a specific application and a specific workload and by 35% on average across all benchmarks (compared to the default configuration). We evaluated our approach for 3 different garbage collectors on the DaCapo and SPECjbb benchmarks, as well as on a real-world industrial application.

Categories and Subject Descriptors

D.3.4 [**Programming Languages**]: Processors—*Memory Management (Garbage Collection)*

General Terms

Performance, Experimentation, Measurement

Keywords

Garbage Collection, Configuration, Optimization, Java

1. INTRODUCTION

Garbage collection (GC) relieves programmers from reclaiming unused heap objects manually. This convenience has led to a wide-spread use of managed execution environments. Moreover, compacting garbage collectors allow for faster allocations because allocating an object is as simple as appending it to the end of the used heap, making expensive searches for a fitting memory block unnecessary.

ICPE'14, March 22–26, 2014, Dublin, Ireland.
Copyright 2014 ACM 978-1-4503-2733-6/14/03 ...$15.00.
http://dx.doi.org/10.1145/2568088.2568091.

However, while object allocations produce a direct and easy to understand performance impact, the costs of garbage collections are easily overlooked. Programmers are often unaware of the proportion their application spends on collecting garbage. They often also do not know that the lifetime and the modification patterns of objects can have a big influence on GC behavior. This unawareness may result in bad throughput, long response times, or even in applications that are completely unresponsive, due to long GC pauses.

Managed environments such as the Java virtual machine (VM), which we used in our research, often provide hundreds of parameters for tuning the garbage collector to the needs of a specific application. Each of these parameters comes with a default value that has been selected to fit the 'average application'. However, defining an average application is hard considering today's application diversity. Brecht et al. [8] observed that the default configuration of a garbage collector is rarely perfect for any given application. As only a few parameters come with guidelines on how to choose appropriate values, most operators stick to tuning only this small set of parameters, ignoring others which might lead to additional improvements. Due to the lack of documentation, they often exhaustively profile their application with different GC configurations, having only a faint clue of what they are doing. This attempt is tedious, and might even be futile, due to the sheer number of parameters, the lack of knowledge about the GC implementation, and the unknown influence of each parameter. Thus, operators have to spend a lot of time for tuning their application, often without finding a configuration that provides a significant improvement.

In this paper, we propose to use iterated local search to automatically find an application-tailored GC configuration in a black-box manner. We also present experiments showing that our approach decreases GC time and thus overall run time significantly on well-known Java benchmarks and on a real-world industrial application. Furthermore, we provide explanations on why an optimized configuration is well-suited for the respective application.

Our scientific contributions are a method for automatically tuning a Java garbage collector for a specific application as well as an empirical evaluation for a large set of benchmarks and three widely used garbage collectors.

We conducted our research in cooperation with Compuware Austria GmbH. Compuware develops leading-edge performance monitoring tools for multi-tier Java and .NET applications. In their own applications as well as in applications of their customers, high GC times are a problem that currently cannot be resolved with Compuware's tools.

This paper is structured as follows: Section 2 provides a basic understanding of garbage collection; Section 3 describes the problem we want to address in more detail; Section 4 illustrates our optimization approach; Section 5 describes our research method and experimental setup as well as detailed results; Section 6 discusses related work; Section 7 shows open research questions; and Section 8 concludes the paper.

2. GARBAGE COLLECTION IN HOTSPOT

This section provides a basic understanding of the garbage collectors available in the Java 8 Hotspot™ VM.

The *Serial GC* is the oldest of them and was designed for single-core machines with a small heap. It is a stop-the-world collector, meaning that it suspends the entire VM during garbage collection. Furthermore, it is a generational collector [16, 24], i.e., it divides the heap into a young generation and an old generation of objects. The young generation consists of a *nursery* and two survivor spaces, called *from space* and *to space*. New objects are allocated in the nursery. When the nursery is full, i.e., when there is not enough free space for a new object, all live objects are marked recursively (mark phase) based on the root pointers (i.e., static variables, local variables and pointers originating from other heap spaces). Subsequently, all marked objects in the nursery and in the from space are copied to the to space, and the two survivor spaces are swapped, resulting in an empty nursery and an empty to space (copy phase). Copying collectors waste memory because one survivor space is always empty, but they allow for fast collections because the collection time only depends on the number of live objects and not on the amount of garbage. When an object has survived a certain number of garbage collections in the young generation, it is tenured, i.e., it is copied into the old generation. If the old generation becomes full, it must be garbage collected as well. For the old generation, the Serial GC uses a mark-and-compact scheme. First, all live objects are marked; then all marked objects are moved towards the beginning of the heap, while all pointers to them are adjusted. Mark-and-compact collection is significantly slower than copying collection but it does not waste memory for empty semi-spaces. Furthermore, collections of the young generation (minor collections) are done much more frequently than collections of the old generation (major collections) because most objects die young, and thus the old generation does not fill up so quickly.

The *Parallel GC* uses the same heap layout and the same algorithms as the Serial GC. However, each phase is done in parallel by multiple threads, decreasing the garbage collection time considerably on multi-core processors.

The *Concurrent Mark and Sweep GC* is again generational and is based on the Parallel GC. However, it is not a stop-the-world collector. Rather, it reduces the time of major collections by doing parts of its work (e.g., marking) concurrently in the background while the application (the mutator) runs in the foreground and might even modify references, thus interfering with the collector. Using the Concurrent Mark and Sweep GC increases application responsiveness, especially if all available cores are used by the mutator. On the other hand, if the mutator is under heavy load and thus interferes with the collector heavily, the collector might have to revisit parts of the heap because references were modified by the mutator.

The *Garbage First GC* [10] is a generational collector. It divides the heap into a number of small regions; the young generation (i.e., the nursery and the survivor spaces) and the old generation are logical sets of such regions and are not contiguous. The marking phase is done concurrently, similar to the Concurrent Mark and Sweep GC, but regions with only a few live objects are collected first in order to free as much memory as possible per collection. Thus, this collector can deal with large heaps efficiently, because long collections of many regions arise rarely.

3. PROBLEM

The Hotspot™ VM [20] comes with 681 parameters (1338 with a debug build), most of them documented only by sparse comments in the VM's source code. These parameters are only exposed with the `PrintFlagsFinal` VM flag.

To get an overview of this mass of parameters, we categorized them into several groups, e.g., compiler parameters, memory parameters, or threading parameters. As our goal was to parameterize the garbage collector, we focused on the memory group. This group was again split into one subgroup for each garbage collector of the Hotspot™ VM. We also introduced an additional group of parameters affecting all garbage collectors, e.g., parameters setting the field layout of an object or the size of allocation buffers. Every group is stripped from all tracing and debugging flags so that only performance-relevant parameters remain.

Table 1 shows all subgroups of the memory group and their respective sizes.

Group	Parameters
Generic Memory	17
Parallel GC (Parallel Old GC)	37
Garbage First GC (G1)	45
Concurrent Mark and Sweep (CMS)	103
Parallel New GC (ParNew)	41
Serial GC	37
	280

Table 1: Memory parameter groups

Some parameters, such as the preferred heap size and just-in-time compiler, are chosen automatically at startup by the virtual machine. This mechanism, called *Ergonomics* [17], takes the underlying hardware (e.g., the number of processors) as well as a pause-time goal into account to choose values for a small set of parameters automatically. For example, the parameter `ParallelGCThreads` is automatically set to the number of available processors when using a parallel stop-the-world collector. Unfortunately, this mechanism takes only static information into account and cannot adjust parameters in response to program characteristics.

Furthermore, parameters are often added or removed from one VM release to the next, making previous tuning results obsolete. If an application is executed on different VMs, the GC parameters might differ entirely. Tuning GC parameters automatically counteracts these problems in addition to improving performance.

4. APPROACH

Our approach is to use iterated local search for tuning a garbage collector to the specific needs of a given application.

The core of this method is an optimization algorithm that adjusts parameter values so that the performance is maximized. For the optimization, we need a parameter model describing the available parameters and their respective legal values, as well as an objective function able to evaluate a given configuration by returning a single value describing the induced performance. This function will profile the application with the given parameter values because it cannot compute or guess the induced performance in advance. Figure 4 shows the individual elements of our approach.

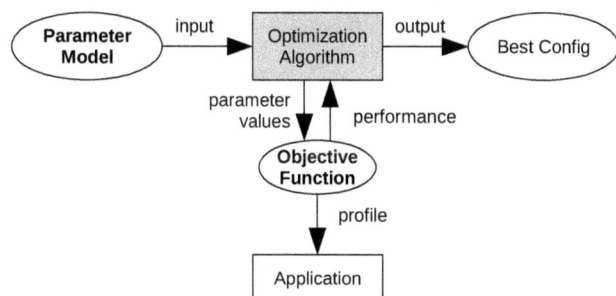

Figure 1: Approach

For the optimization algorithm we decided to use ParamILS [14], an existing optimization framework that is publicly available and easy to use. In the future, however, we also plan to try other optimization frameworks.

4.1 Parameter Model

The input of the optimization algorithm defines the parameter model, with the names of all available parameters, their valid values, and their start values. Furthermore, it includes a description of the relationships between parameters, e.g., parameter A must not be set if parameter B has a certain value. Figure 2 shows a partial model of four GC parameters in ParamILS-specific syntax.

```
XX:TargetSurvivorRatio {25, 50, 75} [50]
XX:?DisableExplicitSystemGC {0, 1} [0]
XX:?UseAdaptiveSizePolicy {0, 1} [0]
XX:?UseAdaptiveSizePolicyWithSystemGC {0,
    1} [0]

Conditionals:
XX:?UseAdaptiveSizePolicyWithSystemGC |
    XX:?DisableExplicitSystemGC in {0}
XX:?UseAdaptiveSizePolicyWithSystemGC |
    XX:?UseAdaptiveSizePolicy in {1}
```

Figure 2: ParamILS input example

The parameter XX:TargetSurvivorRatio is a numeric parameter with the legal values 25, 50, and 75, and a start value of 50. The parameters XX:?DisableExplicitSystemGC, XX:?UseAdaptiveSizePolicy, and XX:?UseAdaptiveSizePolicyWithSystemGC are boolean parameters, 0 being false and 1 being true. As the names suggest, UseAdaptiveSizePolicy enables an adaptive heap-resizing policy during garbage collection. XX:?UseAdaptiveSizePolicyWithSystemGC enables this policy also when System.gc() is called, whereas System.gc() calls can be disabled by setting XX:?DisableExplicitSystemGC to true. Obviously, allowing

adaptive resizing with System.gc() makes no sense if adaptive resizing was disabled in the first place. Such constraints are defined in the last section of the input file, headed by the Conditionals keyword. Each line in this section describes that the first parameter is only to be set if the value of the second parameter is within the specified values. This can reduce the search space for the optimization algorithm significantly, producing better results faster.

4.2 Objective Function

In addition to the parameter model, we need an objective function translating given parameter values into a performance metric. In our case, the objective function is implemented by a script that starts a Java application several times and extracts its garbage collection time via *Java Management Beans* and returns the median to the optimization algorithm. As we extract the aggregated garbage collection time, the optimization algorithm will optimize for overall throughput. Other optimization goals that could be considered will be briefly discussed in Section 7.

4.3 ParamILS

When provided with a parameter description (i.e., a parameter model) and an appropriate problem launcher (i.e., an objective function), ParamILS can optimize the parameter settings for any kind of problem. For finding an optimum, the solution space (i.e., all sets of parameter values) is searched using an iterated local search plus a heuristic for making random changes to the configuration from time to time in order to avoid getting stuck in local minima. To determine the quality of a configuration, the quality metric value returned by the objective function is used. This approach is very similar to *hill climbing*, i.e., it changes one parameter at a time until no more improvement is observed, then it repeats the same with the next parameter, and so on. Furthermore, ParamILS introduces a technique called adaptive capping, which aborts runs as soon as they become obvious to not yield any improvement. The optimization algorithm and its implementation are explained in more detail in Hutter et al. [14].

5. EXPERIMENTS

We used our approach described in Section 4 to find the best GC parameter settings for several Java benchmarks using an iterated local search algorithm that tunes parameter values in order to find the smallest overall GC time for a given application and a given input. This section describes our experiments and their results for three different GCs.

5.1 Setup and Research Method

Figure 3 shows the setup of our experiment. As described in Section 4, we use ParamILS as a configuration optimizer. The output of the optimizer, i.e., the best configuration found, is piped to the configuration minimizer, which eliminates all parameters that retained their default values. This minimum configuration is used by the validator to execute several runs, both with the default configuration and with the minimum configuration, to make more detailed quality measurements.

Since the number of possible parameter configurations is huge, the optimizer cannot explore them all. So we have to stop after a certain number of runs or after a certain time. We decided to stop the optimization of an application after

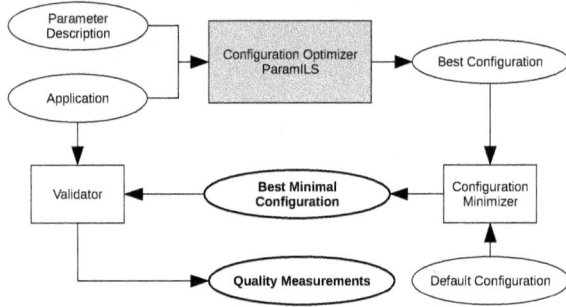

Figure 3: Experiment setup

4 hours. Experiments showed that not much improvement is to be expected after that time for most of our benchmarks, but of course different termination criteria could be used for other experiments. Our experiments optimize for throughput, i.e., the quality metric to be minimized is the overall GC time in an application. Other optimization objectives are discussed in Section 7.

The following subsections describe our research method in more detail, i.e., the selection of benchmarks, the selection of garbage collectors, and the definition of quality metrics.

5.1.1 Benchmarks

To get a broad set of benchmarks, we used applications from various sources. We looked at the DaCapo 2009 benchmark suite, based on Blackburn et al. [7, 1], and selected seven GC-intensive benchmarks, i.e., eclipse, h2, jython, sunflow, tomcat, tradesoap and xalan. Unfortunately, eclipse crashes on Java 8 [20] and was therefore excluded from our selection. In addition to that, we selected the SPECjbb 2005 benchmark which puts a lot of pressure on the garbage collector. The DaCapo benchmarks were always executed with the largest input supported and the SPECjbb benchmark was executed with eight warehouses. For each of these benchmarks, we experimentally determined the minimum heap required for execution. Table 2 shows our benchmarks as well as their minimum heap sizes and average run times when using Java 8 and the Parallel GC.

Benchmark	Min. Heap [MB]	Run Time [s]
DaCapo h2	300	36.89
DaCapo jython	40	11.03
DaCapo sunflow	10	6.49
DaCapo tomcat	75	6.08
DaCapo tradesoap	25	18.18
DaCapo xalan	10	11.00
SPECjbb	300	451.68

Table 2: Benchmarks used for the experiments

5.1.2 Garbage Collectors

To show that our approach is applicable to any garbage collector, we conducted our experiments with three different garbage collectors and their respective parameters:

- The *Parallel GC* is the default garbage collector, making it one of the most frequently used GCs.

- The *Concurrent Mark and Sweep GC* was selected because the customers of our industrial partner make heavy use of it.

- The *Garbage First GC* (also called G1 GC) was included because is uses a relatively new algorithm, and is therefore quite different from the other garbage collectors. Furthermore, it enjoys increasing popularity with large server applications.

We excluded parameters setting the heap size because there is ample evidence (e.g., Yang et al. [27], Brecht et al. [8]) that the heap size has a significant impact on garbage collector performance. Furthermore, if we enable the optimizer to adjust the heap size as well, it will always choose the biggest allowed value.

5.1.3 Quality Metrics

We defined four quality metrics for determining the quality of a garbage collector configuration:

- The *garbage collection time* is the overall time the benchmark spent on collecting garbage. Minimizing this metric is the main goal of our optimization.

- The *run time* or *throughput* determines the impact of the optimized configuration on the overall application behavior. The DaCapo benchmarks process a given input and terminate subsequently, making the run time a good performance indicator. The SPECjbb benchmark, on the other hand, runs for a fixed amount of time, making the run time a useless metric. In this case, we rather measure the throughput.

- The *garbage collection frequency* describes the number of garbage collection cycles that occurred during the benchmark execution. Together with the garbage collection time, this metric can be used to estimate the average length of garbage collection pauses.

- The *peak heap usage* indicates the maximum amount of live memory during benchmark execution.

Whenever these metrics were measured, we executed a number of warm-ups first in order to stabilize the caches and to JIT-compile all the hot spots.

We examined all optimized configurations and their induced behavior by injecting custom agents into the VM, which extract information such as the GC frequencies and the GC times. These agents use the *Java Virtual Machine Tool Interface* (JVMTI) to access VM-internal information.

In order to better understand the results and offer detailed interpretations, we also used the built-in GC logging mechanism as well as VM instrumentation to collect additional data, e.g., the run time of individual GC phases or the average object ages. Our custom VM does not introduce any costly computations, but rather aggregates and exposes already existing information. For example, the average object age is computed during the marking phase, because the GC has to traverse all objects anyway. Nevertheless, to reduce the risk of tainted results, all figures in the following subsections have been created without GC logging and with an unmodified VM.

5.1.4   Hardware and Software

We ran our experiments on an Intel® Core™ i7-3770 CPU @ 3.40GHz×4 (8 Threads) on 64-bit with 18GB RAM running Ubuntu 12.10 Quantal Quetzal with the Kernel Linux 3.5.0-38-generic. All unnecessary services were disabled and the experiments were always executed in text-only mode. We used the OpenJDK 8 Early Access Release b100 [20], because significant changes were made to the garbage collectors compared to Java 7, e.g., the permanent generation was removed.

5.2   Results

This subsection provides an overview of the results of our experiments. A detailed discussion will follow in Section 5.3.

Figures 4 - 7 show the measured quality metrics for all benchmarks with a specific garbage collector. Each subfigure is a histogram with 2 bars per benchmark; the left (dark) bars indicate the results of the default parameter configurations; the right (light) bars show the results of the optimized parameter configurations. All values are medians of multiple runs, normalized with respect to the value of the default configuration. We used the median because it is more realistic than the peak performance, more stable with respect to outliers than the arithmetic mean, and more meaningful for our metrics than the geometric mean. The error interval on top of each bar indicates the standard deviation. Due to the normalization, a large error interval on a long running benchmark might indicate the same standard deviation as a smaller error interval in a shorter running benchmark (cf. Table 2). For benchmarks that execute for a fixed amount of time, i.e., SPECjbb, the throughput is normalized by dividing the default configuration throughput by the optimized throughput. The rightmost two bars represent the arithmetic mean of the individual speedups.

Figure 4 shows the results of the parameter optimization for the Parallel GC without any memory pressure applied, i.e., the VM is allowed to increase the heap size arbitrarily. Please note that the heap usage diagram has a different scale and that the heap size is not explicitly set but is a result of the optimized configuration. The results show that the overall run time is decreased by 9% in the tradesoap benchmark and shows slight speedups for almost all other benchmarks. Of course, the impact on the overall run time depends on how much time a benchmark spends for garbage collection. The GC time, on the other hand, has been reduced significantly for all benchmarks. With the optimized parameter configuration, the tradesoap benchmark does not need any garbage collection at all, reducing the GC frequency and the GC time to zero. Sure enough, these results are mostly due to the fact that the heap size has been increased by a factor of 13. Large heaps lead to less garbage collections, because it takes longer to fill the heap. Furthermore, the GC time depends only on the number of live objects which is independent of the heap size.

To show that the GC time depends on more than just the heap size and that it can be reduced by optimizing the GC configuration, we decided to artificially apply memory pressure to all benchmarks. This was done by experimentally determining the minimum heap size for a benchmark and setting the actual heap size to a multiple of that value. Table 2 shows the determined minimum heap sizes of our benchmarks. For the following experiments, we decided to use a maximum heap size that is twice the minimum heap size

for every benchmark because this seems to create a realistic memory pressure. When the memory pressure is decreased, i.e., the heap is increased, measurements have shown that the results converge to the values shown in Figure 4.

5.2.1   Parallel GC

Figure 5 shows the results of optimizing the Parallel GC with twice the minimum heap size. Due to the memory pressure, the heap cannot grow arbitrarily but the memory manager must get along with the space available. In some cases, i.e., in h2, jython, and tomcat, the heap usage is higher than with the default configuration, although it is below the allowed maximum heap size. Thus, the optimized configuration obviously uses the available space more efficiently than the default configuration, e.g., by choosing better sizes for the survivor spaces. The GC time and the GC frequency have both been reduced on all benchmarks. Compared to the results without memory pressure (Figure 4) the overall run time speedup is significantly higher (by up to 42% for xalan) because the garbage collection ratio is bigger, i.e., due to memory pressure the application spends a larger percentage of its run time on garbage collection. The h2 and the SPECjbb benchmarks show less improvement than the others, because due to their larger execution time, fewer runs could be executed by the optimizer in the fixed time frame.

5.2.2   Concurrent Mark and Sweep GC

The results of optimizing the Concurrent Mark and Sweep GC (Figure 6) show only small improvements, indicating that the default parameter settings were more or less adequate for our benchmarks. One might also question the statistical significance of the results considering the small speedups and their standard deviations.

5.2.3   Garbage First GC

Optimizing the Garbage First GC yields results (Figure 7) that are similar to those of the Parallel GC. Some benchmarks show a remarkable reduction in GC time, which is, however, not observable in the overall run time, because GC time seems to be only a small fraction of the run time in this configuration. Nevertheless, the overall run time of SPECjbb could be reduced by 10%. The sunflow benchmark uses only a fraction of the heap space available with the default configuration. The optimized configuration utilizes the available space better, resulting in a spike in the heap usage. Furthermore, the standard deviation is much higher compared to the Parallel GC. This indicates that, due to the large number of small heap regions, the Garbage First GC is easily influenced by external factors, such as the object allocation order or the heap layout. The optimization on tradesoap does not find a configuration resulting in a significant speedup, indicating that the default configuration is already well suited for this application. The GC frequency of h2 increased whereas the GC time dropped, meaning that although the application ended up collecting garbage more often, the individual GC pauses where shorter, resulting in an overall reduction of GC time.

5.3   Detailed Results and their Interpretation

We have selected two benchmarks for which we will discuss the results in more detail. These benchmarks have been selected based on their differing optimum configurations.

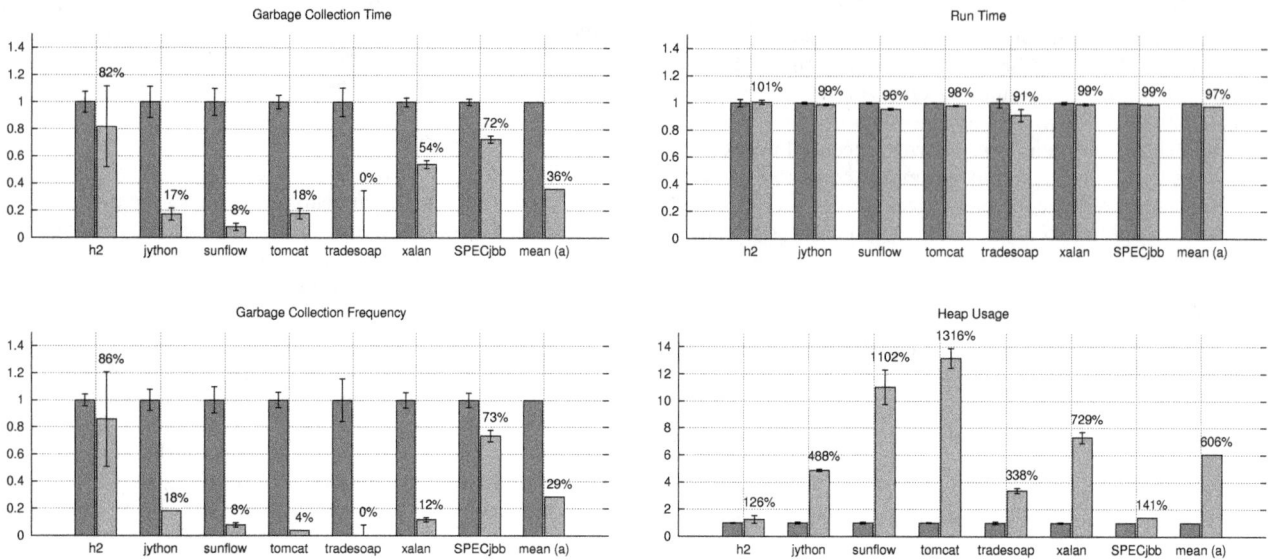

Figure 4: Optimization results for the Parallel GC (normalized, without memory pressure)

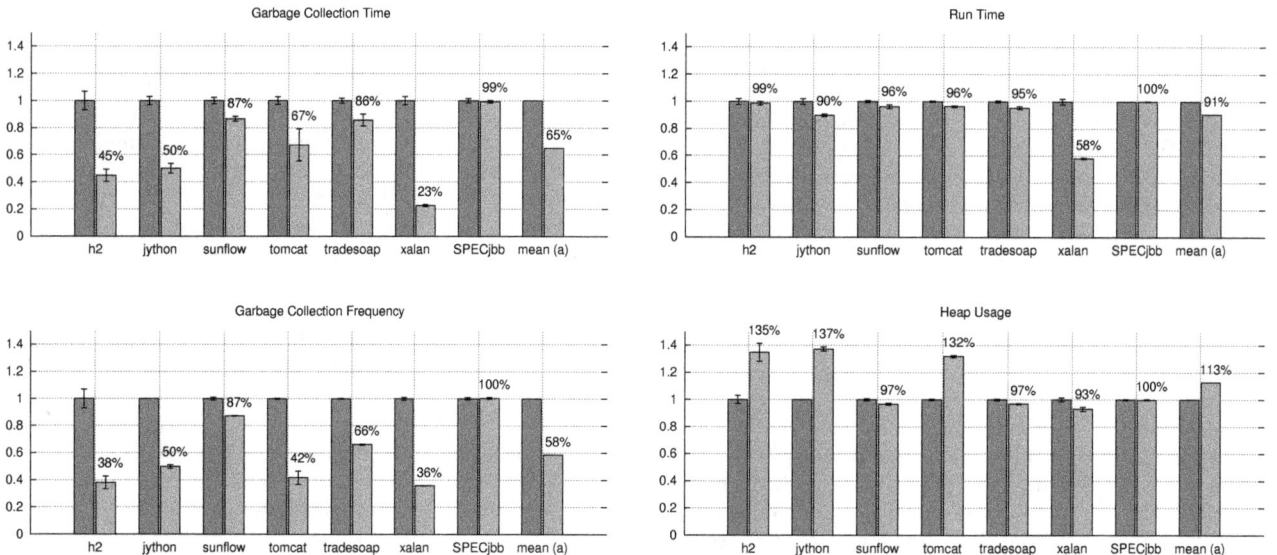

Figure 5: Optimization results for the Parallel GC (normalized, with memory pressure)

5.3.1 Parallel GC applied to xalan

This section looks at the optimization of the Parallel GC when running the DaCapo xalan benchmark. Figure 8 shows the GC frequencies, the GC times, and the heap usage for the xalan benchmark broken down into different heap subspaces and their respective GC algorithms. The left (dark) bars are the values produced by the default configuration, and the right (light) bars are produced by the optimized configuration. *Scavenge* denotes the collection of the young generation and *MarkSweep* the collection of the old generation. *Eden Space* and *Survivor Space* together make up the young generation (the second survivor space required by the scavenge algorithm is not shown as it is always empty). Please note that this figure shows the peak space usage and

not the actual space size. However, the peak usage is equal to the size in the eden space and the old generation because GCs mostly occur when a space is full. The size of the survivor space depends on the usage and the value of the *TargetSurvivorRatio* parameter. The default value for this parameter is 50, i.e., the survivor space is sized so that up to 50% are occupied after a minor GC, meaning that the size of the survivor space is approximately twice the usage. Figure 8 shows that both the GC frequency and the GC time dropped dramatically in the optimized configuration when more space was given to the young generation. If the young generation is larger it needs less frequent collections and thus gives young objects more time to die between collections. If objects die before they are tenured, the old generation be-

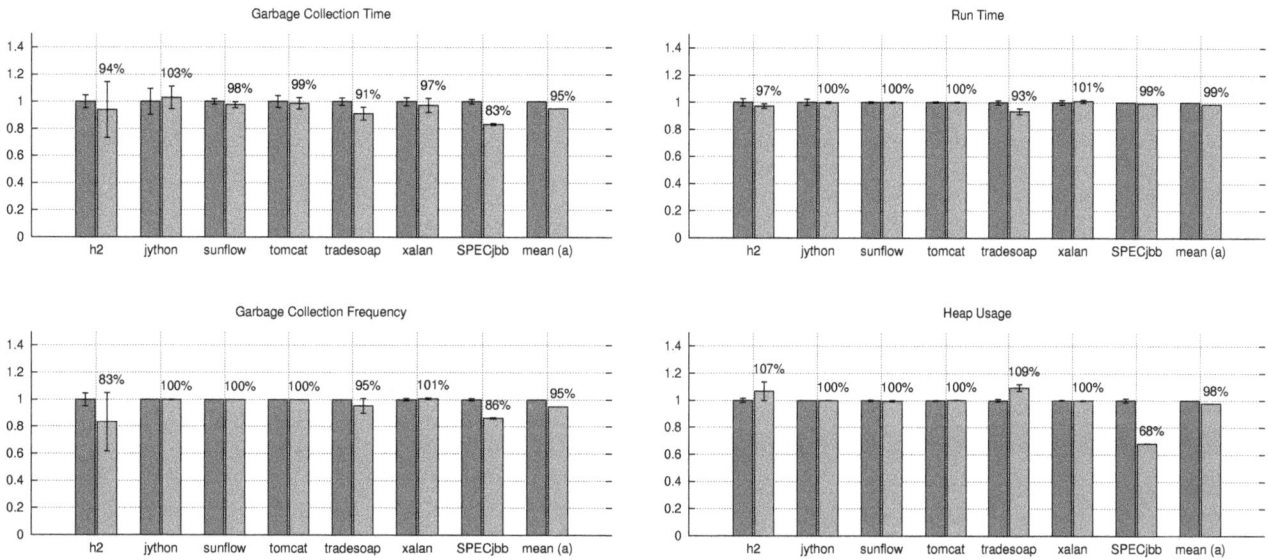

Figure 6: Optimization results for the CMS GC (normalized, with memory pressure)

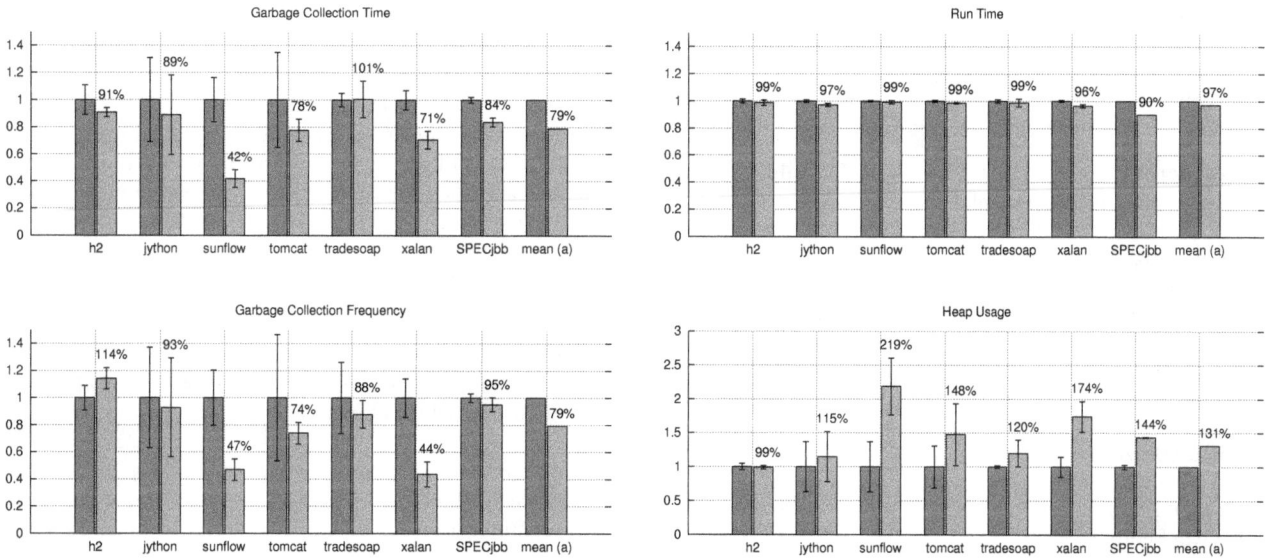

Figure 7: Optimization results for the G1 GC (normalized, with memory pressure)

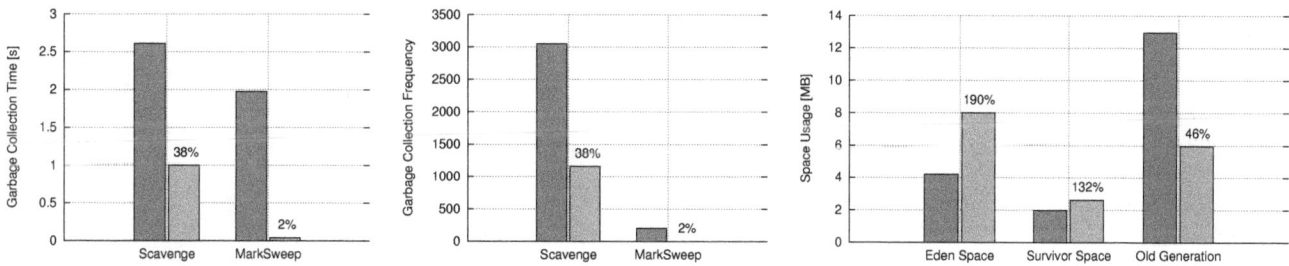

Figure 8: Detailed optimization results for xalan (Parallel GC with memory pressure)

117

comes smaller and the expensive *MarkSweep* GC can run less frequently. Obviously, the xalan benchmark has many short-living objects ([7]) so that the optimized configuration is beneficial here.

Figure 9 shows that with the optimized configuration every *Scavenge* run frees more than four times as much memory as with the default configuration. This confirms our conjecture that in the optimized configuration most objects die before the next GC run.

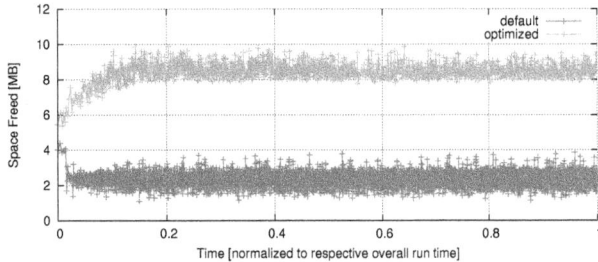

Figure 9: Amount of memory freed in the young generation for xalan (Parallel GC with memory pressure)

The optimized configuration and its interpretation.
Table 3 compares the optimized (new) parameter values with their default (old) values for the xalan benchmark. Parameters that retained their default values are excluded.

Parameter	old	new
AdaptiveSizeDecrementScaleFactor	4	2
AdaptiveSizeMajorGCDecayTimeScale	10	5
AdaptiveSizePolicyCollectionCostMargin	50	40
AdaptiveSizeThroughPutPolicy	0	1
BindGCTaskThreadsToCPUs	-	+
CollectGen0First	-	+
MinHeapFreeRatio	40	20
MinSurvivorRatio	3	1
NewRatio	2	1
OldPLABSize	1024	2048
PLABWeight	75	80
ResizeOldPLAB	+	-
SurvivorPadding	3	2
TargetSurvivorRatio	50	70
TenuredGenerationSizeIncrement	20	30
TenuredGenerationSizeSupplement	80	85
TenuredGenerationSizeSupplementDecay	2	16
UseAdaptiveGCBoundary	-	+
UseAdaptiveGen.SizePolicyAtMajor	+	-
UseAdaptiveGen.SizePolicyAtMinor	+	-
UseAdaptiveSizeDecayMajorGCCost	+	-
UseAdaptiveSizePolicyFootprintGoal	+	-
YoungGenerationSizeIncrement	20	30
YoungPLABSize	4096	1024
YoungGenerationSizeSupplement	80	75
YoungGenerationSizeSupplementDecay	8	2

Table 3: Optimized parameter configuration for xalan (Parallel GC with memory pressure)

The *NewRatio* parameter configures the size ratio between the old generation and the young generation, i.e., a default

value of 2 results in an old generation that is twice as big as the young generation. Changing this value to 1 doubles the size of the young generation, thus cutting the GC frequency of the young generation at least in half. Enabling the *UseAdaptiveGCBoundary* flag allows the VM to move the boundary between heap spaces, making it easier to further increase the size of the young generation. Decreasing the *MinSurvivorRatio* from 3 (i.e., the eden space is at least three times as big as a single survivor space) to 1 results in bigger survivor spaces. Therefore, more objects can be kept in the young generation for a longer time before they are promoted to the old generation. Additionally, increasing the *TargetSurvivorRatio* enables a bigger fraction of the survivor space to be occupied and thus allows more live objects in the survivor spaces without forcing a premature promotion. *CollectGen0First* forces a collection of the young generation just before collecting the old generation, avoiding a major GC immediately followed by a minor GC. Furthermore, the *YoungPLABSize* (i.e., the size of the young-to-old promotion buffer) is decreased because it is hardly used in xalan. The *OldPLABSize* (i.e., the size of the promotion buffer used for compacting objects in the old generation), is increased to reduce the frequency of buffer overflows during major GCs. Furthermore, the optimized configuration disables several adaptive policies (e.g., *UseAdaptiveGenerationSizePolicyAt-Minor*, *UseAdaptiveGenerationSizePolicyAtMajor*, and *Use-AdaptiveSizePolicyFootprintGoal*) that would interfere with other chosen parameter values. Please note that these dependencies were not in our parameter model, but were found automatically during optimization. The optimized configuration also contains some false positives, such as *Adaptive-SizeThroughPutPolicy*, *AdaptiveSizeDecrementScaleFactor*, and *AdaptiveSizeMajorGCDecayTimeScale*. These parameters were modified by the optimization algorithm before it disabled the corresponding policies. There was not enough time for the optimization algorithm to determine that these parameters are now without any impact.

Note that this parameter configuration is specific for the xalan benchmark and would not necessarily produce good results for other benchmarks.

Optimization.
Figure 10 shows the progress when optimizing the parameter configuration for xalan. The horizontal axis represents

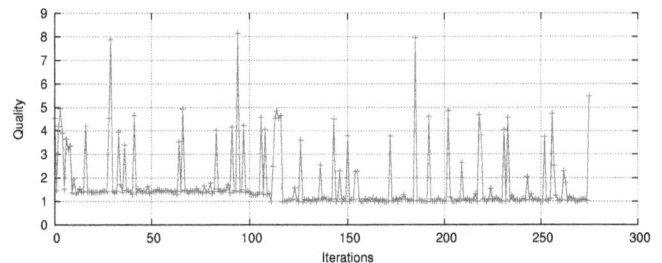

Figure 10: Optimization progress for xalan (Parallel GC with memory pressure)

the number of iterations, the vertical axis represents the quality of the respective iterations (i.e., GC time in seconds). As expected, a relatively good configuration is found very early. Afterwards, the algorithm tries to further optimize the configuration, occasionally making a bad choice resulting in spikes, but returning immediately if a change does not show an improvement. In all our benchmarks, a good configuration was already found after a few iterations, and no further significant improvements were made after a total optimization time of 4 hours.

5.3.2 Garbage First GC applied to SPECjbb

This section looks at the optimization of the Garbage First GC when running the SPECjbb benchmark. In terms of allocation rates and absolute GC times, this benchmark puts significantly more pressure on the garbage collector than the xalan benchmark. Moreover, measurements have shown that, although many objects die young, the average object age at death is considerably higher than in xalan. Figure 11 shows the GC time and the GC frequency per generation as well as the heap space usages. It turned out that the default parameter configuration kept almost all objects in the young generation. However, tenuring long-living objects earlier would decrease the GC time of the young generation at the expense of the old generation. The optimized configuration has found the sweet spot, or at least an approximation of it, for the object distribution between generations.

The optimized configuration and its interpretation.

Table 4 compares the optimized parameter values with their default values for the SPECjbb benchmark. Values marked with a '*' are chosen at start-up time for our machine by the GC ergonomics.

Parameter	old	new
G1ConfidencePercent	50	40
G1ConcRefinementGreenZone	8*	4
G1ConcRefinementServiceIntervalMillis	300	150
G1ConcRefinementYellowZone	24*	32
G1ConcMarkStepDurationMillis	10	5
G1ConcRSHotCardLimit	4	16
G1HeapRegionSize	1MB*	4MB
G1HeapWastePercent	10	15
G1MixedGCCountTarget	8	16
G1ReservePercent	10	5
G1RSetUpdatingPauseTimePercent	10	15
G1RSetScanBlockSize	64	128
G1SATBBufferEnqueueThresholdPercent	60	30
G1UseAdaptiveConcRefinement	+	-

Table 4: Optimized parameter configuration for SPECjbb (G1 GC with memory pressure)

The parameter *G1RSetUpdatingPauseTimePercent* defines a limit for the time used updating the remembered sets. This limit affects the concurrent refinement and when a GC is triggered. These sets contain all root pointers per heap region, i.e., all pointers into the region originating from other regions. Increasing this parameter enables the garbage collector to process more updates to this set necessary for the heavy load of the SPECjbb benchmark. Increasing the *G1ConcRSHotCardLimit* allows more pointer updates in a memory card before the card is considered hot, thus triggering a garbage collection later than usual. If code with many pointer updates but only few allocations is executed, a higher limit prevents unnecessary collections. The *G1-ConcRefinementGreenZone* and *G1ConcRefinementYellow-*

Zone define how many update buffers for the remembered set will be left in the queue (see Detlefs et al. [9]) and at which queue size how many concurrent refinement threads are triggered. Reducing the green zone results in fewer buffers left in the queue whereas increasing the yellow zone results in concurrent processing being triggered later as usual. Therefore, less concurrent refinement threads are triggered less often but have to process a bigger queue, reducing the interference between the concurrent refinement and the mutator. This behavior is favorable for heavy load with many pointer updates, as observed in the SPECjbb benchmark. The *G1ConcMarkStepDurationMillis* is decreased, resulting in smaller incremental steps in the marking phase. Thus, if many pointers are modified (as it is the case with SPECjbb) the necessary re-marking steps due to the mutator interference are also shorter, decreasing the time spent on re-marking and thus the overall GC time. To reduce parallelization overhead, the *G1RSetScanBlockSize* is increased, resulting in bigger chunks for each worker thread. An increased *G1SATBBufferEnqueueThresholdPercent* leads to more SATB (Snapshot At The Beginning) buffers to be enqueued, enabling the garbage collector to handle pointer updates more quickly. Finally, the *G1HeapRegionSize* is increased, resulting in improved locality of sequentially allocated objects (i.e., it is more likely that sequentially allocated objects are in the same heap space) and in longer intervals between garbage collections. Therefore, objects have more time to die and each garbage collection can free a bigger fraction of a heap region.

Similarly to xalan, this parameter configuration was optimized to fit the exact needs of the SPECjbb benchmark.

5.4 Real-world Experiment

In addition to the DaCapo and SPECjbb benchmarks, we conducted our experiments also on a real-world industrial application. This subsection describes the modified setup and the results of this experiment.

5.4.1 Modified Setup and Research Method

The application for which we tuned the garbage collector is the dynaTrace Server 5.5 from our industrial partner Compuware. The dynaTrace Server receives monitoring information, such as stack traces, allocation events, garbage collector information, and captured parameter values, from agents that are injected into other real-world applications in order to monitor them. This information has to be processed and aggregated in real time and has to be stored into a performance warehouse (i.e., a database) to be accessible via the dynaTrace Client.

When the load is too high, i.e., when the agents send too much data per time unit to the server, it starts to ignore incoming data. Compuware has experimentally determined the maximum data rate that the server is able to handle without having to skip anything for a given hardware setting and given VM parameters. For our experiment, we used 68 agents to send data at that rate, resulting in a server that is used up to its maximum capacity but is still handling the received data correctly.

Due to the typical environment characteristics of Compuware's customers, the heap size was fixed at 8GB. Until now, Compuware achieved the best performance with the Concurrent Mark and Sweep GC. Therefore, we optimized the configuration of this GC.

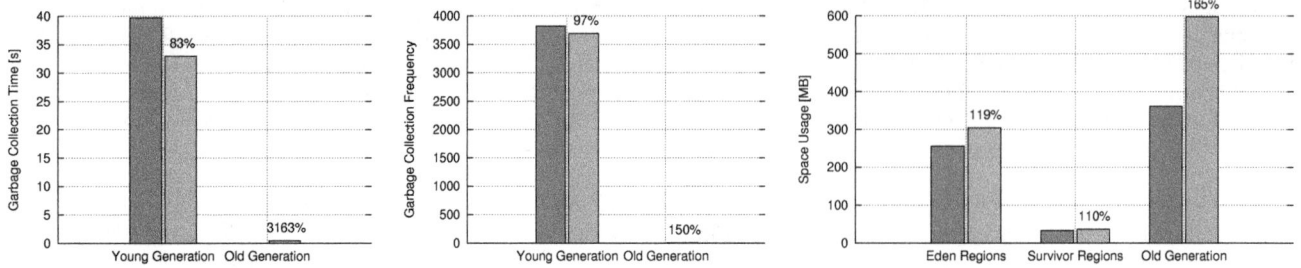

Figure 11: Detailed optimization results for SPECjbb (G1 GC with memory pressure)

As the server is handling requests continuously, we fixed a single optimization iteration, i.e., a single run with a given configuration, to 15 minutes. The optimization was conducted for 2.5 days, resulting in about 600 iterations.

Similar to the other benchmarks, the objective function was defined as the aggregated GC time during 15 minutes under load. We had to add additional safeguards to the objective function because some configurations, while leading to an overall GC time improvement, had significantly longer GC pauses. Such configurations resulted in a decreased responsiveness, forcing the server to skip data. Thus, the objective function continuously reads the server logs and reports a configuration as crashed when the server starts skipping data or when it loses the connection to the agents due to long GC pauses. Such effects arise early, which enables the optimization algorithm to save time because it can prematurely abort runs with such configurations.

The server ran on $4 \times$ MJ3GK E7540 @ 2.4GHz$\times$6 Intel® Xeon® Multi Core Dunnington D0 on 64-bit with 96GB RAM running Linux Ubuntu 10.10 Maverick Meerkat. The agents creating the load ran on separate machines in the same network in order to avoid biased results.

5.4.2 Results

Figure 12 shows the aggregated GC time and the GC frequency before (left, dark) and after (right, light) the optimization. Although the GC frequency increased up to

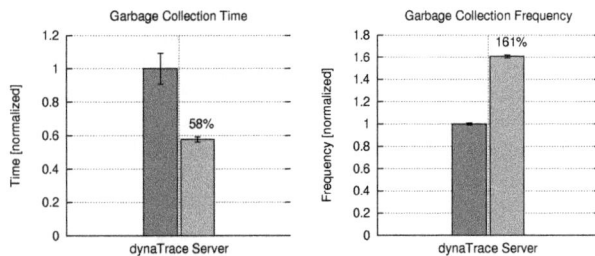

Figure 12: Optimization results for the dynaTrace Server (normalized, with the CMS GC)

161%, the GC time dropped to 58%. We do not show the run time or the throughput because the agents were configured to send requests at the same fixed rate before and after the optimization.

The detailed results (Figure 13) show that the eden space (*Par Eden Space*) has been cut in half, resulting in an increased minor collection frequency, whereas the old gener-

ation space (*CMS Old Gen*) was increased by 26%. Most objects allocated by the dynaTrace Server are temporary objects that are created during request processing. These objects usually die before the first GC cycle. Therefore, 73% of the GC time was spent on minor collections (*ParNew*). However, there are also long-living objects which the dynaTrace Server keeps in memory to enable fast access for dynaTrace Clients. As these objects are usually stored in caches, they can be collected within the first few major collections. Increasing the old generation space gives them more time to die and thus speeds up collections in the old generation.

The optimized configuration leads to a better balance of short-living and long-living objects between the two generations. As most objects die before the first collection, the size of the young generation can be safely reduced and objects that survive the first collection are promoted to the old generation. Increasing the size of the old generation reduces the major GC frequency and gives long-living objects more time to die there before the next major collection. Preliminary tests have shown that, in this scenario, the transaction throughput can be increased by as much as 14%.

These results show that our approach of automatically tuning GC parameters not only works for smaller benchmarks but also for real-world industrial applications

5.5 Threats to Validity

Impact of individual parameters Although we examined the GC logs carefully and performed additional runs with our instrumented VM in order to be able to explain the optimization effects, more experiments would be required to better understand the impact of each parameter in isolation as well as in combination with others.

Applicability to other VMs Our approach is applicable to any VM that exposes parameters to control garbage collection behavior. In order to verify this, experiments would have to be conducted for other VMs. However, we are confident that our approach yields similar results because they use similar garbage collection algorithms and parameters.

Hardware diversity All benchmarks were executed on the same machine. Although we expect most parameters to be hardware independent, additional experiments would be required to verify this assumption and to analyze potentially different result configurations for the same benchmark.

6. RELATED WORK

To the best of our knowledge, no work has been published on automatically tuning a GC considering *all* parameters. There is some research, though, on choosing proper sizes for

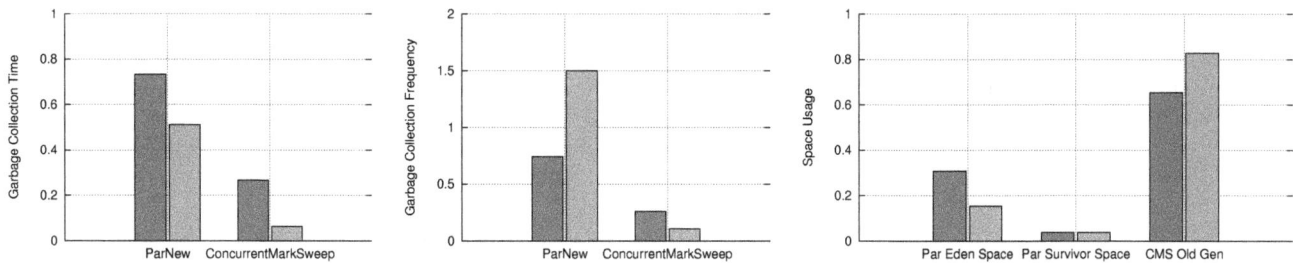

Figure 13: Detailed optimization results for the dynaTrace Server (normalized, with the CMS GC)

the entire heap or for individual spaces, for manual tuning, GC performance, and parameter value selection in general:

Heap space sizes Yang et al. [27] implemented a heap size analysis to minimize paging while maximizing throughput by adjusting the heap size accordingly. Only moderate changes to the garbage collector are necessary to employ their approach, which can reduce the GC time considerably. Brecht et al. [8] experimentally examined the performance impact (e.g., the overall run time, GC pause times, and footprint) of changing the heap size for Java applications. Furthermore, they devised a heuristic algorithm to resize the heap with respect to the observed application behavior. Guan et al. [12] investigated the performance effects of different nursery sizing policies. They proposed a hybrid policy for handling different memory pressure scenarios efficiently, enabling server applications to deal with higher workloads. Balsamo et al. [3] used a queuing model for predicting the optimal activation rate, i.e., the GC frequency to minimize the mean response time. Vengerov [26] developed a mathematical analysis to maximize the throughput based on the sizes of the young and the old generation, as well as on the tenuring threshold. He showed that, using his definition, the heap size and the tenuring threshold converge to their optimal values, achieving the optimal throughput. Valesco et al. [25] proposed a method for dynamic reorganization of the heap in a generational collector. They present two techniques for choosing the percentage of reserved space and show that these techniques can reduce the collection time substantially. Singer et al. [22] introduced the allocation curve as a special form of the demand curve from economics as well as the term allocation elasticity to control heap growth.

Manual tuning Gousios et al. [11] examined the impact of GC tuning on Java server applications. Using the results of their experiments, they devised a number of guidelines to tune the Sun and the IBM virtual machines. However, these guidelines refer only to the heap size and to the selection of a garbage collector. Hirt et al. [13] described some parameters of the JRockit VM and the capability of the JRockit Mission Control to provide statistics about heap space usage. The described parameters are mostly about individual heap space sizes and their resizing, and the selection of GC algorithms. Moreover, the interpretation of the provided heap space statistics is left to the user as only little guidance on tuning is provided.

GC performance Blackburn et al. [6] identified key algorithmic features of three GC algorithms and developed a function for expressing their performance costs based on the heap size.

GC selection Singer et al. [21] implemented a method to select a garbage collection algorithm based on a single profiling run, achieving a significant speedup over choosing the default GC each time. However, they focus on choosing the garbage collector only, ignoring the GC parameters.

GC parameters Singer et al. [23] suggest using decision trees to predict a small set of parameters, i.e., the GC algorithm and one of two new-to-old generation ratios. However, they do not consider the entire set of available parameters. Other sources provide guidelines on how to select values for certain parameters of the Java VM. Oracle [19, 18] provides information about some parameters of the Hotspot^{TM} VM and explains their effect on the garbage collector. However, this description is limited to parameters controlling the size of individual heap spaces, the size of the entire heap, the heap growth, and the GC algorithm. Lee [15] offers similar instructions about choosing the heap size. Beckwith [4] provides more insight into the Garbage First collector and its most important parameters [5]. However, some of the suggested parameter values are experimental and most of them remain unexplained.

7. FUTURE WORK

Optimizing other VM parameters As our approach is of a black-box manner, it is not limited to garbage collection, but could also be applied to other VM parameters such as compiler heuristics or threading behavior.

Choosing other optimization frameworks We used ParamILS because it is easy to adapt and publicly available for academic use. However, one might consider other optimization frameworks as well (e.g., Heuristic Lab [2]) in order to check whether they can find better optima.

Changing the optimization goal Our optimization goal was the overall throughput of an application. Therefore, we used the aggregated GC time as an objective function for the optimization algorithm. However, one could also think of other optimization goals such as the average or maximum GC pause time.

8. CONCLUSIONS

In this paper we proposed a technique for the automatic tuning of GC parameters for specific applications using an optimization tool that applies a modified hill climbing approach. We conducted detailed experiments with a variety of GC-intensive benchmarks from the DaCapo benchmark suite and from SPECjbb 2005 as well as with a real-world industrial application (the dynaTrace Server). The experiments were performed for 3 widely used garbage collectors of the Hotspot™ VM.

Our measurements show that for some benchmarks, the GC time can be reduced by up to 77% leading to an overall run-time speedup of up to 42% relative to the default configuration. The average reduction of GC time across all benchmarks was 35% and the average speedup on overall run time was 9% (for the Hotspot™ default GC).

With dozens of GC parameters, which are scarcely documented and hard to understand, the manual tuning of applications is a tedious task which is often guided by trial and error. Automatic tuning can be an attractive alternative that exploits otherwise hidden GC potential based on the characteristics of specific applications.

9. ACKNOWLEDGMENTS

This work was supported by the Christian Doppler Forschungsgesellschaft, and by Compuware Austria GmbH.

10. REFERENCES

[1] DaCapo. http://www.dacapobench.org/, 2013.
[2] M. Affenzeller. Architecture and Design of the HeuristicLab Optimization Environment. In *Advanced Methods and Applications in Computational Intelligence*, pages 197–261, 2014.
[3] S. Balsamo, G.-L. D. Rossi, and A. Marin. Optimisation of Virtual Machine Garbage Collection Policies. In *Proc. of the Intl. Conf. on Analytical and Stochastic Modeling Techniques and Applications*, pages 70–84, 2011.
[4] M. Beckwith. G1: One Garbage Collector to Rule Them All. http://www.infoq.com/articles/G1-One-Garbage-Collector-To-Rule-Them-All, 2013.
[5] M. Beckwith. Garbage First Garbage Collector Tuning. http://www.oracle.com/technetwork/articles/java/g1gc-1984535.html, 2013.
[6] S. M. Blackburn, P. Cheng, and K. S. McKinley. Myths and Realities: the Performance Impact of Garbage Collection. In *Proc. of the Joint Intl. Conf. on Measurement and Modeling of Computer Systems*, pages 25–36, 2004.
[7] S. M. Blackburn, R. Garner, C. Hoffmann, A. M. Khang, K. S. McKinley, R. Bentzur, A. Diwan, D. Feinberg, D. Frampton, S. Z. Guyer, M. Hirzel, A. Hosking, M. Jump, H. Lee, J. E. B. Moss, A. Phansalkar, D. Stefanović, T. VanDrunen, D. von Dincklage, and B. Wiedermann. The DaCapo Benchmarks: Java Benchmarking Development and Analysis. In *Proc. of the Annual ACM SIGPLAN Conf. on Object-oriented Programming Systems, Languages, and Applications*, pages 169–190, 2006.
[8] T. Brecht, E. Arjomandi, C. Li, and H. Pham. Controlling Garbage Collection and Heap Growth to Reduce the Execution Time of Java Applications. *Trans. Program. Lang. Syst.*, 28(5):908–941, 2006.
[9] D. Detlefs. Concurrent Remembered Set Refinement in Generational Garbage Collection. In *USENIX Java VM Research and Technology Symp.*, 2002.
[10] D. Detlefs, C. Flood, S. Heller, and T. Printezis. Garbage-First Garbage Collection. In *Proc. of the Intl. Symp. on Memory Management*, pages 37–48, 2004.
[11] G. Gousios, V. Karakoidas, and D. Spinellis. Tuning Java's Memory Manager for High Performance Server Applications. In *Proc. of the 5th Intl. System Administration and Network Conf.*, pages 69–83, 2006.
[12] X. Guan, W. Srisa-an, and C. Jia. Investigating the Effects of Using Different Nursery Sizing Policies on Performance. In *Proc. of the Intl. Symp. on Memory Management*, pages 59–68, New York, NY, USA, 2009.
[13] M. Hirt and M. Lagergren. *Oracle JRockit: The Definitive Guide*. 2010.
[14] F. Hutter, H. H. Hoos, K. Leyton-Brown, and T. Stutzle. ParamILS: An Automatic Algorithm Configuration Framework. *Journal of Artificial Intelligence Research*, 36:267–306, 2009.
[15] S. Lee. How to Tune Java Garbage Collection. http://www.cubrid.org/blog/textyle/428187, 2012.
[16] H. Lieberman and C. Hewitt. A Real-time Garbage Collector Based on the Lifetimes of Objects. *Commun. ACM*, 26(6):419–429, 1983.
[17] Oracle. Garbage Collector Ergonomic. http://docs.oracle.com/javase/7/docs/technotes/guides/vm/gc-ergonomics.html, 2013.
[18] Oracle. Java HotSpot VM Options. http://www.oracle.com/technetwork/java/javase/tech/vmoptions-jsp-140102.html, 2013.
[19] Oracle. Java SE 6 HotSpot[tm] Virtual Machine Garbage Collection Tuning. http://www.oracle.com/technetwork/java/javase/gc-tuning-6-140523.html, 2013.
[20] Oracle. OpenJDK 8 Early Access Release b100. http://jdk8.java.net/archive/8-b100.html, 2013.
[21] J. Singer, G. Brown, I. Watson, and J. Cavazos. Intelligent Selection of Application-specific Garbage Collectors. In *Proc. of the Intl. Symp. on Memory Management*, pages 91–102, 2007.
[22] J. Singer, R. E. Jones, G. Brown, and M. Luján. The Economics of Garbage Collection. In *Proc. of the Intl. Symp. on Memory Management*, pages 103–112, 2010.
[23] J. Singer, G. Kovoor, G. Brown, and M. Luján. Garbage collection auto-tuning for java mapreduce on multi-cores. In *Proc. of the Intl. Symp. on Memory Management*, pages 109–118, 2011.
[24] D. Ungar. Generation Scavenging: A Non-disruptive High Performance Storage Reclamation Algorithm. In *Proc. of the ACM SIGSOFT/SIGPLAN Software Engineering Symp. on Practical Software Development Environments*, pages 157–167, 1984.
[25] J. Velasco, A. Ortiz, K. Olcoz, and F. Tirado. Dynamic Management of Nursery Space Organization in Generational Collection. In *INTERACT-8, workshop*, pages 33–40, 2004.
[26] D. Vengerov. Modeling, Analysis and Throughput Optimization of a Generational Garbage Collector. In *Proc. of the Intl. Symp. on Memory Management*, pages 1–9, 2009.
[27] T. Yang, M. Hertz, E. D. Berger, S. F. Kaplan, and J. E. B. Moss. Automatic Heap Sizing: Taking Real Memory into Account. In *Proc. of the Intl. Symp. on Memory Management*, pages 61–72, 2004.

Constructing Performance Model of JMS Middleware Platform

Tomáš Martinec, Lukáš Marek,
Antonín Steinhauser, Petr Tůma
Faculty of Mathematics and Physics
Charles University
Prague, Czech Republic
last.name@d3s.mff.cuni.cz

Qais Noorshams, Andreas Rentschler,
Ralf Reussner
Chair Software Design and Quality
Karlsruhe Institute of Technology
Karlsruhe, Germany
last.name@kit.edu

ABSTRACT

Middleware performance models are useful building blocks in the performance models of distributed software applications. We focus on performance models of messaging middleware implementing the Java Message Service standard, showing how certain system design properties – including pipelined processing and message coalescing – interact to create performance behavior that the existing models do not capture accurately. We construct a performance model of the ActiveMQ messaging middleware that addresses the outlined issues and discuss how the approach extends to other middleware implementations.

Categories and Subject Descriptors

D.2.8 [**Software Engineering**]: Metrics—*Performance Measures*

General Terms

Performance

Keywords

Software Performance; Performance Analysis; Measurement; Modeling; JMS

1. INTRODUCTION

Software performance engineering (SPE) is a discipline that focuses on incorporating performance concerns into the software development process, aiming to reliably deliver software with particular performance properties [36]. Among the tools employed by SPE are predictive performance models. Constructed in the early phases of the software development process, the models help predict the eventual software performance and thus guide the development [3].

To deliver the expected guidance, the predictive performance models must capture all relevant system components.

For modern software applications, this may entail modeling complex system layers such as the virtual machine or the messaging middleware. Composing such complete performance models directly is necessarily expensive and inefficient. Instead, the abstract application model can be constructed first, with the models of standard system components added later [39, 8]. This gives rise to the need for composable performance models of standard system components.

Our work focuses on the construction of such performance models for messaging middleware, specifically messaging middleware that implements the Java Messaging Service (JMS) standard [37]. Although JMS performance models were published before [26, 14, 30, 9, 13, 11, 34], we illustrate that the existing models often fail to capture important elements of middleware behavior. In turn, this omission results in reduced performance prediction accuracy, especially where processor utilization and message latency are concerned. Our contribution is as follows:

– Using code analysis and experimental measurements of a mainstream JMS implementation, we illustrate situations where observed performance is not accurately predicted by common models.

– We provide a detailed technical analysis of the observed effects as an essential basis for further modeling.

– We design a performance model that captures these effects and validate the model using experimental measurements.

We have decided to organize our presentation in a way that familiarizes the reader with the necessary platform-specific background as soon as possible. This helps avoid potentially inaccurate generalizations in the introductory text. In Section 2, we introduce our modeling context and describe our experimental platform. Section 3 explains the issues that complicate accurate performance modeling of our platform. We show how to construct a performance model that addresses these issues in Section 4, and follow by evaluating and discussing the model results in Section 5. This is where we pay particular attention to explaining how our results, so far presented in a platform-specific context, can be generalized. Section 6 relates our modeling efforts to the existing research, and finally Section 7 summarizes our conclusions.

2. MODELING CONTEXT

The expectations put on a performance model are closely related to the intended model use. We therefore start by describing such uses, paying particular attention to the inputs that are available to the modeler and the outputs that the modeler would seek in each context.

As noted in the introduction, middleware performance models are needed as building blocks in application performance models. Such models are used in early stages of the software development process to guide important design decisions, or in software maintenance activities when a change impact analysis can be conducted to choose among multiple modification directions [21]. On the input side, the modeler can usually collect information about the timing (or more generally resource demands) of the operations used as atomic elements of the model. Restrictions on the ability to instrument particular operations may require using specialized microbenchmarks or deriving detailed information from aggregate statistics such as overall system throughput. On the output side, the modeler would require the model to accurately predict general design feasibility and overall scalability trends with respect to performance. The model should also suffice for comparing design alternatives.

Middleware performance models can also be understood as a description of the expected performance (rather than an approximation of the actual performance). Besides simple software documentation purposes, this use can also benefit software performance testing [5, 15]. In this context, the models can be provided with the same inputs as in the early stages of the software development process, with one important addition – the models can be automatically calibrated against the actual performance in selected benchmarks. Such calibration makes the question of absolute prediction accuracy mute, the modeler instead evaluates the ability to fit the model to the measurements with reasonable values of the calibrated parameters.

It is also possible to use the models at runtime to plan system adaptation [7]. Particular to this context is the need to maintain low overhead in both collecting the inputs and evaluating the model. The output of the model is used to make adaptation decisions, reliable estimation of trends or reliable comparison of alternatives is therefore preferred to absolute prediction accuracy.

In summary, the three modeling contexts all put emphasis on predicting trends, which are used to make relative comparisons or to assess system scalability. Where absolute prediction accuracy is important, model calibration is performed on the timing information collected through measurement.

2.1 Modeling Messaging Brokers

Our work focuses on the construction of performance models for JMS middleware [37]. The JMS architecture envisions multiple clients communicating by sending and receiving application specific messages. The messages travel either through queues in a point-to-point pattern or through topics in a publish-subscribe pattern. The JMS standard provides multiple quality-of-service settings, especially important from performance perspective is deciding whether the JMS middleware should keep messages in transient buffers or persistent storage and whether the message delivery should be subject to transaction processing.

The model we construct should be a suitable building block in application performance models. It must be able to predict basic performance metrics relevant for the JMS middleware – especially resource utilization, message throughput and message latency – that would be observed for a given workload on a given platform. The middleware model does not describe the workload itself, that is the task of the application performance models that would incorporate the middleware model.

2.2 Experimental Platform

In our experience, the process of building and validating a performance model is necessarily platform-dependent. Although the individual steps can follow a common overall approach, the modeling accuracy depends on multiple technical details that need to be considered. We therefore introduce our experimental platform and continue the presentation in a platform-specific context. Generalizations are discussed as appropriate.

Our code analysis and experimental measurements are performed on the ActiveMQ 5.4.2 messaging middleware [2], which implements the JMS standard [37]. Central to the middleware is the message broker, a process that manages messaging channels, which are either queues or topics. Message producers and message consumers connect to the broker using sockets. We isolate broker performance by executing it on a dedicated computer, a single-core 2.33 GHz Intel Xeon machine with 4 GB RAM running Fedora Linux with kernel 3.9.2-200 x86_64 and OpenJDK 1.6.0-24 x86_64. The producers and consumers run on two additional computers connected through a dedicated gigabit Ethernet network with accelerated Broadcom network adapters, chosen so that they can saturate the broker while at low load themselves – the producer is an eight-core (two chips four cores each) 2.30 GHz AMD Opteron machine with 16 GB RAM and the consumer is an eight-core (two chips four cores each) 1.86 GHz Intel Xeon machine with 8 GB RAM.

From the many quality-of-service settings available, we focus on the transient message passing mechanism with acknowledgments. This setting targets applications that require low-latency high-throughput reliable message delivery and is therefore a natural performance modeling subject. We do not model quality-of-service settings that require persistent message storage, because with such settings, the storage performance tends to dominate the observations. Existing storage performance modeling methods are then likely better suited for capturing the observed performance [38].

The transient message passing mechanism is implemented in four broker threads that process a message passing through a broker queue, as shown on Figure 1:

– The first thread blocks waiting for messages arriving through a network socket. On message arrival, the thread reads the message, selects the destination queue and stores the message in a container associated with this queue. This thread is blocked when the container is full.

– The second thread blocks waiting for messages arriving in the container filled by the first thread. On message arrival, the thread locates the message consumer and passes the message to the third thread, responsible for communicating with that consumer.

- The third thread blocks waiting for messages and sends them on to the consumer through a network socket.

- The fourth thread blocks waiting for acknowledgments arriving from the consumer through a network socket. On acknowledgment arrival, the corresponding message is recognized as processed.

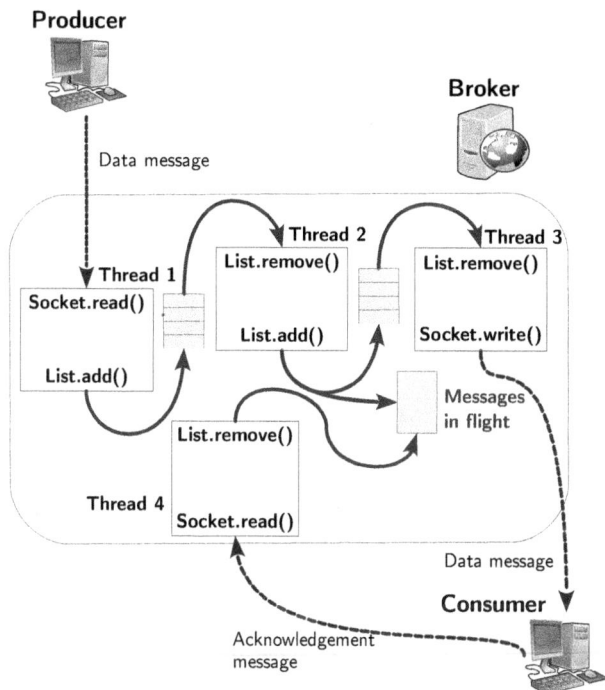

Figure 1: Transient message passing architecture in ActiveMQ 5.4.2.

3. MODELING ISSUES

Existing models of messaging middleware[1] typically belong to one of two broad classes, here called *models with queues* and *fitted models*:

- A typical model with queues relies on the fact that messaging channels resemble service queues. The model would represent resources such as processor or storage with service queues and approximate a message passing through a messaging channel with a single service request in each of the queues.

  Models with queues were shown to achieve high accuracy especially in complex systems with multiple messaging channels, where the mean resource demands at the bottleneck resources determine the achievable throughput and the accumulated effects of queueing at the messaging channels dominate the observed latencies [18, 34].

- A fitted model is typically used when the observed performance is determined through interactions at the implementation level that are either not understood in

---

[1]We discuss the existing models in depth in the related work section. We avoid the discussion here to maintain text flow.

sufficient detail or simply too complex. After quantifying the workload properties that impact performance, the model would derive a function that predicts performance from the workload properties by fitting a function template to the observed measurements.

Fitted models were successfully used with workload properties such as message size or filter count [13, 11], whose impact is otherwise difficult to predict because it consists of many minuscule implementation effects.

Despite their many strong points, both model classes exhibit accuracy issues in certain situations inherent to our modeling context. We describe these issues next.

3.1 Pipelined Message Processing

The ActiveMQ broker processes messages in several phases that form a pipeline. When any of the phases limits concurrent processing – as is the case with the thread-per-connection and thread-per-destination patterns in our broker – messages may queue inside the pipeline. Such queueing has a relatively benign impact on throughput but a very significant effect on latencies, as illustrated on Figure 2.

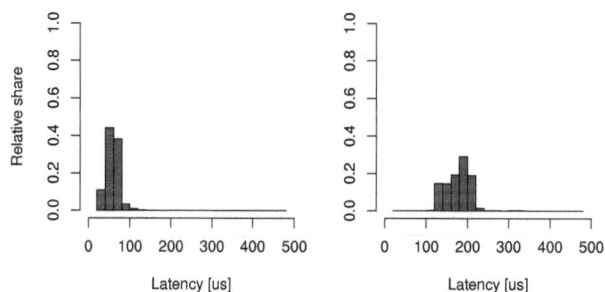

Figure 2: Impact of bursts on latency distribution. Constant throughput 5000 msg/s, left workload sending individual messages, right workload sending bursts of ten messages.

Figure 2 shows the distribution of message latencies observed at the throughput of 5000 msg/s in two workload configurations, regular and bursty. In the regular configuration, the producer emits one message every 200 μs. In the bursty configuration, the producer emits a burst of ten messages every 2 ms.

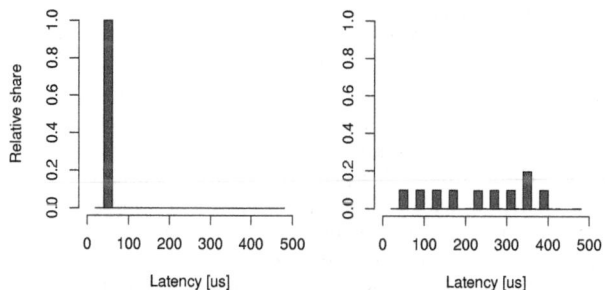

Figure 3: Predicting impact of bursts on latency distribution with G/G/1 queue. Constant throughput 5000 msg/s, left workload sending individual messages, right workload sending bursts of ten messages.

Figure 3 shows that approximating the broker with a single service queue – as a model with queues might do – is not enough when modeling the bursty workload latency. The model used the same distribution of the arrival times and the service times as Figure 2. For the regular workload, the predicted latency matches the measurement reasonably well. For the bursty workload, the predicted latency shows several regular clusters from 40 μs to 420 μs but the measurement forms a single cluster from 120 μs to 240 μs – the model not only failed to predict the absolute latency, it also failed to approximate the overall trend.

Section 5 shows how our model improves the prediction accuracy by reflecting the pipeline architecture in the model structure. A fitted model that would capture the latency would have to include the information quantifying the bursts in the workload properties. Unfortunately, adding new independent variables into the workload properties increases the cost of building a fitted model.

3.2 Thread Scheduling Overhead

The use of multiple threads in the ActiveMQ broker introduces the opportunity for context switching, that is, the act of handing control of the processor from one thread to another. Although the design intent is to make context switch a fast operation, the accumulated overhead of context switching can impact performance.

Two major reasons for a context switch are the scheduling policies enforced by the operating system and the blocking behavior exhibited by the executing threads. The scheduling policies are usually only enforced after a thread has run for some time – 750 μs on our platform – which makes them unlikely to impact relatively fast message processing – tens of microseconds on our platform. In contrast, the thread blocking behavior may trigger context switches arbitrarily fast.

The cost of a context switch can vary significantly [35, 23]. On our platform, a simple benchmark where two threads take turns blocking each other on a synchronization variable estimates the context switch duration to be 3.3 μs. The pipelined message processing, which involves four threads operating on each message, further multiplies the context switch overhead. Even more importantly, the amount of context switching per message varies. When messages arrive far from each other in time, the threads finish processing a message before the next one arrives and therefore block waiting once per message. But when messages arrive close to each other, the threads have a new message to process by the time they finish processing the previous one and therefore do not block waiting. This effect is shown on Figure 4.

Figure 4 illustrates that on our broker, the relative amount of context switching changes from about 20 switches per message for low throughput to about 1 switch per message for high throughput. The peak throughput can be deduced from Figure 5, which shows the dependency between the target throughput and the actual throughput (the producer attempts to generate messages at the target throughput rate, but the broker flow control restricts the producer to avoid message loss). Also worth noting is the implied fact that peak processor utilization does not coincide with peak throughput – a practically important effect because high processor utilization is often taken to indicate a bottleneck.

To model this thread scheduling effect, a model with queues would require a special load dependent service queue. A fit-

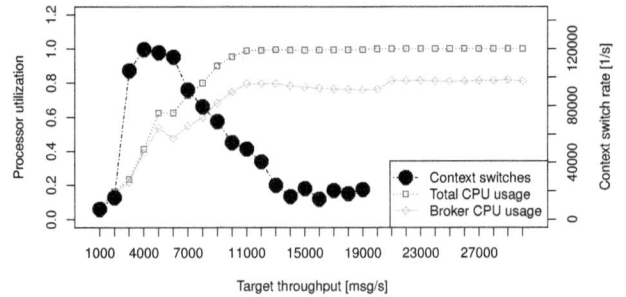

Figure 4: Dependency of broker processor utilization and context switch rate on target throughput.

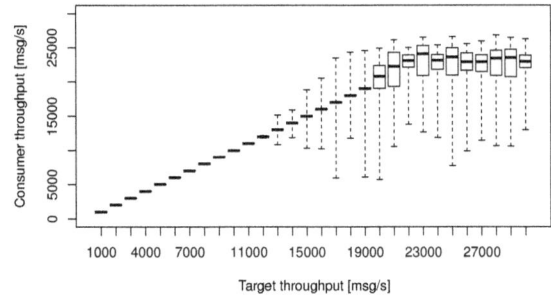

Figure 5: Dependency of actual throughput on target throughput.

ted model can probably capture the effect more easily, but we are not aware of any work doing so.

3.3 Message Coalescing

The performance impact of both the pipelined processing and the thread scheduling is more pronounced in bursty workloads than in regular workloads. Besides bursts that are inherent to the workload from the application perspective, more bursts can be introduced as the broker processes the messages, again influencing the observed performance. One source of such message bursts in our broker is the implementation of the TCP protocol in the network stack, which is used to transport messages between the producers and consumers and the broker. The protocol minimizes the processing overhead by coalescing smaller messages into larger packets, both in software and in hardware. Coalescing in software follows RFC 896 [16] and is disabled by default – because this is a sensible default, we leave it disabled in our experiments. Coalescing in hardware is done as a part of the Generic Receive Offload (GRO) [41] and Generic Segmentation Offload (GSO) [40] features.

Both GRO and GSO are enabled by default, and although they can also be disabled, keeping the default makes the experimental platform more realistic. We believe existing simulation tools such as the **ns** simulator [31] are more suitable for modeling the message coalescing behavior at the TCP protocol level than the performance models considered here. To avoid the need for modeling this behavior, we collect the information quantifying the bursts on the broker machine. Figure 6 illustrates message coalescing on our platform – the producer uses the **sendto** socket function to transmit 1030 B long messages at a rate of 20000 msg/s, the two graphs show the statistical distribution of packet sizes observed through the `pcap` monitoring interface when departing the producer and when arriving at the broker. Without message coalescing, the graphs would show all messages having 1030 B plus the TCP protocol header.

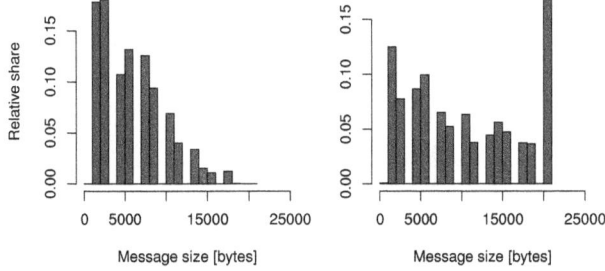

Figure 6: Packet sizes observed when departing the producer (left) and arriving at the broker (right).

Another opportunity for message coalescing arises in connection with the garbage collection. On our platform, the garbage collector occasionally stops the broker threads to free heap space. Messages received while the broker threads wait are held in the operating system buffers and processed by the broker as soon as the garbage collector finishes. From the perspective of the broker, this has the same effect as if the messages arrived in one burst. Figure 7 displays the latencies during a garbage collection pause. With pluses, we show latencies measured at the points where messages enter and leave the broker – the cluster of pluses at the end of the garbage collection pause shows the broker reading the messages held in the operating system buffers during the pause. With circles, we show latencies estimated at the points where messages enter and leave the operating system buffers – the slope of circles during the garbage collection pause shows how the messages accumulate. Section 4 explains how this effect is captured by our model.

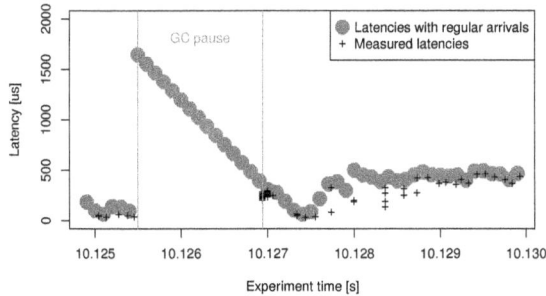

Figure 7: Effect of garbage collection pause on latency.

4. PERFORMANCE MODEL CONSTRUCTION

To address the modeling issues outlined in Section 3, we construct a performance model that directly reflects the broker structure as shown on Figure 1. We use Queueing Petri Nets (QPN) [20] as the modeling formalism, both because it offers modeling abstractions that match the architecture elements and because it has extensive tooling support [19].

QPN combines the modeling concepts of Petri Nets and Queueing Networks. The essential elements of a QPN model

are immediate and timed places and immediate and timed transitions. As usual, places can hold colored tokens, transitions consume tokens in input places and produce tokens in output places. Immediate places always make their tokens available to transitions, timed places only make tokens available after they pass an internal service queue. Tokens can also be subject to departure discipline that imposes ordering restrictions. Immediate transitions have weights and are considered to happen instantaneously, timed transitions have firing rates and are considered to happen after a random delay. QPN models can be nested, a timed place can represent a nested QPN model, tokens arriving at the nested place are submitted to the nested model, tokens departing the nested model are made available to transitions.

4.1 Broker Model

We model the broker by a QPN model shown on Figure 8, which is nested in the QPN model of the measurement harness. This nesting is the reason why the model has a single input place and a single output place – tokens representing all incoming network traffic arrive at the input place, tokens representing all outgoing network traffic depart from the output place. Colors are used to distinguish messages from acknowledgments.

The path a message takes through the broker, implemented by multiple threads described in Section 2.2, is modeled as follows:

- A new message is represented by a token of the `msg` color that arrives in the `input` place. The `msg` token immediately transitions to the `accept-msg` place, with another token deposited in the `queue` place to model the storage occupied by the message.

- The `accept-msg` place represents the thread that reads the message from the network socket and stores it in a destination container. After processing, the `msg` token transitions to the `process` place.

- The `process` place represents the thread that reads the messages from the destination container and locates the message consumer. After processing, the `msg` token transitions to the `dispatch` place.

- The `dispatch` place represents the thread that sends the messages to the consumer through the network socket. After processing, the `msg` token transitions to the `system` place.

- The `system` place represents processing done by the operating system outside the broker, which does not count towards latency measured as messages enter and leave the broker, but still contributes to processor utilization. After processing, the `msg` token departs the broker network.

An acknowledgment will eventually confirm the reception of the message. The path the acknowledgment takes through the broker is modeled as follows:

- A new acknowledgment is represented by a token of the `ack` color that arrives in the `input` place. The `ack` token immediately transitions to the `accept-ack` place.

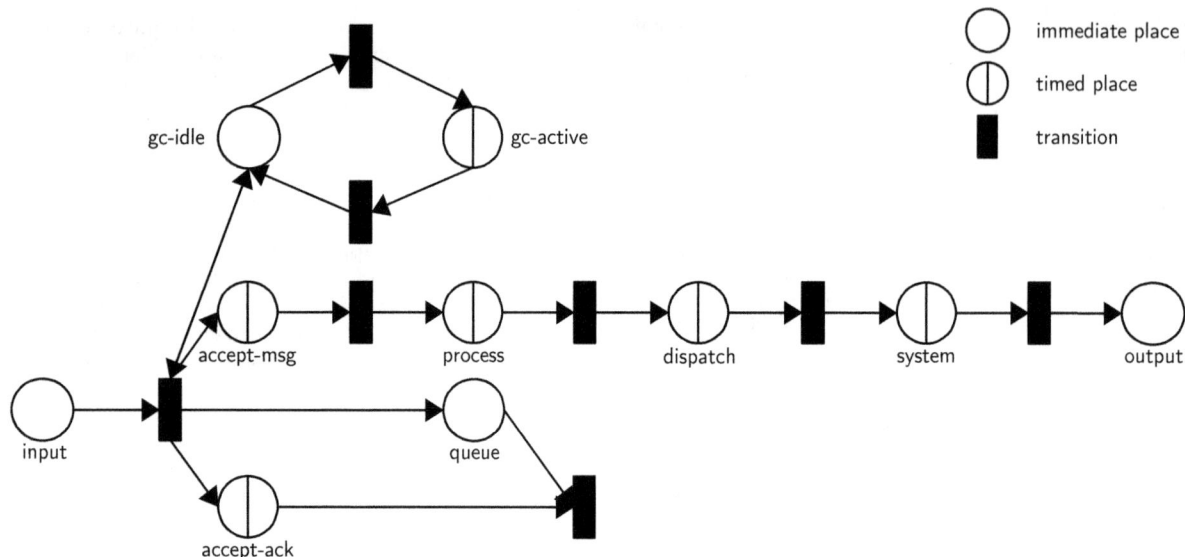

Figure 8: Nested broker QPN model

– The accept-ack place represents the thread that reads the acknowledgment from the network socket and recognizes the corresponding message as processed. After processing, the ack token is discarded by a transition that also removes one token from the queue place to indicate no storage is occupied by the message anymore.

4.2 Garbage Collection

Section 3.3 explains how garbage collection causes message coalescing in the operating system buffers. To model this behavior, we need to represent the garbage collection pauses. To do this, we observe how the broker allocates memory.

The objects maintained by the broker are primarily concerned with clients and messages and destinations. Individual instances of the objects represent individual clients and messages and destinations. The lifetime of these objects is necessarily related to the lifetime of the concepts they represent, simply because keeping them around for longer would cause memory leaks. This arrangement makes messages most important from the garbage collection perspective – objects related to messages have high allocation rates (on par with throughput rates) and short lifetimes (on par with roundtrip times).

Our experimental platform uses a generational garbage collector that will never promote message-related objects beyond the young generation (except if the young generation lifetime was shorter than the message roundtrip time, which is not common [24]). We can therefore imagine that each message passing through the broker will require allocating objects of certain average size. When the accumulated size of these objects reaches the young generation size, a young generation collection will be triggered and all these objects will be collected.

In the model on Figure 8, the garbage collector state is modeled using the gc-idle and gc-active places and a single collector token. The transition from the input place is enabled only when the collector token resides in the gc-idle place. Once the collector token transitions into the

gc-active place, no tokens transition to the accept-msg and accept-ack places, simulating a garbage collection pause. Multiple garbage tokens are used to represent allocated objects. The garbage tokens accumulate in the gc-idle place with each message, the transition from the gc-idle place to the gc-active place requires that enough garbage tokens accumulate.

4.3 Context Switching

Section 3.2 explains how the thread scheduling overhead impacts performance. We model this effect by introducing a new processor scheduling strategy into the QPN formalism. The strategy assumes each timed place represents a thread that keeps executing until no more work remains or until the scheduler executes another thread instead. In this context, we mimic two elements of a typical thread scheduler behavior – the overhead of switching from one thread to another and the limit on the time a thread is allowed to execute when other threads wait.

The strategy accepts the context switch duration c and the quantum duration q as parameters. Tokens from one timed place are processed until the accumulated execution time reaches q. At that moment, the strategy switches to executing tokens from another timed place, extending the execution time of the first token in that place by c.

4.4 Model Calibration

Before use, the model must be populated with a number of parameters. These are the resource demands of the processing performed by the broker threads, the resource demands related to processing outside the broker, and additional constants – the quantum duration, the context switch duration, the garbage collection threshold.

To collect the processor demands of the broker threads, we insert measurement probes into the broker source code, collecting time needed to execute the relevant code fragments. As a technical complication, the collected time may include passive waiting, which is not a processor demand. In our case, excluding passive waiting by the usual means (mea-

128

suring and subtracting the waiting duration or using clock that stops while waiting) was burdened by excessive overhead. We have therefore decided to measure the broker when near saturation and discard the upper decile of the processor demand measurements. Running near saturation makes passive waiting rare and because the times we measure are short, measurements that are distorted by waiting are easily identified by their extreme value. Our outlier filtering choice may have a slight systematic impact on modeled latencies.

To measure the processor demand related to processing outside the broker, we look at the difference between the overall processor utilization and the processor utilization due to the broker threads. From the data used in Figure 4, we estimate the processor demand of the `system` place to be 20 % of the total processor demand used in the other timed places in the model.

The collected processor demands are necessarily burdened by measurement overhead. To assess and compensate, we scale the average processor demand per message to match the peak throughput. The data used in Figure 5 place the peak throughput at 22400 msg/s, this gives us an average processor demand per message of $1/22400$ or 45 μs, of which 20 % or 9 μs is related to processing outside the broker. Without overhead compensation, the average total demand of the timed places in the model is 46 μs, we compensate by multiplying each broker demand by 0.96 to give the average total demand of 45 μs.

Section 3.2 explains how the amount of context switching per message changes between rates that generate peak utilization and peak throughput – the data used in Figure 4 shows these rates to be 11000 msg/s and 22400 msg/s. Our model is constructed to involve five context switch penalties at rates close to peak utilization and zero context switch penalties at rates close to peak throughput, we can therefore calculate a single context switch penalty to be $(1/11000 - 1/22400)/5$ or 11 μs. This is a model parameter only, more context switches with shorter duration actually happen in reality. The other parameter related to scheduling – the quantum duration – is a part of the operating system settings.

Finally, we measure the number of messages that trigger garbage collection by looking at the garbage collection log. To avoid interference due to the virtual machine ergonomics [17], we fix the young generation size.

5. PERFORMANCE MODEL RESULTS

We show the behavior of our performance model on the same workloads that were used to illustrate the modeling issues in Section 3. We use transient message passing mechanism with acknowledgments to transport 975 B long byte array messages between the producer and the consumer. We vary the throughput rate, generating messages either in a regular pattern (producing one message every $1/r$ for throughput r) or in a bursty pattern (producing ten messages every $10/r$ for throughput r), and observe (and model) processor utilization and message latency at the given throughput rate. The model is fed the same distribution of the arrival times as the broker in the measurement experiments.

To measure message latency, we use dynamic library wrappers that intercept calls to the `recvfrom` and `sendto` socket functions at the points where messages enter and leave the broker. We use unique message identifiers embedded in the message body to associate the calls with individual mes-

sages. Our measurements indicate the overhead of wrapping the socket calls does not influence the achievable throughput noticeably, however, we collect the latency information separately from other measurements as a precaution.

The broker processor utilization information is collected through the `cpu` controller of the control group subsystem [29]. While more accurate than other sources, this method does not include the network processing part of the workload that occurs inside the kernel rather than the broker. We therefore also plot the information in the `proc` pseudo file system, which includes the kernel interrupt processing.

Our measurement harness, based on the performance tests included with the messaging middleware, uses dedicated producer and consumer machines to generate message traffic. We check throughput and utilization at both machines, making sure no bottlenecks limit the traffic. We collect the essential measurements for 10 minutes at each throughput rate and discard observations distorted by the warmup and shutdown phases (some measurements are timed and inspected manually).

5.1 Processor Utilization

Figure 9 shows how our model approximates the processor utilization. The measured values are the same as shown on Figure 4.

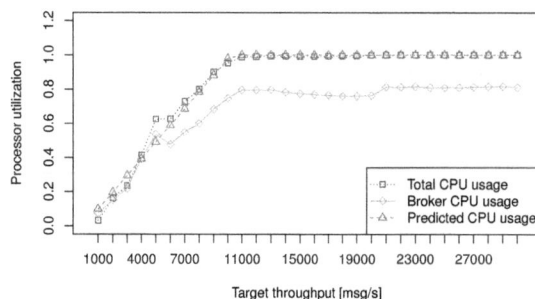

Figure 9: Prediction of broker processor utilization.

The fact that the model captures the linear increase of utilization with throughput is relatively mundane. As a more important contribution, the model also captures the fact that processor utilization peaks much sooner than at maximum throughput – in our measurements, the processor utilization exceeds 95 % at 10000 msg/s, but the maximum throughput is around 22400 msg/s.

Compared to measurements, the model does not explain the increase of processor utilization around 5000 msg/s. To explain this effect, we show the outbound network traffic information on Figure 10. We see that although the broker transmits an almost constant amount of bytes per message, at 5000 msg/s it suddenly uses about 25 % more packets per message than at 4000 msg/s. This increase in network traffic is reflected directly in the increase of processor utilization.

The reason for the network traffic increase is related to detailed behavior the TCP protocol, which can be observed by capturing the network traffic between the broker and the consumer. At 4000 msg/s, the delay between sending a message and receiving an acknowledgment is smaller than the delay between sending two messages – at the TCP protocol level, packets carrying messages from broker to consumer and packets carrying acknowledgments from consumer to broker therefore alternate and each acts as a TCP ACK for

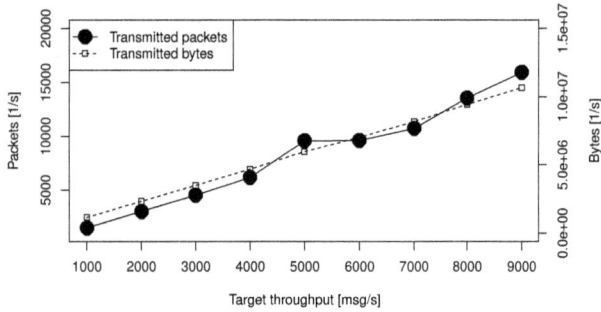

Figure 10: Network traffic from broker to consumer measured in packets and bytes.

the previous packet. At 5000 msg/s, the delay between sending a message and receiving an acknowledgment is close to the delay between sending two messages, which means that the broker sometimes manages to send two messages and then receive two acknowledgments – at the TCP protocol level, this means packets in the two directions no longer alternate and the flow control mechanism mandates sending extra TCP ACK packets, causing the increase in network traffic. While an interesting phenomenon per se, we believe this increase is outside a reasonable scope of performance modeling.

5.2 Message Latency

Message latency consists of the time spent processing and the time spent waiting. At low throughput, processing tends to dominate and latencies are relatively low. At high throughput, waiting tends to dominate and latencies are relatively high. To avoid losing detail due to scale, we examine several ranges separately.

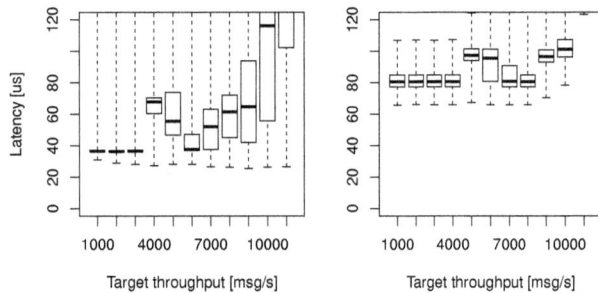

Figure 11: Measured (left) and predicted (right) message latencies at low throughput with regular workload.

Figure 11 shows the measured and predicted message latencies for low throughput rates generated in the regular pattern. Both the measurement and the model show the same trend, which starts with mostly constant latencies and gradually introduces variation. In absolute terms, the model overestimates the latency roughly by a factor of two. One reason for this difference is our calibration procedure, which removes outliers and scales the remaining values to maintain throughput – because throughput is sensitive to outliers in resource demands, removing outliers requires scaling the remaining values towards higher resource demands, which yield higher latency estimates.

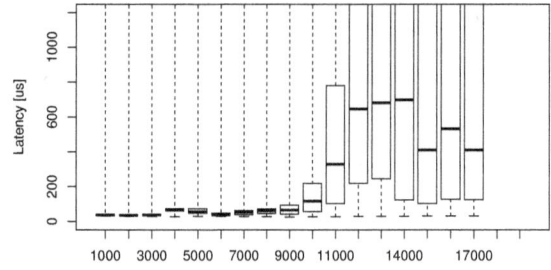

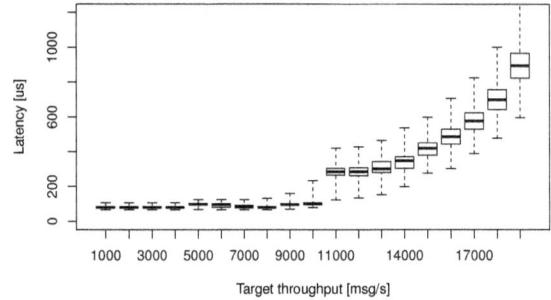

Figure 12: Measured (upper) and predicted (lower) message latencies at low to medium throughput with regular workload.

Figure 12 shows the measured and predicted message latencies for low to medium throughput rates. Again, both the measurement and the model show the same trend, with latencies increasing by about an order of magnitude around the point where the throughput rate exceeds 10000 msg/s, which also happens to be the point where the processor utilization nears the peak. In absolute terms, the model does not exhibit the variation apparent in the measurements. We attribute this to the differences between our scheduler model and the real scheduler. While our scheduler model handles timed places in a round-robin fashion, the real scheduler on our platform enforces strict fairness. More complex scheduler models may help here [10].

Figure 13 completes the latency prediction information for all throughput rates generated in the regular pattern. When the producer attempts to generate messages at rates above peak throughput, the broker flow control restricts the producer to avoid message loss. In this situation, the message latency is determined by the storage threshold that triggers flow control – approximated by the maximum capacity of the queue place in our model. The fact that the model successfully estimates the very high latency is therefore due to a trivial model parameter, more important is the fact that the model estimates the throughput at which the flow control is triggered.

We point out that the behavior of the broker near peak throughput is unstable, with long periods of degraded performance. At high throughput rates, there is only little spare capacity to deal with backlog that may form due to minor disruptions. The broker therefore takes a long time to recover from such disruptions, which leads to large accumulated impact on latencies. Figure 14 illustrates this lack of stability.

As the sole exception to the rule that the model is fed the same distribution of the arrival times as the broker in the measurement experiments, Figure 13 uses modeled arrival

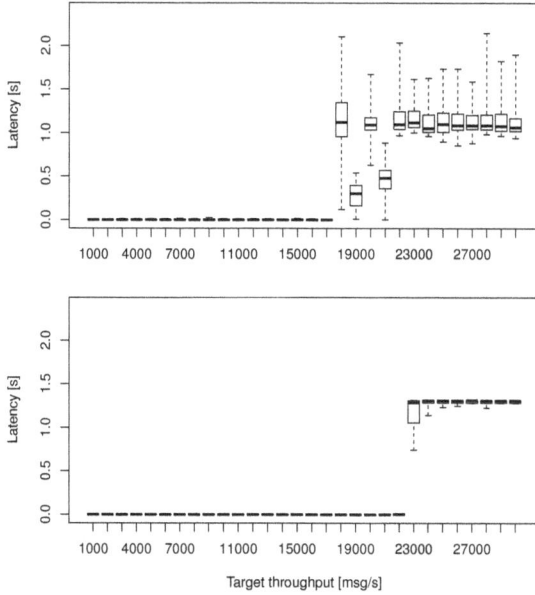

Figure 13: Measured (upper) and predicted (lower) message latencies at low to high throughput with regular workload.

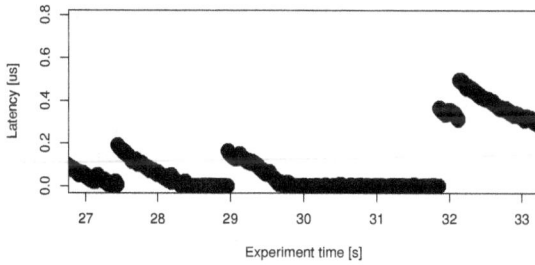

Figure 14: Unstable broker latencies at 19000 msg/s.

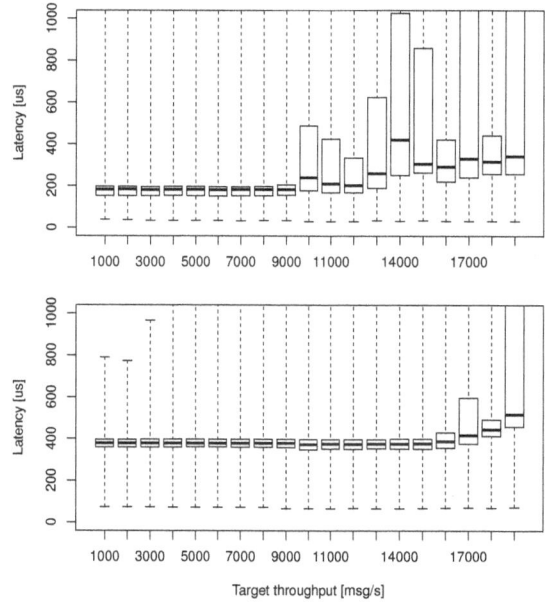

Figure 15: Measured (upper) and predicted (lower) message latencies at low to medium throughput with bursty workload.

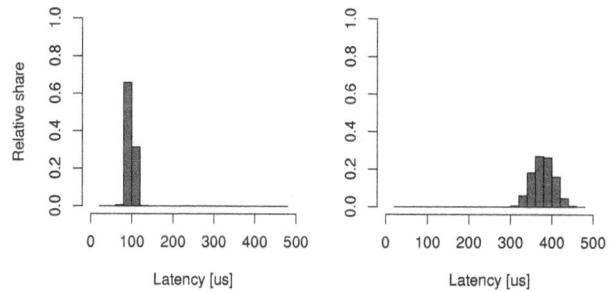

Figure 16: Predicting impact of bursts on latency distribution. Constant throughput 5000 msg/s, left workload sending individual messages, right workload sending bursts of ten messages.

times that match the target throughput. This is necessary because at high throughput rates, the measured arrival times include broker flow control and therefore reflect the observed throughput rate rather than the target throughput rate.

Figure 15 shows the measured and predicted message latencies for low to medium throughput rates generated in the bursty pattern. Similar to the regular workload results, the bursty workload results show the same trend, with some overestimation of latency and some underestimation of variation. As an important factor, the model correctly predicts that introducing burstiness results in shifting the cluster of observed latencies en bloc, rather than creating multiple clusters as Section 3.1 illustrates. Compare Figure 16 with Figures 2 and 3.

5.3 Discussion

The results show that our model is capable of addressing the issues outlined in Section 3 as far as the trends are concerned – we predict that pipelined processing of message bursts results in a tight cluster of latencies, we show that varying thread scheduling overhead leads to utilization and throughput peaking at very different rates, and we do both

in presence of realistic message coalescing. To our knowledge, these effects were not captured by JMS models before.

The prediction of processor utilization is also very accurate in absolute terms. The same cannot be said about latency, where our predictions at low throughput are somewhat pessimistic and predictions at high throughput do not fluctuate as much as measurements – as we explain, this is in part due to model calibration and in part due to realistic scheduling being more complex than the scheduling disciplines of our model. The accuracy of latency prediction is very reasonable for uses outlined in Section 2. We should note that we do not use measured latencies to calibrate the model and still predict latencies of individual messages at very high resolution. Again, we believe this was not done in JMS models before.

An important question that we address in this discussion is whether our results can be generalized beyond our experiments. We present arguments for why we believe our work is not strictly limited to our experimental platform. We also provide the source code and the data we have collected and used, so that more experiments are possible [1].

The most visible concern in generalizing our results is the range of workloads used in the experiments. While we vary both the throughput rate and the distribution of message arrival times, we use messages of equal size and type exchanged between a single producer and a single consumer. This contrasts especially with work that experiments on complex workloads such as SPECjms2007 [34].

The existing body of work on JMS performance provides a reliable summary of how individual workload parameters influence performance, and in fact suggests that extending the workload along many parameter axes would bring little principal benefit. Work such as [33, 13] shows there usually is a linear dependency between the message size and the associated processor demand, in contrast there usually is almost no dependency on the number of clients and destinations as long as messages are not replicated. Our model can be extended to support multiple message sizes and types by using multiple token colors with different associated processor demands, as used in [34]. Support for multiple clients and destinations should not require principal changes to our model either – the relevant message processing paths in our broker are reasonably similar to the message processing path of our workload. On the other hand, workloads that require persistent message storage would represent a challenge, due to the dominating nature of storage latencies in the model that otherwise deals in microseconds.

Experiments with limited workloads provide an important benefit in that they help isolate individual modeling concerns. Tracking the performance issues that we focus on in a complex workload is virtually impossible – although they are still likely to exist (there is no reason why context switching or garbage collection would go away with more complex workloads), their performance impact is combined with the performance impact of workload variability.

As one item, our work covers the impact of thread scheduling overhead on performance. The exact impact is both workload-dependent and platform-dependent – in general, we can expect the need for context switching to increase with more clients and destinations (because clients and destinations are served by separate threads) and to decrease with more cores (because threads will not compete for cores as much). As long as there are more clients and destinations (and therefore internal broker threads) than cores, the thread scheduling overhead should be present. The performance impact of individual context switches is also likely to increase with heavier workload, because such workload is associated with heavier memory cache traffic and context switches may flush memory cache content.

As another item, our work describes pipelined message processing. This is an architectural decision that concerns the broker implementation, one that is apparently reasonable but certainly not the only one possible. Brokers that use different architectures may require different models – unfortunately, determining the broker architecture for performance modeling purposes is a demanding endeavor even when broker sources are available, and not likely to get easier with closed source brokers.

Finally, our work requires measuring durations of operations that occur inside the broker. This is again easier when broker sources are available, but with current instrumen-

tation techniques [28, 27], instrumenting major control flow locations such as network communication or thread synchronization inside closed source brokers is also possible.

6. RELATED WORK

Performance modeling of distributed systems based on messaging is a frequent research subject. Some authors choose to work at a relatively high abstraction level, modeling complex networks of computers that communicate through messaging. At this level, details of individual node performance are typically simplified and the modeling efforts investigate important high level properties such as system capacity limits. Some high level modeling work is very close to our research, for example [18] proposes a method of constructing models that approximates communicating nodes with $M/M/1$ queues and uses QPN for experimental evaluation. Our model can improve this approximation – the possibility is actually mentioned by the authors, but there is not enough technical information in the paper to estimate the contribution of such model change to accuracy.

In [34], the SPECjms2007 benchmark is modeled with QPN, using $G/M/8$ queues to approximate processors and $G/M/1$ queues to approximate storage. The authors achieve significant modeling accuracy on a variety of workloads – in contrast with our work, the authors cover a wide variety of message sizes and types and quality-of-service settings, but keep the broker processor utilization below 80 %. The authors use a nested QPN model with three timed places in tandem representing the processor, the storage and the network resources – our model can again improve this approximation when exploring workloads that lead to high broker utilization, provided it is extended with more quality-of-service settings.

In [26], the broker is approximated with an $M/M/*$ queue, similar queues are used to model a component container and a database. The authors predict throughput and latency in a closed workload with zero think time – a situation which exercises the ability of the broker to serve individual clients fairly, leading to a linear dependency between the number of clients and the latency.

In a broader context, other formal tools are used to model messaging networks – for example, probabilistic timed automata are used to capture behavior in presence of message loss in [12]. We observe that high level modeling is considered valuable even when validation against a real system is not done.

Some studies focus on explorative evaluation of broker performance. Among early examples is [6], where performance of two JMS brokers were evaluated. The measurements focus on maximum sustainable throughput with various quality-of-service settings. A thorough study of JMS performance is [33], where one JMS broker is examined using the SPECjms2007 benchmark. Although these studies do not construct performance models (and sometimes do not even name the examined brokers due to licensing restrictions), they are a valuable source of common performance trends that can be observed across brokers. One typical observation is that message size is an important factor, increase in message size causes linear increase in processor demand. In contrast, the number of clients and destinations does not seem to be important when the total traffic remains constant. These observations support our discussion on including additional validation workloads in our work.

Explorative evaluation of broker performance can help create fitted models. This is the case in a large range of experiments summarized in the doctoral thesis [13]. In a number of separate publications, these experiments investigate parameters such as throughput [14] or latency [30] and construct fitted models that approximate the measurements. Interestingly, some of the experiment parameter ranges are chosen with the assumption that peak processor utilization implies peak throughput, which we show is not necessarily true.

A thorough process of building a fitted JMS model through explorative experiments is described in [11]. The experiments are carried on the ActiveMQ 5.3 messaging middleware, which makes the results even closer to ours. Again, the choice of experiment parameter ranges equals peak utilization workload with peak throughput workload. The work also demonstrates the difficulties of building an accurate model for the range of workloads we consider – the processor utilization in the experiments used to create the fitted model never exceeds 50 %, and the parameter dependencies are collected in experiments that assume no resource contention, which may limit suitable parameters.

Another work that creates a fitted JMS model is [9], the authors show how the model can be integrated into a larger performance model that captures particular SPECjms2007 interactions. The focus is on the integration process, technical details of the JMS model are not investigated. Similar approach in the context of component systems was investigated in [25].

Our work also touches on the issue of constructing a performance model with limited knowledge of the modeled system. Other authors have tackled this problem, in [4] an enterprise application model is constructed from partial architectural information and collected execution traces.

The problem of determining resource demands with limited measurement ability in the context of workload with multiple request types was addressed in [32] and [22], the authors of [42] estimate and adjust performance model parameters by tracking the prediction error. Using similar techniques in combination with artificial workloads crafted to exercise particular elements of the broker architecture can likely provide enough information to calibrate the performance model even when measurements based on instrumentation are not available.

As a summary to our related work survey, we believe our model can provide accuracy improvement in the context of existing modeling work, which mostly acknowledges that broker performance is implementation specific and provides mechanisms for plugging detailed broker models into platform independent application models. Where fitted models are used, our work highlights important effects related to pipelined processing and message coalescing that should be considered when selecting the model parameters. We also believe our work is the first to attract attention to the significant impact of pipelined processing and message coalescing in the context of broker performance modeling.

7. CONCLUSION

Our work is based on observing performance of the ActiveMQ messaging middleware. We attract attention to the fact that pipelined processing (the act of handling messages in stages by multiple broker threads) and message coalescing (the act of processing several adjacent messages together at some stage) can interact even with very simple workloads to create performance effects of significant magnitude that the existing performance models do not capture. We provide technical explanation for these effects and design a broker model that describes them.

We show that our model provides a reasonably accurate approximation of the identified effects. As an important distinction – where the existing JMS models may capture the effects by calibrating for a particular workload, our JMS model is built by analyzing and reflecting the reasons behind the effects. Our work therefore touches upon a broader question of how calibrating and validating the model against the same workload – something that is regularly done in model validation experiments – contributes to perceived model accuracy.

Although our work has used a specific platform and specific workloads, we argue that the effects we observe can reasonably occur on other platforms. We provide the source code and the data we have collected and used to make more experiments possible [1].

Acknowledgement

This research has been funded by the EU project ASCENS 257414, by the German Research Foundation (DFG) grant RE1674/5-1, by the Czech Science Foundation (GAČR) grant P202/10/J042, and Charles University institutional funding.

8. REFERENCES

[1] Complementary material.
http://d3s.mff.cuni.cz/papers/jms-modeling-icpe.

[2] Apache Software Foundation. *Apache ActiveMQ*.
http://activemq.apache.org.

[3] F. Brosch, H. Koziolek, B. Buhnova, and R. Reussner. Architecture-Based Reliability Prediction with the Palladio Component Model. *Transactions on Software Engineering*, 38(6), 2011.

[4] F. Brosig, S. Kounev, and K. Krogmann. Automated Extraction of Palladio Component Models from Running Enterprise Java Applications. In *Proceedings of ROSSA 2009*, 2009.

[5] L. Bulej, T. Bures, J. Keznikl, A. Koubková, A. Podzimek, and P. Tuma. Capturing performance assumptions using stochastic performance logic. In *Proceedings of ICPE 2012*. ACM, 2012.

[6] S. Chen and P. Greenfield. QoS Evaluation of JMS: An Empirical Approach. In *Proceedings of HICSS 2004*. IEEE, 2004.

[7] I. Epifani, C. Ghezzi, R. Mirandola, and G. Tamburrelli. Model Evolution by Run-Time Parameter Adaptation. In *Proceedings of ICSE 2009*. IEEE, 2009.

[8] J. Happe, S. Becker, C. Rathfelder, H. Friedrich, and R. H. Reussner. Parametric Performance Completions for Model-Driven Performance Prediction. *Performance Evaluation*, 67(8), 2010.

[9] J. Happe, H. Friedrich, S. Becker, and R. Reussner. A Pattern-Based Performance Completion for Message-Oriented Middleware. In *Proceedings of WOSP 2008*. ACM, 2008.

[10] J. Happe, H. Groenda, M. Hauck, and R. Reussner. A Prediction Model for Software Performance in Symmetric Multiprocessing Environments, 2010.

[11] J. Happe, D. Westermann, K. Sachs, and L. Kapova. Statistical Inference of Software Performance Models for Parametric Performance Completions. In *Proceedings of QOSA 2010*. Springer, 2010.

[12] F. He, L. Baresi, C. Ghezzi, and P. Spoletini. Formal Analysis of Publish-Subscribe Systems by Probabilistic Timed Automata. In *Proceedings of FORTE 2007*. Springer, 2007.

[13] R. Henjes. Performance Evaluation of Publish/Subscribe Middleware Architectures, 2010.

[14] R. Henjes, M. Menth, and C. Zepfel. Throughput Performance of Java Messaging Services Using WebSphereMQ. In *Proceedings of ICDCS 2006 WORKSHOPS*, 2006.

[15] V. Horky, F. Haas, J. Kotrc, M. Lacina, and P. Tuma. Performance Regression Unit Testing: A Case Study. In *Proceedings of EPEW 2013*. Springer, 2013.

[16] Internet Engineering Task Force. *Congestion Control in IP/TCP Internetworks*. http://tools.ietf.org/html/rfc896.

[17] R. Jones and R. Lins. Java SE 6 HotSpot Virtual Machine Garbage Collection Tuning. http://www.oracle.com/technetwork/java/javase/gc-tuning-6-140523.html.

[18] S. Kounev, K. Sachs, J. Bacon, and A. Buchmann. A Methodology for Performance Modeling of Distributed Event-Based Systems. In *Proceedings of ISORC 2008*. IEEE, 2008.

[19] S. Kounev, S. Spinner, and P. Meier. QPME 2.0 - A Tool for Stochastic Modeling and Analysis Using Queueing Petri Nets. In *From Active Data Management to Event-Based Systems and More*, 2010.

[20] S. Kounev, S. Spinner, and P. Meier. Introduction to Queueing Petri Nets: Modeling Formalism, Tool Support and Case Studies (Tutorial Paper). In *Proceedings of ICPE 2012*. ACM, 2012.

[21] H. Koziolek, B. Schlich, C. Bilich, R. Weiss, S. Becker, K. Krogmann, M. Trifu, R. Mirandola, and A. Martens. An Industrial Case Study on Quality Impact Prediction for Evolving Service-Oriented Software. In *Proceedings of ICSE 2011*. ACM, 2011.

[22] S. Kraft, S. Pacheco-Sanchez, G. Casale, and S. Dawson. Estimating Service Resource Consumption from Response Time Measurements. In *Proceedings of VALUETOOLS 2006*. ACM, 2006.

[23] C. Li, C. Ding, and K. Shen. Quantifying The Cost of Context Switch. In *Proceedings of ExpCS 2007*. ACM, 2007.

[24] P. Libič, P. Tůma, and L. Bulej. Issues in Performance Modeling of Applications With Garbage Collection. In *Proceedings of QUASOSS 2009*. ACM, 2009.

[25] Y. Liu, A. Fekete, and I. Gorton. Design-Level Performance Prediction of Component-Based Applications. *IEEE Transactions on Software Engineering*, 31(11), 2005.

[26] Y. Liu and I. Gorton. Performance Prediction of J2EE Applications Using Messaging Protocols. In *Proceedings of CBSE 2005*. ACM, 2005.

[27] C.-K. Luk, R. Cohn, R. Muth, H. Patil, A. Klauser, G. Lowney, S. Wallace, V. J. Reddi, and K. Hazelwood. Pin: Building Customized Program Analysis Tools with Dynamic Instrumentation. In *Proceedings of PLDI 2005*. ACM, 2005.

[28] L. Marek, A. Villazón, Y. Zheng, D. Ansaloni, W. Binder, and Z. Qi. DiSL: A Domain-Specific Language for Bytecode Instrumentation. In *Proceedings of AOSD 2012*. ACM, 2012.

[29] P. Menage. Linux Control Groups. https://www.kernel.org/doc/Documentation/cgroups/cgroups.txt.

[30] M. Menth and R. Henjes. Analysis of the Message Waiting Time for the FioranoMQ JMS Server. In *Proceedings of ICDCS 2006*, 2006.

[31] NS-3 Project. *NS-3*. http://www.nsnam.org/.

[32] G. Pacifici, W. Segmuller, M. Spreitzer, and A. Tantawi. Dynamic Estimation of CPU Demand of Web Traffic. In *Proceedings of VALUETOOLS 2006*. ACM, 2006.

[33] K. Sachs, S. Kounev, J. Bacon, and A. Buchmann. Performance Evaluation of Message-Oriented Middleware Using the SPECjms2007 Benchmark. *Performance Evaluation*, 2009.

[34] K. Sachs, S. Kounev, and A. Buchmann. Performance Modeling and Analysis of Message-Oriented Event-Driven Systems. *Journal of Software and Systems Modeling*, 2012.

[35] B. Sigoure. How Long Does It Take To Make A Context Switch ? http://blog.tsunanet.net/2010/11/how-long-does-it-take-to-make-context.html.

[36] C. U. Smith and L. G. Williams. *Performance Solutions: A Practical Guide to Creating Responsive, Scalable Software*. Addison-Wesley, 2002.

[37] Sun Microsystems. *Java Message Service Specification Version 1.1*, 2002.

[38] E. Varki, A. Merchant, J. Xu, and X. Qiu. Issues and Challenges in the Performance Analysis of Real Disk Arrays. *IEEE Transactions on Parallel and Distributed Systems*, 15(6), 2004.

[39] T. Verdickt, B. Dhoedt, F. Gielen, and P. Demeester. Automatic Inclusion of Middleware Performance Attributes into Architectural UML Software Models. *IEEE Transactions on Software Engineering*, 31(8), 2005.

[40] H. Xu. GSO: Generic Segmentation Offload. http://lwn.net/Articles/188489/.

[41] H. Xu. net: Generic Receive Offload. http://lwn.net/Articles/311357/.

[42] T. Zheng, C. M. Woodside, and M. Litoiu. Performance Model Estimation and Tracking Using Optimal Filters. *IEEE Transactions on Software Engineering*, 2008.

Performance Awareness

Keynote Abstract

Petr Tůma
Department of Distributed and Dependable Systems
Faculty of Mathematics and Physics
Charles University, Prague, Czech Republic
petr.tuma@d3s.mff.cuni.cz

ABSTRACT

The talk will take a broad look at performance awareness, defined as the ability to observe performance and to act on the observations. The implicit question posed in the talk is what can be done to improve various aspects of performance awareness – be it our awareness of the various performance relevant mechanisms, our awareness of the expected software performance, our ability to attain and exploit performance awareness as software developers, and our options for implementing performance aware applications.

Keywords

Performance Awareness, Development, Documentation, Measurement

Categories and Subject Descriptors

D.4.8 [**Performance**]: Measurements

General Terms

Performance

1. OVERVIEW

In broad terms, performance awareness can be defined as the ability to observe performance and to act on the observations. Performance awareness should permeate software development – at many levels, from architectural design through implementation to eventual maintenance, decisions need to be made that balance performance against factors such as development effort or maintenance cost – and without performance awareness, this balance cannot be achieved.

Performance awareness is often gained through experimental performance evaluation. Observation of live systems is used to learn about actual performance and to discover and analyze potential performance anomalies ; experimental benchmarks of various complexity are used to evaluate software and hardware designs ; theoretical performance models are often validated against experimental measurements.

Because thorough experimental performance evaluation can be both difficult and expensive, software development may rely on an evaluation that is accidentally or intentionally limited. A limited evaluation may contribute to incomplete awareness, which in turn increases the potential for less-than-ideal development decisions that yield less-than-optimal software systems.

Using examples of performance evaluation experiments, the talk will argue that opportunities for relatively simple improvements exist in the methods and tools we use to achieve performance awareness. The talk structure will look at four performance awareness topics:

Mechanisms. Contemporary systems include complex performance relevant mechanisms that interact to determine the observed performance. Performance awareness requires learning about these mechanisms in an efficient manner.

Expectations. The observed performance of a system is a result of both deliberate design and accidental interactions. Compared to awareness of the observed performance, awareness of the design intent can be more convenient in some software development tasks.

Developers. It is difficult to anticipate which steps in the software development process will significantly influence system performance. Besides working on automated optimizations that tend to hide performance relevant mechanisms, we should work on efficient methods and tools that provide developers with performance awareness to complement the optimizations.

Applications. Dynamic nature of performance often requires adaptive applications that possess performance awareness. Despite this need, performance awareness is still not treated the same as other forms of software reflection.

ICPE'14, March 22–26, 2014, Dublin, Ireland
ACM 978-1-4503-2733-6/14/03.
http://dx.doi.org/10.1145/2568088.2576097.

Figure 2: Instrumentation overhead.

2. MEASUREMENTS

The keynote abstract reproduces several of the experimental measurements from the talk for better readability. Figure 1 illustrates the impact of heap object placement on the SPEC CPU2006 results. Figure 2 shows the overhead of instrumenting all exported functions of SPEC CPU2006 with timestamping. The measurements were conducted on a server with two Intel Xeon E5-2660 processors, 48 GB RAM, running the latest packages from Fedora 18 and Fedora 20 distributions of Linux.

3. ACKNOWLEDGMENTS

Collaboration with my current and former colleagues, for which I remain ever grateful, has naturally contributed to the presented results. The EU and GAČR funding was essential for much of our activities.

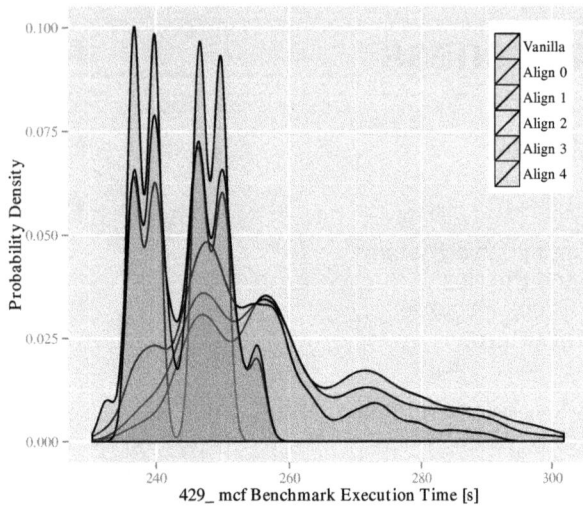

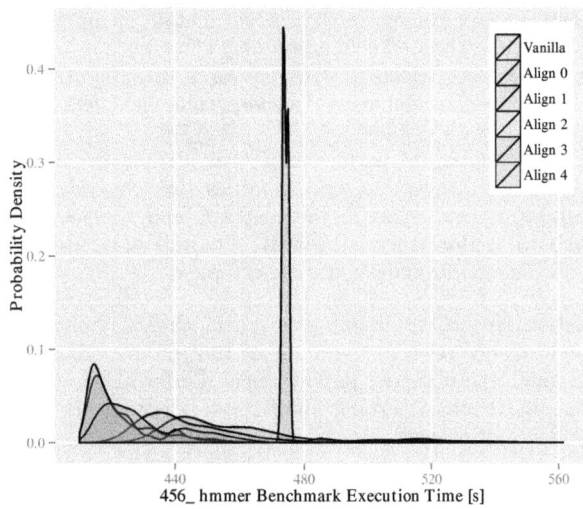

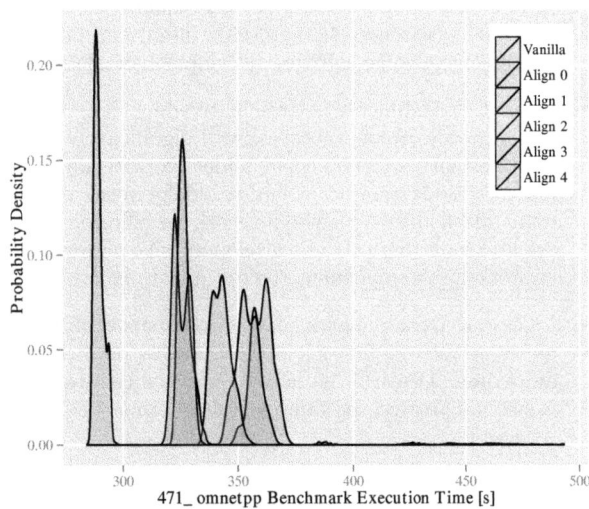

Figure 1: Allocation alignment impact.

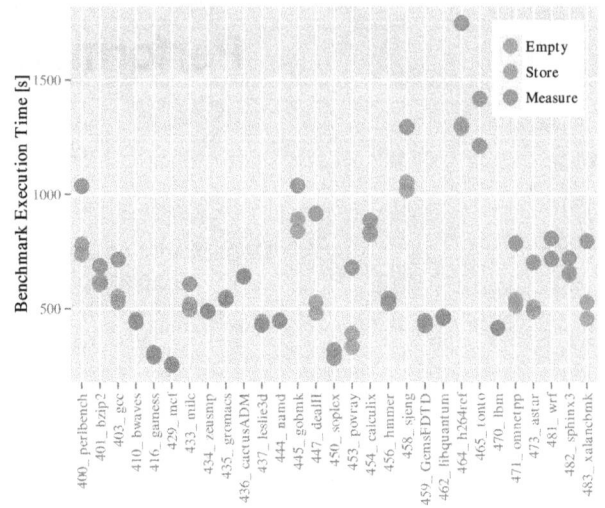

Test-Driving Intel Xeon Phi[*]

Jianbin Fang
TU Delft, the Netherlands
j.fang@tudelft.nl

Henk Sips
TU Delft, the Netherlands
h.j.sips@tudelft.nl

Lilun Zhang
NUDT, China
llzhang@nudt.edu.cn

Chuanfu Xu
NUDT, China
xuchuanfu@nudt.edu.cn

Yonggang Che
NUDT, China
ygche@nudt.edu.cn

Ana Lucia Varbanescu
UvA, the Netherlands
a.l.varbanescu@uva.nl

ABSTRACT

Based on Intel's Many Integrated Core (MIC) architecture, Intel Xeon Phi is one of the few truly many-core CPUs - featuring around 60 fairly powerful cores, two levels of caches, and graphic memory, all interconnected by a very fast ring. Given its promised ease-of-use and high performance, we took Xeon Phi out for a test drive. In this paper, we present this experience at two different levels: (1) the microbenchmark level, where we stress "each nut and bolt" of Phi in the lab, and (2) the application level, where we study Phi's performance response in a real-life environment. At the microbenchmarking level, we show the high performance of five components of the architecture, focusing on their maximum achieved performance and the prerequisites to achieve it. Next, we choose a medical imaging application (Leukocyte Tracking) as a case study. We observed that it is rather easy to get functional code and start benchmarking, but the first performance numbers can be far from satisfying. Our experience indicates that a simple data structure and massive parallelism are critical for Xeon Phi to perform well. When compiler-driven parallelization and/or vectorization fails, programming Xeon Phi for performance can become very challenging.

Categories and Subject Descriptors

H.4 [**Information Systems Applications**]: Miscellaneous; D.2.8 [**Software Engineering**]: Metrics—*complexity measures, performance measures*

Keywords

Experience with Xeon Phi, Microbenchmarking, Performance Analysis, Optimization.

---

[*]Part of the work was done by Jianbin Fang during an internship, funded by the Natural Science Foundation of China under Grant No.11272352, at NUDT in January 2013.

1. INTRODUCTION

Intel Xeon Phi (Phi) is the newest high-throughput architecture targeted at high performance computing (HPC). Without a doubt, Phi will be part of the very next generation of supercomputers that will challenge TOP500[1].

To achieve its theoretical high performance (around 1 TFlop), Intel Xeon Phi [15] uses around 60 cores and 30 MB of on-chip caches, and relies on traditional many-core features like vector units or SIMD/SIMT, high throughput, and high bandwidth [17]. It adds to that some "unconventional" features, such as the overall L2 cache coherency and the ring interconnect, all for the sake of performance and usability.

By taking Phi as a black-box with over 200 hardware threads, we ran Leukocyte Tracking (a medical imaging application [21]) on it. We found that (1) the sequential application (a single thread) on Phi runs about 5× slower than the same sequential execution on a "traditional" multi-core processor, and (2) that the Phi version scales only up to 40 threads (Figure 13, more details in Section 5). To explain this (observed) performance behavior, as well as to eventually improve it, we require a deeper understanding of the architecture and its parameters.

Moreover, previous experiences with massively parallel high performance platforms such as NVIDIA GPUs or the Cell-/BE showed that a trade-off between performance and ease-of-use is necessary: "simple" programming often leads to disappointing performance [22,27]. Therefore, given Phi's promise of breaking this pattern, this work focuses on a test drive of the platform: we have conducted a two-stage empirical study of the Xeon Phi, stressing its high-performance features both in isolation (aiming to quantify their maximum achievable performance), and in the real-life case-study (aiming to understand its regular performance).

To this end, we have implemented and used dedicated microbenchmarks - gathered in a suite called *MIC-Meter* [2] - to measure the performance of four key architectural features of Xeon Phi: the processing cores, the memory hierarchies, the ring interconnect, and the PCIe connection. Following these experiments "in isolation", we propose a conceptual model of the processor that facilitates the performance analysis and optimization of the real-life case-study.

Such a thorough evaluation can benefit two different classes of Phi users: the *experts*, who are interested in in-depth architectural knowledge, and the *production users*, interested

---

[1]In June 2013, two Xeon Phi supercomputers - TIANHE-2 from NUDT and STAMPEDE from TACC - were ranked first and sixth in TOP500: http://www.top500.org.
[2]https://github.com/haibo031031/mic-meter

in simple and effective ways to use processors. For expert users - like most high performance computing (HPC) programmers and compiler developers are - knowing the requirements for density and placement of threads per cores, the optimal utilization of the core interconnections, or the difference in latency between the different types of memories on chip are non-trivial details that, when properly exploited, can lead to significant performance gains. For production users, a simplified view of the Xeon Phi machine is mandatory to help exploring different parallelism strategies. Such a model is simplified view of the machine, including the most important functionality and performance constraints.

The main contributions of our work are as follows:

- We present our hands-on experience achieved while microbenchmarking the Xeon Phi (Section 3). This experience also leads to interesting numerical results for the capabilities of Phi's cores, memories, interconnects (i.e., the ring and the PCIe).

- We synthesize four essential platform-centric performance guidelines, aimed at easing the development and tuning of applications for the Xeon Phi (Section 4).

- We propose a conceptual model of Phi ($SCAT$), which strips off the performance irrelevant architectural details, presenting the programmers with a simple, functionality-based view of the machine (Section 4).

- Using a case study (leukocyte tracking), we analyze the application and optimize it, discussing the lessons to be learned from this experience (Section 5).

2. BENCHMARKING INTEL XEON PHI

In this section, we introduce Intel Xeon Phi - with its novel features and typical programming models, and we present our benchmarking methodology.

2.1 The Architecture

Intel Xeon Phi has over 50 cores (the version used in this paper belongs to the 5100 series and has 60 cores) connected by a high-performance on-die bidirectional interconnect (shown in Figure 1). In addition to these cores, there are 16 memory channels (supported by memory controllers) delivering up to 5.0 GT/s [12]. When working as an accelerator, Phi can be connected to a host (i.e., a device that manages it) through a PCI Express (PCIe) system interface - similar to GPU-like accelerators. Different from GPUs, a dedicated embedded Linux μOS (version: 2.6.38.8) runs on the platform.

Each core contains a 512-bit wide vector unit (VPU) with vector register files (32 registers per thread context). Each core has a 32KB L1 data cache, a 32KB L1 instruction cache, and a core-private 512KB unified L2 cache. In total, a 60-core machine has a total of 30MB of L2 cache on the die. The L2 caches are kept fully coherent by the hardware, using DTDs (distributed tag directories), which are referenced after an L2 cache miss. Note that the tag directory is not centralized, but split up into 64 DTDs, each getting an equal portion of the address space and being responsible for maintaining it globally coherent. Another special feature of Xeon Phi is the fast bidirectional ring interconnect. All connected entities use the ring for communication purposes, using special controllers called *ring stops* to insert requests and receive responses on the ring.

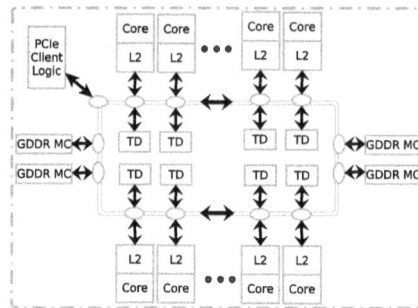

Figure 1: The Intel Xeon Phi Architecture.

The novelties of the Xeon Phi architecture relate to five components : (1) the vector processing cores, (2) the on-chip memory, (3) the off-chip memory, (4) the ring interconnect, and (5) the PCIe connection. As these are the features that differ, in one way or another, from a typical CPU - vectors are wider, there are many more cores, cache coherency and shared memory are provided with low penalty for 60 or more cores, and a ring interconnect holds tens of agents that can interchange messages/packets concurrently -, we focus our benchmarking efforts on these features.

2.2 Programming

In terms of usability, there are two ways an application can use Intel Xeon Phi: (1) in *offload mode* - the main application is running on the host, and it only offloads selected (highly parallel, computationally intensive) work to the coprocessor, or (2) in *native mode* - the application runs independently, on the Xeon Phi only, and can communicate with the main processor or other coprocessors [13] through the system bus. In this work, we benchmark Xeon Phi in both modes.

Finally, to program applications on Xeon Phi, users need to capture both functionality and parallelism. Being an x86 SMP-on-a-chip architecture, Xeon Phi offers the full capability to use the same tools, programming languages, and programming models as a regular Intel Xeon processor. Specifically, tools like Pthreads [5], OpenMP [2], Intel Cilk Plus [1], and OpenCL [24] are readily available. Given the large number of cores on the platform, a dedicated MPI version is also available. In this work, all the experiments we present are programmed using C/intrinsics/assembly with OpenMP/Pthreads; we also use Intel's icc compiler (V13.1.1.163).

2.3 MIC-Meter

We show our MIC-Meter in Figure 2. The goal of our benchmarking is two-fold: to show how the special capabilities of Xeon Phi can and should be measured, to quantify the performance of this novel many-core architecture, and eventually to identify the impacting factors. To this end, we choose a microbenchmarking approach: we measure each capability in isolation, under variable loads, and we quantify its performance in terms of both latency-oriented and throughput-oriented metrics.

Simply put, *latency* is the time required to perform an operation and produce a result. As latency measurement focuses on a single action from its beginning to its end, one needs to isolate the operation to be measured and use

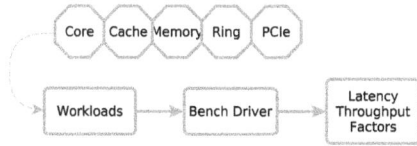

Figure 2: The MIC-Meter Overview.

a highly accurate, non-intrusive timing method. Alternatively, we can measure a long enough sequence of operations with an accurate timer, and estimate latency per operation by dividing the measured time by the number of operations. In this paper, latency measurements are done with a single thread (for individual operations) or two threads (for transfer operations) with Pthreads. All latency benchmarks are written in C (with inline assembly).

Throughput is the number of (a type of) operations executed in a given unit of time. As higher throughput means better performance, microbenchmarking focuses on measuring the *maximum achievable throughput* for different operations, under different loads; typically, the benchmarked throughput values are slightly lower than the theoretical ones. Thus, to measure maximum throughput, the main challenge is to build the workload such that the resource that is being evaluated is fully utilized. For example, when measuring computational throughput, enough threads should be used to fully utilize the cores, while when measuring memory bandwidth, the workload needs to have sufficient threads to generate enough memory requests. For all the throughput measurements in this paper, our multi-threaded workloads are written in C and OpenMP.

We note that the similarities between Phi and a regular multi-core CPU allow us to adapt existing CPU benchmarks to the requirements of Xeon Phi. In most cases, we use such "refurbished" solutions, that prove to serve our purposes.

3. EMPIRICAL EVALUATION

In the following sections, we present in detail the MIC-Meter and the results for each of the components: (1) the vector processing cores, (2) the on-chip and off-chip memory, (3) the ring interconnect, and (4) the PCIe connection.

3.1 Vector Processing Cores

We evaluate the vector processing cores in terms of both instruction latency and throughput. For latency, we use a method similar to those proposed by Agner Fog [7] and Torbjorn Granlund [9]: we measure instruction latency by running a (long enough) sequence of dependent instructions (i.e., a list of instructions that, being dependent on each other, are forced to be executed sequentially - *an instruction stream*).

The same papers propose a similar approach to measure throughput in terms of *instructions per cycle (IPC)*. However, we argue that a measurement that uses all processing cores together, and not in isolation, is more realistic for programmers. Thus, we develop a `flops` microbenchmark to explore the factors for reaching the theoretical maximum throughput on Xeon Phi (Section 3.1.2).

3.1.1 Vector Instruction Latency

Xeon Phi introduces 177 vector instructions [11]. We roughly divide these instructions into five classes [3]: mask instructions, arithmetic (logic) instructions, conversion instructions, permutation instructions, and extended mathematical instructions.

The benchmark for measuring the latency of vector instructions is measuring the execution time of a sequence of 100 vector operations using the same format: $zmm1 = op(zmm1, zmm2)$, where $zmm1$ and $zmm2$ represent two vectors and op is the instruction being measured. By making $zmm1$ be both a source operand and the destination operand, we ensure the instruction dependency - i.e., the current operation will depend on the result of the previous one.

For special classes of instructions - such as the `conversion` instructions `vcvtps2pd` and `vcvtpd2ps` - we have to measure the latency of the conversion pair ($zmm2 = op12(zmm1)$; $zmm1 = op21(zmm2)$) in order to guarantee the dependency between contiguous instructions (i.e., it is not possible to write the result of the conversion in the same source operand, due to type incompatibility). Similarly, we measure the latency of extended mathematical instructions such as `vexp223ps` and `vlog2ps` in pairs, to avoid overflow (e.g., when using 100 successive `exp()`'s).

The interesting results for vector instruction latency are presented in Table 1. With these latency numbers, we know how many threads or instruction streams we need to hide the latency on one processing core.

Table 1: The vector instruction latency (in cycles).

Instruction	Category	Latency
kand, kor, knot, kxor	mask instructions	2
vaddpd, vfmadd213pd, vmulpd, vsubpd	arithmetic instructions	4
vcvtdq2pd, vcvtfxpntdq2ps, vcvtfxpntps2dq, vcvtps2pd	convert instructions	5
vpermd, vpermf32x4	permutation instructions	6
vexp223ps, vlog2ps, vrcp23ps, vrsqrt23ps	extended mathematical instructions	6

3.1.2 Vector Instruction Throughput

The Xeon Phi 5100 has 60 cores working at 1.05 GHz, and each core can process 8 double-precision data elements at a time, with maximum 2 operations (`multiply-add` or `mad`) per cycle in each lane (i.e., a vector element). Therefore, the theoretical instruction throughput is 1008 GFlops (approximately 1 TFlop). But **is this 1 TFlop performance actually achievable?** To measure the instruction throughput, we run 1, 2, 4 threads on a core (60, 120, and 240 threads in total). During measurement, each thread performs one or two instruction streams for a fixed number of iterations: $b_{i+1} = b_i$ op a, where i represents the iteration, a is a constant, and b serves as an operand and the destination. The loop was fully unrolled to avoid branch overheads. The microbenchmark is vectorized using explicit intrinsics, to ensure a 100% vector usage.

---

[3]Note that we choose not to measure the latency of memory access instructions because the latency results are highly dependent on the data location(s).

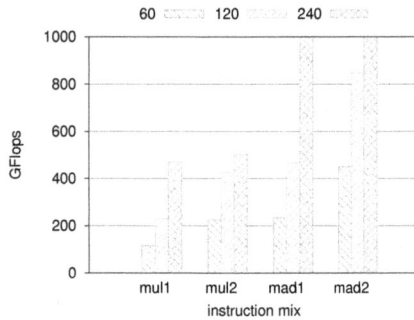

Figure 3: Arithmetic throughput using different numbers of threads (60, 120, 240), different instruction mixes (`mul` versus `mad`), and issue widths (using one and two independent instruction streams).

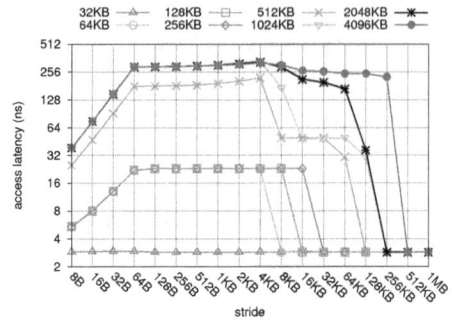

Figure 4: Average memory latency when changing strides and datasets. The x-axis is logarithmic and it represents the pointer chasing stride.

The results are shown in Figure 3. We note that the peak instruction throughput - i.e., one vector instruction per cycle (1TFlops in total) - can be achieved when using 240 threads and the multiply-add instruction. As expected, the `mad` throughput is twice larger than the `mul` throughput. Further, two more observations can be added. First, when using 60 threads (one thread per core), the instruction throughput is low compared with the cases when using 120 or 240 threads. This is due to the fact that it is not possible to issue instructions from the same thread context in back-to-back cycles [12]. Thus, programmers need to run at least two threads on each core to be able to fully utilize the hardware resources. Second, when a thread is using only one instruction stream, we have to use 4 threads per core (240 threads in total) to achieve the peak instruction throughput. This is because the latency of an arithmetic instruction is 4 cycles (Table 1), and we need no less than four threads to totally hide this latency (i.e., fill the pipeline bubbles [10]). To comply, programmers need to either use 4 threads per core or have more independent instruction streams.

To summarize, for a given instruction mix (`mul` or `mad`), the achievable instruction throughput depends not only on the number of cores and threads, but also on the issue width (i.e., the number of independent instruction streams). We also benchmarked the EMU (extended math unit) and see [6] for more details.

3.2 Memory Latency

Available benchmarks, such as `BenchIT` [25] and `lmbench` [18] use *pointer-chasing* to measure the on-chip and off-chip memory access latency. This approach has the advantage of not only determining the latency itself, but also exposing the differences between consecutive layers of a memory hierarchy (i.e., different layers of caches and main memory will have significantly different latencies). Thus, we use a similar approach to measure the latency for an Xeon Phi core (i.e., the latency for accessing local caches and main memory - see Section 3.2.1).

When more than two cores communicate, measuring latency is complicated. For this, Daniel Molka et al. proposed an approach to quantify cache-coherency effects [19]. In our

work, we adapt this approach to Xeon Phi using the correct memory fences and cache flushing instructions [4].

3.2.1 Access Latency on a Single Core

To reveal the local access latency, we use a *pointer-chasing* benchmark similar to those used by `BenchIT` and `lmbench`. Essentially, the application traverses an array A of size S by running $k = A[k]$ in a fully unrolled loop. The array is initialized with a *stride*, i.e., $A[k] = (k + stride)\%S$. By measuring the execution time of the traversal, we can easily obtain an estimate of the average execution time for one iteration. This time is dominated by the latency of the memory access. The traversal is done in one thread and utilizes only one core. Therefore, the memory properties obtained here are local and belong to one core.

The results are shown in Figure 4. We see that the Xeon Phi has two levels of data caches (L1 and L2). The L1 data cache is 32KB, while the L2 data caches should be smaller than 512KB. Furthermore, the accessing latency of L1 and L2 data caches is around 2.87 ns (3 cycles) and 22.98 ns (24 cycles), respectively. With a stride of 64 bytes, Xeon Phi takes 287.51 ~ 291.18 ns (302 ~ 306 cycles) to finish a data access in the main memory (when the dataset is larger than 512KB). We note that when traversing the array in a larger stride (e.g., 4KB), the latency of accessing data in off-chip memory is slightly larger. This is because the contiguous memory accesses fall into different pages. Furthermore, we can observe (from the upper trend) that threads operate the data in a batch manner, i.e., a 64-byte cache-line. Information about cache associativity can also be seen in Figure 4 (see [23] for the calculation approach).

3.2.2 Remote Cache Latency

We have illustrated our measurements and results for memory latency on a single core in Section 3.2.1. In this section, we focus on measuring remote cache latency. For these measurements, we use an approach based on that proposed for a traditional multi-core processor by Daniel Molka [19]. Our setup is built as follows: prior to the measurement, the to-be-transferred cache-lines are placed in different locations (cores) and in a certain coherency state (`modified`, `exclusive`, or `shared`). In each measurement, we use two threads

---

[4]Since Xeon Phi has no `mfence` or `clflush`, we need to change the benchmark by searching and replacing them with equivalent instructions.

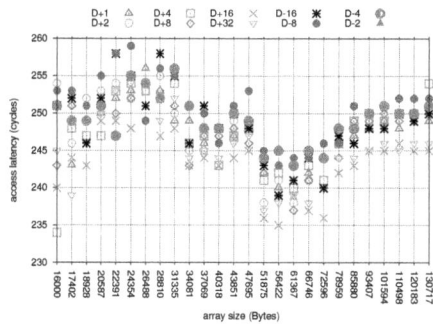

(a) Modified

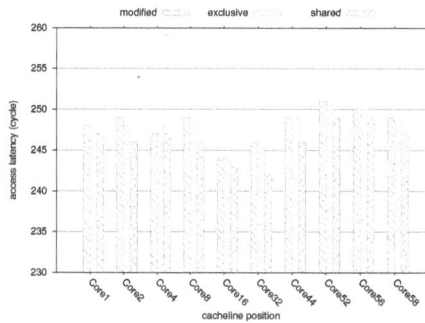

(b) Overall

Figure 5: Read latencies of Core 0 accessing the cache lines on Core 1 (D+1), Core 2 (D+2), Core 4 (D+4), Core 8 (D+8), Core 16 (D+16), Core 32 (D+32), Core 44 (D-16), Core 52 (D-8), Core 56 (D-4),and Core 58 (D-2).

(T0, T1), with T0 pinned to Core 0 and T1 pinned on another core (Core X). The latency measurement always runs on Core 0, transferring a predefined number of cache lines from Core X to Core 0.

Figure 5 shows our results for remote cache accesses latency on Xeon Phi. In Figure 5(a), we see that when the cache line is in modified state, the overall latency of remote access averages around 250 cycles, which is much larger than the local cache access latency (by an order of magnitude) but still smaller than the off-chip memory access latency (by 17%). By getting the *median* value of all the input data sets (up to 128 KB), we get the overall remote latency shown in Figure 5(b). We note no relationship between the remote access latency and the cache-line states, except that accessing remote shared cachelines takes a few less cycles. This is because in whichever state a cacheline is, when a core accesses it, a transfer is needed from a remote core (different from a traditional multi-core CPU with cores sharing the last-level cache). Furthermore, Xeon Phi adopts the MOESI cache coherence protocol [12] to share a cacheline before writing it back, and thus Figure 5(b) shows no penalty of writing data back. In [6], our experiments have shown that there is a relation between the latency and the core distances on an older version of the Xeon Phi (namely, 31S1P), but this effect seems to have disappeared on the newer Xeon Phi 5110.

3.3 Memory Bandwidth

McCalphin's stream benchmark [16] includes a memory bandwidth benchmark and presents results for a large number of high-end systems. However, his solution is based on a combination of both read and write operations. In this paper, we want to separate *reads* and *writes* so as to quantify the impacting factors. In BenchIT, Daniel Molka et al. presents a solution to measure bandwidth in a similar way with that of latency measurement (see Section 3.2.2). His microbenchmark requires compiler optimizations to be disabled (i.e., the code should be compiled with the -OO option), thus disabling the software prefetching on Xeon Phi. As a result, this measurement will underestimate bandwidth. In this section, we present our own OpenMP implementation of a memory bandwidth microbenchmark, considering hardware/software prefetching, streaming stores, ECC effects and off-chip/on-chip differences.

3.3.1 Off-Chip Memory Bandwidth

The Xeon Phi used in this work has 16 memory channels, each 32-bits wide. At up to 5.0 GT/s transfer speed [5], it provides a theoretical bandwidth of 320 GB/s. But **is this theoretical bandwidth really achievable in real cases?** To answer this question, we use separate benchmarks to measure the memory bandwidth for both read and write operations. The read benchmark reads data from an array A ($b = b + A[k]$). The write benchmark writes a constant value into an array A ($A[k] = C$). Note that A needs to be large enough (e.g., 1 GB) such that it cannot fit in the on-chip memory. To avoid the impact of "cold" TLBs, we start with two "warm-up" iterations of the benchmarks, before we measure a third one. We use different numbers of running threads - from 1 to 240.

Our results are shown in Figure 6 (HWP+SWP) (we plot the median value of ten runs of the benchmarks). Overall, we see that the maximum bandwidth for both read and write is far below the theoretical peak of 320 GB/s. Moreover, both the read and write memory bandwidth increases over the number of threads - which happens because when using more threads, we can generate more requests to memory controllers, thus making the interconnect and memory channels busier. Thus, if aiming to achieve high memory bandwidth, programmers need to launch enough threads to saturate the interconnect and the memory channels. Figure 6(a) shows that the read bandwidth peaks at 164 GB/s, achievable with using 60 threads or more (pinning at least one thread to a core). However, we can obtain the maximum write bandwidth (76 GB/s, as seen in Figure 6(b)) only when using 240 threads. In general, the write bandwidth is around half of the read bandwidth. This happens because Xeon Phi implements a write-allocate cache policy and the original content has to be loaded into caches before we overwrite it completely. To avoid the memory bandwidth waste, programmer can use *streaming stores* [6] on Xeon Phi [14]. We see that using *streaming store* instructions speeds up write operations up to 1.7 times (Figure 6(b):HWP+SWP+SS), with memory write bandwidth now peaking at 120 GB/s. Thus, programmers must consider using *streaming stores* to optimize the memory bandwidth.

---

[5]GT/s stands for Giga Transfers per second.
[6]Streaming stores do not require a prior cache line read for ownership (RFO) but write to memory "directly".

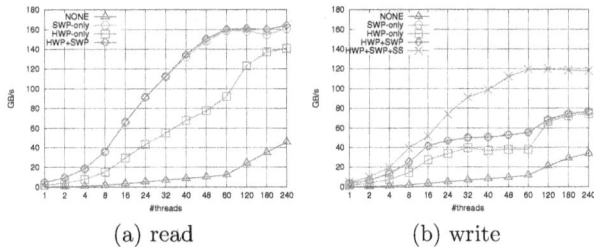

(a) read   (b) write

Figure 6: Read and write memory bandwidth.

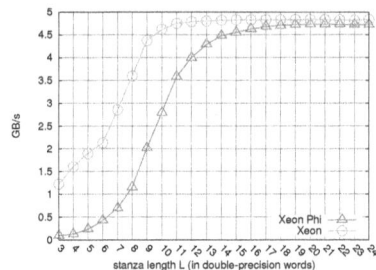

Figure 7: Performance of STriad on the Xeon Phi (the x-axis is in log scale and the results on Xeon are normalized to those on Xeon Phi).

Prefetch Effects: Xeon Phi supports both hardware prefetching (HWP) and software prefetching (SWP). The L2 cache has a streaming hardware prefetcher that can selectively prefetch code, read, and RFO (Read-For-Ownership) cachelines into the L2 cache [12]. Figure 6 shows the memory bandwidth of four different configurations: no prefetching, HWP or SWP only, or both. When disabling both HWP and SWP, the memory bandwidth is low (45 GB/s for reading and 33 GB/s for writing). With only SWP, we already achieve similar memory bandwidth to that achieved when enabling both of them. This similarity indicates that the hardware prefetcher will not kick in when software prefetching performs well. Furthermore, enabling only HWP delivers about half of the bandwidth achieved when enabling only SWP (the bandwidth is roughly $1.9\times$ smaller, on average).

To further evaluate the efficiency of prefetching on Xeon Phi, we use the Stanza Triad (STriad) [4] benchmark with a single thread. STriad works by performing a DAXPY (Triad) inner loop for a length L stanza, then jumps over k elements, and continues with the next L elements, until reaching the end of the array. We set the total array size to 128 MB, and set k to 2048 double-precision words. For each stanza, we ran the experiment 10 times, with the L2 cache flushed each time, and we calculate median value of the 10 runs to get the memory bandwidth for each stanza length. Figure 7 shows the results of the STriad experiments on both Xeon Phi and a regular Xeon processor (Intel Xeon E5-2620). We see an increase in memory bandwidth over stanza length L, and we note it eventually approaches a peak of 4.7 GB/s (note that this is achieved per core). Further, we see the transition point (from the bandwidth-increasing state to the bandwidth-stable state) appears earlier on Xeon than on Xeon Phi. Therefore, we conclude that non-contiguous access to memory is detrimental to memory bandwidth efficiency, with Xeon Phi showing more restrictions on the stanza length when prefetching data than the regular Xeons. To comply, programmers have to create the longest possible stanzas of contiguous memory accesses, improving prefetching and memory bandwidth.

ECC Effects: The Xeon Phi coprocessor supports ECC (Error Correction Code) to avoid software errors caused by naturally occurring radiation. Enabling ECC adds reliability, but it also introduces extra overhead to check for errors. We examined the bandwidth differences with and without disabling ECC. With ECC disabled, we noticed a 20% to 27% bandwidth increase [6]. Note that all the experiments in this paper are performed with ECC enabled. Furthermore, the new μOS kernel on Phi adds support of the transparent huge pages (THP) functionality, which is enabled by

default and often improves application performance without any code or environmental changes.

3.3.2 Aggregated On-Chip Memory Bandwidth

The available on-chip memory bandwidth is always essential in performance tuning and analysis. So, **how large is the on-chip memory bandwidth that can be achieved?** To answer this question, we measure the cache bandwidth on a single core [7] and calculate the *aggregated* cache bandwidth by multiplying it with the number of cores. We first use a set of vmovapd instructions to measure the native **read** or **write** bandwidth. Our results show that the L1 access (read or write) throughput is 64 bytes per cycle. Thus, the aggregated L1 bandwidth is 4032 GB/s for **read** or **write**. Then we measure the maximum achieved bandwidth from programmers' point of view for scale1 ($O[i] = a \times A[i]$), scale2 ($O[i] = a \times O[i]$), saxpy1 ($O[i] = a \times A[i] + B[i]$), and saxpy2 ($O[i] = a \times A[i] + O[i]$) operations. To avoid overheads from the high-level code, we use intrinsics in the kernel code. We also disable the software prefetching due to the fact that the data is located in caches after warming up.

The results are shown in Figure 8. We see that the maximum achieved bandwidth on a core is 73 GB/s, 96 GB/s, 52 GB/s, 69 GB/s for scale1, scale2, saxpy1, saxpy2, respectively. The bandwidth of scale2 and saxpy2 is $1.3\times$ larger (than scale1 and saxpy1, respectively) because the data cache allows a read/write cache-line replacement to happen in a single cycle [8]. The L1 bandwidth on a single core could be larger when further unrolling the loops or better scheduling instructions for each dataset. The aforementioned numbers are achieved by unrolling the loops 16 times without changing the assembly code.

Furthermore, it is difficult to exactly measure the L2 bandwidth due to the presence of the L1 cache. The bandwidth depends on the memory access patterns. Specifically, when we use a L2-friendly memory access pattern, the compiler will identify the stream pattern and prefetch data to the L1 cache in time. By this, we will get a much larger bandwidth due to the common efforts of L1 and L2. On the other hand, an unfriendly memory access will experience many L1 misses

---

[7]Note that we choose not to measure the inter-core communication bandwidth because we assume that cache-line transfers occur rather scattered, and not in a large volume. Thus, the measurement of inter-core (remote) access latency is of greater use.

[8]http://software.intel.com/en-us/articles/intel-xeon-phi-core-micro-architecture

(a) scale1 bandwidth.

(b) scale2 bandwidth.

(c) saxpy1 bandwidth.

(d) saxpy2 bandwidth.

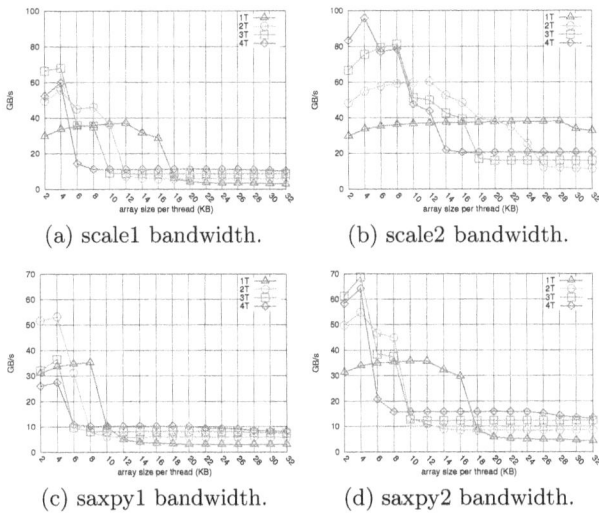

Figure 8: Cache bandwidth on a single core.

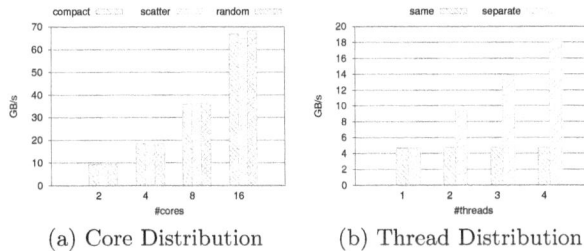

(a) Core Distribution

(b) Thread Distribution

Figure 9: Core and thread distribution effects (we use the `read` kernel and the array size is 1 GB).

and result in cache thrashing. Our benchmarking results are obtained when disabling the software prefetching. When using 4 threads on a core, we notice a bandwidth of 11 GB/s, 20 GB/s, 10 GB/s, 16 GB/s for `scale1`, `scale2`, `saxpy1`, `saxpy2`, respectively (Figure 8).

3.4 Ring Interconnect

On Xeon Phi, the cores and memory controllers are interconnected in a bi-directional ring. When multiple threads are requesting data simultaneously, shared components like the ring stop or DTDs can become performance bottlenecks. In order to check this hypothesis, and its eventual performance impact, we use *thread affinity* to fix threads on cores, and we run the bandwidth microbenchmarks to quantify potential bandwidth changes (in GB/s) for different thread-to-core mapping scenarios.

3.4.1 Core/Thread Distribution

First, we measure the `read` memory bandwidth by distributing threads onto separate cores in three different patterns: (1) *compact* - the cores are located close to each other, (2) *scattered* - the cores are evenly distributed around the ring, and (3) *random* - the core IDs are selected randomly with no repeats. The bandwidths are measured using 2, 4, 8, and 16 cores and the results are presented in Figure 9(a). We see that the three approaches achieve very similar memory bandwidths. Thus, the cores around the ring are *symmetric*

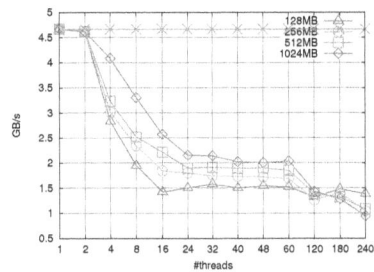

Figure 10: The memory bandwidth when the threads read the same memory space.

on Xeon Phi, and the distance between has practically no impact on the achieved bandwidth.

Second, as each Xeon Phi core supports up to four hardware threads, we investigate whether there is any impact on bandwidth if the threads are all gathered on the same core (thus, less interconnect traffic) or distributed among different cores. Figure 9(b) shows that when the threads run on the same core, the bandwidth stabilizes at 4.7 GB/s. We also note that running threads on separate cores results in a linear bandwidth increase with the number of threads. We conclude that when multiple threads on the same core request data simultaneously, they will compete for the shared hardware resources (e.g., the ring stops), thus serializing the requests. On the bright side, the threads located on the same core share cache data and have faster data accesses (see Section 3.2).

3.4.2 Accessing Shared-Data

Section 3.4.1 focuses on the achieved bandwidth when threads access separate memory spaces. In this section we investigate **what is the bandwidth when different threads access the same memory space simultaneously?** We expect that the bandwidth would resemble that obtained by a single thread, assuming the memory requests are served by *broadcasting*. Figure 10 presents the measured bandwidth, showing that the `read` bandwidth decreases over the number of threads until 24 (or 16). Thereafter, the bandwidth is constant around 1.5-2.0 GB/s (i.e., one third of the single thread bandwidth). When using more threads than cores, the bandwidth drops even further. This behavior is different from the linear increase trend (shown in Figure 9(a)) seen when accessing separate memory spaces. We assume the bottleneck lies in the simultaneous access to the DTDs. Therefore, for bandwidth gain, applications should strive to keep threads accessing different parts/cachelines of the shared memory space (for as much as possible), to avoid the effects of contention at the interconnect level.

3.5 PCIe Data Transfer

When used as a coprocessor, Xeon Phi is connected via PCIe to a host (e.g., a traditional CPU). When offloading computation to the Xeon Phi, the tasks and the related data need to be transferred back and forth between the two processors. As seen for GPUs [?], these transfers can be expensive in terms of overall application performance. Thus, we have designed a benchmark to measure the data transfer bandwidth. To do so, we use the `offload` pragma (specifying `in` and `out` for the transfer direction) to transfer datasets

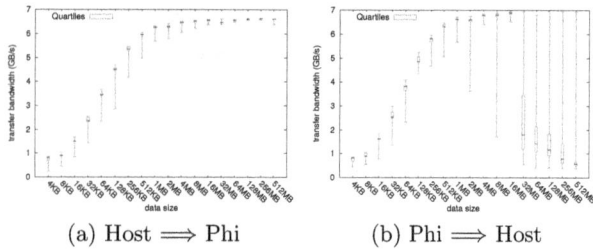

(a) Host $\Longrightarrow$ Phi   (b) Phi $\Longrightarrow$ Host

Figure 11: Achieved data transfer bandwidth (over PCIe) between a host and an Xeon Phi.

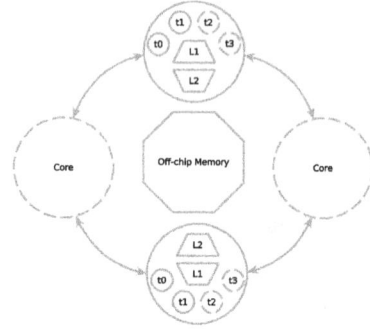

Figure 12: The SCAT model of Intel Xeon Phi.

of different sizes from host to Xeon Phi and back. The transferred data is allocated with a 4KB alignment, for optimal DMA performance [12].

The achieved bandwidth between host and Xeon Phi is presented in Figure 11 (we report the results over 1000 times). We note that the bandwidth increases with data size, and it is relatively stable for different runs, for both directions. However, for data transfers larger than 32 MB, the Phi to host bandwidth shows a large variation, with the `median` bandwidth value decreasing sharply (up to 6 times!). The reasons for this large variance are still under investigation.

4. SCAT: AN XEON PHI MODEL

We compare our results with the information provided by the Intel Software Development Guide (SDG) in Table 2. We note that we did improve on the content of the official data: instruction latency data, local and non-local memory access bandwidth and latency data, an interconnect study, and a PCIe offload evaluation. We also have the following key observations, which lead to optimization guidelines.

High Throughput: Xeon Phi is indeed a high-throughput platform. The peak instruction throughput is achievable, but it depends on the following factors: (1) the number of threads and threads/core occupancy, (2) the utilization of the 512-bit vectors, (3) the issuing width (i.e., the number of independent instruction streams), (4) the instruction

mix. Furthermore, single-precision data leads to better performance for math-intensive kernels.

Memory Selection: Accessing the local L1 cache is 8 times faster than accessing the local L2 cache, which is again an order of magnitude faster than accessing the remote caches or the off-chip memory. However, the difference between a remote cache access and an off-chip memory access is relatively small (17%). Furthermore, the remote access latency does not depend on the cache-line state.

Efficient Memory Access: Data is read and written from/to the off-chip memory in cache lines (64 bytes). The maximum achievable bandwidth is 164 GB/s for `read` operations and 76 GB/s for `write` operations - a lot lower than the theoretical peak of 320 GB/s. With `streaming store` instructions, the `write` bandwidth can increase up to 1.7 times. Further, programmers need many threads (at least 60 - one per core) to issue enough memory requests to saturate the ring interconnect and the memory channels. The hardware and software prefetching can improve bandwidth; their efficiency increases with the length of the `stanzas` of contiguous memory accesses. Finally, disabling ECC leads to an average of 20% increase in bandwidth.

Ring Interconnect: All cores can be seen as *symmetrical* peers, and the distance between cores has little impact on performance. However, memory requests from threads running on the same core are serialized, provided that the bandwidth reaches 4.7 GB/s. Furthermore, when threads (on different cores) are accessing the same data, the simultaneous access to the DTD leads to bandwidth loss.

Overall, we believe our results are complementary to the SDG, and, being backed up by more practical guidelines, be of added value for programmers using this platform.

SCAT Model: Based on the numbers and the observations, we attempt to build a simple view of the Xeon Phi, providing production users with a platform model for reasoning about parallel algorithm design and performance optimization. Figure 12 shows the machine model for Xeon Phi. The machine has 60 symmetrical cores, each of which contains 1/2(/3/4) vector threads working on 8 double-precision or 16 single-precision data elements in a lock-step manner. `Family threads` (threads suited in the same core) differ from `remote threads` (threads suited in another core) in that they share and compete local resources. Furthermore, compared with accessing local caches, remote caches and off-chip memory are slow (see the numbers in Table 2). We

Table 2: A comparison with the data in SDG ('N/A' stands for "not available" in SDG).

Metric	SDG	Measured
VPU		
Latency	general statement	cycles/instruction
Throughput	1008 GFlops	1008 GFlops
EMU evaluation	general statement	quantified
L1 Cache (32KB)		
Latency (local)	1 cycle	3 cycles
bandwidth (local)	N/A	R=64B/c;W=64B/c
L2 Cache (<512KB)		
Latency (local)	11 cycles	24 cycles
Bandwidth (local)	N/A	quantified
Latency (remote)	N/A	250 cycles
Off-chip memory		
Latency	N/A	302 cycles
Bandwidth	320 GB/s	R=164GB/s;W=76GB/s
Prefetching	general statement	quantified
ECC factor	general statement	quantified
Interconnections		
Ring Traffic Contention	N/A	ring stops, DTDs
PCI Express Bandwidth	N/A	up to 7 GB/s

summarize the model as *SCAT* (symmetric cores and asymmetric threads).

This machine model limits itself to those architectural details that are important for performance. For example, programmers do not have to keep the ring interconnect in mind because the cores perform symmetrically. On the other hand, the threads on the same core share and compete the shared resources, putting up `asymmetry` and impelling us to take care of `thread affinity`. Therefore, this platform model captures the key performance features of the processor, ensuring good performance with relatively low programming effort (i.e., using high-level programming tools).

5. LEUKOCYTE TRACKING

In this section, we focus on our case-study application, Leukocyte Tracking. Specifically, we aim to evaluate the gap(s) between the achieved performance of the application and the performance indicated by the microbenchmarks.

Leukocyte Tracking is a medical imaging application which detects and tracks rolling leukocytes (white blood cells) in vivo video microscopy of blood vessels. The velocity of rolling leukocytes provides important information about the inflammation process, which aids biomedical researchers in the development of anti-inflammatory medications [21].

In the application, cells are detected in the first video frame and then tracked through subsequent frames [21]. Tracking accounts for around 90% of the total execution time and thus we focus on this procedure. Tracking is accomplished by first computing, in the area surrounding each cell, a Motion Gradient Vector Flow (MGVF) matrix. The MGVF is a gradient field biased in the direction of blood flow, and it is computed using an iterative Jacobian solution procedure. After computing the MGVF, an active contour is used once again to refine the shape and determine the new location of each cell. Unfortunately, leukocyte tracking is computationally expensive, requiring more than four and a half hours to process one minute of video. Boyer et al. have translated the tracking algorithm from Matlab to C and OpenMP [3].

5.1 Performance Analysis

Without any code changes, we compile and run the kernel on both Phi and SNB (Intel Xeon E5-2620, a dual 6-core processor with hyper-threading disabled), and show their performance in Figure 13. We see that, on SNB, the execution time decreases when increasing the number of threads. On Phi, the execution time decreases when the number of threads is less than 40. Using more than 40 threads brings no further performance gain. Overall, we note that the performance on Phi (with 40 threads) is 2× worse than that on SNB (with 12 threads), while the sequential execution of the same application (i.e., running on a single thread) on Xeon Phi is 5× slower than on SNB.

To further understand these results, we analyze the overall performance by taking both parallelism and per-thread performance into account, and focus on two aspects: (1) the single-thread performance and (2) scalability. The analysis includes the interactions between kernel characteristics and processor features.

Single thread: When tracking a leukocyte, we use 18 data structures/matrix (1 input sub-image, 1 motion gradient vector field, 8 neighbours to store intensity differences, and 8 neighbours to store the heaviside value). For the given input dataset, each matrix has 41×81 elements (in

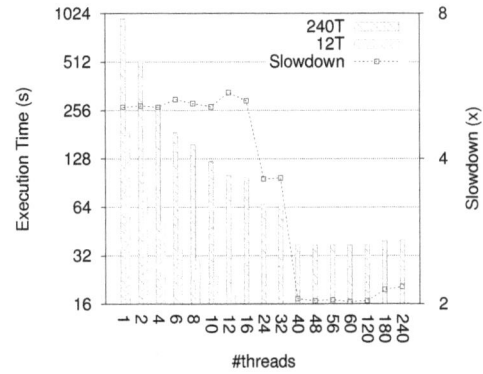

Figure 13: The initial performance results of Leukocyte Tracking on an Xeon Phi processor (240 threads) and an Xeon processor (12 threads).

double-precision). In total, tracking a leukocyte needs 467 KB ($18 \times 41 \times 81 \times 8$), which is smaller than the size of a local L2 cache (Figure 12 and Table 2). Thus, the iterative Jacobian solver will work intensively on tracking a leukocyte with data located on-chip, and the tracking speed is not limited by the memory access.

As for computation without vectorization, a thread on Phi (working at 1.05 GHz and issuing an instruction every two cycles, see Section 3.1) runs 4× slower than one on SNB (working at 2.0 GHz and issuing instructions every cycle). With vectorization, the difference is lowered to roughly 2×. In our practical experience, the single thread performance on Phi is around 5× worse than that on SNB, an indication that vectorization is not applied on both platforms. Indeed, the compiler reports an auto-vectorization failure (consequently, only 12.5% of the SIMD lanes are used).

Scalability: Figure 13 shows that the performance on Phi varies little when using over 40 threads. Through code analysis, we observed that parallelization is performed over the number of leukocytes. As the number of leukocytes from the input datasets is 36, increasing the number of threads to more than 36 brings no performance gain. In other words, the kernel parallelism does not match Phi's massive hardware parallelism (36 << 240, see Figure 12). On the other hand, SNB has only has 12 threads, showing much better scalability. To fully utilize the hardware resources on Phi, we *must* increase the paralellism of the application.

5.2 Performance Optimization

5.2.1 Vectorizing the Kernel

When tracking a leukocyte, the kernel loops over a fixed-sized portion of a frame (a sub-image with 41×81 pixels). A typical loop is shown in Figure 14 ($m = 41$, $n = 81$). As we have mentioned, the compiler fails to vectorize this code due to the assumption of data dependency (the original code uses `pointers to pointers` and dereferencing the data structure is too complex for the compiler to automate).

We note that enabling vectorization for these cases requires an intervention from the programmer. The typical approach for manual vectorization is to add low-level intrinsics in the high-level C code, thus specifically instructing the compiler to use the vector units.

```
input: MAT* z, double v, double e
output: MAT* H
double one_over_pi = 1.0 / PI;
double one_over_e = 1.0 / e;
for (i = 0; i < m; i++) {
    for (j = 0; j < n; j++) {
        double z_val=m_get_val(z, i, j)*v;
        double H_val=one_over_pi * \
            atan(z_val*one_over_e)+0.5;
        m_set_val(H, i, j, H_val);
    }
}
```

Figure 14: The Heaviside step function.

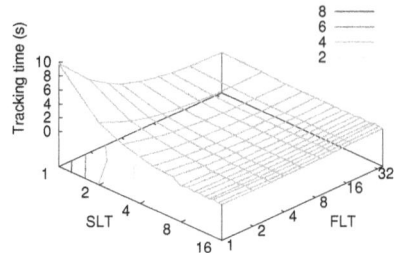

Figure 15: The selection of FLT and SLT.

We identify three main factors that make code vectorization for leukocyte tracking cumbersome. First, `data alignment`: when vectorizing the code, data accesses should start with an address aligned at 64 bytes (512 bits). This must be insured with specific memory allocation (i.e., dedicated APIs). Second, the `non-unit-strided memory access`: when the 8 elements in a vector are non-contiguous, the offset for each element must be specified. This occurs when calculating the gradient in the tracking kernel. Third, and final, vectorizing a loop requires special care when the number of iterations is not a multiple of the vector length. Thus, we also need to deal with the `remainder` of the inner-loop (i.e., because $n\%8 \neq 0$). Therefore, we use two loops in the tracking kernel: a vector loop (for the bulk of the computation), and a scalar loop (used to deal with the loop remainder).

Fixing all these problems (and thus manually vectorizing this code using intrinsics) takes an expert programmer two days. Moreover, the kernel code doubles in size (from ∼200 lines to ∼400 lines). Correspondingly, the tracking time per frame decreases to 8.5s from 31s (∼4× faster) on Phi. The remaining optimization space is roughly 2×. The limiting factor is that the kernel uses trigonometric operations, which can be further optimized by using EMU (Section 3.1 and [6]).

5.2.2 Changing Parallelism

As we have mentioned, the parallelism of leukocyte tracking is limited by the number of leukocytes (36 in the given data set). For the traditional multi-core processors, this number is still larger than that of the hardware threads. But on a Phi with 240 hardware threads, running the tracking kernel with 36 parallel threads can never fully utilize the platform.

We attempt to improve on this situation by increasing parallelism. Thus, we spawn a second-level parallelism over the outer loop of the sub-image in Figure 14. Next, we need to tune the dimensions of the two parallel levels by specifying the number of first-level threads (FLT) and the number of second-level threads (SLT). We select these two numbers from those that satisfy the following constraints: (1) $FLT \times SLT \leq 240$, (2) $FLT \leq 36$, (3) $SLT \leq 41$. We autotune the kernel using $FLS \in \{1, 2, 3, 4, 6, 9, 12, 18, 36\}$ and $SLT \in \{1, 2, 3, 4, 5, 6, 7, 8, 9, 10, 11, 12, 13, 14, 15, 16\}$ [9]. Figure 15 shows the tracking time per frame for different combinations. We see that the best performance achieved by Phi is around 0.1s per frame when $FLT = 4$ and $SLT = 8$, indicating that using more threads does not mean a faster tracking

($4 \times 8 < 240$). According to the SCAT model (Figure 12), it is of no use binding multiple threads to the same core due to little data reuse.

5.2.3 Overall Performance

We compare the execution time of tracking leukocytes per frame on Phi against the ones achieved by SNB (using a higher clock and better performing cores, but a lot less parallelism), and on an NVIDIA Kepler GPU (K20m, a GPU with a similar peak performance and more massive parallelism, programmed in CUDA implementation [10]). The comparison is illustrated in Table 3. We notice that Xeon Phi is 6× faster than SNB, while it is around 40% slower than K20. Admittedly, optimizing the tracking kernel on SNB (by hand-tuning for enabling vectorization) can lead to a performance increase (a maximum 4×, most likely, with SNB-specific intrinsics). K20 performs better than Phi due to the more efficient reduction implemented in the GPU shared memory [3]. Specifically, at the second level of parallelism, we use multiple threads that are bound to separate cores on Phi, while the CUDA implementation runs the same amount of work on a block (and a multi-processor). Thus, when performing reduction, the shared (reduction-)variable on Phi has to be transferred back and forth at the second-level cache. As we have measured, the remote cache access is as slow as accessing the off-chip memory (Figure 12 and Table 2). With CUDA on K20, this reduction happens in shared memory, with much higher performance. The final code of leukocyte tracking for Phi is publicly available [11].

Table 3: Tracking time per frame (in seconds). 'VEC' represents 'vectorization'; 'FMT/SMT' is 'to use the first-level/second-level multi-threading', respectively. The optimizations are incrementally added.

	1T	+VEC	+FMT	+SMT	Overall
Phi	31	8.5	0.7	0.1	0.1
SNB	6	–	0.6	–	0.6
K20	–	–	–	–	0.06

---

[9]SLT can be as large as 41, but our results show a large SLT is not necessary due to the limited per-thread work.

[10]We change the original Rodinia single-precision version to the double-precision version for a fair comparison.

[11]`https://github.com/haibo031031/mic-apps`

5.3 Discussion

One of the important selling points of Phi is the continuity of programming models from the traditional multi-core processors - the OpenMP and MPI models and codes are functionally compatible. Ideally, programmers should obtain high performance without a lot of investment in programming model learning (e.g., OpenCL), tuning and hacking low-level code (e.g., assembly code with pthreads). Effectively, the expectation is that re-compiling the code with the `-mmic` option will do. Our experience leads to a different conclusion: porting legacy code or developing new code still needs a lot of developer interventions.

Note 1. Using intrinsics indeed brings us a significant performance gain, but it exposes low-level implementation details to users, conflicting with the principles of encapsulation and high-level programming. It also requires code specialized for Phi, which will further fail to run the on traditional multi-core processors. This deviates from the original design goal of Phi, i.e., to keep using traditional programming models. A possible solution is to provide a high-level vector template/library/model (e.g., ispc [12]). The template can present users with the required operations (e.g., multiply and reduction). When implementing the template, we translate the operations into their equivalent intrinsics specialized to a platform. Thus, we can keep code portable and not hinder performance.

Note 2. Xeon Phi truly needs massive parallelism to fully use the hardware threads. This observation makes a significant difference between SNB and Phi. SNB has a dozen of hardware threads, while Phi has over a two hundred. Only those applications with abundant parallelism can fully utilize the machine. When lacking parallelism, applications can either look for finer grain parallelism (atypical for OpenMP, but useful when available), or find a way to load multiple (independent) tasks on the platform. However, note that the number of required threads depends on applications and their run-time contexts.

Note 3. On Xeon Phi, using OpenMP can perform global reduction on the globally shared caches, but this proves to be less efficient than expected (apparently due to frequent memory transfers). When using CUDA/OpenCL on GPUs, an efficient reduction can be performed in shared memory (or local memory in OpenCL) at the block (or work-group in OpenCL) level. Further, our experience shows that the leukocyte tracking maps more naturally to the GPU architecture: mapping a leukocyte to a multi-processor. While on Phi, we need to map a leukocyte to multiple processing cores. Thus, we believe that a multiprocessor on GPUs is equivalent to multiple processing cores on Phi, at least in the context of leukocyte tracking.

To summarize, we conclude that (1) although it often destroys portability, manual vectorization is mandatory for exploiting Phi's performance; a high-level library can be used to hide the platform-dependent details, but vectorization *must* be enabled as much as possible, and (2) massive parallelism is needed on Phi to fully use the hardware. In a nutshell, merely relying on compilers with traditional programming models to achieve high performance on Phi is still far from reality.

---

[12] http://ispc.github.io/

6. RELATED WORK

In this section, we survey and briefly discuss the work related to our (micro)benchmarking approach. We focus mainly on existing CPU and GPU benchmarking methods, as there are no other comprehensive studies of Xeon Phi - yet.

In [23], the authors develop a high-level program to evaluate the cache and TLB for any machine. Part of our work is based on their approaches (targeting uni-core processors, though). Multiple studies are also performed on multi-core CPUs. In [20], the authors report performance numbers from three multi-core processors , including not only execution time and throughput, but also a detailed analysis on the memory hierarchy performance and on the performance scalability between single and dual cores. Daniel Molka et al. [19] revealed many fundamental details of the Intel Nehalem using benchmarks for latency and bandwidth between different locations in the memory subsystem. We use similar approaches for the access latency of remote caches.

For GPUs, Volkov et al. [28] presented detailed benchmarking of the GPU memory system that reveals sizes and latencies of caches and TLB. Later, Wong et al. [29] presented an analysis of the NVIDIA GT200 GPU and their measurement techniques. They used a set of micro-benchmarks to reveal architectural details of the processing cores and the memory hierarchies. Their results revealed the presence of some undocumented hardware structures. While these microbenchmarks are in CUDA and targeted NVIDIA GPUs, Thoman et al. [26] develop a set of OpenCL benchmarks targeting a large variety of platforms. They include code designed to determine parameters unique to OpenCL, like the dynamic branching penalties prevalent on GPUs. They also demonstrate how their results can be used to guide algorithm design and optimization

Garea et al. [8] developed an intuitive performance model for cache-coherent architectures and demonstrated its use on Intel Xeon Phi. Their model is based on latency measurements, which match well with our latency results. In addition to the cache access latency, we have shown how we benchmark the instruction throughput, the memory bandwidth at different levels, and the interconnect performance.

7. CONCLUSION AND FUTURE WORK

Given its performance promises, Intel Xeon Phi is very likely to become popular for both low-end high performance computing applications (smaller scale scientific applications like Leukocyte Tracking), and the next generation of supercomputers. In this paper, we presented our hands-on experience with this processor - in both the "lab" and using a real application - and discussed several key insights into the performance of this new many-core processor. By using a set of self-designed microbenchmarks, we characterized the major components of this architecture - cores, memory, and interconnections - summarizing them into four machine-centric observations (potential optimization guidelines). We also made a first attempt to provide a simple machine view (*SCAT*) to facilitate application design and performance tuning on the Xeon Phi.

In general, our benchmarking results are consistent with Xeon Phi's published data. However, the data we have added through this benchmarking effort allowed us to expose more accurately the expected key performance factors for the Xeon Phi. We have shown that the platform is able to deliver its performance promises in terms of computation, but programmers will need to find the right parallelization strategy to fill 240 hardware threads with compute-intensive tasks, while finding the right balance between data partitioning and coherent memory requests to achieve sufficient memory bandwidth. Thus, we believe the number of applications that can easily use Xeon Phi's potential in their existing, naive form is, for now, very limited. And for high performance, our and other experience show that programmers need to take a lot of efforts on parallelization, analysis, and optimization.

In terms of future work, we are extending our hands-on experience with more application studies. As a long term plan, we are targeting a quantified performance model for Xeon Phi, which could be used in identifying performance bottlenecks and guiding performance optimization. This model would build upon the microbenchmarks and application characteristics for its foundations, but expose different complexity layers depending on the user requirements.

8. ACKNOWLEDGMENTS

The authors would like to thank Sabela Ramos Garea from University of A Coruña and Evghenii Gaburov from SURF-sara for the numerous on-line discussions. This work is partially funded by CSC (China Scholarship Council), and the National Natural Science Foundation of China under Grant No.61103014 and No.11272352.

9. REFERENCES

[1] R. D. e. a. Blumofe. Cilk: an efficient multithreaded runtime system. *SIGPLAN Not.*, 30(8):207–216, Aug. 1995.

[2] O. A. R. Board. OpenMP application program interface (version 4.0). Technical report, July 2013.

[3] M. Boyer et al. Accelerating leukocyte tracking using CUDA: A case study in leveraging manycore coprocessors. In *IPDPS'09*, May 2009.

[4] K. Datta et al. Optimization and performance modeling of stencil computations on modern microprocessors. *SIAM Rev.*, 51(1):129–159, Feb. 2009.

[5] David. *Programming with POSIX Threads*. May 1997.

[6] J. Fang et al. Benchmarking intel xeon phi to guide kernel design. Technical Report PDS-2013-005, Delft University of Technology, Apr. 2013.

[7] A. Fog. Lists of instruction latencies, throughputs and micro-operation reakdowns. Technical report, Copenhagen University, Feb. 2012.

[8] S. R. Garea and T. Hoefler. Modeling Communication in Cache-Coherent SMP Systems - A Case-Study with Xeon Phi. 2013. HPDC'13.

[9] T. Granlund. Instruction latencies and throughput for AMD and intel x86 processors. Technical report, KTH, Feb. 2012.

[10] J. L. Hennessy and D. A. Patterson. *Computer Architecture, Fifth Edition: A Quantitative Approach.* Morgan Kaufmann, 5 edition, Sept. 2011.

[11] Intel. *Intel Xeon Phi Coprocessor InstructionSet Architecture Reference Manual*, Sept. 2012.

[12] Intel. *Intel Xeon Phi Coprocessor System Software Development Guide*, Nov. 2012.

[13] Intel. *An Overview of Programming for Intel Xeon Processors and Intel Xeon Phi Coprocessors*, Oct. 2012.

[14] Intel. *Streaming Store Instructions in the Intel Xeon Phi coprocessor*, 2012.

[15] Intel. Intel Xeon Phi Coprocessor. http://software.intel.com/mic-developer, April 2013.

[16] John D. McCalpin. STREAM: Sustainable Memory Bandwidth With High Performance Computers, April 2013.

[17] V. W. Lee et al. Debunking the 100X GPU vs. CPU myth: an evaluation of throughput computing on CPU and GPU. *SIGARCH Comput. Archit. News*, 38(3), June 2010.

[18] L. McVoy et al. lmbench: portable tools for performance analysis. In *USENIX ATEC'96*, 1996.

[19] D. Molka et al. Memory performance and cache coherency effects on an intel nehalem multiprocessor system. In *PACT'09.*, Sept. 2009.

[20] L. Peng et al. Memory hierarchy performance measurement of commercial dual-core desktop processors. *Journal of Systems Architecture*, 54(8):816–828, Aug. 2008.

[21] N. Ray et al. Motion gradient vector flow: an external force for tracking rolling leukocytes with shape and size constrained active contours. *Medical Imaging, IEEE Transactions on*, Dec. 2004.

[22] A. Sclocco et al. Radio astronomy beam forming on Many-Core architectures. In *IPDPS*, 2012.

[23] A. J. Smith et al. Measuring cache and TLB performance and their effect on benchmark runtimes. *IEEE Trans. Comput.*, (10), Oct. 1995.

[24] J. E. Stone et al. OpenCL: A parallel programming standard for heterogeneous computing systems. *Computing in science & engineering*, 12(3):66–72, May 2010.

[25] Technical University of Dresden. BenchIT: Performance Measurement for Scientific Applications, August 2013.

[26] P. Thoman et al. Automatic OpenCL device characterization: Guiding optimized kernel design. In *Euro-Par'11*. 2011.

[27] A. L. Varbanescu, A. S. van Amesfoort, T. Cornwell, G. van Diepen, R. van Nieuwpoort, B. G. Elmegreen, and H. J. Sips. Building high-resolution sky images using the Cell/B.e. *Scientific Programming*, 17(1-2):113–134, 2009.

[28] V. Volkov and J. W. Demmel. Benchmarking GPUs to tune dense linear algebra. In *High Performance Computing, Networking, Storage and Analysis, 2008. SC 2008. International Conference for*, pages 1–11. IEEE, Nov. 2008.

[29] H. Wong, M.-M. Papadopoulou, M. Sadooghi-Alvandi, and A. Moshovos. Demystifying GPU microarchitecture through microbenchmarking. In *2010 IEEE International Symposium on Performance Analysis of Systems & Software (ISPASS)*, pages 235–246. IEEE, Mar. 2010.

A Power-Measurement Methodology for Large-Scale, High-Performance Computing

Thomas R. W. Scogland
Virginia Tech
tom.scogland@vt.edu

Craig P Steffen
University of Illinois
csteffen@ncsa.illinois.edu

Torsten Wilde
Leibniz Supercomputing Ctr
Torsten.Wilde@lrz.de

Florent Parent
Calcul Québec
florent.parent@calculquebec.ca

Susan Coghlan
Argonne National Laboratory
smc@anl.gov

Natalie Bates
Energy Efficient HPC Working
Group
natalie.jean.bates@gmail.com

Wu-chun Feng
Virginia Tech
feng@cs.vt.edu

Erich Strohmaier
Lawrence Berkeley National
Laboratory
EStrohmaier@lbl.gov

ABSTRACT

Improvement in the energy efficiency of supercomputers can be accelerated by improving the quality and comparability of efficiency measurements. The ability to generate accurate measurements at extreme scale are just now emerging. The realization of system-level measurement capabilities can be accelerated with a commonly adopted and high quality measurement methodology for use while running a workload, typically a benchmark.

This paper describes a methodology that has been developed collaboratively through the Energy Efficient HPC Working Group to support architectural analysis and comparative measurements for rankings, such as the Top500 and Green500. To support measurements with varying amounts of effort and equipment required we present three distinct levels of measurement, which provide increasing levels of accuracy. Level 1 is similar to the Green500 run rules today, a single average power measurement extrapolated from a subset of a machine. Level 2 is more comprehensive, but still widely achievable. Level 3 is the most rigorous of the three methodologies but is only possible at a few sites. However, the Level 3 methodology generates a high quality result that exposes details that the other methodologies may miss. In addition, we present case studies from the Leibniz Supercomputing Centre (LRZ), Argonne National Laboratory (ANL) and Calcul Québec Université Laval that explore the benefits and difficulties of gathering high quality, system-level measurements on large-scale machines.

Categories and Subject Descriptors

C.4 [**Performance of Systems**]: Measurement Techniques

ICPE'14, March 22–26, 2014, Dublin, Ireland.
Copyright is held by the owner/author(s). Publication rights licensed to ACM.
ACM 978-1-4503-2733-6/14/03 ...$15.00.
http://dx.doi.org/10.1145/2568088.2576795.

General Terms

Measurement, Performance, Energy, Power, Methodology

Keywords

Power-measurement methodology, Green500, Top500, high-performance computing, datacenter

1. INTRODUCTION

The energy efficiency of large-scale, high-performance computing (HPC) systems has become a key factor in design, procurement, and funding decisions. While many benchmarks exist for evaluating the computational performance of supercomputers, there remains a lack of standard methods for the accurate evaluation of energy efficiency at scale. In early 2011, the Energy Efficient HPC Working Group (EE HPC WG) [5] undertook a survey of power submissions to the Green500 [8] and Top500 [16] lists. The survey demonstrates that there is a wide variation in the quality of the measurements [6]. Some of the power submissions were very comprehensive and reflected a high level of quality. A number of the submissions were based on sampling and extrapolation and reflected a moderate level of quality. Even so, nearly half of the Green500 list power numbers were not based on measured power; rather they were derived from vendor specifications.[1] The survey identified the following methodology complexities and issues:

- Fuzzy lines of demarcation between the computer system and the data center infrastructure, e.g., fans, power supplies, liquid cooling

- Shared resources, e.g., storage and networking

- Limitations on data center and system instrumentation for system level power measurement

This paper describes the results of a collaborative effort led by the EE HPC WG with the Green500 [8], the Top500 [25] and The Green Grid [24] to address the complexities and

---

[1]Because submissions for power use in the Top500 were more sparse, the Green500 list was used as the larger sample set.

issues identified in the survey. The output of this collaborative effort is an improved power and energy measurement methodology for use with any system-level HPC benchmark. There are increasingly rigorous levels of measurement described by the methodology.

Few HPC systems today possess the instrumentation required to measure their power in its entirety without including other unrelated systems or subsystems in their datacenters. Further, adding large-scale or facility-level measurement equipment to existing systems and facilities is a difficult proposition. To accommodate systems that cannot feasibly be instrumented with the equipment necessary to produce the highest quality measurement, the methodology specifies three levels of measurement of increasing quality and complexity. Level 1 is similar to the Rev0.9 Green500 run rules, a single average power measurement extrapolated from a subset of a machine. Level 2 is more comprehensive, but remains a power measurement based on a subset of the overall system. Level 3 is the most rigorous of the three but only possible at a few sites. However, it offers a verifiably accurate full system measurement at any scale.

A broad community-based process was followed for developing the improved power measurement methodology [3]. The EE HPC WG has almost 400 members with 50% from government agencies, 30% from industry, and 20% from academic institutions. There are members from 20 different countries, mostly the United States and Europe. This methodology was generated and went through review with multiple opportunities for participation from the entire EE HPC WG. It also went through a review and approval from the Green500, the Top500 and The Green Grid. The methodology has gone through two testing phases with feedback from alpha testing resulting in modifications for the revision that went though beta testing. Both test phases included reporting on the test results to the broader community at major supercomputing conferences (ISC12 and SC12). The Green500 implemented this improved methodology as of its June 2013 List.

The rest of the paper is laid out as follows. Section 2 presents related work in measurement methodologies. Section 3 describes the methodology along with each of the levels. Sections 4 though 6 describe the experiences of the Leibniz Supercomputing Centre (LRZ), Argonne National Laboratory (ANL), and Calcul Québec Université Laval as illustrative case studies for the methodology. We present our conclusions in Section 7. Finally, in Section 9, we recognize as additional authors the invaluable contributions of the many people who participated in this collaborative and largely volunteer effort.

2. RELATED WORK

Benchmarking efforts have three inter-related and yet distinct elements: workload, metrics, and methodology. This paper focuses on the methodology, specifically the methodology used to measure system power while running an HPC workload.

There are several benchmarking efforts that attempt to characterize HPC architectural trends and that include a power measurement (some required and others optional). The most widely recognized benchmarking efforts are the Top500 [25] and Green500 [8], both of which use High Performance Linpack (HPL) [15] as the workload; additionally the Graph500 [1] has begun to gain traction with a workload

that is focused on graph analysis and accepts power measurements as the Green Graph500 [2]. The Top500 accepts an optional power measurement, whereas it is the key thrust of the Green500. Since the inception of the Green500 [18], much work has been done to describe and evaluate a power-measurement methodology to use while running an HPC workload. Most of this work has been done for the Green500, but most recent and comprehensive is the exploration of the Green500's power measurement methodology limitations by Subramaniam and Feng [22].

The power-measurement methodology of the Standard Performance Evaluation Corporation (SPEC) [21] is likely the most cited methodology and framework for evaluating power and energy efficiency tied to a workload. This methodology was developed alongside the SPECpower benchmark, which evaluates the energy efficiency of a server, or set of servers, running the SPEC Java Business Benchmark (SPECjbb). Though it was developed for server workloads, the SPEC power measurement methodology and tools can be applied to others, as Hackenberg [10] demonstrates with his analysis of SPECMPI workloads run on a small cluster of nodes. The SPEC High Performance Group [19] has recently included the option and specification for power submissions as part of the SPEC OMP2012 benchmark suite [20] as an optional add-on and has since been analyzed by Muller [17]. While SPEC's methodology is precise and widely applied in multiple domains, it is not designed with supercomputer-scale systems in mind.

Whatever methodology it may be, the importance of having a common method goes beyond the benefit of an apples-to-apples comparison. One of the main purposes of benchmarking, particularly for the Green500 and Top500, is to analyze trends of the results over time or across designs. Analyses, such as Subramaniam and Feng's analysis of trends from the Green500 [23] and Hsu and Poole's analysis of trends in SPECpower [12], reveal information that would be at least obscured without a common methodology in each set of data. Yet more such trends might be found in far larger sets of data if a widespread common methodology can be established.

The intent of this effort is to push the envelope from prior related work with respect to power-measurement methodology and to do so along several dimensions, including the fraction of the machine that is instrumented, the time span for the measurement, and the machine boundary. In addition to improving the accuracy of the power-measurement methodology, we seek to accelerate the pace at which power-measurement capabilities evolve. For example, Hsu describes the evolving power measurement capabilities of HPC facilities and systems at seven levels (from the site all the way down to components) [11]. Our three-tiered quality levels are meant to raise the bar and accelerate the pace of evolution and adoption of high-fidelity, power-measurement capabilities.

In particular, this paper recommends a full-system, power measurement whereas Subramaniam [22] and Kamil [13] do not consider it a practical option and recommend extrapolating from a fractional system measurement. However, Laros [14] shows that there is value to full system measurements beyond improving the accuracy of the benchmarking effort. Benefits like those demonstrated by Laros partially motivated the full-system measurement encouraged by the EE HPC WG methodology.

3. MEASUREMENT METHODOLOGY

The methodology defined by the EE HPC WG defines three quality levels; essentially a *good*, *better*, or *best* rating system with Level 3 being the best. The quality ratings impose requirements on four different aspects of the power measurement:

1. The measurement itself, including the time span over which the measurement is taken, the time granularity, and the measurements reported

2. The fraction of the system that is instrumented

3. Subsystems that must be included in the measurement

4. Where in the power distribution network the measurements are taken

Increasingly stringent measurements are required in each of the four aspects for higher quality levels. Each level increases the measurement quality as well as its coverage of the machine infrastructure. For a measurement to qualify for a certain quality level, all aspects of the measurement must meet the requirements for that level, though they are allowed to exceed those requirements.

Level 1 is based on version 0.9 of the Green500 run rules [9]. We propose Level 3 as an enhanced energy measurement methodology that augments the ability to monitor and manage energy use. However, we understand that not all existing systems have the infrastructure to obtain Level 3 measurements. Hence, we define a Level 2 methodology as an intermediate step between Levels 1 and 3.

While each of the aspects listed above shifts for each level, there are several commonalities as well. All three levels require that you specify the power meter used. There are currently no requirements on the type or quality of power meter other than their sampling granularity. All levels also require that the power measurement is taken upstream of alternating current to direct current conversion, or accounted for by modeling or measuring the power lost during conversion.

The methodology distinguishes between the core phase of a workload and the entire workload. The core phase is the section of the workload that performs the main body of work evaluated or performed by the workload. The core phase does not include job launch and teardown time. While Level 2 and Level 3 require measurements across the entire run of an application, the span and frequency of measurements at all levels is defined in terms of the core phase. This decision was made in order to reasonably account for workloads with long setup and teardown times and short core phases that might otherwise focus the measurement on unimportant parts of the run.

Levels 2 and 3 require an idle power measurement. Idle power is defined as the power used by the system when it is not running a workload, but it is in a state where it is ready to accept a workload. The idle state is not a sleep or a hibernation state. As such, the idle measurement should be a near constant for a system given constant datacenter conditions, and the idle measurement need not be linked to a particular workload. The idle measurement may be made just before or after the workload is run, or independently so long as it is taken in the ready state. The idle measurement, while not a function of the workload being measured, serves as a baseline allowing the analysis of metrics such as

static and dynamic power, energy proportionality, and others. These each offer important insights into the system as well as its interaction with the workload, revealing not only the energy consumed, but the amount consumed *because the workload is running*.

Table 1 summarizes the aspect and quality levels, with each defined in greater detail below.

3.1 Level 1

Level 1 requires at least one calculated power value. This value is the average of individual power measurements sampled at one-second intervals and taken over the required timespan. The required timespan is at least 20% of the workload's core phase or one minute, whichever is longer.

The requirement to sample at one-second intervals may be satisfied internally by the meter. All values reported by the meter need to be used in the calculation, though they may be aggregated at time scales larger than the sampling interval. For example, the meter may sample at one second intervals and report a value every minute, in that case measurements must be read once per minute and used in the calculation of the overall average power.

Level 1 requires that all the subsystems participating in the workload be listed, but that only the compute-node subsystem be measured. Level 1 requires that at least 1/64 of the compute-node subsystem or at least 1kW be measured, whichever is larger. The contribution from the remaining compute nodes is estimated by scaling up the sampled portion by the fraction that is monitored. If the compute node subsystem contains more than one type of compute nodes, at least one member from each type must be included in the measurement. The full system power should then be scaled proportionally for each type to determine the full system power.

In some circumstances it may be impossible to avoid a power contribution from other subsystems, such as integrated networking infrastructure in blade systems. In this case, subtracting an estimated value for the included subsystem is not allowed, but a list of what subsystems are included in this fashion may be included with the measurement.

3.2 Level 2

Level 2 requires two calculated average power values, one for the core phase of the workload and another for the entire workload. In addition, the complete set of measurements used to calculate these average values must be provided.

The complete set of measurements used to calculate the power values must be a series of equally spaced measurements taken during the run. These measurements must be included in the submission for verification purposes. The measurements must be spaced close enough so that at least 10 measurements are reported during the core phase of the workload, and a minimum of one each before and after the core phase. The reported average power for the core phase of the run is the numerical average of the measurements collected during the core phase. The reported average power for the whole run will be the numerical average of the power measurements for the whole run. As with Level 1, all reported measurements must be read, and all must be included in the average. Idle power must also be included, but may be taken as a separate event.

For Level 2, all subsystems participating in the workload must be measured or estimated. At least 1/8 of the compute-

Table 1: Summary of aspects and quality levels

Aspect	Level 1	Level 2	Level 3
1a: Granularity	One power sample per second	One power sample per second	Continuously integrated energy
1b: Timing	The longer of one minute or 20% of the run	Equally spaced across the full run	Equally spaced across the full run
1c: Measurements	Core phase average power	• 10 average power measurements in the core phase • Full run average power • idle power	• 10 energy measurements in the core phase • Full run average power • idle power
2: Machine fraction	The greater of 1/64 of the compute subsystem or 1 kW	The greater of 1/8 of the compute-node subsystem or 10 kW	The whole of all included subsystems
3: Subsystems	Compute-nodes only	All participating subsystems, either measured or estimated	All participating subsystems must be measured
4: Point of measurement	Upstream of power conversion **OR** Conversion loss modeled with manufacturer data	Upstream of power conversion **OR** Conversion loss modeled with off-line measurements of a single power supply	Upstream of power conversion **OR** Conversion loss measured simultaneously

node subsystem or at least 10 kW of power be measured, whichever is larger. The remaining part of the compute-node subsystem is extrapolated, and all types must be included, as with Level 1.

Other subsystems may be measured or estimated. If estimated, the submission must include the relevant manufacturer specifications and formulas used for power estimation.

3.3 Level 3

Level 3 submissions include the total energy over the course of the run, energy in the core phase, and the average power over those regions as computed from the energy. Each of these numbers is taken from a continuously integrated energy measurement as the total energy consumed to that point, each measurement will be the sum of the previous measurement and the energy consumed since it was taken, not as instantaneous power. In order to calculate the average power, the energy consumed in a given phase is computed by subtracting the total energy at the end of the phase from the energy at the start, and dividing by the time. The complete set of total energy readings used to calculate average power (at least 10 during the core computation phase) must be included in the submission, along with the execution time for the core phase and the execution time for the full run. At least one measurement must fall before and one after the core phase. These must also be reported along with idle power. Unlike Levels 1 and 2, Level 3 need not be concerned about different types of compute nodes because Level 3 measures the entire system as a single unit. In addition to including the entire compute-node subsystem, all subsystems participating in the workload must be measured.

The measurements in the following sections of the paper are placed here as illustrations of the principles outlined in the power measurement specification. Normally, submissions would present one set of data targeted at the submission level desired by the submitter. These sections instead list multiple levels as illustrations of the constraints and ramifications of submitting at different quality levels with the intent of encouraging higher quality level measurements.

4. CASE STUDY FROM BADW-LRZ

The SuperMUC supercomputer at the Leibniz Supercomputing Center of the Bavarian Academy of Sciences and Humanities (BADW-LRZ) is one of the 10 fastest supercomputers in the world according to the June 2013 Top500 list. The data center housing SuperMUC was designed with an extensive monitoring infrastructure and provides many state-of-the-art measuring capabilities. This system is an ideal candidate to demonstrate the differences between the different levels described in the methodology.

The system consists of 18 islands, each of which are comprised of seven compute racks plus one network rack, and a total of 9,288 compute nodes. There are 2 power distribution units (PDUs) per rack; a PDU has 6 outlets and each outlet can power anywhere from 4 to 8 compute nodes.

SuperMUC is equipped with IBM 46M4004 Power Distribution Units, which are capable of sampling voltage, current and power at 120 Hz. Power values are averaged over 60 seconds and have a one minute readout interval. RMS current and voltage measurements have +/-5% accuracy over the entire range of supported voltages. For the SuperMUC tests, Level 1 and 2 power measurements are taken from the PDUs, sampled 120 times per second and recorded at ten equally spaced points once every 50 minutes.

Level 3 measurements used a Socomec Diris A40/A41 meter. This meter is a multi-function digital power and continuously integrating energy meter with a one-second internal measurement updating period and a 15-minute readout interval. The meter takes measurements up to the 63rd harmonic. The meter is International Electrotechnical Commission (IEC) 61557-12 certified. The energy accuracy is defined by IEC 62053-22 accuracy class index 0,5S. The power measurements have 0.5% accuracy. The meter is located after the transformers and after the dynamic UPS system and measures the power consumption for the entire room containing SuperMUC.

In order to provide easy comparison with widely available measurements, each case study is constructed around a run of the High Performance Linpack (HPL) [15] benchmark according to the version 1.0a EE HPC WG methodology

SuperMUC HPL Power Consumption (Machine Room + PDU Measurement)

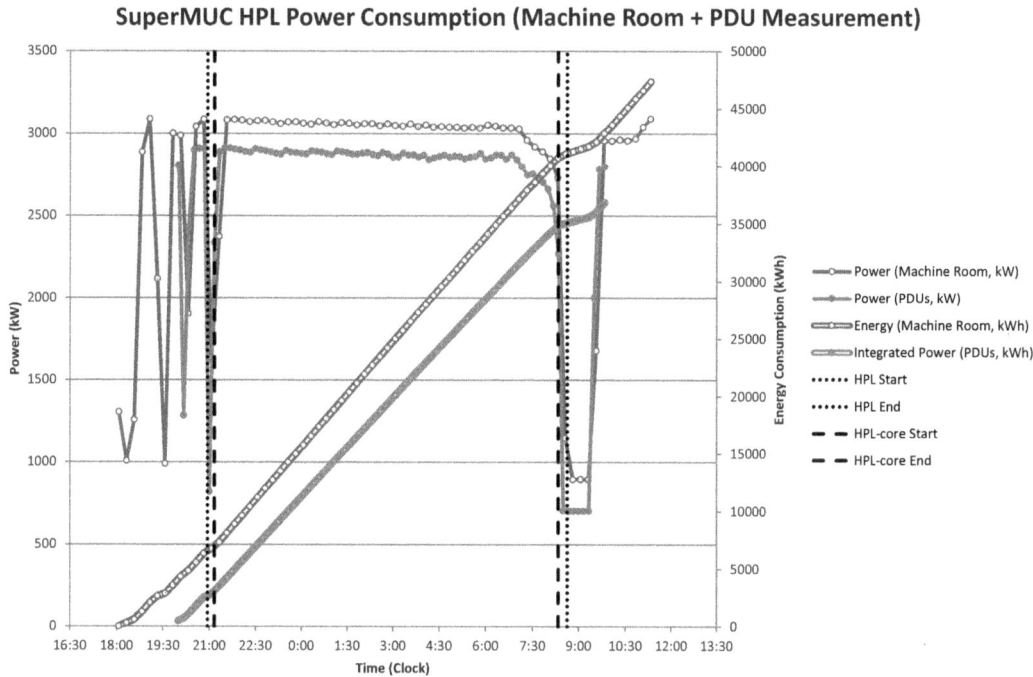

Figure 1: SuperMUC HPL power consumption ([machine room - Level 3] and [PDU - used for Level 1 and 2] measurement)

Table 2: SuperMUC: Level 1 results from one PDU outlet with 8 nodes

Average Power Location	Average Power Value
Average power for PDU outlet #6 with 8 nodes	2.126118kW
Average power per node	0.265765kW
Average power for the full machine during HPL core phase	2468.425kW

document [4].[2] The HPL run for SuperMUC is graphically represented in Figure 1. The run starts at 20:56 and ends at 8:37, for a duration of 701 minutes. The core phase, which is clearly visible in the power consumption of the benchmark as a long consistently high plateau of power consumption, starts at 21:10 and ends at 8:20 for a duration of 670 minutes. Given that length, the 20% of core phase runtime required for a level one measurement is 134 minutes.

4.1 Level 1

For Level 1, the reported value is the average over 140 minutes (23:20 - 01:40) which is just slightly more than 20% of the core phase. The power from one PDU outlet servicing 8 nodes is measured as 2126.118W, which is 265.77 watts/node. The extrapolated value for the entire machine (9288 compute nodes) is 2468.43 kW. Table 2 lists Level 1 power measurements.

---

[2]The current version of the methodology [3] requires the greater of 1/64th of the machine or 1kW for Level 1, and all measurements available during the run to be included at Level 2, when this study was conducted those requirements did not exist.

4.2 Level 2

Recall that Level 2 requires 1/8 of the system or 10kW, whichever is larger plus an additional system idle measurement. Fifteen power measurements were taken. The elapsed time of the Linpack run goes from 0 to 701 minutes with a measurement recorded every 50 minutes ending at 700min. The core phase begins at 14min and ends at 684min, placing 13 measurements within the core phase and satisfying the requirement for more than ten in that phase. The idle power is separately measured as 703kW for all of SuperMUC.

Level 2 also requires the measurement or estimation of all used subsystems (for example, networking). The two Ethernet switches in each compute rack of SuperMUC are automatically included when averaging over all PDU measurements for a rack. Additionally we must account for the power used by the InfiniBand and BNT-Ethernet switches which are located in a separate networking rack in each island. Recall that SuperMUC has 18 islands and hence 18 network racks, each of which has 10 PDU outlets; the system then has a total of 180 networking PDU outlets.

The power for one of these PDUs averaged over the full run is 415.15W and over the core phase is 416.08W. The value for the full system, all 180 networking racks, for the full run is 74.73kW, and the value for the core phase only is 74.89kW. The average power consumed by the IB switches does not depend significantly on the compute load of the system; it increases only by about 0.23%. This contrasts with the compute node behavior where the average power per node changes by about 10% between HPL core phase only and the full run.

In order to determine the skew introduced by choosing one or another of the minimum requirements for Level 2, either 1/8th of the system or greater than 10 kilowatts, each of the two is explored separately below.

4.2.1 Level 2 (1/8 System)

To measure 1/8 of the system, the power of 16 racks was measured. Of those fourteen contain 12 PDU outlets and 74 nodes, while the remaining two racks contain 72 nodes with the same number of PDU outlets. The total number of nodes measured come to 1,180 nodes, which is greater than 1/8 (1,161) of the total compute nodes (9288). The average power for a PDU is measured for both the full run, finding 1,670.04W, and for the core phase as 1848.36W.

To extrapolate to the entire compute subsystem, we multiply the average power for a PDU outlet by the number of PDU outlets measured, 192, divide by the number of nodes measured, 1,180, and multiply by the total number of compute nodes, or 9,288. Then, to extrapolate for the entire system, add the power measured for the network racks. Table 3 lists the details of the Level 2 power measurements.

4.2.2 Level 2 (>10 KW)

As compared to the 16 racks and 1,180 nodes required to conform to the 1/8th of the system requirement, the 10kW fraction of SuperMUC is miniscule. The power for just one rack with 2 PDUs, consisting of 6 outlets each, for a total of 12 PDU outlets and 74 nodes is measured. Since the fraction is so much smaller, a more efficient subset of the machine can be counted. The average power for a PDU outlet is lowered to 1,645.5W over the full run and 1,819.6 over the core phase only. Power consumption at the PDU outlet level is lowered by 24.54W and 28.76W respectively, changing nothing but the size of the machine fraction instrumented.

Extrapolating full-system power as before, the shifts seen in the PDU outlet-level measurements are magnified. At the full-system level, the smaller machine fraction consumes 2,553.1kW on average over the full run and 2,815.5 over the core phase. Counting the full system, the drop in power consumption shown by decreasing the fraction instrumented is 45.5 kilowatts over the full run or 52.75kW over the core phase. While the shift is less than 1/50 (i.e., 0.02) of the overall consumption, it is significant for large-scale systems. Therefore, the methodology requires the larger of the two to be used.

4.3 Level 3

Level 3 requires continuously integrated energy measurements of the complete system and as such, the data consist of accumulated energy reported every fifteen minutes. Figure 1 shows power and energy measurements vs. time. Over the full run the average power is computed to be 2,910.618kW, and 3,019.315kW over the core phase of the run. The Level 3 measurement is materially higher than either of the Level 2 measurements (357kW in the worst-case). Part of that difference comes from including portions of the system not included in the Level 2 measurement, for example the system data storage, and from really measuring all nodes. Another part comes from including infrastructure components such as the cooling system. This is in contrast to differences between the two different Level 2 measurements. There the main factor is the extrapolation of the final value from different system sizes.

4.4 Performance

When running on the entire SuperMUC system, all 9,288 nodes, the HPL benchmark reports an RMax of 2.582 Pflops.

Table 4: SuperMUC: Calculated megaflops/watt for the different quality levels

Quality Level	Mflops/Watt full run	Mflops/Watt core phase
L1	1055	1055
L2 (>10kW)	1011	917
L2 (>1/8)	994	900
L3	887	855

Table 4 lists the calculated efficiencies in Mflops/watt based on the power measurements gathered at each level.

Level 3 delivers the most accurate values, as it was obtained using a revenue-grade meter and measures the entire system including:
- Compute nodes
- Interconnect network
- GPFS mass storage systems
- Storage network
- Head/login and management nodes
- Internal warm water cooling system (machine room internal cooling such as water pumps, heat exchangers, etc.)
- PDU power distribution losses

Measurements for the lower levels were obtained using the PDUs, resulting in lower accuracy and additionally based only on the power of the compute and networking subsystems.

Since all requirements for each level were fulfilled, Table 4 illustrates the effect of attempting to compare results across disparate accuracy levels. As can be seen from the table the efficiency of the Level 1 core phase differs from that of Level 3 by 200Mflops/Watt or around 23% (1055 Mflops/Watt vs. 855 Mflops/Watt). This result is obtained without looking for the most energy efficient nodes for the Level 1 measurement. It is not hard to imagine that the difference could increase further if they were carefully selected for efficiency.

Level2 is closer to Level 3 (about 12% for the full run and about 5% for the HPL core run). But cherry picking would still be possible. Looking at the two possible requirements for a Level 2 the measurements show a difference of about 1.7%.

The comparison of the different measurement quality levels, that were all taken during the same run, shows that ranking different levels in one list would strongly favor lower level submissions. As a result of this, the Green500 has opted to require a level one measurement with every submission even if the submission also includes a higher level measurement to ensure comparability on the main list. We urge any other ranking organizations or procedures to perform separate rankings for each quality level, and discourage comparison across levels.

5. CASE STUDY FROM ARGONNE NATIONAL LABORATORY

The Argonne Leadership Computing Facility's (ALCF) new Mira supercomputer, sited at Argonne National Laboratory, debuted as the 3rd fastest supercomputer in the world (Top500, June-2012). Mira is a forty-eight rack IBM Blue Gene[3]/Q (BG/Q) with a peak compute performance of 10 PetaFlop/s (PF). The system has 49,152 compute nodes,

---

[3]Copyright 2013 by International Business Machine Corporation

Table 3: SuperMUC: Level 2 power measurements

| | 1/8th system | | >10kW | |
	Full run	HPL core phase	Full run	HPL core phase
Average power for one PDU outlet	1,670.039W	1,848.355W	1,645.500W	1,819.592W
Machine average power	2,523.875kW	2,793.357kW	2,478.391kW	2,740.601kW
Full machine + network	2,598.601kW	2,868.252kW	2,553.117kW	2,815.496kW

each with 16 cores and 16 gigabytes of memory, for a total of 786,432 cores and 786 terabytes of memory. The BG/Q is 93% water-cooled and 7% air-cooled, and, through innovative computer, network, and water-cooling designs, is one of the top energy efficient supercomputer architectures in the world.

The most challenging aspect of implementing the EE HPC WG power measurement methodology for Mira was inherently social/political and not technological. The ALCF BG/Q computers are located in the data center of the Theory and Computing Sciences (TCS) building. The TCS building is managed by a 3rd party. Because the building is not owned by ANL, the data from the building management system (BMS), which tracks energy usage over time, are not readily available to the tenants of the data center. Modifications to the system to add trending, gather data more frequently, etc., are infeasible for the same reason.

Because of these difficulties, ALCF was unable to measure Mira's HPL run at Level 3 for all aspects for an attempted submission in June 2012 to the Top500. Some Level 3 aspects were achieved. Table 5 shows the levels achieved for each aspect.

5.1 Measurement Specifications

As originally delivered, the IBM Blue Gene/Q provides several interesting power monitoring capabilities within the system, both at a coarse-grained level, with the Bulk Power Modules (BPMs) measuring one quarter of a rack each, and at a more fine-grained level, e.g. voltage domains within a node board (DCAs).[4] Figure 2 shows the locations of the monitors from the 480V distribution panels through to the fine-grained power monitor at the node board level.

Eaton Digitrip Optim 1050 meters measure the 480V power at the electrical distribution panels (Mira's racks are directly wired to these panels) mounted on the data center walls. The Eaton data are part of the BMS and are only readily accessible to the building management company. BPMs provide power measurements both upstream and downstream of the AC/DC power conversion. BPM data are gathered, along with other environmental data, into the overall control system database and are generally only accessible to the system administrator. The DCAs provide power measurements for the seven voltage domains on each node board and can be accessed by users from a running job. To determine overall power usage, the DCA power data would have to be adjusted for the power loss due to the AC/DC conversion using the BPM data.

The choice of measuring location depends not only on access but also on the planned usage for the data. For example, measurements at the distribution panels are impractical because measurements are taken every five minutes, one for each phase of their 3-phase AC input power supplies, resulting in only 30 data points per time step for the full Mira

---

[4]See [26] for more information on the DCA power measurement capabilities

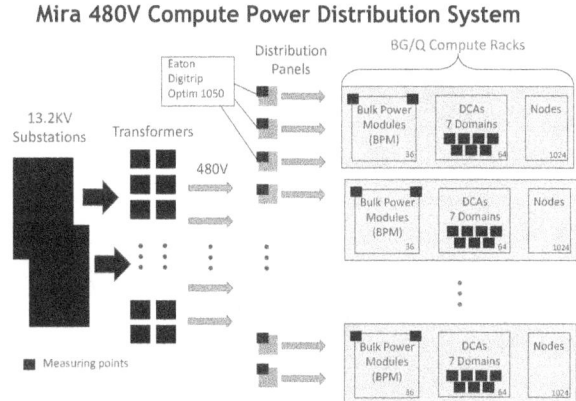

Figure 2: Power measurement locations for the Mira supercomputer

system. The data are also not kept beyond a few days, as the system tracking the data has very little storage space. The BPM measurements are primarily used to look at BPM efficiency and to monitor for potential problems with the BPMs. There are 36 BPMs in every rack (nine in a n+1 configuration for every 256 nodes), with four data points at each measurement (input and output current, input and output voltage), resulting in a total of 6,912 data points at each five-minute time step for Mira. The measurements are taken approximately every five minutes, for a total of 82,944 data points each hour. Users may request access to the BPM data, but the data are stored in a fire-walled database and are only provided as historical data. Therefore, if a user is interested in realtime power measurements, the user would use the DCA data, which are accessible from within a running job and provide much finer measurements both in time, measured every 560ms, and in space, 2 DCAs per every 32 nodes, for a total of 64 per rack. The DCA current and voltage are measured for each of seven voltage domains (described in Section 5.3) totaling 43,008 data points per time step, or 276,480,000 data points per hour. The DCA data would be appropriate for developing an application power signature, evaluating the impact of changes to an algorithm, or performing research into power management and reduction techniques for the next generation of computer systems.

Because data at the different locations are measured at different time scales and granularities, it can be challenging to compare the data between them. In addition, the panel measurements include other BG/Q racks, and, as such, cannot be accurately compared to the BPM and DCA data.

5.2 Mira Linpack Data

The Mira HPL run and evaluation is summarized in Figure 3, where the job starts at 23:21:30 and ends at 15:24:37

Table 5: Mira HPL aspect levels achieved

Aspect	Level Achieved	Notes
1a: Granularity	2	Bulk Power Modules (BPMs) sample instantaneously every 200us, but only measure average power and do not provide energy computed by continuously integrating power as required by Level 3
1b: Timing	2	195 point-in-time power averaged measurements were taken at equally spaced 5 minute intervals; Unable to measure integrated total energy values
1c: Measurements	2	Idle power measurement taken; more than 10 power measurements were taken within the core phase;
2: Machine fraction	3	All 48 racks (whole machine) were measured
3: Subsystems	3	Whole system
4: Point of measurement	3	Power measurements were taken both upstream and downstream of power conversion; power conversion measured simultaneously during the same run

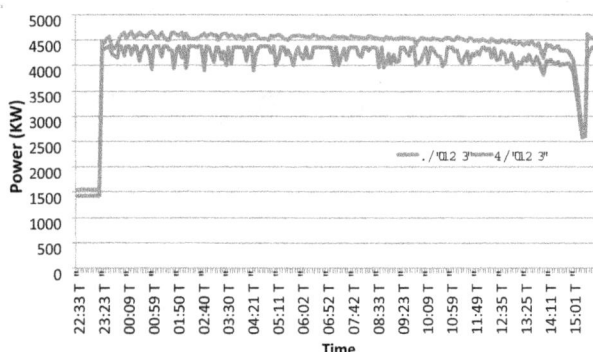

Figure 3: Power measurements during Mira Linpack run

Table 6: Mira Linpack data

Data Item	Value
Start Time	23:21:30
End Time	15:24:37
Performance (TFlops)	8,201
Mflops/Watt full run	1,824
Duration (s)	57,787.7
Idle power (kW)	1,549.10
Full run power (avg kW)	4,496.44

the next day for a duration of 963.1 minutes. BPM power measurements were automatically pulled by the control system and uploaded to the control system database every five minutes; these are plotted in Figure 3. Input power, specifically AC power at the entry to each BPM, is shown in blue, and output power (DC power at the exit of each BPM) is shown in red. The overall efficiency of the AC/DC power conversion across the entire time period measured was 93.3%.

Because the HPL code used was not modified to produce a timestamp at the start and end of the core phase [5], we do not know exactly when the core phase began and ended. From the Linpack output data, time was 57559.8 seconds; dgemm wall-time was 52784.8 seconds, and dtrsm wall-time was 342.1 seconds. The total time from the start of the job to the timestamp at the end of the job was 57787.7 seconds. Table 6 shows the Linpack measurements.

---

[5]Although HPL has since released this functionality, it was not readily available at the time of the test.

5.3 Reaching Level 3

Because the BPMs do not measure total energy, the Mira HPL power calculations were unable to reach Level 3. To address this issue, IBM, with a goal of achieving Level 3, has developed a firmware upgrade that can provide total energy measurements with sample rates over 2000 times per second at the DCAs. This modification was the direct result of IBM working with the EE HPC WG to determine the appropriate methodology.

The DCAs can be used by end users to measure CPU, memory, and network usage. The data gathered are downstream of the AC/DC conversion, and for a Level 3 full-system measurement these data would need to be adjusted for AC to DC conversion loss using measurements from the BPMs. Gathering DCA measurements requires modification of the code, and because the available DCA data at the time of the Mira HPL run was not Level 3 compliant, DCA measurements were not taken. At this time, installation of the firmware is not officially supported by IBM. With Mira in production, ALCF will not install the firmware until it becomes officially supported.

6. CASE STUDY FROM Calcul Québec Université Laval

Colosse is a Compute Canada cluster at Calcul Québec Université Laval. Installed in 2009 by Sun Microsystems, this cluster consists of 960 nodes (x6275 Sun blades with X5560 Nehalem processors) with 24 GB RAM, totaling 7,680 cores. The cluster also includes a Lustre filesystem offering one petabyte of storage (total of 28 OSS and MDS servers), and an Infiniband QDR fat-tree network built using two Sun M9 DSC648 core switches and 42 leaf switches.

Colosse is an air-cooled cluster installed in a three-level silo building. The site's cylindrical topology offers an outer cold air plenum in front of all racks, and the generated heat is captured in a central hot core cylinder. While the computer is air-cooled, the facility uses chilled water cooling at the infrastructure level. Chilled water input temperature is typically 5 °C, and the heated water is returned to the system at temperatures ranging from 25 to 28 °C. The cold air plenum temperature is maintained at 19 °C, at a relative humidity between 45% and 55%.

A 2 MW site transformer provides 3-phase 600 V. A Siemens 9330 power meter is connected on the 600 V power grid. This meter's accuracy specification complies with the IEC 687

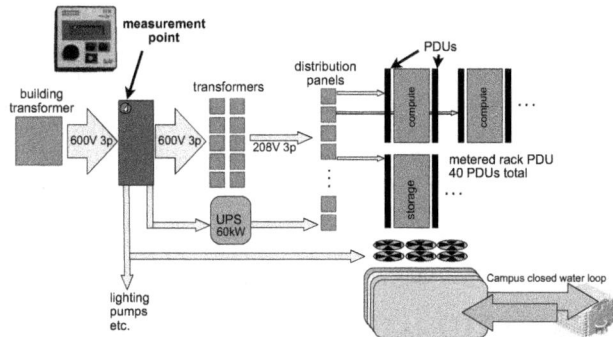

Figure 4: Power measurement points for the Colosse super-computer

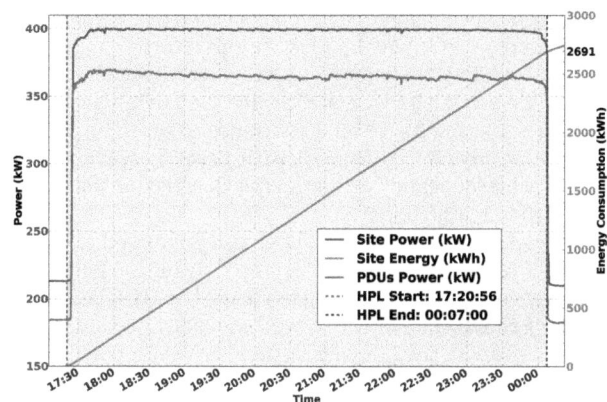

Figure 5: Power and energy measurements during the Colosse run

Class 0.5 specification and ANSI 12.20 Class 0.5. Ten 112 kVA transformers provide 3-phase 208 V to ten distribution panels.

The Colosse cluster uses about 30 % of the site's electrical and cooling capacity. It contains ten computer racks with 96 nodes per rack. Each rack is powered from two metered APC (Schneider Electric) AP7866 16.2 kW PDUs. The storage system, management servers, Infiniband and Ethernet switches are installed in ten computer racks. These racks are powered from two metered APC (Schneider Electric) AP7868 12.5 kW PDUs. Overall, the system has a total of 40 PDUs. The metering on these PDUs measures instantaneous current for each input phase and outlets. Continuously integrated total energy measurement, as required for a Level 3 measurement, is not available from these PDUs.

As an early adopter of the new measurement methodology, we set a goal to achieve a Level 3 measurement. The Siemens power meter was used since this meter provides the required energy measurement. This power meter is reachable through a TCP/IP connection, so we are able to adjust the measurement period according to the measurement requirements; the meter is capable of measuring up to 1,920 times per second. The integrated energy and power measurements are reported every 30 seconds.

Figure 4 shows the location of the Siemens power meter.

A drawback to using this power meter is that measurements include subsystems that are not required by the methodology (such as power transformers, UPS, site lightning, water pumps, fans).

Figure 5 and Table 7 show the Level 3 measurement results from May 2012. The energy measurement shows that 2691 kWh was consumed during the HPL run. By comparing the site power (measured from the Siemens power meter) and the PDU power (measured from instantaneous power measurements on the 40 PDUs), we note that the power transformers, water pumps, fans, and lighting consumed between 30 kW and 35 kW during the run.

The Colosse cluster has been in operation for over three years. Running HPL requires a significant maintenance window to get all systems working correctly. While this is usually not a problem for new systems under deployment (usually this is part of acceptance testing), it has an important impact for production systems. The power and energy requirements highlight the need for better instrumentation. New supercomputer deployments (or major renovations) should require power and energy sensors in the rack.

Table 7: Colosse power data

Data Item	Value
Start time	17:20:56
End time	00:07:40
Performance (TFlops)	77.89
Mflops/Watt full run	196
Duration (s)	24,404
Idle power (kW)	213.38
Full run power (avg, kW)	396.75

7. CONCLUSIONS

The energy consumption of larger HPC systems is an ever-growing concern. This paper described a more refined and rigorous power measurement methodology for HPC systems under workload runs. The methodology was developed by the Energy Efficient HPC Working Group in collaboration with Green500, Top500, and the Green Grid.

This paper considered three levels of quality of measurements: Level 1, which is similar to the Green500 version 0.9 run rules, and Levels 2 and 3, which include more comprehensive and integrated energy-usage measurements.

Case studies at LRZ, ANL, and Calcul Québec showed how this methodology can help these centers pinpoint the energy "hot spot" in a much clearer way than was previously possible. In particular, Level 3 measurements were indeed found to be both more precise and more accurate than Level 1 and Level 2 measurements. However, Level 3 measurements today require HPC-center, infrastructure-level instrumentation.

The challenges for attaining Level 3 measurements are not only technical, but also organizational and economic. Our case studies illustrated these challenges as well as demonstrated that measurements at different quality levels yielded different reuslts. Comparison of test results are best for data taken at the same quality level.

This is an important result. There are two main reasons for performance metrics. The first is to track a site's performance over time. The second is to be able to compare one site to another. The ability to do the latter is greatly enhanced by defining the levels.

Comparisons between sites at the same level are now meaningful. In the past, power measurements at different sites could be argued to have been different enough to not be meaningful. For example, note LRZ's difference between L1 (1055 Mflops/Watt) and L3 (905 MFlops/Watt).

When trending an individual site over time, the worst thing to do would be to not measure the energy, claiming that one is waiting for Level 3 instrumentation to be added. The best approach is is to start with Level 1, which is reasonably achievable and then trend the cluster over time with a repeatable methodology.

The work of the EE HPC WG is also paying off in other aspects. Previously, the start and stop time for the HPL (HP Linpack) "core phase" was also not clear. The HPL code now includes a timestamp for the "core phase" start and stop time to better support the power measurement methodology. All sites are encouraged to use these timestamps.

Challenges also remain for larger installations regarding how to get to Level 3. At Argonne, IBM BG/Q responded to user desire for Level 3 measurements with a firmware upgrade, but it is not yet officially supported. The power meter installed at Calcul Québec for Level 3 measurements also had its issues in that it included power consumed by power transformers, water pumps, fans, and lighting, which consumed between 30 kW and 35 kW during the run, originally not part of Level 3. These examples point out the difficulties of getting to Level 3. These are best avoided by new cluster installations including the right measurement capability at the time of installation.

Future Work

Building more energy efficient HPC systems continue to be a major concern. In Europe, the EU COST Action IC0805 Open Network for High-performance Computing on Complex Environments and EU COST Action IC0804 Energy Efficiency of Large Scale Distributed Systems recently combined efforts proposing further work in this area [7].

The measurement quality level needs to be included when reporting power data for ranking sites such as the Green500 and Top500, because the different levels produce different results. The validity of comparing across sites is enhanced when reporting values and stating the Level used.

Level 3 measurement capabilities could be made a feature of HPC systems, as demonstrated by the IBM BG/Q. It is recommended that users ask for these kinds of capabilities from their vendors.

The EE HPC WG continues to develop and refine the methodologies, while at the same time exploring their applicability to measure the energy used in other performance metrics. In the near future, we are investigating the elimination or adjustment of Level 1 and increasing the specificity of Levels 2 and 3.

The focus on improving the ability to take precise and accurate power measurements is important for understanding architectural trends such as those provided for the Top500 and Green500. With these advanced measurement capabilities, larger HPC centers (such as LRZ) are more able to effectively drive energy efficiency programs.

8. ACKNOWLEDGMENTS

Portions of this research used resources of the Argonne Leadership Computing Facility at Argonne National Laboratory, which is supported by the Office of Science of the U.S. Department of Energy under contract DE-AC02-06CH11357.

Portions of this research used resources of Calcul Québec and Compute Canada, which is funded by the Canada Foundation for Innovation (CFI) and the Gouvernement du Québec.

Portions of this research have been carried out within the PRACE project, which has received funding from the European Community's Seventh Framework Program (FP7/2007-2013) under grant agreements no. RI-261557 and RI-283493, and at the Leibniz Supercomputing Centre (BADW-LRZ) with support of the State of Bavaria, Germany, and the Gauss Centre for Supercomputing (GCS), Germany.

9. ADDITIONAL AUTHORS

Anna Maria Bailey, LLNL
John Baron, SGI
Sergio Barrachina, UJI
Paul Coteus, IBM
Anne C. Elster, NTNU
Ladina Gilly, CSCS
Robin Goldstone, LLNL
Chung-Hsing Hsu, ORNL
Ted Kubaska, IEEE
James Laros, SNL
Yutong Lu, NUDT
David Martinez, SNL
Michael Patterson, Intel
Stephen Poole, ORNL
James H. Rogers, ORNL
Greg Rottman, ERDC
Mehdi Sheiklhalishahi, UNICAL
Daniel Tafani, LRZ
William Tschudi, LBNL

10. REFERENCES

[1] The Graph 500. http://www.graph500.org/.
[2] The Green Graph 500. http://green.graph500.org/.
[3] Energy Efficient High Performance Computing Power Measurement Methodology. http://green500.org/sites/default/files/eehpcwg/EEHPCWG_PowerMeasurementMethodology.pdf.
[4] Energy Efficient High Performance Computing Power Measurement Methodology version 1.0a. http://green500.org/sites/default/files/eehpcwg/EEHPCWG_PowerMeasurementMethodology.pdf.
[5] Energy Efficient HPC Working Group. http://eehpcwg.lbl.gov/.
[6] Energy Efficient HPC Working Group, Green500 and Top500 Power Submission Analysis. http://eehpcwg.lbl.gov/documents.
[7] EU COST Action IC0805: Open Network for High-Performance Computing on Complex Environments. http://www.complexhpc.org.
[8] Green500. http://www.green500.org/.
[9] Green500 Run Rules. http://green500.org/docs/pubs/RunRules_Ver0.9.pdf.
[10] D. Hackenberg and et al. Quantifying power consumption variations of hpc systems using spec mpi benchmarks. *Computer Science Research and Development*, 25:155–163, 2010.
[11] C. H. Hsu and S. Poole. Power measurement for high performance computing: State of the art. In *Proceedings of the International Green Computing Conference*, 2011.

[12] C. H. Hsu and S. Poole. Power signature analysis of the SPECpower_ssj2008 benchmark. In *Proceedings of the International Symposium of Performance Analysis of Systems and Software (ISPASS)*, 2011.

[13] S. Kamil, J. Shalf, and E. Strohmaier. Power Efficiency in High Performance Computing. In *Proceedings of the High Performance, Power Aware Computing Workshop (HPPAC)*, 2008.

[14] J. Laros. Topics on measuring real power usage on high performance computing platforms. In *Proceedings of the International Conference on Cluster Computing (CLUSTER)*, 2009.

[15] HPL A Portable Implementation of the High-Performance Linpack Benchmark for Distributed-Memory Computers. www.netlib.org/benchmark/hpl/.

[16] H. W. Meuer, E. Strohmaier, and H. D. Simon. Top500. www.top500.org.

[17] M. S. Müller, J. Baron, W. C. Brantley, H. Feng, D. Hackenberg, R. Henschel, G. Jost, D. Molka, C. Parrott, J. Robichaux, P. Shelepugin, M. van Waveren, B. Whitney, and K. Kumaran. SPEC OMP2012 — An Application Benchmark Suite for Parallel Systems Using OpenMP. In *Lecture Notes in Computer Science*, pages 223–236. Springer Berlin Heidelberg.

[18] S. Sharma, C. H. Hsu, and W.-c. Feng. Making a case for a green500 list. In *Proceedings of the High Performance Power Aware Computing Workshop*, 2006.

[19] SPEC High Performance Group. http://www.spec.org.

[20] SPEC OMP2012. http://www.spec.org/omp2012/.

[21] SPEC Power Committee. SPEC power and performance benchmark methodology. Technical report, Standard Performance Evaluation Corporation, June 2010. Tech. Rep. Version 2.0.

[22] B. Subramaniam and W. Feng. Understanding power measurement implications in the green500 list. In *Proceedings of the IEEE/ACM International Conference on Green Computing and Communications (GreenCom)*, 2010.

[23] B. Subramaniam, T. Scogland, and W. Feng. Trends in Energy-Efficient Computing: A Perspective from the Green500. In *roceedings of the 4th International Green Computing Conference, Arlington, VA*, June 2013. (to appear).

[24] The Green Grid. http://www.thegreengrid.org/.

[25] Top 500 Supercomputing Sites. http://www.top500.org.

[26] K. Yoshii, K. Iskra, R. Gupta, P. Beckman, V. Vishwanath, C. Yu, and S. Coghlan. Evaluating Power-Monitoring Capabilities on IBM Blue Gene/P and Blue Gene/Q. In *2012 IEEE International Conference on Cluster Computing (CLUSTER)*. IEEE.

Engineering Resource Management Middleware for Optimizing the Performance of Clouds Processing MapReduce Jobs with Deadlines

Norman Lim
Dept. of Systems and Computer
Engineering
Carleton University
Ottawa, ON, Canada
nlim@sce.carleton.ca

Shikharesh Majumdar
Dept. of Systems and Computer
Engineering
Carleton University
Ottawa, ON, Canada
majumdar@sce.carleton.ca

Peter Ashwood-Smith
Huawei Technologies Canada
Kanata, ON, Canada
Peter.AshwoodSmith@
huawei.com

[Industrial and Experience Paper]

ABSTRACT

This paper focuses on devising efficient resource management techniques used by the resource management middleware in clouds that handle MapReduce jobs with end-to-end service level agreements (SLAs) comprising an earliest start time, execution time, and a deadline. This research and development work, performed in collaboration with our industrial partner, presents the formulation of the matchmaking and scheduling problem for MapReduce jobs as an optimization problem using: Mixed Integer Linear Programming (MILP) and Constraint Programming (CP) techniques. In addition to the formulations devised, our experience in implementing the MILP and CP models using various open source as well as commercial software packages is described. Furthermore, a performance evaluation of the different approaches used to implement the formulations is conducted using a variety of different workloads.

Categories and Subject Descriptors

C.2.4 [**Computer-Communication Networks**]: Distributed Systems. C.4 [**Performance of Systems**]: *performance attributes, modeling techniques.*

Keywords

Resource management on clouds, MapReduce with deadlines, Optimization, Mixed integer linear programming (MILP), Constraint programming (CP).

1. INTRODUCTION

Cloud computing, which concerns improving the way Information Technology (IT) is managed and consumed is receiving a great deal of interest from researchers and practioners from academia and industry. Cloud computing makes computational (hardware and software) resources accessible as scalable and on-demand services over a network such as the Internet [1]. To accomplish this goal, the cloud computing paradigm employs a wide-range of concepts and technologies such as virtualization, service-orientation, elasticity, scalability, and pay-as-you-go. Using the virtualization technology, cloud computing is able to deliver an on-demand, service-oriented model that offers: Infrastructure-as-a-Service (IaaS), Platform-as-

a-Service (PaaS), and Software-as-a-Service (SaaS). IaaS delivers basic computational resources (virtual machines) as an on-demand service whereas PaaS offers a higher-level service (e.g. application framework with development tools) where consumers can create and deploy their own scalable Web applications without having to invest in and maintain their own physical infrastructure. Lastly, SaaS provides consumers with complete end-user Web applications. Communication and social applications such as Customer Relationship Management (CRM) systems, email, and Facebook are examples of SaaS. Along with an on-demand service-oriented model, cloud computing also offers *scalability*, *elasticity*, and *pay-as-you-go* features. The scalability and elasticity characteristics of the cloud provide the ability to grow or shrink the number of resources allocated to a consumer's request dynamically with time. With the pay-as-you-go model, consumers can lease resources on-demand from the service provider and pay only for the time the resources are used.

In addition to researchers and service consumers, cloud computing that is based on resources acquired on demand is generating a great deal of interest among service providers and system builders as well. Cloud service providers typically own a large pool of resources that include computing, storage, and communication resources. Effective resource management strategies and performance optimization techniques need to be developed for harnessing the power of the underlying resource pool. The important operations performed by a resource manager deployed in the resource management middleware for a cloud include: *matchmaking* and *scheduling*. When a request arrives, the resource manager invokes a *matchmaking* algorithm that selects the resource or resources (from a given a pool of resources) to be allocated to the request. Once a number of requests get allocated to a specific resource, a *scheduling* algorithm is used to determine the order in which these requests are to be executed. Both matchmaking and scheduling are well known as computationally hard problems because they need to satisfy a user's requirements for a quality of service that is often captured in a service level agreement (SLA); while also achieving the desired system objectives for the service providers, such as generating a high resource utilization and adequate revenue. Matchmaking and scheduling decisions can be made in one joint step (see [2] and [3] for example). The resource management technique presented in this paper makes such a joint decision on matchmaking and scheduling. Note that in this paper the term *output schedule* is used to define the task to resource mapping, and when each task runs on their assigned resource.

Both performance optimization and performance modeling are important components of performance engineering. This

ICPE'14, March 22–26 2014, Dublin, Ireland
Copyright 2014 ACM 978-1-4503-2733-6/14/03...$15.00.
http://dx.doi.org/10.1145/2568088.2576796

research concerns engineering resource management middleware that has two primary objectives: reducing the overhead of making resource management decisions and making decisions that achieve high system performance. This paper focuses on the investigation of techniques for management of resources on clouds in which the workload includes requests characterized by an end-to-end SLA [1] that comprises an earliest start time, execution time, and (soft) deadline [4] specified by the user. On systems with soft deadlines, jobs are permitted to miss their deadlines; however, the desired system objective is to minimize the number of jobs that do miss their deadlines. In addition, these requests also require *multiple stages of execution* with potentially different resources used in each stage. Considering these types of requests poses a new challenge to the resource management problem. Most of the works on resource management on clouds for workloads characterized by SLAs have only considered requests that require a single resource (i.e. single stage of execution). A scenario that involves reserving multiple resources simultaneously is important in the context of applications that require multiple system components, and can also arise from workflows that require the interaction of multiple applications that run on different resources. In this context, the workloads that are considered in this paper consist of *MapReduce* jobs.

MapReduce is a programming model that is characterized by multiple stages of execution and requires that the user define two functions [5]: a *map function* and a *reduce function*. Google proposed the use of MapReduce for processing large amounts (e.g. terabytes) of raw data in a distributed (parallel) manner to generate or derive more meaningful data [5]. The map function generates a set of intermediate key/value pairs from a set of input key/value pairs. These intermediate key/value pairs are grouped together and then passed to the reduce function where the values with identical keys are merged. A typical MapReduce job consists of a set of map tasks and a set of reduce tasks. The reduce tasks generally do not start executing until all map tasks are completed. Many computations can be expressed using MapReduce. For example, a MapReduce application can be deployed to count the number of URL accesses on a web server [5]. In this application, the map function processes the web server logs and produces a data set with an intermediate key/value pair of the form: {URL, 1}. This new data set is then processed by the reduce function, which sums all the values with identical keys to emit a new data set with the following key/value pair: {URL, total count}.

A popular implementation of MapReduce is Apache Hadoop [6], which is used by many companies and institutions for a variety of applications such as data processing (e.g., sorting, indexing, and grouping), data analysis, data mining (e.g. web crawling), machine learning, and scientific research (e.g. bioinformatics) [7]. In all these cases, there may be situations where a batch of MapReduce jobs needs to be executed either on a private cluster, or a cloud (such as Amazon EC2). On both systems, matchmaking and scheduling a batch of MapReduce jobs needs to be performed by the resource management middleware. Completing each job in the batch within a specific period of time (characterized by a deadline) is often a user requirement [4][8]. Resource management on such an environment is the focus of attention in this paper. Similar systems that map and schedule a batch of MapReduce jobs are investigated in [8], [9], and [10].

The goal of our research, performed in collaboration with Huawei Technologies, Canada, is to devise a cloud resource manager that can effectively perform matchmaking and scheduling of MapReduce jobs each of which is characterized by an end-to-end SLA comprising an earliest start time, execution time, and a deadline specified by the user. In this paper, we focus on describing our investigation and experiences with using various techniques and technologies to formulate and solve the matchmaking and scheduling problem. Figure 1 displays the three different approaches that are used for solving the matchmaking and scheduling problem. As shown in Figure 1, we formulate the matchmaking and scheduling problem as an optimization problem, and solve the matchmaking and scheduling problem jointly. More specifically, we describe our investigation/ experience in formulating the problem using: (1) *Mixed Integer Linear Programming* [11][12] (MILP), and (2) *Constraint Programming* [13] (CP) techniques. Both MILP and CP are well-known theoretical techniques that can solve optimization problems and find *optimal* solutions. See Section 2 for a further discussion on MILP and CP. Various implementations of our solutions based on MILP and CP using different software packages are considered: *Approach 1*: MILP model implemented and solved using LINGO [14] (commercial software); *Approach 2*: CP model implemented using MiniZinc/FlatZinc [15] and solved using Gecode [16] (both open source software); and *Approach 3*: CP model implemented and solved using IBM ILOG CPLEX Optimization Studio (CPLEX) [17] (commercial software). This paper is motivated by issues such as:

- How to employ the existing theory on MILP and CP for devising efficient resource management algorithms that minimize the number of jobs missing their deadlines on a closed system subjected to a batch workload comprising MapReduce jobs with deadlines.

- Development of efficient implementations of the algorithms using Commercial-Off-The-Shelf (COTS) packages that produce an acceptable system overhead accrued during the execution of the resource management algorithms.

- Getting an understanding of the relationship between the size of the workload and system performance.

A separate set of experiments is performed for evaluating the performance of each approach. The inputs used for a given set of experiments include a set of Jobs, J, and a set of resources, R, on which to execute J (see Figure 1). The MILP/CP solver program corresponding to the embodiment of an approach is executed on a desktop PC (described in Section 5). As captured in Figure 1 the *output schedule* (the mapping of tasks on resources and their assigned start times), along with the time required to complete the execution of the batch of MapReduce jobs, and the number of jobs missing their deadlines are obtained as an output at the end of a given experiment. The processing time required by the solver to produce the output is also measured by using the solver's built-in timing utilities. A performance evaluation was conducted to compare the three approaches using various system and workload parameters. Our goal is to determine which of these approaches is able to solve the matchmaking and scheduling problem for MapReduce jobs efficiently, and understand the trade-off between processing time and the quality of the output schedule in terms of the number of jobs missing their deadlines, and the completion time of the workload. The main contributions of this paper include:

- Devising a technique for generating an optimal solution that minimizes the number of jobs missing their deadlines. The formulation of two models, one using MILP and one using CP, for achieving the optimal solution for matchmaking and scheduling MapReduce jobs with SLAs are presented.
  - A comparison of MILP and CP, focusing on the differences in using these two techniques for achieving the resource management technique.

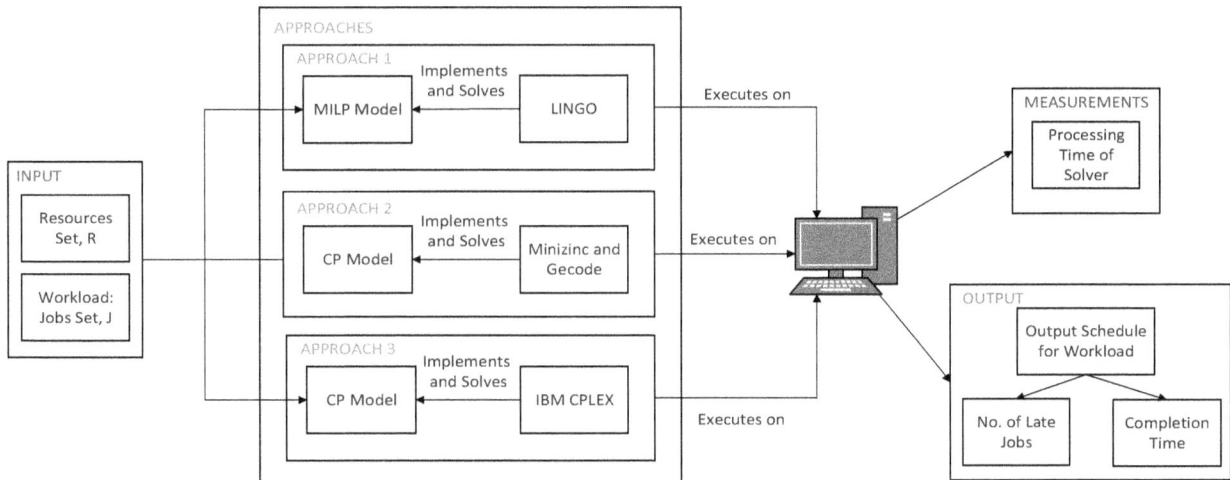

Figure 1. Overview of our approach.

- A discussion of the three approaches used to implement the MILP and CP models is presented.
- A performance evaluation of the three approaches using a variety of different system and workload parameters is presented. Insights gained into system behavior from the results of the performance evaluation are described.

The results of this research will be useful to researchers, designers, and users of the resource management middleware, including system developers and cloud service providers.

The rest of the paper is organized as follows. Section 2 provides a brief introduction to MILP and CP, and presents related work. Section 3 presents the problem description, and the formulations of the MILP and CP models. The design and implementation of the MILP and CP models using the three software packages are discussed in Section 4. In Section 5, the results of the performance evaluation, and a comparison of the performance of the three approaches are presented. Lastly, Section 6 concludes the paper and provides directions for future work.

2. BACKGROUND AND RELATED WORK

MILP [11] and CP [13] are well-known techniques that are used to solve optimization problems, and are capable of finding *optimal* solutions with regards to maximizing or minimizing an objective function. Both techniques have the same general modeling structure. There are a set of *decision variables* that need to be assigned values that ensure an *objective function* is optimized (maximized or minimized) subject to *constraints*—conditions that cannot be violated. In addition, both MILP and CP have been shown to be effective in solving planning and scheduling problems, such as the traditional job shop scheduling problem [3]. MILP is a subfield of mathematical programming (MP) (also called mathematical optimization) where the model has the following characteristics: (1) some of the decision variables must be integers, and (2) the objective function and constraints are mathematically linear [12]. The theoretical basis for MILP and mathematical optimization in general is numerical algebra [18]. To solve MILP models, techniques such as cutting-planes (constraint relaxations) and Branch and Bound are used.

CP was developed by computer science researchers in the mid-1980s by combining knowledge and techniques from artificial intelligence, logic and graph theory, and computer programming languages [13]. This theoretical foundation for CP is different than the theoretical foundation for MP techniques, such as MILP [18]. Unlike MILP models, CP models natively support a variety of arithmetic operators and logical constraints such as integer division, and the 'implies' constraint [19]. To

formulate logical constraints in a MILP model, the 'big-M' formulation technique [11] is typically used [19]. CP also defines a general set of specialized constraints, called *global constraints* that model frequently used patterns seen in optimization problems [20]. For example, one such constraint is the *cumulative* constraint which is used in scheduling problems to ensure that the capacity of each resource is not violated at any point in time.

The main limitation of CP models is that, natively, the decision variables can only be discrete (i.e. integer or Boolean) [13], whereas MP models support both discrete and continuous decision variables. The theoretical basis for solving MP models is numerical algebra; in contrast, for CP models the theoretical basis is logical inference including logic and graph theory. Search algorithms, including back-tracking and local search [13], are commonly used to solve CP models. The general idea in these search algorithms is to use logical inferences to assign values to the decision variables, and then to evaluate if the new values of the decision variables produce a better output (higher value if maximizing or lower value if minimizing) for the objective function.

A significant body of knowledge exists in the area of resource management on grids and clouds. More recently, researchers have also started investigating the problem of scheduling and matchmaking MapReduce jobs with deadlines. Due to space limitations, a representative set of work is presented. Development of a resource management middleware for clouds that is able to make smart and global decisions for achieving high system performance is being considered in OpenStack [21], which is collaborative open-source cloud software project. The authors of [8], propose a Deadline Constraint Scheduler for Hadoop [6] to handle jobs with deadlines. A job execution cost model that considers parameters including the execution time of map and reduce tasks, and input data sizes is developed. Dong et al. [9] focus on the scheduling of workloads comprising of MapReduce jobs with deadlines (real-time jobs) and jobs with no deadlines (non-real-time jobs). They integrate techniques such as Tasks Forward Scheduling (TFS) and Approximately Uniform Minimum Degree of Parallelism (AUMD) into the existing Hadoop scheduler to form a two-level scheduler that is capable of scheduling both real-time and non-real-time jobs. In [4], Verma et al. propose two resource allocation policies based on the earliest deadline first (EDF) strategy for Hadoop. The first policy is *MinEDF*, which allocates the minimum number of task slots required for completing a job before its deadline. The second policy, called *MinEDF-WC*, enhances MinEDF by adding the ability to dynamically allocate and de-allocate resources (task slots) from active jobs according to demand.

Similar to our research, the works discussed in [4], [8], and [9] investigate matchmaking and scheduling MapReduce jobs with deadlines. However, these works propose heuristic-based schedulers whereas our work describes using optimization techniques that can generate optimal solutions. These works also do not consider jobs characterized with earliest start times, which can be important in the context of advance reservation requests. In addition, the focus of [4], [8], and [9], is on improving the Hadoop [6] scheduler, which is an open source framework that implements the MapReduce programming model. The research described in this paper describes solutions for the general matchmaking and scheduling problem for MapReduce jobs with deadlines.

3. PROBLEM DESCRIPTION AND MODEL FORMULATIONS

This section describes the modeling of matchmaking and scheduling MapReduce jobs with end-to-end SLAs comprising an earliest start time, execution time, and a deadline. First, a model of the MapReduce matchmaking and scheduling problem is presented (Input box of Figure 1). The formulations of the MILP and CP models are then described in Sections 3.1 and 3.2, respectively. A general matchmaking and scheduling problem requires two components for input data: a *workload* component, and a *system* component [2]. The workload data component outlines the characteristics of the jobs, whereas the system data component defines the attributes of the resources that the jobs will be executed on.

In our model, each MapReduce job j in the set of jobs, J, needs to mapped and scheduled on a cloud environment with m resources (or computing nodes), which is represented by a set $R = \{r_1, r_2, ..., r_m\}$. Each resource r in the set R has: (1) a map task capacity (or number of map slots), c_r^{mp}, and (2) a reduce task capacity (or number of reduce slots), c_r^{rd}. The map and reduce task capacities specify the number of map and reduce tasks, respectively, that each of the resources can execute in parallel at a point in time. In addition, the map task slots are independent from the reduce tasks slots, which means that a map task can be run at the same time that a reduce task is executing.

The workload comprises a set (batch) of MapReduce jobs to schedule, $J = \{j_1, j_2, ..., j_n\}$ where n is the number of jobs in the set. Each job j in the set J has the following:

- A set of map tasks $T_j^{mp} = \{t_{j,1}^{mp}, t_{j,2}^{mp}, ... t_{j,k_j^{mp}}^{mp}\}$ where k_j^{mp} denotes the number of map tasks that are in job j.
- A set of reduce tasks $T_j^{rd} = \{t_{j,1}^{rd}, t_{j,2}^{rd}, ... t_{j,k_j^{rd}}^{rd}\}$ where k_j^{rd} denotes the number of reduce tasks in job j.
- A set $T_j = \{T_j^{mp}, T_j^{rd}\}$ contains all tasks for job j.
- Earliest start time for the job, s_j
- Deadline for the job, d_j, by which the job should be completed (i.e. soft deadline).

Each task t in T_j has the following attributes: (1) a required execution time, e_t, and (2) a resource capacity requirement, q_t. Note that typical map and reduce tasks only require executing on one resource slot [4]. As such, q_t is typically set to one. All the tasks of all jobs are placed in a master set T.

The requirements for mapping and scheduling the set of jobs J on to the set of resources R are summarized. Each task t in T_j can only be scheduled to start at, or after job j's earliest start time, s_j. Secondly, each task t in T can only be mapped to a single resource r where t executes on r for e_t time units. Map tasks and reduce tasks can be executed in parallel, however, all the map tasks have

to be completed before the reduce tasks can start executing. Furthermore, at each point in time, the capacity limits of the resources cannot be violated (i.e. a resource cannot be assigned to run more tasks in parallel than it can handle). The system objective for the resource manager (objective function) is to minimize the number of jobs that miss their deadlines (i.e. minimize the number of late jobs).

3.1 Formulation of the MILP Model

The MILP model uses a time-indexed formulation [22], which is a commonly used model for formulating scheduling problems that considers discrete time (i.e. integer values for time). The discrete time values are contained in a set I called the *time range*. Although, time is a continuous variable, discrete time values can be considered by changing the unit of time. For example, if the execution of a task takes 5.1 seconds, the time can be converted into a discrete time value by changing it to 5100 milliseconds. In some cases, if the length of times are very different (e.g., 0.1s versus 10^3s), it may not best to change the unit of time because the converted values can be quite large (e.g. 0.1s becomes 100ms and 10^3s becomes 10^6ms). In these cases, it may be more appropriate to round the non-discrete time values to the nearest higher integer. For instance, the 0.1s can be rounded up to 1s.

Table 1 presents the formulation of the MILP model. Recall that the input of the MILP model comprises a set of resources R on which to execute a set of jobs J, and that a set T contains all tasks of all jobs in J. The following decision variables are defined in the MILP model:

- A binary variable, x_{tri} where $x_{tri} = 1$ if task t is assigned to start executing on resource r at time i; otherwise, $x_{tri} = 0$. There is an x_{tri} variable for each combination of tasks in T, resources in R, and times in I.
- A binary variable, N_j, that denotes if a job misses its deadline, d_j. The variable $N_j = 1$ if job j misses its deadline; otherwise $N_j = 0$. There is an N_j variable for each job in J. N_j is initially set to zero for all jobs.

Table 1: Formulation of the MILP Model

$$Minimize \sum_{j \in J} N_j \quad such \ that$$

$$\sum_{i \in I} \sum_{r \in R} x_{tri} = 1 \quad \forall t \in T \tag{1a}$$

$$\left((i \mid x_{tri} = 1) \geq s_j \quad \forall t \in T_j^{mp}, \forall r \in R, \forall i \in I\right) \quad \forall j \in J \tag{2a}$$

$$\left(i \mid x_{tri} = 1 \geq \max_{t' \in T_j^{mp}, r' \in R, i' \in I} ((i' \mid x_{t'r'i'} = 1) + e_{t'}) \atop \forall t \in T_j^{rd}, \forall r \in R, \forall i \in I\right) \quad \forall j \in J \tag{3a}$$

$$\left(N_j d_j \geq \max_{t \in T_j^{rd}, r \in R, i \in I} ((i \mid x_{tri} = 1) + e_t) - d_j\right) \quad \forall j \in J \tag{4a}$$

$$\sum_{t \in T^{mp}} \sum_{i' \in I_{tri}^*} x_{tri'} q_t \leq c_r^{mp} \quad \forall r \in R, \forall i \in I \tag{5a}$$

$$where \ I_{tri}^* = \{i' \mid i - e_t < i' \leq i\}$$

Same as (5) but for reduce tasks. (6a)

$$x_{tri} \in \{0, 1\} \quad \forall t \in T, \ \forall r \in R, \forall i \in I \tag{7a}$$

$$N_j \in \{0, 1\} \quad \forall j \in J \tag{8a}$$

$$i \in \mathbb{Z} \tag{9a}$$

Constraint (1a) specifies that each task t in T is executed only on a single resource. This is accomplished by summing all the x_{tri} variables for each task t, and ensuring that the sum is equal to one. Guaranteeing that the assigned start time of all the map tasks is after the job's earliest start time (s_j) is captured by constraint (2a). Constraint (2a) requires iterating through all the x_{tri} variables, specifically focusing on the variables that represent map tasks of the jobs (T_j^{mp}). Furthermore, only the variables where $x_{tri} = 1$ are of interest because these are the variables that define the assigned start time i of task t on resource r. Recall that constraint (1a) ensures that each task t has only one x_{tri} variable equal to one. Thus, the term $(i \mid x_{tri} = 1)$ identifies the scheduled start time of task t, which is at time i.

Constraint (3a) ensures that the reduce tasks are scheduled to start only after all map tasks are completed. This is accomplished by iterating through all reduce tasks of a job j (T_j^{rd}), and ensuring that the start time of the reduce task is after the completion time of the latest finishing map task (LFMT) of job j. To calculate the completion time of the LFMT, the equation $\max_{t' \in T_j^{mp}, r' \in R, i' \in I} ((i' \mid x_{t'r'i'} = 1) + e_{t'})$ is used. This equation iterates through all map tasks and calculates the completion time of the task: sum of start time $(i' \mid x_{t'r'i'} = 1)$ and the execution time ($e_{t'}$). The max function returns the maximum value from a given set of values. Constraint (4a) states that N_j, which is initially set to zero, should be changed to one if job j misses its deadline. A job j misses its deadline if the completion time of the latest finishing reduce task (LFRT) in job j is after the job's deadline (d_j). To ensure that N_j is set to one if j misses its deadline, the left-hand side (LHS) is the product of N_j and d_j, and this value must not be less than the right-hand side (RHS), which is equal to the completion time of the LFRT minus d_j. For example, if job 1 has d_1=30s, and the LFRT is 35s, which means job 1 missed its deadline, the RHS is equal to 5s, and the LHS evaluates to 0 since N_j is initially set to zero. To ensure that the LHS is greater than or equal to the RHS, N_j will have to be changed to one, such that the LHS=30, which is greater than the RHS=5.

Making sure that the map and reduce task capacities of each resource are not violated at any point in time is captured by constraints (5a) and (6a), respectively. Constraints (5a) and (6a) use an integer set I^*_{tri} that is defined to contain the assigned start time of task t, if and only if, at time point i, t is still executing on resource r. This set I^*_{tri} is used to ensure that only tasks still executing at a point in time i are included in the calculations to determine the number of tasks that are executing on a resource at time i. The total number of tasks executing on a resource r, at any point in time, must not exceed the capacity of the resource (c_r). As shown in Table 1, I^*_{tri} is a set of integers defined as follows: $\{i' \mid i - e_t < i' \le i\}$ where i' represent the values in the set I^*_{tri}. The following example task is used to explain the use of I^*_{tri} set. A task, denoted $t1$, has an execution time e_{t1}=5s, and the decision variable x_{tri}=1 (task t is assigned to start executing on resource r at time i) has the following values for its indices: $t=t1$, $r=r1$, $i=23$, and thus, $x_{t1,r1,23} = 1$. Given the values for $t1$ described, and the current time of interest is i=25s, the set $I^*_{tri} = I^*_{t1,r1,25}$ will have the following values $\{21, 22, 23, 24, 25\}$. As shown, this set does contains the assigned start time of $t1$, i=23s. Lastly, constraints (7a) to (9a) specify the valid domain of the decision variables, which restrict the values that the respective variables can have.

3.2 Formulation of the CP Model

The formulation of the CP model is presented in Table 2. Similar to the MILP model, the input of the CP model comprises a set of resources R on which to execute a set of jobs J. Recall, also that a set T contains all tasks of all the jobs in J. The CP model has the following decision variables:

- A binary variable, x_{tr}, which is set to one if task t is assigned to resource r; otherwise, $x_{tr} = 0$ (used for *matchmaking*). There is an x_{tr} variable for each combination of tasks in T, and resources in R.
- An integer variable, a_t, specifies the assigned (or scheduled) start time of a task t (used for *scheduling*). There is an a_t variable for each task in T.

- A binary variable, N_j, which is set to one if job j misses its deadline; otherwise, N_j is set to zero. An N_j variable is defined for each job in J.

The CP constrains are expressed differently than the MILP constraints, but perform the same role as the constraints for the MILP model. The reason for the differences is because the CP model defines a separate decision variable for the assigned start time of the tasks (a_t), as well as makes use of CP's global constraints, and native support for mathematical operators. Constraint (1b) iterates through all tasks in T and ensures that each task is mapped to only one resource. Similar to constraint (1a), this is done by summing all the x_{tr} variables of a given task t, and ensuring the sum is equal to one. Constraint (2b) specifies that the scheduled start time of each map task in a job j (a_t) is at or after job j's start time (s_j). Constraint (3b) states that the scheduled start time of each reduce task of a job j (denoted $a_{t'}$) is at or after the completion time of the LFMT, which is calculated using the *max* function in a similar manner as explained for constraint (3a).

Table 2: Formulation of the CP Model

$$\text{Minimize} \sum_{j \in J} N_j \quad \text{such that}$$

$$\sum_{r \in R} x_{tr} = 1 \quad \forall t \in T \tag{1b}$$

$$\left(a_t \ge s_j \quad \forall t \in T_j^{mp} \right) \quad \forall j \in J \tag{2b}$$

$$\left(a_{t'} \ge \max_{t \in T_j^{mp}} (a_t + e_t) \quad \forall t' \in T_j^{rd} \right) \forall j \in J \tag{3b}$$

$$\left(\max_{t \in T_j^{rd}} (a_t + e_t) > d_j \Rightarrow N_j = 1 \right) \quad \forall j \in J \tag{4b}$$

$$\left(cumulative((a_t \mid x_{tr} = 1), (e_t \mid x_{tr} = 1), (q_t \mid x_{tr} = 1), c_r^{mp}) \, \forall t \in T_j^{mp} \right) \forall r \in R \tag{5b}$$

$$\left(cumulative((a_t \mid x_{tr} = 1), (e_t \mid x_{tr} = 1), (q_t \mid x_{tr} = 1), c_r^{rd}) \, \forall t \in T_j^{rd} \right) \forall r \in R \tag{6b}$$

$$(x_{tr} \in \{0,1\} \quad \forall t \in T) \; \forall r \in R \tag{7b}$$

$$N_j \in \{0,1\} \quad \forall j \in J \tag{8b}$$

$$a_t \in \mathbb{Z} \quad \forall t \in T \tag{9b}$$

The CP model simplifies the expression of constraint (4a), which ensures that N_j should be changed to one (from zero) if job j misses its deadline, by using the 'implies' operator (see constraint (4b)). A job j misses its deadline if the completion time of the LFRT exceeds the deadline of the job (d_j). The completion time of the LFRT is calculated in a similar manner as in the case of constraint (4a). In addition, constraints (5b) and (6b), which enforce that the map and reduce task capacities of the resources are not violated, are simplified by formulating the constraints using the CP global constraint, *cumulative* [20]. For each point in time, the cumulative function sums up the number of executing tasks at the given time point, and ensures that this number does not exceed the resource capacity limit. Four parameters are required by the cumulative constraint: the assigned start time, execution time, and resource requirement of the tasks, as well as the capacity of the resource. There is one cumulative constraint for each resource, and only the tasks that are assigned to that resource (i.e. x_{tr}=1) are of interest for that particular constraint. The remaining constraints, (7b) to (9b), define the domain of the decision variables used in the formulation.

Overall, it can be seen that the constraints in the CP model are expressed in a more intuitive and simple manner. For example, in the formulation of the CP model, constraint (4b) simply uses the logical operator, implies ($\Rightarrow$) to set N_j to 1 if job j misses its deadline. Furthermore, to formulate constraint (5b) and (6b), the CP model uses CP's global constraint, *cumulative*. Conversely, as shown in Table 1, the formulation of constraints (4a), (5a), and (6a) for the MILP model requires using more complex mathematical formulas that are not as straightforward.

4. DESIGN AND IMPLEMENTATION EXPERIENCE

Three approaches are used to implement the MILP and CP models presented in Section 3. For all three approaches, after solving the respective MILP or CP model, an output schedule that shows the mapping of tasks to resources, and the scheduled start time of the tasks, is generated. In other words, values are assigned to all the decision variables such that the constraints are *satisfied*, and the objective function is *optimized*. The use of MILP [11] and CP [13] in our resource management techniques led to an optimal solution. Thus, the output schedule that is produced is optimal with regards to the number of jobs that miss their deadlines. This means that there is no other output schedule that can produce a lower number of jobs missing their deadlines.

4.1 Approach 1: MILP Model with LINGO

LINGO is a tool used to build, model, and solve optimization problems (through mathematical programs) developed by LINDO Systems Inc. [23]. LINGO provides a built-in algebraic modeling language for expressing optimization models, and a powerful and efficient solving engine capable of solving a range of mathematical optimization problems including linear, non-linear, and integer problems.

This section briefly discusses how the MILP model was implemented in LINGO v13.0. More detail on how to use LINGO can be found in [23]. The LINGO modeling language provides a data type called *Sets* that can be used to model a group of related objects. By using Sets, constraints on the decision variables can be efficiently and compactly expressed using a single statement. Each set can have a number of attributes associated with each member of the set. In the implementation of the MILP model, sets were used to represent the jobs set J, tasks set T, resources set R, and time range set I. For example, the task set T is implemented as follows:

```
SETS: TASKS: parentJob, type, execTime, resReq;
```

The *parent job* attribute identifies which job the task belongs to. For example, if the parent job attribute of a task is 2, it means that this task belongs to the job with an id equal to 2. The *type* attribute indicates whether the task is a map task (type=0) or a reduce task (type=1). The execution time and resource requirement attributes represent e_t and q_t, respectively.

A representative set of examples of how the constraints of the MILP model (defined in Table 1) are implemented using LINGO are presented. Constraint (1a) is implemented as follows:

```
@FOR( TASKS(t):
    @SUM( TIME(i):
        @SUM( RESOURCES(r): x(t,r,i) )) = 1 );
```

The @FOR construct is used to iterate the members of a given set, and can be used to generate constraints for each member of the set. As the name suggests, the @SUM construct is a looping function that calculates the sum of all members in the given set. The variable x used in the LINGO model has the same role as the x decision variable discussed in Section 3.1.

The implementation of Constraint (5a) using LINGO is presented:

```
@FOR( RESOURCES(r):
  @FOR(TIME(i):
    @SUM( TASKS(t)| type(t) #EQ# 0:
      @SUM( TIME(i2|(i-execTime(t)) #LT# i2 #AND#
                    i2 #LE# i:
        x(t,r,i2)*resReq(t) ) ) <= mapCapacity(r))
);
```

The @SUM construct uses LINGO's conditional qualifier operator ('|'), which limits the scope of the looping function and restricts the members of the set that are processed. More specifically, only the members of the set that evaluate the conditional qualifier equation to true will be processed. For example, the first @SUM construct specifies that only tasks with a *type* attribute equal to zero (i.e. map tasks) are processed.

An important feature in this implementation is captured in how constraint (4a) is implemented. LINGO provides an *If-Then-Else* flow of control construct, which performs a similar role to the *if-else* statements used in general programming languages. The *If-Then-Else* construct could have been used to simplify the implementation of constraint (4a) whose purpose is to set the decision variable N_j to 1 if the job j misses its deadline. However, it was determined that using the *If-Then-Else* construct to implement constraint (4a) changed the program from a MILP into a Mixed Integer Non-linear Program (MINLP). MINLPs are generally more difficult and require more processing time to solve compared to MILPs [23], and this leads to a longer time before a solution can be found. Thus, the use of the *If-Then-Else* construct was avoided.

4.2 Approach 2: CP Model with MiniZinc and Gecode

In Approach 2, the CP model is implemented with MiniZinc 1.6 [15], which is an open-source CP-based modeling language that is designed to efficiently model and express constraint programming problems. To solve the MiniZinc model, it is first converted to a FlatZinc [15] model. FlatZinc is a low-level language that is designed to be easily translated to a form which CP solving engines can use. One such solving engine that supports solving FlatZinc models is Gecode 3.7.3 (short for Generic Constraint Development Environment) [16]. Gecode is an open-source tool implemented in C++ for solving CP problems.

This section briefly discusses how the CP model was implemented using MiniZinc. More detail on how to use the MiniZinc modeling language can be found in [24]. Similar to LINGO, MiniZinc also provides a mechanism to group together closely related data called *Sets and Arrays*. In MiniZinc, the data set for tasks is implemented as follows:

```
set of int: Jobs = 1..NUM_JOBS;
set of int: Tasks = 1..NUM_TASKS;
array [Tasks] of Jobs: parentJob;
array [Tasks] of 0..1: type;
array [Tasks] of int: execTime;
array [Tasks] of int: resourceReq;
```

First a set of integers, called *Tasks*, is defined to represent the indices of the arrays. Next, the attributes of the tasks, which are the same as those discussed in Section 4.1, are declared using arrays. The domain of each of the attributes, which is the range of acceptable values that an attribute can have, is also declared here. For example, the domain of the parent job attribute is equal to the set of integers called Jobs, which has a range from 1 to *NUM_JOBS* where *NUM_JOBS* is the number of jobs in the batch that needs to be executed. As shown, the implementation of data sets in MiniZinc requires using two data types (sets and arrays), and is not as compact as the one used in LINGO, but performs the same function.

A representative set of examples of how the CP constraints (defined in Table 2) are implemented using MiniZinc is presented. In MiniZinc, constraint (2b) is expressed as follows:

```
constraint forall(j in Jobs) (
    forall(t in Tasks where parentJob[t] == j /\
                            type[t]==0) (
      startTime[t] >= releaseTime[j]  )
);
```

All constraints in MiniZinc, start with the keyword *constraint*. The *forall* construct performs an identical function to LINGO's @FOR construct. Similarly, the *where* keyword in the forall statement is MiniZinc's conditional qualifier operator. The ∧ operator performs a logical conjunction (logical *and*) operation.

A novelty of this implementation is the devising of a modified cumulative constraint for implementing constraints (5b) and (6b). The original cumulative constraint provided by MiniZinc [15] could not be used because it was not able to handle the two different task types present in MapReduce jobs: map tasks and reduce tasks. Thus, a modified cumulative constraint, called *mycumulative*, is developed that ensures that map tasks and reduce tasks are only scheduled on the map slots and reduce slots of the resources, respectively, and also the capacities of the resources are not violated. The function prototype for the *mycumulative* constraint is presented:

```
predicate mycumulative(array[int] of var int:
    startTime, array[int] of int: execTime,
    array[int] of int: resourceReq, array[int] of
    int: resourceCapacity, array[int,int] of var
    int: x, array[int] of int: type, int: taskType)
```

The first four parameters: start time of the tasks, execution time of the tasks, resource requirement of the tasks, and the capacity of the resources, are the parameters in the original cumulative function provided by MiniZinc. The new parameters added include: the matchmaking variable x (discussed in Section 3.2), the *type* attribute of the tasks, and a variable *taskType* which indicates if the constraint should be computed for map tasks (taskType=0), or for reduce tasks (taskType=1). Another change made in *mycumulative* is that it ensures that the resource capacities are not violated for all the resources in R, within the function, which means that the *mycumulative* constraint needs to be invoked only once. The cumulative constraint provided by MiniZinc checks only a single resource within the function, and thus needs to be invoked separately for each resource.

A code snippet of the *mycumulative* constraint is shown:

```
forall (r in Resources) (
  forall( i in Times ) (
    resourceCapacity[r] >=
      sum( t in Tasks where type[t]==taskType) (
        x[t,r]*resourceReq[t]*bool2int(
        startTime[t] <= i /\ i < startTime[t] +
        execTime[t]) )
) );
```

The range of times in the *Times* set is calculated from the lower bound of the task start times to the upper bound of the task completion times. The matchmaking variable, x, is used to ensure that only tasks mapped to the resource of interest are included in the sum. The *bool2int* library function converts a Boolean value to an integer, where true is equal to one, and false is equal to zero. The bool2int component of the equation is used to ensure that only tasks that are still executing at the time of interest, i, are included in the resource capacity calculations.

4.3 Approach 3: CP Model with CPLEX

In Approach 3, the CP model is implemented and solved using IBM CPLEX 12.5 [17]. More specifically, CPLEX's *Optimization Programming Language* (OPL) [25] is used to implement the CP model. OPL is an algebraic language specifically designed for expressing optimization problems, and therefore is able to provide a natural representation of optimization models that is more compact and less complex than using general-purpose programming languages. The OPL model is then solved using CPLEX's *CP Optimizer* constraint programming solving engine, which provides specialized variables, constraints, and other mechanisms for modelling and solving scheduling problems efficiently [26][27]. For example,

the CP Optimizer provides a built-in decision variable data type called *interval* that can be used to represent tasks (or activities) that need to be executed. The interval data type has five attributes: start time, duration, end time, optionality, and intensity. The optionality attribute is used to indicate whether or not the interval is required to be present in the solution. For example, the optionality attribute can be used to represent optional tasks that are not required to be executed for the solution to be valid, but can be executed if the constraints are not violated. The intensity attribute defines the resource usage or utility of a task over its interval.

The implementation of the CP model using CPLEX is briefly discussed. Additional information for expressing CP models in OPL can be found in [25] and [26]. Similar to the other approaches, OPL supports using sets and a data type called *tuple* which allows related data to be grouped together. For example, the *Tasks* set is expressed in OPL as follows:

```
tuple Task {
    key string id;  int parentJob;  int type;
    int execTime; int resReq; };
{ Task } Tasks = ...;
```

First a task tuple is defined, and then this tuple is used to define a set of *Tasks*. The task tuple has the same attributes as those discussed for Approaches 1 and 2, except for an additional field called *id* which is required in OPL to uniquely identify the task.

A key feature of this implementation is that it makes use of CPLEX's *tuple* sets and *interval* decision variable data type, which allows the system to use the optimized library functions and constraints that CPLEX provides, such as the *alternative* constraint and *pulse* function [26]. This in turn allows the system to efficiently solve the matchmaking and scheduling problem by reducing processing time and memory requirements [27]. More specifically, the CP model's decision variables: a_t and x_{tr} are implemented using CPLEX's *interval* data type, and are named *taskInterval* and *xtr*, respectively:

```
dvar interval taskInterval [t in Tasks] size
                t.execTime
dvar interval xtr [o in Options] optional
```

There is a *taskInterval* variable for each task that needs to be mapped and scheduled, and this interval defines the task's start time, end time, and execution time. There is also an x_{tr} variable for each tuple in the Options set, which is a derived set that contains all the possible combinations of tuples of the form <Task, Resource>. Note that this interval is *optional*, which allows only a subset of the intervals to be present in the final schedule. By using the interval data type, the implementation can make use of the optimized library functions that CPLEX provides.

A representative set of examples of the implementation of the constraints of the CP model (defined in Table 2) is presented. For instance, in the OPL model, constraint (1b) is expressed using the *alternative* constraint as follows:

```
forall (t in Tasks)
    alternative(taskInterval[t], all(o in Options:
                o.task.id==t.id) xtr[o]);
```

The *alternative* constraint is a synchronization constraint that requires two parameters: an interval i, and a set of intervals S. The alternative constraint states that the interval i will only be present in the solution if and only if there is exactly one interval in S (denoted j) that is also present in the solution. Both intervals i and j are synchronized meaning they both start and end at the same time. Thus, it is appropriate to use the alternative constraint to express constraint (1b), which ensures that each task is assigned to only one resource. In the example, the set S is produced by using the *all* construct invoked with a conditional qualifier (':' operator). More specifically, S is a subset of x_{tr} variables that have the same id as the task of interest, t.

In the OPL model, constraint (5b) is expressed as follows:

```
forall (r in Resources) {
    sum (o in Options: o.resource.id ==r.id &&
        o.task.type == 0)
        pulse(xtr[o],o.task.resReq)<=r.mapCapacity; }
```

The *pulse* function is used to generate the resource usage of a task, and requires two parameters: an interval i to represent the task, and a height value h to indicate the resource usage (i.e. capacity requirement) required by the task. The pulse function produces a value as a function of time. When the task is active (i.e. during the interval between the start and end times), the pulse function generates a value equal to the supplied value h to indicate the amount of resource usage of the task, and at all other points in time, the pulse function generates a value of zero. The expression for constraint (5b) states that for each resource r, the sum of all the values produced by the pulse function at each point in time, must be less than or equal to the map capacity of resource r.

5. PERFORMANCE EVALUATION

To evaluate the system performance achieved with the three approaches discussed in Section 4, experiments were performed on a closed system using various batch workloads where each batch comprised of multiple jobs to execute. Each experiment concluded after successfully mapping and scheduling all the jobs in the batch, and an output schedule and completion time of the batch is determined. Such an experimental environment, based on a closed system is similar to what is used by [8], [9], and [10], and is apt for evaluating and comparing the performance (e.g. processing time) of the modeling techniques and solvers. In future work, we will investigate techniques to handle an open system with a stream of job arrivals.

To compare the performance of the three approaches the following metrics are used:

- *Completion time* (C): time at which all jobs in the batch finish executing.
- *Processing time* (P): time it takes for the solver to read the input data (job, task, and resource sets), generate the model, and produce the output schedule that minimizes the number of late jobs.
- Number of jobs that miss their deadlines (N).
- Size of workload (number of tasks) the approach could successfully handle.

Note that the system focuses on meeting deadlines of the jobs in the workload and its primary objective is to minimize N. Ensuring that C is small is a secondary objective that can be considered given that the primary objective is achieved.

The experiments were conducted on a PC with a 3.2GHz Intel Core 2 Duo CPU and 6.00GB of RAM running under Windows 7 Professional. Lower processing times for obtaining the solutions can be expected to be achieved by running the solvers on a system with a faster CPU and more memory. Each experiment was repeated ten times and the confidence intervals, which were all less than 8% at a confidence level of 95%, are shown on the figures as bars originating from the mean value.

5.1 Description of Workloads

Table 3 presents the system and workload parameters for the experiments used to compare the three approaches. The workloads are synthetic workloads, each of which is characterized by a number of parameters. Similar workloads have been used by other researchers. For example, the Large 2 workload is adopted from [10], whereas the other workloads are derived by using the same distributions as those used in [10].

A walkthrough of Table 3 is provided. In the 'Jobs' column, the first row defines the number of jobs in the batch (n). The second and third rows define the earliest start time (s_j) and deadline (d_j) of each job j, respectively. The last row(s) of the Job's column denotes the number of map tasks (k_j^{mp}) and reduce tasks (k_j^{rd}), respectively, for job j. The next column, 'Task Execution Times', specifies the execution times of map tasks (e_t^{mp}) and reduce tasks (e_t^{rd}), respectively. The last column, 'Resources', defines the number of resources (m) in the resource set, R. In addition, for each resource r in R, the number of map slots (c_r^{mp}) and reduces slots (c_r^{rd}) are defined. Since the workload and system parameters are integers, discrete uniform distributions (DU) are used to generate the values for all parameters except d_j. The calculation of d_j uses a uniform distribution (U), which produces real values, for generating a *multiplier* for e_j^{max}—the execution time (in seconds) of job j when all tasks are executed sequentially (i.e. max execution time of job j). To ensure that d_j is an integer, the *ceiling* function is used at the end of the calculation. Note that in the 'Large 2' row, $e_j^{tot\_mp}$ (in seconds) denotes the total execution time of all map tasks of job j.

Table 3: System and Workload Parameters

Workload	Jobs, J (s_j and d_j in seconds, s)	Task Execution Times (in seconds, s)	Resources, R
Small 1	$n = 5$: $s_j \sim$ DU(1,50) $d_j \sim s_{j+}(e_j^{max})*$ U(1,5) $k_j^{mp}=10, k_j^{rd}=3$	$e_t^{mp} \sim$ DU(1,15) $e_t^{rd} \sim$ DU(1,50)	$m = 10$: $c_r^{mp}=2$ $c_r^{rd}=2$
Small 2	$n = 5$: $s_j \sim$ DU(1,50) $d_j \sim \lceil s_j + e_j^{max} *$ U(1,2)$\rceil$ $k_j^{mp} \sim$ DU(1,15) $k_j^{rd} \sim$ DU(1, k_j^{mp})	$e_t^{mp} \sim$ DU(1,15) $e_t^{rd} \sim$ DU(1,75)	$m = 25$: $c_r^{mp}=2$ $c_r^{rd}=2$
Medium	$n = 10$: $s_j \sim$ DU(1,50) $d_j \sim \lceil s_j + e_j^{max} *$ U(1,2)$\rceil$ $k_j^{mp}=10$ $k_j^{rd}=5$	$e_t^{mp} \sim$ DU(1,25) $e_t^{rd} \sim$ DU(1,75)	$m = 15$: $c_r^{mp}=2$ $c_r^{rd}=2$
Large 1	$n = 2$: $s_1= 0, s_2= 500$ $d_j \sim \lceil s_j + e_j^{max} *$ U(1,2)$\rceil$ $k_j^{mp}=100$ $k_j^{rd}=30$	$e_t^{mp} \sim$ DU(1,15) $e_t^{rd} \sim$ DU(1,50)	$m = 25$: $c_r^{mp}=4$ $c_r^{rd}=4$
Large 2 (adopted from [10])	$n = 50$: $s_j \sim$ DU(1,1500) $d_j \sim \lceil s_j + e_j^{max} *$ U(1,2)$\rceil$ $k_j^{mp} \sim$ DU(1,100) $k_j^{rd} \sim$ DU(1, k_j^{mp})	$e_t^{mp} \sim$ DU(1,10) $e_t^{rd} = \frac{e_j^{tot\_mp}}{k_j^{rd}}$	$m = 50$: $c_r^{mp}=2$ $c_r^{rd}=2$

The goal of the experiments is to use various workloads with different characteristics such as the size of the batch, the number of tasks in a job, and the execution times of tasks, for analyzing the impact of workload characteristics on performance. For example, in the Small 1 workload there are five jobs, each job with 10 map tasks with execution times varying from 1s to 15s, and three reduce tasks with execution times varying from 1s to 50s. The Large 2 workload comprises 50 jobs with each job having a varying number of map tasks from 1 to 100, and a varying number of reduce tasks from 1 to k_j^{mp}. Thus, on average the Large 2 workload has about 3750 tasks compared to the Small 1 workload, which has 65 tasks.

5.2 Results of Experiments

5.2.1 Small and Medium Workloads

Figure 2 and Figure 3 present the C and P results, respectively, for the three approaches when using the small and medium workloads. In all the experiments performed, the optimal solution is found in the sense that N is zero. As expected, the results show that for all three approaches: as the size of workload increases giving rise to a larger number of tasks, P and C also increase. From Figure 3, it can be observed that Approach 3 achieves the lowest P (note that the bars are quite small and may not be visible); however, it also generated an output schedule that produced the highest C. This can be attributed to the fact that in Approach 3 the solver produces the first output schedule that optimizes the objective function (minimizing N) and does not focus on the minimization of C. The lower P achieved by Approach 3 can be attributed to the mechanisms that CPLEX's CP Optimizer solving engine provides to efficiently solve matchmaking and scheduling problems, including the use of the interval decision variables, and functions to operate on those variables [26] (as discussed in Section 4.3).

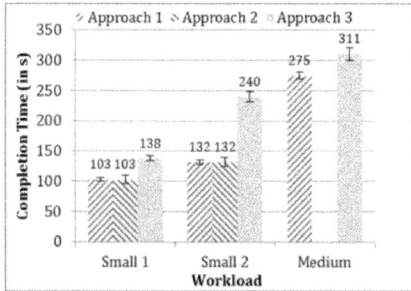

Figure 2. Completion time for the small & medium workloads.

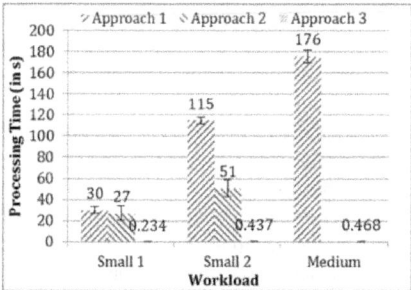

Figure 3. Processing time for the small & medium workloads.

Another observation that can be made from Figure 3 is that the approaches that implement the CP model (i.e. Approaches 2 and 3) attained a lower P compared to Approach 1, which implements the MILP model. The reason for this behavior can be due to the large number of decision variables that the solver for the MILP model has to generate and solve. Recall that the MILP model uses a decision variable x_{tri}, and that there is an x_{tri} variable for each combination of tasks in T, resources in R, and time points in I. In the CP model there are less decision variables because there are separate decision variables for matchmaking, x_{tr}, and scheduling, a_t. Note that Approach 2 was not able to handle the Medium workload after a couple of hours of solving. This may be due to the limitations of the solver from being able to handle such a large number of tasks to map and schedule on our system, which leads to a model that contains a large number of decision variables.

5.2.2 Large Workloads

The C and P results for the three approaches when handling the large workloads are shown in Figure 4. Approach 2 was not able to handle these larger workloads for the same reasons as discussed in Section 5.2.1, and Approach 1 was only able to generate an output schedule for the Large 1 workload. When attempting to generate solutions for the larger workloads with Approaches 1 and 2, the system would eventually run out of memory, and the solver would crash. The solvers of Approach 1 and 2 could not handle such a large number of decision variables on our system. The results show that Approach 3 outperforms Approach 1 for similar reasons as discussed in Section 5.2.1.

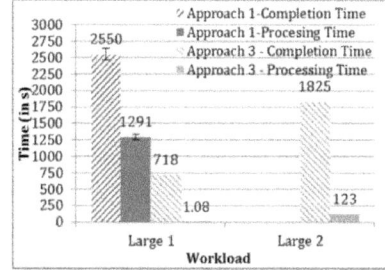

Figure 4. Completion time and processing time for the large workloads.

In order, for Approach 1 to handle the Large 1 workload, the granularity of I was reduced to decrease the number of decision variables in the model. Recall from Section 3.1 that Approach 1 requires specifying a set of integers, I, which defines the range of time (or time slots) during which jobs can be scheduled to start executing on a resource. The time range can be chosen from time $i=0$ to $i=MAX\_COMP\_TIME$ where MAX_COMP_TIME is the maximum completion time of the workload given that each job executes sequentially on the m resources. The granularity of I can be changed to restrict when jobs can be executed. For example, the granularity of a set $I_1=\{1, 2, 3, …, 100\}$ can be reduced to $I_2=\{2, 4, 6, …, 100\}$. Note that such a change reduces the number of members of I by 50%. The more values in I, the longer it takes for the solver to generate and solve the MILP model used in Approach 1 because more decision variables are present. The MILP model has a decision variable, x_{tri}, for each combination of tasks t in T, resources r in R, and time i in I. As such, the number of variables that are present in MILP model increases as the number of tasks, number of resources, or number of time slots increase.

For the experiment where Large 1 was being used, the set I for Approach 1 was set to have 100 time slots with an interval of 25 seconds between each slot: $\{0, 25, …, 2500\}$. If reducing the granularity of I was not done, the MILP model would contain a very large number of decision variables, and the system would not have enough memory to find a solution and generate an output schedule. A disadvantage of reducing the granularity of I is that this procedure can increase C because some tasks cannot be scheduled to start executing at their earliest start times. For example, if a job j has s_j =27s, and the time slots have intervals of 25s, the tasks of j cannot be executed until time 50s. Figure 4 shows C for Approach 1 is over 2500s, which is about three times longer than Approach 3's C. Therefore, the results show that for Approach 1, there is tradeoff between being able to handle larger workloads, and achieving a lower C.

5.2.3 Effect of Workload Parameters

In this section, the effect of varying different workload parameters on system performance is discussed. The experiments conducted in this section are based on the Large 2 workload (adopted from [10]). Approach 3 was the only approach capable of handling the larger workloads with up to 100 jobs and 7000 tasks that were experimented with. As discussed in Section 5.2.2,

Approaches 1 and 2 could not handle larger workloads because the system would crash due to lack of memory. Approach 3's use of CPLEX's CP Optimizer solving engine provides mechanisms and functions to efficiently solve scheduling problems [26]. As discussed in Section 4.3, implementing the CP model using CPLEX's interval decision variables allows the solver to efficiently use the system memory, which in turn allows larger workloads to be handled by Approach 3. Note that for all the experiments discussed in this section N was zero.

Effect of number of jobs (n): Figure 5 shows C and P when n is varied for the Large 2 workload. As expected, C increases with n because there are more jobs to execute. In addition, P also increases because there are more tasks to map and schedule on the resources. It is observed P/C, a measure of resource management overhead, increases with n. This shows that P is increasing at a faster rate than C. For example, the results show that the highest P/C is 0.26 (26%), and is achieved when $n=100$. In some systems, this scheduling overhead may be too high; however, the overhead can be tolerated in situations where the task to resource mapping and scheduling for the batch of jobs is performed offline and the execution of the batch takes place at a later point in time. When n is less than 100, P/C is much smaller (0.0196 and 0.06074 for $n = 25$ and 50, respectively), and thus, in these situations, online mapping and scheduling can be considered: the solver can be run as soon as the batch of jobs becomes available on the system followed by the execution of the batch.

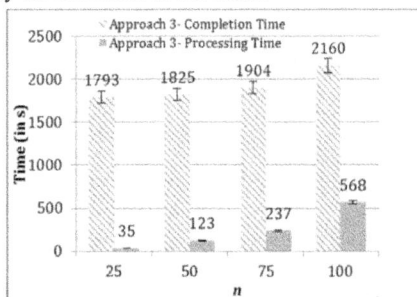

Figure 5. The effect of number of jobs on performance.

Effect of task execution time: Figure 6 shows P and C when the upper-bound of the discrete uniform distribution used for generating task execution times, denoted ___, is varied for the Large 2 workload. As shown in Figure 6, P increases with ___ because there is now a higher chance of tasks having overlapping execution. Thus, the solver requires more time to decide at what time and on which resource to execute a task in order to generate an output schedule that minimizes N. As expected, C also increases because jobs require more time to execute. However, it can be observed that P increases at a slower rate compared to C, and thus, the P/C decreases as ___ increases. The resource management overhead is observed to be small: P/C varies from 0.0674 to 0.0320 as ___ is changed from 10 to 100 seconds.

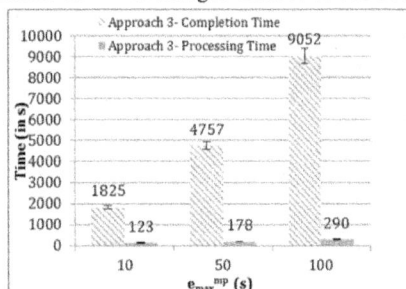

Figure 6. The effect of task execution time on performance.

A number of experiments were performed to analyze the effect of changing the other workload and system parameters, including: s_j, d_j, and m on system performance. Due to space limitations, only a representative set of results is presented. The following modified versions of the Large 2 workload were used: (1) *Large 2a*: same as Large 2, but increases s_j to ~DU(1,*3000*); (2) *Large 2b*: same as Large 2, but increases d_j to ~ $s_{j + (e_{max})}$* U(1,*4*); and (3) *Large 2c-1, 2c-2, and 2c-3:* same as Large 2, but sets m to 10, 25, and 100, respectively. Figure 7 shows the results for these additional Large 2 workloads.

Effect of earliest start time (s_j): Figure 7 shows that increasing s_j (see Large 2 and Large 2a) increases C because on an average, jobs tend to start executing at a later time. Conversely, increasing s_j reduces P. Having a larger range of s_j decreases the chance of jobs having overlapping execution times, and also reduces the contention for resources. This means that at a given point in time, there may not be as many concurrent tasks that the solver has to map and schedule compared to the situation where the s_js are closer to one another. Thus, the solver is able to quickly determine an output schedule that ensures that N is minimized.

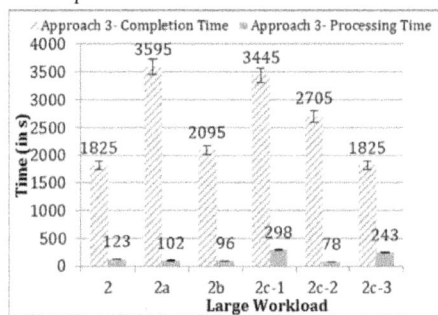

Figure 7. System performance for the additional Large 2 workloads.

Effect of deadline (d_j): When comparing the Large 2 and Large 2b workloads of Figure 7, it is observed that increasing d_j reduces P, but increases C. When the deadlines of the jobs are not as stringent, jobs will have more *slack time* (also called laxity), which is defined as the difference between the deadline, and the sum of the execution time and the earliest start time of the job: $d_j - (s_j + $ ___ $)$. The slack time is the extra time a job has to complete its execution before its deadline. When the slack time is higher, the solver does not need to spend as much time to generate an output schedule that minimizes N. The increase in C can be attributed to the fact that the solver returns the first output schedule that is able to minimize N, and does not focus on minimizing C. When the jobs have smaller slack times, the solver has to ensure that jobs are completed in shorter periods of time, which in turn reduces C.

Effect of number of resources (m): Figure 7 shows that increasing m from 10 to 25 (see Large 2c-1 and Large 2c-2), both P and C decrease because there are more resources in which to map and schedule the tasks. Even though there are less decision variables to generate and solve when m is smaller, the solver requires more time to determine the best task to map and schedule on the resources at a given time so that N is minimized. It is observed that when m is increased from 25 to 50 (Large 2c-2 and Large 2), P increases because the solver has more decision variables to generate and solve. However, there are more resources available to execute the tasks, which leads to a lower C. Lastly, when increasing m from 50 to 100 (Large 2 and Large 2c-3), P increases, whereas C stays the same. In this case, the additional resources cannot be used to further decrease N or C because both N and C are already minimized, and thus increasing

m just increases the number of decision variables that the solver has to generate and solve, which adds unnecessary overhead, and leads to higher P. Therefore, it can be observed that for a given workload, changing m to a value that is too high or too small can lead to an increase in P. In addition, increasing m tends to reduce C until m is significantly high and no further improvement in C is observed.

5.2.4 Summary of Experimental Results

This section summarizes the key observations made from analyzing the results of the experiments. Recall that solving an MILP [11] and CP [13] generates optimal solutions, and therefore all three approaches generated optimal output schedules with regards to minimizing N. For the system and workload parameters experimented with, and for the workloads that the approaches could handle, optimal output schedules where $N=0$ were generated. For workloads in which N was not be zero, a task mapping and schedule that minimizes N is generated.

Approach 1: did not perform well in the experiments compared to the other two approaches. Along with Approach 2, Approach 1 did generate a schedule that produced the lowest C for the small workloads; however, for a given workload, Approach 1 was measured to have a higher P compared to Approach 2. In addition, for the Medium workload, Approach 1 generated an output schedule with 11.5% lower C compared to Approach 3, but P was also 375% higher. Lastly, for the Large 1 workload, Approach 1 was outperformed and had higher C and P compared to Approach 3. Thus, for the system and workload parameters experimented with, it is not recommended that Approach 1 be used unless P is not a concern. If, in addition to meeting deadlines, reducing the completion times for the batch is important, Approach 1 may be suitable to use in situations in which the mapping and scheduling for the jobs can be performed ahead of time (e.g. offline).

Approach 2: is only able to handle the smaller workloads (less than 150 tasks) on our system. For a larger value for the total number of tasks in the batch, Approach 2 could not generate a schedule because the system used would eventually run out of memory, and the solver would crash. As discussed, along with Approach 1, Approach 2 generated an output schedule with the lowest C for the small workloads. Even though, P was lower compared to Approach 1, Approach 2's P is still over 100 times larger than the P measured for Approach 3. Thus, for the small workloads, there is a trade-off between having a lower C (using Approach 2) versus a lower P (using Approach 3). Similar to Approach 1, Approach 2 can be considered for small workloads when the resource management can be performed ahead of the time at which the batch becomes ready to execute.

Approach 3: In general, the experimental results showed that Approach 3 performed the best. Regardless of workload size, it was able to achieve a much lower P compared to the two other approaches. However, it also generated an output schedule with slightly higher C. For example, for the Small 2 workload, the C is 1.8 times larger compared to Approaches 1 and 2, however; the P is over 100 times smaller. On many systems satisfying the deadlines is sufficient and achieving a small batch completion time is only a secondary objective. Furthermore, Approach 3 is able to handle the larger workloads (i.e. Large 2 and above) that the other two approaches could not handle. In fact, the experiments described in this paper indicate Approach 3 is able to handle workloads containing up to 7000 tasks (see Figure 5).

Overall, the experimental results indicated that Approach 3 would be the best candidate to implement a resource manager that is capable of handling an open stream of requests arriving on the system that is being considered for our future research. Approach 3 was the only approach capable of handling the larger workloads, and was measured to have the lowest P. Having a low P is important to consider when handling an open stream of job requests, because a low matchmaking and scheduling overhead is key to efficiently process incoming requests.

6. CONCLUSIONS

This paper concerns resource management on clouds in which the workload includes requests characterized by multiple stages of execution, and an end-to-end SLA. More specifically, our work focuses on engineering resource management middleware that can effectively perform matchmaking and scheduling of MapReduce jobs, each of which is characterized by an end-to-end SLA comprising an earliest start time, execution time, and a (soft) deadline specified by the user. Both the reduction of resource management overhead as well as achieving high system performance are objectives of this research. The problem of matchmaking and scheduling MapReduce jobs with SLAs was formulated using MILP and CP. The MILP and CP models were implemented and solved using three approaches: (1) MILP model implemented and solved using LINGO [6], (2) CP model implemented using MiniZinc/FlatZinc [7] and solved using Gecode [8], and (3) CP model implemented and solved using IBM CPLEX. All three approaches have an associated learning curve period; however, configuring, implementing, and executing the models using Approaches 1 and 3 were easier compared to Approach 2 because both LINGO and CPLEX provide a feature-rich integrated development environment (IDE), whereas MiniZinc and Gecode only provide command-line interfaces.

Solving an MILP or CP model generates optimal solutions, and therefore all three approaches are able to produce optimal output schedules with regards to minimizing the number of jobs missing their deadlines. Our investigation and experiences with using the various techniques and software packages to formulate and solve the matchmaking and scheduling problem were discussed. A number of experiments were performed using different workloads and parameters to compare the performance of the three approaches in terms of metrics such as completion time (C): time at which all jobs in the workload finish executing, and processing time of the solver (P). Insights into system behaviour gained from the experimental results for the workload and system parameters we experimented with are presented.

- Approach 3 is observed to achieve the lowest P compared to the two other approaches; however, it also generated an output schedule that produced the highest C. In addition, Approach 3 was the only approach able to handle the larger workloads (over 1000 tasks in the workload, described in Section 5.2.3).

- Approaches 1 and 2 each had a case where they were able to generate an output schedule that had the lowest C; however, the P in these cases is much higher compared to Approach 3.

- The results show that Approaches 2 and 3, which use CP, have lower P compared to Approach 1, which uses MILP.

- Approach 3 was observed to effectively handle the Large 2 workload that was adopted from [10]: the processing time was only 6.7% of the batch completion time.

A more detailed analysis of Approach 3 that includes the effect of larger workloads was performed and the insights gained are discussed.

- Both P and C are observed to increase when the number of jobs (n) in the workload increases. The P to C ratio, denoted P/C, which is an indicator for the mapping and scheduling overhead, also increases with n. However, when $n <=75$ it was found that P/C was reasonably small: less than 0.13.

- When execution time of tasks increases, both P and C increase as well; however, in this case, P/C decreases as execution time of tasks increase.
- For a given workload, if the number of resources in the system (m) is too small or too high, P tends to increase, but having a higher m typically can generate an output schedule with lower C until a point where C can no longer be decreased. Increasing m when the workload does not require it (i.e. number of tasks is not sufficiently large), tends to increase P.
- Increasing the deadline of the jobs (d_j) reduces P, but increases C. Similarly, increasing the earliest start times of the jobs (s_j) decreases P, and tends to increase C as well.

If minimizing the number of jobs missing their deadlines is the sole objective, Approach 3 that is able to handle workloads with over 1000 tasks seems to be the most suitable because of the lower P. However, it was observed that using Approach 3 leads to a slightly higher C in comparison to the other approaches. Based on the results of the experiments described in this paper, it was found that Approaches 1 and 2 are most useful in cases where the workloads are smaller (a few hundred tasks), and there is sufficient time to perform the resource management decisions (e.g. offline, where processing time is not a concern). Approach 3 would be best suited to implement a resource manager that can perform matchmaking and scheduling of an open stream of MapReduce jobs with end-to-end SLAs. Such a resource manager warrants further investigation. Our plans for future research also includes refining the optimization models to consider more advanced features for resource management of MapReduce jobs including data locality and speculative execution (backup tasks) [5]. Evaluation of the three approaches in the context of more complex and real workloads, and investigating techniques for handling node failures, which are important for large systems, form important directions for future research as well.

7. ACKNOWLEDGMENTS

We are grateful to Huawei Technologies, Canada, and the Government of Ontario for supporting this research.

8. REFERENCES

[1] Buyya, R., Yeo, C.S., Venugopal, S., Broberg, J., and Brandic, I. 2009. Cloud computing and emerging IT platforms: Vision, hype, and reality for delivering computing as the 5th utility. *Future Generation Computer Systems*. 25, 6 (June 2009), 599-616.

[2] Heinz, S., and Beck, J.C. 2011. Solving resource allocation/scheduling problems with constraint integer programming. *In Proc. of Workshop on Constraint Satisfaction Techniques for Planning and Scheduling Problems (COPLAS)* (12-13 June 2011). 23–30.

[3] Hooker, J.N. 2005. Planning and scheduling to minimize tardiness. *In van Beek, P., ed., Principles and Practice of Constraint Programming*. Vol. 3709 of LNCS (2005). 314–327.

[4] Verma, A., Cherkasova, L., Kumar, V.S., and Campbell, R.H. 2012. Deadline-based workload management for MapReduce environments: Pieces of the performance puzzle. In *Proc. of Network Operations and Management Symposium (NOMS)* (16-20 April 2012). 900-905.

[5] Dean, J. and Ghemawat, S. 2004. MapReduce: Simplified data processing on large clusters. *International Symposium on Operating System Design and Implementation* (December 2004). 137–150.

[6] The Apache Software Foundation. Hadoop. Available: http://hadoop.apache.org.

[7] Apache. Hadoop Wiki. Available: http://wiki.apache.org/hadoop/PoweredBy

[8] Kc, K., and Anyanwu, K. 2010. Scheduling Hadoop Jobs to Meet Deadlines. In *Proc. of International Conference on Cloud Computing Technology and Science (CloudCom)* (Nov. 30 2010-Dec. 3 2010). 388-392.

[9] Dong, X., Wang, Y., and Liao, H. 2011. Scheduling Mixed Real-Time and Non-real-Time Applications in MapReduce Environment. In *Proc. of International Conference on Parallel and Distributed Systems (ICPADS)* (7-9 Dec. 2011). .9-16.

[10] Chang, H., Kodialam, M., Kompella, R.R., Lakshman, T.V. Lee, M., and Mukherjee, S. 2011. Scheduling in mapreduce-like systems for fast completion time. In *Proc. of IEEE INFOCOM* (10-15 April 2011). 3074-3082.

[11] Bosch, R. and Trick, M. 2005. Integer programming. *Search Methodologies*. Springer US (2005). 69-95.

[12] Chinneck, J.W. 2004. Chapter 13: Binary and Mixed-Integer Linear Programming. *Practical Optimization: a Gentle Introduction* (2004). Available: http://www.sce.carleton.ca/ faculty/chinneck/ po.html

[13] Rossi, F., Beek, P., and Walsh, T. 2008. Chapter 4: Constraint Programming. *Handbook of Knowledge Representation* (2008). 181-211.

[14] Lindo Systems Inc. Lindo Systems – Optimization Software. Available: http://www.lindo.com/.

[15] NICTA. MiniZinc and FlatZinc. Available: http://www.MiniZinc.org/.

[16] Gecode. Generic Constraint Development Environment. Available: http://www.gecode.org/.

[17] IBM. IBM ILOG CPLEX Optimization Studio. Available: http://www-03.ibm.com/software/products/us/en/ ibmilogcpleoptistud

[18] Lustig, I. J., and Puget, J.-F. 2001. Program Does Not Equal Program: Constraint Programming and Its Relationship to Mathematical Programming. *INTERFACES*. 31, 6 (Nov.-Dec. 2001). 29-53.

[19] Refalo, P. 2000. Linear formulation of constraint programming models and hybrid solvers. *Principles and Practice of Constraint Programming–CP 2000*. Springer Berlin Heidelberg (2000). 369-383.

[20] Beldiceanu, N. and Demassey, S. Global Constraint Catalog. Available: http://www.emn.fr/z-info/sdemasse/gccatold/ Ccumulative.html.

[21] Udupi, Y. and Dutta, D. Business Rules and Policies driven Constraints-based Smart Resource Placement in Openstack. White Paper. Cisco.

[22] Van den Akker, J. M., Hurkens, C., and Savelsbergh, M. 2000. Time-indexed formulations for machine scheduling problems: Column generation. *INFORMS Journal on Computing*. 12.2 (2000). 111-124.

[23] LINDO Systems Inc. 2011. LINGO 13.0: User's Guide.

[24] Marriott, K., Stuckey, P.J., Koninck, L.D., and Samulowitz, H. 2012. An Introduction to MiniZinc Version 1.6.

[25] IBM. 2009. IBM ILOG OPL Language Reference Manual. White Paper. IBM Corporation (2009).

[26] IBM. 2010. Detailed Scheduling in IBM ILOG CPLEX Optimization Studio with IBM ILOG CPLEX CP Optimizer. White Paper. IBM Corporation (2010).

[27] Dong, T. 2009. Efficient modeling with the IBM ILOG OPL-CPLEX Development Bundles. White Paper. IBM Corporation (December 2009).

A Meta-Controller Method for Improving Run-Time Self-Architecting in SOA Systems

John M. Ewing and Daniel A. Menascé
Department of Computer Science, MS 4A5
Volgenau School of Engineering
George Mason University
4400 University Dr., Fairfax, VA 22030
{jewing2,menasce}@gmu.edu

ABSTRACT

This paper builds on SASSY, a system for automatically generating SOA software architectures that optimize a given utility function of multiple QoS metrics. In SASSY, SOA software systems are automatically re-architected when services fail or degrade. Optimizing both architecture and service provider selection presents a pair of nested NP-hard problems. Here we adapt hill-climbing, beam search, simulated annealing, and evolutionary programming to both architecture optimization and service provider selection. Each of these techniques has several parameters that influence their efficiency. We introduce in this paper a meta-controller that automates the run-time selection of heuristic search techniques and their parameters. We examine two different meta-controller implementations that each use online learning. The first implementation identifies the best heuristic search combination from various prepared combinations. The second implementation analyzes the current self-architecting problem (e.g. changes in performance metrics, service degradations/failures) and looks for similar, previously encountered re-architecting problems to find an effective heuristic search combination for the current problem. A large set of experiments demonstrates the effectiveness of the first meta-controller implementation and indicates opportunities for improving the second meta-controller implementation.

Categories and Subject Descriptors

G.1.6 [**Optimization**]: Global optimization, Simulated annealing; I.2.8 [**Artificial Intelligence**]: Problem solving, Control methods, and Search; D.2.11 [**Software Architectures**]: Patterns; D.4.8 [**Performance**]: Stochastic analysis; C.4 [**Modeling Techniques**]: Experimentation

Keywords

automated run-time software architecting, autonomic computing, meta-controlled QoS optimization, combinatorial search techniques, heuristic search, metaheuristics, SOA

1. INTRODUCTION

Service Oriented Architectures (SOA) present many interesting potential benefits and challenges [10]. SOA software systems can be composed on the fly through service discovery. We assume an environment in which there are many functionally equivalent service providers (SPs) that may exhibit different quality of service (QoS) attributes at different cost. In recent work, the authors of this paper and colleagues at George Mason University developed a framework called Self-Architecting Software Systems (SASSY) [26, 27] that allows domain experts to specify the requirements of an SOA software system using a visual activity-based language [11]. SASSY automatically finds a software architecture and a selection of SPs that maximizes a given utility function of various QoS attributes subject to cost constraints. SASSY monitors the operation of the system at run-time and performs adaptation by re-architecting and selecting new SPs as needed. The general adaptation performed by SASSY follows the MAPE-K autonomic model [17] as well as the Kramer and McGee three-layer adaptation model [20].

Many autonomic controllers are based on search methods supported by performance models [15]. The models enable prediction of the performance of any potential system configuration [1, 12, 25, 26]. Then, a search algorithm is employed to explore the system configuration space in a quest for the most suitable system configuration. Typically, the most suitable configuration is the one that maximizes utility. The search algorithms employed range from simple exhaustive search to complex heuristics. Heuristic search supported by modeling has proven robust even in certain cases where the assumptions of the performance model do not hold [1].

Parameter tuning was an early application of adaptive systems employing heuristic search [25], which has proven to be a popular choice for resource allocation [12, 16, 29, 31]. Recent work with these methods has focused on selecting optimal software architectures [26] and service selections [4, 7, 23, 24] at run-time.

An excellent roadmap that summarized the state-of-the-art and identified critical challenges for the systematic software engineering of self-adaptive systems was presented by Cheng et. al. [5]. The approach to self-adapting software systems presented here is based on software architectures, i.e., it is a white box approach. A different approach, which falls in the category of black box approaches, is based on adaptation by selectively enabling and disabling software features. An example of this approach is the FeatUre-oriented

Self-adaptatION (FUSION) framework, which learns the impact of adaptation decisions on the system's goals [8, 9].

This paper builds on SASSY, which automatically re-architects an SOA software system when services fail or degrade. Optimizing both architecture and SP selection presents a pair of nested NP-hard problems. Here we significantly extend SASSY in two ways: (1) we adapt hill-climbing, beam search, simulated annealing, and evolutionary programming to both architecture optimization and SP selection; and (2) we introduce a meta-controller to automate the run-time selection of heuristic search techniques and their parameters.

We examine two different meta-controller implementations that each use online learning. The first implementation identifies the best heuristic search combination from various prepared combinations. The second implementation analyzes the current self-architecting problem (e.g. changes in performance metrics, service degradations/failures) and looks for similar, previously encountered re-architecting problems to find an effective heuristic search combination for the current problem. A large set of experiments demonstrates the effectiveness of the first meta-controller implementation and indicates opportunities for improving the second meta-controller implementation.

The rest of this paper is organized as follows. Section two presents definitions used in the paper. Section three defines the optimization problem to be solved by the self-adapting self-architecting framework. The next section discusses the framework and all its modules. Section five presents four heuristic algorithms and the challenges of heuristic search. Section six presents two different approaches to the meta-controller. The next section presents and discusses the experimental results. Section eight considers the related work. Finally, section nine presents concluding remarks.

2. DEFINITIONS

This section defines the terms used in this paper. These definitions are not meant to define a new software architectural description language [15] but to establish the concepts required in the paper at a sufficient level of abstraction.

Definition 1 (basic software component): a piece of software that has a well-defined interface that specifies the functions performed by the component. A software component can be composed with other components, can be reused, and independently implements its functions.

Definition 2 (composite software component): an atomic composition of components (basic or composite) that has an interface equivalent to a basic software component. The interface of a composite component is called a *connector*.

Definition 3 (link): a tuple (v, w) where v and w are either basic or composite software components and v invokes a function provided by w.

Definition 4 (software architecture, $\mathcal{A}$): the tuple $(\mathcal{C}, \mathcal{L}, \mathcal{S})$ where $\mathcal{C}$ is a set of basic or composite software components, $\mathcal{L} = \{(v, w) \mid v, w \in \mathcal{C}\}$ is a set of links, and $\mathcal{S}$ is a set of service sequence scenarios defined below.

Definition 5 (service sequence scenario, SSS): an SSS of the software architecture, $\mathcal{A}$, is the tuple $(\Theta, q, U(q))$ where (1) $\Theta = (\mathcal{C}_s, \mathcal{L}_s)$ is such that $\mathcal{C}_s \subseteq \mathcal{C}, \mathcal{L}_s \subseteq \mathcal{L}$, and $\forall (v, w) \in \mathcal{L}_s, v, w \in \mathcal{C}_s$; (2) q is a QoS metric, and (3) $U(q)$ is an attribute utility function, discussed below, of metric q.

Figure 1 provides a pictorial example of a software architecture, $\mathcal{A}$, where $\mathcal{C} = \{C_1, C_2, C_3, C_4, C_5\}$, $\mathcal{L} = \{L_1, L_2, L_3, L_4, L_5\}$, and $\mathcal{S} = ((\mathcal{C}_s, \mathcal{L}_s), r, U(r))$ where $\mathcal{C}_s = \{C_1, C_2, C_3\}$, $\mathcal{L}_s = \{L_1, L_3\}$, r is the response time metric, and $U(r)$ is a utility function of r.

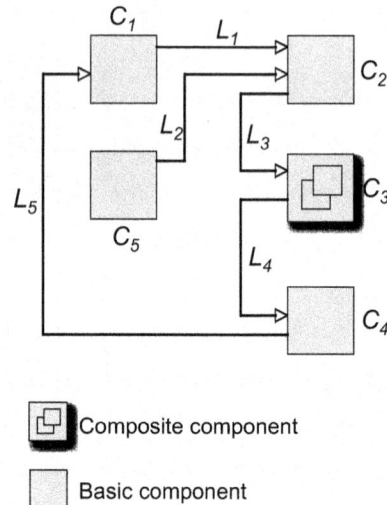

Figure 1: Depiction of an architecture.

Definition 6 (SOA software system): the result of instantiating a software architecture $\mathcal{A} = (\mathcal{C}, \mathcal{L}, \mathcal{S})$ in which the basic software components, including those that are part of composite software components, in $\mathcal{C}$ are instantiated by SPs available in an SOA environment. The selection of SPs to instantiate the basic software components of an architecture is denoted by Z.

Definition 7 (attribute utility function, $U(q)$): a function that maps a value of q to a number $u \in [0, 1]$ in a way that larger values of u correspond to better values of q. A performance model for q can be used to predict q from a given $\mathcal{A}$ and Z.

Definition 8 (global utility function, $U_g(U_1(q_1), \cdots, U_m(q_m))$): a function of the attribute utility functions of all the SSSes. The value of the function U_g must $\in [0, 1]$.

Definition 9 (SSS performance model, $\mathbb{E}(q)$): a performance model for the SSS $(\Theta, q, U(q))$ that is a function (or algorithm) used to compute the value of the performance metric q for the SSS.

3. THE OPTIMIZATION PROBLEM

In SASSY, a domain expert describes data flows between activities for a new SOA application in a visual language [26]. The domain expert can specify multiple QoS requirements which are then expressed as SSSes and attribute utility functions defined in the previous section. SSSes and attribute utility functions can also be used to specify different security options and the utility payoff for achieving specific levels of security on each component in the SSS. The domain expert then specifies a global utility function that combines the attribute utility functions.

When these requirements are finalized, SASSY generates a base software architecture that consists of a coordinator and a basic software component for each activity described in the data flow. Each basic software component is linked to the coordinator, and SSS performance models are automatically generated using an expression tree and the set of rules described in [26].

More sophisticated architectures can be derived from the base architecture by substituting composite components for basic components. Specific architectural patterns can be used as templates for composite components. SASSY employs load-balancing and fault-tolerant architectural patterns to improve the QoS in the specified SSSes [28]. SASSY seeks to find an architecture that can provide the greatest U_g.

To make the architecture executable, the coordinator must bind a set of SPs to the basic components in the architecture. Different SPs may offer the same service with varying levels of performance and cost. For a given architecture, SASSY searches for a combination of SPs that maximizes U_g.

The coordinator is able to substitute patterns and components to the architecture at run-time [14]. This enables the system to re-architect at run-time when new services become available or a service currently bound to the architecture fails.

The self-architecting optimization problem is to find the software architecture $\mathcal{A}^*$ and the SP selection Z^* such that U_g is optimized. More formally, the optimization problem can be expressed as:

Find an architecture $\mathcal{A}^*$ and a corresponding SP allocation Z^* such that

$$(\mathcal{A}^*, Z^*) = \operatorname{argmax}_{(\mathcal{A}, Z)} U_g(\mathcal{A}, Z). \quad (1)$$

$U_g(\mathcal{A}, Z)$ is the global utility function of architecture $\mathcal{A}$ and service selection Z.

This optimization problem may be modified by adding a cost constraint. In the cost-constrained case, one assumes that there is a cost associated with each SP for providing a certain QoS level [26].

The number of different architectures is $O(p^n)$ where p is the average number of architectural patterns that can be used to replace any component and n is the number of components in the architecture. The number of possible SP selections for an architecture with n components is $O(s^n)$ where s is the average number of SPs that can be used to implement each component. Thus, the size of the solution space for this optimization problem is $O((p \times s)^n)$. The solution space is huge even for small values of $p, s,$ and n; in fact, the problem is NP-hard. For example, for $p = 5, s = 2,$ and $n = 10$, the size of the solution space is on the order of 10^{10}, i.e., 10 billion possible solutions [26].

Without an accompanying service selection, Z, performance models cannot predict the performance of an architecture, $\mathcal{A}$. Thus, each evaluation of an architecture $\mathcal{A}$ requires a new NP-hard search of the service selection space for the service allocation Z that maximizes the U_g of $\mathcal{A}$.

A search for a near-optimal architecture $\mathcal{A}$ requires a sequence of transformations from one architecture to another. We restrict these transformations to those that replace the initial basic components with functionally equivalent architectural patterns, i.e., composite components. More precisely, the only allowed transformations from an architecture $\mathcal{A}_i = (\mathcal{C}_i, \mathcal{L}_i, \mathcal{S}_i)$ into a different architecture $\mathcal{A}_j = (\mathcal{C}_j, \mathcal{L}_j, \mathcal{S}_j)$ are those that replace a basic component $c \in \mathcal{C}_i$ with a composite component c' or replace a composite component $c' \in \mathcal{C}_i$ with a basic component c. The replacement of

components is driven by the goal to optimize U_g of the architecture. We select composite components from a library of QoS architectural patterns [28]. We also consider changes to the security level to be architecture transformations rather than changes to the selection of SPs.

The presence of nested NP-hard optimization problems in the software architecture optimization problem suggests the need for effective heuristic search. The optimal selection of SPs for a given architecture is similar to the problem of optimal service allocation for business processes in SOAs described in [7].

Most research on NP-hard optimization problems has focused on local search algorithms and evolutionary algorithms [30]. It should be noted that local search algorithms and evolutionary algorithms are not guaranteed to find the global optimum; however in most cases they find near-optimal solutions. Sacrificing an optimal solution for a near-optimal solution is usually an acceptable tradeoff to avoid a costly exhaustive search of the exponentially-sized solution spaces found in NP-hard problems.

For autonomic computing systems, the time and resources available for heuristic search may be substantially limited. Often, an optimization search will be spurred by changes in the autonomic controller's environment, and the controller will need to respond to these changes within a matter of seconds. Therefore, good heuristic search performance is essential for the autonomic controller.

Two particular characteristics are of concern in heuristic search performance: 1) the ability to avoid entrapment in local optima and 2) the convergence rate. The convergence rate measures improvement in the best predicted U_g with respect to either the number of evaluations or processing time consumed by the search.

For the autonomic controller presented here, the utility landscapes of the configuration spaces may vary widely due to differences in utility functions, application designs, and environments. The behaviors of heuristic search algorithms vary considerably and often interact with the ruggedness of the utility landscape. All search heuristics seek to balance *exploration* of previously unvisited portions of the search space with *exploitation* of promising areas of the search space. On smoother utility landscapes, exploitative heuristic search algorithms are likely to experience higher convergence rates than exploration-oriented algorithms. On rougher utility landscapes, exploration-oriented algorithms are more likely to avoid entrapment in local optima than exploitative algorithms.

4. ARCHITECTURAL SELF-ADAPTATION FRAMEWORK

This section describes our framework for self-adaptation and architecture/component selection optimization. Figure 2 shows the modules and data flows in the proposed monitoring and optimization framework. An architecture optimization search is started when either:

- the performance monitor (box 1) detects that a decline in U_g has crossed some threshold or

- the service registry (box 7) notifies the meta-controller that a new SP has become available.

The performance monitor sends a message to the meta-controller (box 2). The meta-controller selects an appropri-

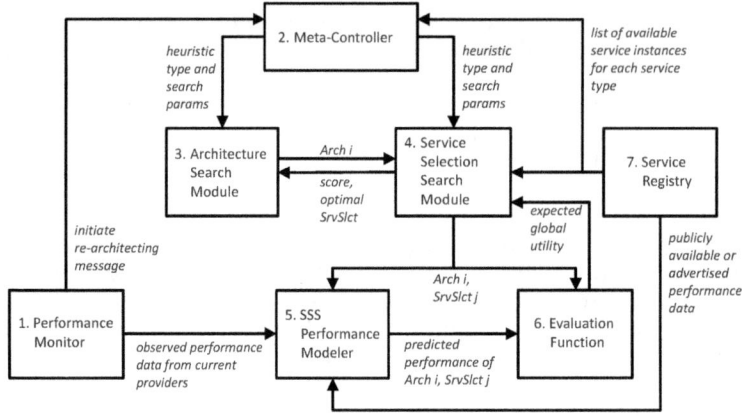

Figure 2: Data flows in the meta-controller monitoring and optimization framework.

ate heuristic search procedure, $\mathcal{H}_{Arch}$ for the architecture search module (box 3) and a potentially different heuristic search procedure, $\mathcal{H}_{SrvSlct}$, for the service selection search module (box 4).

The architecture search module (box 3) commences the execution of the heuristic search procedure, $\mathcal{H}_{Arch}$. Whenever $\mathcal{H}_{Arch}$ requests an evaluation (i.e., prediction of U_g) for a specified architecture, $\mathcal{A}_i$, the architecture search module (box 3) passes $\mathcal{A}_i$ to the service selection search module (box 4).

At this point, the service selection search module (box 4) initiates a new search that takes $\mathcal{A}_i$ as input and executes the heuristic search procedure $\mathcal{H}_{SrvSlct}$. Whenever $\mathcal{H}_{SrvSlct}$ requests an evaluation of service selection, Z_j, the service selection search module (box 4) passes a copy of $\mathcal{A}_i$ and Z_j to each of the SSS performance modeler (box 5) and the evaluation function (box 6).

The SSS performance modeler (box 5) predicts the QoS metrics for each SSS and passes the results to the evaluation function (box 6). The evaluation function applies the attribute utility functions of each SSS to the QoS metrics. The resulting SSS utility values are fed into the U_g function.

The evaluation function (box 6) returns $U_g(\mathcal{A}_i, Z_j)$ to the service selection search module (box 4), and $\mathcal{H}_{SrvSlct}$ uses this as the fitness score for Z_j and continues the search. The heuristic $\mathcal{H}_{SrvSlct}$ persists searching until some exit criterion is met (e.g. threshold utility is achieved or evaluation budget consumed). When $\mathcal{H}_{SrvSlct}$ completes, the service selection search module (box 4) returns $U_g^{best}(\mathcal{A}_i, Z_{best})$ and Z_{best} to the architecture search module (box 3).

With the completion of a service selection search instance, $\mathcal{H}_{Arch}$ uses $U_g^{best}(\mathcal{A}_i, Z_{best})$ as the fitness score for $\mathcal{A}_i$ and continues the search. The heuristic $\mathcal{H}_{Arch}$ persists searching until some exit criterion is met (e.g. threshold utility is achieved or evaluation budget consumed). When $\mathcal{H}_{Arch}$ completes, the architecture search module (box 3) sends $\mathcal{A}_{best}$ and Z_{best} to the change planner/manager (not shown in Fig. 2). The change planner/manager then executes a plan for online evolution or adapation of the running system.

This framework assumes the existence of a service registry (box 7) that includes QoS levels of the service instances listed in the registry [6]. This information is required by three modules: the meta-controller (box 2) that uses this information when selecting $\mathcal{H}_{Arch}$ and $\mathcal{H}_{SrvSlct}$, the service selection search module (box 4) that needs to know which

SPs are available for the search, and the SSS performance modeler (box 5) that uses the advertised performance of the SPs.

The performance monitor (box 1) continuously collects QoS metrics and tracks U_g in real-time. As mentioned at the start of this section, the performance monitor (box 1) can initiate a new architecture search if U_g (most likely represented as a moving average) declines below a threshold utility level that was set upon completion of the last architecture search. The performance monitor (box 1) continuously sends performance data updates to the SSS performance modeler (box 5), which stores near term performance data so that it is prepared to support optimization searches.

5. HEURISTIC ALGORITHMS EMPLOYED

This section describes one of the main contributions of this paper, i.e., the adaptation of well-known heuristic algorithms to architecture search and service selection. In particular, we have adapted the following heuristic algorithms: hill-climbing, beam search, simulated annealing, and evolutionary programming. Hill-climbing, beam search, and simulated annealing belong to the local search family of heuristic algorithms. Local heuristic search algorithms (known as direct search in the operations research community [18]) start with one or more solutions (referred to as the *visited solutions*) and then evaluate similar solutions called neighbors. In an effort to find better solutions, a local search algorithm will then visit one or more promising neighbor solutions and generate new neighborhoods to evaluate from those visited solutions. The search proceeds until either the search budget has been exhausted or a local optimum has been found. Most local search algorithms, after identifying a local optimum, will restart the search from a randomly selected solution(s) in an attempt to locate a better optimum.

5.1 Hill-Climbing

Hill-climbing is a relatively simple local search method that visits only one solution at a time. Hill-climbing can operate in either a greedy mode or an opportunistic mode. A greedy hill-climber evaluates an entire neighborhood before visiting one of the neighboring solutions. The greedy hill-climber will visit the highest utility solution in the neighborhood so long as that solution offers a utility improvement over the currently visited solution. The greedy hill-climber then generates a new neighborhood when it visits this new neighbor. An opportunistic hill-climber evaluates members of the neighborhood one at a time in a randomly selected order. If any neighbor offers an improvement in score over the currently visited solution, the opportunistic hill-climber will move to visit that solution and generate a new neighborhood, neglecting the evaluation of the rest of the former neighborhood. In either mode, when the hill-climber becomes stuck in local optima, it may select a random solution and recommence the search.

5.2 Beam Search

Beam search is similar to hill-climbing but visits multiple solutions at the same time. The currently visited solutions in beam search are referred to as the *level-list*. The maximum size of the level-list is called the *beam width*. The beam search algorithm generates neighbors for each member of the level-list. The best solutions from the combined neighborhood are then selected for the next level-list. Optional selection requirements may also be applied to the new level-list. Our implementation of beam search stores previously used level-list solutions in a hash table, so that no solution makes more than one appearance on the level-list. This allows beam search to move down the utility landscape and potentially out of a local optimum.

5.3 Neighborhood Filtering (Hill-Climbing and Beam Search)

The definition of the neighboring solutions is a key to the success of local search heuristic algorithms. For configuration optimization problems, local search typically will define the neighborhood as any configuration that has a single change from the currently visited solution. For many medium to large configuration optimization problems, such a neighborhood definition could lead to large, unwieldy neighborhoods that reduce the effectiveness of the search.

In our previous work [26], we applied heuristic filtering to reduce the size of the neighborhood. A neighborhood heuristic filter examines the shortcomings of the currently visited solution and identifies and visits only those neighboring solutions that are most likely to have an improved U_g score.

Filtered neighborhood construction in architecture search attempts to improve U_g by addressing the k SSSs with the largest negative impact on U_g. In some of the neighborhood generation rules, only candidate components are considered for modification. The j worst performing components for the given SSS metric are designated as the candidate components.

For non-security SSSs, neighbors are produced in the following ways:

- For each of the j candidate components: 1) neighbors are produced by substituting architectural patterns [28] that are expected to improve the metric of the SSS and 2) neighbors are produced by incrementing/decrementing the number of service instances in that component.

- If the non-security SSS has a common component with a security SSS, a neighbor is produced by decrementing the security option level along the entire path of the security SSS.

If the SSS is a security SSS (i.e., the SSS metric is a security option), then a neighbor is produced by incrementing the level of that option along the entire SSS path.

Neighborhood construction in service selection search also considers the k non-security SSSs with the largest negative impact on U_g. For each of the k SSSs and for each of their j candidate components, the lowest performing service instance is identified according to the SSS metric. If an unused service instance offers a performance improvement in the SSS metric, a neighbor is produced by substituting in the superior service instance.

5.4 Simulated Annealing

Simulated annealing is a stochastic local search heuristic that operates like opportunistic hill-climbing with one key difference: simulated annealing may stochastically decide to visit inferior (i.e., lower predicted U_g) neighbors [30]. The probability of visiting an inferior neighbor i is determined as follows [30]:

$$p\left(V_i^{inf}\right) = e^{\left(\frac{-\Delta U_g^i}{T}\right)} \tag{2}$$

where ΔU_g^i is the difference in global utilities between the currently visited solution and neighbor i, and T is the temperature variable. When T is large, the probability that simulated annealing will decide to visit a significantly inferior neighbor is high. When T is small, simulated annealing is less likely to visit inferior neighbors and its behavior will start to resemble a deterministic hill-climber. To simulate the cooling process, T is gradually reduced as the search proceeds. The process by which T is reduced is referred to as the cooling schedule. In this work, we employ an exponential cooling schedule:

$$T_{i+1} \leftarrow \alpha T_i \tag{3}$$

where α is a constant between 0 and 1, and i is the number of completed evaluations. An accepted rule of thumb for determining the initial temperature, T_0, is to ensure at the start of the search a roughly 40% to 60% chance that a significantly inferior neighbor will be visited. When using an exponential cooling schedule, T_0 can be calculated by:

$$T_0 \leftarrow \frac{-\Delta U_g^*}{\ln x_0} \tag{4}$$

where ΔU_g^* is a significant difference in global utility, and x_0 is the desired probability of visiting a significantly inferior neighbor at the start of the search. The exponential cooling parameter, α, can be computed by:

$$\alpha \leftarrow \left(\frac{-\Delta U_g^*}{T_0 \ln x_{b-1}}\right)^{\frac{1}{b-1}} \tag{5}$$

where b is the number of evaluations in the search budget and x_{b-1} is the desired final probability of visiting a significantly inferior neighbor.

5.5 Evolutionary Programming

Evolutionary programming employs the paradigm of evolution to evolve improved solutions. The algorithm uses a parent population (size M) to generate an offspring population. The first step in this algorithm is to generate an initial population. In the architecture search, the initial population is comprised of mutated copies of the starting architecture.

In the service selection search, the initial population is randomly generated. Then evolutionary programming enters a loop of the following steps:

1. Select the M solutions with the highest fitness (predicted U_g).

2. Move surviving solutions to parent population.

3. Parent solutions reproduce to generate offspring population of size K.

4. Mutate offspring solutions.

5. Determine fitness (predicted U_g) of offspring solutions.

This loop continues until the search budget is consumed. If the populations are *overlapping*, offspring and parent solutions compete for survival in step 1. If the populations are *non-overlapping*, only offspring are eligible for being selected in step 1. Reproduction in evolutionary programming is asexual and an offspring is initially an identical copy of the parent.

Evolutionary programming uses a phenotypic representation, so the features of the solution are mutated directly. The size of the mutation is influenced by a parameter called the *step size*. When a solution mutates, the number of changes made to the architecture is randomly generated from a normal distribution $N(\mu, \sigma)$ with μ set to the step size and σ set to 0.5μ (a minimum of one change per mutation is enforced). The type of change made to a software architecture $\mathcal{A}$ is randomly selected from the following list:

- A change in the level of a security option.

- A change to the architectural pattern of one component.

- Increasing by one the number of service instances in a composite component.

- Decreasing by one the number of service instances in a composite component.

The changes made in service selection mutation are substitutions of SPs. We use an adaptive step size in service selection search. This means that the step size itself is modified by adding a randomly selected value from a normal distribution with μ set to zero and σ set to a parameter called the *adaptive step factor*. Employing adaptive step size allows the search to make large jumps through the space at the start of the search. When a near-optima is located, individuals with more modest mutations will tend to have the highest fitness, and consequently individuals with smaller step sizes are likely to be favored. As the step sizes shrink, the search converges on the near-optima and moves from exploration to exploitation.

5.6 Challenges of Heuristic Search

Each heuristic search algorithm has its own strengths and weaknesses. The global utility landscape of the architecture and service selection solution spaces can vary in ruggedness (i.e., the number of local optima and the shapes of these optima). This ruggedness is difficult to quantify and may change with each re-architecting event. Each heuristic algorithm will strongly interact with the ruggedness of the utility landscape in a different way. The parameter selection (e.g., filter settings, population settings, step sizes) will have its own interactions with the landscape.

In a SASSY system with no meta-controller, a system administrator would need to select a heuristic algorithm for both the architecture search and the service selection search. The system administrator would have three options:

1. use an educated guess to select heuristic algorithms,

2. tinker with heuristic settings until adequate performance is achieved, or

3. run detailed time-consuming tests to find optimal heuristic settings.

Guessing runs the risk of making a poor choice in heuristic algorithms that would consequently lead to poor performance in re-architecting. The second and third options are labor intensive and require a skilled system administrator, which is antithetical to the goals of autonomic computing. Therefore, we propose automating the selection of heuristic algorithms and their parameters with a meta-controller.

6. META-CONTROLLER

The primary function of the meta-controller, the second major contribution of this paper, is to decide the heuristic algorithms and their parameters at the start of a re-architecting event. The meta-controller has two auxillary functions to support its decision-making process: 1) training on previously encountered problems and 2) analyzing the collected performance data from the training process. The meta-controller contains a *candidate list* of pre-existing heuristic search combinations (one for architecture selection and the other for service selection) that were found to be successful in other SASSY applications. Ideally, the candidate list should contain a variety of search algorithms.

When the meta-controller makes a heuristic selection decision in a re-architecting event, the meta-controller stores an optimization problem, $\mathcal{P}$, consisting of the starting architecture and a list of all the SPs with their current QoS metrics. After the re-architecting search completes, the meta-controller stores a *result tuple* of $\mathcal{P}$: $(\mathcal{H}_{arch}, \mathcal{H}_{SrvSel}, U_g^{best})$. After the re-architecting process completes, the meta-controller begins a preemptive training process testing other heuristic search combinations from the candidate list against $\mathcal{P}$ and storing the outcome in the result tuple.

Below we present two different designs for the meta-controller, each with its own analytic method and decision-making process.

6.1 Overall Best Heuristic Pair

The `Overall Best` meta-controller attempts to determine the overall best candidate heuristic combination over the entire range of re-architecting optimization problems encountered by a SASSY application. Each time a result tuple is stored, the `Overall Best` meta-controller updates the average U_g^{best} for the given heuristic combination. When it is time for the `Overall Best` meta-controller to make a decision, it chooses the heuristic combination that has produced the highest average U_g^{best}.

6.2 Context Best Heuristic Pair

It is unlikely that there is a single heuristic search combination that outperforms all other heuristic search combinations over the potential optimization problem space. A certain heuristic combination may dominate a portion of the optimization problem space, while other heuristic combinations dominate other portions of the space. The `Context Best` meta-controller attempts to determine the overall best candidate heuristic combination given specific features of $\mathcal{P}$.

In many architecture search problems, a near-optimal architecture may be nearby the starting architecture. When facing such problems, the autonomic controller is best served by using heuristic search algorithms that intensely scan the architecture space surrounding the starting point. In other architecture search problems, the closest near-optima are relatively far away from the starting architecture. With these problems, the autonomic controller is better served using heuristic search algorithms that can travel some distance from the starting architecture.

Changes in the service environment that have occurred since the previous re-architecting can impact the expected distance of near-optimal architectures from the starting architecture. Thus, measurements of service environment changes may offer insight into the likelihood of proximate near-optimal architectures. These metrics can be used as features in a machine learning problem. If the meta-controller can successfully train on these features via a machine learning approach, the meta-controller may be able to predict whether an exploitative (e.g., beam search) or exploratory heuristic search algorithm (e.g., simulated annealing) is more likely to be successful.

Changes in QoS metrics and utility scores may be useful features in predicting whether the architecture search and service selection searches should employ neighborhood filtering for the local search algorithms. It is possible that machine learning approaches may make other connections between optimization problem features and heuristic combinations.

6.2.1 Characterizing the Optimization Problem

An accurate and relevant representation of the optimization problem is required for a machine learning approach to successfully train. The representation used for the `Context Best` meta-controller presented in this paper is shown in Table 1. The features in the *Component* group and *Security Option* group reflect the starting architecture of the system and some statistics on the service environment. The BSC architectural pattern stands for a basic component in the architecture, while the LB architectural pattern represents a load-balancing composite component in the architecture, and the fFT architectural pattern indicates a fast fault-tolerant composite component [26]; one and only one of these three fields must be set to true for each component. The current level field in the *Security Option* group is set to the level of security enabled on a component for that particular security option (multiple security options may be specified by the domain expert). The *Overall, SSS utility*, and *QoS Metric* groups reflect the performance of the architecture and service selection in the current service environment.

6.2.2 Processing the Training Set

Whenever a result tuple is stored, the `Context Best` meta-controller extracts the features of the problem, $\mathcal{F}(\mathcal{P})$, in Table 1. A training set record, keyed to $\mathcal{F}(\mathcal{P})$, is created that contains an empty linked-list of result tuples. The training set record is then added to the training set's specialized data structure (this data structure has both hash table and array

properties). If the training set already contains a matching training record, the new results are appended to the pre-existing record in the training set.

6.2.3 Decision Making

When the `Context Best` meta-controller needs to select a candidate heuristic combination, it extracts $\mathcal{F}(\mathcal{P}_{current})$ for the current re-architecting problem. If a training record with a matching $\mathcal{F}(\mathcal{P})$ is found in the training set, the `Context Best` meta-controller determines which candidate heuristic combination has the best recorded performance in that training record.

If no such training record exists, the `Context Best` meta-controller employs the k-nearest neighbor (KNN) algorithm [13] as follows:

1. Calculate the Euclidean distance between $\mathcal{F}(\mathcal{P}_{current})$ and the key of each training record.

2. Select top k closest training records.

3. Each of the k training records votes for the candidate heuristic that performed best on its problems.

4. If one heuristic combination received more votes than any other, select that heuristic combination. If there is a tie in the voting, select the heuristic combination from the training record closest to $\mathcal{F}(\mathcal{P}_{current})$.

7. EXPERIMENTAL EVALUATION

This section describes experiments used to assess the two different meta-controllers: `Overall Best` and `Context Best`. A third meta-controller that randomly selects a heuristic pair was used as a control.

7.1 Problem Application and Environment

Each meta-controller was assigned to manage an SOA application of 25 components. Each component is considered to have its own service type. For each component, we randomly generated about six possible SPs. No component had fewer than three possible SPs. Fig. 3 shows the data-flow diagram of the managed application. Each meta-controller was given a cost constraint that afforded roughly 2.25 SPs per component. Each SP has the following attributes:

- capacity (i.e., the maximum transaction rate for the provider),
- execution time,
- availability, and
- cost.

No SP was dominated in all four attributes by another provider.

7.2 SSSes and Utility Functions

The SSSes and utility functions were randomly generated for the application depicted in Fig. 3. The random generation process ensures that no two SSSes share both the same QoS metric and the same pathway through the application. Table 2 shows the SSSes used in the experimental evaluation.

Each security option has three levels. The lowest level has no impact on an SP's capacity or execution time. Increases in security levels reduce an SP's capacity and lengthen the execution time.

Group	Value	Type	Number of Features
Overall	U_g	floating point	1
Overall	$\Delta(U_g)$	floating point	1
SSS Utility	$U(q)$	floating point	n_{SSS}
SSS Utility	$\Delta(U(q))$	floating point	n_{SSS}
Component	BSC Arch. Pattern	boolean	n_{cmp}
Component	LB Arch. Pattern	boolean	n_{cmp}
Component	fFT Arch. Pattern	boolean	n_{cmp}
Component	number of SPs used	integer	n_{cmp}
Component	number of SPs available	integer	n_{cmp}
Component	number of SPs changed	integer	n_{cmp}
QoS Metric	current q for component	floating point	$n_{cmp} \times n_{QoS}$
QoS Metric	$\Delta(q)$ for component	floating point	$n_{cmp} \times n_{QoS}$
Security Option	current level	integer	$n_{cmp} \times n_{sec}$

Table 1: Features of the machine learning problem.

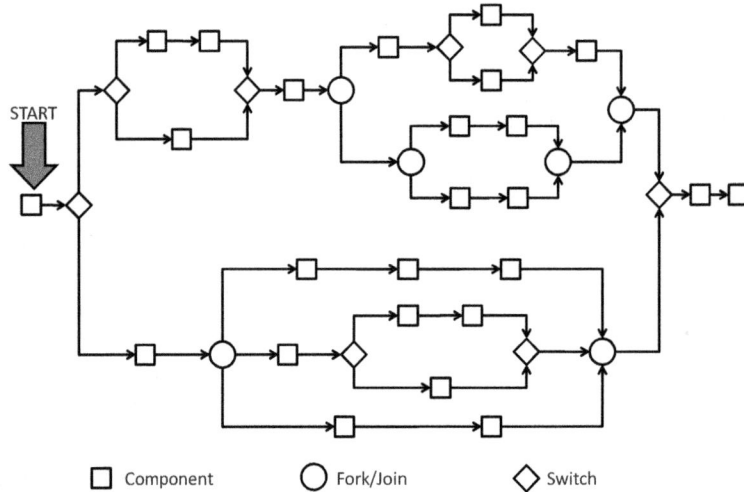

Figure 3: SOA application for experimental evaluation.

QoS Metric	Weight	Number of Components
Security Option 1	0.13	14
Security Option 2	0.06	13
Security Option 2	0.06	13
Security Option 2	0.07	14
Security Option 2	0.10	17
Throughput	0.11	16
Throughput	0.17	13
Throughput	0.05	13
Availability	0.17	16
Execution Time	0.08	14

Table 2: SSSes used in experimental evaluation.

Each security option SSS considers its current security level to be the lowest level found on any member component. To determine their utility, security option SSSes use a discrete utility payoff table.

The throughput, availability, and execution time SSSes use sigmoidal utility functions similar in form to those found in [26].

7.3 Candidate Heuristic Combinations and Other Meta-Controller Settings

During the development process, the heuristic search algorithms and meta-controller procedures were tested and debugged with a 30-component SOA application not pre-

sented here. Using the development SOA application, a metaheuristic genetic algorithm was employed to find the following four near-optimal heuristic search algorithms for the architecture search:

1. an opportunistic hill-climber (HC) with SSS filter, $k = 5$, and component filter, $j = 2$,

2. beam search (BS) with beam width of two, SSS filter, $k = 5$, and component filter, $j = 2$,

3. evolutionary programming (EP) with non-overlapping populations, parent population size $M = 6$, offspring population size $K = 30$, and a step size of 2.0, and

4. simulated annealing (SA) with $p(V_{init}^{inf})$ set to 66% and $p(V_{last}^{inf})$ to 0.0023% (V^{inf} is defined here as a move with a -0.1 change in U_g.)

A similar metaheuristic genetic algorithm, also not presented here, was employed to find two near-optimal heuristic search parameters for the service selection search:

1. an opportunistic hill-climber (HC) with no neighborhood filtering and

2. evolutionary programming (EP) with overlapping populations, parent population size $M = 3$, offspring population size $K = 19$, initial step size of 3.5, and an adaptive step factor of 4.5.

The four architecture heuristic search algorithms were combined with the two service selection heuristic algorithms to make eight heuristic search combinations: 1) HC-HC, 2) HC-EP, 3) BS-HC, 4) BS-EP, 5) EP-HC, 6) EP-EP, 7) SA-HC, and 8) SA-EP.

Each of the architecture searches was configured to run with 5 threads, and each of the service selection searches was configured to run with 25 threads. Composite components were limited to a maximum size of five basic components. The architecture search budget was set to 100 architecture evaluations. The service selection search budget was set to 1,200 service selection evaluations. With these budget settings, a re-architecting search should take less than 1 minute on most modern computers.

In both Overall Best and Context Best, the number of training replications for each problem encountered was set to one. The Context Best KNN algorithm was run with $k = 5$. The re-architecting threshold was set to 80% of U_g predicted during the last re-architecting.

To provide a baseline for comparison, we built a third meta-controller, Random, that randomly selects one of the eight heuristic search combinations described above to employ whenever a re-architecting event occurs. We also tested simple autonomic controllers (i.e., no meta-controller used) that always use the same heuristic search combination.

7.4 Simulation

Each simulation commenced with the SOA application in a near-optimal architecture determined a priori by an offline heuristic search. The simulation time is divided into discrete intervals called *controller intervals* of duration ϵ time units.

The following actions take place at the end of each controller interval:

- SPs that are active and up will be scheduled to go down t_{fail} time units after they become operational. The time t_{fail} is drawn from an exponential distribution with an average equal to the SP's MTTF (Mean Time To Failure). This exponentially distributed number is rounded up to the closest multiple of ϵ. Thus, at the end of each controller interval, if any SP is scheduled to go down at that time, the SP is flagged as down, and the software system's U_g is computed and recorded.

- For each SP that failed at the end of a controller interval, an exponentially distributed number t_{recover} with average equal to the SP's MTTR (Mean Time To Repair) is selected. The value of t_{recover} is rounded up to the closest multiple of ϵ. Thus, at the end of a controller interval, if any SP is scheduled to recover, the SP is flagged as operational again. The meta-controller conducts a re-architecting search to see if the new SP can be used to attain a higher U_g.

- Compute the U_g. If it falls below a certain set threshold, initiate rearchitecting.

Separate Mersenne Twister random number streams were used for the generation of simulation events and for heuristic search calculations. The duration of each simulation was 500 ϵ. We conducted 100 simulations for each meta-controller.

7.5 Experimental Results

The meta-controllers encountered about 230 re-architecting events on average over the course of a single simulation run.

We calculated the average U_g over the course of each simulation experiment. Figure 4 shows the distribution of average global utilities in each set of 100 experiments produced by the eight simple controllers and three meta-controllers. The boxes in this figure show the three population quartiles, while the whiskers show the maximum and minimum. Next we assess the statistical significance of the results.

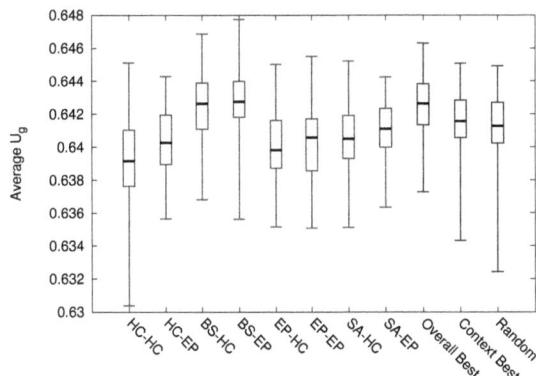

Figure 4: Box plot showing the quartiles of the simulation runs.

Table 3 shows the mean of the average global utility for each of the meta-controllers along with 95% confidence intervals. The meta-controller Overall Best clearly outperforms the other two meta-controllers; its lower confidence bound is greater than the upper bounds of the others.

The small range of average U_g is due to the meta-controllers keeping the systems at near-optimal U_g most of the time. Occasionally, a critical SP will fail, and it is either not possible or very difficult to achieve near-optimal U_g. The overall duration of failure events causing more than a 10% reduction in U_g was observed to be less than 15 ϵ in the average simulation run. Though uncommon, the differences in meta-controller response to these failures result in some statistical differences in the average U_g.

Controller	Lower Bound	Mean	Upper Bound
HC-HC	0.63858	0.63910	0.63962
HC-EP	0.63994	0.64035	0.64076
BS-HC	0.64194	0.64234	0.64273
BS-EP	0.64225	0.64268	0.64311
EP-HC	0.63960	0.64001	0.64043
EP-EP	0.63987	0.64028	0.64069
SA-HC	0.64014	0.64054	0.64095
SA-EP	0.64062	0.64098	0.64134
Ovrll Bst	0.64228	0.64263	0.64297
Cntxt Bst	0.64129	0.64164	0.64200
Random	0.64081	0.64119	0.64157

Table 3: 95% confidence intervals for net overall average U_g.

We applied the Tukey-Kramer procedure to perform a simultaneous pair-wise comparison of the eleven controllers (eight simple controllers and three meta-controllers) in Table 3. We determined that Overall Best was significantly better than Random and six of the eight simple controllers (those employing HC-HC, HC-EP, EP-HC, EP-EP, SA-HC, and SA-EP) at the 95% confidence level. This procedure also demonstrated that Context Best was better than five of the simple controllers (HC-HC, HC-EP, EP-HC, EP-EP, and SA-HC). We further applied the Tukey-Kramer procedure on just the results of the three meta-controllers, and we were able to conclude that `Overall Best` was significantly better than `Context Best` and that `Context Best` was significantly better than `Random` at the 95% confidence level.

Figure 5 shows the U_g over time. All three meta-controllers do well in maintaining U_g over the course of the simulation runs. As can be seen by the size of the error bars, the experimental variance makes it difficult to compare the different meta-controllers; this variance cancels out to some degree when computing the overall average for each simulation experiment.

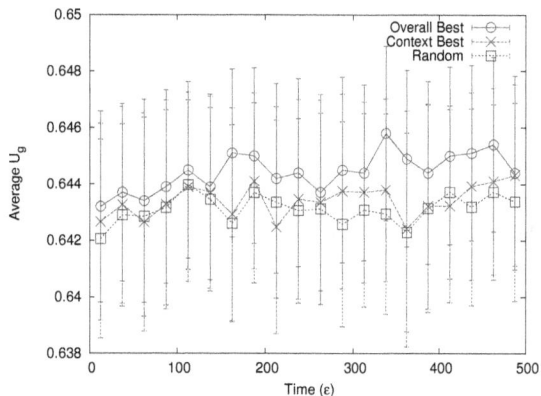

Figure 6: Percentage of time a heuristic combination was selected by the meta-controllers.

To better understand the differences in heuristic combination selection between `Context Best` and `Overall Best`, we collected 2,000 re-architecting problems encountered in our simulations. Each heuristic combination was tested against each problem 30 times. For each problem, the average U_g found by all the heuristic combinations was calculated. Then, the relative performance of each heuristic combination on each problem was determined.

Figure 7 shows a scatter plot of the relative performance of BS-EP vs EP-EP on each re-architecting problem. The thin black line shown in Fig. 7 indicates where the performance of BS-EP and EP-EP are equal; a large concentration of problems are close to this line. EP-EP outperformed BS-EP on 78.2% of the problems. However, as can be seen in Fig. 7, when BS-EP outperforms EP-EP, it is typically by a larger margin. The average difference in U_g between EP-EP and BS-EP when EP-EP is better equals 0.00048 whereas when BS-EP is better the difference is 0.01268, approximately 25 times greater.

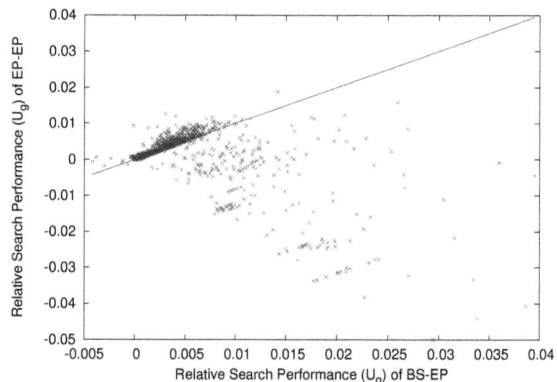

Figure 5: The average global utility over time with 95% error bars.

Table 4 shows the heuristic combination performance data collected by the `Overall Best` meta-controller. Heuristic combinations employing hill-climbing for service selection search perform poorly in comparison to heuristic combinations employing evolutionary programming for service selection search. The best heuristic combination is BS-EP, using beam search in the architecture search and evolutionary programming in the service selection search.

Heuristic Search Combination	Lower Bound	Mean	Upper Bound
HC–HC	0.6305	0.6310	0.6314
HC–EP	0.6412	0.6415	0.6419
BS–HC	0.6367	0.6370	0.6374
BS–EP	0.6429	0.6432	0.6435
EP–HC	0.6402	0.6405	0.6408
EP–EP	0.6414	0.6417	0.6420
SA–HC	0.6377	0.6381	0.6385
SA–EP	0.6414	0.6417	0.6420

Table 4: Average heuristic combination peformance tables collected by `Overall Best` with 95% confidence intervals.

The evolving behavior of the meta-controllers can be seen in Fig. 6. The data series labeled *early* in Fig. 6 were collected from just the first half of the simulation, while the data series labeled *late* were collected from only the second half of the simulation. We can see that by the second half of the simulation, `Overall Best` has clearly converged on to the most overall effective heuristic combination, BS-EP.

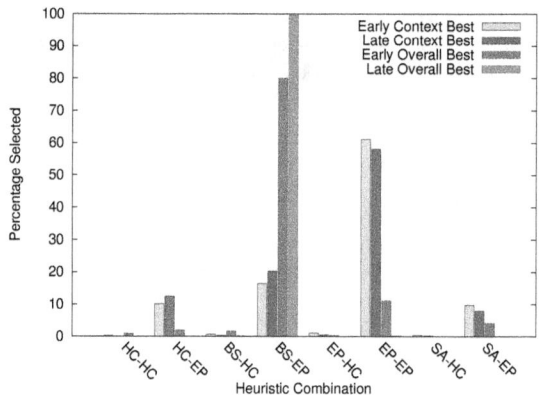

Figure 7: Scatter plot of relative heuristic combination performance on 1,935 re-architecting problems.

The KNN algorithm used in the `Context Best` meta-controller does not account for the risk that picking incorrectly EP-EP over BS-EP could lead to a relatively large drop in performance. The `Context Best` meta-controller would need to correctly identify the best heuristic combination about 85% of the time to equal the performance of `Overall Best`. It is unlikely that simple KNN can achieve such accuracy in the face of the following challenges presented by the use of online training sets:

- a relatively small number of training problems,

- one training replication per heuristic combination for each problem, and

- a relatively large number of fields in the problem characterization.

The experiments were performed on systems with two 2.4 GHz quad-core hyper-threading Intel Xeon processors. Re-architecting searches using hill-climbing for service selection took an average of 15.0 seconds to complete, while re-architecting searches using evolutionary programming for service selection took an average of 6.9 seconds to complete. The choice of architecture heuristic algorithm had less impact on re-architecting search times.

8. RELATED WORK

In [2], Calinescu et al. present QoSMOS, a system for online performance management of SOA systems. Like SASSY, this system employs utility functions to combine multiple QoS objectives and optimizes the selection of SPs. Unlike SASSY, QoSMOS considers some SPs to be white boxes, and it can modify the configuration parameters and resource allocations for those white box SPs. QosMOS does not consider architectural patterns for improving QoS. Optimization in QoSMOS is conducted through exhaustive search, a technique that would not scale well to the problems considered by SASSY.

Cardellini et al. devise a framework, MOSES, for optimizing SOA systems in [3]. Similar to SASSY, MOSES uses SP selection and architectural patterns for improving the QoS of a SOA service or application. MOSES adapts the optimization problem such that it can be solved through linear programming (LP) techniques. The use of LP limits the form of the objective function in MOSES. SASSY does not face similar restrictions on the form of the utility function. On larger problems, MOSES must restrict the space of substitutions considered to keep the problem solvable in near real-time.

Mani et al. in [21] develop a system using Role Based Modeling Language to model the performance impact of design pattern changes in SOA systems. As the SOA application implements a new design pattern, the changes in the systems are passed to the system's performance model.

Other researchers have investigated using multi-objective optimization techniques to reduce effort and increase the quality of software architecture designs. When the optimization search completes, these systems present human decision makers with a set of Pareto optimal architecture candidates. PerOpteryx, introduced by Koziolek et al. in [19], employs architectural tactics in a multi-objective evolutionary algorithm to expedite the multi-objective search process. Martens et al. present a similar system in [22] that starts quickly by using LP on a simplified version of the problem to prepare a starting population for a multi-objective evolutionary algorithm.

9. CONCLUSION

The `Overall Best` meta-controller showed a statistically significant benefit over the other two meta-controllers. Although `Overall Best` did not outperform simple controllers using `BS-HC` and `BS-EP`, it was not known a priori which

heuristic search combinations would provide the best performance. The `Overall Best` meta-controller was able to identify `BS-EP` as the best heuristic search combination without having to run its own large batch of simulation experiments. The cost of training the `Overall Best` meta-controller is very small. Therefore, using this meta-controller for non-trivial SOA software systems would provide a net measurable benefit, improving the performance of the system and reducing the burden on human administrators.

The relatively poor performance of the `Context Best` meta-controller was initially surprising. Further analysis revealed that the `Context Best` meta-controller was unable to adjust for the risk presented by disparities in relative heuristic combination performance.

If the `Context Best` meta-controller could identify appropriate heuristic search combination with a high level of accuracy while accounting for risk, `Context Best` would likely provide superior performance. The `Context Best` meta-controller may be improved by upgrading the machine-learning technique employed from simple KNN to a more advanced method. Machete and similar methods provide advanced versions of the KNN algorithm [13]. Another possibility would be to substitute either a neural network or an SVM. These have the disadvantage of requiring time to train, but SVM allows the use of penalty weights to control the risk of selecting the wrong heuristic search combination.

In future work, we plan to test our approaches on a wider variety of SOA applications. We also plan to model the lifetime utility U_l, which would reflect the utility produced by an architecture over its expected lifetime. Modeling U_l and incorporating adaptation costs would provide a more holistic approach to assessing architectures and service selections.

Acknowledgements

The work of D. Menascé is partially supported by NIST grant No. 70NANB12H277.

10. REFERENCES

[1] M. N. Bennani and D. A. Menascé. Assessing the robustness of self-managing computer systems under highly variable workloads. In *Proc. 1st IEEE International Conference on Autonomic Computing (ICAC '04)*, pages 62–69, New York, NY, May 2004.

[2] R. Calinescu, L. Grunske, M. Kwiatkowska, R. Mirandola, and G. Tamburrelli. Dynamic QoS management and optimization in service-based systems. *Software Engineering, IEEE Transactions on*, 37(3):387–409, 2011.

[3] V. Cardellini, E. Casalicchio, V. Grassi, S. Iannucci, F. Lo Presti, and R. Mirandola. Moses: A framework for QoS driven runtime adaptation of service-oriented systems. *Software Engineering, IEEE Transactions on*, 38(5):1138–1159, 2012.

[4] E. Casalicchio, D. A. Menascé, V. Dubey, and L. Silvestri. Optimal service selection heuristics in service oriented architectures. In *Quality of Service in Heterogeneous Networks*, pages 785–798. Springer, 2009.

[5] B. H. Cheng, R. de Lemos, H. Giese, P. Inverardi, J. Magee, J. Andersson, B. Becker, N. Bencomo, Y. Brun, B. Cukic, et al. *Software engineering for*

self-adaptive systems: A research roadmap. Springer, 2009.

[6] A. D'Ambrogio. Model-driven WSDL extension for describing the QoS of web services. In *IEEE International Conference on Web Services (ICWS '06)*, pages 789–796, Chicago, IL, Sept. 2006.

[7] V. Dubey and D. A. Menascé. Utility-based optimal service selection for business processes in service oriented architectures. In *IEEE International Conference on Web Services*, pages 542–550, Miami, FL, July 2010.

[8] A. Elkhodary. A learning-based approach for engineering feature-oriented self-adaptive software systems. In *Proc. 18th ACM SIGSOFT international symposium on Foundations of software engineering*, FSE '10, pages 345–348, 2010.

[9] A. Elkhodary, N. Esfahani, and S. Malek. Fusion: a framework for engineering self-tuning self-adaptive software systems. In *Proc. 18th ACM SIGSOFT international symposium on Foundations of software engineering*, FSE '10, pages 7–16, 2010.

[10] T. Erl. *Service-Oriented Architecture: Concepts, Technology, and Design.* Prentice Hall, Upper Saddle River, NJ, 2005.

[11] N. Esfahani, S. Malek, D. A. Menascé, J. P. Sousa, and H. Gomaa. A modeling language for activity-oriented composition of service-oriented software systems. In *Proc. 12th ACM/IEEE International Conference on Model Driven Engineering Languages and Systems MODELS '09*, pages 591–605, Denver, CO, Oct. 2009.

[12] J. M. Ewing and D. A. Menascé. Business-oriented autonomic load balancing for multi-tiered web sites. In *IEEE International Symposium on Modeling, Analysis, and Simulation of Computer and Telecommunication Systems (MASCOTS '09)*, pages 279–288, London, United Kingdom, Sept. 2009.

[13] J. Friedman. Flexible metric nearest neighbor classification. Technical report, Stanford University Statistics Department, 1994.

[14] H. Gomaa, K. Hashimoto, M. Kim, S. Malek, and D. A. Menascé. Software adaptation patterns for service-oriented architectures. In *Proc. 2010 ACM Symposium on Applied Computing*, pages 462–469, Sierre, Switzerland, Mar. 2010.

[15] M. C. Huebscher and J. A. McCann. A survey of autonomic computing–degrees, models, and applications. *ACM Computing Surveys*, 40(3):1–28, Aug. 2008.

[16] G. Jung, K. R. Joshi, M. A. Hiltunen, R. D. Schlicting, and C. Pu. Generating adaptation policies for multi-tier server applications in consolidated server environments. In *Proc. 5th IEEE International Conference on Autonomic Computing (ICAC '08)*, pages 23–32, Chicago, IL, June 2008.

[17] J. O. Kephart and D. M. Chess. The vision of autonomic computing. *IEEE Computer*, 36(1):41–50, Jan. 2003.

[18] T. G. Kolda, R. M. Lewis, and V. Torczon. Optimization by direct search: New perspectives on some classical and modern methods. *SIAM Review*, 45(3):385–482, Sept. 2003.

[19] A. Koziolek, H. Koziolek, and R. Reussner. Peropteryx: automated application of tactics in multi-objective software architecture optimization. In *QoSA-ISARCS '11*, pages 33–42, 2011.

[20] J. Kramer and J. Magee. Self-managed systems: an architectural challenge. In *Future of Software Engineering (FOSE '07)*, pages 259–268, Minneapolis, MN, May 2007.

[21] N. Mani, D. C. Petriu, and M. Woodside. Propagation of incremental changes to performance model due to soa design pattern application. In *Proc. ACM/SPEC international conference on International conference on performance engineering*, pages 89–100. ACM, 2013.

[22] A. Martens, D. Ardagna, H. Koziolek, R. Mirandola, and R. Reussner. A hybrid approach for multi-attribute QoS optimisation in component based software systems. In G. Heineman, J. Kofron, and F. Plasil, editors, *Research into Practice–Reality and Gaps*, volume 6093 of *LNCS*, pages 84–101. Springer Berlin Heidelberg, 2010.

[23] D. A. Menascé, E. Casalicchio, and V. Dubey. A heuristic approach to optimal service selection in service oriented architectures. In *Proc. 7th International Workshop on Software and Performance (WOSP 2008)*, pages 13–24, Princeton, NJ, June 2008.

[24] D. A. Menascé, E. Casalicchio, and V. Dubey. On optimal service selection in service oriented architectures. *Performance Evaluation Journal*, 67(8):659–675, Sept. 2009.

[25] D. A. Menascé, R. Dodge, and D. Barbará. Preserving QoS of e-commerce sites through self-tuning: A performance model approach. In *Proc. 3rd ACM Conference on E-commerce*, pages 224–234, Tampa, FL, Oct. 2001.

[26] D. A. Menascé, J. M. Ewing, H. Gomaa, S. Malek, and J. P. Sousa. A framework for utility-based service oriented design in SASSY. In *Workshop on Software and Performance*, pages 27–36, San Jose, CA, Jan. 2010.

[27] D. A. Menascé, H. Gomaa, S. Malek, and J. Sousa. Sassy: A framework for self-architecting service-oriented systems. *IEEE Software*, 28(6):78–85, Nov. 2011.

[28] D. A. Menascé, J. P. Sousa, S. Malek, and H. Gomaa. QoS architectural patterns for self-architecting software systems. In *Proc. 7th International Conference on Autonomic Computing (ICAC '10)*, pages 195–204, Washington, DC, June 2010.

[29] N. Poggi, T. Moreno, J. L. Berral, R. Gavaldá, and J. Torres. Self-adaptive utility-based web session management. *The International Journal of Computer and Telecommunications Networking*, 53(10):1712–1721, July 2009.

[30] V. J. Rayward-Smith, I. H. Osman, C. R. Reeves, and G. D. Smith, editors. *Modern Heuristic Search Methods.* Wiley, Hoboken, NJ, 1996.

[31] L. Zhang and D. Ardagna. SLA based profit optimization in autonomic computing systems. In *Proc. 2nd International Conference on Service Oriented Computing (ICSOCŠ04)*, pages 173–182, New York, NY, Nov. 2004.

Agile Middleware for Scheduling: Meeting Competing Performance Requirements of Diverse Tasks

Feng Yan
College of William and Mary
Williamsburg
VA, USA
fyan@cs.wm.edu

Shannon Hughes
College of William and Mary
Williamsburg
VA, USA
srhughes@cs.wm.edu

Alma Riska
EMC Corporation
Cambridge
MA, USA
alma.riska@emc.com

Evgenia Smirni
College of William and Mary
Williamsburg
VA, USA
esmirni@cs.wm.edu

ABSTRACT

As the need for scaled-out systems increases, it is paramount to architect them as large distributed systems consisting of off-the-shelf basic computing components known as compute or data nodes. These nodes are expected to handle their work independently, and often utilize off-the-shelf management tools, like those offered by Linux, to differentiate priorities of tasks. While prioritization of background tasks in server nodes takes center stage in scaled-out systems, with many tasks associated with salient features such as eventual consistency, data analytics, and garbage collection, the standard Linux tools such as `nice` and `ionice` fail to adapt to the dynamic behavior of high priority tasks in order to achieve the best trade-off between protecting the performance of high priority workload and completing as much low priority work as possible. In this paper, we provide a solution by proposing a priority scheduling middleware that employs different policies to schedule background tasks based on the instantaneous resource requirements of the high priority applications running on the server node. The selection of policies is based on off-line and on-line learning of the high priority workload characteristics and the imposed performance impact due to low priority work. In effect, this middleware uses a *hybrid* approach to scheduling rather than a monolithic policy. We prototype and evaluate it via measurements on a test-bed and show that this scheduling middleware is robust as it effectively and autonomically changes the relative priorities between high and low priority tasks, consistently meeting their competing performance targets.

Categories and Subject Descriptors

C.4 [**Computer Systems Organization**]: Performance of Systems

General Terms

Performance, Algorithms

Keywords

priority scheduling; performance guarantee; background throughput; learning performance patterns; decision map; Linux priority utilities; workload characterization

1. INTRODUCTION

Scaling of web services is mostly achieved by deploying distributed systems in large data centers or even across them. Traditional computer systems, particularly those supporting enterprise applications, do not scale well, especially with regard to cost. To mitigate cost at a large scale, the industry is increasingly turning to commodity hardware and open-source software to accomplish large-scale services and computation. In order to scale-out and still operate effectively, the building blocks are off-the-shelf server nodes that operate mostly independently, while exchanging messages with other participating nodes [20]. This goal, exemplified by the *Open Compute* [2] initiative which has been widely adopted by the broader tech community, is to keep down the cost of systems that host big data and provide large scale analytics and other important web services.

One of the salient characteristics of the large distributed systems hosting a wide range of web services is supporting a wide range of features, including eventual consistency of data, data replication, garbage collection, and log data analysis, that run asynchronously in the background, at the level of the individual server node. The goal is to serve user workload as fast as possible and handle most of the management tasks *only when system resources are moderately utilized*. To illustrate the existence of opportunities for effective scheduling of background tasks in real systems, we illustrate in Figure 1 the arrival intensity of requests to store new data or read existing ones in one of the nodes of a large scale web service over a three day period. The strong daily pattern in the arrival intensity allows the system to schedule other important but less time sensitive tasks, e.g., garbage collection, during periods of low user activity, ensuring that these tasks do not affect the user quality of experience.

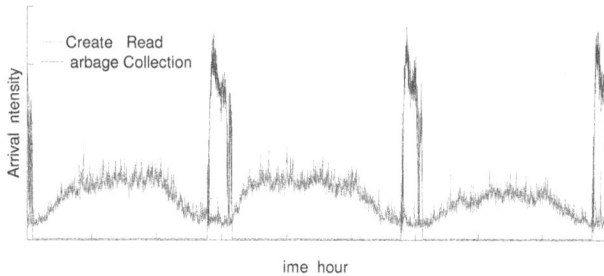

Figure 1: Overtime plot of arrival intensity for a large scale web service .

Here, we develop scheduling middleware that builds upon standard scheduling prioritization tools that are available in any Linux distribution, which often is the operating system of choice in the individual nodes of scaled-out systems. Standard distributions provide monolithic tools for priority scheduling but these are usually not reactive to changing workload conditions as those depicted in Figure 1. The scheduling middleware that we propose is based on effectively launching `nice` and `ionice`, the most common prioritization tools, with the appropriate priority levels that best match the existing system conditions. Furthermore, these priority levels are *continuously adjusted* throughout the lifetime of the system to control relative priorities between the user (or foreground) traffic and the background system features in order to guarantee quality of service targets for foreground work while maximizing completion levels of background features.

While prioritization features have been proposed at the kernel level [26, 18] or at the application level [19, 17, 15], our focus is to provide middleware that is built upon standard tools that are available in any Linux distribution and most importantly operate in user-space. By utilizing `nice` and `ionice` as building blocks, we ensure that at fine time scales (i.e., microseconds) there is correct differentiation of the processes based on their priorities. At coarse time scales (i.e., minutes), we control and manage these priorities (i.e., via `renice` and other utilities) to ensure that foreground performance is protected and background work is completed as efficiently as possible. The middleware that we propose is based on several standard monolithic scheduling policies (e.g., `nice` and `ionice`) but also on `smart`, a new (but still monolithic) mechanism that suspends background work briefly when foreground load spikes [23]. During the lifetime of the execution of the background work, the proposed middleware switches among the various basic policies as considered best fit.

Using the web-driven TPC-W benchmark [1, 5] as a representative foreground application, we experiment with a range of background tasks, as defined by controllable micro benchmarks. Our extensive set of experiments shows that we can effectively utilize system resources by scheduling background jobs with the *best* monolithic policy depending on resource availability, maintaining an overall uniform utilization of the system. We stress that the selection of the best

policy is left to the middleware and this can change during the course of the execution.

The rest of the paper is organized as follows. In Section 2, we provide results from characterizing the behavior of `nice` under several scenarios. Section 3 develops our new prioritization scheme which determines the priority of the background tasks. The new framework is evaluated via extended experiments in Section 4. We discuss related work in Section 5. We conclude the paper and summarize future work in Section 6.

2. PRELIMINARIES

In this section, we first present an overview of the available off-the-shelf scheduling tools for priority scheduling and continue with an overview of resource demands across time for a typical workload to illustrate how background scheduling can become truly opportunistic. Finally, we show with evidence that a single background scheduling policy cannot be effective under all circumstances, which further corroborates the need for agile middleware that continuously adjusts priority scheduling parameters in a transparent and autonomic way.

2.1 Prioritizing Background Work

Proprietary systems often have their own priority scheduling algorithms that allow them to maintain performance of user workload while other lower priority jobs are running in the background. For systems built of off-the-shelf Unix components, the readily available tools for priority scheduling are `nice`, which prioritizes access to the CPU resource, and `ionice`, which prioritizes access to the disk resource. While different distributions of Unix have different implementations of `nice` and `ionice`, they operate similarly: when enabled, they allow users to adjust the execution priority of processes.

A process that is invoked via `nice` can have a scheduling priority between -20 (the highest priority) and 19 (the lowest priority). A process invoked with nice 0 or without nice command runs with the default (i.e., normal) priority. `nice` determines the chunk of CPU time for a specific process, i.e., the higher the priority the larger the chunk of CPU time the process gets. The exact relation between the `nice` parameter and the amount of CPU time dedicated to a process is implementation dependent and varies between Unix/Linux distributions. The mechanism is generally simple to use and depends on fine-grained CPU consumption. A user can change the priority of a process via `Eunice`.

Similarly, `ionice` allows ranking the priority of a process from 0 to 3, where 3 is meant to designate a process that should be given IO resources only when the IO system is idle. Adding `ionice` can help boost `nice`'s performance in cases of memory-intensive background tasks.

A user may select to invoke both `nice` and `ionice` together. Combining `nice 19` with `ionice 3` gives the lowest priority setting for both resources. We label this combination as **allnice** and it represents the most straightforward way for the background work to minimally effect the performance of foreground work using commodity utilities.

In [23], a scheduling policy named `smart` is developed that focuses on adapting background job scheduling to foreground work with demands that are variable across time. The basic premise is to observe and effectively *predict* periods of low and high utilization of the foreground work and launch or suspend background work based on monitoring system utilization levels. Suspending and resuming utilizes system resources by scheduling background work only when resources are lightly to moderately utilized by high priority processes. Additionally, it better isolates the foreground performance than `nice` or `allnice`, as well as doing so more consistently than either of the off-the-shelf options.

In this paper, we develop a middleware that utilizes `smart` in [23] as well as the Linux priority scheduling tools `nice` and `ionice` and further enhances their capabilities by defining a set of policies which are automatically invoked within the same application run. The policies that are automatically selected by the middleware are the following:

- **nice 0**: the background work and the foreground application are running at the same priority for both CPU and IO resources.

- **allnice**: the background work runs at the lowest priority but it is never suspended, i.e., it is executed using `nice 19` with `ionice 3`.

- **smart+**: the background work is suspended briefly if load spikes using `smart` [23]. Once load returns back to its previous level, **allnice** is used here, unlike to the policy in [23].

- **FGonly**: the background work is suspended completely if high load for an extended period (i.e., at the hour-level granularity) is detected.

Additional policies can be added according to the specific system and application scenarios. In general, more scheduling policies give finer control, but may also result in more overhead. Intermediate policies with different `nice` parameters can be used, as well as more policies between the two extremes of **nice 0** and **FGonly**. For ease of presentation and with no loss of generality, we focus here on the four policies outlined above. More details are given in Section 3.

2.2 Scheduling Background Work: Perils and Opportunities

To illustrate the ample opportunities and perils of background scheduling, we show in Figure 2 the CPU utilization and response time as a function of elapsed time for TPC-W [1], a classic multi-tiered benchmark[1] that has significant variability across time in its CPU and memory demands [22]. The figure illustrates three scenarios: one with only 10 emulated browsers (EBs) (top graph), one with 40 emulated browsers (middle graph), and one with 70 emulated browsers (bottom graph). The figure clearly shows many opportunities to schedule background jobs when there are only 10 emulated browsers: the CPU utilization is consistently low, with the exception of a few short time periods. Similarly, average response times are low across the entire experiment. The middle graph shows a different situation: with 40 EBs several bursts of short but high CPU activity that are usually clustered together, interspersed with periods of low CPU usage. The average user response time follows closely the CPU usage patterns. The bottom graph, where there are 70 EBs, shows longer periods of high utilization intermixed with periods of low utilization. The figure illustrates that there are

[1] For the exact description of the experimental and measurement setting see Section 4.

plenty of opportunities to schedule background tasks when there are only 10 EBs, but higher load situations require more care, lest background work is scheduled during periods of high utilization and TPC-W performance is compromised.

2.3 Monolithic Background Scheduling

Figure 3 illustrates a first proof-of-concept of the relative advantages and disadvantages of scheduling background jobs using **nice 0**, **allnice**, **smart+**, and **FGonly**. The last policy gives the norm of the ideal response time. The background work that we launch here is explained in detail in Section 4. The figure illustrates the cumulative distribution histogram (CDH) of response times for TPC-W (first row) and the throughput of background jobs (second row), presented as the number of completed iterations. The CDH figures clearly illustrate that the ranking of the various policies with respect to foreground performance are consistent for 10, 40, and 70 EBs and reflect how conservatively the background work is scheduled, ditto for the respective amount of completed background work. Yet, if there is a certain service level objective, e.g., if the 80th percentile of response time needs to be less than 600 ms, then background scheduling can be tuned to be more or less aggressive, such that it takes into account the load in the system as expressed by the number of EBs is able to guarantee better background throughput. If the system operates with 10 EBs, then **nice 0** is sufficient for performance and maximizes the completed iterations but if the system operates with 40 EBs then **allnice** can offer performance guarantees while keeping iterations at a maximum. When EBs rise to 70, then **any** background scheduling must be stopped. The figure clearly shows that effective background scheduling needs to be agile and hybrid, i.e., *continuously change its priority parameters* (e.g., switch from **nice 0** to **allnice** to **smart+** to **FGonly**) depending on the system operating conditions. In the following section we define how to develop and launch such middleware.

3. METHODOLOGY

The basic premise of the proposed middleware is that if load from the high priority (or foreground) application is light, then running background tasks with the same priority should not violate the foreground performance target. As load from the foreground application increases, the priority of background work should decrease. If the system foreground load is high then the background should be suspended until the high load period passes. We aim to consistently meet the system's foreground performance target while serving as much background work as possible. To achieve this goal, we learn the corresponding performance for different foreground load levels and monitor the latter to decide at what priority (if at all) to schedule background tasks.

3.1 Foreground Load Levels Relative to the Target

Load levels are defined relative to the foreground performance target, which, without loss of generality, we define as the percentile of requests whose response time is less than a target value (e.g., 80% of foreground requests are served in less than 600 ms). The system then is said to be under high load if it closely meets the target. If the target is violated, then the system is in overload. If the load results in better performance than the target, then we consider the load to

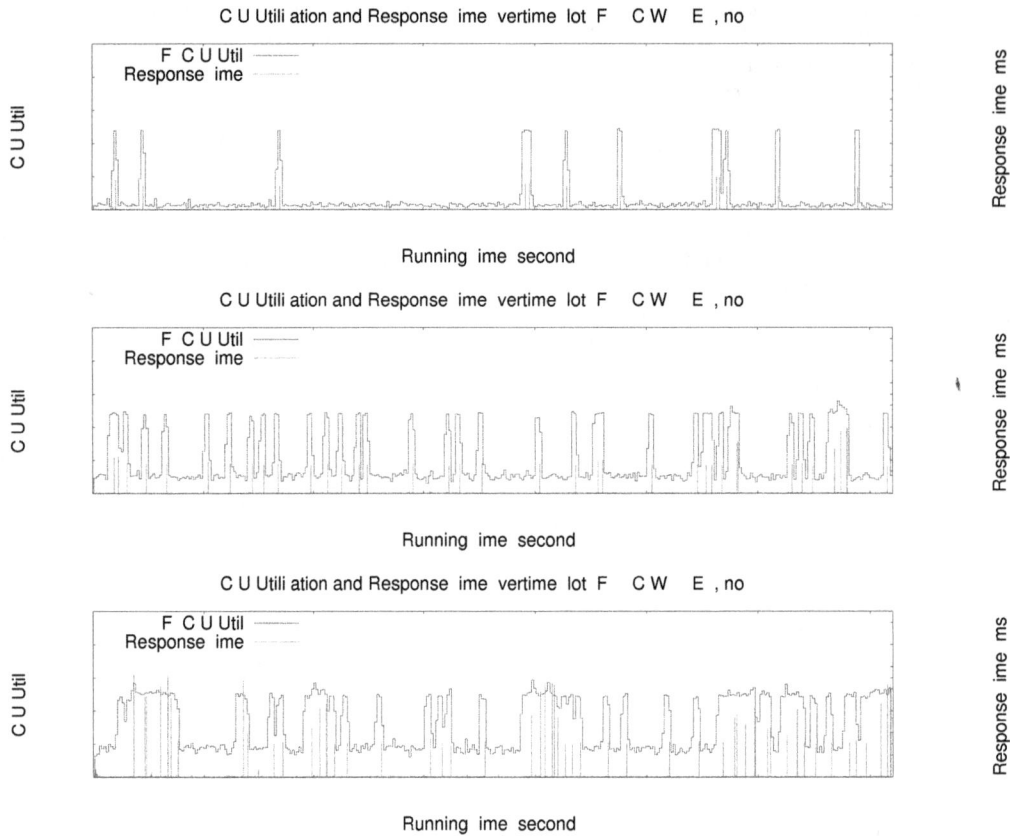

Figure 2: Overtime comparison of CPU utilization and average response times for 10, 40, and 70 emulated browsers. The duration of of this experiment is one hour.

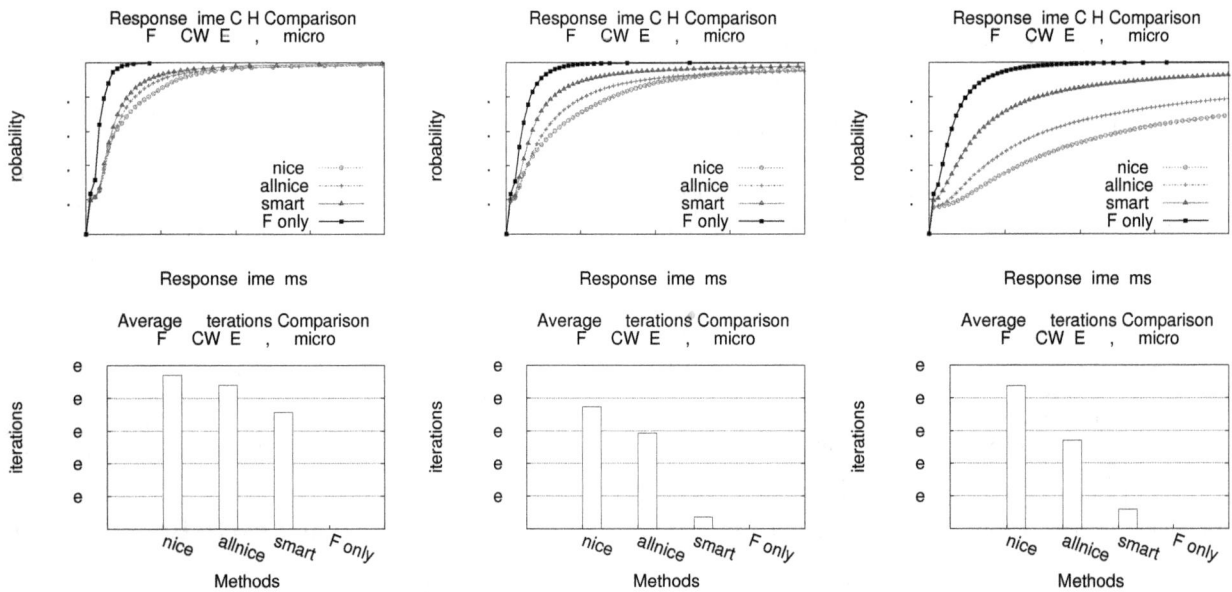

Figure 3: Performance results for TPC-W (CDH of response times) and background work completed (measured in number of iterations).

be light to moderate and background work can be scheduled without violating the target. The lighter the load, the higher the priority of the background work.

In Figure 4, we plot the cumulative distribution histogram (CDH) of TPC-W response times when load varies from light to heavy. In TPC-W the load is measured by the number of emulated browsers - EBs - (which corresponds to the number of network connections). In general, the load of a web service (which is the application type of interest given our focus on the individual nodes of a scaled-out system) can be measured similarly, although other metrics of load can be trivially defined and applied to our methodology.

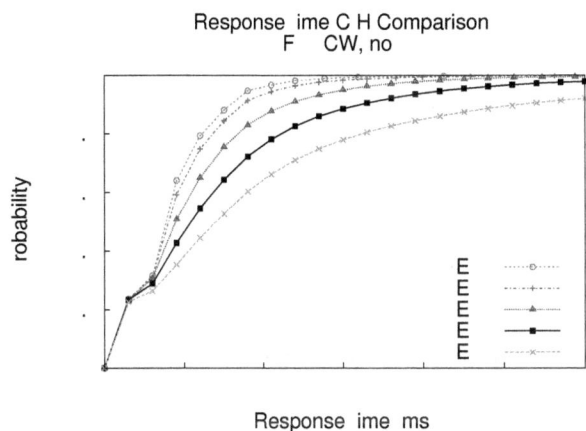

Figure 4: CDH of response times for different system load (EBs).

For a given target, we define the "high load" level based on the measurements captured in Figure 4. For example, the target of 80th percentile being at most 600 ms would result in "high-load" being 80 EBs, because it is the highest load level meeting this target. If the foreground performance target for the 80th percentile is to be at most 300 ms, then 70 EBs would be the "high load" in the system, while a load of 80 EBs would put the system into overload. For a target of 300 ms the system should serve background work alongside foreground only if the foreground load is less than 70 EBs.

The measurement data present in Figure 4 can be collected off-line in a test environment or it can be collected in the system as it comes on-line and kept up-to-date over time. Collecting such data should be possible with minimal effort, since the systems we are focusing on are provided by the general Linux distribution with an array of monitoring and logging tools.

3.2 Priority Policy Decision

The proposed middleware requires identifying the relation between current load and performance target for the foreground application (as described in Subsection 3.1), in order to identify the availability of resources to execute background tasks and set correctly the relative priority of the background tasks. As a result, similarly to the learning described in Subsection 3.1, we learn the foreground performance with a single representative background task (see more details in Section 4) treated with one of the four priority policies defined in Subsection 2.1. We again generate the distribution of foreground response times. For example, for

each of the evaluated TPC-W loads and **nice 0**, we generate the same set of response time distributions as captured in Figure 4.

We learn foreground performance behavior through a number of representative cases. The background tasks that we use for *training* run concurrently with TPC-W are described in Section 4 and can be tuned to demand more or less CPU and memory resources. Specifically, during learning, we measure the system under the foreground application plus heavy background load, i.e., demanding more than 100% CPU utilization and memory, so that the impact on foreground performance would hold for *any* background task that may be served in the system. Because of these choices during the learning period, we consider the measurements conducted as a baseline that can be used reliably to guide our decision on the priority policy for a given foreground load (and its performance target) and *any* background task. Results shown in Section 4 support these choices. Our reliance on fine-grained priority scheduling done by **nice** and **ionice** adds to the robustness of our decisions.

To help visualize the data we collect during our learning process, as well as to clarify our decision-making process with regard to dynamically changing background priorities, we plot the collected data, i.e., the distribution of response times for different load levels and priority policies, as stacked bars, see Figure 5. The x-axis of Figure 5 consists of all possible (*system load, priority policy*) pairs. The y-axis in Figure 5 represents the response time percentiles of the foreground requests, measured in milliseconds. The different colors used in each bar mark a specific, i.e., 50, 70, 80, and 90th, percentile of the response time distribution for a specific pair.

The data structure visualized in Figure 5 is paired with the foreground performance target which we illustrate with a horizontal line which represents the expected response time percentile. In this figure we have marked performance targets for the 80th percentile of response times to be equal to or less than 600ms. In this case, more than 70 EBs is considered "high load", since the target is met under the **FG-only** policy only. As the foreground load decreases, the 80th percentile of foreground response times is met also by several priority policies that serve background work. For example, for 50 EBs, the 80th percentile of foreground response time is less than 600ms under the **smart+** policy, while for 40 EBs the target is still met if we schedule background work via **allnice**. At 30 EBs or less that background work can be scheduled with the same priority as foreground work via **nice-0** without violating the target. The benefit of increasing the priority of background work (from **FG-only** to **nice-0**) as foreground load reduces is to serve more background work while ensuring that the foreground performance target is met. The map in Figure 5 is used by the scheduling middleware that we propose here as the decision making engine to automatically adjust priorities as foreground load conditions change over time.

A schematic view of information interchange in our priority scheduling hybrid middleware is provided in Figure 6. We reiterate that the learning is done in such a way that it can either be complete off-line or on-line as the system comes up and can be updated overtime with more observations. As we provide more details on our prototype in Section 4, we also highlight the standard Linux utilities that we use.

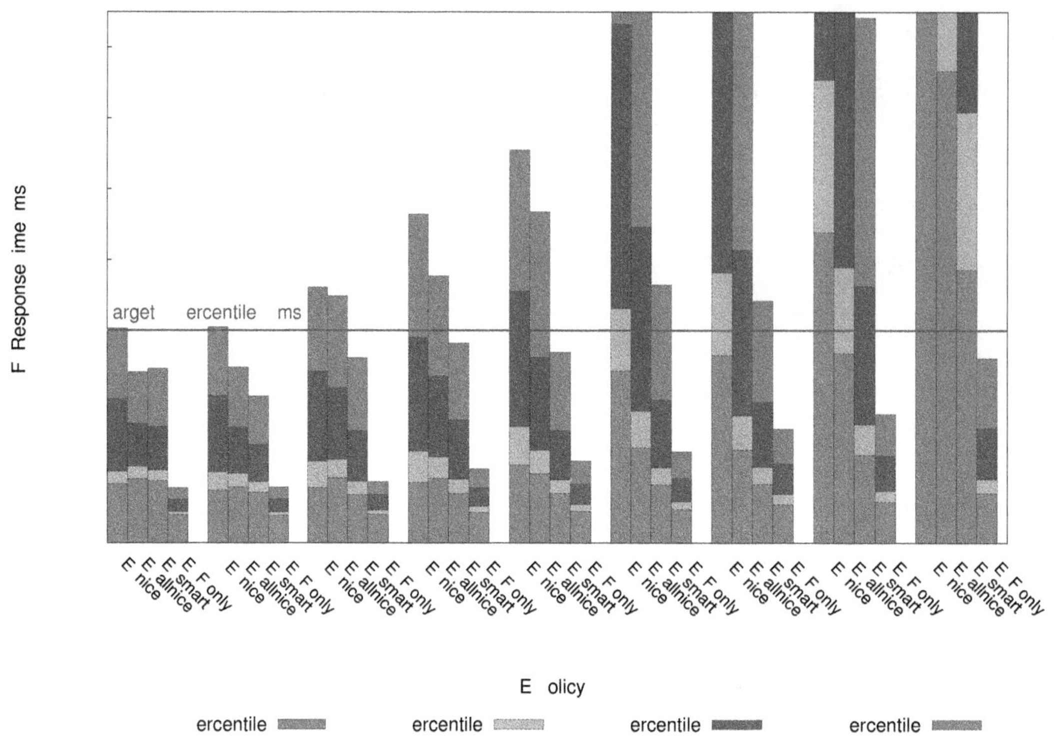

Figure 5: Decision map.

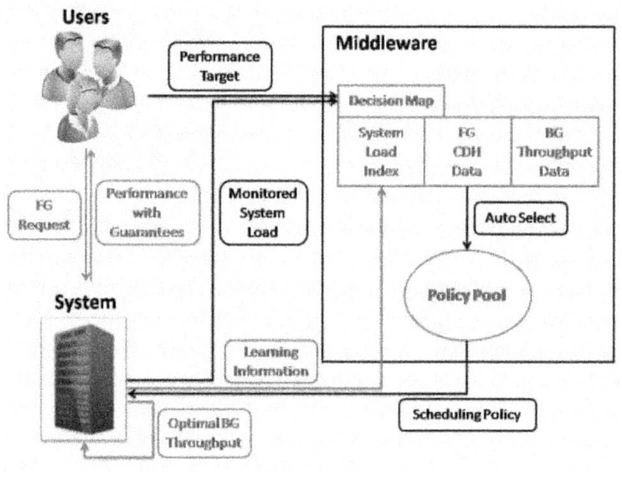

Figure 6: Schematic view of the middleware scheme.

4. EXPERIMENTAL EVALUATION

All experiments presented here are conducted on a Dell Precision WorkStation with Intel Pentium Dual Core 2.4GHz processor, 1GB memory, Seagate 7.2K SATA hard drives, running openSUSE 11.4 (64 bit). As foreground workload, we use a Java implementation of the TPC-W benchmark. For background work we use our own micro benchmark in order to do control the experiments and ensure representative data with regard to learning.

We consider TPC-W to be a challenging workload, because it is characterized by variability in its resource de-

mands across time [5], as also shown in Figure 2. TPC-W is a web server and database performance benchmark [1] and in our prototype we use to drive the system the java distribution in [4]. We use tomcat as the application server and mysql as the database server. TPC-W provides a large number of parameters. We use the browsing mix on a 100000 items in the database.

We develop our own micro benchmark to use as background work, which is built upon the Isolation Benchmark Suite [13]. The micro-benchmark performs multiplications in a tight loop which is embedded in a larger one containing array initializations and file writes. The micro benchmark allows to experiment with a broader range of CPU, memory, and IO background demands. In the results reported in this section, we have used three different variations of the micro benchmark. In each of the three scenarios, four instances of the micro-benchmark are run concurrently, each consuming approximately 20% of memory capacity and some IO traffic. The micro benchmarks parameters are scaled to change the CPU demand across as shown below:

- micro1: consumes approximately 100% of the system's total CPU resource.

- micro2: consumes approximately 45% of the system's total CPU resource.

- micro3: consumes approximately 160% of the system's total CPU resource (i.e., uses almost both cores).

In order to provide a simple and easily portable implementation, our monitoring and scheduling algorithms are implemented entirely in user space, making use of readily available Linux commands (e.g., `pidstat` and `kill`). For monitoring, we launch a shell script to call `pidstat` every 10 seconds and extract the CPU utilization for all running processes, classifying the results into three main categories: foreground (TPC-W related) processes, background (micro benchmark related) processes, and other system processes. The coarse granularity of these intervals differs from the fine-grained handling generally used in real-time scheduling algorithms in the literature, but we emphasize that we delegate the fine-grained decisions to `nice` and `ionice`.

To control the execution of background work, we use the STOP and CONT signals and pass them to process by the `kill` command to "pause" and "resume" the background tasks. The process is suspended by being starved of resources, but because it is not actually killed, it can be immediately resumed from where it is paused. We stress all these native system tools make our method easy to deploy and with low overhead.

4.1 Results

Initially, we evaluate our hybrid scheduling middleware by running the TPC-W as the foreground task and four micros for a total of 100% additional CPU utilization (i.e., variant *micro1* above) as background tasks for different foreground performance targets. We choose two scenarios to present here. Scenario 1's performance target is the 80th percentile to be equal or smaller than 600 ms and Scenario 2's performance target is the 90th percentile to be equal or smaller than 650 ms. Based on the decision map of Figure 5 the scheduling strategy is devised and summarized in Table 1. The policy transition parameters in Table 1 are obtained from our off-line learning. As robustness of this learning approach is key to our evaluation, we run all our tests for 14 hours, during which the foreground load varies from 0 to 80 EBs, including load levels that were not used in learning. For those cases, the decision is done based on the next higher load tested.

We evaluate our hybrid priority scheduling middleware by comparing it with the monolithic scheduling methods for the same scenario. Our experiments are run 14 hours long to ensure enough instances of foreground workload changes occur to demonstrate the robustness of our hybrid middleware. We plot the results for Scenario 1 and Scenario 2 in Figures 7 and 8, respectively. In each figure, we plot the system load measured by both CPU utilization and number of EBs (see top plot). As load varies over time, so do the opportunities to schedule background work. For each hour, we report in the top plot of Figures 7 and 8 along the x-axis, the decision of our hybrid middleware based on the parameters devised in Table 1 and monitoring of foreground load levels. Figures 7 and 8 also plot the CDH and CCDF of the response times for the different monolithic policies and our hybrid middleware (see the second row).

As expected, the **FG-only** and **nice-0** achieve the best and worst foreground performance, respectively, because **FG-only** suspends background work while **nice-0** treats foreground and background work the same. The other two policies, **allnice** and **smart+** maintain better foreground performance at the cost of background throughput (bottom right plot in Figures 7 and 8). The bottom left plot in Figures 7 and 8 shows how hybrid meets the foreground performance target (see vertical line) while achieving highest background throughout among all policies that do meet the performance target (**FG-only**, **smart+**, and **hybrid**

for Scenario 1 and **FG-only** and **hybrid** for Scenario 2). (see right plot in the bottom row).

We also evaluate the resiliency of our hybrid middleware to the learning methodology. Recall that learning was done with background tasks adding up to 100% CPU utilization. We run the same 14 hours test for Scenario 1 and Scenario 2, but now the background work follows the variant micro2 (45% total CPU demand) and micro3 (total 160% CPU demand). For micro2 background workload, we show the respective results for Scenario 1 and Scenario 2 in Figures 9 and 10. For micro3 background workload, we show respective results for Scenario 1 and Scenario 2 in Figure 11 and Figure 12. The decisions on policy transitions are done according to Table 1 for both cases.

These experiments confirm that the hybrid middleware meets the foreground performance target under all these different combinations of foreground performance targets and background workload and that the learning approach is effective. The reason behind this is that the low priority workload is only scheduled during low system load periods, where the foreground impact is well controlled. In addition, we are always conservative by approximating the untrained foreground intensity to the higher nearest intensity entry in the decision map. Another critical aspect that contributes to the resiliency of our hybrid middleware is the fact that the scheduling policies used in our scheme are based on `nice` and `ionice`, which control priorities at very fine granularities.

5. RELATED WORK

There has been a large volume of related work, that can be roughly classified as scheduling that requires kernel modification, application modification, real time scheduling, or scheduling for quality of service. Yet, to the best of our knowledge, there is no mechanism that is available at the user space as the one proposed here, that relies on automatic usage of pause/resume of background execution as well as automatic usage of the various `nice` and `ionice` options, or `renice` thereof.

Traditional work on real-time scheduling relies on strictly or semi-strictly predictable periodic tasks, such as media players, and requires kernel modification, changes to application code in order to take advantage of the scheduling, and keeping track of specific deadline information for every task [19, 17, 15]. Cucinotta et. al. focus on meeting acceptable throughput for "soft real-time" applications, specifically media streaming [7]. To do this, they take a signal processing approach to characterize the activity periodicity behavior of the blackbox legacy applications they are attempting to control, and use the results to budget resources for each application. Their implementation requires kernel modification and does not explicitly stop low priority background tasks in order to better protect foreground tasks, as ours does. Meehean et. al. propose a very flexible system which requires kernel modification and demonstrate a scenario similar to ours [14]. Our work does know rely on periodicity or any modifications to kernel or application code.

Scheduling that provides quality is service to individual customers has been developed in [26], which look to provide kernel support for differentiating quality of service for individual customers. We are focused on preventing background tasks on the server from interfering with any response-time-sensitive tasks without again requiring any kernel modification. Indeed, the proposed mechanism to background task

Table 1: Scheduling Computed from Decision Map for different Scenarios.

Scenario 1: Target: $Prt(80\%) <= 600ms$			Scenario 2: Target: $Prt(90\%) <= 650ms$		
System Load	EB Range	Policy Selection	System Load	EB Range	Policy Selection
low	0-30	nice0	low	0-10	nice0
medium	31-40	allnice	medium	11-19	allnice
high	41-60	smart+	high	20-40	smart+
extreme	61-80	FGonly	extreme	40-80	FGonly

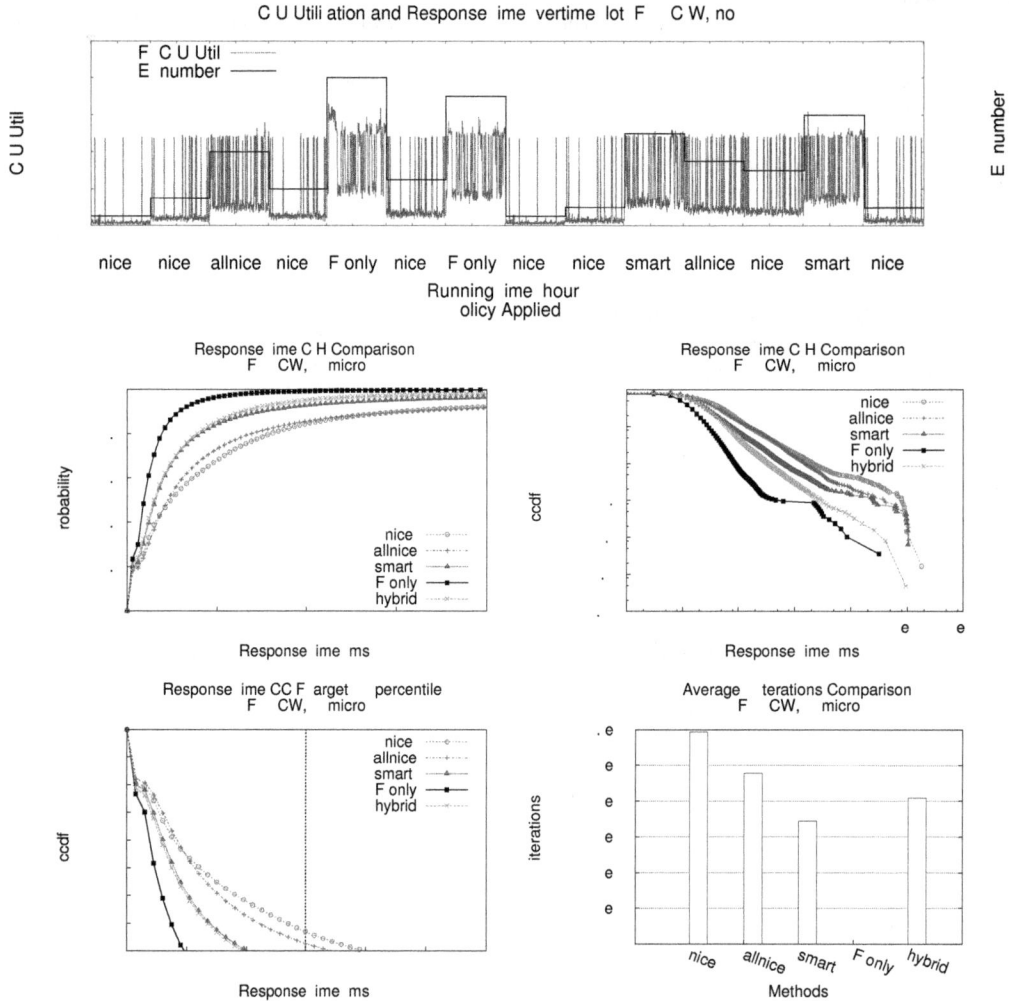

Figure 7: Scenario 1 - BG: CPU total demand: 100% .

management could be combined with QoS differentiation schemes by using different thresholds to protect higher QoS processes.

Recent scheduling research has often focused on the particular problems of scheduling jobs on multicore machines and computing clusters [10, 25]. When priority schedulers are considered, it is generally with the intention of improving their fairness or maintaining fairness when adapting a scheduler to more complex circumstances [25, 11]. The individual characteristics of particular tasks are often taken into account for scheduling purposes, for instance to save energy during periods of low utilization [21] or to spread out intensive tasks to prevent thermal damage to a machine [6]. In some cases the non-linear interaction of different co-located jobs is taken into account [12]. In this work, we look to use as much of the spare capacity as possible for time-insensitive background tasks, as in the case of a server handling the continuous and bursty workload of foreground user traffic while also intending to perform replication, integrity checking, data analysis, or other work [16, 24].

Virtual machines (VMs) can also be used to isolate high priority tasks [18]. VM management is not straightforward either and requires significant overhead to manage, monitor, and adjust resource allocation. In contract to traditional VM managing solutions our approach is simpler to use as it does not require the deployment of any additional software. We provide a more precise sharing of resources since it adjusts based on percentage of total CPU usage and may

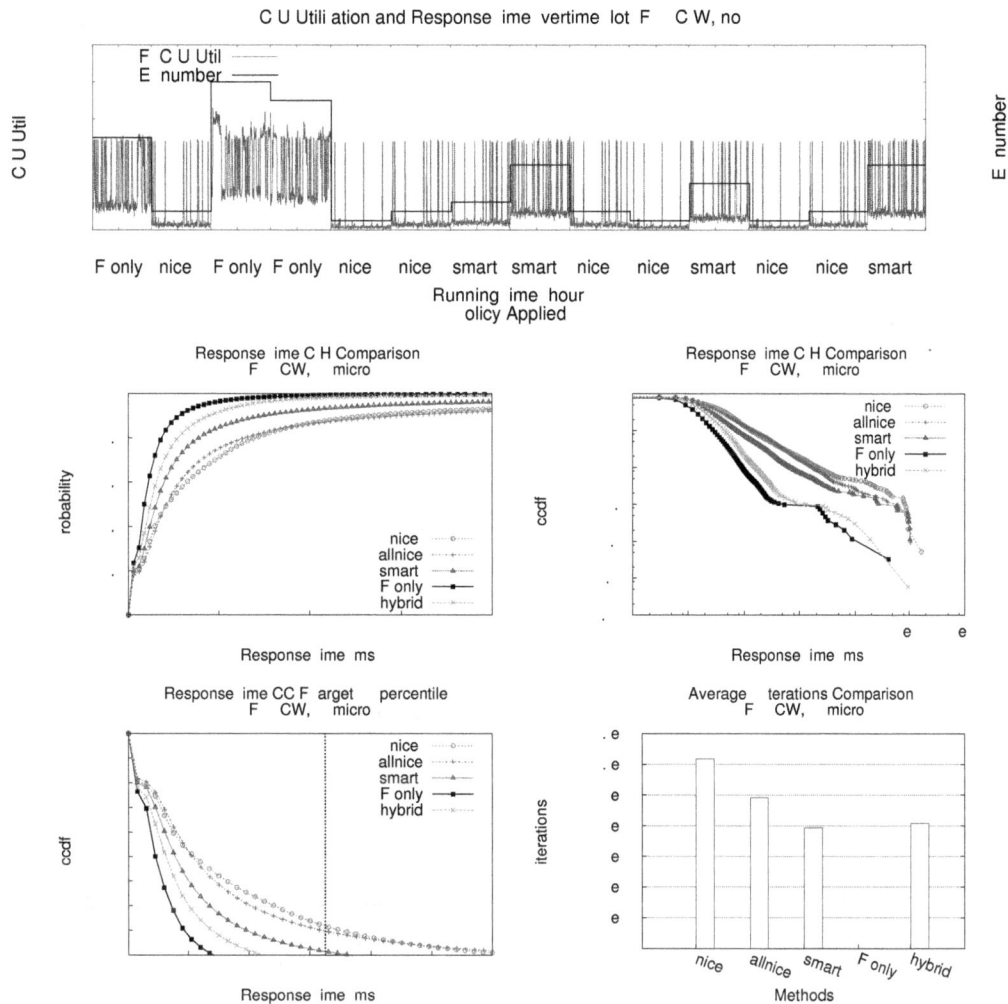

Figure 8: Scenario 2 - BG: CPU total demand: 100% .

allow the high and low priority processes to share cores, whereas the virtual machine approach generally assigns a whole number of cores to each virtual machine, although the exact number may change dynamically [18].

Other researchers have focused on the progress rate of applications to determine appropriate resource sharing between them [8, 9]. Ferguson et. al. describe a weighted fair-sharing system that uses the progress rate to effectively balance between jobs with specific deadlines of varying importance [9]. Douceur and Bolosky share our goal more clearly, identifying very low priority tasks that should not be allowed to impact the foreground task [8]. To determine whether the background task should be run or temporarily stopped, they monitor the progress rate of the background applications, assuming that when the progress rate falls below a particular threshold, it must be because of foreground process contention for shared resources. The background tasks are then stopped for a window of time, then tried again. Inspired by the TCP congestion control mechanism, the sleep window increases exponentially as resource contention is repeatedly observed. These approaches work well, but require a way to monitor the progress rate of background applications by the foreground application themselves.

Closely related to our work, Abe et. al. consider distributed computing projects like SETI@home, which allow individuals to donate computing time to scientific calculations when their computer is otherwise idle [3]. Similar to our work, Abe et. al. find built-in priority scheduling insufficient to protect foreground performance and choose to turn off background processing when the system detects resource contention with foreground processes. They monitor the background process to detect this contention and apply an exponential back off to reduce the impact on the foreground. Instead of attempting to measure the progress of the background tasks, however, they monitor the share of resources given to the background process. If the share drops, they assume that the foreground processes are now demanding more resources and could benefit from the background dropping altogether. In contrast, we focus on the behavior of the foreground task, looking for the best periods in which to perform background work.

To sum up, the proposed middleware for background scheduling differs from all the above work in that it does not require changing the kernel or depend on complex software. It does not require making changes to the foreground application or its processes, it can be even deployed without

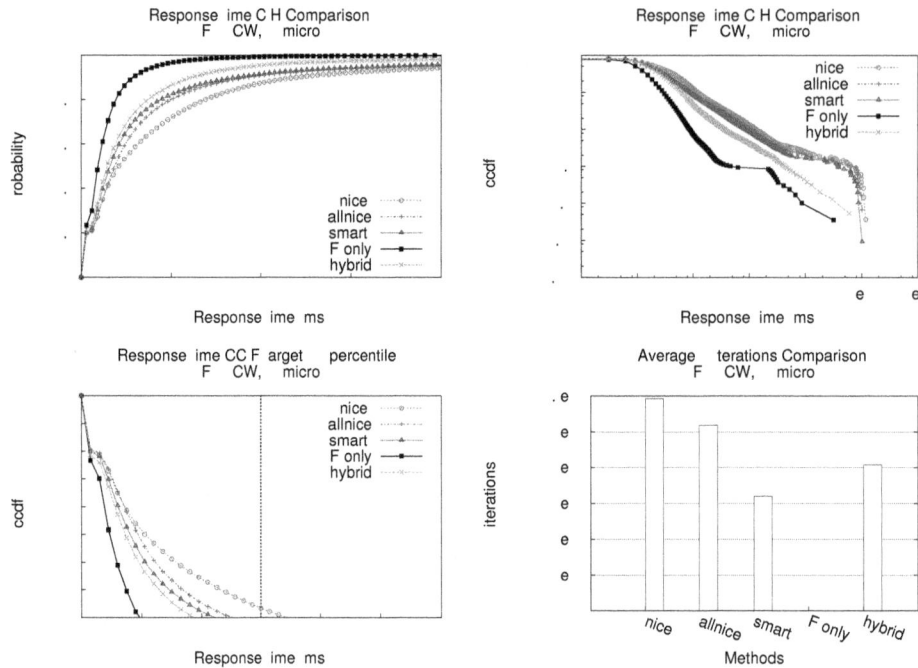

Figure 9: Scenario 1 - BG: CPU total demand: 45% .

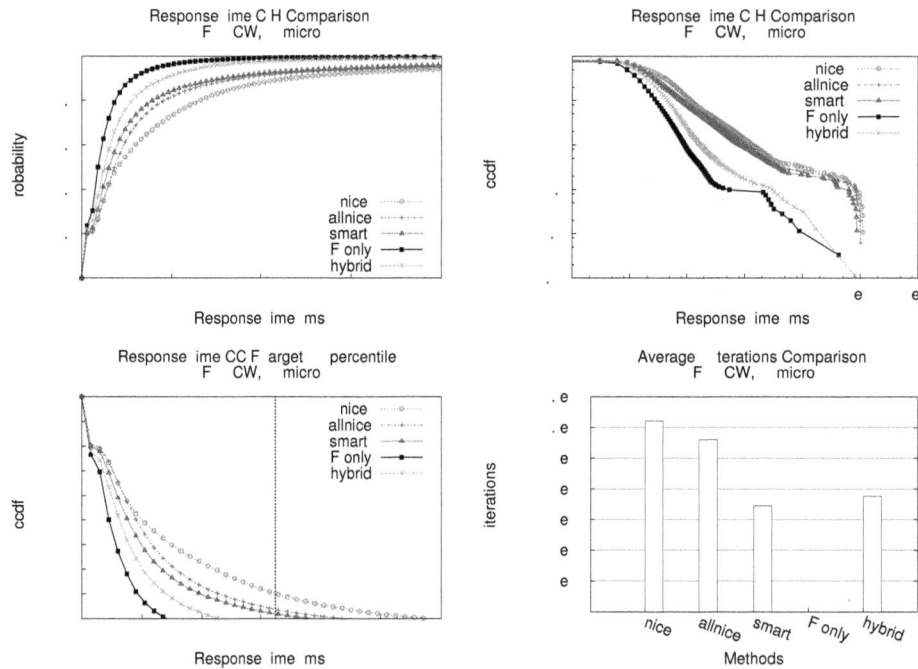

Figure 10: Scenario 2 - BG: CPU total demand: 45% .

interrupting the current services. To deploy it, a learning phase is required to characterize the statistical distribution of the foreground traffic's busy periods to determine the optimal periods to suspend the background job execution, and based on this information it launches *different* background job scheduling policies that can best fit the current system conditions. Therefore, it is lightweight, portable, and flexi-ble as it manages to take advantage of the benefits of several monolithic background scheduling policies while minimizing their respective shortcomings.

6. CONCLUSIONS

In this paper, we proposed a middleware scheme that remedies the shortcomings of monolithic background schedul-

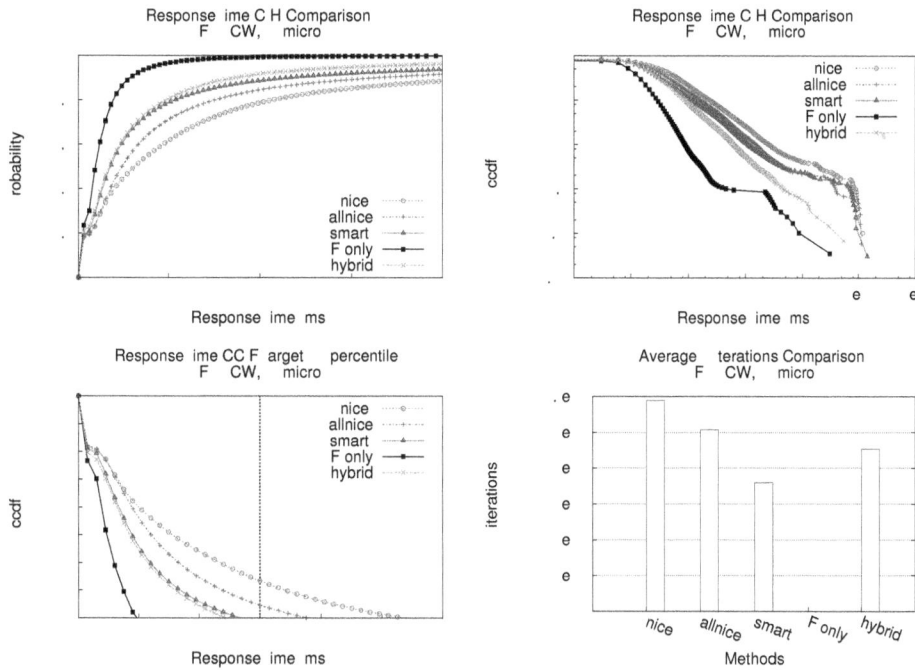

Figure 11: Scenario 1 - BG: CPU total demand: 160% .

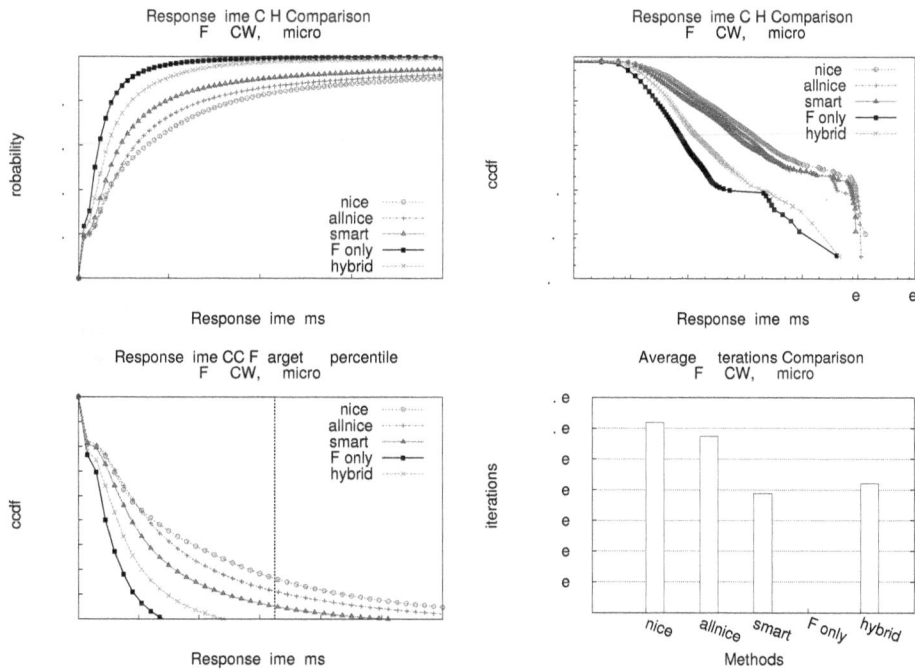

Figure 12: Scenario 2 - BG: CPU total demand: 160% .

ing and provides strong performance guarantees on foreground work. Our middleware scheme learns the foreground resource requirements and stores such information in a compact way, in the form of a cumulative data histogram. This learning allows the scheme to determine the appropriate scheduling policy based on pre-specified performance targets and current system load levels. The scheduling middleware is built above standard system tools, ensuring that is portable, with low overhead, and that can be deployed easily at a node level within large scaled-out systems. Detailed experimental results verified its effectiveness and robustness. In the future, we plan to add more policies and experiment with a wider array of different applications. We also plan to explore the case of meeting background work targets (e.g., close to a deadline) but still with minimum foreground performance impact.

7. ACKNOWLEDGMENTS

This work is supported by NSF grant CCF-0937925. The authors thank EMC for providing the enterprise data used for this work.

8. REFERENCES

[1] TPC-W. http://www.tpc.org/tpcw/.

[2] The open compute project. http://www.opencompute.org/, 2011.

[3] Y. Abe, H. Yamada, and K. Kono. Enforcing appropriate process execution for exploiting idle resources from outside operating systems. In *EuroSys*, pages 27–40, 2008.

[4] T. Bezenek, T. Cain, R. Dickson, T. Heil, M. Martin, C. McCurdy, R. Rajwar, E. Weglarz, C. Zilles, and M. Lipasti. Java tpc-w implementation distribution. http://pharm/ece.wisc.edu/tpcw.shtml, 2011.

[5] E. Cecchet, A. Ch, S. Elnikety, J. Marguerite, and W. Zwaenepoel. A comparison of software architectures for e-business applications. Technical report, In Proc. of 4th Middleware Conference, Rio de, 2002.

[6] A. K. Coskun, R. D. Strong, D. M. Tullsen, T. S. Rosing, and T. S. Rosing. Evaluating the impact of job scheduling and power management on processor lifetime for chip multiprocessors. In *SIGMETRICS/Performance*, pages 169–180, 2009.

[7] T. Cucinotta, F. Checconi, L. Abeni, L. Palopoli, and L. Palopoli. Self-tuning schedulers for legacy real-time applications. In *EuroSys*, pages 55–68, 2010.

[8] J. R. Douceur, W. J. Bolosky, and W. J. Bolosky. Progress-based regulation of low-importance processes. In *SOSP*, pages 247–260, 1999.

[9] A. D. Ferguson, P. Bodak, S. Kandula, E. Boutin, R. Fonseca, and R. Fonseca. Jockey: guaranteed job latency in data parallel clusters. In *EuroSys*, pages 99–112, 2012.

[10] M. Isard, V. Prabhakaran, J. Currey, U. Wieder, K. Talwar, A. Goldberg, and A. Goldberg. Quincy: fair scheduling for distributed computing clusters. In *SOSP*, pages 261–276, 2009.

[11] C. Krasic, M. Saubhasik, A. Sinha, and A. Goel. Fair and timely scheduling via cooperative polling. In *EuroSys*, pages 103–116, 2009.

[12] S.-H. Lim, J.-S. Huh, Y. Kim, G. M. Shipman, C. R. Das, and C. R. Das. D-factor: a quantitative model of application slow-down in multi-resource shared systems. In *SIGMETRICS*, pages 271–282, 2012.

[13] J. N. Matthews, W. Hu, M. Hapuarachchi, T. Deshane, D. Dimatos, G. Hamilton, M. McCabe, and J. Owens. Quantifying the performance isolation properties of virtualization systems. In *Experimental Computer Science*, page 6, 2007.

[14] J. Meehean, A. Arpaci-Dusseau, R. Arpaci-Dusseau, and M. Livny. CPU Futures: Scheduler support for application management of cpu contention. Technical Report at: http://research.cs.wisc.edu/techreports/2010/TR1684.pdf, 2011.

[15] C. W. Mercer, S. Savage, and H. Tokuda. Processor capacity reserves: Operating system support for multimedia applications. In *ICMCS*, pages 90–99, 1994.

[16] N. Mi, A. Riska, X. Li, E. Smirni, and E. Riedel. Restrained utilization of idleness for transparent scheduling of background tasks. In *Proceedings of the Eleventh International Joint Conference on Measurement and Modeling of Computer Systems, SIGMETRICS/Performance*, pages 205–216, 2009.

[17] J. Nieh and M. S. Lam. A smart scheduler for multimedia applications. pages 117–163, 2003.

[18] P. Padala, K.-Y. Hou, K. G. Shin, X. Zhu, M. Uysal, Z. Wang, S. Singhal, and A. Merchant. Automated control of multiple virtualized resources. In *EuroSys*, pages 13–26, 2009.

[19] L. Sha, T. F. Abdelzaher, K.-E. ÃĔrzÃľn, A. Cervin, T. P. Baker, A. Burns, G. C. Buttazzo, M. Caccamo, J. P. Lehoczky, and A. K. Mok. Real time scheduling theory: A historical perspective. pages 101–155, 2004.

[20] M. Stonebraker. The case for shared nothing. *IEEE Database Eng. Bull.*, 9(1):4–9, 1986.

[21] E. Thereska, A. Donnelly, D. Narayanan, and D. Narayanan. Sierra: practical power-proportionality for data center storage. In *EuroSys*, pages 169–182, 2011.

[22] Q. Wang, Y. Kanemasa, M. Kawaba, and C. Pu. When average is not average: large response time fluctuations in n-tier systems. In *Proceedings of the 9th international conference on Autonomic computing*, ICAC '12, pages 33–42, New York, NY, USA, 2012. ACM.

[23] F. Yan, S. Hughes, A. Riska, and E. Smirni. Overcoming limitations of off-the-shelf priority schedulers in dynamic environments. In *Proceedings of the 21st International Symposium on Modeling, Analysis, and Simulation On Computer and Telecommunication Systems*, MASCOTS 13, 2013.

[24] F. Yan, A. Riska, and E. Smirni. Fast eventual consistency with performance guarantees for distributed storage. In *ICDCS Workshops*, pages 23–28, 2012.

[25] M. Zaharia, D. Borthakur, J. S. Sarma, K. Elmeleegy, S. Shenker, I. Stoica, and I. Stoica. Delay scheduling: a simple technique for achieving locality and fairness in cluster scheduling. In *EuroSys*, pages 265–278, 2010.

[26] R. Zhang, T. Abdelzaher, and J. Stankovic. Kernel support for open qos-aware computing. In *Real-Time and Embedded Technology and Applications Symposium, 2003. Proceedings. The 9th IEEE*, pages 96–105, 2003.

Understanding, Modelling, and Improving the Performance of Web Applications in Multicore Virtualised Environments

Xi Chen, Chin Pang Ho, Rasha Osman, Peter G. Harrison, William J. Knottenbelt

Department of Computing, Imperial College London, United Kingdom, SW7 2AZ

{x.chen12, c.ho12, rosman, pgh, wjk}@imperial.ac.uk

ABSTRACT

As the computing industry enters the Cloud era, multicore architectures and virtualisation technologies are replacing traditional IT infrastructures. However, the complex relationship between applications and system resources in multicore virtualised environments is not well understood. Workloads such as web services and on-line financial applications have the requirement of high performance but benchmark analysis suggests that these applications do not optimally benefit from a higher number of cores.

In this paper, we try to understand the scalability behaviour of network/CPU intensive applications running on multicore architectures. We begin by benchmarking the Petstore web application, noting the systematic imbalance that arises with respect to per-core workload. Having identified the reason for this phenomenon, we propose a queueing model which, when appropriately parametrised, reflects the trend in our benchmark results for up to 8 cores. Key to our approach is providing a fine-grained model which incorporates the idiosyncrasies of the operating system and the multiple CPU cores. Analysis of the model suggests a straightforward way to mitigate the observed bottleneck, which can be practically realised by the deployment of multiple virtual NICs within our VM. Next we make blind predictions to forecast performance with multiple virtual NICs. The validation results show that the model is able to predict the expected performance with relative errors ranging between 8 and 26%.

Categories and Subject Descriptors

C.4 [**Computing Systems Organisation**]: Performance of Systems—*Modeling Techniques*; G.3 [**Mathematics of Computing**]: Probability and Statistics

Keywords

Benchmarking, Performance Modelling, Multicore, Virtualisation, Web Applications

1. INTRODUCTION

Cloud computing has received intensive attention from academia and industry. Two major techniques which are heavily used in this context are virtualisation and multicore architectures. Major cloud service providers, such as Amazon or Microsoft, provide a variety of virtual machines (VMs) that offer different levels of computing power. This computing paradigm provides improved performance, reduced application design and deployment complexity, elastic handling of dynamic workloads, and lower power consumption compared to traditional IT infrastructures [10, 38, 37].

Applications running in cloud environments exhibit a high degree of diversity; hence, strategies for allocating resources to different applications and for virtual resource consolidation increasingly depend on understanding the relationship between the required performance of applications and system resources [39]. To increase resource efficiency and lower operating costs, cloud providers resort to consolidating resources, i.e. packing multiple applications into one physical machine [8]. Understanding the performance of these applications is important for cloud providers to maximise resource utilisation and augment system throughput while maintaining individual application performance targets. Performance is also important to end users, because they are keen to know their applications are provisioned with sufficient resources to cope with varying workloads. Instead of increasing or decreasing the same instances one by one [17, 23], a combination of multiple instances might be more efficient to deal with the burstiness of dynamic workloads [48, 40, 29]. To handle the resource scaling problems, a model that can appropriately express, analyse, and predict the performance of applications running on multicore VM instances is necessary.

There are at least three observations we can make in light of present research. First, not all workloads/systems benefit from multicore CPUs [13, 44] as they do not scale linearly with increasing hardware. Applications might achieve different efficiency based on their concurrency level, intensity of resource demands, and performance level objectives [12]. Second, the effects of sharing resources on system performance are inevitable but not well-understood. The increased overhead and dynamics caused by the complex interactions between the applications, workloads and virtualisation layer introduce new challenges in system management [22]. Third, modelling of low-level resources, such as CPU cores, are not generally captured by models [16, 25] or models are not comprehensive enough to support dynamic resource allocation and consolidation [35, 43].

Many benchmarking studies suggest that each individual core performs differently across the cores of one multiprocessor [24, 32, 21]. Veal et al. [45] and Hashemian et al. [21] observe a CPU single core bottleneck and suggest methods to distribute the bottleneck to achieve better performance. However, most modelling work treats each core of a multicore processor equally by using $M/M/k$ queues [7, 5], where k represents the number of cores. To the best of our knowledge, the problem of modelling the imbalance between cores and the performance of applications in multicore virtualised environment has not been adequately addressed.

This paper presents a simple performance model that captures the virtual software interrupt interference in network-intensive web applications on multicore virtualised platforms. We first conduct some benchmark experiments of a web application running across multiple cores, and then introduce a multi-class queueing model with closed form solution to characterise aspects of the observed performance. Target metrics include utilisation, average response time and throughput for a series of workloads. The key idea behind the model is to characterise the imbalance of the utilisation across all available cores, model the processing of software interrupts, and correctly identify the system bottleneck. We validate the model against direct measurements of response time, throughput and utilisation based on a real system. We take steps to alleviate the bottleneck, which turns out to involve at a practical level the deployment of multiple virtual NICs. Thereafter, we predict the performance of the system with the same workload parameters after tuning the system configuration for improved performance.

The rest of the paper is organised as follows. Section 2 provides context and background. Section 3 presents our testbed setup and performance scaling results. Section 4 introduces our performance model and validates it. Section 5 extends our model for new hardware configurations. Section 6 surveys related work and Section 7 concludes.

2. BACKGROUND

In this section, we briefly recap multicore architectures, then explain the basic steps involved in receiving/transmitting traffic from/to the network and finally discuss the overhead introduced by virtualisation. We aim to understand the most important properties of workloads and systems in order to incorporate them in an analytical model.

Multicore & Scalability: To exploit the benefits of a multicore architecture, applications need to be parallelised [31, 33, 45]. Parallelism is mainly used by operating systems at the process level to provide seamless multitasking [14]. We assume that the following two factors are inherent to web applications which scale with the number of cores: (1) the workload of a web application typically involves multiple concurrent client requests on the server and hence, is heavily parallel; (2) they can exploit the multithreading and asynchronous request services provided by modern web servers (such as Nginx). Each request is usually processed by a separate *thread* and threads can run simultaneously on different CPUs. As a result, modern web servers can efficiently utilise multiple CPU cores. However, scalability of web servers is not in practice linear as other factors, such as sharing cache between cores, communication overhead, call-stack depth, synchronization between threads, or sequential work-flows [29, 45, 8, 24] limit the performance.

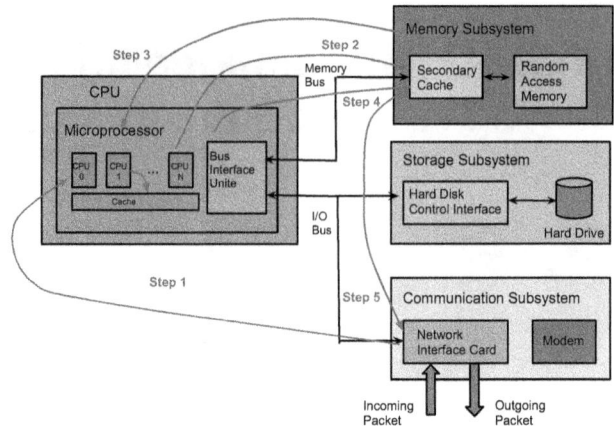

Figure 1: Context Switching Inside a Multicore Server

Linux Kernel Internals & Imbalance of Cores: Modern computer architectures are interrupt-driven. If a device, such as a network interface card (NIC) or a hard disk, requires CPU cycles, it triggers an interrupt which calls a corresponding handler function. As we look at web applications, we focus on interrupts generated by NICs. As packets from the network arrive, the NIC stores these in an internal packet queue and generates an interrupt to notify the CPU to process the packet. By default, an interrupt is handled by a single CPU (usually *CPU 0*). Figure 1 illustrates the process of passing a packet from the network to the application then sending a response back to the network (step 1 to 5). The NIC driver copies the packet to memory and generates a *hardware interrupt* to signal the kernel that a new packet is readable. A previously registered interrupt handler is called which generates a *software interrupt* to push the packet down to the appropriate protocol stack layer or application (step 2) [47]. By default, a NIC software interrupt is handled by *CPU 0 (core 0)* which induces a non-negligible load and, as processing rates increase, creates a major bottleneck for web applications (*interrupt storm*) [45].

Virtualisation & Hypervisor Overhead: Since we focus on the performance modelling of web applications running in virtualised environments, the relationship between performance cost and virtualisation overhead must be taken into account. The virtualisation overhead greatly depends on what guest workloads are doing on the host hardware [15]. With technologies like VT-x/AMD-V and nested paging, CPU-intensive guest code runs at very close to 100% native speed while I/O might take considerably longer due to virtualisation [15]. For example, Barham et al. [3] show that the CPU-intensive SPECweb99 benchmark and the I/O-intensive Open Source Database Benchmark suite (OSDB) perform differently in native Linux and XenoLinux (based on the Xen hypervisor). PostgreSQL in OSDB places considerable load on the disk resulting in many protection domain transitions which is reflected in the substantial virtualisation overhead. SPECweb99 on the other hand, does not require these transitions and hence performs 99.2% of the performance of the bare machine.

Considering the aspect of virtualisation overhead is an important factor for building accurate performance models. However, we include it into parameters in this work and will not further discuss it but rather leave this to future research.

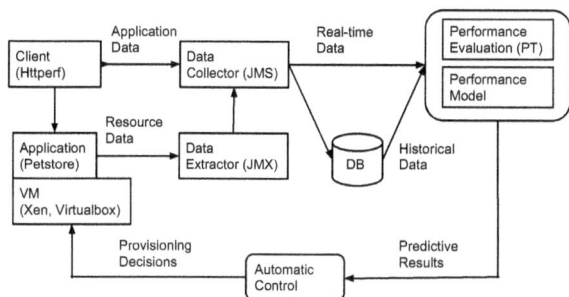

Figure 2: Testbed Architecture

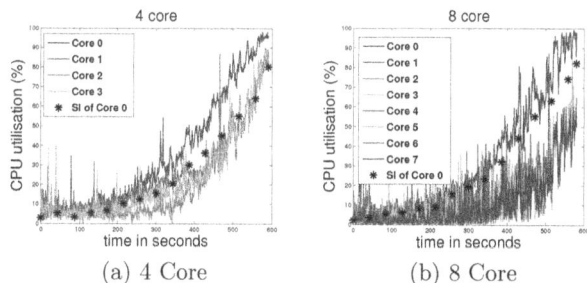

Figure 3: CPU Utilisation and Software Interrupt Generated on CPU 0 of 4 Core and 8 Core VM Running the Petstore Application on VirtualBox

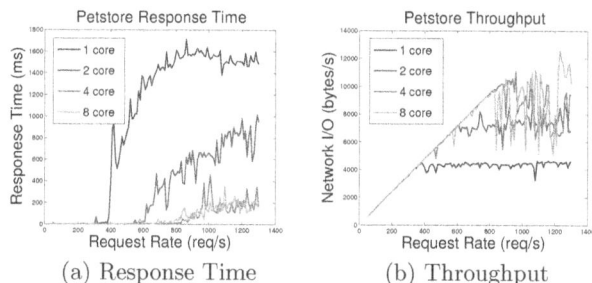

Figure 4: Response Time and Throughput of 1 to 8 Core VMs Running the Petstore Application on VirtualBox

3. BENCHMARKING

In this section, we conduct an initial benchmarking experiment to study the impact of multiple cores and software interrupt processing on a common HTTP-based web application. Requests do not involve database access and hence, no disk I/O is required during a response. Our application is the Oracle Java Petstore 2.0[1] which uses GlassFish[2] as the HTTP server. We run the Petstore application on Virtual-Box and Xen hypervisor, respectively. The Oracle Java Petstore 2.0 workload is used to expose the VM to high HTTP request volumes which cause intensive CPU activity related to processing of input and output network packets as well as HTTP requests. Autobench[3] was deployed to generate the HTTP client workload.

Testbed Infrastructure. We set up two virtualised platforms: Xen and Virtualbox, using the default configurations. The hypervisors are running on an IBM System X 3750 M4 with four Intel Xeon E5-4650 eight-core processors at 2.70GHz to support multicore VM instances comprising 1 to 8 cores. The server has a dual-port 10 Gbps Ethernet physical network interface card (pNIC), which can operate as a virtual 1 Gbps Ethernet NIC (vNIC). The physical NIC interrupt handling is distributed across the cores, providing maximum interrupt handling performance. The machine is equipped with 48 GB memory and connected to sockets with DDR3-1333MHz channels. Other resources (e.g. disk and network bandwidth) are over-provisioned.

Testbed Setup. The system used to collect the performance data of our tests consists of several components as shown in Figure 2. The *data collector* (Java Message Service) extracts a set of application statistics, e.g. response time and throughput. This is combined with the output of the *data extractor* (Java Management Extension), which provides hardware characteristics, i.e. utilisation of each core of the VM, memory bandwidth, etc. The data collector can either feed this data directly to the *performance evaluator* or store it a database for future analysis. The performance evaluator is based on the concept of Performance Trees [42, 11], which translate the application and system characteristics into parameters that can be directly used by our performance model. The performance model is then analysed and performance indices of the system are derived and compared

to actual measurements. The *automatic controller* optimises the resource configuration for specific performance targets. The system is designed for both on-line and off-line performance evaluation and resource demand estimation, which can be applied in areas such as early stage deployment and run-time management on cloud platforms. In this paper, we do not employ the *automatic controller* in our experiments.

Benchmark. Each server VM is configured with one vCPU with a number of virtual cores (from 1 core up to 8 cores for eight experiments) with 4 GB of memory and one vNIC. To mitigate the effect of physical machine thread switching and to override hypervisor scheduling, each virtual core (vCore) was pinned to an individual physical core. For each experiment, Autobench sends a fixed number of HTTP requests to the server at a specific request rate. The mean request rate incrementally increases for each experiment by 10 req/sec from 50 (e0.02)[4] to 1400 (e0.00071). Figure 3 presents the vCore utilisation for the 4 and 8 core VMs running on Virtualbox at increasing request rates for a total duration of 600s. Figure 4 shows the corresponding response time and throughput for the VM from 1, 2, 4 and 8 cores. The utilisation, response times, and throughput for the Xen hypervisor are not shown; however, they exhibit similar performance trends.

From Figure 3(a) and 3(b), we observe that the utilisation of vCore 0 reaches 90% and 98% at 500 secs (corresponding to 1200 req/sec) for 4 and 8 vCore servers respectively, while the utilisation of the other vCores are under 80% and 60% for the same setup. Figure 4(a) shows that the sys-

---

[1]http://www.oracle.com/technetwork/java/index-136650.html
[2]https://glassfish.java.net/
[3]http://www.xenoclast.org/autobench/

---

[4]e0.02 refers to an exponential distribution with a mean interarrival time of 0.02s, http://www.hpl.hp.com/research/linux/httperf/httperf-man-0.9.txt

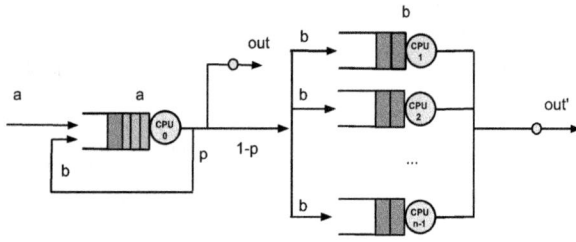

Figure 5: Modelling a Multicore Server Using A Network of Queues

tem becomes overloaded at 400 req/s for a single vCore and at 600 req/s for a dual core. The saturation points for 4 vCores (800 req/s) and 8 vCores (900 req/s) do not reflect the doubling of vCPU capacity. Figure 4 also shows that for the single and dual core cases, the improvement of system throughput asymptotically flattens with a higher request rate and finally saturates around 4000+ bytes/sec and 7000+ bytes/sec. However, the capacity of the VM servers does not increase linearly when the number of vCores changes from 4 to 8 vCores.

When investigating the imbalance of vCore utilisation and lack of scalability across vCores, we have observed that the software interrupt processing causes 90% of the *vCore 0* utilisation, as shown in Figure 3. This saturates *vCore 0* as network throughput increases and it becomes the bottleneck of the system. This bottleneck has also been observed in network-intensive web applications executing on non-virtualised multicore servers [21].

In summary, Figures 3 and 4 show that, when using the default configurations of VirtualBox, the multicore VM server exhibits poor performance *scalability* across the number of cores for network intensive workloads. Additionally, the *utilisation* of each vCore behaves differently across the cores and as vCore 0 deals with *software interrupts*, it saturates and becomes the bottleneck of the system.

4. PROPOSED MODEL

This section describes our proposed model for the performance of a web application running in a multicore virtualised environment. We first give the specification of the model and then present an approximate analytical solution followed by the description of our method to estimate the model parameters. Finally, we validate our model with the testbed from Section 3. Here we refer to vCore 0, ..., vCore $n-1$ as CPU 0, ..., CPU $n-1$.

4.1 Model Specification

Consider a web application running on an n-core VM with a single NIC (eth0), as in our set-up in Section 3.

Modelling Multiple Cores: We model the symmetric multicore processor using a network of queues where each queue (CPU 0, ..., CPU $n-1$) represents a single core (Figure 5). The interrupts generated by eth0 are handled by CPU 0. In a Linux system, one can see that CPU 0 serves an order of magnitude more interrupts than any other core in */proc/interrupts*. We assume that two classes are served under processor sharing (PS) queueing policy in CPU 0; the other queues are M/M/1-PS with single class, which reflects

the scheduling policy in most operating systems (e.g. Linux CPU time sharing policy).

When a request arrives from the network:

1. eth0 detects the associated packet and generates an interrupt, which is represented by job class a for CPU 0 (see Figure 5).

2. The interrupt is processed and the packet is forwarded to the application which reads the request. From the model perspective, a class a job turns into a class b job, which reflects that the interrupt triggers the scheduling of a request process.

3. Jobs of class b are either scheduled to CPU 0 with probability p or to one of the remaining CPUs with probability $1 - p$. Class a and b jobs are served at service rate μ_1 and μ_2, respectively.

4. After a class b job has been processed, the response is sent back to the client. Note that we naturally capture output NIC interrupts by including them into the service time of class a jobs.

In our model, the arrival of jobs is a Poisson process with arrival rate λ and job service times are exponentially distributed. The system has a maximum number of jobs that it can process as shown in Figure 4, which is also very common for computer systems. For each experiment, an arrival is dropped by the system if the total number of jobs in the system has reached a specified maximum value N.

The preemptive multitasking scheme of an operating system, such as Windows NT, Linux 2.6, Solaris 2.0 etc., utilises the interrupt mechanism, which suspends the currently executing process and invokes the kernel scheduler to reschedule the interrupted process to another core. Otherwise, when a class a job arrives, a class b job executing in CPU 0 could be blocked. However, in a multicore architecture, the blocked processes could experience a timely return to execution by a completely fair scheduler, shortest remaining time scheduler, or some other CPU load-balancing mechanism. To simplify the model, class a and class b jobs are processed separately with a processor sharing policy in CPU 0.

4.2 CPU 0

The proposed queueing model in Figure 5 abstracts the process of serving web requests on a multicore architecture. In this model, CPU 1 to CPU $n-1$ are modelled as standard M/M/1-PS queues, the arrivals to which emanate at CPU 0 as class b jobs. An M/M/1-PS queue is one of the common queue types in the literature [30]. The nontrivial part of the model, however, is CPU 0. CPU 0 processes two classes of jobs, a and b, and the number of jobs can be described as a two dimensional Markov chain $X = (i, j)$, where i is the number of class a job and j is the number of class b job. Figure 6 illustrates the state transitions corresponding to the generator matrix of its stochastic process, $\mathbf{Q}$.

One can compute the stationary distribution numerically by solving the normalised left zero eigenvector of $\mathbf{Q}$. However, as the capacity of the system, N, is a very large number in the real system, the size of $\mathbf{Q}$, is combinatorially large and hence, computing the zero eigenvector becomes infeasible. In the next section, we obtain the stationary distribution of the Markov chain.

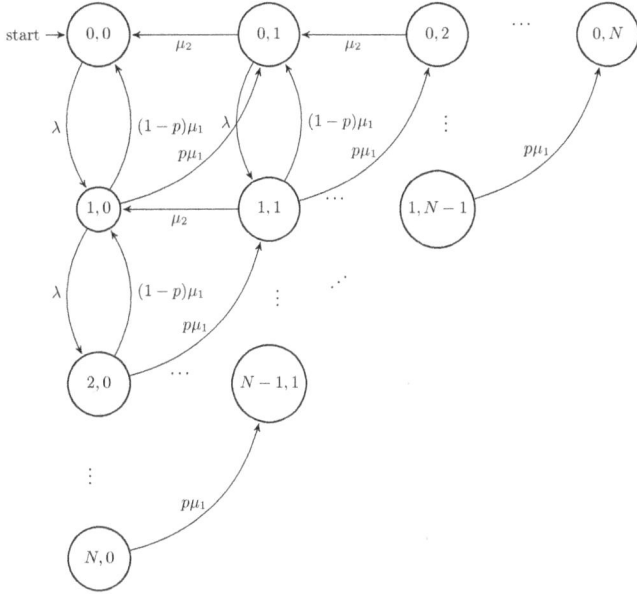

Figure 6: State Transition Diagram for CPU 0

4.2.1 Two-class Markov Chain and its Stationary Distribution of CPU 0

The model specification given in Section 4.1 and the state transition diagram of Figure 6 make the approximating assumption that the total service rate for each class (a and b) does not degrade as the population of the network increases, remaining at the constant values μ_1 and μ_2. Therefore the classes behave independently and the modelled behaviour of CPU 0 is equivalent to a tandem pair of single-class PS queues with rates μ_1 (for class a) and μ_2 (for class b) respectively. The arrival rate at the first queue is λ and at the second $p\lambda$ (since we are considering only CPU 0). This is a standard BCMP network [30] with a population constraint and so has the product-form given in equation (2)[5]. Moreover, the result is a trivial application of the Reversed Compound Agent Theorem (RCAT), see for example [19] [20]. The normalising constant can be obtained as a double sum of finite geometric series and gives the value of $\pi_{0,0}$ shown in equation (1).

We therefore have the following product-form solution:

PROPOSITION 1. *Assuming that a steady state exists, let the steady-state probability of state (i,j) in Figure 6 be denoted $\pi_{i,j}$. Then,*

$$\pi_{0,0} = \frac{(\alpha - 1)(\alpha - \beta)(\beta - 1)}{\alpha^{N+2}(\beta - 1) + \beta^{N+2}(1 - \alpha) + \alpha - \beta}, \quad (1)$$

and

$$\pi_{i,j} = \alpha^i \beta^j \pi_{0,0}, \quad (2)$$

where

$$\alpha := \frac{\lambda}{\mu_1} \quad and \quad \beta := \frac{p\lambda}{\mu_2}. \quad (3)$$

[5]We thank a referee for pointing out that the result was first derived in [41]

PROOF. By the proceeding argument, the BCMP Theorem yields,

$$\pi_{i,j} = C\pi_1(i)\pi_2(j).$$

where C is a normalising constant. The marginal probabilities are,

$$\pi_1(k) = \alpha^k \pi_1(0), \pi_2(k) = \beta^k \pi_2(0) \quad \forall k = 0, 1, \dots, N.$$

Therefore,

$$\pi_{i,j} = C\pi_1(i)\pi_2(j) = C\alpha^i\beta^j\pi_1(0)\pi_2(0) = \alpha^i\beta^j\pi_{0,0}.$$

Normalizing, we have

$$\sum_{i,j} \pi_{i,j} = 1$$

$$\sum_{i,j} \alpha^i \beta^j \pi_{0,0} = 1$$

$$\pi_{0,0} \sum_{i=0}^{N} \sum_{j=0}^{N-i} \alpha^i \beta^j = 1$$

Since

$$\sum_{i=0}^{N} \sum_{j=0}^{N-i} \alpha^i \beta^j = \frac{\alpha^{N+2}(\beta - 1) + \beta^{N+2}(1 - \alpha) + \alpha - \beta}{(\alpha - 1)(\alpha - \beta)(\beta - 1)},$$

we obtain

$$\pi_{0,0} = \frac{(\alpha - 1)(\alpha - \beta)(\beta - 1)}{\alpha^{N+2}(\beta - 1) + \beta^{N+2}(1 - \alpha) + \alpha - \beta}.$$

$\square$

4.2.2 Average Sojourn Time

Proposition 1 provides the stationary distribution of the Markov chain associated with CPU 0. With that information, we can find the average number of jobs in the system.

PROPOSITION 2. *Let the random variable k denote the total number of jobs at CPU 0. Then,*

$$E(k) = \frac{g(\alpha,\beta) - g(\beta,\alpha) + (\beta - \alpha)(2\alpha\beta - \alpha - \beta)}{[\alpha^{N+2}(\beta - 1) + \beta^{N+2}(1 - \alpha) + \alpha - \beta](\alpha - 1)(\beta - 1)}, \quad (4)$$

where $g(x,y) := x^{N+2}(y - 1)^2(xN - N - 1)$.

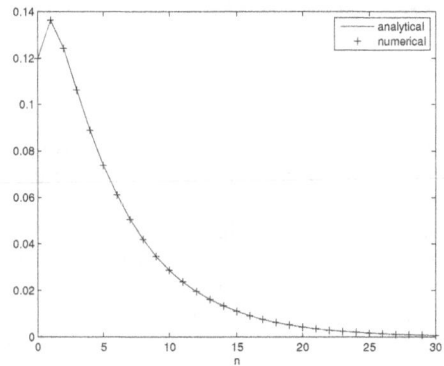

Figure 7: Comparing Numerical and Analytical Solution of E(k)

201

The proof of Proposition 2 can be found in Appendix A. Figure 7 plots the value of $E(k)$ against N.

Consider again CPU 0 with two job classes a and b. Arrivals will be blocked if the total number of jobs reaches N. The probability function of the total number of jobs at CPU 0 can be calculated as,

$$P_N = P[n_a + n_b = N] = \sum_{i,j}^{i+j=N} \pi_{i,j}$$

Using Proposition 2, a job's expected sojourn time $E(T)$ can be calculated from the long-term average effective arrival rate λ and the average number of jobs $E(k)$, using *Little's Law* for the system as follows:

$$E(T) = \frac{E(k)}{\lambda(1 - P_N)}$$

4.2.3 Average Service Time and Utilisation

PROPOSITION 3. *Let T_s be the random variable denoting the service time of a job γ entering service. The expected service time is*

$$E(T_s) = \frac{1}{\mu_1}n_a^0 + \frac{1}{\mu_1}\frac{\lambda}{\lambda + p\mu_1}(1 - n_a^0) + \frac{1}{\mu_2}\frac{p\mu_1}{\lambda + p\mu_1}(1 - n_a^0),$$
(5)

where

$$n_a^0 = \pi_{0,0}\frac{1 - \beta^{N+1}}{1 - \beta}.$$

The proof of the proposition is provided in Appendix B. With the result above, the utilisation of a single core can be derived by the *Utilisation Law*,

$$U = \lambda E(T_s)$$

4.3 Likelihood for Estimating Parameters

The stationary distribution π of the Markov process in Figure 6 with generator matrix $\mathbf{Q}$ and the expected number of jobs $E(k)$ are given in Propositions 1 and 2. There are three corresponding parameters, μ_1, μ_2, and p. We assume that the average response time for a certain request arrival rate λ_i can be estimated from real system measurements. From our previous observations, for example, when a one core system receives 100 req/sec, on average, 2.9% of the CPU utilisation are spent for processing software interrupts while for 200 req/sec, this amount increases to 7.2%. We can obtain μ_1 from utilisation law,

$$\frac{\bar{\lambda}}{\mu_1} = \bar{U}_{si}$$
(6)

where $\bar{U}_{si}$ denotes the average utilisation of software interrupts (si) processed by CPU 0 during a monitoring window of size t and $\bar{\lambda}$ is the average λ_i during t. Then the reciprocal of μ_1 is the mean service time of CPU 0 handling si. Note that by using the average utilisation for software interrupts to calculate μ_1, the service time for a class a job includes the service time for *all* software interrupts involved to successfully process the corresponding class b job (see Section 4.1). Here, we find μ_1 to be 3301 req/sec. In the single core case, p is 1. However, for multiple core cases, p can be obtained by the inverse proportion of the utilisation as a load balancing across multiple cores.

Let T_i be the average response time estimated for a certain arrival rate from the model and T_i' be the average time from the real system measurements when the arrival rate is $\lambda_i, i = 1, \ldots, m$. Since the estimated response time T' is the mean of samples, it is approximately a normally distributed random variable with mean T and variance $\frac{\sigma_T^2}{n}$ when the number of samples n is very large [6]. Hence μ_2 can be estimated by maximising the log-likelihood function,

$$\log \prod_{i=1}^m \frac{1}{\sqrt{2\pi\sigma_i^2/n_i}}\exp\left[\frac{(T_i' - T_i)^2}{2\pi\sigma_i^2/n_i}\right]$$
(7)

Maximising the log-likelihood function above is equivalent to minimising the weighted sum of squared errors:

$$\sum_{i=1}^m \frac{(T_i' - T_i)^2}{2\pi\sigma_i^2/n_i}$$
(8)

Now the problem of finding the parameters becomes an optimisation problem,

$$\mu_2 = \arg\min_{\mu_2} \sum_{i=1}^m \frac{(T_i' - T_i)^2}{2\pi\sigma_i^2/n_i}$$
(9)

The optimisation problem can be solved in different ways, such as steepest descent and truncated Newton [6]. We carried out the experiments in the single core case with λ varying from 10 req/s to 500 req/s. For each λ we sent requests from 300 to 30 000 req/s and measured the mean response time and the corresponding standard deviation.

4.4 Combined Model

In the previous section, we analysed the properties of CPU 0, which gives us a better understanding of how its performance is affected by interrupts. To build the entire model, we will combine the previous results of CPU 0 and the results of CPU 1 to CPU $n-1$ given in [30].

For K jobs arriving in the system, we expect Kp of them will stay in CPU 0 and $K(1-p)$ of them will be sent to CPU 1, ..., CPU $n-1$. Given request arrival rate λ, we approximate the arrival rate of jobs at CPU 1, ..., CPU $n-1$ as $\lambda(1-p)$. We further assume that those jobs are uniformly assigned to different cores and so for CPU i, the corresponding (class b) job arrival rate is $\lambda_i = \lambda(1-p)/(n-1)$. Given the service rate of class b jobs is μ_2, the expected number of jobs at these CPUs is $\lambda_i/(\mu_2 - \lambda_i)$, $\forall i = 1, \ldots, n-1$.

	CPU 0	CPU 1, ..., CPU n-1
Arrival Rate	λ $p\mu_1(a \to b)$	$\lambda(1-p)$
Service Rate	μ_1 (a) μ_2 (b)	μ_2
Mean Jobs	Proposition 2	$\lambda_i/(\mu_2 - \lambda_i)$

Table 1: Summary of Key Model Parameters

Table 1 gives the brief summary of key model parameters. Let k_i denote the number of jobs in the queue of CPU i; then by Little's Law, the expected sojourn time of a request in the whole system is,

$$
\begin{aligned}
E(T_{\text{sys}}) &\approx \frac{E(k_0 + k_1 + \cdots + k_{n-1})}{\lambda} \\
&= \frac{E(k_0) + E(k_1) + \cdots + E(k_{n-1})}{\lambda}.
\end{aligned}
$$

202

Values of μ_2 (req/sec)			
1 core	2 core	4 core	8 core
367	345	300	277

Table 2: Likelihood Estimation of the Mean Service Time for Class b Job

4.5 Validation

We validate our model against real system measurements of response time and throughput, focusing on benchmarks running on the VirtualBox hypervisor and using the system set-up of Section 3.

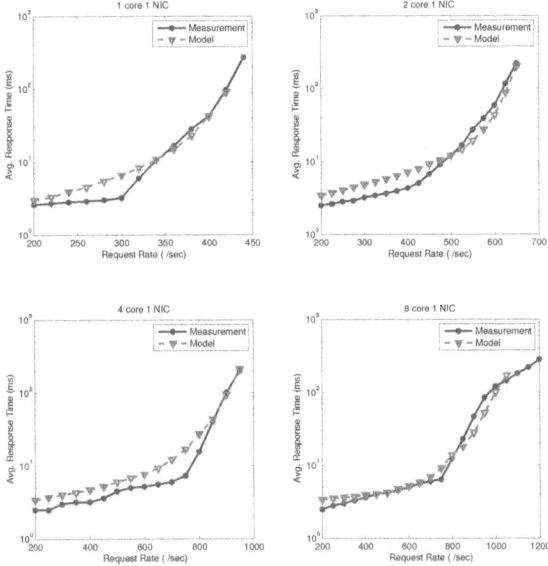

Figure 8: Response Time Validation

Prior to validation, we conducted baseline runs of the benchmark in our test-bed system. For each run, we varied the number of cores and collected information about workload and response time for the parameter estimation (see Section 4.3). The parameters we obtained for class b decrease from 1 core to 8 cores as shown in Table 2. The decreasing μ_2 captures the fact that the web server scales poorly on multiple cores because of (i) the virtualisation overhead; (ii) the inherent problem of multicore, such as context switching overhead. Figure 8 shows the validation of response time.

5. SCALABILITY AND MODEL ENHANCEMENT

In this section, we first describe a set of complementary techniques of system and hardware configurations aimed to prevent the single core bottleneck discussed in Section 3. We apply one of the techniques to increase parallelism and improve performance for multicore web applications. Second, we derive our model for performance under an improved configuration. We then validate our model under the new configurations and show that the results fit with the obtained performance improvements.

5.1 Scalability Enhancement

Multiple network interfaces can provide high network bandwidth and high availability [24, 21, 45]. Enforcing CPU affinity for interrupts and network processing has been shown to be beneficial for SMP systems [45] and the same benefits should apply to virtualised multicore systems. Combining multiple NICs and CPU affinity allows us to distribute the software interrupts for different NICs to different cores and hence mitigate load imbalance. In real systems, installing multiple network interfaces might cause space and power issues; however, in virtualised environments, this can be trivially achieved by using virtual NICs. For our enhanced configuration, we configure multiple vNICs as follows:

- Fix the number of web server threads to the number of cores and assign each web server thread to a dedicated core to avoid the context switching overhead between two or more threads [21].

- Distribute the NIC interrupts to multiple cores by assigning multiple virtual NICs, i.e. vboxnet, to the VM.

5.2 Model Enhancement

Since we model the imbalance of multicore system by distinguishing two different types of queues, we can derive the model for the new configuration by increasing the number of leading two-class queues to match the number of cores m which deal with NIC interrupts. Recall that our baseline model assumes a single core (queue) handling NIC interrupts (job a). Consider the situation when job a comes to m two-class queues (equals to m CPU 0), in which m represents the number of cores that handle NIC interrupts. Then, a class a job transfers into a class b job and either returns to the queue with probability p or proceeds to CPU m, ..., CPU $n - 1$ with probability $1 - p$.

5.3 Blind Prediction with Previous Parameters and Model Limitations

We apply the model for the enhanced configurations with the same parameters as shown in Table 2. The revalidation results are shown in Figure 9. The results show that the performance of the application improves with the new configurations, and exhibits better scalability. For example, with 4 cores and 1 NIC, the knee-bend in system performance occurs at around 800 req/sec; using 2 NICs this increases to around 1000 req/sec and for 4 NICs to around 1200 req/sec.

The summary of the error found in all validation results of Figure 8 and Figure 9 are shown in Table 3. The average relative modelling error is around 15%. This shows a tendency to decrease with an increasing number of NICs. We see a relative error of e.g. 7.9% and 7.4%, for a 4 core machine with 2 NICs and a 4 core machine with 4 NICs, respectively. Since distributing the NIC interrupts in the real system causes extra context switching overhead, the response time of relatively low intensity workloads (i.e. 200 to 600 req/sec) is round 10-20% higher than that for the default configuration.

We identify several factors that affect model accuracy:

1. The *routing probability* p: we use a simple load balancing policy as we discussed in Section 4.3, which cannot represent the Linux kernel scheduling algorithm used in our testbed, which is a completely fair scheduler. More advanced scheduling policies like O^2 [46] can also not be described with this simple model.

203

	1 NIC				2 NICs			4 NICs		Overall
Num. of Core	1	2	4	8	2	4	8	4	8	
Response Time	23.8	23.2	25.8	11.3	19.4	7.9	10.3	7.4	14.2	15.9
Throughput	14.1	12.9	13.4	16.5	14.5	11.9	15.6	10.6	16.7	14.02
Util. Core 0 to m-1	10.5	7.9	8.4	9.8	8.4	8.9	12.9	11.4	13.4	10.2
Util. Core m to N-1	-	-9.4	-14.6	-23.7	-	-10.4	- 16.7	-	-17.8	-15.4

Table 3: Relative Error between Model and Measurements (%)

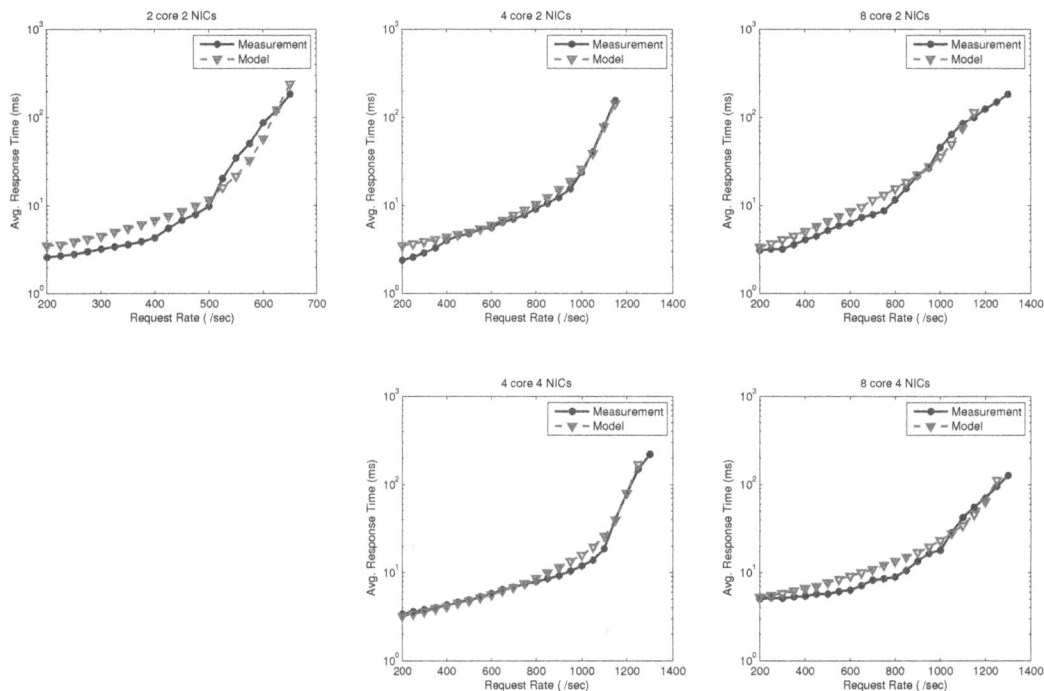

Figure 9: Revalidation of Response Time with Multiple NICs

2. *Interrupt priority*: in general, NIC interrupts (job a) have higher priority than system and user processes (job b). In the single core case, job b is blocked when a new job a arrives. However, in the multicore case, the scheduler will assign it to another core. To simplify the model, we do not consider priorities and interference between job classes a and b.

3. *Context switching overhead*: an operating system executes a context switch by loading a new context, i.e. registers, memory mappings, etc., in one CPU. Though we try to reduce the context switching overhead by assigning each web server thread statically to a distinct core, other context switches, such as register, task, and stack, need to be considered.

4. *Hypervisor overhead*: our model implicitly considers virtualisation overhead, e.g. via the decrease of service rate with increasing number of cores. However, how the overhead of processing requests at the different virtualisation layers has yet to be accounted for.

6. RELATED WORK

Multicore Benchmarking. Veal and Foong [45] identified that scaling of web applications on multicore systems requires distributing the affinity of NICs to different cores. Harji et al. [18] examined in-memory and disk I/O static web application performance on a quad-core system. Their experiments reveal that "the implementation and tuning of web servers is perhaps more important than server architecture". Hashemian et al. [21] characterised the performance of dynamic and static network intensive Web applications on a two quad-core system. The authors have shown that achieving efficient scaling behaviour entails application specific configurations to achieve high utilisation on multiple cores. In addition, the authors observed the CPU's single core bottleneck caused by the default configuration of the NIC interface. We have now identified that the NIC interrupt bottleneck is present in default virtual machine configurations. Peternier et al. [31] profile the execution of parallel multi-threaded benchmarks on multicore systems and use the collected parallel profile to predict the wall time execution of the benchmarks for a target number of cores.

Virtual Machine Performance. Cherkasova and Gardner [9] examined the performance of web applications on the Xen VM monitor on a single processor system, identifying the effect of network interrupts on physical CPU utilisation. Pu et al. [34] measured the performance of co-located web applications on virtualised clouds. Most of the work related to virtual network interfaces is concerned with optimising the packet delivery between the physical NIC and the hosted virtual machines, e.g. [4, 36]. VM migration optimisation and performance has been studied using a variety of approaches including analytical models [1, 28], regression-based models [22, 27] and benchmarking [26].

Multicore Modelling. Most queueing network models represent k-core processors as M/M/k queues. M/M/k models have also been used when modelling virtualised applications running on multicore architectures. Cerotti et al. [7] benchmark and model the performance of virtualised applications on a multicore environment using an M/M/k queue. Brosig et al. [5] model the overhead of virtualised applications using multi-server queueing Petri-nets similar to an M/M/k queue with additional scheduling mechanisms for overlapping resource usage. The authors assume that the VM-specific CPU demands and the VM-specific overhead in terms of induced CPU demand on Domain-0 are known. Brosig et al. reported accurate prediction of server utilisation; however, large errors were present for response time calculations for multiple guest VMs. Bardhan et al. [2] developed an approximate two-level single-class Queueing Network model to predict the execution time of applications on multicore systems. The model captures the memory contention caused by multiple cores and incorporates it into an application-level model.

7. CONCLUSION

This paper has presented a performance model for web applications deployed in multicore virtualised environments. The model is general enough to capture the performance of web applications deployed on multicore VMs and can account for hardware idiosyncrasies such as CPU bottlenecks and interrupt influences. We gave an approximate analytical solution and validated our model in our testbed using an open-source web application running on multicore VMs. In addition, we presented a simple approach to achieve better scalability for multicore web servers through use of virtual hardware. We also demonstrated the applicability of our model in the enhanced configurations.

In future, we will refine our model to overcome the approach limitations we discussed and extend our model to multi-granularity multiple VM instances. We also plan to investigate how the model fits multiple applications (e.g. I/O-intensive) deployed on heterogeneous VM instances. Another direction is to develop a multi-objective optimisation policy to support more comprehensive resource management.

Acknowledgements

We would like to thank Lukas Rupprecht and the anonymous reviewers for insightful comments. We greatly appreciated the help with test-bed setup from Duncan White, Lloyd Kamara, Thomas Joseph and other CSG team members. Thanks also to Eva Kalyvianaki and members of AESOP group. Xi Chen is supported by an Imperial Faculty of Engineering International Scholarship.

8. REFERENCES

[1] A. Aldhalaan and D. A. Menascé. Analytic performance modeling and optimization of live VM migration. *Proc. EPEW*, pages 28–42, 2013.

[2] S. Bardhan and D. A. Menascé. Analytic performance models of applications in multi-core computer. *Proc. MASCOTS*, 2013.

[3] P. Barham, B. Dragovic, K. Fraser, S. Hand, T. Harris, A. Ho, R. Neugebauer, I. Pratt, and A. Warfield. Xen and the art of virtualization categories and subject descriptors. *Proc. SOSP*, 2003.

[4] M. Bourguiba, K. Haddadou, and G. Pujolle. Packet aggregation based network I/O virtualization for cloud computing. *Proc. Computer Communications*, pages 309–319, Feb. 2012.

[5] F. Brosig, F. Gorsler, N. Huber, and S. Kounev. Evaluating approaches for performance prediction in virtualized environments. *Proc. MASCOTS*, 2013.

[6] J. Cao, M. Andersson, C. Nyberg, and M. Kihl. Web server performance modeling using an M/G/1/K*PS queue. *Proc. Telecommunications*, 2:1501–1506, 2003.

[7] D. Cerotti, M. Gribaudo, P. Piazzolla, and G. Serazzi. End-to-End performance of multi-core systems in cloud environments. *Proc. EPEW*, pages 221–235, 2013.

[8] L. Y. Chen, G. Serazzi, D. Ansaloni, E. Smirni, and W. Binder. What to expect when you are consolidating: effective prediction models of application performance on multicores. *Proc. Cluster Computing*, May 2013.

[9] L. Cherkasova and R. Gardner. Measuring CPU overhead for I/O processing in the Xen virtual machine monitor. *Proc. USENIX ATEC*, pages 387–390, 2005.

[10] J. D. Deng and M. K. Purvis. Multi-core application performance optimization using a constrained tandem queueing model. *Journal of Network and Computer Applications*, 34(6):1990–1996, Nov. 2011.

[11] N. J. Dingle, W. J. Knottenbelt, and T. Suto. PIPE2: A tool for the performance evaluation of generalised stochastic Petri nets. *Proc. ACM SIGMETRICS*, 2009.

[12] H. Esmaeilzadeh, E. Blem, R. St. Amant, K. Sankaralingam, and D. Burger. Dark silicon and the end of multicore scaling. *Proc. ISCA*, pages 365–376, 2011.

[13] M. Ferdman, A. Adileh, and O. Kocberber. Clearing the clouds: a study of emerging scale-out workloads on modern hardware. *Proc. ASPLOS 2012*, pages 1–11, 2012.

[14] P. Gepner and M. Kowalik. Multi-Core processors: new way to achieve high system performance. *Proc. PARELEC*, pages 9–13, 2006.

[15] D. Gupta, L. Cherkasova, R. Gardner, and A. Vahdat. Enforcing performance isolation across virtual machines in Xen. *Proc. Middleware*, 2006.

[16] V. Gupta, R. Nathuji, and K. Schwan. An analysis of power reduction in datacenters using heterogeneous chip multiprocessors. *Proc. ACM SIGMETRICS*, pages 87–91, 2011.

[17] R. Han, L. Guo, M. M. Ghanem, and Y. Guo. Lightweight resource scaling for cloud applications. *Proc. CCGrid*, pages 644–651, May 2012.

[18] A. S. Harji, P. A. Buhr, and T. Brecht. Comparing high-performance multi-core web-server architectures. *Proc. SYSTOR*, pages 1–12, 2012.

[19] P. G. Harrison. Turning back time in Markovian process algebra. *Journal of Theoretical Computer Science*, 290:1947–1986, Jan. 2003.

[20] P. G. Harrison, C. M. Lladó, and R. Puigjaner. A unified approach to modelling the performance of concurrent systems. *Journal of Simulation Modelling Practice and Theory*, 17:1445–1456, Oct. 2009.

[21] R. Hashemian, D. Krishnamurthy, M. Arlitt, and N. Carlsson. Improving the scalability of a multi-core web server. *Proc. ACM/SPEC ICPE*, pages 161–172, 2013.

[22] N. Huber, M. V. Quast, M. Hauck, and S. Kounev. Evaluating and modeling virtualization performance overhead for cloud environments. *Journal of CLOSER*, pages 563–573, 2011.

[23] W. Iqbal, M. Dailey, and D. Carrera. SLA-driven adaptive resource management for web applications on a heterogeneous compute cloud. *Proc. CloudCom*, pages 243–253, 2009.

[24] H. C. Jang and H. W. Jin. MiAMI: Multi-core aware processor affinity for TCP/IP over multiple network interfaces. *Proc. HPI*, pages 73–82, Aug. 2009.

[25] N. Khanyile, J. Tapamo, and E. Dube. An analytic model for predicting the performance of distributed applications on multicore clusters. *Proc. IAENG*, 2012.

[26] S. Kikuchi and Y. Matsumoto. Performance modeling of concurrent live migration operations in cloud computing systems using PRISM probabilistic model checker. *Proc. Cloud Computing*, pages 49–56, 2011.

[27] H. Liu, H. Jin, C. Z. Xu, and X. Liao. Performance and energy modeling for live migration of virtual machines. *Proc. HPDC*, pages 249–264, Dec. 2011.

[28] D. A. Menascé. Virtualization: concept, application, and peformance modeling. *Proc. CMG conference*, 2005.

[29] Q. Noorshams, D. Bruhn, S. Kounev, and R. Reussner. Predictive performance modeling of virtualized storage systems using optimized statistical regression techniques categories and subject descriptors. *Proc. ACM/SPEC ICPE*, pages 283–294, 2013.

[30] Peter G. Harrison, Nareth M. Patel. *Performance modeling of communication networks and computer architecture*. Addison-Wesley, 1992.

[31] A. Peternier, W. Binder, A. Yokokawa, and L. Chen. Parallelism profiling and wall-time prediction for multi-threaded applications. *Proc. ACM/SPEC ICPE*, pages 211–216, 2013.

[32] R. Prasad, M. Jain, and C. Dovrolis. Effects of interrupt coalescence on network measurements. *Passive and active network measurement*, pages 247–256, 2004.

[33] G. Prinslow and R. Jain. Overview of performance measurement and analytical modeling techniques for multi-core processors, 2011. http://www.cse.wustl.edu/~jain/cse567-11/ftp/multcore/.

[34] X. Pu, L. Liu, Y. Mei, S. Sivathanu, Y. Koh, C. Pu, and Y. Cao. Who is your neighbor: Net I/O performance interference in virtualized clouds. *Proc. Services Computing*, pages 314–329, 2012.

[35] A. Rai, R. Bhagwan, and S. Guha. Generalized resource allocation for the cloud. *Proc. ACM SoCC*, pages 1–12, 2012.

[36] K. K. Ram, J. R. Santos, Y. Turner, A. L. Cox, and S. Rixner. Achieving 10 Gb/s using safe and transparent network interface virtualization. *Proc. ACM SIGPLAN/SIGOPS VEE*, 2009.

[37] C. Reiss, A. Tumanov, and G. Ganger. Heterogeneity and dynamicity of clouds at scale: Google trace analysis. *Proc. SoCC*, 2012.

[38] G. Shanmuganathan, A. Gulati, and P. Varman. Defragmenting the cloud using demand-based resource allocation categories and subject descriptors. *Proc. ACM SIGMETRICS*, pages 67–80, 2013.

[39] A. Sharifi and S. Srikantaiah. Mete: meeting end-to-end qos in multicores through system-wide resource management. *Proc. ACM SIGMETRICS*, pages 13–24, 2011.

[40] U. Sharma, P. Shenoy, and D. F. Towsley. Provisioning multi-tier cloud applications using statistical bounds on sojourn time. *Proc. ICAC*, pages 43–52, 2012.

[41] S.S.Lam. Queuing Networks with Population Size Contraints. *IBM Journal of Research and Development*, pages pp 370–378, July, 1977.

[42] T. Suto, J. Bradley, and W. Knottenbelt. Performance trees: A new approach to quantitative performance specification. *Proc. MASCOTS*, pages 303–313, 2006.

[43] B. M. Tudor and Y. M. Teo. On understanding the energy consumption of ARM-based multicore servers. *Proc. ACM SIGMETRICS*, pages 267–278, 2013.

[44] A. Tumanov and J. Cipar. alsched: algebraic scheduling of mixed workloads in heterogeneous clouds. *Proc. SoCC*, 2012.

[45] B. Veal and A. Foong. Performance scalability of a multi-core web server. *Proc. ANCS*, pages 57–66, 2007.

[46] D. Wentzlaff, K. Modzelewski, and J. Miller. An operating system for multicore and clouds : mechanisms and implementation categories and subject descriptors. *Proc. SoCC*, 2010.

[47] W. Wu, M. Crawford, and M. Bowden. The performance analysis of Linux networking - packet receiving. *Proc. International Journal of Computer Communications*, 2006.

[48] F. Wuhib, R. Stadler, and H. Lindgren. Dynamic resource allocation with management objectives implementation for an OpenStack cloud. *Proc. CNSM*, pages 309–315, 2012.

APPENDIX

A. PROOF OF PROPOSITION 2

PROOF. By definition, the expected number of jobs is

$$E(k) = \sum_{i,j}(i+j)\pi_{i,j}.$$

Using results from Proposition 1, we have

$$
\begin{aligned}
E(k) &= \sum_{i,j}(i+j)\pi_{i,j}, \\
&= \pi_{0,0}\sum_{i,j}(i+j)\alpha^i\beta^j, \\
&= \pi_{0,0}\sum_{i=0}^{N}\sum_{j=0}^{N-i}(i+j)\alpha^i\beta^j, \\
&= \pi_{0,0}\frac{g(\alpha,\beta)-g(\beta,\alpha)+(\beta-\alpha)(2\alpha\beta-\alpha-\beta)}{(\alpha-1)^2(\alpha-\beta)(\beta-1)^2}, \\
&= \frac{g(\alpha,\beta)-g(\beta,\alpha)+(\beta-\alpha)(2\alpha\beta-\alpha-\beta)}{[\alpha^{N+2}(\beta-1)+\beta^{N+2}(1-\alpha)+\alpha-\beta](\alpha-1)(\beta-1)},
\end{aligned}
$$

where $g(x,y) := x^{N+2}(y-1)^2(xN-N-1)$. $\square$

B. PROOF OF PROPOSITION 3

PROOF. Let n_a be the current number of class a job in the system, we have

$$
\begin{aligned}
E(T_s) &= E(T_s|\gamma \text{ is job a})P(\gamma \text{ is job a}) \\
&\quad + E(T_s|\gamma \text{ is job b})P(\gamma \text{ is job b}) \\
&= \frac{1}{\mu_1}P(\gamma \text{ is job a}) + \frac{1}{\mu_2}P(\gamma \text{ is job b}) \\
&= \frac{1}{\mu_1}P(\gamma \text{ is job a}|n_a=0)P(n_a=0) \\
&\quad + \frac{1}{\mu_1}P(\gamma \text{ is job a}|n_a>0)P(n_a>0) \\
&\quad + \frac{1}{\mu_2}P(\gamma \text{ is job b}|n_a=0)P(n_a=0) \\
&\quad + \frac{1}{\mu_2}P(\gamma \text{ is job b}|n_a>0)P(n_a>0).
\end{aligned}
$$

Since

$$P(\gamma \text{ is job b}|n_a=0)=0, \qquad P(\gamma \text{ is job a}|n_a=0)=1,$$

we have

$$
\begin{aligned}
E(T_s) &= \frac{1}{\mu_1}P(n_a=0) \\
&\quad + \frac{1}{\mu_1}P(\gamma \text{ is job a}|n_a>0)P(n_a>0) \\
&\quad + \frac{1}{\mu_2}P(\gamma \text{ is job b}|n_a>0)P(n_a>0). \\
&= \frac{1}{\mu_1}P(n_a=0) + \frac{1}{\mu_1}\frac{\lambda}{\lambda+p\mu_1}P(n_a>0) \\
&\quad + \frac{1}{\mu_2}\frac{p\mu_1}{\lambda+p\mu_1}P(n_a>0) \\
&= \frac{1}{\mu_1}P(n_a=0) + \frac{1}{\mu_1}\frac{\lambda}{\lambda+p\mu_1}(1-P(n_a=0)) \\
&\quad + \frac{1}{\mu_2}\frac{p\mu_1}{\lambda+p\mu_1}(1-P(n_a=0)).
\end{aligned}
$$

Notice that from previous results,

$$
\begin{aligned}
P(n_a=0) &= \sum_{j=0}^{N}\pi_{0,j} \\
&= \pi_{0,0}\sum_{j=0}^{N}\alpha^0\beta^j \\
&= \pi_{0,0}\frac{1-\beta^{N+1}}{1-\beta}.
\end{aligned}
$$

Therefore,

$$E(T_s) = \frac{1}{\mu_1}n_a^0 + \frac{1}{\mu_1}\frac{\lambda}{\lambda+p\mu_1}(1-n_a^0) + \frac{1}{\mu_2}\frac{p\mu_1}{\lambda+p\mu_1}(1-n_a^0),$$

where

$$n_a^0 = \pi_{0,0}\frac{1-\beta^{N+1}}{1-\beta}. \qquad \square$$

An Evaluation of ZooKeeper
for High Availability in System S

Cuong M. Pham,
Zbigniew Kalbarczyk,
Ravishankar K. Iyer
University of Illinois at Urbana-Champaign
{pham9, kalbarcz, rkiyer}@illinois.edu

Victor Dogaru
IBM Software Group
Oakland, CA, USA
vdogaru@us.ibm.com

Rohit Wagle,
Chitra Venkatramani
IBM T.J Watson Research Center,
Yorktown Heights, NY, USA
{rwagle, chitrav}@us.ibm.com

ABSTRACT

ZooKeeper provides scalable, highly available coordination services for distributed applications. In this paper, we evaluate the use of ZooKeeper in a distributed stream computing system called System S to provide a resilient name service, dynamic configuration management, and system state management. The evaluation shed light on the advantages of using ZooKeeper in these contexts as well as its limitations. We also describe design changes we made to handle named objects in System S to overcome the limitations. We present detailed experimental results, which we believe will be beneficial to the community.

Categories and Subject Descriptors

D.2.8 [**Software Engineering**]: Metrics – *performance measures*

D.2.4 [**Software Engineering**]: Software/Program Verification – *reliability*

General Terms

Reliability, Performance

Keywords

Distribute systems, high availability, stream processing, distributed coordination.

1. INTRODUCTION

ZooKeeper (ZK) [1] is a scalable, highly available, and reliable coordination system for distributed applications. The primitives exposed by ZK can be leveraged for providing dynamic configuration management, distributed synchronization, group and naming services in large-scale distributed systems. This paper evaluates the use of ZK as the coordination backbone for System S (commercialized as InfoSphere Streams [4][8], a distributed streaming middleware system. We present our findings from a detailed experimental study to understand the application of ZK in System S, both to replace some of the existing services and to provide new capabilities. We also detail the design changes we made to System S to better utilize ZK capabilities. We expect the findings will be useful to distributed systems designers looking to leverage ZooKeeper as the coordination backbone.

System S applications are developed to analyze high-volume, continuous data from a variety of sources. The programming model supports application specification in the form of a dataflow graph, with analytics components or operators interconnected by streams, which carry tuples of a fixed schema. The System S runtime hosts applications from multiple users, deploys the compiled operators (called Processing Elements or PEs) across a distributed system, manages their streaming interconnections, monitors and manages their resource usage and lifecycle. Some requirements of the system that make ZK a good candidate as a coordination backbone include:

- **High Availability**: System S applications are long running, and process data continuously. High availability is a crucial requirement both from an infrastructure and an application point of view. If any of the components fail, the system has to detect it and take appropriate recovery actions [3].

- **High Performance**: System S is a high-performance system supporting a dynamic application execution environment. An application can change its topology during runtime based on analysis results, and new applications that connect to existing ones can be launched and removed dynamically. Supporting these features requires a high-performance control and coordination backbone.

- **Scalability**: System S can support a very large set of applications and is scalable over hundreds of nodes. This requires a scalable coordination service to manage a large number of named entities, and a large number of clients.

- **Management Simplicity**: Currently System S leverages different services to provide system recovery (DB2), system coordination and configuration (file-system). Simplifying this to a single system makes management in terms of deployment and troubleshooting easier.

The ZK architecture satisfies these requirements for System S and is a good candidate due to its scalability, resiliency, in-memory implementation, event-based interface, and a wait-free data-object interface. In this paper, we evaluate ZK for the set of functions outlined below:

- Resilient name server – providing a highly available name service, which stores information about all named entities in the system, such as PEs, and stream end-points, supporting a dynamic execution environment.

- Dynamic System Configuration – providing a configuration service that supports dynamic updates and notifications to configuration parameters.

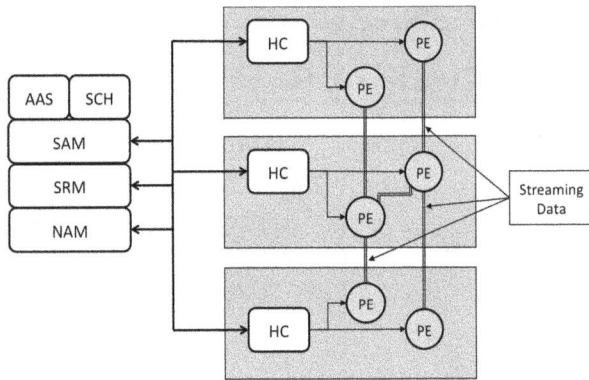

Figure 1: System S Runtime Architecture

- System state management and update notifications for the runtime state of system entities such as PEs, streams, and applications.

In this study, we designed and carried out a set of performance measurements for ZK in conditions which simulate specific System S application workloads. We report our findings on the advantages and shortcomings of using ZK in the System S context. We also report on changes to the System S runtime design to better leverage ZK capabilities. Specifically, we run experiments, which align our performance measurements with existing benchmarks, and compare existing System S performance to an alternative implementation using ZK for each of the functions outlined above.

Based on our experiments, we find that:

- ZK is a better alternative to the current name services in System S, which is either based on a shared file system or a non-recoverable service. ZK does not impact the system performance, while providing crash tolerance and eliminating the dependency on a shared file system across the System S cluster.
- ZK is a more easily manageable and higher performance alternative to the current system recovery feature in System S based on DB2 [3]. Although using DB2 is more reliable, configuring DB2 HADR is onerous. In the course of applying ZK to the above two scenarios, we had to make appropriate design choices to get the required functionality while maintaining high performance. One of the limitations in ZK is the size of each zNode. We had to ensure that System S state objects were appropriately sized and organized to get the best performance from ZK. We also discovered that the ZK C++ client significantly outperforms the Java client. Since most System S infrastructure components are written in C++, we could clearly leverage this benefit. In this paper, we quantify this difference for the awareness of application writers, when they design high-performance System S applications.

The rest of the paper is organized as follows. Section 2 provides background information and presents related work. Section 3 presents our experimentation methodology and setup. Sections 4, 5, and 6 present the results from the evaluation of ZK for the three functions outlined before. Section 7 concludes the paper.

2. BACKGROUND AND RELATED WORK

2.1 ZooKeeper Overview

ZK is a service, which provides wait-free coordination for large-scale systems. ZK can be used as the kernel for building more complex coordination services at clients.

ZK uses client-server architecture. The server side, called *ensemble*, consists of one *leader* and several *followers* to provide a replicated service. It requires that a majority of servers has not crashed, to provide continuous service. Crashed servers are able to recover and rejoin the ensemble. If the leader server crashes, the rest will elect a new leader. Only the leader can perform update operations; it then propagates the incremental state changes to the followers using the Zab protocol [2]. Each server keeps a copy of the data in its memory, but saves the transaction logs and snapshots of the data in persistent storage for recovery.

Application clients implement their logic on top of ZK client libraries, which handle network connection and provide APIs for invoking ZK primitive operations. Currently ZK supports C/C++, Java and Python bindings for clients. A ZK client can establish a session with a ZK service, and sessions enable clients to move transparently among the servers. Sessions have timeouts to keep track of the liveness of the client and server.

The ZK *data model* provides its clients an abstraction of a hierarchical name space, like a virtual file system. The data node is called *zNode*. ZK *consistency model* guarantees that write operations are linearizable, but read operations are not. All write operations have to go through the leader, which is then responsible for propagating the updates to other followers. To boost the performance, read requests are handled locally by the server that the client is connected to. As a result, a read might return a stale value.

The ZK *consistency model* guarantees that write operations are linearizable, but read operations are not. All write operations have to go through the leader, which is then responsible for propagating the updates to other followers. To boost the performance, ZooKeeper has local reads. That means read requests are handled locally by the server that the client is connected to. As a result, a read might return a stale value.

ZK implements a useful feature for coordination, called *watches*. The idea is to allow the client to monitor, or watch for modifications on zNodes. Clients set watches on zNodes they want to monitor, and then they will be notified asynchronously when watched zNodes are modified.

2.2 ZooKeeper in Other Systems

Many distributed applications have adopted ZK as an integral part of their systems, such as Distributed HBase [5]. Distributed HBase [5], which can consist of thousands of nodes, uses ZK to manage cluster status. For instance, HBase clients can query ZK to find the cluster to connect to. In addition, ZK is used to detect and trigger repairing process for node failures. HBase also intends to extend the usage of ZK for other purposes, such as monitoring table state and schema changes.

Several other real-time streaming analytics systems, such as Stormy [6] and Twitter Storm [7], have also integrated ZK in their implementations. While Stormy [6] employs ZK to provide consistent leader election, Twitter Storm uses ZK to implement Reliable Runtime with auto restart, and Dynamic Configuration changes.

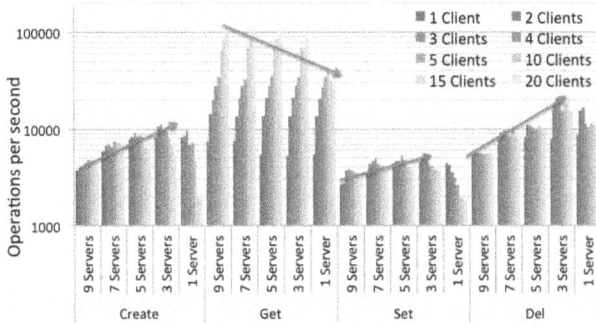

Figure 2: ZK basic operations throughput

This paper describes in details the intended use cases of ZK in System S, as well as presents our in-depth performance and availability analysis of these use cases.

2.3 System S Overview

System S [4][8] comprises of a middleware runtime system and an application development framework, geared towards supporting the development of large-scale, scalable and fault-tolerant stream processing applications. An application is essentially a flowgraph in which operators carry out portions of the data processing analytics by consuming and producing new streams, leading to the extraction of relevant results [9]. Once an application is compiled, a set of runnable processing elements is created. A processing element (PE) is a runtime container for portions of the flowgraph, i.e., a collection of operators and their stream interconnections. PEs belonging to an application can be logically grouped together to form jobs. A System S user can then start up the application by submitting it to the middleware runtime system, thereby creating one or more jobs. The jobs can then be monitored, moved and canceled using system management tooling.

The System S middleware runtime architecture (Figure 1) separates the logical system view from the physical system view. The runtime contains two distinct sets of components – the centralized components are responsible for accepting job management and monitoring requests, deploying and tracking streaming applications on the runtime environment and the distributed components, which are responsible for managing application pieces deployed on individual hosts. Specifically, the Streams Application Manager (SAM) is the centralized gatekeeper for logical system information related to the applications running on System S. SAM pro- vides access to this information to the administration and visualization tooling. SAM also functions as the system en- try point for job management tasks. The Streams Resource Manager (SRM) is the centralized gatekeeper for physical system information related to the software and hardware components that make up a System S instance. SRM is the middleware bootstrapper, carrying out the system initialization upon an administrator request. In the steady-state, SRM is responsible for collecting and aggregating system-wide metrics, including the health of hosts that are part of a System S instance and the health of the System S componentry itself, as well as relevant performance metrics necessary for scheduling and system administration.

The runtime system also includes additional components, which we briefly describe here. The Scheduler (SCH) is the component responsible for computing placement decisions for applications to be deployed on the runtime system [10][11]. The Name Service

(NAM) is the centralized component responsible for storing service references enabling inter-component communication by associating symbolic names with resource endpoints that can be registered, unregistered and remotely queried. The Authentication and Authorization Service (AAS) is the centralized component that provides user authentication as well as inter-component cross authentication, vetting interactions between the components.

The runtime system has two distributed management components. The Host Controller (HC) is the component running on every application host and is responsible for carrying out all local job management tasks including starting, stopping and monitoring processing elements on behalf of requests made by SAM. The HC is also responsible for acting as the distributed monitoring probe on behalf of SRM ensuring that the distributed pieces of applications remain healthy. Finally, a System S runtime instance typically includes several instances of the Processing Element Container (PEC), which hosts the application user code embedded in a processing element. To ensure physical separation, there is one PEC per processing element running on the system.

Some System S components (SAM, AAS, SRM and NAM) maintain an internal state in order to carry out their operations. Each component's internal state reflects a partial view of the overall System S instance state to which the component belongs. This internal state must be durable if the component is to recover from failure.

Stateful centralized services currently save their state in DB2 to support recovery from failure. Distributed services recover state either by querying the centralized servers or the environment.

3. EXPERIMENTAL SETUP

All experiments are conducted on a selected group of RedHat 6 hosts. Each host contains one Intel Xeon 3.00 GHz CPU (4 cores) and 8GB RAM. All the hosts are interconnected via 1 Gigabit Ethernet with approximate ping time is steady at 0.095-millisecond round-trip. ZK server hosts also have local hard-disks where the ZK snapshots and transaction logs are stored.

3.1 Primitive Operations Throughput

In order to establish the baseline of ZK's performance on our experimental cluster, we present the following experiment, which examines the throughput of ZK primitive operations under varying workloads and varying the number of servers in a quorum. The number of clients in each test ranges from 1 to 20. Each client issues 100,000 asynchronous requests and then waits for all of them to finish at the server side to report the throughput independently from other clients. The throughput of a server ensemble is the aggregated throughput of all the clients running concurrently. The result is shown in Figure 2.

As expected, the throughputs of Write request, including Create, Set, and Delete, increase as the number of servers in a quorum decreases, except in the case of standalone server. This behavior is expected as ZK is using primary-backup model [2]: only the leader can make updates, then broadcast atomically to other following servers; the more following servers, the greater the time to complete the broadcast.

As Read requests are distributed evenly to all the available servers, where they are processed locally, the throughput increases as the number of server increases. However, when the servers are under-utilized, adding more servers does not improve the throughput. As shown in Figure 2, the throughputs of ensembles, containing from 1 to 9 servers are the same with 1 to 4 clients, as even the standalone server is underutilization. Read throughput is one order of magnitude faster than the Write throughput.

In summary, adding more servers into the quorum, on one hand, increases Read throughput and number of tolerable server crashes. But on the other hand, it consumes more compute resources and decreases the Write throughput.

4. ZOOKEEPER AS A NAME SERVICE SERVER

4.1 Use Case Description

The Name Service (NAM) is responsible for presenting an interface where System S components and applications can register and locate remote resource endpoints. The space in NAM is organized in a directory-based hierarchy, where an object can be placed anywhere in the directory structure.

Currently System S offers two implementations for NAM: Distributed NAM and File System NAM. Distributed NAM is a scalable daemon suitable for large deployments. The service is not backed by durable storage; therefore it is a single point of failure in the system. The File System NAM implementation is suitable for simple deployments as well as development and testing environments. This implementation relies on an NFS shared file system to store and propagate entries, which is intrinsically recoverable.

Although NAM does not significantly impact the performance of the stream applications, it plays a critical role in the availability of the streaming system. According to our performance profiling, even during then job submission time when NAM experiences a peak of activity, the applications spend only about 1% of their execution time invoking NAM. However, System S cannot tolerate NAM unavailability, as this service is in the critical path of inter-component communication. During job submission, SAM contacts the HCs in order to start PE instances on a subset of the instance hosts. During initialization, each PE is responsible for establishing data connections with the other PEs in order to send data streams, which results in a large number of NAM requests. Specifically, a PE (i) registers its data input ports with NAM; (ii) queries NAM for the host and port of the PE it has to connect to.

To test this use case, we developed a ZK-based NAM implementation and integrated it with System S. System S's components are linked against the ZK client library to make requests to the ZK NAM. Current NAM operations translate into zNode Create, Get, and Delete operations.

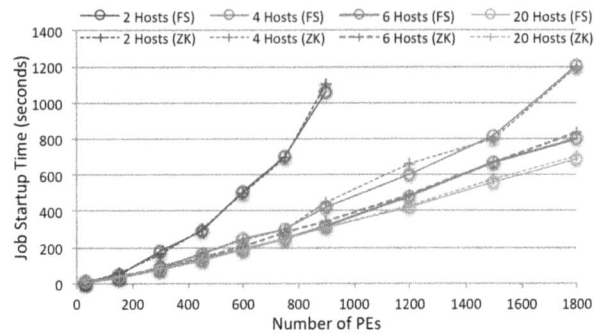

Figure 3: Job startup time File System vs. ZK NAM

We compared the startup time of a Streams job using ZK NAM under normal working conditions, versus during ZK leader crashes. We also compared ZK NAM and file-based NAM under normal conditions but not during server failures, since the underlying NFS implementation was not configured for high availability.

4.2 Failure Free Execution

This experiment examined the performance of ZK NAM in normal working conditions. Particularly, we compared the *startup time* of stream jobs using ZK and File System NAM. We also inspected closer at the Read and Write request arrival rates at NAM during stream job startup.

We used the Long Chains performance benchmark to generate workload for the experiment. Each Long Chains job consists of one input operator and one output operator joined using a set of relay operators linked in chains. The input operator sends tuples to a given number of operator chains. Each chain has a configurable length. All the chains are joined at the output operator. The number of chains is also customizable for each job.

Figure 3 shows the comparable startup times of ZK NAM and File System NAM under varying number of PEs and varying computing resources (number of hosts running the job). This result confirms the expectation mentioned above, as NAM should not significantly impact the performance of the application.

Figure 4a shows the Write and Read request arrival rate at NAM during job startup time. At peak, NAM receives >350 Read requests and >50 Write requests per second. These rates are low compared to ZK throughput (Section 3.1), which shows that the load posed by job submission is under the capacity of our ZK

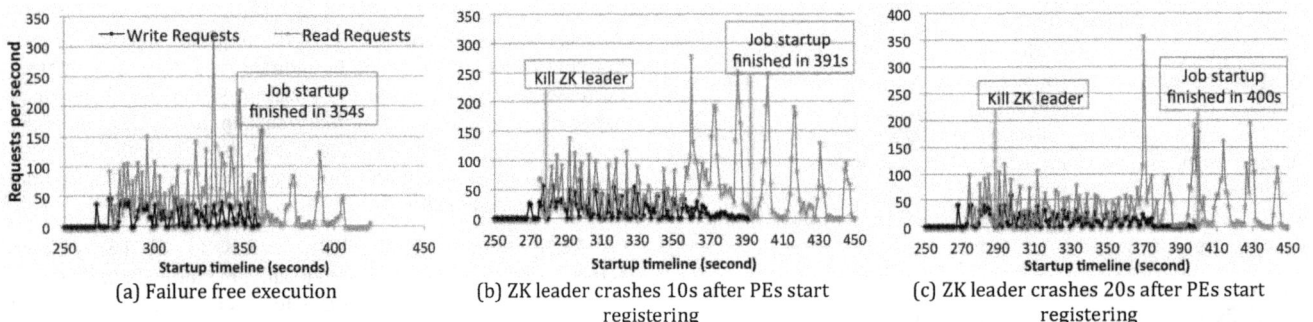

(a) Failure free execution

(b) ZK leader crashes 10s after PEs start registering

(c) ZK leader crashes 20s after PEs start registering

Figure 4: Request arrival rate at NS during job submission (Long Chains benchmark with 900 PEs running on 4 hosts)

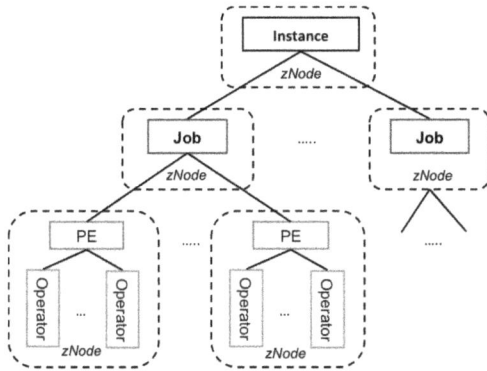

Figure 5: Persisting the model of a System S job to ZooKeeper zNodes

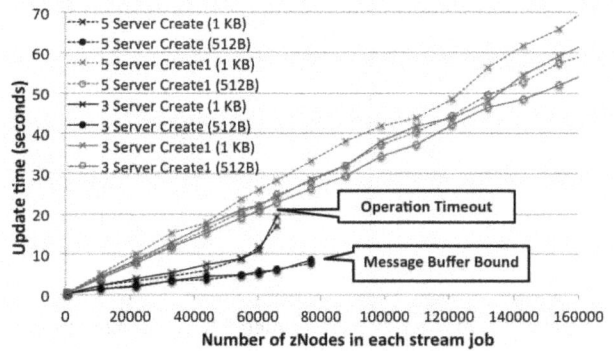

Figure 6: Multi-op performance
Create (black lines): one Multi-Op per job; Create1 (blue lines): multiple Multi-Op per job. Experimented with two sets of three and five ZK servers. zNode size is 512B or 1KB in each experiment.

installation. One ZK server ensemble can accommodate multiple job submissions at the same time, and still has available bandwidth for other tasks as well.

Figure 4a also shows that Read requests arrive at NAM about three times faster than Write requests. This is a good ratio for ZK. The number of Write requests depends on the number of PEs, as each PE needs to register its input ports once. The number of Read requests depends on the topology of the PEs: how many neighbors each PEs needs to query. This ratio is aligned with Long Chains topology. In general, this ratio tends to be greater, which makes it a good workload pattern for ZK.

While delivering similar performance, ZK can tolerate server failures and reduce stress to the file system, which is often the IO bottleneck to many distributed system. The next section examines NAM's behavior under ZK server crashes.

4.3 ZooKeeper Server Failure Execution

Figure 4b and 3c demonstrate that NAM can sustain ZK Server crashes. A ZK leader crash impacts a streaming job start time by increasing the total duration of the start operation.

Two possible causes of the additional delay are: (i) increasing workload for the rest of the servers; and (ii) execution stalled during session migrations from failed server to other servers. The first cause does not happen in this case. Because adding additional requests, that other servers have to handle for the failed server, does not exceed each server's capacity. That rules out the possibility that increasing workload on each active server causes increasing the running time. The second cause is what really happens in this case. In order to confirm this argument, we experimented with different server crash duration, or Mean-Time-To-Repair (MTTR), and different crash points.

When varying the MTTR of the server failure, we did not observe any changes in the startup time. For example, if the crashed server is restarted after 60 seconds, while the job is still starting-up, the startup time is the similar to the startup time when the crashed server is not restarted. This experiment also confirms the observation in section 3.1: once ZK servers are underutilized, adding one ZK server to the ensemble does not impact the application performance.

However, the crash point in time of the server does affect the performance. As showed in Figure 4c, where the crash point was

moved further 10 seconds back in comparison with Figure 4b, we see a slight increase in the startup time. The further away we are from the startup time, the more PEs have established connections with NAM. Therefore, if a server crashes, there are more ZK clients which have to migrate their sessions to the other servers. That causes a longer delay for name registering and querying.

These two experiments again confirm the cause of the increasing running time is the session migration due to server crashes.

5. ZOOKEEPER AS A RECOVERY DATABASE

5.1 Use Case Description

A System S instance runs one or more streaming applications logically managed as jobs [3]. An application is essentially a graph in which the vertices are the data flows and the nodes are operators running the Streams application code. A PE is a runtime container, which can host one or more operators. Operators and PEs have ports, which are connected to create data streams. These entities are structured in a hierarchical model, which for the purpose of our experiments is mapped to a hierarchy of zNodes, as illustrated in Figure 5.

In the System S architecture, SAM has two responsibilities:

- *Instance Management*: accepting job management requests for deploying streaming applications and updating the associated instance state.

- *Instance State Access*: providing access to logical system information related to the applications running on System S (the instance model) to administration and visualization clients.

SAM processes job submission requests in stages, which generate updates to the System S instance model. The current System S implementation uses two building blocks, which together provide system-wide fault tolerance: a reliable communication infrastructure (CORBA), and a relational database (IBM DB2). Instance model updates and messages to remote components within each stage are persisted within a single transaction.

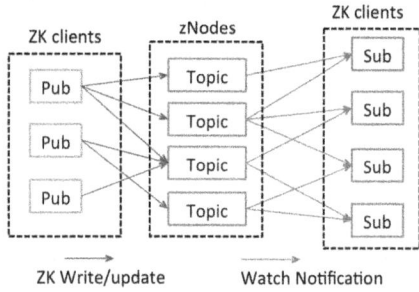

Figure 7: Publisher-subscriber model for Dynamic System Configuration

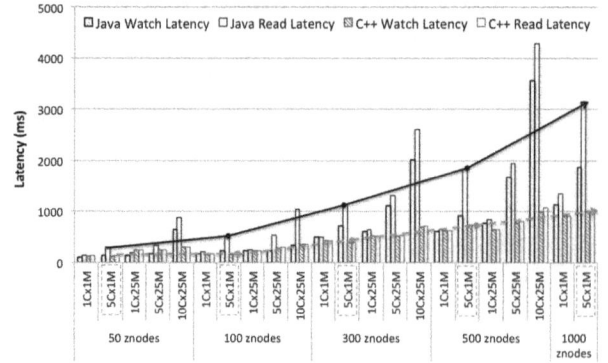

Figure 8: Watch & Read latency

C: number of subscriber clients per machine. M: number of machines running the subscriber. The black (for Java clients) and red (for C++ clients) arrows show the increasing trend of latencies when increasing the number of zNode each client monitors

With ZK, a set of related state updates can be executed using a ZK multi-operation (multi-op), which allows a batch of create, delete, update or version-check operations to succeed or fail together.

To help evaluate multi-op performance when using ZK, we want to measure the maximum zNode multi-op rate achievable for various node numbers.

5.2 Single Multi-op for One Stream Job

Multi-ops are submitted to ZK as one single request. Even though the request contains a list of operations, ZK applies the same *message size boundary* and *operation timeout* as for a single primitive operation request, which sets a limit for the number of operations packed in each multi-op.

In order to increase the number of operations batched in one multi-op, we configured ZK server to accept a message size up to 45MB, as well as extend the operation timeout to 30 seconds.

The black lines in **Figure 6** show that the multi-op execution time depends on both the number of batched operations packed into one message and the data size of each operation. The time taken for the multi-ops, which creates multiple 1KB zNodes per request, starts growing quickly after reaching approximately 50,000 zNodes per request due to CPU bound at the server. We start encountering operation timeouts on reaching 66,000 zNodes per request. When operating with a 512B sized nodes, the number of zNodes created by each Multi-Op is limited by the message buffer size.

5.3 Multiple Multi-ops For One Streams Job

To ensure the scalability, a ZK-based implementation would have to use a combination of the following techniques:

- Structure instance model changes such that properties, which do not change during the life of a job, are grouped into a small number of "constant" zNodes. This technique simplifies the zNode management (for example, "constant" zNodes can be created in a separate multi-op).

- Split job submissions into several stages, which are atomically executed. In this case, the responsibility of restoring the system to the state prior to the job submission in case of a failure will partially fall onto the client.

The blue lines in **Figure 6** illustrate the execution time where the execution of a job submission is split into several multi-ops. We believe that the extra overhead of the multi-op logic causes longer overall update times for the same number of nodes (about three times longer than in the extreme case where each multi-op updates a single node). In a real-life implementation, we expect that combining multiple operations in the same multi-op can shorten

the overall update time. Further, where possible, by combining asynchronous execution of stage N with preparation of update operations for stage N+1, total execution time can be reduced.

6. ZOOKEEPER AS A PUBLISH-SUBSCRIBE MIDDLEWARE FOR DYNAMIC SYSTEM CONFIGURATION

6.1 Use Case Description

In this use case, we evaluate ZK as a mechanism for Dynamic System Configuration. System S contains tools, which help users inspect the state of an instance and retrieve PE-based and operator-based data flows for the set of applications running on that instance. The tools can depict the runtime environment using a topological visualization perspective with overlaid performance metrics. In order to provide a fresh view of the system, these tools run the following query types: (i) Retrieving instance topology and state; and (ii) Monitoring instance performance.

The tools periodically query SAM to retrieve the system state and topology and refresh their stream graph view. In an implementation based on ZK, instead of periodically polling SAM, clients would set watches on nodes of interest and let ZK send notifications when nodes are updated.

To simulate this usage pattern, we implemented a simple publish-subscribe system using ZK watches as illustrated in Figure 7. ZK servers act as the publish-subscribe middleware, where each topic is represented by one zNode, while the Subscribers and Publishers are ZK clients. The subscriber sets watches on the zNodes (the topics) that they wish to monitor. Meanwhile the publishers update the topics' content by writing to the corresponding zNodes. Upon each update, ZK servers send out notifications to the subscribers that have set watches on the updated zNode. Upon receiving a notification, each subscriber sends a Read request to the ZK servers to query the content of the zNode, and then resets the watch on that zNode.

The semantics is slightly different from a regular publish-subscribe system, where the middleware sends the updated content to the subscribers upon each notification. ZK only sends notifications telling the subscribers that there is a recent change in the watched zNode, and then the subscribers are responsible for retrieving the updated content. In addition, the subs have to re-set the watch if they still want to monitor that zNode.

6.2 Failure Free Execution

It is of importance to know how much time it takes for the watch notifications and the updated data to reach all the subscribers under normal execution conditions.

In this experiment, we setup one publisher that updates N zNodes at the same time. There are M subscribers evenly distributed on P number of hosts. Each subscriber sets watches on all N zNodes. We measured:

- *The watch latency*: the time from a publisher starts updating all N zNodes until all the watch notifications arrive at all the M subscribers.

- *The read latency*: the time from a publisher starting to update all N zNodes until all the data (after subscribers issue read requests) arrive at all the M subscribers.

Since each subscriber performs a considerable amount of processing in this use case, we examined the performance of both C++ and Java implementations of the subscriber. The results of these experiments are shown in Figure 8.

C++ subscribers outperform the Java ones, and the gaps become more significant when increasing either the number of subscribers running on each machine or the number of zNodes monitored by each subscriber. When each machine has only one subscriber, and each subscriber monitors less than 1000 zNodes, the watch and read latencies of C++ and Java subscribers are comparable. However, as clearly shown by the trend lines in Figure 8, the watch and, especially, read latencies of Java subscribers increase faster than for C++. The same trend can be observed when keeping the number of zNodes constant, but increasing the number of subscribers running on each machine. With five subscribers on each machine and up to 1000 zNodes monitored by each client, read latency of the Java implementation is from 2 to 3 times slower than that of the C++ implementation.

Figure 9b shows the average CPU utilization of Java and C++ subscribers across 25 machines; each machine has 30 subscribers; each subscriber monitors 1000 zNodes. The C++ lines are shorter because the C++ subscribers finished receiving the update faster than the Java ones. The CPU utilization peaks of ZK servers (the dashed lines) are similar when serving C++ and Java subscribers. However, while 30 C++ subscribers utilize at most 22% of the CPU resource, 30 Java subscribers consume the entire CPU resource of the machine. Java subscribers are the scalability bottleneck of the ZK based publisher-subscriber system.

It is also worth to note that each subscriber (in both C++ and Java implementations) runs as a single-threaded user process. Thus each Java subscriber requires a Java Virtual Machine (JVM). It could be more efficient to implement each subscriber as a thread, so that its footprint would be smaller. But we did not explore that proposal, because our design requires relatively isolation and independence between subscribers.

Figure 9a-b further visualize the latency differences between C++ and Java subscribers in the same setup. As we can see the watch notifications start arriving about 2 seconds after the update for both C++ and Java subscribers. However, as C++ subscribers are able to accommodate more requests at the same time, they finish faster than the Java subscribers. The performance of C++ subscribers is stable, as they all finished after 4-9 seconds. On the

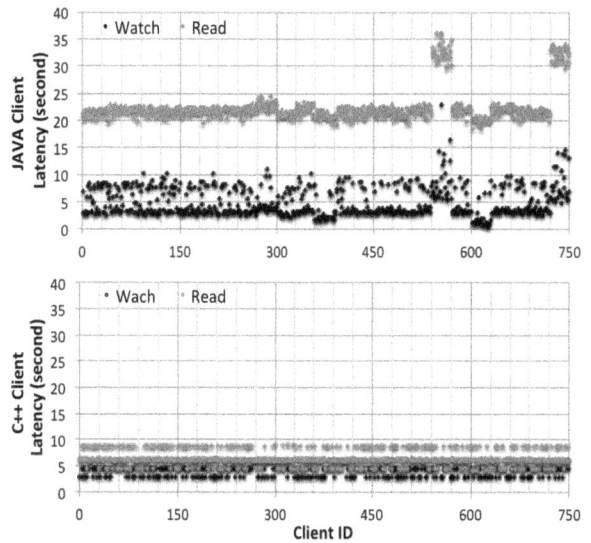

(a) Detailed latencies on each client. The black dots and the red dots show the watch arrival time and read data completion time, respectively. Each machine hosts 30 clients (therefore each grid column represents the clients of one machine)

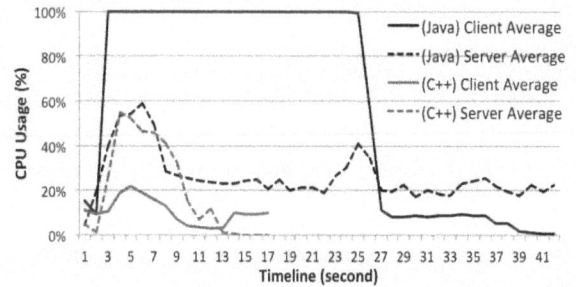

(b) Average CPU utilizations across 25 machines

Figure 9: Java vs. C++ clients (1000 watches/client)

other hand, there is a wide gap (~10 seconds) between watch arrival time and read completion in Java subscribers. It is also noticeable that Java clients are relatively unstable due to the fact that they are exhausting the resources of the machines. Therefore the performance of Java clients is more sensitive to the noise in the system (e.g. created by other system background services).

We did not compare Java and C++ clients in the other two use cases because these use cases mostly exercise the servers, therefore we anticipated that the performance of the clients would not significantly impact the performance of the overall service. On the other hand, since this particular use case involves the execution of the clients most heavily, we decided to examine the differences between Java and C++ clients.

6.3 ZooKeeper Failure Execution

In this experiment, we quantified the impact of ZK server crashes on the availability of our system. We used C++ clients in this experiment to achieve the highest server utilization.

In order to reduce the performance and network overhead, watches are managed locally in each server. The caveat of this

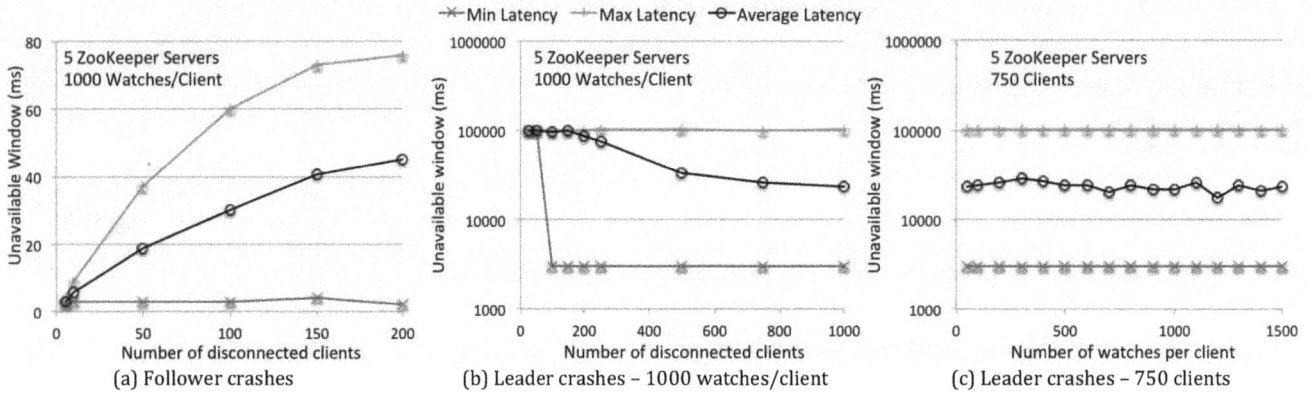

Figure 10: Unavailable window after (a) Follower crashes and (b, c) Leader crashes

design is that the other servers are not aware of the watches that the crashed server was managing. Therefore, not only do the clients have to reconnect to the other servers, they have to resubmit all the active watches to the newly connected server. From when the server crashes to when the watches are resubmitted successfully, the clients will lose all the watch notifications that occur during that period. We call this period *watch unavailable window*, as depicted in Figure 11.

6.3.1 Zookeeper follower crashes

Figure 10a illustrates the watch unavailable window of the clients when a following ZK server crashes. In this experiment, the server ensemble consists of 5 servers; and each client monitors 1000 watches. Because the clients are evenly distributed to 5 servers, the number of disconnected clients due to one, follower crashes is one fifth of the total number of clients.

The *min latency* and *max latency* are the read latencies of the first and the last clients, respectively, that receive all the updated data. The chart shows that the min latency is constant (3 milliseconds), and the max latency increases gradually as the number of disconnected clients increases. This latency is negligible for many applications. For example interactive Stream Console users would not be able to notice this latency of update.

6.3.2 Zookeeper leader crashes

Figure 10b-c illustrate the watch unavailable window of the clients when a ZK leader crashes. This window ranges from 3 to 100 seconds. This is a considerable impact on the availability of the service. The reason for this long unavailable window is: ZK leader crashes force the rest of the servers to re-elect a new leader. During this re-election time, all clients are disconnected, thus no

request is severed. After the new leader is elected, all the servers start accepting connections. That also means there is a burst of watch resubmission requests initiated from all the clients.

7. CONCLUSION

This paper describes three intended use cases of ZooKeeper in System S: Resilient Name Service, Dynamic System Configuration using publish-subscribe model, and Recovery Database. Our in-depth analysis has shown that ZooKeeper is a viable coordination backbone, which will potentially improve the performance, reliability and availability of the next generation of System S Infrastructure.

ACKNOWLEDGMENTS

We would like to thank Michael Spicer of the IBM Software Group for giving considerable direction and comments throughout our experiments. We would like to thank the IBM Research team member, Richard King, for his effort in explaining current System S performance tests. We would like to thank Shu-Ping Chang and Wesley Most for their efforts in maintaining the research cluster in IBM Hawthorne, NY and servicing our requests.

REFERENCES

[1] Hunt, Patrick, Mahadev Konar, Flavio P. Junqueira, and Benjamin Reed. "ZooKeeper: Wait-free coordination for Internet-scale systems." In *USENIX ATC*, vol. 10. 2010.

[2] Junqueira, Flavio P., Benjamin C. Reed, and Marco Serafini. "Zab: High-performance broadcast for primary-backup systems." In *Dependable Systems & Networks (DSN), 2011 IEEE/IFIP 41st International Conference on*, pp. 245-256. IEEE, 2011.

[3] Wagle, Rohit, Henrique Andrade, Kirsten Hildrum, Chitra Venkatramani, and Michael Spicer. "Distributed middleware reliability and fault tolerance support in system S." In *Proceedings of the 5th ACM international conference on Distributed event-based system*, pp. 335-346. ACM, 2011.

[4] IBM InfoSphere Streams: http://www-01.ibm.com/software/data/infosphere/streams/

[5] Apache HBase: http://hbase.apache.org/

[6] Loesing, Simon, Martin Hentschel, Tim Kraska, and Donald Kossmann. "Stormy: an elastic and highly available

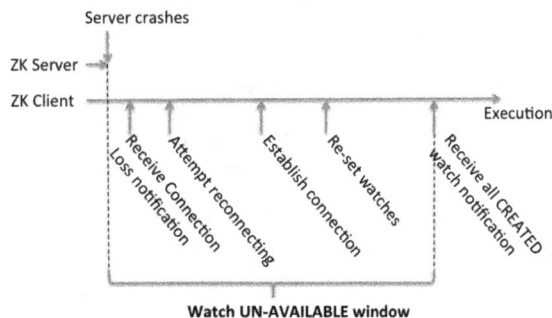

Figure 11: ZooKeeper watch un-available window

streaming service in the cloud." In*Proceedings of the 2012 Joint EDBT/ICDT Workshops*, pp. 55-60. ACM, 2012.

[7] Marz, N., "A Storm is coming" http://engineering.twitter.com/2011/08/storm-is-coming-more-details-and-plans.html, August 2011

[8] Amini, Lisa, Henrique Andrade, Ranjita Bhagwan, Frank Eskesen, Richard King, Philippe Selo, Yoonho Park, and Chitra Venkatramani. "SPC: A distributed, scalable platform for data mining." In Proceedings of the 4th international workshop on Data mining standards, services and platforms, pp. 27-37. ACM, 2006.

[9] Wu, Kun-Lung, Kirsten W. Hildrum, Wei Fan, Philip S. Yu, Charu C. Aggarwal, David A. George, Buğra Gedik et al.

"Challenges and experience in prototyping a multi-modal stream analytic and monitoring application on System S." InProceedings of the 33rd international conference on Very large data bases, pp. 1185-1196. VLDB Endowment, 2007.

[10] Wolf, Joel, Nikhil Bansal, Kirsten Hildrum, Sujay Parekh, Deepak Rajan, Rohit Wagle, Kun-Lung Wu, and Lisa Fleischer. "SODA: An optimizing scheduler for large-scale stream-based distributed computer systems." In Middleware 2008, pp. 306-325. Springer Berlin Heidelberg, 2008.

[11] Wolf, Joel, Nikhil Bansal, Kirsten Hildrum, Sujay Parekh, Deepak Rajan, Rohit Wagle, and Kun-Lung Wu. "Job admission and resource allocation in distributed streaming systems." In *Job Scheduling Strategies for Parallel Processing*, pp. 169-189. Springer Berlin Heidelberg, 2009.

Scalable Hybrid Stream and Hadoop Network Analysis System

Vernon K. C. Bumgardner
Department of Computer Science
University of Kentucky
Lexington, Kentucky, USA
cody@uky.edu

Victor W. Marek
Department of Computer Science
University of Kentucky
Lexington, Kentucky, USA
marek@cs.uky.edu

ABSTRACT

Collections of network traces have long been used in network traffic analysis. Flow analysis can be used in network anomaly discovery, intrusion detection and more generally, discovery of actionable events on the network. The data collected during processing may be also used for prediction and avoidance of traffic congestion, network capacity planning, and the development of software-defined networking rules. As network flow rates increase and new network technologies are introduced on existing hardware platforms, many organizations find themselves either technically or financially unable to generate, collect, and/or analyze network flow data. The continued rapid growth of network trace data, requires new methods of scalable data collection and analysis. We report on our deployment of a system designed and implemented at the University of Kentucky that supports analysis of network traffic across the enterprise. Our system addresses problems of scale in existing systems, by using distributed computing methodologies, and is based on a combination of stream and batch processing techniques. In addition to collection, stream processing using Storm is utilized to enrich the data stream with ephemeral environment data. Enriched stream-data is then used for event detection and near real-time flow analysis by an in-line complex event processor. Batch processing is performed by the Hadoop MapReduce framework, from data stored in HBase BigTable storage. In benchmarks on our 10 node cluster, using actual network data, we were able to stream process over 315k flows/sec. In batch analysis were we able to process over 2.6M flows/sec with a storage compression ratio of 6.7:1.

Categories and Subject Descriptors

C.2.3 [**Network Operations**]: Network Management, Network Monitoring; C.2.4 [**Distributed Systems**]: Distributed applications

Keywords

NetFlow, SDN, Stream Processing, Hadoop, Complex Event Processing

1. INTRODUCTION

The University of Kentucky, a large public university in Lexington, KY has extensive IT operations, serving to over 30,000 students (both undergraduate and graduate students), and over 16,000 faculty and staff. Both the instruction of students, research of the faculty and significant administrative functions of the university must be supported. Significant network operations have to be supported, administered and supervised to provide 24/7 smooth operation of the university. An additional burden on the IT is created by the Medical Campus, a number of research hospitals and clinics that provide one of the main facilities for the Eastern part of the Commonwealth of Kentucky.

Since a significant number of students resides in the university housing, the university must provide uninterrupted service 24/7, with the only periods of decreasing demand during parts of vacation period (although additional sessions are still meeting), and inter-session breaks. On any weekday one expects of up to 17,000 separate networks (most of them small) within the large Campus community. The number of wireless access points on Campus exceeds 5000.

With the rapid growth of student personal computing equipment (laptops, tablets, and intelligent phones), networking operations are under constant demand (varying over time with significant peaks and valleys). The equipment is used often during the instruction, creating an additional demand. Faculty support is also time-of-the-day dependent, concentrating primarily over the working hours.

For that reason the IT operations have to maintain an adequate and up-to-date picture of the demand and, in a bigger detail, the information about the traffic patterns on the campus network. The amount of traffic is significant; We estimate it at 282GB/sec (of the order 1PB/hour) and the storage capabilities and processing power required for off-line processing do not allow to store the entire traffic even for limited period of time. In particular only limited forms of an audit of the traffic are possible. Moreover, the data collected (flows) does not provide the information *ex post* to react to the events occurring within the network.

Instead, we report on the distributed processing and analysis of the network traffic. Such analysis is done in *real-time*, using the distributed computation within MapReduce/Hadoop paradigm. The flows collected during a specific period of time are analyzed and the results used for assignment of resources to the networks that need them. Additionally, some auditing capabilities that are, for all practical reasons, also *real-time* become available to react to events that may interfere with normal IT operations.

By collecting and analyzing the data the university is able to abstract from specific short-time events and create a more complete picture of the data processing on campus and the associated network traffic. Having such data allows to predict the future trends and thus needs of the network needs that are required by the university community.

The main part of this paper, Section 2.1, describes the procedure and technical means applied in our research. The problem of collecting the data and the obstacles that appear in the process are described in Section 2.1.1. The main software tool used in this phase of the generation collection, and processing is *Fprobe* [8]. The collection of flows is described in Section 2.1.2. Custom code has been written to receive flows generated by Fprobe and submit flow bundles to an AMQP-compatible queue. These operations are executed on the host, with the flow generation, collection and message serving on the same physical machine.

The stream processing included in our experiments is described in Section 2.2. A variation on MapReduce suitable for stream processing, Storm [24] is used to process flows. The workflow of the stream processing is described as a spout/bolt process with the specific steps used in the process described in some detail. Specifically, the AMPQ Spout translates the AMPQ queue data into a format that is used by Storm Bolts. This stream is then processed by the Combiner Bolt, which merges multiple queues into a single stream. The Resolver Bolt consumes the merged stream and injects state information into the records. A Complex Event Processing Bolt using ESPER [5], provides discovery of security incidents and the traffic information. Additional bolts allow for reporting and storing the data in HBase.

Time-related data, in particular time series is stored in HBase and due to the nature of the flow information (ip-addresses, ports and router information) is stored in compressed form. Availability of MapReduce framework (Hadoop) allows for parallel processing of information. We report the experimental results found in the process and indicate how experimental data found during the processing allows us to get the useful and practically usable information about the flow.

Section 3 describes our perspective on the results of the paper and possibilities of further research.

2. TRAFFIC COLLECTION AND ANALYSIS

There will be a projected [19] 18-fold growth in mobile network traffic from 2011-2016, and by 2017 there will be a predicted [12] five network devices per person. Hardware devices equipped with ASICs will be capable of generating line-rate flow exports, even on very high throughput links. At the time of this writing, no single appliance exist that can collect hundreds of thousands of flows per second. Commercial distributed collectors, claim to collect millions of flows per second. These claims are based on the aggregate processing of the distributed collectors, which does not elevate the limitations of a single flow exporter to a single collection device. Methods of collection and analysis are needed that allow for both distributed processing and central visibility.

Table 1: Network Devices

Device	Count
Core	6
Distribution	44
Access	1176
Wireless Controllers	47
Wireless Access Points (AP)	5442
Virtual Switchs	42

2.1 Flow Generation and Collection

Simply generating NetFlows from high traffic links, is in itself, a highly computational task [6]. With the introduction of advance network technologies, such as Multi-protocol Label Switching (MPLS) [17], often embedded hardware does not have the ability to generate discrete flows and sampling methods are used. In our environment, the network topology is based on a hierarchical network design model [15]. In this model, the Access layer operates on the OSI [29] Layer 2 (Data Link) and so NetFlow generation is not possible on these devices. Both Core and Distribution layer devices typically have the ability to generate NetFlows, however in our environment due to the presence and computational overhead of MPLS, NetFlow generation on these routers is not vendor-supported.

While we were not able to generate NetFlows from our network hardware, we were able to generate flows in our virtual environments. NetFlows for all network traffic on our VMware vSphere [27] virtual machine farm, including intra-node communication, is exported by the vSphere virtual distributed switch.

2.1.1 NetFlow Generation from Monitor Ports

NetFlow generation was not possible on our network hardware, so we distributed software-based probes at the Core layer. The probes ingest aggregates of distribution links from the Core routers, effectively monitoring all traffic passing from distribution to distribution. This probe point also allows for the observation of all traffic between cores and on the network Edge. Due to link aggregation the overall potential monitor capacity exceeds the monitoring link, so dropped packets will occur if this limit is exceeded. Additional probes can be added to prevent packet loss due to link aggregation.

The probe boxes run an instance of Fprobe [8] for each monitored network interface. In Fprobe we are able to specify the Link layer header size, so MPLS header information is ignored and a NetFlow is generated from the correct IP diagram. The monitored data is used to generate NetFlows which are directed toward a collector.

2.1.2 NetFlow Collection

NetFlow collection is largely dependent on the host networking stack and how quickly flows can be removed from the UDP buffer. In Linux, the UDP maximum receive buffer size is set as a kernel option. The default buffer size is far too small for high rate flow collection, so on our collectors we increased the receive buffer to 16MB. There are many NetFlow collectors and libraries available in the common domain, unfortunately most collectors have been developed to record flows to either a relational database or a flat file. The available libraries proved to be complete and accurate, but were either too slow, or the program language made in-application augmentation difficult. To solve those problems we wrote our own NetFlow version 5 and 9 collectors. These collectors run on the probe nodes and stream a pertinent subset of NetFlow information to a Advanced Message Queuing Protocol (AMPQ) [26] queues. Every Fprobe instance has a related collector and every collector has a set of AMPQ queues. There is an AMPQ queue for the data stream and a queue for log information. NetFlows are sequenced by the flow generator, so if a missed flow is detected, a warning message is placed in the log queue specific to that stream. The AMPQ server is hosted on the same node as the collector. We run the flow generator, collector, and AMPQ server all on the same host, however all of these functions can be distributed. This model keeps the data collection fully distributed and allows for horizontal and vertical scaling of probes based on load.

2.2 Complex Event (Stream) Processing

In Section 2.1.1 we described a distributed method of collecting NetFlows, but there is an even larger computational problem in analyzing that distributed aggregation of data. In our campus environment, we average from 5k to 25k flows per second. At that rate we process and record over a billion flows per day. Traditionally, single threaded applications analyzed collections of flow logs. Using traditional methods flow analysis could not possibly keep up with flow generation. Recently, researchers [14, 22] have started using Hadoop [10] to process these massive logs, however this method is still batch in nature. In addition to simply processing flow logs, there are additional benefits to processing streams of flows as they are generated. The obvious benefit of stream processing is the ability to react in near real-time to observed network events. Perhaps not so obvious, is the benefit of injecting state (machine name, network, subnet, etc) information in the flow logs, even if report generation will ultimately be a batch process.

Analysis of NetFlow data can be involved, among other things, for security applications [18, 31, 4, 20], including anomaly and intrusion detection. In addition, performance [25, 13] and planning information can be obtained from this analysis. With the introduction of Software Defined Networking (SDN) [16], we are now able control the network in near real-time. As we analyze streams of flows we can now preempt and react to actionable events as they occur. If a security anomaly is detected, a copy of the anomalous flow can be directed to a payload analyzer for deep packet inspection. Similarly, congestion can be predicted and detected through flow stream analysis. SDN controllers can be reconfigured to avoid and correct performance problems.

To process our aggregate of flows generated from our distributed probes, we use Storm, an complex event processor and distributed computation framework. Storm applications create topologies of interfaces to ingest and transform tuple streams. Similar to MapReduce [3], Storm distributes and processes tuples of information on multiple nodes and processes. However, unlike MapReduce, Storm will process tuples until the job is manually terminated. The primary topology components of Storm are Spouts and Bolts. Spouts, as the name suggest, are used to ingest data streams and emit tuples consumable by the application topology. On the other hand, Bolts read tuples from either Spouts or other Bolts, and also typically emit a tuple stream. Normally, tu-

Table 2: AMPQ Spout Tuple

Element Name	Description
timestamp	Time of flow creation
srcIp	Source IP address
srcPort	Source Port
dstIp	Destination IP
dstPort	Destination Port
byteCount	Sum of bytes in flow
proto	IP protocol
first_t	Router uptime at flow start
last_t	Router update at flow end
collector	Probe Queue Name

ple transformations, operations, and external data drains occur in Bolts.

2.2.1 AMPQ Spout

We have developed spouts that subscribe to AMPQ queues on the probe nodes. The AMPQ service, which is provided by RabbitMQ [21], ensures an interoperable, flow-controlled, message passing service with guaranteed delivery. The spout, unpackages bundles of NetFlows generated by the probes and creates a discrete tuple for each flow. Along with building the Storm tuple, the spout also injects a element identifying the originating probe and related coverage area. In effect, AMPQ Spout produces a stream of database records; the attribute names are in the Column 1 of Table 2, AMPQ Spout Tuple, the meaning of these attributes is provided by Column 2.

2.2.2 Combiner Bolt

The combiner bolts accept tuples emitted by the *AMPQ Spouts*. The first three elements of the tuple defined in Table 2 are combined in the new element *srcIp-dstIp-TS* and the source elements are removed. The *srcIp-dstIp-TS* element will be used later as a tuple key. The modified tuple stream with the new flow key is then emitted by the combiner bolt. The purpose of this bolt is to take the output of the probe-specific spouts, combine them in a common output, and assign a key value to the emitted tuple. Output from this bolt is typically consumed by the *Resolver Bolt*.

2.2.3 Resolver Bolt

The resolve bolt is one of the most important components in the flow processing system. This bolt reads tuples from the *Combiner Bolt* and injects known state (internal networks) information into the tuple. At the time of this writing flow state information includes: internal or external network, host subnet router, router interface, and host subnet VLAN for both the source and destination addresses in the flow. These elements are concatenated and injected in the tuple stream under the element names *srcInfo* and *dstInfo*.

In order to trace source and destination network information we must first have a list of subnets with related state information. The next step is to calculate for each subnet on you list to check if source or destination address exist in that subnet. Subnet matching can be calculated in $O(n)$ time. One needs to realize, however, we have over 17k subnets on our campus, so near real-time processing was challenging. As stated earlier, our flow rate averages from 5k to 25k flows per second, so at that rate we must process a flow on

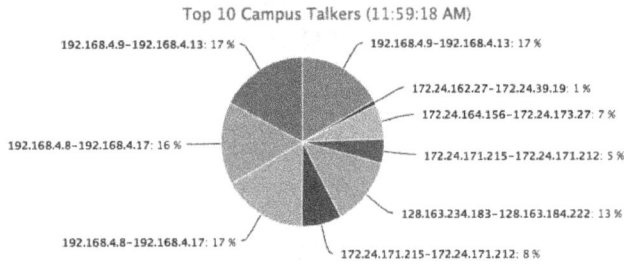

Figure 1: Live CEP Report

Table 3: Stream Process Rates

Source → Destination	Processed Flows/sec
$AMPQ \rightarrow Spout$	318672
$AMPQ \rightarrow ResolverBolt$	315208
$AMPQ \rightarrow DrainBolt$	233864

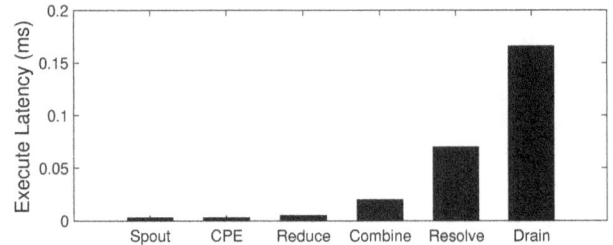

Figure 2: Topology Component Latency

average every 0.04ms. Initial tests show that the resolver bolts execution latency is 2ms per bolt process. In an attempt to improve performance we increased the number of processes to 20 (across 10 computers) and sorted the subnet list on update, which placed most used subnets in the front of the list. While these changes improved performance, we still could not keep up with the flow rate. In our test we found that the majority of the execution overhead involved in the creation of subnet objects used to compare flow addresses with known subnets. The bolt was rewritten using the Google Guava [9] object caching libraries. The Guava-cached *Resolver Bolt* had an execution latency of 0.08ms, so over 20 processes that gave us a theoretical limit of 250k resolutions per second. The *Resolver Bolt* consumes all tuples and elements emitted by the *Combiner Bolt* and injects state elements. Output from this bolt is typically consumed by all other downstream bolts.

2.2.4 Reducer and CEP Bolts

While distributed remote call procedures (RPC) are possible in Storm, often it is easier to simply reduce a subset of tuples to a single process. *Reducer bolts* can either receive all tuples emitted by a large number of bolts or they can receive a reduced tuple stream based on a field-grouping filter. Most often these bolts are used in near real-time reporting or Complex Event Processing (CEP) where a specific subset of system wide elements is needed.

Complex Event Processing (CEP) [2] is the term used to describe a collection of methods used in the analysis of unbounded streams of information. A CEP engine will continuously process information streams in an attempt to identify, and react to, meaningful events. In the *CEP Bolt* we have implemented the ESPER [5] event stream processing (ESP) and event correlation engine (CEP). With this bolt we can detect any event that can be defined using the ESPER event processing language (EPL). We have implemented several *CEP Bolts* including bot detection, network scan detection, top talkers, top connections, highest transfer rates, lowest transfer rates, total flows per second, and total bandwidth per second. *CEP Bolts* are specific to a single EPL query, so they most often take input from a *Reducer Bolt* and emit a value specified by the query, on a user specified interval.

2.2.5 Report Bolt

Due to the distributed nature of the Storm framework there is no method to "query" the application topology for information. Luckily, we can get information out of the system the same way we put it in, by making use of AMPQ queues. RabbitMQ, our AMQP server, provides a Simple Text-Orientated Messaging Protocol (STOMP) [28] plugin,

which is directly consumable by web browsers using WebSockets [7]. The near real-time bi-directional capabilities of WebSockets, allows us to observe CEP events as they occur in our application topology. An example of this type of reporting is found in the CEP "Top Talkers" bolt, shown in Figure 1.

2.2.6 Drain Bolt

Once all state elements have been injected into the tuple stream and all CEP events have been calculated for a given tuple, we are ready to record the tuple. We have implemented an HBase [11] client into the *Drain Bolt*, which allows us to keep a running log of all flows processed by the system. All flows are recorded in a single HBase table for post-processing. In Section 2.3.1 we describe the benefits of using Hbase tables for this process. The *Drain Bolt* records all output emitted from the *Resolver Bolt* and does not emit a tuple stream.

2.2.7 Stream Load Testing

Due to the queue-based architecture of our flow collection system we have a good way to load-test the overall system using real data. If we disable or kill the Storm application topology there will be nothing to clear the AMPQ queues on the probe boxes and they will continue to grow. In our test we disabled our topology for several hours allowing millions of flows to be queued on the probe servers. We then enabled our topology, processed the awaiting queues, and calculated the transfer rates across the topology as shown in Table 3. Under load the topology actually performed 20% better than we had predicted, based on calculations in Section 2.2.3 *Resolver Bolt*.

2.3 Hadoop Processing

Not all information about networks can be extracted from streaming CEP. The application topologies we develop to analyze flows of network data are continuous by nature, however a large number of CEP detection rules are time-dependent. Due to resource constraints, even in a distributed system, the window of time available for in-memory processing is often insufficient for event modeling.

We have developed a method of storing and analyzing network flow data using Hadoop and HBase. Hadoop is an ideal system for log processing. We take advantage of HBase for flow storage and Hadoop MapReduce for data processing.

2.3.1 HBase

HBase is particularly suited for sparse, time-dependent, structured, and highly compressible data. For data collection, a single database is used. HBase is capable of storing multiple records with the same key, as long as the timestamp is different, however our database it limited to a single row per key. Our database is configured with no block level caching, since random repeated reads are unlikely. Unlike file-based batch processing methods, we can retrieve HBase data based on a specific time range. This greatly improves job startup time since all data does not have to be scanned to process a specific range. To do this efficiently, we must take steps to avoid monotonically increasing row keys [30] due to the time series nature of our data. This is caused by using a increasing value, like a timestamp, for the first part of the key. When this occurs data piles up on certain nodes, which prevents the efficient distribution and processing of data. When storing time series information in an HBase key, one should stick with the form *[metric_type][event_timestamp]* to prevent performance problems related to data distribution. As described in Section 2.2.2, our key (*srcIp-dstIp-TS*) is constructed as a concatenation of address information and timestamp, which balances well across nodes.

The data we are storing is highly structured and we know that there is a relatively small amount of fixed information (ip addresses, tcp/udp ports, and router information) that we will be recording many times. This type of data compresses very well, so we have configured our database to use Google's Snappy [23] compression. Our sample HBase table contains over a billion records which relates to a database size of 118GB. If we dump our database to sequence files on the HDFS file system, the resulting sequence file size is 789GB. Under a compressed HBase table a flow generates 125 bytes of data as opposed to 836 bytes for the sequence file, which is a 6.7X reduction in size. The HDFS file system and batch flow processors outside of Hadoop also provide several compression options [1]. HBase has the advantage of automatic table compression updates, which will periodically evaluate and compact the entire table.

2.3.2 MapReduce

The MapReduce framework, provided by Hadoop, is well suited to process large datasets in parallel on distributed clusters of commodity servers. We have developed several MapReduce jobs as shown in Table 4, to analyze flows based on count, size, and rate. Since our flow data has been enriched with environmental state data, we have a rolling historical record of network utilization. Not only can we analyze traditional source and destination ip traffic, but we can analyze information about network routers, interfaces, subnets, and VLANs. With this additional information, analysis can be extended from our campus network topology to its building geography. Information such as, under provisioned wireless areas, can be determined by relating the interface flow rate with the service access point, at the time the flow was generated. As shown in Table 5, our MapReduce jobs were able to process between 1.5 - 2.6M flows/sec at a rate of 1.2 - 2.1GB/sec, depending on job type. For highly parallel tasks, such as flow processing, the aggregate throughput is largely a sum of the through of the individual parts. It

Table 4: MapReduce Jobs

Job Type	Description
1	Flow count per router subnet
3	Flow count between router subnets
4	Observed unknown subnet count
5	IP $Src \rightarrow Dst$ count
6	IP $Src \rightarrow Dst$ Bytes
7	Router subnet $Src \rightarrow Dst$ Bytes
8	Bytes per router subnet
9	Bytes per router
14	IP $Src \rightarrow Dst$ Bytes/sec
15	Router subnet $Src \rightarrow Dst$ Bytes/sec

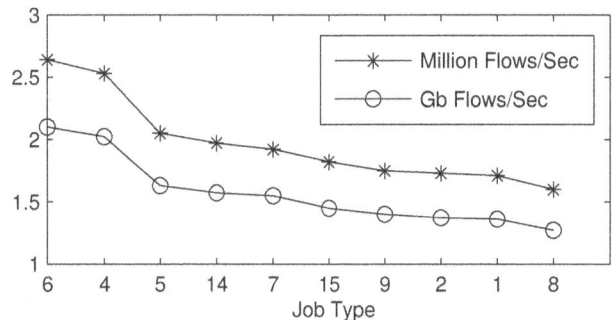

Figure 3: Performance information for MapReduce Jobs

is worth note that we achieved a per node throughout of 211MB/sec compared to 72MB/sec in a similar [14] Hadoop based flow processing system.

3. CONCLUSIONS

In this paper we reported the results of our work on processing the flow information at a medium-size educational institution. We showed how the paradigm of Storm can be used to process the flow data through the sequence of spouts and bolts. One benefit of this approach is that the data can be processed further with MapReduce on HBase. Our results have a practical aspect; the data thus obtained can be used in a variety of applications that trace both security of the system and also provide the data that can be used for predictions of the future IT needs of the university.

---

[1]FPS: Flows Per Second FPN: Flows Per Node,MBS: Total Throughput/Sec in MB, MBS: Node Throughput/Sec in MB

Table 5: Hadoop Process Rates

Job	FPS	FPN	MBS	MBN
1	1708906	170891	1363	136
3	1726783	172678	1377	138
4	2533070	253307	2020	202
5	2045258	204526	1631	163
6	2641174	264117	2106	211
7	1915686	191569	1528	153
8	1596946	159695	1273	127
9	1759167	175917	1403	140
14	1972324	197232	1573	157
15	1822925	182293	1454	145

1

We are in the process of developing *CEP Bolts* that interface with SDN controllers for security and performance functions. In the future, we plan on adding server performance metric information to our stream, when values are known. We will further develop analytical methods to make informed decision around the choice of movements of workloads or movements of data, based on network, system, and job profile data.

4. ACKNOWLEDGMENTS

The system described in this document, was initially developed to analyze network traffic in support of *NSF Grant OCI-1246332, U. of Kentucky, "CC-NIE Integration: Advancing Science through Next Generation SDN Networks", PI: V. Kellen, co-PI J. Griffioen.*

5. REFERENCES

[1] Y. Chen, A. Ganapathi, and R. H. Katz. To compress or not to compress-compute vs. io tradeoffs for mapreduce energy efficiency. In *Workshop on Green networking*, pages 23–28. ACM, 2010.

[2] G. Cugola and A. Margara. Processing flows of information: From data stream to complex event processing. *ACM Computing Surveys (CSUR)*, 44(3):15, 2012.

[3] J. Dean and S. Ghemawat. Mapreduce: simplified data processing on large clusters. *Comm. of the ACM*, 51(1):107–113, 2008.

[4] L. Ertoz, E. Eilertson, A. Lazarevic, P.-N. Tan, V. Kumar, J. Srivastava, and P. Dokas. Minds-minnesota intrusion detection system. *Next Generation Data Mining*, pages 199–218, 2004.

[5] Esper. http://esper.codehaus.org/, 9 2013.

[6] C. Estan, K. Keys, D. Moore, and G. Varghese. Building a better netflow. *SIGCOMM Comput. Commun. Rev.*, 34(4):245–256, Aug. 2004.

[7] I. Fette and A. Melnikov. The websocket protocol. *IETF*, 2011.

[8] Fprobe. http://sourceforge.net/projects/fprobe, 9 2013.

[9] Guava, http://code.google.com/p/guava-libraries/, 9 2013.

[10] Hadoop. http://hadoop.apache.org/, 8 2013.

[11] Hbase. http://hbase.apache.org, 9 2013.

[12] C. V. N. Index. Forecast and methodology, 2012–2017. *White Paper*, 2013.

[13] M. A. Kolosovskiy and E. N. Kryuchkova. Network congestion control using netflow. *arXiv preprint arXiv:0911.4202*, 2009.

[14] Y. Lee and Y. Lee. Toward scalable internet traffic measurement and analysis with hadoop. *ACM Comp. Comm.Rev.*, 43(1):5–13, 2012.

[15] L. Li, D. Alderson, W. Willinger, and J. Doyle. A first-principles approach to understanding the internet's router-level topology. *SIGCOMM Comput. Commun. Rev.*, 34(4):3–14, Aug. 2004.

[16] N. McKeown. Software-defined networking. *INFOCOM keynote talk, Apr*, 2009.

[17] MPLS. http://www.cisco.com/en/US/products/ps6557/products_ios_technology_home.html, 9 2013.

[18] J.-P. Navarro, B. Nickless, and L. Winkler. Combining cisco netflow exports with relational database technology for usage statistics, intrusion detection, and network forensics. In LISA 2000, pages 285–290, 2000.

[19] Cisco. Global mobile data traffic forecast update, 2012–2017. http://www.cisco.com/en/US/solutions/.../white_paper_c11-520862.html, 2013.

[20] T.-L. Pao and P.-W. Wang. Netflow based intrusion detection system. In *Networking, Sensing and Control, 2004 IEEE International Conference on*, volume 2, pages 731–736. IEEE, 2004.

[21] RabbitMQ. http://www.rabbitmq.com, 9 2013.

[22] RIPE. https://labs.ripe.net/Members/wnagele/large-scalepcap-data-analysis-using-apache-hadoop, 10 2011.

[23] Snappy http://code.google.com/p/snappy/, 9 2013.

[24] Storm. http://storm-project.net/, 9 2013.

[25] T. Telkamp. Traffic characteristics and network planning. In *Proc. Internet Statistics and Metrics Analysis Workshop*, 2002.

[26] S. Vinoski. Advanced message queuing protocol. *Internet Computing, IEEE*, 10(6):87–89, 2006.

[27] Vmware vsphere. https://www.vmware.com/products/vsphere/, 9 2013.

[28] V. Wang, F. Salim, and P. Moskovits. *The Definitive Guide to HTML5 WebSocket*. Apress, 2012.

[29] D. Wetteroth. *OSI Reference Model for Telecommunications*. McGraw-Hill Professional, 2001.

[30] T. White. *Hadoop: the definitive guide*. O'Reilly, 2012.

[31] X. Yin, W. Yurcik, M. Treaster, Y. Li, and K. Lakkaraju. Visflowconnect: netflow visualizations of link relationships for security situational awareness. In *ACM workshop on Visualization and data mining for computer security*, pages 26–34. ACM, 2004.

LIMBO: A Tool For Modeling Variable Load Intensities
Demo Paper

Jóakim v. Kistowski
Karlsruhe Institute of
Technology, Germany
joakim.kistowski
@student.kit.edu

Nikolas Herbst
Karlsruhe Institute of
Technology, Germany
herbst@kit.edu

Samuel Kounev
Karlsruhe Institute of
Technology, Germany
kounev@kit.edu

ABSTRACT

Modern software systems are expected to deliver reliable performance under highly variable load intensities while at the same time making efficient use of dynamically allocated resources. Conventional benchmarking frameworks provide limited support for emulating such highly variable and dynamic load profiles and workload scenarios. Industrial benchmarks typically use workloads with constant or stepwise increasing load intensity, or they simply replay recorded workload traces. In this paper, we present LIMBO - an Eclipse-based tool for modeling variable load intensity profiles based on the Descartes Load Intensity Model [3] as an underlying modeling formalism.

Categories and Subject Descriptors

C.4 [**Computer Systems Organization**]: Performance of Systems—*Modeling Techniques*

General Terms

Benchmarking, Workload, Modeling

Keywords

Load Intensity Variation, Load Profile, Open Workloads, Meta-Modeling, Transformation, Model Extraction

1. INTRODUCTION

Today's cloud and web-based IT services need to handle huge amounts of concurrent users. Customers access services independently of one another and expect reliable quality-of-service under highly variable and dynamic load intensities. In this context, any knowledge about a service's load intensity profile is becoming a crucial information for managing the underlying IT resource landscape. Load profiles with large amounts of concurrent users are typically strongly influenced by human habits, trends, and events. This includes strong deterministic factors such as time of the day, day of the week, common working hours and planned events.

Common benchmarking frameworks such as Faban[1], Rain [1], and JMeter[2] allow job injection rates to be configured either to constant values, stepwise increasing rates (e.g., for stress tests), or rates based on recorded workload traces.

The tool we present in this paper aims at closing the gap between highly dynamic load intensity profiles observed in real life and the current lack of support for flexible handling of variable load intensities in benchmarking frameworks.

In [3], we introduce two modeling formalisms at different abstraction levels: At the lower abstraction level, the *Descartes Load Intensity Model* (DLIM) offers a structured and accessible way of describing the load intensity over time by editing and combining mathematical functions. The *High-Level DLIM* (HLDLIM) allows the description of load variations using few defined parameters that characterize the seasonal patterns, trends, as well as bursts and noise elements.

In this demo paper, we present LIMBO[3] - an Eclipse-based tool for handling and instantiating load intensity models based on DLIM. LIMBO offers an accessible way of editing DLIM instances and extracting them from existing traces. It also supports using HLDLIM parameters for easy creation of new DLIM instances through a model creation wizard. An example load profile of a DLIM instance is shown in Fig.1.

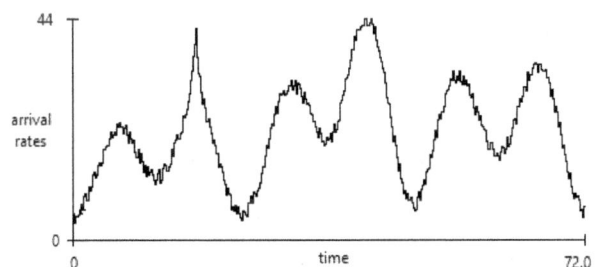

Figure 1: **An example load profile of a DLIM instance plotted by LIMBO.**

ICPE'14, March 22–26, 2014, Dublin, Ireland.
ACM 978-1-4503-2733-6/14/03.
http://dx.doi.org/10.1145/2568088.2576092.

2. DEFINITION OF LOAD INTENSITY

In this work, *load intensity* is a discrete function describing *arrival rates* of workload units over time. We assume

---

[1]Faban http://faban.org
[2]JMeter http://jmeter.apache.org
[3]LIMBO http://www.descartes-research.net/tools/

that the work units are of a homogeneous type and define the *arrival rate* $r(t)$ at time t as follows:

$$r(t) = R'(t)$$
$$\text{with } R(t) = |\{u_{t_0}|t_0 \leq t\}|$$

where $R(t)$ is the amount of all *work units* u_{t_0}, with their respective *arrival time* t_0, that have arrived up until time t.

3. LIMBO

LIMBO allows editing of load intensity models based on DLIM and supports guided model creation using the parameters defined in HLDLIM.

3.1 Descartes Load Intensity Model

DLIM describes request arrival rates over time and offers a way to define a piece-wise mathematical function for the approximation of variable arrival rates with support for (partial) periodicity, flexibility and composability.

3.2 High-Level DLIM

HLDLIM offers abstracted knowledge about load intensity variations modeled through a limited number of workload parameters. Inspired by the time series decomposition approach in BFAST [2], a HLDLIM instance describes a *Seasonal* and *Trend* part. Additionally, it features a *Burst* and *Noise* part.

3.3 Implementation

The tooling for DLIM and HLDLIM models is realized as a plug-in for the Eclipse IDE. It provides an editor for the creation and modification of model instances, as well as additional utilities for using the created models. Using DLIM's EMF-generated code base as a basis, the following features have been implemented:

Model Evaluation: Support for the DLIM function output calculation and manual refinement of model instances.

Modeling Process Assistance: We are currently implementing an automated process for the creation and extraction of DLIM instances. So far, LIMBO provides a model instantiation guidance by means of a wizard.

Utilities: Additional functionality is provided for existing DLIM instances. Including functionality for the generation of arrival rate series from a time-stamp series, and a tool that calculates the difference between an arrival rate trace and a model instance.

LIMBO consists of five individual plug-ins as visualized in Fig. 2:

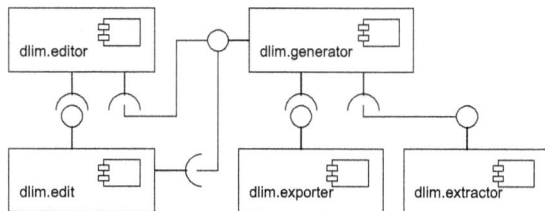

Figure 2: LIMBO architecture.

1. **DLIM Generator** The `dlim.generator` plug-in contains the DLIM element interfaces and implementations, as well as their default utilities (e.g., for validation). It also contains model evaluation tools, as well

as arrival rate and time-stamp series generators. It features two extension points:

Exporter extension points supports custom implementations by implementing the `dlim.exporter.IDlimExporter` interface. Default exporters are contained in the `dlim.exporter` plug-in.

Extractor extension point allows the addition of extractors for deriving a model instance from an existing trace. Extractors must implement `dlim.reader.IDlimArrivalRateReader` for their trace parser and `dlim.extractor.IDlimExtractor` for the model instance creator. Default extractors are contained in the `dlim.extractor` plug-in.

2. **DLIM Generator Edit**
This plug-in contains the providers used by the editor, which provide display specific information, such as the display images and labels of model elements.

3. **DLIM Generator Editor**
The `dlim.editor` plug-in contains all GUI elements and their utilities. It also contains implicit modeling process knowledge in its GUI.

4. **DLIM Exporter**
The `dlim.exporter` plugin offers default implementations of the `dlim.generator` plugin's `dlim.exporter.IDlimExporter` interface and the `exporter` extension point.

5. **DLIM Extractor**
The `dlim.extractor` plug-in offers default implementations of the `dlim.extractor.IDlimExtractor` interface and the `extractor` extension point.
Both `extractor` extension point implementations in this plug-in use the provided default `dlim.reader.ArrivalRateReader` provided by the `dlim.generator` plug-in.

4. CONCLUSIONS

In this demo paper, we introduce LIMBO: A toolkit for creating and editing of DLIM instances. By enabling the flexible handling of load intensity profiles, we address a strong need in the areas of benchmarking and elastic capacity management. Currently, we are extending LIMBO to support an automatic model-from-trace extraction process.

5. REFERENCES

[1] A. Beitch, B. Liu, T. Yung, R. Griffith, A. Fox, and D. A. Patterson. Rain: A workload generation toolkit for cloud computing applications. Technical Report UCB/EECS-2010-14, EECS Department, University of California, Berkeley, Feb 2010.

[2] J. Verbesselt, R. Hyndman, G. Newnham, and D. Culvenor. Detecting trend and seasonal changes in satellite image time series. *Remote Sensing of Environment*, 114(1):106 – 115, 2010.

[3] J. G. von Kistowski, N. R. Herbst, and S. Kounev. Modeling Variations in Load Intensity over Time. In *Proceedings 3rd International Workshop on Large-Scale Testing (LT 2014), co-located with the 5th ACM/SPEC International Conference on Performance Engineering (ICPE 2014)*. ACM, March 2014. Accepted for Publication.

LibReDE: A Library for Resource Demand Estimation

[Demonstration Paper]

Simon Spinner
Karlsruhe Institute of
Technology (KIT)
Karlsruhe, Germany
simon.spinner@kit.edu

Giuliano Casale
Imperial College London
London, UK
g.casale@imperial.ac.uk

Xiaoyun Zhu
VMware, Inc.
Palo Alto, US
xzhu@vmware.com

Samuel Kounev
Karlsruhe Institute of
Technology (KIT)
Karlsruhe, Germany
kounev@kit.edu

ABSTRACT

When creating a performance model, it is necessary to quantify the amount of resources consumed by an application serving individual requests. In distributed enterprise systems, these resource demands usually cannot be observed directly, their estimation is a major challenge. Different statistical approaches to resource demand estimation based on monitoring data have been proposed, e.g., using linear regression or Kalman filtering techniques. In this paper, we present LibReDE, a library of ready-to-use implementations of approaches to resource demand estimation that can be used for online and offline analysis. It is the first publicly available tool for this task and aims at supporting performance engineers during performance model construction. The library enables the quick comparison of the estimation accuracy of different approaches in a given context and thus helps to select an optimal one.

1. INTRODUCTION

A resource demand is the time a unit of work (e.g., request or transaction) spends obtaining service from a resource (e.g., CPU or hard disk) in a system. Resource demands are input parameters of widely used stochastic performance formalisms (e.g., Queueing Networks or Queueing Petri Nets). In order to obtain accurate performance predictions for a system, a performance engineer needs to determine representative values for the resource demands during performance model construction.

State-of-the-art monitoring tools can only provide aggregate resource usage statistics on a system- or per-process-level. However, in many applications one process may serve requests of different types with varying resource require-

ments (due to different computations, caching, etc.). As a result, the resource demands usually cannot be observed. Instead, we need to estimate resource demands based on the available aggregate monitoring data. Different approaches to resource demand estimation using statistical techniques, e.g., linear regression [4], Kalman filtering [6, 5], or non-linear optimization [3, 2], have been proposed. These approaches differ in their expected input measurements and their robustness to data anomalies. Furthermore, the approaches need to be parameterized correctly to yield good results. The selection of a suitable estimation approach and the optimization of its parameters usually requires experiments to validate the resulting resource demands.

Given that there are no publicly available implementations of estimation approaches, a performance engineer is currently forced to implement estimation approaches on his own. This is a time-consuming and error-prone task. In this paper, we present LibReDE, a library supporting performance engineers to determine resource demands by providing a set of ready-to-use implementations of estimation approaches. Based on the actual system and the available monitoring data, the estimation library can automatically determine a set of candidate estimation approaches and execute them. A performance engineer can then validate the resulting resource demand estimates and select the approach that yields the best results. Furthermore, the library also provides a framework that can be used as a basis by developers of estimation approaches. Through reuse, the effort for adapting existing estimation approaches or for implementing new ones, can be significantly reduced.

2. USAGE AND FEATURES

The library can be either executed as a standalone program or integrated in other programs as a Java library. The standalone program can be either called through a console interface or through a Matlab function. It is designed for offline analyses where the measurement traces are available beforehand. If executed on the console, the user must provide the monitoring data as comma-separated values stored in a file. If executed within Matlab, it is possible to pass Matlab arrays directly to the library without conversion. The shared library offers the same functionality through a

ICPE'14, March 22–26, 2014, Dublin, Ireland.
ACM 978-1-4503-2733-6/14/03.
http://dx.doi.org/10.1145/2568088.2576093.

Java API. Additionally, it contains functions to continuously add new measurement data to an estimator and update the estimates recursively over time. This makes the library also applicable for online analyses, e.g., in a self-adaptive system that uses a performance model for planning reconfigurations.

The library currently provides implementations of seven estimation approaches: (a) a least squares regression approach based on the Utilization Law [4], (b) a Kalman filter estimator based on observed average response times and utilization [6], (c) a Kalman filter estimator based on the Utilization Law [5], (d) a non-linear optimization algorithm minimizing the difference between observed and calculated average response times [3], (e) a non-linear optimization algorithm relying on utilization and average response time observations [2], (f) an approach based on the Service Demand Law apportioning the aggregate utilization based on the observed response times [1], and (g) an approach that approximates the demands with the observed response times (applicable in low load scenarios) [1]. The user can select one or more estimation approaches to execute. If none is specified, the library will automatically select a set of applicable approaches based on the structure of the estimation problem and the available monitoring data. All selected approaches are then executed to estimate the resource demands. The user gets an overview of the estimates from each approach.

The monitoring data must be available as time series data with associated timestamps for each sample. The library can work on time series with individual events (e.g., arrival times and response times of individual requests) or on fixed sampled time-aggregated data (e.g., average response times or average throughput). If the input data consists of time series with individual events, the library automatically computes the required time-aggregated data.

The behavior of the estimation approaches can be controlled by a set of parameters. The *step size* parameter determines the sampling interval over which the input data is aggregated. If the estimator is executed recursively, it also determines the interval in which the estimates are updated. The *estimation window* parameter defines a sliding window controlling how many samples are included when updating the estimates. A *start time* and *end time* for the estimation can be specified. Additionally, there may be parameters specific to a certain estimation approach.

3. LIBRARY DESIGN

Figure 1 shows the major components of LibReDE. The *estimation approach* instantiates concrete instances of an estimation algorithm, an observation model, and a state model. It then triggers and coordinates the estimation procedure. The *estimation algorithm* component implements the underlying statistical technique of an estimation approach (e.g., non-negative least squares regression or non-linear optimization). The *state model* component encodes apriori knowledge about the resource demands as state constraints and contains functions to determine initial estimates. The *observation model* component defines the relationship between the observed system metrics and the hidden resource demands. The state model and the observation model both access the *monitoring repository* and the *workload description* components. The monitoring repository stores the user-provided monitoring data and provides functions to query and aggregate this data. The workload description component provides information about the system services

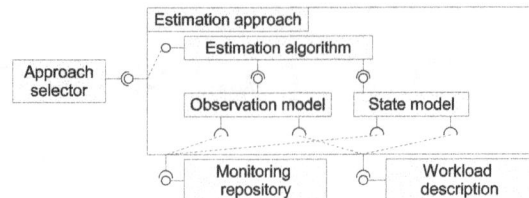

Figure 1: UML component diagram

and resources (including scheduling strategies and number of CPU cores). Finally, the *approach selector* instantiates all available estimation approaches and executes a subset verified to be applicable to a given estimation problem.

The library design enables a high level of reuse between different estimation approaches. The same estimation algorithms, observation models or state models can be shared between different estimation approaches. Thus the component-based structure facilitates the implementation of new estimation approaches.

4. CONCLUSION AND FUTURE WORK

In this paper, we presented a library for resource demand estimation. The library provides ready-to-use implementations of estimation approaches and can be used as a framework to implement new approaches. The source code of the library is open-source and publicly available[1]. The future development of the library will focus on integrating additional estimation approaches and supporting automatic cross-validation for the estimated resource demands. Furthermore, we also plan to implement techniques to automatically search for optimal parameter values (e.g., the step size) for an estimation approach.

5. REFERENCES

[1] F. Brosig, N. Huber, and S. Kounev. Automated extraction of architecture-level performance models of distributed component-based systems. In *26th IEEE/ACM Intl. Conf. On Automated Software Engineering*, Nov 2011.

[2] Z. Liu, L. Wynter, C. Xia, and F. Zhang. Parameter inference of queueing models for it systems using end-to-end measurements. *Perf. Eval.*, 63(1):36–60, 2006.

[3] D. Menascé. Computing missing service demand parameters for performance models. In *Proc. of the 2008 Computer Measurement Group (CMG) Conference*, pages 241–248, 2008.

[4] J. Rolia and V. Vetland. Parameter estimation for performance models of distributed application systems. In *Proc. of the 1995 conf. of the Centre for Advanced Studies on Collaborative research*, page 54. IBM Press, 1995.

[5] W. Wang, X. Huang, X. Qin, W. Zhang, J. Wei, and H. Zhong. Application-level cpu consumption estimation: Towards performance isolation of multi-tenancy web applications. In *2012 IEEE 5th Intl. Conf. on Cloud Computing*, pages 439–446, Jun 2012.

[6] T. Zheng, M. Woodside, and M. Litoiu. Performance model estimation and tracking using optimal filters. *IEEE Trans. on Soft. Eng.*, 34(3):391–406, 2008.

---

[1]http://www.descartes-research.net/tools

Server Efficiency Rating Tool (SERT) 1.0.2: An Overview

Hansfried Block
Fujitsu Technology Solutions GmbH
hansfried.block@ts.fujitsu.com

Jeremy A. Arnold
IBM Corporation
arnoldje@us.ibm.com

John Beckett
Dell Inc.
john_beckett@dell.com

Sanjay Sharma
Intel Corporation
sanjay.sharma@intel.com

Mike G. Tricker
Microsoft Corporation
mike.tricker@microsoft.com

Kyle M. Rogers
Hewlett-Packard Company
kyle.rogers@hp.com

ABSTRACT

The Server Efficiency Rating Tool (SERT) has released the Standard Performance Evaluation Corporation (SPEC) and the EPA released Version 2.0 of the ENERGY STAR for Computer Servers program in early 2013 to include the mandatory use of the SERT. Other governments world-wide that are concerned with the growing power consumption of servers and datacenters are also considering adoption of the SERT. This poster-paper provides an overview of the current release of 1.0.2 version of SERT.

Categories and Subject Descriptors

H.3.4 [**Systems and Software**]: Performance evaluation (efficiency and effectiveness)

General Terms

Design, Experimentation, Measurement, Performance, Reliability, Standardization.

Keywords

SPEC, Benchmark, Energy Efficiency, Server, System Performance, Performance Engineering, Memory, System Discovery, Affinitization, Framework, Reporting, Energy Star, Environmental Protection Agency (EPA).

1. SERT OVERVIEW

The SERT [2] is designed to be an architecture-neutral rating tool for measuring the overall energy efficiency of servers. It is highly scalable and has been tested on servers with up to eight sockets (or processors) and on up to 64 homogeneous multi-node servers (or blade servers). It is supported on servers based on the Intel and AMD x64 family of processor, IBM POWER, Oracle SPARC (all 64-bit) and ARM Cortex-A9 & A15 (32-bit).

The use of multiple power analyzers and temperature sensors is supported by the SERT in order to measure a large scope of system configurations. The most basic SERT measurement configuration requires one **power analyzer**, one **temperature sensor**, a system under test (**SUT**), and a **Controller** system.

The SERT's test harness, named **Chauffeur** [7], controls the software installed on the SUT and **Controller**. Chauffeur also handles the logistical side of measuring and recording the power consumption and inlet temperature of the SUT.

The SUT gets instructions from the **Director** (Chauffeur instance) to execute the suite, which is comprised of a set of **workloads**. The workload consists of a set of **Worklets**, which exercise the SUT while Chauffeur collects the power and temperature data. The Worklets are the actual code designed to stress a specific system resource or resources, such as the CPU, memory, or storage IO [3].

Each power analyzer and temperature sensor interacts with its dedicated instance of the **SPEC PTDaemon**, which gathers their readings while the Worklets are executed.

The **Reporter**, executed after all measurement phases are completed, compiles all of the environmental, power, and performance data for a complete test run into an easy-to-read HTML report as well as an extensible markup language (XML) report; the HTML report includes a graphical visualization of the results.

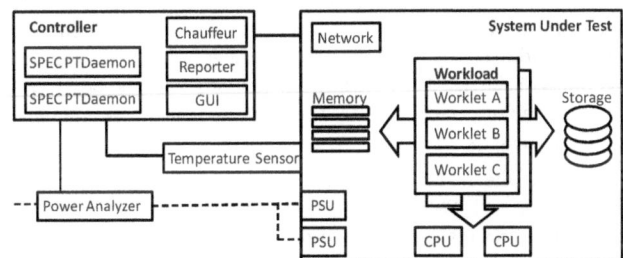

Figure 1 - Discovery Workflow

2. GRAPHICAL USER INTERFACE

The SERT includes a graphical user interface (GUI) in order to simplify the configuration and setup of test runs, allow real-time monitoring and to review the final results. The GUI is provided to enable test engineers with minimal power consumption and efficiency experience to more easily configure the SUT, including hardware and software detection and configuration, selecting the correct tests and initiating the test sequence.

The GUI offers ease of navigation with tabbed screens via a navigation menu and Back/Next buttons, per screen Help, and the ability to review/edit/save fields which are automatically populated via the automated discovery support. This also allows a specific configuration to be saved for subsequent re-use when re-testing the same or a similar SUT.

The GUI can automatically select the appropriate command-line options and number of clients, based on the processor, operating system and Java Virtual Machine (JVM) being used.

The GUI also supports selecting the correct power analyzer and temperature sensor for the list of supported devices, performing the necessary configuration and creating and testing the connections between PTDaemon and the selected devices.

3. SERT OUTPUT

The SERT produces a final HTML report [4] that looks like this:

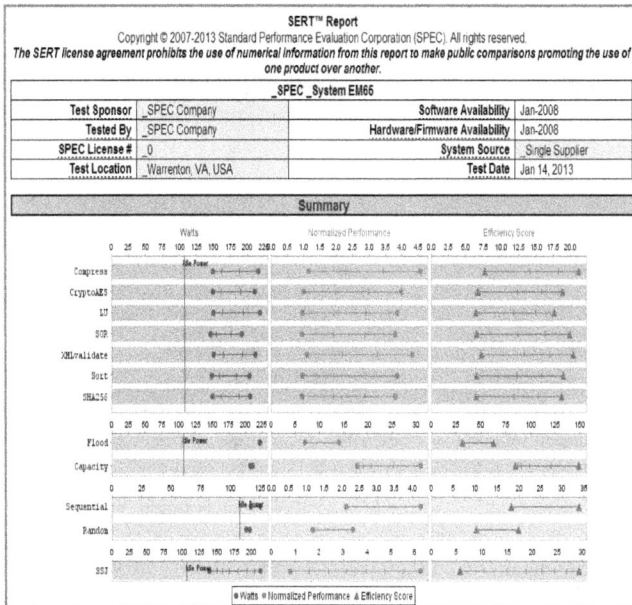

The main SERT report is generated in XML format. This contains all the information regarding the SERT run including all hardware and software configurations of the Controller, the SUT, and the SERT workloads. It includes all relevant information about the Worklets, such as JVM affinity & options, and other launch settings, along with the resulting performance, power and efficiency results.

As well as the XML, there are also four more human readable reports, two in HTML and two more in formatted text, covering higher level results (as shown in the included image) and the full detailed drill-down of all possible parameters and results

4. WORKLOADS and WORKLETS

The SERT includes five workloads (CPU, Memory, Storage, Hybrid and Idle) which in turn comprise a total of thirteen Worklets that focus on specific areas of processor, memory or storage IO behavior.

Due to the complexity and potential cost of creating a highly performant networking environment the Network IO is handled by a configuration modifier that simulates steady state efficiency of an ideal network adapter.

A detailed examination of all the SERT Worklets is included in the SERT Design Document [6]. This includes a section describing what they do, how they work and why they were selected for the final release.

5. NEXT STEPS

Development of the SERT is on-going, with regular enhancements being provided to further simplify configuration and use, as well as adding support for more hardware platforms and power analyzers.

SPEC is planning to create a Worklet construction kit, enabling 3rd parties to develop new Worklets and workloads, and initially

targeting academic partners. There is also significant on-going work to define metrics, making use of the initial data that has been acquired during the development and initial public use of the SERT [5].

6. CONCLUSIONS

The SERT was released in February 2013, for use in Version 2.0 of the EPA ENERGY STAR for Computer Servers program [1]. Updates are already underway to support simplified test configuration, and to add additional processor support. Use of the SERT became mandatory as part of acquiring ENERGY STAR for Computer Servers Version 2 in December 2013.

7. ACKNOWLEDGEMENTS

The authors also wish to acknowledge current and past members of the SPECpower Committee who have contributed to the design, development, testing, and overall success of the SERT: Greg Darnell, Karl Huppler, Van Smith, Paul Muehr, David Ott, Nathan Totura, Klaus-Dieter Lange, Cathy Sandifer, Jason Glick, and Dianne Rice, as well as the late Alan Adamson and Larry Gray.

SPEC and the names SERT, and SPEC PTDaemon, are registered trademarks of the Standard Performance Evaluation Corporation. Additional product and service names mentioned herein may be the trademarks of their respective owners.

8. REFERENCES

[1] ENERGY STAR Enterprise Servers Specification Version 2.0: http://www.energystar.gov/products/specs/node/142

[2] Lange, K. D., and Tricker, M. G. 2011. The Design and Development of the Server Efficiency Rating Tool (SERT). In *Proceedings of the second joint WOSP/SIPEW international conference on Performance engineering* (Karlsruhe, Germany, March 14 - 16, 2011). DOI= http://dx.doi.org/10.1145/1958746.1958769

[3] Lange, K. D., Tricker, M. G., Arnold, J. A., Block, H., and Koopmann, C. 2012. The Implementation of the Server Efficiency Rating Tool (SERT). In *ICPE '12 Proceedings of the third joint WOSP/SIPEW international conference on Performance Engineering* (Boston, USA, April 22 - 25, 2012). DOI= http://dx.doi.org/10.1145/2188286.2188307

[4] Lange, K.D., Arnold, J.A., Block, H, Totura, N, Beckett, J and Tricker, M.G. 2013. Further Implementation Aspects of the Server Efficiency Rating Tool (SERT). In *ICPE '13 Proceedings of the fourth joint WOSP/SIPEW international conference on Performance Engineering* (Prague, Czech Republic, April 21 - 24, 2013). DOI= http://dx.doi.org/10.1145/2479871.2479926

[5] Server Efficiency Rating Tool - Home Page: http://www.spec.org/sert/

[6] Server Efficiency Rating Tool - Design Document (Section 7 describes the current set of Worklets): http://www.spec.org/sert/docs/SERT-Design_Document.pdf

[7] Arnold, J.A. Master's Project 2013. Chauffeur: A Framework for Measuring Energy Efficiency of Servers

SPECjbb2013 1.0: An Overview

Charles Pogue
Hewlett-Packard Company
charles.pogue@hp.com

Anil Kumar
Intel Corporation
anil.kumar@intel.com

Douglas Tollefson
IBM Corporation
dougrt@us.ibm.com

Steve Realmuto
Oracle Corporation
steve.realmuto@oracle.com

ABSTRACT

SPECjbb2013 [1] is an entirely new version of the industry standard benchmark for evaluating Java server business performance from Standard Performance Evaluation Corporation (SPEC) [2]. It is designed with three categories which allow multiple configurations (Composite/single host, MultiJVMs/ single host, Distributed/single or multi hosts), enabling the user to systematically analyze their system. Additionally, the status of published results is summarized and a series of research project configurations are suggested.

Categories and Subject Descriptors

H.3.4 [**Systems and Software**]: Performance evaluation (efficiency and effectiveness)

General Terms

Design, Experimentation, Measurement, Performance, Reliability, Standardization

Keywords

SPEC, SPECjbb2013, Benchmark, Server, System Performance, Performance Engineering, Responsiveness, Java

1. SPECJBB2013 DESIGN

SPECjbb2013 is designed from the ground up to support distributed deployment using the latest data formats (e.g. XML), communiction using compression, messaging with security as well as the latest Java Development Kit (JDK) 7 features. No code was reused from earlier SPECjbb versions.

It models the infrastructure of a world-wide supermarket company, exercises point of sales in local supermarkets as well as online purchases, by processing related to user and supply chain management and by data mining operations in the company headquarters.

Reflecting the need of modern production environments where responsiveness is critical, this benchmark is designed to show response time details across gradually increasing load levels until the maximum capacity is reached, making the benchmark very useful for a comprehensive evaluation of system responsiveness. Utilization of the Java 7 fork / join framework exploits the parallelism utilized on modern multi-core processor architecture and serves as a good example to emulate in many applications. Other Java platform features like java.util.concurrent and NIO.2 are also exercised.

ICPE'14, March 22–26, 2014, Dublin, Ireland.
ACM 978-1-4503-2733-6/14/03.
http://dx.doi.org/10.1145/2568088.2576095

2. CONFIGURATION OVERVIEW

SPECjbb2013 has 3 benchmark components. The **Controller** (CTRL) directs the execution of the benchmark. The **Transaction Injector** (TxI) issues requests to the Backend and measures the end-to-end response time for each request. The business logic resides inside the **Backend** (BE) which is comprised of three main entities: the Supermarkets (SM), the Suppliers (SP) and the Headquarters (HQ), which mainly exercises intra-JVM communication. The BE processes these requests from the TxI and notifies the TxI after a request has been processed.

Multiple run configurations that allow diverse users to analyze and overcome bottlenecks at each layer of the system stack (e.g., hardware, OS, JVM, application) are supported.

The simplest configuration is shown in Figure 1, where the three benchmark components are running inside the same JVM (dotted line) on the same server (solid line).

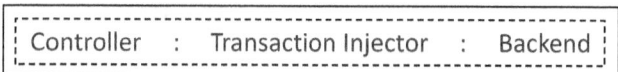

Figure 1. SPECjbb2013 Composite/Single Host Example

Figure 2 shows a configuration example where the CTRL, Txl and BE are running on the same server but each benchmark component resides in its own JVM.

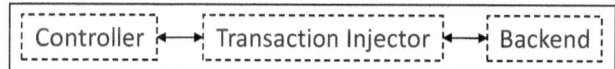

Figure 2. SPECjbb2013 MultiJVM / Single Host Example

SPECjbb2013 also allows the CTRL to reside on a separate unit, adding the complexity of network access between the CTRL and the host (TxL and BE) to the benchmark.

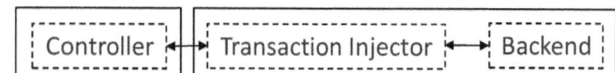

Figure 3. SPECjbb2013 Distributed / Single Host Example

Multiple hosts are also supported for even more complexity.

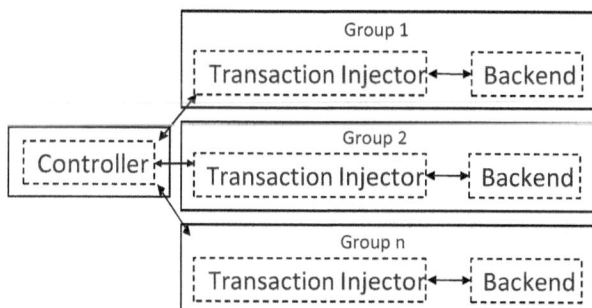

Figure 4. SPECjbb2013 Distributed / Multi Host Example

3. METRIC

SPECjbb2013 utilizes two metrics: a capacity throughput metric (max-jOPS) and a throughput under response time constraint metric (critical-jOPS). The max-jOPS metric indicates the sustainable full system throughput without any response time constraints. The higher the max-jOPS performance number, the better the system capacity throughput.

The critical-jOPS metric indicates the maximum level of performance that a system can achieve while meeting specific response time constraints. The higher the critical-jOPS performance number, the better system capacity throughput with minimum service level agreement (SLA) responsiveness requirements.

4. DIFFERENT FROM TYPICAL BENCHMARKS

A typical benchmark exercises a platform near 100% utilization and reports a throughput metric. This does not reflect usual production systems which operate below 50% utilization while ensuring graceful response at full utilization. To reflect production environment deployments, this benchmark exercises the system in gradual increments to max sustained capacity. In addition to metrics max-jOPS and critical-jOPS, benchmark report shows response time behavior across the gradual load increments in a graph which is very useful to evaluate the systems responsiveness from light load to heavy load [5].

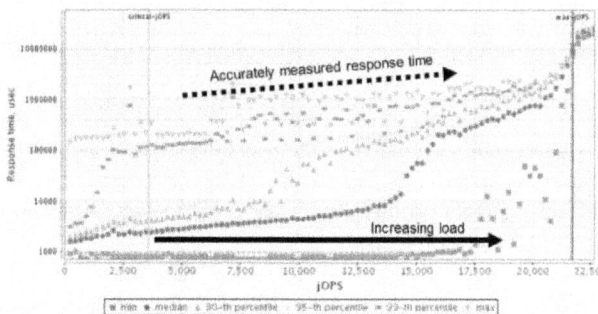

Figure 5. SPECjbb2013 Overall Throughput

5. CURRENT RESULT SUMMARY

Current results for the benchmark include submissions from many major manufacturers, indicating the benchmark's wide reaching appeal. The hardware used for the submissions covers an extensive range of systems including blade servers, rack mount servers and tower servers. A total of 20 different models have been used up to this point, ranging from simple one processor systems to complex systems using 16 processors.

6. RESEARCH OPTIONS

SPECjbb2013 has more than 300 control parameters that may be configured by researchers. While published compliant runs must follow the specified run rules, when used for research or testing, there is flexibility to set hundreds of control parameters to configure the benchmark to emulate different production environments.

Examples of such research options are `specjbb.group.count=1` which sets the number of Backends and `specjbb.forkjoin.workers=2` which sets the number of fork / join workers in the thread pool.

The benchmark can be run at a fixed injection rate for any desired period. This mode is intended for testing requiring a steady state, such as software stack testing as well as stressing the platform for longer durations. User defined load levels of a given injection rate could also be executed.

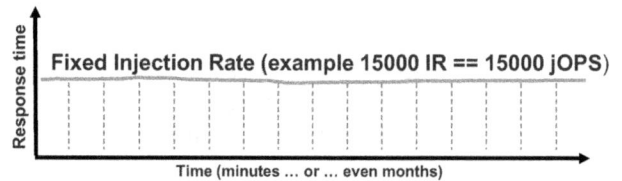

Figure 6. SPECjbb2013 Fixed Injection Rate Example

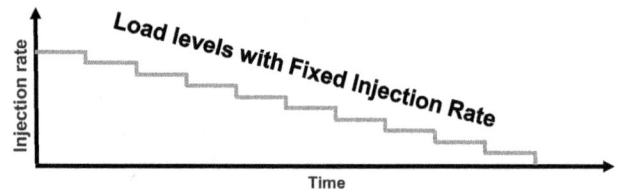

Figure 7. SPECjbb2013 Load Levels Example

Many of the above properties are listed in the SPECjbb2013.props files as part of the benchmark kit.

7. CONCLUSION

SPECjbb2013 is a highly configurable performance benchmark utilizing the latest Java technologies. The benchmark can be used from single server configuration, to virtualized and private cloud environments measuring response time accurately and therefore providing a challenging modern workload that motivates improvements in key components of the system (hardware, OS, JVM) to improve system response times.

8. ACKNOWLEDGMENTS

The authors want to acknowledge the additional members of the SPEC OSG Java Subcommittee who have contributed to the design, development, testing, and overall success of the SPECjbb2013 benchmark: Aleksey Shipilev, Daryl Maier, David Keenan, Elena Sayapina, Seiguei Katkov, Klaus-Dieter Lange, and Vasanth Venkatachalam

SPEC and the benchmark name SPECjbb are registered trademarks of the Standard Performance Evaluation Corporation.

9. REFERENCES

[1] SPECjbb2013 web site: http://www.spec.org/jbb2013/

[2] Standard Performance Evaluation Corporation home page: http://www.spec.org

[3] SPECjbb2013 Design Document: http://www.spec.org/jbb2013/docs/designdocument.pdf

[4] Shipilev, A., and Keenan, D. 2012. SPECjbb2012: updated metrics for a business benchmark. In Proceedings of the ICPE '12 Proceedings of the 3rd ACM/SPEC International Conference on Performance Engineering. DOI= http://dx.doi.org/10.1145/2188286.2188340

[5] Maier, D. and Kumar, A. 2013. Java Interprocess Communication Challenges in Low-Latency Deployments [CON7370] https://oracleus.activeevents.com/2013/connect/sessionDetail.ww?SESSION_ID=7370

System Performance Analyses through Object-oriented Fault and Coupling Prisms

Alessandro Murgia*, Roberto Tonelli,
Michele Marchesi, Giulio Concas
Dept. of Electrical Engineering
University of Cagliari, Cagliari, Italy
*Dept. of Mathematics-Inf., University of Antwerp, Belgium
alessandro.murgia@uantwerpen.be

Steve Counsell, Stephen Swift
Dept. of Information Systems
Brunel University,
Uxbridge, Middlesex, UK
steve.counsell@brunel.ac.uk

ABSTRACT

A fundamental aspect of a system's performance over time is the number of faults it generates. The relationship between the software engineering concept of 'coupling' (i.e., the degree of inter-connectedness of a system's components) and faults is still a research question attracting attention and a relationship with strong implications for performance; excessive coupling is generally acknowledged to contribute to fault-proneness. In this paper, we explore the relationship between faults and coupling. Two releases from each of three open-source Eclipse projects (six releases in total) were used as an empirical basis and coupling and fault data extracted from those systems. A contrasting coupling profile between fault-free and fault-prone classes was observed and this result was statistically supported. Object-oriented (OO) classes with low values of fan-in (incoming coupling) and fan-out (outgoing coupling) appeared to support fault-free classes, while classes with high fan-out supported relatively fault-prone classes. We also considered size as an influence on fault-proneness. The study thus emphasizes the importance of minimizing coupling where possible (and particularly that of fan-out); failing to control coupling may store up problems for later in a system's life; equally, controlling class size should be a concomitant goal.

Categories and Subject Descriptors

D.3.3 [**Programming Languages**]: Language Constructs and Features.

General Terms

Measurement, Performance, Experimentation.

Keywords

Coupling, fan-in, fan-out, faults, refactoring.

1. INTRODUCTION

As an object-oriented facet, excessive coupling [5] is, anecdotally and empirically, an acknowledged contributor to faults [1, 4] and hence a contributor to degradation of system performance. Here, coupling refers to the inter-connectedness of the components in a system. While no large system can exist without some form of coupling, wherever possible, developers should seek to minimize this facet of a system because of the relationship it forms with faults. In this paper, we explore the relationship between faults and coupling where the latter is decomposed into *fan-in* and *fan-out* [12]. We chose these two sub-forms of coupling to make the distinction between inward (fan-in) and outward (fan-out) links belonging to a class and we explore the relationship between fan-in and fan-out for sets of fault-free and fault-prone classes. Two releases from each of three Eclipse projects (six releases in total) were used as an empirical basis of the study and coupling and fault data extracted from those releases. Results showed a stark contrast between the coupling levels of fault-free classes and fault-prone classes. Low fan-in and fan-out appeared to support fault-free classes. Statistical evidence supported that result for four of the six releases studied. Analysis of class size between fault-prone and fault-free classes suggests that faults arise because of relatively high amounts of coupling (particularly fan-out), which in turn is dependent largely on class size. Developers should therefore aim to keep components as small as possible as a first line of defense against faults and pursue re-engineering and refactoring activities which decompose classes and methods.

1.1 Motivation

The motivation for the research comes firstly, from the relative lack of replication studies exploring the relationship between fault data and coupling on a longitudinal (i.e., release-by-release) basis [13]. Secondly, it comes from the fact that the relative merits of fan-in or fan-out (and combinations thereof) are still open research areas. Study of fan-in and fan-out from a fault perspective might lead to novel conclusions about the relationships between faults and other software engineering disciplines such as refactoring [2, 10, 18]. Finally, the work is also motivated by the role that class size plays in class composition. Lessons and conclusions based on class data are of questionable value unless size is taken into consideration [8, 9]. The indirect link between faults and class size (through the medium of coupling) is often neglected by other studies, yet can offer us insights into system behaviour otherwise lost [8]. The remainder of the paper is organised as follows. In the next section, we describe the analysis of the data on a release-by-release basis supported with fault and coupling data. We further support that analysis with statistical correlation. In Section 3, we discuss issues raised by the study including threats to study validity and related work before concluding in Section 4 pointing to further work.

2. DATA ANALYSIS
2.1 Preliminaries

Our analysis is based on two releases from each of three Eclipse projects: jdt.core, jdt.ui and jdt.uiworkbench. We used Eclipse as a basis of our research since it is a large, long-surviving system with more than ten years of development. We took into account faults between six releases. The JHawk tool [14] was used to extract the incoming 'fan-in' coupling and outgoing 'fan-out' coupling metrics for each class. The RefFinder tool [16] was used to extract up to sixty-three refactorings between two releases and the data reported relates to all classes that had been the subject of at least one refactoring between releases. We chose to study classes which had been refactored as opposed to studying every class in the system for two reasons. Firstly, by studying refactored classes, we obtain a mix of those classes that are likely to have been problematic and those that have had refactoring applied to them in a perfective sense. Secondly, because the study presented is part of a wider examination of refactoring, faults and the relationship these two have with coupling [15]. Fault data was collected manually by one of the researchers and subsequently verified by another. In the subsequent analysis, we present tabular data between each release, relevant correlation values, level of significance (1% or 5%) and data for fan-in and fan-out to support relationships between coupling and faults. We define a fault in this paper as an 'observed failure in the system' and marked as such by Eclipse developers using the Bugzilla fault-tracking system. We use parametric correlation measures assuming a normal distribution (Pearson's) and non-parametric measures which make no assumption about the data distribution (Kendall's and Spearman's). Using all three gives a broad and complete set of correlation values that using one alone might not accord. Finally, we note that the set of faults and refactorings collected were disjoint across releases; in other words, double counting of either was not a threat to the collected data.

2.2 Jdt.core_3.0_3.1

Table 1 shows summary statistics for the values of fan-in and fan-out (henceforward called 'FIN' and 'FOUT') for all 1151 classes containing at least one fault and which had been refactored at least once between releases 3.0 and 3.1. It also shows the FIN and FOUT data for the 154 fault-free, refactored classes. For each set, the minimum (Min), maximum (Max), Mean and standard deviation (SD) values are shown. For example, for the set of fault-prone classes, the minimum FIN was 0, maximum FIN was 228 with mean FIN 20.21 and SD 29.91. For fault-prone classes, we see that the mean value of FOUT is greater than the mean for FIN.

Table 1. Coupling data for jdt.core 3.0_3.1

Classes	Min	Max	Mean	SD
Fault-prone				
FIN	0	228	20.21	29.91
FOUT	0	195	30.59	32.69
Faults	1	71	10.44	32.12
Fault-free				
FIN	0	23	6.38	5.81
FOUT	0	34	7.63	6.57

The maximum value of FIN of 228 was for a class with 54 methods and 2 faults. The FOUT value of 195 belonged to a class with 159 methods and which exhibited 28 faults over the period studied. The maximum number of faults (71) belonged to a class called Scope with 81 methods. Its FIN was 66 and FOUT 48.

For the set of fault-free classes in the same table, the maximum values of FIN and FOUT are noticeably lower than those for fault-prone classes presented. The mean FIN value of 6.38 and mean FOUT value of 7.63 are considerably lower than the corresponding mean values for fault-prone classes. The question as to whether 'fault-free' classes over that period (as opposed to fault-prone classes) present a different profile in terms of their FIN and FOUT values also arises. To determine the relationship between FIN and FOUT in each of the categories, we correlated the respective values for the two data sets (fault-prone and fault-free). Correlation values between FIN and FOUT for fault-free classes showed no statistical significance for any of the three coefficients (0.03, 0.05 and 0.08 for Pearson's, Kendall's and Spearman's, respectively). On the other hand, for the set of fault-prone classes, we found correlations of 0.10 for Pearson's (not significant), 0.14 and 0.19 for Kendall's and Spearman's coefficients between FIN and FOUT, the latter both significant at the 1% level (0.01). For this project, FIN and FOUT profiles for fault-prone classes seem to differ significantly from that of fault-free classes. Both the FIN and FOUT values for fault-prone classes are higher. From Table 1, fault-prone classes tend to have a higher mean FOUT than the corresponding FIN value. This would make sense; a class with many incoming couplings (i.e., a high FIN value) is *depended upon* by many classes for the functionality that it offers. This means that it should be maintained very carefully because of the ripple effect of faults that changes to that class would cause to those dependent classes. The same is not true of classes with a high number of outgoing couplings (i.e., high FOUT). In that case, because the dependencies are outgoing, the ripple effects of any faults are likely to be less severe and careless maintenance would have less of an effect on the system.

While the tabular data and correlation results do suggest that fault-prone classes have a higher FIN and FOUT than fault-free classes and this is certainly a feature of the release studied, we cannot overlook the fact that size is also an important factor in the determination of coupling and, indirectly, the number of faults in a system. To this effect, we computed the median and mean number of methods (NOM) for each of fault-prone and fault-free classes. For fault-prone classes, the mean NOM was found to be 44.24 with a median value 23; for fault-free classes, the mean NOM was significantly lower at 10.24 and median 7. In other words, there was a wide variation in the size of the classes between those exhibiting faults and those that did not exhibit faults. Clearly, size is a factor in determining coupling and with that comes faults; restricting class size growth (and with it coupling) may be the major weapon against high fault incidence in classes. We could go further; based on the evidence presented we could hypothesise that the balance of coupling should be in favour of a higher FIN rather than use of FOUT. Developers should thus avoid building classes with high FOUT values.

2.3 Jdt.core_3.1_3.2

Table 2 shows statistics for FIN and FOUT for the 929 fault-prone, refactored classes between releases 3.1 and 3.2. It also shows the FIN and FOUT for the 130 fault-free refactored classes. For fault-prone classes, the mean FOUT is again noticeably larger than the mean of FIN. The maximum value of FOUT is for the same class as the previous release; the FIN value of 194 belonged to class with 52 methods and 11 faults. The maximum number of faults (38) belonged to the same class as in the previous release Scope, which now contained 84 methods. The FIN for this class was 73 and the FOUT 49. As to whether fault-free classes exhibit a different pattern to fault-prone classes, correlating FIN and FOUT for fault-free classes gave a value of 0.05 (not significant) for Pearson's and yet 0.16 and 0.21 for Kendall's and Spearman's, respectively. Both of these values were significant at the 5% level only. This contrasts with 0.07 (significant at the 5% level), 0.20 and 0.29 both significant at the 1% level for Pearson's, Kendall's and Spearman's, respectively for fault-prone classes.

Table 2. Coupling data for jdt core 3.1_3.2

Classes	Min	Max	Mean	SD
Fault-prone				
FIN	0	194	22.72	33.84
FOUT	0	195	28.94	32.69
Faults	1	38	7.06	7.19
Fault-free				
FIN	0	121	5.97	12.71
FOUT	0	33	5.49	7.00

Again, we note a strong difference in the FIN and FOUT relationship depending on whether a class is fault-free or fault-prone. The mean FOUT for fault-prone classes is again higher than that of its corresponding FIN value. When we consider the class size between these releases (given by NOM), we see a similar pattern as that in the previous section. For fault-prone classes, the mean NOM was 46.66 and median 23; for fault-free classes, the mean NOM was 9.2 and median NOM 7. Size is clearly a major factor in the FIN and FOUT values of Table 2; in particular, faults seem to thrive in highly-coupled classes, a feature of large classes. It is interesting to see (from Table 2) a similarity in the FIN and FOUT mean values for fault-free classes (5.97 and 5.49). As noted in the previous section, a balanced coupling profile (avoiding high FOUT values) appears to be a feature of fault-free classes and of fault-free classes here.

2.4 Jdt.ui_3.0_3.1

Table 3 shows summary data for the 1489 fault-prone and 555 fault-free classes between releases 3.0 and 3.1 of jdt.ui. For the former, the maximum value of FIN was 196 belonging to a class with 51 methods and 10 faults (FOUT for this class was 42).

Table 3. Coupling data for jdt.ui 3.0_3.1

Classes	Min	Max	Mean	SD
Fault-prone				
FIN	0	620	8.16	32.29
FOUT	0	51	12.57	10.61
Faults	1	23	3.60	3.37
Fault-free				
FIN	0	287	3.26	13.55
FOUT	0	22	5.19	4.45

The maximum value of FOUT was 51 for a class with 23 methods and 4 faults between releases. The maximum number of faults (23) was for class MoveInnerToTopRefactoring; this class had a FIN of 6 and a FOUT of 39. For FIN and FOUT, for the fault-free set of classes (mean FIN 3.26 and mean FOUT 5.19) we notice a distinct difference in the magnitude of these values compared with those of fault-prone classes.

For the fault-free set of classes, correlations between FIN and FOUT were -0.05 for Pearson's (not significant), 0.10 and 0.14 for Kendall's and Spearman's, respectively (both significant at the 1% level). The correlations for FIN versus FOUT for fault-prone classes on the other hand were 0.06 (significant at the 5% level), 0.09 and 0.11 (both significant at the 1% level). For this release, there is thus a parallel between FIN and FOUT for fault-free and fault-prone classes, in contrast to previous releases. When we again consider class size (given by NOM) we found that for fault-prone classes, the mean NOM was 31.69 and median 21; for fault-free classes, the mean NOM was just 8.53 and median 7. Again, size is a major factor in the FIN and FOUT values and the result extrapolated from Table 3. While we accept that faults arise because of high coupling, it is perhaps allowing class size to grow which is a key contributor to high coupling.

2.5 Jdt.ui_3.1_3.2

Table 4 shows the summary data for the 1187 fault-prone and 390 fault-free classes between releases 3.1 and 3.2. The FIN value of 698 was for the same class as the previous release, with 47 methods and 6 faults between releases.

Table 4. Coupling data for jdt.ui_31_32

Classes	Min	Max	Mean	SD
Fault-prone				
FIN	0	698	12.68	57.17
FOUT	0	70	13.73	12.54
Faults	1	18	3.30	2.69
Fault-free				
FIN	0	84	4.51	11.85
FOUT	0	47	6.40	6.21

The FOUT of 70 belonged to a class consisting of 31 methods with 7 faults over the releases. The class with 18 faults was called JavaEditor and had no methods. Its FIN was 100 and it's FOUT 43, well above the mean of 13.73. From a fault-free class perspective, the mean FIN for the 390 classes was 4.51 and its mean FOUT 6.40. Correlations between FIN and FOUT for those classes were 0.06 (not significant), 0.16 and 0.23, both significant at the 1% level (Pearson's, Kendall's and Spearman's, respectively). This compares with 0.13, 0.15 and 0.20 for fault-prone classes - all significant at the 1% level. Between these two releases, the relationship between fault-free and fault-prone classes was comparable. Considering the class size (given by NOM), we could see this result from a different perspective. For fault-prone classes, the mean NOM was 23.96 and median 17; for fault-free classes, the mean NOM was just 11.82 and the median 8. Again, size would appear to be a major factor in the FIN and FOUT values and from the result from Table 4.

2.6 Jdt.uiworkbench_3.0_3.1

Table 5 shows the summary data for the 695 fault-prone and 154 fault-free classes between 3.0 and 3.1. For the set of fault-prone classes and, as *per* other releases, the mean FOUT of 16.24 exceeds the corresponding value for FIN (9.14). The class with a FIN of 196 was a class with 51 methods and 10 faults over the course of the releases; its FOUT was 42. The maximum value of FOUT was for a class with 99 methods and 24 faults; its FIN was 30. The class with the highest number of faults was a class called WorkbenchPage with 179 methods and 30 faults.

Table 5. Coupling data for jdt.uiworkbench_30_31

Classes	Min	Max	Mean	SD
Fault-prone				
FIN	0	196	9.14	16.91
FOUT	0	83	16.24	18.88
Faults	1	30	4.79	5.91
Fault-free				
FIN	0	23	3.51	7.09
FOUT	0	76	5.34	4.30

The mean FIN for fault-free classes was 3.51 and that for FOUT 5.34. A difference between FIN and FOUT between fault-free and fault-prone classes is thus evident. The correlations for this set of classes were -0.10, -0.03 and -0.07 (Pearson's, Kendall's and Spearman's), none of which were significant. These values contrast starkly with the correlation values for the set of fault-prone classes between FIN and FOUT of 0.59, 0.27 and 0.36, all significant at the 1% level. Considering the class size (given by NOM), for the set of fault-prone classes, the mean NOM was 27.14 and median 16; for fault-free classes, the mean NOM was just 9.56 and median NOM 6. From the data presented, size is a major factor in the determination of FIN and FOUT and, by implication, faults.

2.7 Jdtui.workbench_3.1_3.2

Table 6 shows data between releases 3.1 and 3.2 for the set of 419 fault-prone and 124 fault-free classes. In keeping with the other releases, the mean FOUT for fault-prone classes (18.44) far exceeds that of FIN. The maximum FIN value was 204 and this belonged to same class as in the previous release. It exhibited 4 faults over the period studied. The maximum value of FOUT was 102 - the same class as the previous release with FIN value of 36; faults for this class fell to 19 over the period. The maximum number of faults was 24 for a class called WorkbenchWindow with 144 methods; its FIN was 44 and it's FOUT 89. For the set of fault-free classes, the mean FIN for fault-free classes was 3.68 and for FOUT 5.88. The correlations between FIN and FOUT

were -0.07, 0.09 and 0.12, none of which were significant. Correlations between FIN and FOUT for fault-prone classes, on the other hand, were 0.56. 0.34 and 0.45 (for Pearson's, Kendall's and Spearman's, respectively), all significant at the 1% level. As per most of the releases, there is a clear distinction between the relationship between FIN and FOUT, depending on whether a class is fault-free or fault-prone.

Table 6. Coupling data for jdt.uiworkbench 3.1_3.2

Classes	Min	Max	Mean	SD
Fault-prone				
FIN	0	204	9.04	21.54
FOUT	0	102	18.44	23.23
Faults	1	24	4.47	4.97
Fault-free				
FIN	0	67	3.68	7.99
FOUT	0	28	5.88	6.31

When we once again consider the class size (given by NOM), we found the mean NOM to be 30.00 and median 18; for fault-free classes, the mean NOM was 12.07 and the median 7. Size is once again a major factor in the FIN and FOUT values and from the result from Table 6.

3. DISCUSSION

The study has highlighted the differences between FIN and FOUT for fault-free *vis-a-vis* fault-prone classes. Clearly, developers should try to avoid FOUT becoming excessively high. However, *one guaranteed way of minimizing FOUT is to ensure that a class does not grow in size such that it needs to be coupled to so many other classes. We would condone the use of re-engineering and refactoring techniques to decompose classes should it be felt that a class is growing out of hand.* Of course, we have to be pragmatic; developers only have limited time to devote to such activities. The alternative of faulty classes, however, maybe a worse one. One justification for using FIN and FOUT in this paper is that we could not have emphasized the differences between these two types had we chosen to use CBO metric of Chidamber and Kemerer [6], for example. Figure 1 captures the mean FIN values for fault-prone and fault-free classes across the six releases studied abstracted from Tables 1-6. The dashed line is the set of FIN values for fault-prone classes in the six releases studied; the un-dashed line is that for fault-free classes.

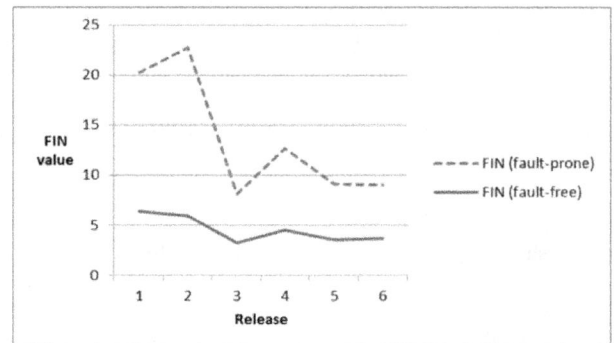

Figure 1. FIN values for fault-prone and fault-free classes (six releases)

There is a clear difference between the set of FIN for the two sets of classes and this applies to all releases. FOUT values for fault-prone classes clearly exceed those of fault-free classes. Figure 2 shows the FOUT mean values for fault-prone and fault-free classes abstracted from Tables 1-6.

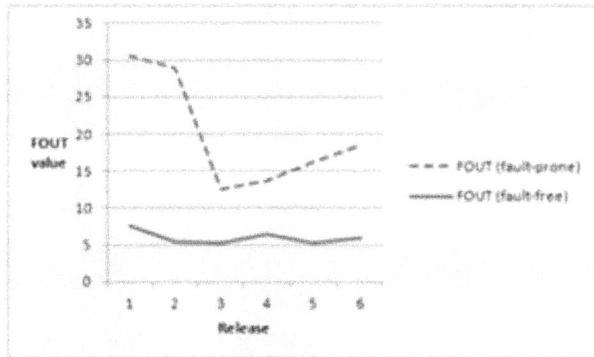

Figure 2. FOUT values for fault-prone and fault-free classes (six releases)

Again, the dashed line represents the set of fault-prone classes and the un-dashed line the set of fault-free classes. Once again the difference between the two sets of classes is clear. It is interesting to note from Figures 1 and 2 that the gap between mean values is most pronounced at earlier releases of the system. While this may be purely chance, it might suggest that re-engineering or refactoring activity [10] may have been put in place to narrow the gap between the two. The extract class and extract method refactorings are just two of the standard set of 72 refactorings proposed by Fowler [10] which may have been applicable here.

On the other hand, the mean values (after falling dramatically in release 3) then start to rise in both Figures 1 and 2. While the results from this data analysis support the view that low FIN and FOUT values contribute to fault-free classes, we need to consider the view that it is the size of a class which may determine a) the level of coupling in a class and b) the fault-proneness of a class. To emphasize the difference, Figure 3 shows just the mean NOM values for fault-prone and fault-free classes as described in Sections 2.2–2.7. There is a clear trend for the number of methods in fault-prone classes to be larger than those that are fault free.

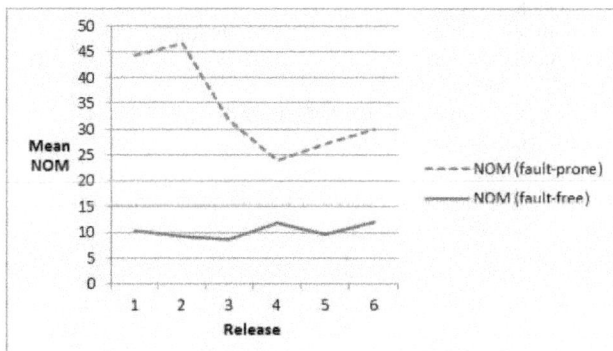

Figure 3. NOM for fault-prone and fault-free classes

3.1 Threats to validity

A number of threats to the validity of the research also have to be considered. Firstly, we only consider one system in our analysis and this could be considered a threat to external validity (i.e., the ability to draw conclusions based on a single system). However, an equal criticism could be applied had we used other systems in terms of our ability to compare results. Second, we have studied only limited releases of that system representing a small time frame in the overall life of the system. Third, in this paper we considered a class to be fault-free if it had not exhibited any faults *up until* that point in time. That is not to say, however, that the class will remain of that status – in a subsequent releases it may become faulty. For the purposes of the study however, this represents a useful benchmark against which we can judge fault-prone classes. Finally, we chose NOM as a mechanism for assessing size, but accept that there are other measures that might have been as appropriate as measures of class size. For example, lines of code (LOC); the problem with using LOC as a measure however is the wide variation with which it can be computed [17]. The NOM metric provides a standard measure of class size.

3.2 Related work

Faults or 'bugs' have been an effective measure of software performance since its inception [9]. The link between fault propensity and software complexity (in this case in the guise of coupling) is also well-understood. Study of fan-in and fan-out in this paper marks a departure from normal studies of the more generic 'coupling' form. In most coupling studies, the Coupling between Objects (CBO) metric of Chidamber and Kemerer [8] has been the standard coupling measure employed. However, while useful, the CBO metric does not distinguish between incoming and outgoing class coupling. This means that conclusions about the *direction* of coupling and the relationship with faults (in the case of the paper presented) cannot be made. Fan in and fan-out were initially presented by [12]. In this paper, we also consider class size as a factor in consideration of the results. This is based on the premises that as classes and methods grow in size, so too do coupling and therefore faults. The relationship between coupling and faults has been empirically shown to exist in OO software by Basili et al., and specifically in the C++ language by Briand et al., [4]; a framework for the measurement of coupling is provided in [3]. The work of El Emam on the influence of size as a confounding factor is also drawn upon herein; in the paper, it is proposed that size should be taken into account as a confounding variable when validating object-oriented metrics [1]. In this paper, we explored fan-in and fan-out but in the context of size also. The link between design patterns and fault-proneness was explored by Gatrell et al. [11]. Design pattern classes (i.e., those forming the pattern's essential structure) were found to be more fault-prone than classes that were not part of the pattern. Finally, much of the research on fault-proneness has focused on fault prediction [13]; the study presented adds weight to the view that size needs to be considered as an essential factor in any study of faults.

4. CONCLUSIONS/FUTURE WORK

The incidence of faults in a system over time is a reflection of the quality of the system and whether its performance continues to match its initial and ongoing requirements. In this paper, data between six releases of Eclipse was analyzed and fault and coupling data collected from each. Results showed that the fan-in and fan-out pattern/profiles for fault-free *vis-a-vis* fault-prone classes showed notable and significant differences. Low values of fan-in/fan-out seem to promote fault-free classes. Equally, a high fan-out value seemed to predominate in fault-prone classes. One explanation for this feature of the data might be that, conceivably, it is easier to make additions and changes to a class which is not dependent on a large number of classes than one that is. The risk of amending a class with many incoming dependencies is significantly higher because of those dependencies. The message it would appear to a developer is to try, whenever possible to minimise coupling both from an incoming and outgoing perspective as would befit good software engineering practice. However, high values of fan-out should be especially avoided since from the evidence presented they are the classes which tend to evolve into fault-prone classes. It would also appear when scrutinising the data more carefully that the main factor in the high fan-in and fan-out classes is the size of a class. Developers should therefore seek to minimise the size of a class (through re-engineering or refactoring) thereby maintaining its cohesion as well as keeping coupling low. In other words, coupling and size co-evolve and *both* should be monitored.

In terms of future work, these emerging results need to be investigated through analysis of more systems and more releases. In this way, a body of evidence can be constructed. The relationship between specific refactorings and faults is one of several lines of research that this study informs as a partial replication to recent work [15]. We encourage further replication studies of this type as collaborative efforts as a means of generating a body of knowledge in this area. To that end, all the data used for the study presented can be made available upon request of the lead of the Brunel team member listed. Future work will explore other class characteristics for relationships with faults. In particular, whether a Zipf (or 80:20) Law exists between faults and other class features [19] such as cohesion [7] as well as fan-in and fan-out.

5. ACKNOWLEDGEMENTS

The research of Alessandro Murgia is sponsored by the Institute for the Promotion of Innovation through Science and Technology in Flanders through a project entitled Change-centric Quality Assurance (CHAQ) with number 120028.

6. REFERENCES

[1] Basili, V., Briand, L., Melo, W., A Validation of Object-Oriented Design Metrics as Quality Indicators, IEEE Transactions on Software Engineering, 22(10), 1996, 751-761.

[2] Bavota, G., De Carluccio, B., De Lucia, A., Di Penta, M., Oliveto, R., Strollo, O., When does a Refactoring Induce Bugs? An Empirical Study Proceedings Working Conference on Source Code Analysis and Manipulation, Riva del Garda, Italy, 2012.

[3] Briand, L., et al. (1999) A unified framework for coupling measurement in OO systems. IEEE Trans. on Soft. Eng., 25(1), 91-121.

[4] Briand, L., Devanbu, P., Melo, W., An investigation into coupling measures for C++, in 19th International Conference on Software Engineering, Boston, USA, pp. 412-421, 1997.

[5] Briand, L., Daly, J. Wust, J., A unified framework for coupling measurement in object-oriented systems, IEEE Transactions on Soft. Engineering, 25: 91-121, 1999.

[6] Chidamber, S.R., Kemerer, C.F., A metrics suite for object oriented design, IEEE Trans. on Soft, Engineering, 20:476-493, 1994.

[7] Counsell, S., Swift, S., Crampton, J., The interpretation and utility of three cohesion metrics for object-oriented design. ACM Transactions on Softw. Eng. Methodol. 15(2): 123-149 2006.

[8] El Emam, K., Benlarbi, S., Goel, N., S. Rai: The Confounding Effect of Class Size on the Validity of Object-Oriented Metrics. IEEE Trans. Software Eng. 27(7): 630-650 (2001).

[9] Fenton, N., Pfleeger, S., Software Metrics: A Rigorous and Practical Approach', International Thomson Computer Press, 1996.

[10] Fowler, M., Refactoring: Improving the Design of Existing Code. Addison-Wesley Professional, 1999.

[11] Gatrell, M., Counsell, S., Design patterns and fault-proneness: a study of commercial C# software, IEEE International Conference on Research Challenges in Information Science, Guadeloupe, 1-8, 2011

[12] Henry, S., Kafura, D., Software Structure Metrics Based on Information Flow, IEEE Transactions on Soft. Engineering 5:510 – 518, 1981.

[13] Hall, T., Beecham, S., Bowes, D., Gray, D., Counsell, S., A Systematic Literature Review on Fault Prediction Performance in Software Engineering IEEE Transactions on Software Engineering, 2012.

[14] JHawk tool: www.virtualmachinery.com/jhawkprod.htm). 2013.

[15] Murgia, A. Tonelli, R., Counsell, S., Concas, G., Marchesi, M., An Empirical Study of Refactoring in the Context of Fan-in and Fan-out: an Empirical Study. Proceedings of European Conference on Software Engineering, Szeged, Hungary, March 2012.

[16] Prete, K., Rachatasumrit, N., Sudan, N., Kim, M., Template-based Reconstruction of Complex Refactorings, International Conference on Software Maintenance, Timisoara, Romania, pp. 1-10, 2010.

[17] Rosenberg, J., Some Misconceptions About Lines of Code, IEEE International Software Metrics Symposium, (METRICS '97), pages 137-143, Bethesda, Maryland, USA, 1997.

[18] Weißgerber, P., Diehl, S., Are refactorings less error-prone than other changes? Proceedings of the International Workshop on Mining software repositories, pages 112–118. ACM, 2006.

[19] Zipf, G., Human Behavior and the Principle of Least Effort, Addison-Wesley, 1949.

Run-Time Performance Optimization of a BigData Query Language

Yanbin Liu, Parijat Dube,
Scott C. Gray
IBM Watson Research Center
Yorktown Heights, USA.
ygliu,pdube,sgray@us.ibm.com

ABSTRACT

JAQL is a query language for large-scale data that connects BigData analytics and MapReduce framework together. Also an IBM product, JAQL's performance is critical for IBM InfoSphere BigInsights, a BigData analytics platform. In this paper, we report our work on improving JAQL performance from multiple perspectives. We explore the parallelism of JAQL, profile JAQL for performance analysis, identify I/O as the dominant performance bottleneck, and improve JAQL performance with an emphasis on reducing I/O data size and increasing (de)serialization efficiency. With TPCH benchmark on a simple Hadoop cluster, we report up to 2x performance improvements in JAQL with our optimization fixes.

Categories and Subject Descriptors

C.4 [**Computer Systems Organization**]: Performance of Systems—*Performance attributes*

Keywords

BigInsights, JAQL, MapReduce, Multi-thread, I/O optimization, Java performance

1. INTRODUCTION

The proliferation of cheaper technologies for collecting and transmitting data of different modalities and formats from different sources such as sensors, cameras, Internet feeds, social networks, mobile phones etc. has rendered the business world with vast amount of data. This plethora of data, if properly processed, can provide significant new insights for tracking markets, customers and business performance. Information management of such vast amount of *Big Data* is critical and technologies for efficient and cost-effective filtering, storing and accessing of data are increasingly sought after. Big Data [2] is typically characterized by having 4 Vs: high Volume, high Velocity, high Variety and Veracity which is a measure of uncertainty in data. Processing of Big Data within reasonable time requires programming

models supporting large-scale, parallel and efficient execution of queries on scale-out infrastructure. The MapReduce programming paradigm, first introduced by Google [10] provides a framework for large-scale parallel data processing. Apache Hadoop [1] is an open-source implementation of MapReduce.

While highly scalable, MapReduce is notoriously difficult to use. The Java API is tedious and requires programming expertise. Query languages like Apache Hive [17], Apache Pig [11] and JAQL [9] provide high-level abstraction to express queries which are then compiled into low-level MapReduce jobs.

IBM InfoSphere BigInsights [4] is a platform for scalable processing of Big Data analytics applications in an enterprise. BigInsights builds on top of open-source Hadoop by adding several features for cost effective management, processing and analysis of enterprise Big Data.

JAQL [9] is an integral part of BigInsights where it provides both the run time and an integration point for various analytics including text analytics, statistical analysis, machine learning, and ad-hoc analysis. Figure 1 shows the BigInsights platform stack. BigInsights applications are executed either entirely in JAQL or JAQL instantiates Hadoop MapReduce jobs for scalable query execution. In BigInsights, JAQL also provides modules to connect to various data sources like local and distributed file systems, relational databases, NoSQL databases. Performance of BigInsights applications is integrally tied with the performance of JAQL and Hadoop run-time.

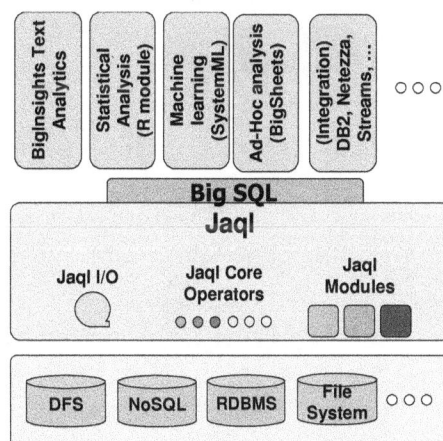

Figure 1: BigInsights Architecture

BigInsights needs a fast run-time to improve performance and needs an ability to run SQL queries. Big SQL is a new and important component of BigInsights providing support for SQL queries execution. Big SQL server is multithreaded supporting multiple sessions and thus can exploit performance scaling offered by multi-thread, multi-core systems. Since JAQL provides run-time environment for BigInsights applications, the focus on run-time efficiency and support for multi-thread execution in JAQL is important for scalable execution of Big SQL and other multi-threaded applications supported by BigInsights including IBM InfoSphere DataStage [5], Tableau [6], and IBM BigSheets [3]. Our work improves JAQL run-time performance in multithread, multi-core environments through: (i) Enabling runtime support for multi-threaded applications running on top of JAQL, and (ii) Speeding-up query execution time by identifying performance bottlenecks and fixing them.

Section 2 provides background information on query processing in BigInsights. Various run-time performance issues of JAQL are highlighted in Section 3. Our solution for enabling multi-thread execution in JAQL run-time is discussed in Section 4. Experiments showcasing improvements in Big SQL/JAQL run-time performance as a result of our optimizations are presented in Section 5. Related work is covered in Section 6 followed by conclusion and future work in Section 7.

2. BACKGROUND

JAQL [9] consists of three major components as shown in Figure 2: a scripting language, a compiler and a runtime component for MapReduce framework to transparently exploit parallelism. JAQL scripting language is designed for analyzing complex/nested semi-structured data. It provides a flexible data model based on JSON (Java Script Object Notation), an easy-to-extend modular design including firstclass functions and a set of syntax for supporting controlflow statements and SQL queries. JAQL compiler is the central-piece that detects parallelism in a JAQL script and translates it into a set of MapReduce jobs. JAQL runtime component for MapReduce framework defines map, combine, reduce, (de)serialization and etc. functions that will be executed in the MapReduce framework.

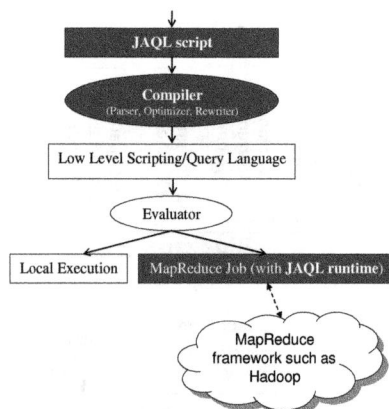

Figure 2: JAQL components

JAQL programming language has been utilized for a number of years for developing large scale analytics on Hadoop clusters. With the release of IBM BigInsights 2.1 (itself a Hadoop distribution) JAQL began to play a more important role by acting as the query parallelization engine and execution runtime for the Big SQL component and, as a result, it was important to dramatically increase the performance of JAQL, particularly when applied to the structured data world of SQL.

The Big SQL component of BigInsights contains a sophisticated SQL optimization and re-write engine that is responsible for taking modern, ANSI SQL, containing complex constructs, such as windowed aggregates, common table expressions, and subqueries, and optimizing the queries via a number of re-write steps. Examples of such optimization include:

- Decorrelation of subqueries

- Lifting of common, repeated queries or query fragments into common table expressions

- Identifying queries that cannot benefit from parallel execution

- Mapping of certain SQL constructs such as interval arithmetic into function calls

The output of the query optimization engine is a re-written SQL query that is then passed to JAQL for processing, at which point JAQL performs the following steps:

1. The SQL statement is immediately re-written into an equivalent JAQL expression. This expression is written in the same fashion that a user of JAQL would have written the query – that is, it contains no indication of how the query should be executed, but is simply an expression of the query that is to be performed.

2. The JAQL rewriter then performs a large number of query re-writes and optimizations, which includes basic activities such as simplifying expressions (e.g. 2 + 2 will be simplified to 4) to more complex re-writes, such as determining whether or not the query can be parallelized and, if so, how to approach the parallelization. Some of these optimizations are directed by the query rewriter via hints that were passed into JAQL via the original SQL statement.

3. The final result of all of these optimizations is a valid JAQL script. In many cases, this script will be decomposed into a series of explicit MapReduce jobs to achieve the end goal of executing the query.

While JAQL has been capable of the majority of the functionality described above for a number of years, in order to utilize it as the runtime for Big SQL, it was necessary to optimize a number of aspects of the language.

3. JAQL PERFORMANCE

3.1 Parallelism

JAQL performance, which includes the performance of both JAQL compiler and JAQL MapReduce runtime, can be influenced by multiple factors. As the multi-core, multiprocessor become the main trend today, the first factor we look at is the parallelism. As we discussed above, by design,

JAQL already explores parallelism by transparently generating MapReduce jobs that can be executed in parallel. In this paper, we explore more parallelism by analyzing the multi-layer software stack of JAQL.

At the top-most level, a JAQL instance, which maintains the state information such as the declared variable and their values, function definitions and etc, can be started either by an interactive shell or an application that submits JAQL statements such as Big SQL. While an interactive shell is used by one user in general and corresponds to one JAQL session naturally, an application may submit JAQL statements on behalf of multiple users who have different objectives. For example, Big SQL supports multi-session and each session represents a separate expression stream from one user. In the past, each process could have at most one JAQL instance. With the changes we have made, we now allow one process to manage multiple JAQL instances (possibly each instance masquerading as a different user in MapReduce). While each JAQL session has at least one executing thread, we are able to improve the performance on a multi-core system with an increased number of threads.

After we have multiple JAQL sessions in one process, we continue with inter-session parallelism. A JAQL session consists of a sequence of JAQL statements, some of which will be rewritten as MapReduce jobs and submitted to a MapReduce framework such as Apache Hadoop [1]. We look at the input and output of the MapReduce jobs and check if there is data dependency among them. When there is no data dependency, we do not wait for the previous jobs to return, but continue with submitting jobs to the MapReduce framework. In this paper, we restrict ourselves to modify JAQL only and will not discuss the scheduling of MapReduce jobs. With ample resources and/or a capable MapReduce scheduler, we are able to improve the performance with submitting MapReduce jobs as early as possible.

3.2 I/O

JAQL is designed for large-scale data analysis and not surprisingly, I/O performance is critical for JAQL performance. This is verified by our experiment that for the benchmark we are running, I/O can be accounted for more than 35% of the total execution time.

3.2.1 I/O Data Size

I/O performance is defined by both I/O speed and I/O data size. When we are discussing the problem in the environment of large-scale data, I/O data size is the first thing that draws our attention. How to reduce the size of the data that needs to be read/write to either the file system or the network is critical for I/O performance. For a MapReduce job executed in Hadoop, its map tasks read input from a distributed file system such as HDFS and reduce tasks write output to HDFS. Inside map and reduce tasks, intermediate results are read from and written to the local file system. In this paper, we are more focused on how to reduce the size of the intermediate data.

3.2.2 I/O (De)Serialization Speed

I/O speed consists of I/O hardware speed, such as the speed of hard disks, and I/O software speed. In this paper, we are concerned about only I/O software speed and especially I/O software speed decided by the JAQL code.

JAQL runtime defines the serialization and de-serialization functions. Inside Hadoop, when data is written to and read from HDFS and local disk or when the data is merged and combined, data is serialized and de-serialized multiple times. We show that we can improve (de)serialization speed by 20%.

3.3 Methodology

Our methodology to analyze and improve JAQL performance is an iterative process as shown in Figure 3. At first, we profile different JAQL components. Then, depending on the profiling results, we identify and locate the performance bottlenecks. After that, we develop solutions to address the performance problems and implement them in the code. To verify the correctness of the solution and to locate new bottlenecks, we profile the new version of the implementation and repeat the process.

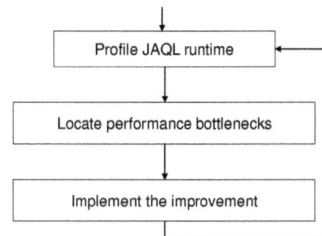

Figure 3: Methodology

4. THREAD-SAFE JAQL RUN-TIME

As we discussed above, JAQL should be able to support multi-session and thus multi-thread to improve its performance on multi-core, multi-processor systems. In general, this problem is a typical textbook problem. However, the problem gets tricky when JAQL sessions share the underlying Hadoop environment including file systems. We will describe it in more details later.

Each JAQL instance supports multiple sessions and each JAQL session has one main thread to parse, compile and evaluate JAQL statement one by one. We save the session resources in the thread local storage of the main thread and call it the session context.

Originally, we make all the shared data as session resources, which are shared among the threads of the same session. That is, we keep a copy of the shared data in the session context. For example, for system properties that describe the environment configuration, we maintain a copy in each session such that each session can configure its environment independently.

Then, we convert some session resources to globally shared resources in the following cases.

- The resource is expensive to initialize. For example, for Hadoop 1.1 we used in this paper, creating a default JobConf [1] involves reading multiple configuration files and is an expensive operation. We make the default configuration a global resource, create it once at the beginning. Each session then makes its own copy of the default JobConf and be able to modify its copy later and thus configure its Hadoop jobs independently.

---

[1] JobConf describes a map-reduce job and needs to be defined when a user submits a job to Hadoop.

- The resource is read-only after initialization. For example, some JAQL specific data structure such as exception handlers falls into this category.

- The resource is not accessed frequently. We make these resources globally shared and synchronize the access to them. The decision is a trade-off between speed and space. For example, we have a variable tz to represent the current time zone. Another variable df represents a date format; a user can call $df.format$ to return a string with the pre-defined date format. The implementation of both variables are from third parties and can not be changed easily. One the one hand, we make tz a global resource to save space since it is not changed frequently. One the other hand, we make df a session resource to avoid synchronizing every call to $df.format$.

The tricky part of making JAQL thread-safe is because of its feature of using Hadoop. The map and reduce functions defined by JAQL read from and write to files. The Hadoop API's, while largely thread safe, do maintain certain global state information, such as the currently active file system, as well as the working and temporary directory within this file system. Without any modification, each JAQL session will use Hadoop APIs to set the active file system as well as working and temporary directories and assuming these global values stay unchanged, use relative paths to locate files later. Unfortunately, it is not the case when there is another JAQL session that may change these values. Thus, as part of the effort to make JAQL thread safe, it was necessary to save each session's settings of the file system and call the Hadoop API carefully to locate the files correctly.

We have implemented the thread-safe JAQL and tested it with a suite of unit tests, which consists of 48 scripts that test different functions provided by JAQL. We have verified the correctness of our implementation by running the suite of tests in three JAQL optimization settings and be able to finish the tests more than 10 times faster.

5. PERFORMANCE ANALYSIS AND OPTIMIZATION

5.1 Profiling JAQL

To improve JAQL performance, we first identify the latency oriented bottlenecks. We accomplish this work by profiling JAQL using JProfiler [16], Hadoop monitoring tools and self-developed monitoring tools.

In this paper, we shall focus on the performance of SQL queries that are issued by Big SQL, which is an important component of BigInsights. JAQL compiler, which is executed inside of the Big SQL process, is responsible of parsing and interpreting SQL query, optimizing the query plan, and forming and submitting the MapReduce jobs. After the job is submitted to Hadoop, JAQL runtime for MapReduce will be executed in the JVMs started by map and reduce tasks. Thus, we shall profile both the Big SQL process and the JVMs of Hadoop map and reduce tasks to analyze JAQL performance.

The first observation we make is that the latency is mostly due to MapReduce job. For a query that takes minutes to finish, the time spent inside Big SQL before the job submission is in milliseconds level. Besides, this time will not change much with a different input and output while the

time of MapReduce job depends greatly on the size of input and output data. Next, we should focus on the JAQL runtime for MapReduce since this is where most time is spent and where we can achieve most improvement of latency.

One SQL query issued by Big SQL can generate multiple MapReduce jobs; one MapReduce job can include multiple map and reduce tasks where each task starts a new JVM by default Hadoop configuration. In order to avoid resource competition of multiple JVMs on the same host, especially the competition over I/O and do a clean profiling, we configure Hadoop such that at any time, there is only one JVM running. Specifically, we set

mapred.tasktracker.map.tasks.maximum=1 and
mapred.tasktracker.reduce.tasks.maximum=1

such that there is only one slot for map task and one slot for reduce task on the host. Then, we set

mapred.reduce.slowstart.completed.maps=1.0

such that Hadoop should start reduce task after all the map tasks are completed. Thus, at any time, we will have only one JVM, at first for map tasks, then for reduce tasks. However, this still give us many JVMs when the number of map and reduce tasks is big. We go one step further to set

mapred.job.reuse.jvm.num.tasks=-1

such that all map tasks will share one JVM instead of starting a new one for each map task and all reduce tasks will share one JVM.

Since we restrict ourselves to JAQL runtime for MapReduce, the configuration discussed above is not only simplifying our profiling work, but also removing the overhead details that are outside of our interest range.

5.2 TPCH Benchmark

We use TPCH benchmark [18] to measure our performance. TPCH is a benchmark consisted of a set of SQL queries, which involves operations such as join, union, filter, sort, aggregate functions and etc, to a database that can be populated to a specified size. For the experiment results in this paper, we populate the database with 1G data and we choose to profile 6 queries which involve different operations as shown in Table 1 and they all involve querying the biggest table, which has 6G rows, in the database.

5.3 Performance Analysis and Optimization

5.3.1 Big SQL

We profile Big SQL server and verify that JAQL performance is critical for Big SQL performance. As shown in Figure 4, more than 70% of the execution time is spent on JAQL runtime, among which 31% is spent on parsing the query, 19% on rewriting and optimizing the query plan, and 22% on evaluating the query plan. One interesting thing to notice is that 15% of the execution time comes from the international component for unicode (com.ibm.icu) that is used to initiate JsonDate.

5.3.2 JAQL Runtime for MapReduce

As we mentioned earlier in the paper, the execution time of MapReduce jobs dominants the total execution time and deserves more attention for performance consideration. We profile the JVMs for map and reduce tasks with the Hadoop

query	operations	# M/R jobs	results
q1	aggregate functions (sum, avg)	2	4 rec with 11 col
q3	join	4	10 rec with 4 col
q5	nested join	4	5 rec with 2 col
q7	join and union all	5	4 rec with 4 col
q21	join and right outer join	7	100 rec with 2 col

Table 1: TPCH queries

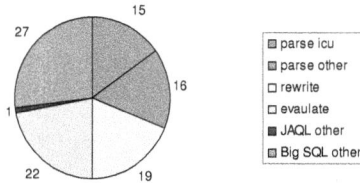

Figure 4: Big SQL Execution Time

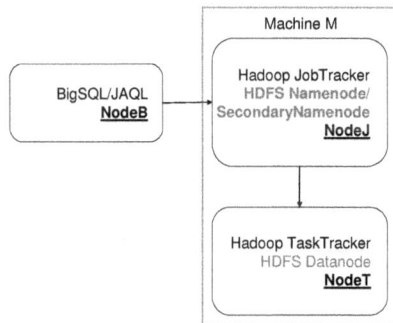

Figure 5: Hadoop Cluster

configuration discussed earlier and in the following, we report our observations and the improvements we made.

To focus on the profiling of JAQL runtime for MapReduce, we set up a simple Hadoop cluster with 2 nodes: one node J as Hadoop job tracker, HDFS Name node and secondary Name node; the other node T as Hadoop task tracker and HDFS Data node. The Big SQL server is on a separate node B. Node J and T are both VMWare virtual machines instantiated on one physical machine, which is a Dual-Core AMD processor with 2.2G CPU. Node B is a Intel Xeco CPU with 24 processors each of which has 1.6G CPU.

We issue the TPCH queries from Big SQL server and profile the map and reduce tasks executed. For the map tasks of the 1st job from query q1 of TPCH benchmark, we find that 50% is spent on JAQL defined map function and 46% is spent on combining and sorting the Mapper̆s output among which 40% is spent on JAQL defined combine function. In total, JAQL runtime accounts to 90% of the execution time of the map task and is obviously crtical for the performance of MapReduce jobs.

We look at the profiling results deeper and observe that I/O serialization is dominant. For the same scenery as above, we observe that 16% is spent on

...binary.temp.TempBinaryFullSerializer.write

, which is responsible of writing the output of mappers, and 19% on

...binary.temp.TempBinaryFullSerializer.read

, which is responsible of the reading the input of mappers.

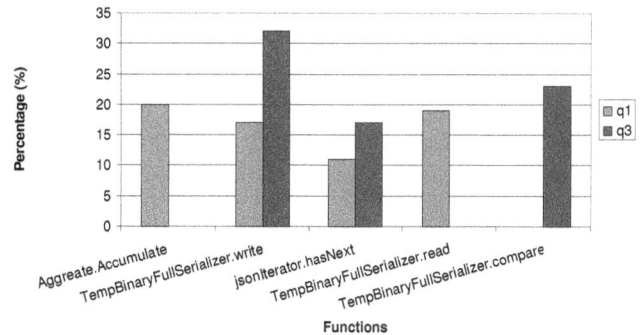

Figure 6: Comparison between Q1 and Q3

The dominance of I/O is not unique for q1, though the exact pattern may be different. As the comparison of q1 and the 1st job of q3 shown in Figure 6, we can see that for q1, the I/O accounts for 35% combining both write and read operations while for q3, the I/O accounts for 32% for write operation only. Besides that, q1 spends 20% on Aggregate.Accumulate which deals with the aggregate functions in the query such as avg, sum, count and etc.; q3 spends 23% on TempBinaryFullSerializer.compare which compares the values. The remaining function jsonIterator.hasNext is used to iterate the expressions and evaluate their values.

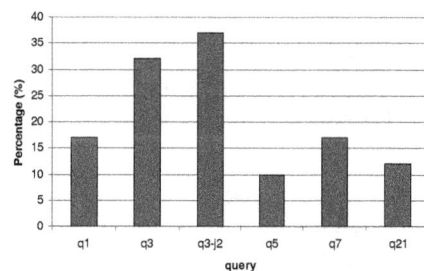

Figure 7: Percentage of Query's write operation

For other queries, we show the comparison result of the I/O write operation in Figure 7. From the figure, we can see that the percentage of

...binary.temp.TempBinaryFullSerializer.write

can be as high as 37% for the map task of the 2nd job of q3 and can be as low as 10% for q5.

5.4 I/O data size

Since I/O performance is dominant in many queries as shown in the above figures, we focus on I/O performance to improve JAQL overall performance. I/O performance is decided by both I/O data size and I/O speed.

We first summarize our effort to reduce I/O data size from different perspectives as follows. Since we cannot reduce the data size of initial input and final output, we check the query plan generated by JAQL and remove unnecessary intermediate data.

5.4.1 Number of Jobs

The goal is to reduce the number of jobs. As fewer jobs are generated, there is no need to pass the data to next job and thus can reduce I/O data size. Also, all the overhead of starting a new job will be eliminated. Both Big SQL and JAQL have optimized the query plan to reduce the number of jobs.

In this paper, we have JAQL dynamically adjust whether or not a particular job should be done locally or submitted to Mapreduce by examining the output of the previous job, which is also the input of the current job. That is, if the input of the current job is smaller than a pre-defined threshold, the job will be done locally to save the overhead of MapReduce framework and remote execution.

5.4.2 Number of Objects

Another goal of optimizing the query plan is to reduce the number of objects that needs to be passed between map and reduce tasks of the same job and the ones passed between jobs of the same query.

The improvement of JAQL on this perspective includes 1) push down the filtering conditions as deep as possible and thus filter out unnecessary objects as early as possible; 2) optimize the order of multiple filtering conditions with hints to do the most effective filtering first; 3) optimize the join order of multiple joins and join methods if they are not explicitly defined with hints to reduce the number of intermediate join results. The hints can be the size of the input tables, the number of rows that may match the join and filter condition, and other operations of the same query.

Another improvement has been reported in [19] which proposes adapting MapReduce to achieve a higher performance. In specific, "situation-aware" map tasks are implemented such that they can communicate through a distributed meta-data store and thus be able to have a global picture of the job. Besides the benefit of load-balancing, another benefit is to generate a smaller number of objects and thus reduce I/O size.

5.4.3 Number of Columns

It is obvious that we should eliminate the columns if they are not needed in the future. The trick is to examine the query plan that was chosen and decide, at any given step, if a particular column is no longer needed after that step, that it is eliminated and the values for the column are not transmitted to the next job in the chain. For example, if a column is only referenced during a single join, but no where else in the query, then after that join has been processed, the column is no longer needed for subsequent steps, such as additional joins, or sorting and grouping.

5.4.4 Number of Encoded Bytes

From both previous experience of other researchers and our experiments, we do not see observable improvement of enabling Hadoop data compression. Thus, we implement our own mechanism to encode the data and reduce the number of encoded bytes.

JAQL, being a language based upon JSON, tends to carry values around in JSON structures that are records [2]. So a given row may look like a record of:

$$\{ \; c1: \; 10, \; c2: \; \text{"bob"}, \; c3: \; \text{"nelson"} \; \}$$

However, in a language like SQL, where you always have a strict schema, it is not necessary to carry around such structures, because the metadata exists externally to the data, the same value as above may be carried around as a simple array [3] of [10, "bob", "nelson"] saving significant space, where the column names don't need to be represented in every row, and processing time, where values are retrieved by position, not name.

The optimization that was performed is to make JAQL more aware of when the data is well formed with a schema, and that all operations performed on the data will result in data that is well formed. In these circumstances, JAQL can treat records as arrays. It can compile out the references to fields of records, such as $t1.c1 > 10$ and replace it with $t1[0] > 10$ and thus can avoid carrying around the associated metadata for the columns in each record.

5.5 I/O (de)serialization overhead

In this paper, for I/O speed, we only consider the I/O overhead imposed by JAQL code, especially the serialization and de-serialization. Besides the de-serialization and serialization of input and output, the intermediate results will need to go through multiple de-serialization and serialization when they are mapped, combined, shuffled, spilled and reduced.

By further analysis, we discovered that we can reduce the number of times when the objects were being de-serialized, especially in the mapper. The problem is that during grouping, Hadoop is de-serializing previously serialized objects in order to compare them to determine which group to place the new object into. To avoid this, JAQL is changed to serialize all of its data in such a fashion that values are binary-collatable. That is, given two buffers full of serialized data, the buffers can have a byte comparison performed in order to collate, rather than having to de-serialize either of the buffers.

By profiling, we are also able to catch the inefficiency points of JAQL implemented serialization and de-serialization functions. We identify RecordSerializer.partition, which deals with record, and ArraySerializer.write, which deals with array, as the hot methods since they are called many times and the total time spent on them is big.

JAQL, being initially designed for loosely structured data, allows for arrays of heterogeneous data, and structures that can be completely different from row to row. As a result, the process of serializing data consists of a significant amount of introspection of a value's type before serialization. To

---

[2] A JAQL record is an un-ordered collection of name-value pairs where name is a literal string and value can be an atomic value, record or list.

[3] A JAQL array is an ordered collection of values.

improve on this situation, we enhance JAQL to recognize situations in which the schema is fully computable, such as in SQL operations, and the general purpose serializers that JAQL would normally use are swapped out with special-purpose serializers that understand, for example, how to serialize only an array of non-nullable long values. These optimizations even include recognizing when a particular value is invariant (for example, could never be anything but the value "3") and avoiding serialization for such values altogether.

5.6 Other improvement

In the following, we describe other improvements we have made into JAQL.

By profiling, we observe that an important portion of execution time is spent on jsonIterator.hasNext as shown in Figure 6. Inside this function, Expr.eval is called to evaluate an expression's value. Once a value is recognized as math expression, MathExpr.evalRaw is called to get the value. However, this function will again call Expr.eval and MathExpr.evalRaw repeatedly, nested to many levels. We also observe that ArrayExpr.evalRaw is expensive due to the fact that it involves many layers of type check.

As with the scenario of serialization, described in the previous section, many operations in JAQL allow for heterogeneous data types. For example, in the expression

$$<prev\ expr> .. \rightarrow filter\ \$.a + \$.b > 10$$

the + and > operators will inspect their values each and every time they are called to determine the input types, how to compute the result, and what type the result should be, thus a significant amount of time is spent during this inspection and making these decisions. This was optimized by, again, recognizing the cases in which the types of the operands are invariant (based upon the schema of the expression) and replacing the general purpose operator with a special purpose operator that only knows how to perform the operation on the specific data type(s) involved in the operation.

5.7 Experiment Results

Next, we demonstrate the performance improvement of the proposed methods discussed above.

In Figure 8, we show the improvement ratio of each job generated by the queries. For example, q7, q7-j2, q7-j3 are the three jobs generated by query q7. The performance improvement of reducing the number of jobs as discussed above is small and is not shown in the figure. The reason is that only the jobs with small input are executed locally and the improvement is in the seconds level while the queries tested here will take minutes to finish. Thus, the improvement ratio is small.

The first set of bars in the figure shows the improvement by reducing the number of objects. The 2nd set of bars shows the improvement by reducing I/O (de)serialization overhead and other improvement. The 3rd set of bars shows the improvement of reducing the number of columns and the number of decoded bytes. We can see that reducing the I/O data size has a bigger effect than reducing (de)serialization overhead in our experiment. And with all the improvements, we are able to improve the performance of queries up to more than 2X.

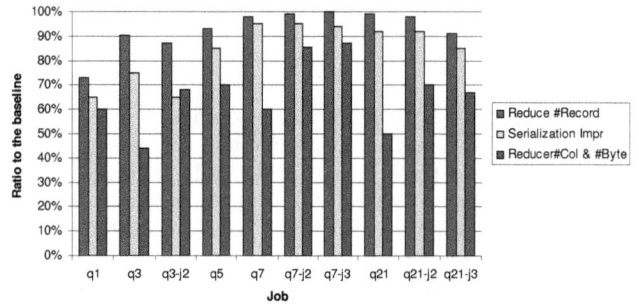

Figure 8: Performance Improvement

6. RELATED WORK

The authors of [15] provide a comparison of three high level query languages for Map reduce, namely, Pig, Hive, and JAQL, on the bases of their functional features and run-time performance. The scalability tests in this study are done using simple non-commercial benchmarks. A qualitative evaluation of these query languages and compilation of their queries into MapReduce jobs is presented in [14]. It was concluded that JAQL, with its expressive power and flexibility, is best suited for large-scale data processing in Big Data analytics. In [13] XQuery language is extended to support JSON data model and the XQuery processor is extended to support MapReduce execution.

MapReduce paradigm is based on isolated execution of individual map tasks (belonging to the same job) which sometimes restrict the choice of algorithms that can be executed in the map-phase. To overcome this limitation, an Adaptive Map-Reduce approach based on Situation-Aware Mappers (SAMs) was introduced in [8, 19]. SAMs which are basically mappers with an asynchronous communication channel between them for exchanging state information. This improves performance of a class of aggregate functions by limiting the output data from map jobs that needs to be shuffled and copied to reduce nodes. They also proposed a new API for developing User Defined Aggregates (UDAs) in JAQL to exploit SAMs.

A technique for run-time performance prediction of JAQL queries (with fixed data flows) over varying input data sets is developed in [12]. Such techniques can be used for optimal resource provisioning and scheduling by MapReduce schedulers like FLEX [20] to meet query performance related Service Level Agreements (SLAs).

The research of [7] describes eXtreme Analytics Platform (XAP), a powerful platform for large-scale data-intensive analytics developed at IBM Research. The main building blocks of XAP are JAQL, FLEX scheduler for optimized allocation of resources to Hadoop jobs, data-warehouses connectors and libraries and tools for advanced analytics. Many of the XAP technologies are incorporated in IBM InfoSphere BigInsights [4] product.

7. CONCLUSION

JAQL is a query language designed for large-scale data analysis. It provides an easy-to-use, flexible and extensible interface to the BigData analytics and explores massive parallelism using MapReduce framework. It is an important component of BigInsights, an IBM flagship product on Big-Data, and its performance is critical for SQL queries submitted by Big SQL and other data analytics applications built on it.

We improve JAQL performance from multiple perspectives. We make JAQL thread-safe and further explore its parallelism; we profile JAQL intensively for performance analysis; we identify that JAQL compiler is dominant in execution time inside Big SQL and JAQL runtime for MapReduce is dominant in execution time inside MapReduce framework; we further identify I/O is critical for performance and be able to improve I/O performance by reducing the I/O data size and increase (de)serialization efficiency.

We profile and measure our improvements in a simple Hadoop cluster with special configuration to reduce the number of JVMs. We show that the performance of TPCH queries can be improved up to 2 times and the biggest improvement comes from the reduction of data size.

In the future, we would like to explore parallelism further inside JAQL. For example, we can check the data dependency beyond the range of one statement (one SQL query) and continue with the statements without data dependency as long as possible. As Hadoop YARN is available, we would like to investigate how JAQL will benefit from the new Hadoop infrastructure. We are also interested in the generation of query plans and investigate if we can reduce I/O data size by a better query plan.

8. REFERENCES

[1] Apache Hadoop. Available at http://hadoop.apache.org.

[2] IBM Big Data & Analytics Hub. Available at http://www.ibmbigdatahub.com/.

[3] IBM BigSheets. Available at http://www-01.ibm.com/software/ebusiness/jstart/bigsheets/.

[4] IBM InfoSphere BigInsights. Available at http://www.ibm.com/software/data/infosphere/biginsights/.

[5] IBM InfoSphere DataStage. Available at http://www-03.ibm.com/software/products/en/ibminfodata/.

[6] Tableau Software. Available at http://www.tableausoftware.com/.

[7] A. Balmin, K. Beyer, V. Ercegovac, J. McPherson, F. Ozcan, H. Pirahesh, E. Shekita, Y. Sismanis, S. Tata, and Y. Tian. A platform for extreme analytics. *IBM Journal of Research and Development*, 57(3/4):4:1–4:11, 2013.

[8] Andrey Balmin, Vuk Ercegovac, Rares Vernica, and Kevin S. Beyer. Adaptive processing of user-defined aggregates in jaql. *IEEE Data Eng. Bull.*, 34(4):36–43, 2011.

[9] Kevin S. Beyer, Vuk Ercegovac, Rainer Gemulla, Andrey Balmin, Mohamed Y. Eltabakh, Carl C. Kanne, Fatma Özcan, and Eugene J. Shekita. Jaql: A Scripting Language for Large Scale Semistructured Data Analysis. *PVLDB*, 4(12):1272–1283, 2011.

[10] Jeffrey Dean and Sanjay Ghemawat. Mapreduce: a flexible data processing tool. *Communications of the ACM*, 53(1):72–77, 2010.

[11] Christopher Olston, Benjamin Reed, Utkarsh Srivastava, Ravi Kumar, and Andrew Tomkins. Pig latin: a not-so-foreign language for data processing. In *Proceedings of the 2008 ACM SIGMOD international conference on Management of data*, SIGMOD '08, pages 1099–1110, New York, NY, USA, 2008. ACM.

[12] Adrian D. Popescu, Vuk Ercegovac, Andrey Balmin, Miguel Branco, and Anastasia Ailamaki. Same queries, different data: Can we predict query performance? In *Proceedings of the 7th International Workshop on Self Managing Database Systems*, Washington DC, USA, April 2012.

[13] Caetano Sauer, Sebastian BÃd'chle, and Theo HÃd'rder. Versatile xquery processing in mapreduce. In Barbara Catania, Giovanna Guerrini, and Jaroslav PokornÃ¡, editors, *Advances in Databases and Information Systems*, volume 8133 of *Lecture Notes in Computer Science*, pages 204–217. Springer Berlin Heidelberg, 2013.

[14] Caetano Sauer and Theo HÃd'rder. Compilation of query languages into mapreduce. *Datenbank-Spektrum*, 13(1):5–15, 2013.

[15] RobertJ. Stewart, PhilW. Trinder, and Hans-Wolfgang Loidl. Comparing high level mapreduce query languages. In Olivier Temam, Pen-Chung Yew, and Binyu Zang, editors, *Advanced Parallel Processing Technologies*, volume 6965 of *Lecture Notes in Computer Science*, pages 58–72. Springer Berlin Heidelberg, 2011.

[16] EJ technologies. Jprofiler manual. 2013.

[17] Ashish Thusoo, Joydeep Sen Sarma, Namit Jain, Zheng Shao, Prasad Chakka, Suresh Anthony, Hao Liu, Pete Wyckoff, and Raghotham Murthy. Hive: a warehousing solution over a map-reduce framework. *Proc. VLDB Endow.*, 2(2):1626–1629, August 2009.

[18] Transaction Processing Performance Council (TPC). Tpc benchmark^{TM} h standard specification revision 2.16.0. 2013.

[19] Rares Vernica, Andrey Balmin, Kevin S. Beyer, and Vuk Ercegovac. Adaptive mapreduce using situation-aware mappers. In *Proceedings of the 15th International Conference on Extending Database Technology*, EDBT '12, pages 420–431, New York, NY, USA, 2012. ACM.

[20] Joel Wolf, Deepak Rajan, Kirsten Hildrum, Rohit Khandekar, Vibhore Kumar, Sujay Parekh, Kun-Lung Wu, and Andrey Balmin. Flex: A slot allocation scheduling optimizer for mapreduce workloads. In Indranil Gupta and Cecilia Mascolo, editors, *Middleware 2010*, volume 6452 of *Lecture Notes in Computer Science*, pages 1–20. Springer Berlin Heidelberg, 2010.

Model-driven Engineering in Practice: Integrated Performance Decision Support for Process-centric Business Impact Analysis

David Redlich
Lancaster University
Lancaster, UK
mr.redlich@gmail.com

Ulrich Winkler
Queen's University
Belfast, UK
uli.winkler@gmail.com

Thomas Molka
University Manchester
Manchester, UK
thomasmolka@gmail.com

Wasif Gilani
SAP Research Centre
Belfast, UK
wasif.gilani@sap.com

ABSTRACT

Modern businesses and business processes depend on an increasingly interconnected set of resources, which can be affected by external and internal factors at any time. Threats like natural disasters, terrorism, or even power blackouts potentially cause disruptions in an organisation's resource infrastructure which in turn negatively impacts the performance of dependent business processes. In order to assist business analysts dealing with this ever increasing complexity of interdependent business structures a model-driven workbench named Model-Driven Business Impact Analysis (MDBIA) has been developed with the purpose of predicting consequences on the business process level for an organisation in case of disruptions. An already existing Model-Driven Performance Engineering (MDPE) workbench, which originally provided process-centric performance decision support, has been adapted and extended to meet the additional requirements of business impact analysis. The fundamental concepts of the resulting MDBIA workbench, which include the introduction of the applied key models and transformation chain, are presented and evaluated in this paper.

Keywords

model-driven engineering, model-driven performance engineering, business process management, business impact analysis

1. INTRODUCTION

Events like the hurricane Katrina, 9/11, or the tsunami in Fukushima have a measurable impact on our society, in general, and organisations, in particular. These consequences are often of a enormous scale, e.g. through direct and indi-

rect impact of 9/11 nearly 18,000 businesses were disrupted, dislocated, or destroyed [1]. Whether disruptions have a huge impact, like 9/11, or are rather small, like the temporary loss of connection to the Internet, an organisation has to be prepared and act accordingly in order to avoid or minimise financial and reputation losses, or even legal consequences.

Business Impact Analysis (BIA) methodologies examine consequences caused by adverse events. In a direct way, resources, such as facilities or an organisation's IT infrastructure, are impacted. These, in turn, may negatively affect the performance of dependent business processes, which eventually leads to a reduced operability of the organisation. Because of performance analysis of business processes being a discipline of the Business Process Management (BPM), only the directly associated resources against the process activities, for example, employees, machines, etc., are considered. Additional resource infrastructure (IT and facility level resources), vital for the directly associated resources to function, are in BPM generally not taken into account. Thus the business processes and resource infrastructures are commonly regarded as two segregated domains, which makes it difficult to perform a thorough impact analysis. A second emerging issue is that in both domains numerous different modelling methodologies and languages are employed, respectively. Thus, a business impact analyst is required to consolidate all the related and potentially interconnected information.

This paper introduces the MDBIA workbench, which has been developed to combine both domains in a generic fashion and provide decision support for BIA on the business process level. Thereby, the resulting workbench reuses an existent model-driven framework, which offers performance related decision support for business processes, and enhances it with modelling and analysis capabilities for resource infrastructures and possible disruptions. The resulting MDBIA workbench enables to answer questions like: "How is the performance of a business process impacted in case of an occurrence of a specific disruption?".

The remainder of this paper is structured as follows: In the Section 2, essential background information of the two domains BPM and BIA is provided. This is followed by a section describing *the Model-driven Performance Engi-*

ICPE'14, March 22–26, 2014, Dublin, Ireland.
Copyright is held by the owner/author(s). Publication rights licensed to ACM.
ACM 978-1-4503-2733-6/14/03$15.00.
http://dx.doi.org/10.1145/2568088.2576797.

neering (MDPE) workbench on which the MDBIA work-bench is based. Then in Section 4, the limitations of the MDPE workbench in terms of BIA are discussed in more detail. These limitations are addressed in the next section which introduces the concepts of the MDBIA workbench, the contribution of this paper. The following section is then evaluating the concepts through a qualitative analysis of a test use case. The paper is concluded thereafter in Section 7, in which also potential future work is proposed.

2. BACKGROUND: BPM AND BIA

BPM is defined by van der Aalst [2] as follows: *"Supporting business processes using methods, techniques, and software to design, enact, control, and analyse operational processes involving humans, organisations, applications, documents, and other sources of information."*. This definition is accompanied with a proposed lifecycle comprising four phases: (1) configure, (2) execute, (3) analyse, and (4) decide. Performance related decision support is, however, considered to be part of the fourth step [3].

When looking upon a business from a process-centric point of view one tends to see and model resources in a quite abstract manner. But nonetheless, resources like employees, facilities, or devices are of importance for any running business. If any of these get damaged or inaccessible, the organisation might not be able to carry out individual tasks anymore or, even worse, it becomes completely dysfunctional. Every year, disruptive events resulting from fire, flood, terrorism, or any other external source seriously harm thousands of businesses [4]. But also small and more frequent disruptions like power interruptions, technical failures, or unavailability of an external service can negatively affect businesses if they are not prepared properly.

In order to have your organisation running smoothly even under unusual circumstances one needs to have a better understanding of the functionality and interconnection of resources and in some cases have backup plans in place. Procedures for sustaining necessary business operations while recovering from a considerable disruption are combined in a so called *Business Continuity Plan* [5]. These plans are part of the overall *Business Continuity Management (BCM)* strategy of an organisation. BCM is standardised by the *British Standards Institution (BSI)* and defined in [6] as *"a holistic management process that identifies potential threats to an organization and the impacts to business operations that those threats, if realized, might cause, and which provides a framework for building organizational resilience with the capability for an effective response that safeguards the interests of its key stakeholders, reputation, brand and value-creating activities."*

Part of the Business Continuity Management standard defined by the BSI is its lifecycle. Similar to the BPM lifecycle it consists of four phases that each serve an individual task [6]: (1) understanding the organisation, i.e. critical business processes, resources, and other entities, plus their respective potential threats are identified and, in case of their occurrence, potential consequences are predicted; (2) determining business continuity strategies, i.e. the minimum level of business operations to mitigate the business impact and specification of time frames until a normal operational level is restored; (3) development and implementation of BCM responses, e.g. accepting the risk, removing it, or installation of a *Recovery Plan*, that defines steps to be

taken back to status quo ante in the given time frame; (4) exercising, maintaining, and reviewing, i.e. exposing flaws of the implemented BCM strategies and plans, which helps to improve them in the next iteration of the lifecycle. However, note that some threats are impossible to simulate in their full extent.

In the first step of the lifecycle the *Business Impact Analysis (BIA)* is addressed. According to [6], BIA is defined as the *"...process of analyzing business functions and the effect that a business disruption might have upon them"*. A more specific description of BIA's purpose is given by [7]: it *"...identifies, quantifies and qualifies the business impacts of a loss, interruption or disruption of business processes on an organisation and provides the data from which appropriate continuity strategies can be determined"*. One difficulty in BIA is to examine and extract resources and, with equal importance, the failure dependencies between them, i.e. if one resource gets unavailable, others do as well. The resulting failure dependency model represents the basis of further impact analyses.

3. STATE OF THE ART

To address the issue of Business Impact Analysis both domains have to be taken into account: business processes and resource infrastructures. However, in recent research they have been mostly regarded separately. Unfortunately, due to the fact that Business Continuity Management is not considered to be in the responsibility of the ICT department [6][13] not much computational support for business impact analysts is provided so far. Though, a couple of theories about resource dependencies in general can be found in exclusively business related literature, e.g. in [8], no modelling approach for their failure dependencies could be found by the author. Until today, business impact analysts still use tools like Microsoft Visio [21] to graphically model and understand the interconnections and possible impacts for an organisation in case a particular resource becomes unavailable.

However, BIA is about analysing the impact on the performance of business processes in the event of a disruption. A number of approaches for analysing the general performance of business processes as a part or as an extension of BPM suits already exist. Many of them, (e.g. [10]), are based on *Monolithic Model Transformation*. The principle of Monolithic Model Transformation is the direct transformation from a particular business process model and performance input parameters to an input for a specified performance analysis tool. Performance input parameters are in the form of historic, assumed, or planned data that is annotated to the business process and its elements to carry out a performance analysis. Examples of these parameters are: the process instance occurrence annotated to a process start element and the resource demand annotated to an activity.

The monolithic approach is restricted to only one single analysis tool and to one specific process model. However, currently networked business processes are composed of parts modelled and managed with different BPM environments. This motivates a more generic approach, namely *Decomposed Model Transformation*, that allows for an integration of multiple process modelling languages and different types of analysis tools. Figure 1 [11] shows its general concept. Note, that M2M stands for Model-to-Model transformation and M2T for Model-to-Text transformation.

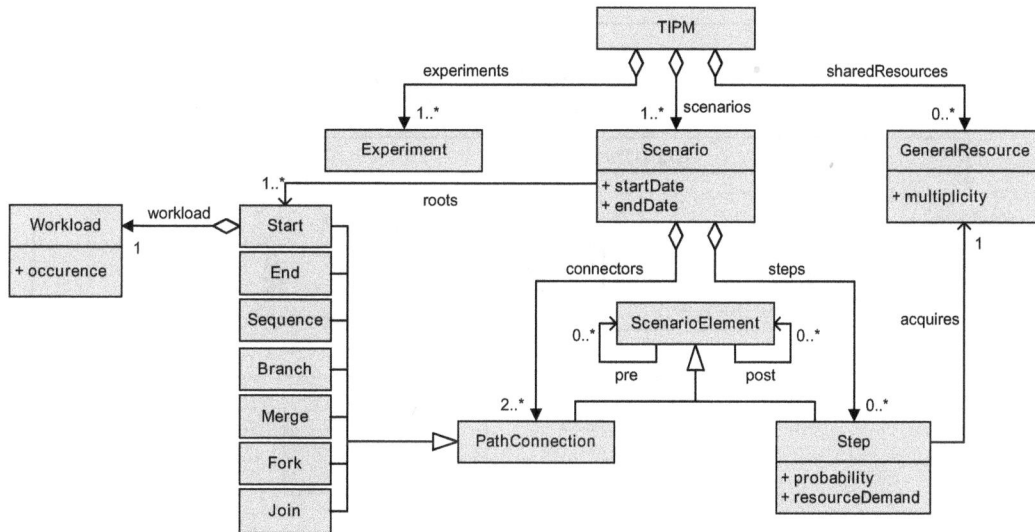

Figure 2: Tool Independent Performance Model (TIPM) Meta-Model

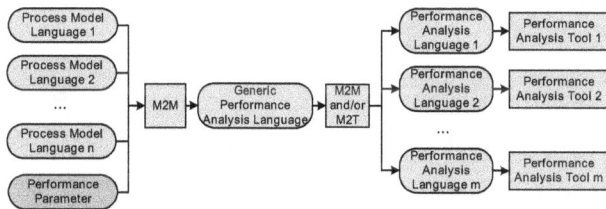

Figure 1: Integration concept via decomposed model transformation

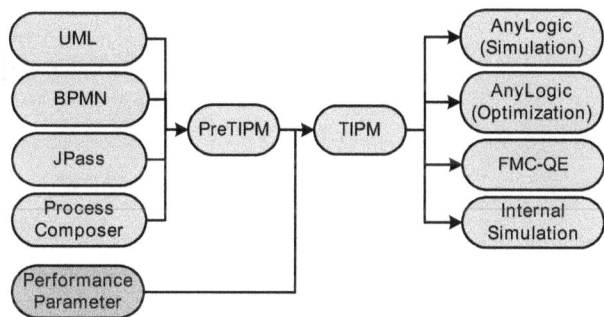

Figure 3: Model transformations in the MDPE workbench

The execution semantic of various different business process models can be abstracted into a unified Petri-Net like behaviour model. This similarity is utilised by a generically usable analysis model depicted as generic performance analysis model in the concept figure. In addition to expressing the process behaviour of a system defined by the input process models, the intermediate model also has to contain the performance parameters necessary for the different types of analyses. In [11], the language *Kernel LAnguage for PErformance and Reliabilty analysis (KLAPER)* is proposed as such a generic performance analysis model language. Other examples are the *Core Scenario Model (CSM)*, introduced in [12], and the *Tool Independent Performance Model (TIPM)* which has derived from CSM [9] and addressed some of its limitations, e.g. static parameter definition replaced by a more generic parameter concept. TIPM, of which a simplified version is depicted in Figure 2, comprises business process behaviour, performance data, and monitors to be filled with the results that are to be computed out of simulations and analytics.

It represents the generic performance analysis language in the Model-Driven Performance Engineering (MDPE) workbench to which every integrated business process modelling language has to be translated and from which a transformation to any analysis model of choice has to be performed.

The MDPE workbench extends existing process modelling tools, for example BPM suits, with performance related decision support [9]. To enable this extension it applies various MDE operations, e.g. decomposed model transformations, model annotations, model weaving, and megamodelling.

The actually implemented model flow of the MDPE workbench from source models to analysis models is depicted in Figure 3, the arrows representing model transformations. As shown, so far adapters for the business process modelling languages BPMN [14] and UML activity diagrams [15], as well as for the tools Process Composer of the Netweaver BPM process environment [16] and JCOM1 jPass [17] exist. The depicted *PreTIPM* is used as an intermediate model to enable the combination of several source models, i.e. models of different languages can yet be interconnected and as a result still be analysed by the MDPE workbench. As such, the PreTIPM model contains all the behavioural business process information extracted from the respective source models but already conforming to the TIPM language.

After merging several distinct process models into one, the integration of the performance parameters into the model is

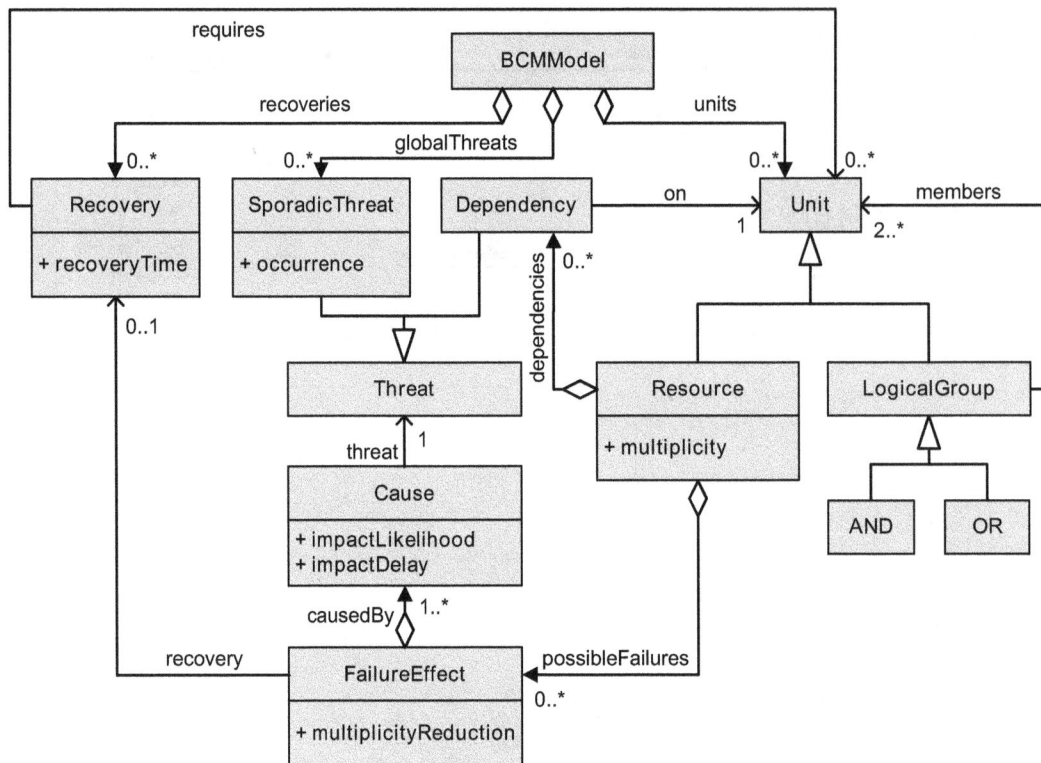

Figure 4: Generic BCM meta-model

performed. The result is then the TIPM model containing the business process data and the respective performance related data. In the last step of the transformation chain the TIPM is translated into the tool-specific performance model of choice. So far, adapters for the AnyLogic tool, suitable for performance simulations and optimisations [18], for the *Fundamental Modeling Concepts for Quantitative Evaluation (FMC-QE)* framework [19], and for an internal simulation tool had been implemented.

4. MOTIVATION TEST WHEN IT WOULD ACTUALLY BREAK

The MDPE workbench has been developed to address performance decision support for business processes. This explicit domain restriction of the tool for business processes leads to fairly limited modelling possibilities for resources. In order to respond to the additional requirements of the resource-centric BIA aspects, the workbench's lack of resource failure dependency and threat modelling abilities has to be addressed. The first identified limitation is the expressiveness restriction of the TIPM model on business processes and their directly related performance data only. In particular, two essential model limitations were identified:

- The first restriction of TIPM is that resources are independent entities only defined by their multiplicity. However, it has been pointed out in Section 2 that resources in practice are usually dependent on each

other. Furthermore, according to the author's knowledge no modelling tool for this purpose is available.

- Another limitation is that no modelling possibility for threats that can cause disruptions in your resource infrastructure is provided.

5. INTEGRATED PERFORMANCE DECISION SUPPORT FOR PROCESS-CENTRIC BUSINESS IMPACT ANALYSIS

First, the model limitations had to be addressed to provide "Integrated Performance Decision Support for Process-centric Business Impact Analysis". Due to the unavailability of failure dependency modelling tools for resources a new language called *Generic Business Continuity Model (GenericBCM)* has been developed and was integrated into the model flow and workbench architecture. The GenericBCM meta-model is depicted in Figure 4. It represents the domain language for modelling resource dependencies in terms of disruption propagation. As such, it has to be able to express the following aspects:

1. The operating ability of a resources can be dependent on the operating ability of other resources. This *operating dependency* has to include also rather complex conditions, like "resource A becomes unavailable if either resource B or resource C together with resource D

is unavailable". The opposite of an operating dependency relation is called *failure dependency*, i.e. an occurring failure is delegated to the dependent resources.

2. The operating ability can not only be limited by other resources. An external event can occur which can force the resource to reduce or completely neutralise its ability to operate. Examples of these *threats* on resources are humans, which become sick, a computer that crashes, or a complete office that has to shut down due to a natural disaster.

3. Furthermore, it is essential to model the loss of the resource's operability. It is a difference if, e.g. a computer gets broken, which would correspond to a multiplicity reduction by one, or the power supply for the whole office breaks down, which would result in an overall computer multiplicity of zero.

4. After a resource suffers an operational mitigation, either caused by a failure dependency or by an external threat, there is the potential to recover after a certain amount of time. Examples are the recovery of a staff member after sickness or a computer getting repaired after a breakdown. The recovery of a resource can be a process itself.

The integration of resource dependency information provided by GenericBCM models entails an adaptation of the decomposed transformation chain of the MDPE approach (see Figure 3) towards an approach with multiple input domains. In particular, the transformation chain of the MDBIA workbench now has to incorporate two distinct but variable input sources, the business process information and the resource dependency information. Figure 5 depicts the applied model flow of the workbench including some of the supported model languages.

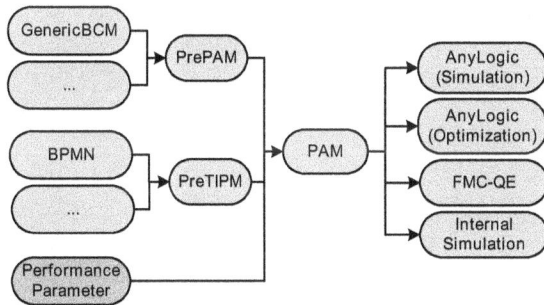

Figure 5: Model transformations in the MDBIA workbench

As a result of the merging of the business process and the resource failure dependency domains, the expressiveness of some of the already involved models has to be extended. The performance parameters have to be modified according to the increased modelling possibilities. In addition, the generic performance analysis model has to be exchanged as TIPM is only able to express business processes in combination with annotated performance information and analysis configuration data. In order to accommodate this request, the new model language *Performance Analysis Model*

(PAM) (see Figure 6) was developed. It is based on the TIPM and extends it in a generic fashion to enable expressing information of resource dependency models, e.g. GenericBCM, without information loss. In PAM dependencies between resources are now modelled as corresponding resource behaviour nets, whose structure is mainly inspired by petrinets and program flow charts. The result is a language in which business processes, threats and resources are the central elements. Business processes are modelled by commonly used units, such as activities and control flow elements. This has been adopted from the TIPM model. In contrast, resources and threats have attributes and behaviour nets containing of states and transitions. The behaviour nets have the purpose of altering these attributes and propagating impacts in the infrastructure during an analysis run.

The transformation chain acts as follows: At first the GenericBCM or any other integrated resource dependency model is translated into a PAM conform model called *Pre-PAM*. The resulting model contains all the information of the GenericBCM but in the more general notation of PAM. Parallel to that, the business process data from the business process models is translated into PreTIPM, just like in the MDPE workbench. Neither the PreTIPM, still conforming to the TIPM model language, nor the transformation towards the model had to be essentially modified. As the PAM extends the TIPM, any model conforming to TIPM is conforming to PAM, as well. Both results, the PreTIPM and the PrePAM are along with the Performance Parameters combined in the next transformation to the *PAM* model, conforming to the PAM model language and the sum of all information provided by these three input models. As the performance parameters contains links to both of the other input models, it is responsible for all the interconnections within the resulting PAM model, i.e. a resource demand defined in the performance parameter model possesses a link to the annotated activity in the process model and a link to the resource that is to be acquired in the dependency model.

The advantage of this generic approach is the reduction of number and complexity of the necessary transformations combining n business process model languages and m resource dependency languages with k performance analysis tools. Using a monolithic integration one would need $m*n*k$ rather complex transformations. The generic approach only needs $m + n$ transformations from the source model languages to the generic model, plus k transformations to the analysis tool models. As these kind of transformations are more functionally specialised their complexity is decreased in terms of lines of code.

In addition to the models, the transformations between them and analysis adapters need to be modified accordingly to enable BIA. Also, it has to be noted that each transformation additionally generates a tracing model, in order to enable an appropriate result management, i.e. results have to be traced back to their original source model elements.

The proposed concepts have been implemented in a workbench called *MDBIA*. It is based on the MDPE workbench[1] and reuses and extends its modelling concepts. In the workbench modelling is done utilising the capabilities of the Eclipse Modeling Framework (EMF) [24] and its extensions; transformations are implemented with the help of ATLAS Transformation Language (ATL) [25][26].

---

[1]The MDPE workbench is an eclipse application (see [23])

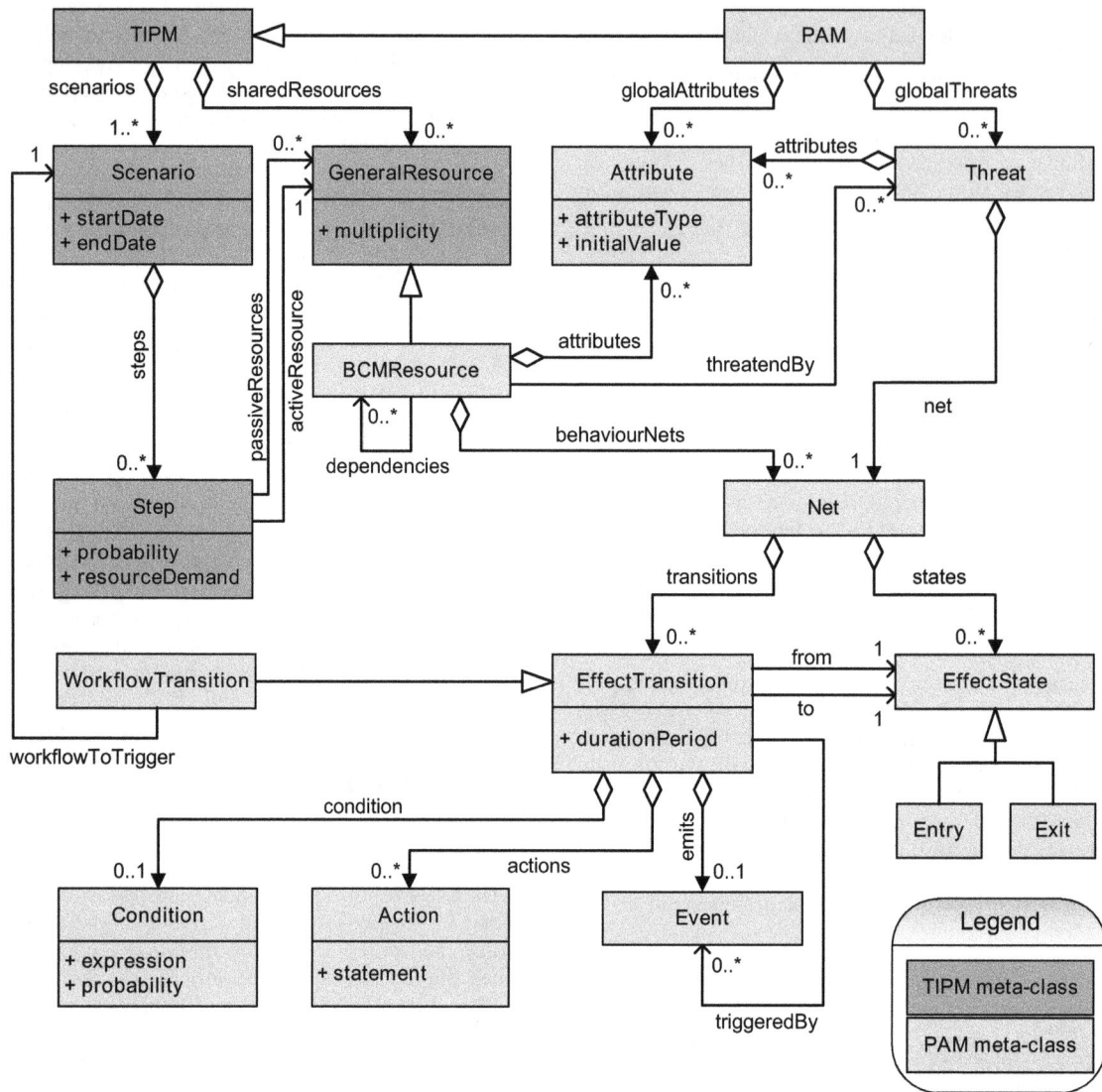

Figure 6: Performance Analysis Model (PAM) extension to TIPM model

6. EVALUATION

After having introduced the MDBIA workbench, its operability is evaluated in this section. This is done by examining a reasonable complex example and discuss the results, i.e. performing a qualitative analysis. First, the example's resource and threat model conforming to the GenericBCM meta-model, as well as a corresponding business process model and performance parameter model are introduced. Then in the intermediate PAM model is presented, which is a result of the transformations and represents all the information provided by the input models at once. Subsequently, the performance results of the analysis is shown and discussed. Thus, the final evaluation is performed by showing that the results are reasonable.

6.1 Input Models

The example case presented here is about the general topic of processing work packages. This use case study may seem simple at first but already produces results complex enough to perform a qualitative analysis of the concept. Note, all parameters correspond to the time unit *day*, e.g. a recovery time of 5 actually means five days.

Resource and Threat Model (GenericBCM).

Five resources are modelled, two actually carrying out work of the business process, "Technical Staff" and "Desktop PC", plus three indirectly involved resources, which are required by the others: "Power", "Office", and "UPS" (Uninterrupted Power Source). The example GenericBCM model is shown in Figure 7. In the use case the availability of the

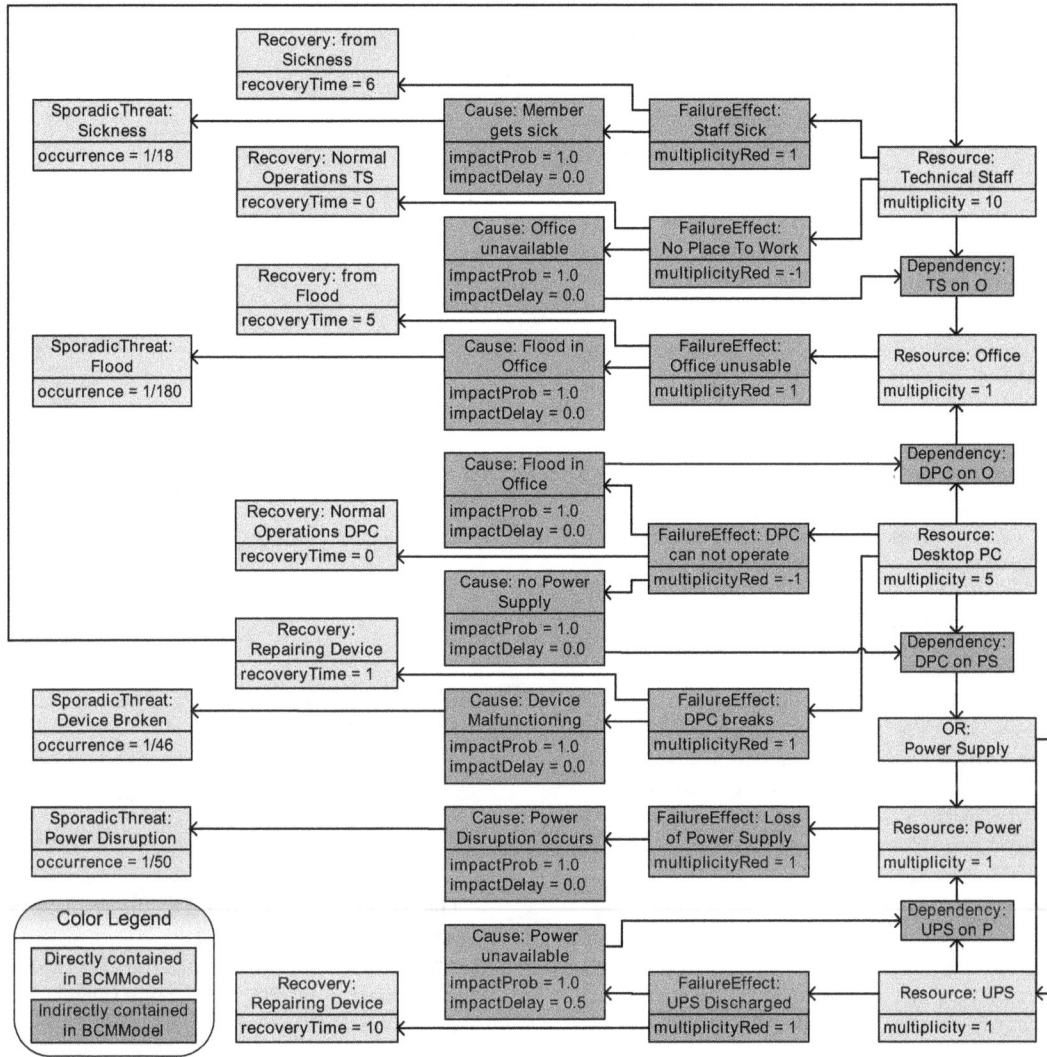

Figure 8: Complete GenericBCM model

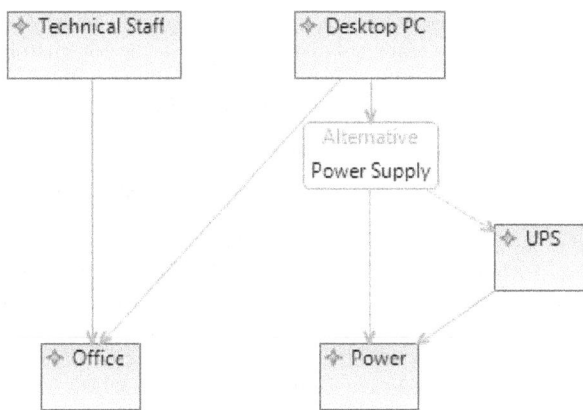

Figure 7: Simplified GenericBCM model in the editor

"Office" resource impacts the operability of both, "Technical Staff" and "Desktop PC". Furthermore, the latter one is dependent on "Power Supply" which is a LogicalGroup of the type OR and as such represents the availability of at least one of the resources "UPS" or "Power". "UPS" in turns is also dependent on "Power" as it has to be recharged after each usage.

However, many elements of the GenericBCM meta-model, such as Causes, Threats, and FailureEffects, are not displayed in the simple overview. The complete model is depicted in Figure 8. For clarity reasons, the BCMModel element is not displayed in the figure, but every element coloured in light grey is directly contained in it. The others are indirectly contained.

Notable features of the model sorted by resource are the following:

- Resource "Technical Staff" has a multiplicity of 10 and contains two FailureEffects that impact its operability: (1) "Staff sick", which is caused by the SporadicThreat "Sickness", occurring every 18 days, and reduces the multiplicity by 1; (2) "No Place To Work", which is caused by "Office unavailable", expressed by the Dependency "TS on O" ("Technical Staff" on "Office"), and reduces the multiplicity to 0, which is expressed by "−1". The recovery from FailureEffect (2) happens instantly right after the "Office" is available again. In contrast, the Recovery "from Sickness" takes 6 days.

- Resource "Office" has a multiplicity of 1 and is threatened by "Flood", which occurs every 180 days and causes the multiplicity to be reduced to 0. The Recovery "from Flood" takes 5 days.

- Resource "Power" has a multiplicity of 1 and is threatened by "Power Disruption", which occurs every 50 days and causes the multiplicity to be reduced to 0. The Recovery "of Power" takes 1 day.

- Resource "UPS" (Uninterrupted Power Supply) is to provide power even though a "Power Disruption" occurred. This is expressed in the model through the FailureEffect "UPS discharged", which reduces the Resource's multiplicity from 1 to 0 after an impactDelay of 0.5 days. The impactDelay is modelled in the Cause "Power unavailable", which further defines the relation between the FailureEffect "UPS discharged" and the Dependency "UPS on P" ("UPS" on "Power"). The recovery process of "UPS charging" takes then 10 days. This means. after "Power" becomes unavailable, the UPS is still up and running for half a day in order to provide power for the system and is recharged another 10 days later.

- Resource "Desktop PC" has a multiplicity of 5 and contains two FailureEffects that impact its operability: (1) "DPC breaks", which is caused by the SporadicThreat "Device Broken", occurring every 46 days, and reduces the multiplicity by 1; (2) "DPC can not operate", which is caused by either "Office not usable", expressed by the Dependency "DPC on O" ("Desktop PC" on "Office"), or "no Power Supply", expressed by the Dependency "DPC on PS" ("Desktop PC" on "Power Supply"). The second FailureEffect consequently reduces the multiplicity to 0 if one of these Causes are triggered. As soon as these threats passed the recovery of this FailureEffect happens instantly. In contrast, the Recovery "Repairing Device" of FailureEffect (1) takes 1 day and, on top of it, needs a member of the "Technical Staff" to carry out the process.

Annotated Business Process Model.
The business process data of the example use case is available in the form of a BPMN model and displayed in Figure 9. It can be seen that the model consists of four activities, two of which are processed in parallel. Additionally to the plain process data, performance parameters have been annotated to the model. These are not shown in the figure but instead informally listed:

- The instance occurrence of the process is modelled by a normal distribution with the parameters 10.0/15.0/7.0 (most likely/worst case/best case) per day.

- The working time demand of the activity "Preparation" is modelled by a normal distribution with the

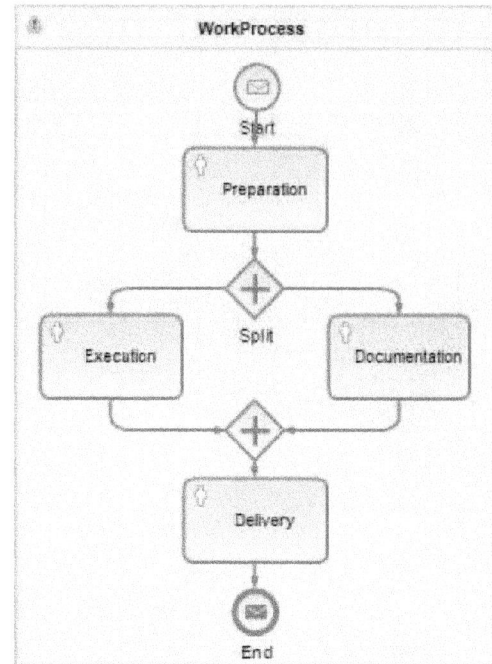

Figure 9: Example business process model conforming to the BPMN standard

parameters 0.1/0.2/0.05 days. The resources "Technical Staff" and "Desktop PC" are acquired in order to carry out this activity.

- The working time demand of the activity "Execution" is modelled by a normal distribution with the parameters 0.4/0.5/0.25 days. The resource "Technical Staff" is acquired in order to carry out this activity.

- The working time demand of the activity "Documentation" is modelled by a normal distribution with the parameters 0.2/0.25/0.15 days. The resources "Technical Staff" and "Desktop PC" are acquired in order to carry out this activity.

- The working time demand of the activity "Delivery" is modelled by a normal distribution with the parameters 0.1/0.2/0.05 days. The resource "Technical Staff" is acquired in order to carry out this activity.

6.2 Intermediate Model

The previously described input models, namely, the threat and resource dependency model (GenericBCM), the business process model (BPMN), and the performance parameter model, are processed by applying the appropriate transformations described in Section 5. Before being handed over to the performance analysis adapter, in this case the internal simulation tool adapter, a generic intermediate model conforming to the PAM meta-model is built, of which a simplified version is shown in Figure 10.

Here, all the information provided by the input models is represented at once. The PAM model depicted comprises the original business process, now conforming to PAM meta-model, the recovery process "RepairingDevice", and the five resources, introduced by the threat and resource dependency model, along with their behaviour nets. As each of the

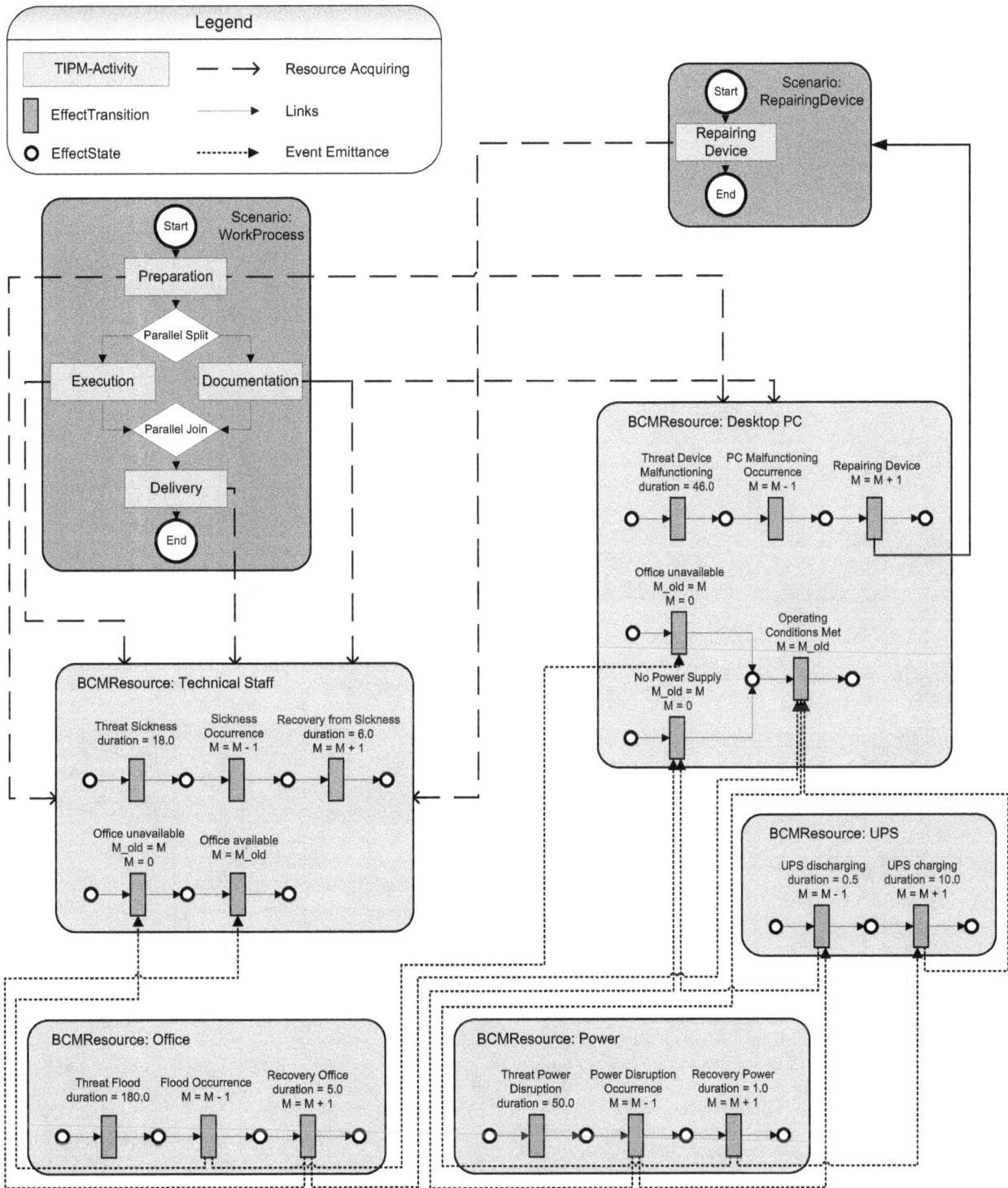

Figure 10: Simplified view on the PAM model resulting from the example input

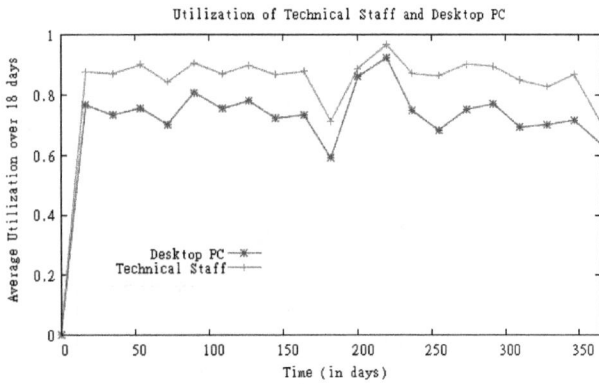

Figure 11: Utilisation of "Technical Staff" and "Desktop PC"

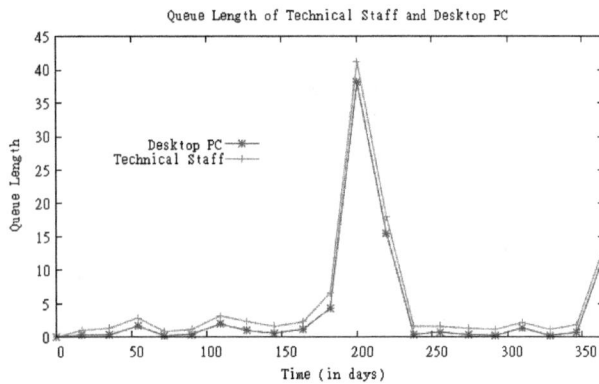

Figure 12: Queue Length of "Technical Staff" and "Desktop PC"

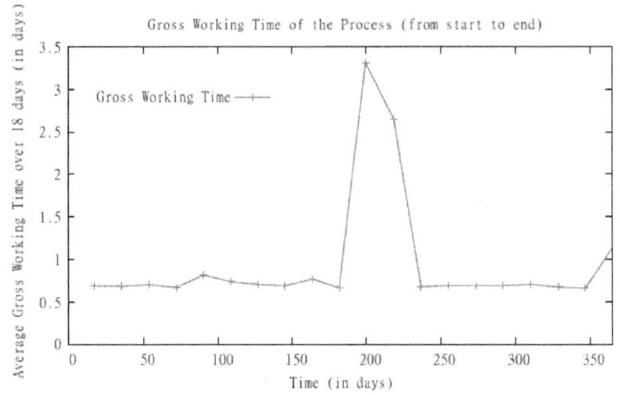

Figure 13: Gross Working Time of the Process

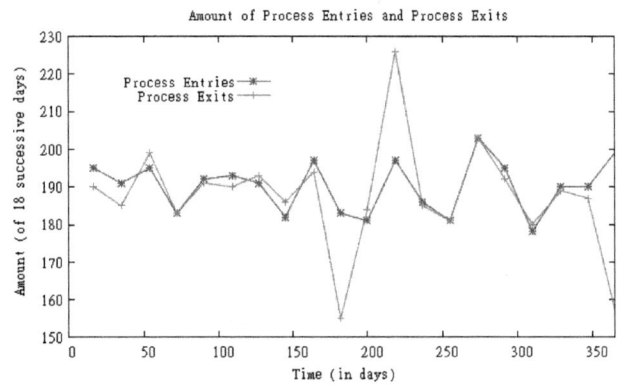

Figure 14: Comparing the numbers of process entries and process exits

threats modelled were only impacting single resources, they have been included into the behaviour nets. Hence, no global threat can be found in the model.

Note that in order to improve the comprehension only essential parts of the PAM model are shown, so it is easier to grasp which relations between the individual elements exist. Examples for not depicted data are: some performance parameters, like working time demand and process instance occurrence.

6.3 Performance Results

The PAM model is the input for the internal simulation tool, which produces performance results. Selected performance output parameters are presented in this section, namely: the utilisation of the two resources "Technical Staff" and "Desktop PC" in Figure 11, the queue length of these resources in Figure 12, the gross working time of the process in Figure 13, and the process entries and process exits in Figure 14.

The time from 01/03/2013 to 01/03/2014 was simulated. The graphs are showing the results of the simulation.

6.4 Discussion

Taking a closer look at the results, a couple of effects become obvious. One of them is, that the simulation has a warm up phase of about twenty days, due to the initial idle state of the process and resources. After that short period, reasonable values can be extracted that are examined in the remainder of this section.

A significant impact on the performance results is caused by the occurrence of the "Flood" event, which influences both of the operating resources "Technical Staff" and "Desktop PC", at times 180.0 and 360.0. The impact of this threat on the resources's utilisations is a nosedive down to 0.6. In contrast, the corresponding queue length rises up to a number of almost 50, which is reasonable taking the forced unavailability over five successive days of both resources into account. The same effect is in some extent noticeable regarding the gross working time depicted in Figure 13: While the average time to complete the process from start to end is about 0.75 days, this value rises up to 3.5 in the period right after a "Flood" occurrence. With respect to the average number of process exits shown in Figure 14, it can be seen that a first reaction is a drop from 190.0 to 160.0 due to the process being blocked for five days. Right after that, the system reacts with a significant increase up to 225.0 as it has to additionally process the bottled-up workload in order to make up for the omissions of the five-day disruption. After approximately forty days, the system has fully recovered from the "Flood" incident.

Another, rather smaller, impact on the system can be recognised for the "Power Disruption" threat. Especially, in the queue length parameter a reaction is noticeable: after each period of 50 days, which corresponds to the occurrence rate of this threat, a slight increase of the resources's queue length can be identified. Because of the "UPS" is reducing the off-time of power supply to only half a day, the effect is almost imperceptible with respect to the other displayed result parameters.

Generally, the performance results for the resources "Technical Staff" and "Desktop PC" appear to be almost identical. The reason for that is identified in the first process activity "Preparation", which acquires both resources. Hence, if only one of the resources is not available, this activity cannot be processed and thus represents a bottle neck of the system. As the first activity is blocking the execution of the successive activities, the rest of the system stays mostly idle.

Some of the frequently reoccurring threats, like "Sickness" or "Device Malfunctioning" seem to have no effect on the system at all. In order to examine if they are actually happening, it is sufficient to have a look at specific events of the simulation event log. In the following box an excerpt of the log is shown, only including events representing changes of the resources's multiplicities. Thereby, "mult" is the new adapted multiplicity of the resource "res". Additionally, with "ql" the queue length of the resource at this point of time (first value) is given.

Excerpt of the Simulation Adapter Event Log

> 180.0; res: Office; act: MULTIPLICTY_CHANGE; mult: 0; ql: 0
> 180.0; res: TechnicalStaff; act: MULTIPLICTY_CHANGE; mult: 0; ql: 0
> 180.0; res: DesktopPC; act: MULTIPLICTY_CHANGE; mult: 0; ql: 0
> 185.0; res: Office; act: MULTIPLICTY_CHANGE; mult: 1; ql: 0
> 185.0; res: TechnicalStaff; act: MULTIPLICTY_CHANGE; mult: 10; ql: 63
> 185.0; res: DesktopPC; act: MULTIPLICTY_CHANGE; mult: 5; ql: 53
> 198.0; res: TechnicalStaff; act: MULTIPLICTY_CHANGE; mult: 9; ql: 26
> 200.0; res: Power; act: MULTIPLICTY_CHANGE; mult: 0; ql: 0
> 200.5; res: UPS; act: MULTIPLICTY_CHANGE; mult: 0; ql: 0
> 200.5; res: DesktopPC; act: MULTIPLICTY_CHANGE; mult: 0; ql: 24
> 201.0; res: Power; act: MULTIPLICTY_CHANGE; mult: 1; ql: 0
> 201.0; res: DesktopPC; act: MULTIPLICTY_CHANGE; mult: 5; ql: 33
> 204.0; res: TechnicalStaff; act: MULTIPLICTY_CHANGE; mult: 10; ql: 29

In the excerpt of the event log the behaviour of the system is demonstrated, when, for example, the "Office" becomes unusable due to an occurring "Flood" at time 180.0. Instantly, the two depending resources "Technical Staff" and "Desktop PC" become unavailable and recover five days later after the "Office" has recovered. Also, the multiplicity reduction due to "Sickness" at time 198.0 and the corresponding recovery at day 204 can be seen.

Another effect demonstrated by the event log excerpt is the occurrence of "Power Disruption" at time 200.0. Half a day later, also the "UPS" along with the "Desktop PC" is affected. Their multiplicity decreases to zero, which represents a complete loss of their operability. Right after "Power" recovered, the operability of "Desktop PC" is restored at time 201.0.

Considering the provided discussion in this section, the performance results have been determined to be reasonable. To conclude the evaluation, it is therefore suggested the PAM model as well as the simulation adapter are operating in a reasonable fashion.

7. CONCLUSION AND FUTURE WORK

This paper introduced a solution for integrated performance decision support for process-centric business impact analysis, namely the MDBIA workbench. Its main purpose is the prediction of involved consequences on the business process level, taking into account occurring disruptions in the resource infrastructure. This has been implemented by adopting concepts of the MDPE workbench along with its generic approach of analysing the performance of various business processes. For reasons highlighted in Section 4, these concepts do not fully meet the requirements of Business Impact Analysis. Thus, the identified limitations of the MDPE workbench have been addressed by extending it with modelling and analysis possibilities for complex resource infrastructures. The resulting workbench integrates a new modelling language called GenericBCM, which allows to model resources, operability dependencies and threats. Furthermore, a new generic intermediate model language, called PAM, has been designed with the purpose of addressing the additional requirements of Business Impact Analysis.

The MDBIA workbench is used in the context of real world industrial use-cases provided by the EU-funded project TIMBUS, namely in the areas of dam safety and eHealth. However, when applying the method presented in this paper to the use cases a few limitations and possible improvements became apparent. This is why we propose the following modifications and extensions to be future work:

1. In the current GenericBCM model parameters are expressed as static values. To increase model accuracy and model expressiveness it is suggested to introduce more advanced parameter representations, e.g. distribution functions, to achieve improved results.

2. Although, there is currently no other language than GenericBCM for the explicit purpose of modelling resource failure dependencies, a number of resource landscape modelling possibilities are available, e.g. the Topology Editor of IBM RSA [20]. From these models the dependencies could potentially be imported.

3. The intermediate PAM model is domain-specific. But with regards to PAM's behaviour net semantic it is to some extent already close to a General Purpose Language (GPL). One promising modification would be to replace this model language with a well researched GPL, for example Coloured-Petri-Nets [22], for which a number of analysis tools can be readily be deployed.

4. The internal simulation tool uses a single-thread execution model to avoid concurrent access to the PAM

model. A future implementation could provide a multi-threaded execution of the internal simulation tool. Another alternative to speed up the current analysis is to replace the simulation, which can be slow for large models, with a more direct and faster analytical approach.

5. The MDBIA workbench is used as a design-time tool for BIA. A possible extension would be to provide support for real-time monitoring, analysis and disaster management. Therefore real-time events could be captured and consumed for continuous BIAs. This approach would enable short-term decision support in real-time.

8. REFERENCES

[1] Library of Congress. Congressional Research Service: The Economic Effects of 9/11: A Retrospective Assessment. http://www.fas.org/irp/crs/RL31617.pdf (2002)

[2] van der Aalst, W., ter Hofstede, A., Weske, M.: Business Process Management, International Conference, BPM 2003, Eindhoven, The Netherlands, June 26-27, 2003, Proceedings, volume 2678 of Lecture Notes in Computer Science. Springer (2003)

[3] Fritzsche, M., Picht, M., Gilani, W., Spence, I., Brown, J., Kilpatrick, P.: Extending BPM Environments of Your Choice with Performance Related Decision Support. In: Proceedings of the 7th International Conference on Business Process Management, pp. 97–112. Springer-Verlag, Berlin, Heidelberg (2009)

[4] Harris, S.:CISSP All-in-One Exam Guide, Fifth Edition. McGraw-Hill, Inc., New York, NY, USA (2010)

[5] Janchivlamdan, R. Buchanan, T., Tierney, T., Davis, J.: Business Continuity Planning and Development. https://ectd.du.edu/source/uploads/11142668.pdf (2007)

[6] British Standards Institute. BS25999, Code of Practice for Business Continuity Management. BSI (2006)

[7] Smith, D.: Business Continuity Management: Good Practice Guidelines, pp. 0–18. BSI (2002)

[8] Pfeffer, J., Salancik, G.: The External Control of Organizations: A Resource Dependence Perspective. Stanford University Press, Stanford, California (2003)

[9] Fritzsche, M.: PhD Thesis: Performance related Decision Support for Process Modelling. School of Electronics, Electrical Engineering and Computer Science, Queens University Belfast (2010)

[10] Rozinat, A., Wynn, M., van der Aalst, W., Hofstede, A., Fidge, C.: Workflow Simulation for Operational Decision Support Using Design, Historic and State Information. In: Proceedings of the 6th International Conference on Business Process Management (BPM'08). Springer-Verlag (2008)

[11] Grassi, V., Mirandola, R., Sabetta, A.: From design to analysis models: a kernel language for performance and reliability analysis of component-based systems. In: Proceedings of the 5th international workshop on Software and performance, pp. 25–36. ACM, New York (2005)

[12] Petriu, D., Woodside, M.:An intermediate metamodel with scenarios and resources for generating performance models from UML designs. In: Software and Systems Modeling, Volume 6, Issue - 2, pp. 163–184 (2007)

[13] Stranack, T., Cornish, C.: Business Continuity Management - Bridging the divide. In: Business, vol. 6, pp. 1–4 (2009)

[14] Object Management Group. Business Process Modeling Notation Specification, Final Adopted Specification, Version 1.0. http://www.bpmn.org/Documents/BPMN_1-0.pdf (2006)

[15] Object Management Group Inc: Unified Modeling Language 2.0: Superstructure. http://www.omg.org/spec/UML/2.0/Superstructure/PDF.formal/05-07-04, 2005

[16] Snabe, J., Rosenber, A., Molle, C., Scavillo, M.: Business Process Management: The SAP Roadmap (2008)

[17] Metasonic AG. jPASS! - Subjektorientierte Prozessmodellierung. http://www.metasonic.de/ (2009)

[18] XJ Technologies. AnyLogic — multi-paradigm simulation software. http://www.xjtek.com/anylogic/ (2010)

[19] Porzucek, T., Kluth, S., Copaciu, F., Zorn, W.: Modeling and Evaluation Framework for FMC-QE. In: Proceedings of the 2009 16th Annual IEEE International Conference and Workshop on the Engineering of Computer Based Systems, pp. 237–243. IEEE Computer Society, Washington DC, USA (2009)

[20] IBM. Rational Software Architect.http://www-01.ibm.com/software/awdtools/swarchitect/ (2011)

[21] Microsoft, Office Visio, http://office.microsoft.com/en-us/visio/ (2007)

[22] Jensen, K., Kristensen, L. M.: Coloured Petri Nets - Modelling and Validation of Concurrent Systems, Springer (2009)

[23] Eclipse Foundation: The Eclipse Foundation. http://www.eclipse.org/org/ (2013)

[24] Budinsky, F., Brodsky S. A., Merks, E.: Eclipse Modeling Framework. Pearson Education (2003)

[25] Jouault, F., Allilaire, F., Bézivin, J., Kurtev, I.: ATL: A model transformation tool. In journal Science of Computer Programming, vol. 72, pp. 31–39, Elsevier North-Holland (2008)

[26] Allilaire, Bézivin, J., F., Jouault, F., Kurtev, I.: ATL: Eclipse Support for Model Transformation. In: Proc. of the Eclipse Technology eXchange Workshop (eTX) at ECOOP, (2006)

Project partially funded by the European Commission under the 7th Framework Programme for research and technological development and demonstration activities under grant agreement 269940, TIMBUS project (http://timbusproject.net/).

Continuous Validation of Load Test Suites

Mark D. Syer
Software Analysis and Intelligence Lab (SAIL)
Queen's University, Canada
mdsyer@cs.queensu.ca

Zhen Ming Jiang
Department of Electrical Engineering &
Computer Science
York University, Canada
zmjiang@cse.yorku.ca

Meiyappan Nagappan, Ahmed E. Hassan
Software Analysis and Intelligence Lab (SAIL)
Queen's University, Canada
{mei, ahmed}@cs.queensu.ca

Mohamed Nasser, Parminder Flora
Performance Engineering
BlackBerry, Canada

ABSTRACT

Ultra-Large-Scale (ULS) systems face continuously evolving field workloads in terms of activated/disabled feature sets, varying usage patterns and changing deployment configurations. These evolving workloads often have a large impact on the performance of a ULS system. Hence, continuous load testing is critical to ensuring the error-free operation of such systems. A common challenge facing performance analysts is to validate if a load test closely resembles the current field workloads. Such validation may be performed by comparing execution logs from the load test and the field. However, the size and unstructured nature of execution logs makes such a comparison unfeasible without automated support. In this paper, we propose an automated approach to validate whether a load test resembles the field workload and, if not, determines how they differ by compare execution logs from a load test and the field. Performance analysts can then update their load test cases to eliminate such differences, hence creating more realistic load test cases. We perform three case studies on two large systems: one open-source system and one enterprise system. Our approach identifies differences between load tests and the field with a precision of $\geq 75\%$ compared to only $\geq 16\%$ for the state-of-the-practice.

Categories and Subject Descriptors

D.2.9 [**Software Engineering**]: Management—*Software Quality Assurance (SQA)*

1. INTRODUCTION

The rise of Ultra-Large-Scale (ULS) systems (e.g., Amazon.com, GMail and AT&T's telecommunication infrastructure) poses new challenges for the software performance field [26]. ULS systems require near-perfect up-time and support millions of concurrent connections and operations. Failures in such systems are typically associated with an inability to scale, than with feature bugs [15,30,47].

Load testing has become essential in ensuring the problem-free operation of such systems. Load tests are usually derived from the field (i.e., alpha or beta testing data or actual production data). The goal of such testing is to examine how the system behaves under realistic workloads to ensure that the system performs well in the field. However, ensuring that load tests are "realistic" (i.e., that they accurately reflect the current field workloads) is a major challenge. Field workloads are based on the behaviour of thousands or millions of users interacting with the system. These workloads continuously evolve as the user base changes, as features are activated or disabled and as user feature preferences change. Such varying field workloads often lead to load tests that are not reflective of the field [9,46], yet these workloads have a major impact on the performance of the system [15,49].

Performance analysts monitor the impact of field workloads on the system's performance using performance (e.g., response time and memory usage) and reliability counters (e.g., mean time-to-failure). Performance analysts must determine the cause of any deviation in the counter values from the specified or expected range (e.g., response time exceeds the maximum response time permitted by the service level agreements or memory usage exceeds the average historical memory usage). These deviations may be caused by changes to the field workloads [15,49]. Such changes are common and may require performance analysts to update their load test cases [9,46]. This has led to the emergence of "continuous load testing," where load test cases are continuously updated and re-run even after the system's deployment.

A major challenge in the continuous load testing process is to ensure that load test cases accurately reflect the current field workloads. However, documentation describing the expected system behaviour is rarely up-to-date and instrumentation is not feasible due to high overhead [38]. Hence execution logs are the only data available to describe and monitor the behaviour of the system under a workload. Therefore, we propose an automated approach to validate load test cases by comparing system behaviour across load tests and the field. We derive system signatures from execution logs, then use statistical techniques to identify differences between the system signatures of the load tests and the field.

Such differences can be broadly classified as feature differences (i.e., differences in the available features), intensity differences (i.e., differences in how often each feature is exercised) and issue differences (i.e., new errors appearing in the field). These identified differences can help performance analysts improve their load tests in the following two ways.

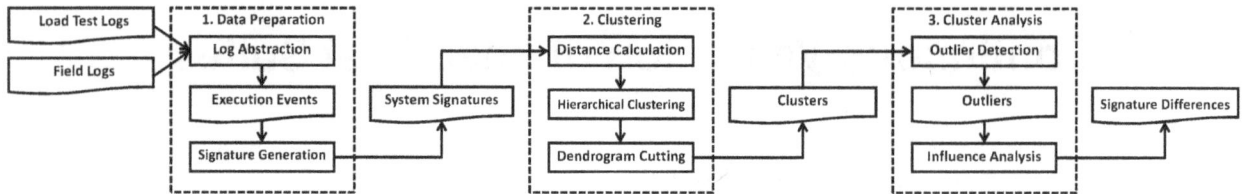

Figure 1: An Overview of Our Approach.

First, performance analysts can tune their load tests to more accurately represent current field workloads. For example, the test workloads can be updated to better reflect the identified differences. Second, new field errors, which are not covered in existing testing, can be identified based on the differences. For example, a machine failure in a distributed system may raise new errors that are often not tested.

This paper makes three contributions:

1. We develop an automated approach to validate the representativeness of load test cases by comparing the system behaviour between load tests and the field.

2. Our approach identifies important execution events that best explain the differences between the system's behaviour during a load test and in the field.

3. Through three case studies on two large systems, one open-source system and one enterprise ULS system, we show that our approach is scalable and can help performance analysts validate their load test cases.

1.1 Organization of the Paper

This paper is organized as follows: Section 2 provides a motivational example of how our approach may be used in practice. Section 3 describes our approach in detail. Section 4 presents our case studies. Section 5 discusses the sensitivity of our case study results to changes in the statistical measures used by our approach. Section 6 outlines the threats to validity and Section 7 presents related work. Finally, Section 8 concludes the paper and presents our future work.

2. MOTIVATIONAL EXAMPLE

Jack, a performance analyst, is responsible for continuously load testing a ULS system. Given the continuously evolving field workloads, Jack often needs to update his load test cases to ensure that the load test workloads match, as much as possible, the field workloads. Jack monitors the field workloads using performance counters (e.g., response time and memory usage). When one or more of these counters deviates from the specified or expected range (e.g., response time exceeds the maximum response time specified in the requirements or memory usage exceeds the average historical memory usage), Jack must investigate the cause of the deviation. He may then need to update his load test cases.

Although performance counters will indicate *if* the field workloads have changed, the only artifacts that Jack can use to understand *how* the field workloads have changed, and hence how his load test cases should be updated, are gigabytes of load test and field logs. Execution logs describe the system's behaviour, in terms of important execution events, during the load test and in the field.

Jack monitors the system's performance in the field and discovers that the system's memory usage exceeds the average historical memory usage. Pressured by time (given the continuously evolving nature of field workloads), management (who are keen to boast a high quality system) and the complexity of log analysis, Jack is introduced to an automated approach that can validate whether his load test cases are actually reflective of the field workloads and, if not, determine how his load test cases differ from the field. This approach automatically derives system signatures from gigabytes of execution logs and compares the signatures from the load test against the signatures in the field to identify execution events that differ between a load test and the field.

Using this approach, Jack is shown key execution events that explain the differences between his load test and field workloads. Jack then discovers a group of users who are using a memory-intensive feature more strenuously than in the past. Finally, Jack is able to update his load test cases to better reflect the users' changing feature preferences and hence the system's behaviour in the field.

3. APPROACH

This section outlines our approach for validating load test cases by automatically deriving system signatures from execution logs and comparing the signatures from a load test against the signatures from the field. Figure 1 provides an overview of our approach, and we describe each phase in detail below. We also demonstrate our approach with a working example of a hypothetical chat application.

3.1 Execution Logs

Execution logs record notable events at runtime and are used by developers (to debug a system) and operators (to monitor the operation of a system). They are generated by output statements that developers insert into the source code of the system. These output statements are triggered by specific events (e.g., starting, queueing or completing a job) and errors within the system. Compared with performance counters, which usually require explicit monitoring tools (e.g., PerfMon [5]) to be collected, execution logs are readily available in most ULS systems to support remote issue resolution and legal compliance (e.g., the Sarbanes-Oxley Act [6] requires logging in telecommunication and financial systems).

The second column of Table 1 and Table 2 presents the execution logs from our working example. These execution logs contain both static information (e.g,. **starts a chat**) and dynamic information (e.g., **Alice** and **Bob**) that changes with each occurrence of an event. Table 1 and Table 2 present the execution logs from the field and the load test respectively. The load test has been configured with a simple use case (from 00:01 to 00:06) which is repeatedly executed at a rate of one request per second.

Table 1: Abstracting Execution Logs to Execution Events: Execution Logs from the Field

Time	User	Log Line	Execution Event	Execution Event ID
00:01	Alice	starts a chat with Bob	starts a chat with ___	1
00:01	Alice	says 'hi, are you busy?' to Bob	says ___ to ___	2
00:17	Bob	says 'yes' to Alice	says ___ to ___	2
00:05	Charlie	starts a chat with Dan	starts a chat with ___	1
00:05	Charlie	says 'do you have file?' to Dan	says ___ to ___	2
00:08	Dan	Initiate file transfer to Charlie	Initiate file transfer (to ___)	3
00:12	Dan	says 'got it?' to Charlie	says ___ to ___	2
00:14	Charlie	says 'thanks' to Dan	says ___ to ___	2
00:14	Charlie	ends the chat with Dan	ends the chat with ___	4
00:18	Alice	says 'ok, bye' to Bob	says ___ to ___	2
00:18	Bob	says 'bye' to Alice	says ___ to ___	2
00:20	Alice	ends the chat with Bob	ends the chat with ___	4

Table 2: Abstracting Execution Logs to Execution Events: Execution Logs from a Load Test

Time	User	Log Line	Execution Event	Execution Event ID
00:01	USER1	starts a chat with USER2	starts a chat with ___	1
00:02	USER1	says 'MSG1' to USER2	says ___ to ___	2
00:03	USER2	says 'MSG2' to USER1	says ___ to ___	2
00:04	USER1	says 'MSG3' to USER2	says ___ to ___	2
00:05	USER2	says 'MSG4' to USER1	says ___ to ___	2
00:06	USER1	ends the chat with USER2	ends the chat with ___	5
00:07	USER3	starts a chat with USER4	starts a chat with ___	1
00:08	USER3	says 'MSG1' to USER4	says ___ to ___	2
00:09	USER4	says 'MSG2' to USER3	says ___ to ___	2
00:10	USER3	says 'MSG3' to USER4	says ___ to ___	2
00:11	USER4	says 'MSG4' to USER3	says ___ to ___	2
00:12	USER3	ends the chat with USER4	ends the chat with ___	5

3.2 Data Preparation

Execution logs are difficult to analyze because they are unstructured. Therefore, we abstract the execution logs to execution events to enable automated statistical analysis. We then generate system signatures that represent the behaviour of the system's users.

3.2.1 Log Abstraction

Execution logs are not typically designed for automated analysis. Each occurrence of an execution event results in a slightly different log line, because log lines contain static components as well as dynamic information (which may be different for each occurrence of a particular execution event). Therefore, we must remove this dynamic information from the log lines prior to our analysis in order to identify similar execution events. We refer to the process of identifying and removing dynamic information from a log line as "abstracting" the log line.

Our technique for abstracting log lines recognizes the static and dynamic components of each log line using a technique similar to token-based code clone detection techniques [28]. The dynamic components of each log line are then discarded and replaced with ___ (to indicate that dynamic information was present in the original log line). The remaining static components of the log lines (i.e., the abstracted log line) describe execution events.

Table 1 and Table 2 present the execution events and execution event IDs (a unique ID automatically assigned to each unique execution event) for the execution logs from the field and from the load test in our working example. These tables demonstrate the input (i.e., the log lines) and the output (i.e., the execution events) of the log abstraction process. For example, the starts a chat with Bob and starts a chat with Dan log lines are both abstracted to the starts a chat with ___ execution event.

3.2.2 Signature Generation

We generate system signatures that characterize a user's behaviour in terms of feature usage expressed by the execution events. Therefore, a system signature represents the behaviour of one of the system's users. We use the term "user" to describe any type of end user, whether a human or software agent. For example, the end users of a system such as Amazon.com are both human and software agents (e.g., "shopping bots" that search multiple websites for the best prices). Signatures are generated for each user because workloads are driven by the combined behaviour of the system's users.

System signatures are generated in two steps. First, we identify all of the unique user IDs that appear in the execution logs. "User IDs" may include email addresses, device IDs or IP addresses that uniquely identify a human or software agent. The second column of Table 3 presents all of the unique user IDs identified from the execution logs of our working example. Second, we generate a signature for each user ID by counting the number of times that each type of execution event is attributable to each user ID. For example, from Table 1, we see that Alice starts one chat, sends two messages and ends one chat. Table 3 shows the signatures generated for each user using the events in Tables 1 and 2.

Table 3: System Signatures

	User ID	(Execution Event ID)			
		1	2	3	4
Field Users	Alice	1	2	0	1
	Bob	0	2	0	0
	Charlie	1	2	0	1
	Dan	0	1	1	0
Load Test Users	USER1	1	2	0	1
	USER2	0	2	0	0
	USER3	1	2	0	1
	USER4	0	2	0	0

3.3 Clustering

The second phase of our approach is to cluster the system signatures into groups of users where a similar set of events have occurred. The clustering phase in our approach consists of three steps. First, we calculate the dissimilarity (i.e., distance) between every pair of system signatures. Second, we use a hierarchical clustering procedure to cluster the system signatures into groups where a similar set of events have occurred. Third, we convert the hierarchical clustering into k partitional clusters (i.e., where each system signature is a member in only one cluster). We have automated the clustering phase using robust and scalable statistical techniques.

3.3.1 Distance Calculation

Each system signature is represented by one point in an n-dimensional space (where n is the number of unique execution events). Clustering procedures rely on identifying points that are "close" in this n-dimensional space. Therefore, we must specify how distance is measured in this space. A larger distance between two points implies a greater dissimilarity between the system signatures that these points represent. We calculate the distance between every pair of system signatures to produce a distance matrix.

We use the Pearson distance (a transform of the Pearson correlation [21]), as opposed to the many other distance measures [1,2,20,21], as the Pearson distance often produces a clustering that is closer to the true clustering (i.e., a closer match to the manually assigned clusters) [25,40]. We find that the Pearson distance performs well when clustering system signatures (see Section 5).

We first calculate the Pearson correlation (ρ) between two system signatures using Equation 1. This measure ranges from -1 to +1, where a value of 1 indicates that two signatures are identical, a value of 0 indicates that there is no relationship between the signatures and a value of -1 indicates an inverse relationship between the signatures (i.e., as the occurrence of specific execution events increase in one system signature, they decrease in the other).

$$\rho = \frac{n \sum_i^n x_i \times y_i - \sum_i^n x_i \times \sum_i^n y_i}{\sqrt{(n \sum_i^n x^2 - (\sum_i^n x)^2) \times (n \sum_i^n y^2 - (\sum_i^n y)^2)}} \quad (1)$$

where x and y are two system signatures and n is the number of execution events.

We then transform the Pearson correlation (ρ) to the Pearson distance (d_ρ) using Equation 2.

$$d_\rho = \begin{cases} 1 - \rho & \text{for } \rho \geq 0 \\ |\rho| & \text{for } \rho < 0 \end{cases} \quad (2)$$

Table 5 presents the distance matrix produced by calculating the Pearson distance between every pair of system signatures in our working example.

3.3.2 Hierarchical Clustering

We use an agglomerative, hierarchical clustering procedure to cluster the system signatures using the distance matrix calculated in the previous step. The clustering procedure starts with each signature in its own cluster and proceeds to find and merge the closest pair of clusters (using the distance matrix), until only one cluster (containing everything) is left. Every time two clusters are merged, the distance matrix is updated. One advantage of hierarchical clustering is that we do not need to specify the number of clusters prior to performing the clustering. Further, performance analysts can change the number of clusters (e.g., to produce a larger number of more cohesive clusters) without having to rerun the clustering phase.

Hierarchical clustering updates the distance matrix based on a specified linkage criteria. We use the average linkage, as opposed to the many other linkage criteria [20,45], as the average linkage is the de facto standard [20,45]. The average linkage criteria is also the most appropriate when little information about the expected clustering (e.g., the relative size of the expected clusters) is available. We find that the average linkage criteria performs well when clustering system signatures (see Section 5).

When two clusters are merged, the average linkage criteria updates the distance matrix in two steps. First, the merged clusters are removed from the distance matrix. Second, a new cluster (containing the merged clusters) is added to the distance matrix by calculating the distance between the new cluster and all existing clusters. The distance between two clusters is the average distance (as calculated by the Pearson distance) between the system signatures of the first cluster and the system signatures of the second cluster [20,45].

Figure 2 shows the dendrogram produced by hierarchically clustering the system signatures using the distance matrix (Table 5) from our working example.

Table 5: Distance Matrix

	Alice	Bob	Charlie	Dan	USER1	USER2	USER3	USER4
Alice	0	0.184	0	1.000	0	0.184	0	0.184
Bob	0.184	0	0.184	0.423	0.184	0	0.184	0
Charlie	0	0.184	0	1.000	0	0.184	0	0.184
Dan	1.000	0.423	1.000	0	1.000	0.423	1.000	0.423
USER1	0	0.184	0	1.000	0	0.184	0	0.184
USER2	0.184	0	0.184	0.423	0.184	0	0.184	0
USER3	0	0.184	0	1.000	0	0.184	0	0.184
USER4	0.184	0	0.184	0.423	0.184	0	0.184	0

3.3.3 Dendrogram Cutting

The result of a hierarchical clustering procedure is a hierarchy of clusters. This hierarchy is typically visualized using hierarchical cluster dendrograms. Figure 2 is an example of a hierarchical cluster dendrogram. Such dendrograms are binary tree-like diagrams that show each stage of the clustering procedure as nested clusters [45].

To complete the clustering procedure, the dendrogram must be cut at some height. This height represents the maximum amount of intra-cluster dissimilarity that will be accepted within a cluster before that cluster is further divided. Cutting the dendrogram results in a clustering where each system signature is assigned to only one cluster. Such a cutting of the dendrogram is done either by 1) manual (visual) inspection or 2) statistical tests (referred to as stopping rules).

Although a visual inspection of the dendrogram is flexible and fast, it is subject to human bias and may not be reliable. We use the Calinski-Harabasz stopping rule [11], as opposed to the many other stopping rules [11, 19, 36, 37, 39], as the Calinski-Harabasz stopping rule most often cuts the dendrogram into the correct number of clusters [36]. We find that the Calinski-Harabasz stopping rule performs well when cutting dendrograms produced by clustering system signatures (see Section 5).

The Calinski-Harabasz stopping rule is a pseudo-F-statistic, which is a ratio reflecting within-cluster similarity and between-cluster dissimilarity. The optimal clustering will have high within-cluster similarity (i.e., the system signatures within a cluster are similar) and a high between-cluster dissimilarity (i.e., the system signatures from two different clusters are dissimilar).

The dotted horizontal line in Figure 2 shows where the Calinski-Harabasz stopping rule cut the hierarchical cluster dendrogram from our working example into three clusters (i.e., the dotted horizontal line intersects with solid vertical lines at three points in the dendrogram). Cluster A contains one user (Dan), cluster B contains four users (Alice, Charlie, USER1 and USER3) and cluster C contains three users (Bob, USER2 and USER4).

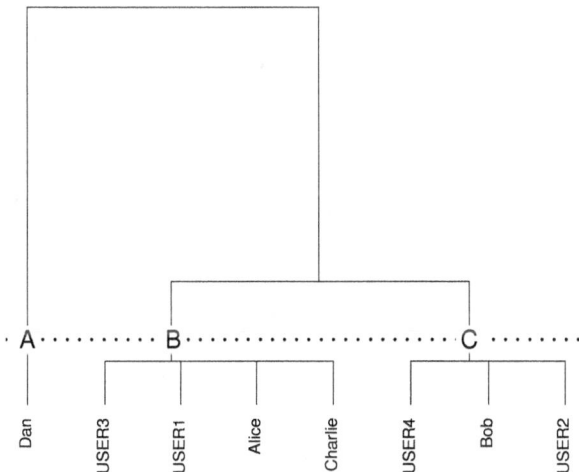

Figure 2: Sample Dendrogram.

3.4 Cluster Analysis

The third phase in our approach is to identify the execution events that correspond to the differences between the load test and field signatures. The cluster analysis phase of our approach consists of two steps. First, outlying clusters are detected. Second, the key execution events of the outlying clusters are identified. We refer to these execution events as "signature differences". Knowledge of these signature differences may lead performance analysts to update their load test cases. "Event A occurs 10% less often in the load test relative to the field" is an example of a signature difference that may lead performance analysts to update a load test case such that Event A occurs more frequently in the load test. We use robust and scalable statistical techniques to automate this step.

3.4.1 Outlier Detection

We identify outlying clusters using z-stats. Z-stats measure an anomaly's deviation from the majority (expected) behaviour [31]. Larger z-stats indicate an increased probability that the majority behaviour is the expected behaviour. Hence, as the z-stat of a particular cluster increases, the probability that the cluster is an outlying cluster also increases. Equation 3 presents how the z-stat of a particular cluster is calculated.

$$z(m,n) = \frac{\frac{m}{n} - p_o}{\frac{p_o \times (1 - p_o)}{n}} \qquad (3)$$

where m is the number of system signatures from the load test or the field (whichever is greater) in the cluster, n is the total number of system signatures in the cluster and p_o is the probability of the errors (by convention, p_o is typically assigned a value of 0.9 [31]).

Table 6 presents the size (i.e., the number of system signatures in the cluster), breakdown (i.e., the number of system signatures from the load test and the field) and z-stat for each cluster in our working example (i.e., each of the clusters that were identified when the Calinski-Harabasz stopping rule was used to cut the dendrogram in Figure 2).

Table 6: Identifying Outlying Clusters

| Cluster | Size | # Signatures from: | | z-stat |
		Field	Load Test	
A	1	1	0	1.111
B	4	2	2	-17.778
C	3	1	2	-18.889

From Table 6, we identify Cluster A as an outlying cluster because its z-stat (1.111) is larger than the z-stats of Cluster B (-17.778) or Cluster C (-18.889).

263

3.4.2 Signature Difference Detection

We identify the differences between system signatures in outlying clusters and the average ("normal") system signature by performing an influence analysis on the signatures. This analysis quantifies the importance of each execution event in differentiating a cluster. Knowledge of these events may lead performance analysts to update their load test cases.

First, we calculate the centre of the outlying clusters and the universal centre. These centres represent the location, in an n-dimensional space (where n is the number of unique execution events), of each of the outlying clusters, as well as the average ("normal") system signature. The centre of a cluster is the average count for each unique event across either 1) all of the signatures in the cluster (for the centre of an outlying cluster) or 2) all of the signatures in all of the clusters (for the universal centre).

Table 7 presents the universal centre and cluster A centre.

Table 7: Universal Centre and Cluster A Centre

	System Signatures (Execution Event ID)			
	1	2	3	4
Universal Centre	0.5	1.875	0.125	0.5
Cluster A Centre	0	1	1	0

Second, we calculate the Pearson distance (d_ρ) between the centre of the outlying cluster and the universal centre. This "baseline" distance quantifies the difference between the system signatures in outlying clusters and the universal average system signature. The Pearson distance between the centre of Cluster A and the Universal Centre is 0.625.

Third, we calculate the change in the baseline distance between the outlying cluster's centre and the universal centre with and without each execution event. This quantifies the influence of each event. When an overly influential event is removed, the outlying cluster becomes more similar to the universal average system signature (i.e., closer to the universal centre) hence these events will have a negative Δd_ρ.

Table 8 presents the change in the distance between the centre of Cluster A and the Universal Centre when each event is removed from the distance calculation.

Table 8: Identifying Influential Execution Events

Event ID	Δd_ρ
1	0.0613
2	0.375
3	-0.625
4	0.0613
$\mu_{\Delta d_\rho}$	-0.0320
$\sigma_{\Delta d_\rho}$	0.422

Finally, we identify the influential events as any execution event that, when removed from the distance calculation, decreases the distance between the outlying cluster and the universal centre by more than twice the standard deviation less than the average. Decreasing the distance between two clusters indicates that they have become more similar. This analysis is similar to how dfbeta residuals are used to iden-

tify observations that have a disproportionate influence on the estimated coefficient values in a regression model [14,17].

From Table 8, the average change in distance ($\mu_{\Delta d_\rho}$) is -0.0320 and the standard deviation of the changes in distance ($\sigma_{\Delta d_\rho}$) is 0.422. Therefore, no execution events are identified as outliers because no change in distance is more than two standard deviations less than the average change in distance (i.e., no Δd_ρ value is $\leq \mu_{\Delta d_\rho} - 2 \times \sigma_{\Delta d_\rho} = -0.877$). For the purposes of this example, we use one standard deviation (as opposed to two standard deviations). Therefore, we identify execution event 3 (i.e., initiating a file transfer) as overly influential.

Our approach identifies one system signature (i.e., the system signature representing the user Dan) as a key difference between the load test and the field. In particular, we identify one execution event (i.e., initiating a file transfer) that is not well represented in the load test (in fact it does not occur at all). Performance analysts should then adjust the load intensity of the file transfer functionality in the load test.

In our simple working example, performance analysts could have examined how many times each execution event had occurred during the load test and in the field and identified events that occur much more frequently in the field compared to the load test. However, in practice, data sets are considerably larger. For example, our first enterprise case study contains over 1,400 different types of execution events and over 17 million log lines. Further, some execution events have a different impact on the system's behaviour based on the manner in which the event is executed. For example, our second enterprise case study identifies an execution event that only causes errors when over-stressed by an individual user (i.e., one user executing the event 1,000 times has a different impact on the system's behaviour than 100 users each executing the event 10 times). Therefore, in practice performance analysts cannot simply examine occurrence frequencies.

4. CASE STUDIES

This section outlines the setup and results of our case studies. First, we present a case study using a Hadoop application. We then discuss the results of two case studies using an enterprise system. Table 9 outlines the systems and data sets used in our case studies.

Our case studies aim to determine whether our approach can detect system signature differences due to 1) feature differences, 2) intensity differences and 3) issue differences between a load test and the field. Our case studies include systems whose users are either human (Enterprise System) or software (Hadoop) agents.

We compare our results with the current state-of-the-practice. Currently, performance analysts validate load test cases by comparing the number of times each execution event has occurred during the load test compared to the field and investigating any differences. Therefore, we rank the events based on the difference in occurrence frequency between the load test and the field. We then investigate the events with the largest differences. In practice, performance analysts do not know how many of these events should be investigated. Therefore, we examine the minimum number of events such that the state-of-the-practice approach identifies the same problems as our approach. We then compare the precision of our approach to the state-of-the-pratice.

Table 9: Case Study Subject Systems.

	Hadoop	Enterprise System	
Application domain	Data processing	Telecom	
License	Open-source	Enterprise	
Load Test Data			
# Log Lines	10,145	17,128,625	11,590,898
Notes	Load test driven by a standard Hadoop application.	Use-case load test driven by a load generator.	Load test driven by a replay script.
Field Data			
Execution Events	15,516	8,194,869	11,745,435
Notes	The system experienced a machine failure in the field.	System experts confirmed that there were no errors in the field.	The system experienced a crash in the field.
Type of Differences	Issue difference	Intensity and differences	Intensity difference
State-of-the-Practice Approach (Best Results)			
Influential Events	4	17	4
Precision	75%	100%	100%
Our Approach			
Influential Events	9	25	19
Precision	56%	60%	16%

4.1 Hadoop Case Study

4.1.1 The Hadoop Platform

Our first system is an application that is built on Hadoop. Hadoop is an open-source distributed data processing platform that implements MapReduce [3,16].

MapReduce is a distributed data processing framework that allows large amounts of data to be processed in parallel by the nodes of a distributed cluster of machines [16]. The MapReduce framework consists of two steps: a Map step, where the input data is divided amongst the nodes of the cluster, and a Reduce step, where the results from each of the nodes is collected and combined.

Operationally, a Hadoop application may contain one or more MapReduce steps (each step is a "Job"). Jobs are further broken down into "tasks," where each task is either a Map task or a Reduce task. Finally, each task may be executed more than once to support fault tolerance within Hadoop (each execution is an "attempt").

4.1.2 The WordCount Application

The Hadoop application used in this case study is the WordCount application [4]. The WordCount application is a standard example of a Hadoop application that is used to demonstrate the Hadoop platform. The WordCount application reads one or more text files (a corpus) and counts the number of times each unique word occurs within the corpus.

Load test: We load test the Hadoop WordCount application on a cluster by attempting to count the number of times each unique word occurs in 3.69 gigabytes of text files. The cluster contains five machines, each with dual Intel Xeon E5540 (2.53GHz) quad-core CPUs, 12GB memory, a Gigabit network adaptor and SATA hard drives.

Field workload: We monitor the performance of the Hadoop WordCount application in the field. We find that the throughput (completed attempts/sec) is much lower than the throughput specified in the system's requirements. We also find that the average network IO (bytes/sec transfered between the nodes of the cluster) is considerably lower than the average historical network IO.

4.1.3 Applying Our Approach

We apply our approach to the execution logs collected from the WordCount application during the load test and from the field. We generate a system signature for each attempt because these attempts are the "users" of the Hadoop platform. Our approach identifies the following system signature differences (i.e., execution events that best describe the differences between the load test and the field):

```
INFO org.apache.hadoop.hdfs.DFSClient: Abandoning
block blk_id

INFO org.apache.hadoop.hdfs.DFSClient: Exception
in createBlockOutputStream java.io.IOException:
Bad connect ack with firstBadLink ip_address

WARN org.apache.hadoop.hdfs.DFSClient: Error Recov-
ery for block blk_id bad datanode_id ip_address

INFO org.apache.hadoop.mapred.TaskTracker:
attempt_id progress
```

4.1.4 Results

Our approach flags only four execution events (out of 25,661 log lines that occur during the load test or in the field) for expert analysis. These execution events indicate that the WordCount application 1) cannot retrieve data from the Hadoop File System (HFS), 2) has a "bad" connection with the node at **ip_address** and 3) cannot reconnect to the datanode (data nodes store data in the HFS) at **ip_address**. Made aware of this issue, performance analysts could update their load tests to test how the system responds to machine failures and propose redundancy in the field.

The last execution event is a progress message. This execution event occurs less frequently than expected because some attempts in the field cannot retrieve data from the Hadoop File System (therefore these attempts make no progress). However, system experts do not believe that this is a meaningful difference between the system's behaviour during the load test and in the field. Hence, we have correctly identified 3 events out of the 4 flagged events. The precision of our approach (i.e., the percentage of correctly identified execution events) is 75%.

265

We also use the state-of-the-practice approach (outlined in Section 4) to identify the execution events with the largest occurrence frequency difference between the load test and the field. In order to produce the same results as our approach and identify the differences between the load test and the field, performance analysts must examine the top 6 events. Although examining the top 6 events will result in the same results as our approach, the precision is only 50% (compared to 75% for our approach).

4.2 Enterprise System Case Study

Although our Hadoop case study was promising, we perform two case studies on an enterprise system to examine the scalability of our approach. We note that these data sets are much larger than our Hadoop data set (see Table 9).

4.2.1 The Enterprise System

Our second system is a ULS enterprise software system in the telecommunications domain. For confidentiality reasons, we cannot disclose the specific details of the system's architecture, however the system is responsible for simultaneously processing millions of client requests and has very high performance requirements.

Performance analysts perform continuous load testing to ensure that the system continuously meets its performance requirements. Therefore, analysts must continuously ensure that the load test cases used during load testing accurately represent the current conditions in the field.

4.2.2 Comparing Use-Case Load Tests to the Field

Our first enterprise case study describes how our approach was used to validate a use-case load test (i.e., a load test driven by a load generator) by comparing the system behaviour during the load test and in the field. A load generator was configured to simulate the individual behaviour of thousands of users by concurrently sending requests to the system based on preset use-cases. The system had recently added several new clients. To ensure that the existing use-cases accurately represent the workloads driven by these new clients, we use our approach to compare a use-case load test to the field.

We use our approach to generate system signatures for each user within the use-case load test and in the field. We then compare the system signatures generated during the use-case load test to those generated in the field. Our approach identifies 17 executions events, that differ between the system signatures of the use-case load test and the field.

These results were then given to performance analysts and system experts who confirmed:

1. Nine events are under-stressed in the use-case load test relative to the field.

2. Six events are over-stressed in the use-case load test relative to the field.

3. Two events are artifacts of the load test (i.e., these events correspond to functionality used to setup the load test cases) and are not important differences between the load test and the field.

In summary, our approach correctly identifies 15 execution events (88% precision) that correspond to differences between the system's behaviour during the load test and in the field. Such results can be used to improve the use-case load tests in the future (i.e., by tuning the load generator to more accurately reflect the field conditions). In contrast, using the state-of-the-practice approach, performance analysts must examine the top 25 execution events in order to uncover the same 17 events that our approach has identified. However, the precision for the top 25 events is 60%, whereas the precision of our approach is 88%.

4.2.3 Comparing Replay Load Tests to the Field

Our second enterprise case study describes how our approach was used to validate a replay load test (i.e., a load test driven by a replay script) by comparing the system behaviour across a load test and the field.

Replay scripts record the behaviour of real users in the field then playback the recorded behaviour during a replay load test, where heavy instrumentation of the system is feasible. In theory, replay scripts can be used to perfectly replicate the conditions in the field during a replay load test [32]. However, replay scripts require complex software to concurrently simulate the millions of users and billions of requests captured in the field. Therefore, replay scripts do not scale well and use-case load tests that are driven by load generators are still the norm [35].

Performance analysts monitoring the system's behaviour in the field observed a spike in memory usage followed by a system crash. To understand the cause of this crash, and why it was not discovered during load testing, we use our approach to generate and compare system signatures for each user in the replay load test and the field. Our approach identifies 4 influential execution events that differ between the system signatures of the replay load test and the field.

These results were given to performance analysts who confirmed that four events are under-stressed in the replay load test relative to the field. Using this information, performance analysts update their load test cases. They then see the same behaviour during load testing as in the field.

In summary, our approach correctly identifies 4 influential execution events that correspond to differences between the system's behaviour during the load test and in the field. Such results provide performance analysts with a very concrete recommendation to help diagnose the cause of this crash.

We also compare our approach to the state-of-the-practice. In order to produce the same results as our approach and identify the differences between the load test and the field, performance analysts must examine the top 19 events. However, the precision of the state-of-the-practice approach is only 16% (compared to 100% for our approach).

The state-of-the-practice approach has an average precision of 44%. However, performance analysts must examine an unknown number of events. Our approach flags events with an average precision of 88%.

---

5. SENSITIVITY ANALYSIS

The clustering phase of our approach relies on three statistical measures: 1) a distance measure (to determine the distance between each system signature), 2) a linkage criteria (to determine which clusters should be merged during the hierarchical clustering procedure) and 3) a stopping rule (to determine the number of clusters by cutting the hierarchical cluster dendrogram). To complement the existing literature, we verify that these measures perform well on our data and evaluate the sensitivity of our results to changes in these measures. We also determine the optimal distance measure, linkage criteria and stopping rule using our Hadoop case study data (similar results hold for our enterprise case study data).

5.1 The Optimal Distance Measure

The hierarchical clustering procedure begins with each system signature in its own cluster and proceeds to identify and merge clusters that are "close." The "closeness" of two clusters is measured by some distance measure. The optimal distance measure will result in a clustering that is closest to the true clustering.

We determine the optimal distance measure by comparing the results obtained by our approach (i.e., the execution events that we flag) when different distance measures are used. Table 10 presents how the number of flagged events, the precision (the percentage of correctly flagged events) and the recall (the percentage of true events that are flagged) is impacted by each of the distance measures in [2, 21]. We calculate recall using the best results in Table 10.

Table 10: Identifying the Optimal Distance Measure

Distance Measure	#Events	Precision	Recall
Pearson distance	4	75%	100%
Cosine distance	2	50%	33%
Euclidean distance	2	50%	33%
Jaccard distance	2	50%	33%
Kullback-Leibler Divergence	2	50%	33%

From Table 10, we find that the Pearson distance produces results with higher precision and recall than any other distance measure. In addition, all five distance measures identify the same two events (the Pearson distance correctly identifies two additional events).

5.2 The Optimal Linkage Criteria

The hierarchical clustering procedure takes a distance matrix and produces a dendrogram (i.e., a hierarchy of clusters). The abstraction from a distance matrix to a dendrogram results in some loss of information (i.e., the distance matrix contains the distance between each pair of system signatures, whereas the dendrogram presents the distance between each cluster). The optimal linkage criteria will enable the hierarchical clustering procedure to produce a dendrogram with minimal information loss.

We determine the optimal linkage criteria by using the cophenetic correlation. The cophenetic correlation measures how well a dendrogram preserves the information in the distance matrix [13]. The cophenetic correlation varies between 0 (the information in the distance matrix is completely lost)

and 1 (the information is perfectly preserved). The optimal linkage criteria will have the highest cophenetic correlation. Table 11 presents the cophenetic correlation for a dendrogram built using each of the four main linkage criteria described in [20, 45].

Table 11: Identifying the Optimal Linkage Criteria

Linkage Criteria	Cophenetic Correlation
Average	0.782
Single	0.522
Ward	0.516
Complete	0.495

From Table 11, we find that the average linkage criteria produces a dendrogram that best represents the distance matrix. We also determine the optimal linkage criteria by applying the cluster analysis phase of our approach (see Subsection 3.4) on a dendrogram that has been built using each of these linkage criteria. Similar to our analysis of the optimal distance measure, Table 12 presents how the number of flagged events, the precision and the recall is impacted by using each of these linkage criteria.

Table 12: Identifying the Optimal Linkage Criteria

Distance Measure	#Events	Precision	Recall
Average	4	75%	100%
Single	6	50%	100%
Ward	2	50%	33%
Complete	3	33%	33%

From Table 12 we find that the average linkage criteria has the highest precision and recall. This is not surprising as the average linkage criteria also had the highest cophenetic correlation. Therefore, the cophenetic correlation may be used in the future to ensure that the average linkage criteria continues to perform well.

5.3 The Optimal Stopping Rule

To complete the clustering procedure, dendrograms must be cut at some height so that each system signature is assigned to only one cluster. Too few clusters will not allow outliers to emerge (i.e., they will remain nested in larger clusters) while too many clusters will lead to over-fitting and many false positives.

We determine the optimal stopping rule measure by applying the cluster analysis phase of our approach (see Subsection 3.4) on a dendrogram that has been cut using different stopping rules are used. Similar to our analysis of the optimal distance measure, Table 13 presents how the number of flagged events, the precision and the recall is impacted by the top 10 automated stopping rules in [36].

From Table 13, we find that the C-Index and Cubic Clustering Criterion stopping rules have 100% recall, but poor precision compared to the Calinski-Harabasz or Gamma stopping rules (75% precision and 75% recall). We select the Calinski-Harabasz stopping rule because the Gamma stopping rule is computationally intensive and does not scale well [12].

Table 13: Identifying the Optimal Stopping Rule

Distance Measure	#Events	Precision	Recall
Calinski-Harabasz	4	75%	75%
Duda and Hart	0	0%	0%
C-Index	7	57%	100%
Gamma	4	75%	75%
Beale	1	0%	0%
Cubic Clustering Criterion	7	57%	100%
Point-Biserial	1	0%	0%
G(+)	1	0%	0%
Davies and Bouldin	2	50%	25%
Stepsize	1	0%	0%

6. THREATS TO VALIDITY

6.1 Threats to Construct Validity

Evaluation

We have evaluated our approach by determining the precision with which our approach flags execution events that differ between the system signatures of a load test and the field. While performance analysts have verified these results, we do not have a gold standard data set. Further, complete system knowledge would be required to exhaustively enumerate every difference between a particular load test and the field. Therefore, we cannot calculate the recall of our approach. However, our approach is intended to help performance analysts identify differences between a load test and the field by flagging execution events for further analysis (i.e., to provide performance analysts with a starting point). Therefore, our goal is to maximize precision so that analysts have confidence in our approach. In our experience working with industry experts, performance analysts agree with this view [23, 24, 27, 43]. Additionally, we were able to identify at least one execution event that differed between the load test and the field in all of our case studies. Hence we were able to evaluate the precision of our approach in all three case studies.

6.2 Threats to Internal Validity

Execution Log Quality/Coverage

Our approach generates system signatures by characterizing a user's behaviour in terms of feature usage expressed by the execution events. However, it is possible that there are no execution logs to indicate when certain features are used. Therefore, our approach is incapable of identifying these features in the event that their usage differs between a load test and the field. However, this is true for all execution log based analysis, including manual analysis.

This threat may be mitigated by using automated instrumentation tools that would negate the need for developers to manually insert output statements into the source code. However, we leave this to future work as automated instrumentation imposes a heavy overhead on the system [34]. Further, Shang et al. report that execution logs are a rich source of information that are used by developers to convey important information about a system's behaviour [41]. Hence, automated instrumentation tools may not provide as deep an insight into the system's behaviour as execution logs.

Defining Users for Signature Generation

In our experience, ULS systems are typically driven by human agents. However, users may be difficult to define in ULS systems that are driven by software agents (e.g., web services [22]) or when users are allowed to have multiple IDs. Defining the users of a particular system is a task for the system experts. However, such a determination only needs to be made the first time our approach is used, afterwards this definition is reused.

6.3 Threats to External Validity

Generalizing Our Results

The studied software systems represent a small subset of the total number of Ultra-Large-Scale software systems. Therefore, it is unclear how our results will generalize to additional software systems, particularly systems from other domains (e.g., e-commerce). However, our approach does not assume any particular architectural details. Hence, there is no barrier to our approach being applied to other ULS systems. Further, we have evaluated our approach on two different systems: 1) an open-source distributed data processing system and 2) an enterprise telecommunications system that is widely used in practice.

Our approach may not perform well on small data sets (where we cannot generate many system signatures) or data sets where one set of execution logs (either the load test or field logs) is much larger than the other. However, the statistical measures that we have chosen are invariant to scale. Further, we have evaluated our approach on small data sets (10,145 load test log lines in our Hadoop study) and data sets where one set of execution logs is much larger than the other (the load test logs are twice as large as the field logs in our first Enterprise case study).

7. RELATED WORK

This paper presented an automated approach to validate load test cases by comparing execution logs from a load test and the field. Load test case design and log analysis are the most closely related areas of research to our work.

7.1 Load Test Case Design

Much of the work in load testing has focused on the automatic generation of load test cases [7, 8, 10, 18, 48]. A survey of load testing (and load test cases) may be found in [27]. Our approach may be used to validate load test cases by comparing the load tests performed with these test cases to the field. We intend to explore how the results of our approach may be used to automatically update load test cases.

7.2 Log Analysis

Shang et al. flag deviations in execution sequences mined from the execution logs of a test deployment and a field deployment of a ULS system [42]. Their approach reports deviations with a comparable precision to traditional keyword search approaches (23% precision), but reduces the number of false positives by 94%. Our approach does not rely on mining execution sequences. We also do not require any information regarding the timing of events within the system, which may be unreliable in distributed systems [33].

Jiang et al. flag performance issues in specific usage scenarios by comparing the distribution of response times for the scenario against a baseline derived from previous tests [30]. Their approach reports scenarios that have performance problems with few false positives (77% precision). To overcome the need for a baseline, Jiang et al. mine execution logs to determine the dominant (expected) behaviour of the system and flag anomalies from the dominant behaviour [29]. Their approach is able to flag <0.01% of the execution log lines for closer analysis by system experts. Our approach is interested in highlighting the differences between a load test and the field, as opposed to just anomalous behaviour. However, our approach can identify anomalous behaviour if such behaviour occurs primarily in the field (Subsection 4.2.3).

In our previous work, we proposed an approach to identify performance deviations in thread pools using performance counters [43, 44]. This approach is able to identify performance deviations (e.g., memory leaks) with high precision and recall. However, this approach did not make use of execution logs. Therefore, we could not identify the underlying cause of these performance deviations. The approach presented in this paper is concerned with highlighting the differences between a load test and the field, as opposed to just performance issues.

8. CONCLUSIONS AND FUTURE WORK

This paper presents an automated approach to validate load test cases by comparing system signatures from load tests and the field using execution logs. Our approach identifies differences between load tests and the field that performance analysts can use to update their load test cases to more accurately represent the field workloads.

We performed three case studies on two systems: one open-source system and one enterprise system. Our case studies explored how our approach can be used to identify feature differences, intensity differences and issue differences between load tests and the field. Performance analysts and system experts have confirmed that our approach provides valuable insights that help to validate their load tests and to support the continuous load testing process.

Although our approach performed well, we intend to explore how well our approach performs when comparing additional data sets as well as data sets from other ULS systems. We also intend to assess whether updating a load test case based on our approach results in the system's performance during the load test becoming more aligned with the system's performance in the field.

Acknowledgement

We would like to thank BlackBerry for providing access to the enterprise system used in our case study. The findings and opinions expressed in this paper are those of the authors and do not necessarily represent or reflect those of BlackBerry and/or its subsidiaries and affiliates. Moreover, our results do not reflect the quality of BlackBerry's products.

9. REFERENCES

[1] Cosine similarity, Pearson correlation, and OLS coefficients. http://brenocon.com/blog/2012/03/cosine-similarity-pearson-correlation-and-ols-coefficients.

[2] Gene Expression Data Analysis Suite: Distance measures. http://gedas.bizhat.com/dist.htm. Last Accessed: 17-May-2013.

[3] Hadoop. www.hadoop.apache.org/. Last Accessed: 17-Apr-2013.

[4] MapReduce Tutorial. http://hadoop.apache.org/docs/stable/mapred_tutorial.html. Last Accessed: 17-Apr-2013.

[5] PerfMon. http://technet.microsoft.com/en-us/library/bb490957.aspx. Last Accessed: 17-Apr-2013.

[6] The Sarbanes-Oxley Act 2002. http://soxlaw.com/. Last Accessed: 17-May-2013.

[7] A. Avritzer and E. J. Weyuker. Generating test suites for software load testing. In *Proceedings of the International Symposium on Software Testing and Analysis*, pages 44–57, Aug 1994.

[8] A. Avritzer and E. J. Weyuker. The automatic generation of load test suites and the assessment of the resulting software. *Transactions on Software Engineering*, 21(9):705–716, Sep 1995.

[9] L. Bertolotti and M. C. Calzarossa. Models of mail server workloads. *Performance Evaluation*, 46(2-3):65–76, Oct 2001.

[10] Y. Cai, J. Grundy, and J. Hosking. Synthesizing client load models for performance engineering via web crawling. In *Proceedings of the International Conference on Automated Software Engineering*, pages 353–362, Nov 2007.

[11] T. Calinski and J. Harabasz. A dendrite method for cluster analysis. *Communications in Statistics*, 3(1):1–27, Jan 1974.

[12] M. Charrad, N. Ghazzali, V. Boiteau, and A. Niknafs. *NbClust: An examination of indices for determining the number of clusters : NbClust Package*. Last Accessed: 13-Sep-2013.

[13] L. Cherkasova, K. Ozonat, N. Mi, J. Symons, and E. Smirni. Automated anomaly detection and performance modeling of enterprise applications. *Transactions on Computer Systems*, 27(3):6:1–6:32, Nov 2009.

[14] J. Cohen, P. Cohen, S. G. West, and L. S. Aiken. *Applied Multiple Regression/Correlation Analysis for the Behavioral Sciences*. Routledge Academic, third edition, 2002.

[15] J. Dean and L. A. Barroso. The tail at scale. *Communications of the ACM*, 56(2):74–80, Feb 2013.

[16] J. Dean and S. Ghemawat. MapReduce: simplified data processing on large clusters. *Communications of the ACM*, 51(1):107–113, Jan 2008.

[17] T. V. der Meera, M. T. Grotenhuisb, and B. Pelzerb. Influential cases in multilevel modeling: A methodological comment. *American Sociological Review*, 75(1):173–178, 2010.

[18] D. Draheim, J. Grundy, J. Hosking, C. Lutteroth, and G. Weber. Realistic load testing of web applications. In *Proceedings of the European Conference on Software Maintenance and Reengineering*, pages 57–68, Mar 2006.

[19] R. O. Duda and P. E. Hart. *Pattern Classification and Scene Analysis*. John Wiley & Sons Inc, 1st edition, 1973.

[20] I. Frades and R. Matthiesen. Overview on techniques in cluster analysis. *Bioinformatics Methods In Clinical Research*, 593:81–107, Mar 2009.

[21] M. H. Fulekar. *Bioinformatics: Applications in Life and Environmental Sciences*. Springer, 1st edition, 2008.

[22] D. Greenwood, M. Lyell, A. Mallya, and H. Suguri. The IEEE FIPA approach to integrating software agents and web services. In *Proceedings of the International Joint Conference on Autonomous Agents and Multiagent Systems*, pages 1412–1418, May 2007.

[23] A. E. Hassan and P. Flora. Performance engineering in industry: current practices and adoption challenges. In *Proceedings of the International Workshop on Software and Performance*, pages 209–209, Feb 2007.

[24] A. E. Hassan and R. C. Holt. Replaying development history to assess the effectiveness of change propagation tools. *Empirical Software Engineering*, 11(3):335–367, Sep 2006.

[25] A. Huang. Similarity measures for text document clustering. In *Proceedings of the New Zealand Computer Science Research Student Conference*, pages 44–56, Apr 2008.

[26] S. E. Institute. *Ultra-Large-Scale Systems: The Software Challenge of the Future*. Carnegie Mellon University, 2006.

[27] Z. M. Jiang. *Automated Analysis of Load Testing Results*. PhD thesis, Queen's University, Jan 2013.

[28] Z. M. Jiang, A. E. Hassan, G. Hamann, and P. Flora. An automated approach for abstracting execution logs to execution events. *Journal of Software Maintenance and Evolution*, 20(4):249–267, Jul 2008.

[29] Z. M. Jiang, A. E. Hassan, G. Hamann, and P. Flora. Automatic identification of load testing problems. In *Proceedings of the International Conference on Software Maintenance*, pages 307–316, Oct 2008.

[30] Z. M. Jiang, A. E. Hassan, G. Hamann, and P. Flora. Automated performance analysis of load tests. In *Proceedings of the International Conference on Software Maintenance*, pages 125–134, Sep 2009.

[31] T. Kremenek and D. Engler. Z-ranking: using statistical analysis to counter the impact of static analysis approximations. In *Proceedings of the International Conference on Static Analysis*, pages 295–315, Jun 2003.

[32] D. Krishnamurthy, J. A. Rolia, and S. Majumdar. A synthetic workload generation technique for stress testing session-based systems. *Transactions on Software Engineering*, 32(11):868–882, Nov 2006.

[33] L. Lamport. Time, clocks, and the ordering of events in a distributed system. *Communications of the ACM*, 21(7):558–565, Jul 1978.

[34] H. Malik, Z. M. Jiang, B. Adams, A. E. Hassan, P. Flora, and G. Hamann. Automatic comparison of load tests to support the performance analysis of large enterprise systems. In *Proceedings of the European Conference on Software Maintenance and Reengineering*, pages 222–231, Mar 2010.

[35] J. A. Meira, E. C. de Almeida, Y. L. Traon, and G. Sunye. Peer-to-peer load testing. In *Proceedings of the International Conference on Software Testing, Verification and Validation*, pages 642–647, Apr 2012.

[36] G. W. Milligan and M. C. Cooper. An examination of procedures for determining the number of clusters in a data set. *Psychometrika*, 50(2):159–179, Jun 1985.

[37] R. Mojena. Hierarchical grouping methods and stopping rules: An evaluation. *The Computer Journal*, 20(4):353–363, Nov 1977.

[38] D. L. Parnas. Software aging. In *Proceedings of the International Conference on Software Engineering*, pages 279–287, May 1994.

[39] P. J. Rousseeuw. Silhouettes: a graphical aid to the interpretation and validation of cluster analysis. *Journal of Computational and Applied Mathematics*, 20(1):53–65, Nov 1987.

[40] N. Sandhya and A. Govardhan. Analysis of similarity measures with wordnet based text document clustering. In *Proceedings of the International Conference on Information Systems Design and Intelligent Applications*, pages 703–714, Jan 2012.

[41] W. Shang, Z. M. Jiang, B. Adams, A. E. Hassan, M. W. Godfrey, M. Nasser, and P. Flora. An exploratory study of the evolution of communicated information about the execution of large software systems. In *Proceedings of the Working Conference on Reverse Engineering*, pages 335–344, Oct 2011.

[42] W. Shang, Z. M. Jiang, H. Hemmati, B. Adams, A. E. Hassan, and P. Martin. Assisting developers of big data analytics applications when deploying on hadoop clouds. In *Proceedings of the International Conference on Software Engineering*, pages 402–411, May 2013.

[43] M. D. Syer, B. Adams, and A. E. Hassan. Identifying performance deviations in thread pools. In *Proceedings of the International Conference on Software Maintenance*, pages 83–92, Sep 2011.

[44] M. D. Syer, B. Adams, and A. E. Hassan. Industrial case study on supporting the comprehension of system behaviour. In *Proceedings of the International Conference on Program Comprehension*, pages 215–216, Jun 2011.

[45] P.-N. Tan, M. Steinbach, and V. Kumar. *Cluster Analysis: Basic Concepts and Algorithms*. Addison-Wesley Longman Publishing Co., Inc., 1st edition, 2005.

[46] J. Voas. Will the real operational profile please stand up? *IEEE Software*, 17(2):87–89, Mar 2000.

[47] E. Weyuker and F. Vokolos. Experience with performance testing of software systems: issues, an approach, and case study. *Transactions on Software Engineering*, 26(12):1147–1156, Dec 2000.

[48] J. Zhang and S.-C. Cheung. Automated test case generation for the stress testing of multimedia systems. *Software: Practices and Experiences*, 32:1411–1435, Dec 2002.

[49] Z. Zhang, L. Cherkasova, and B. T. Loo. Benchmarking approach for designing a mapreduce performance model. In *Proceedings of the International Conference on Performance Engineering*, pages 253–258, Apr 2013.

Application Performance Management using Learning, Optimization, and Control

Xiaoyun Zhu
VMware, Inc.
Palo Alto, California, USA
xzhu@vmware.com

ABSTRACT

In the past decade, the IT industry has experienced a paradigm shift as computing resources became available as a utility through cloud based services. In spite of the wider adoption of cloud computing platforms, some businesses and organizations hesitate to move all their applications to the cloud due to performance concerns. Existing practices in application performance management rely heavily on white-box modeling and diagnosis approaches or on performance troubleshooting "cookbooks"to find potential bottlenecks and remediation steps. However, the scalability and adaptivity of such approaches remain severely constrained, especially in a highly-dynamic, consolidated cloud environment. For performance isolation and differentiation, most modern hypervisors offer powerful resource control primitives such as reservations, limits, and shares for individual virtual machines (VMs). Even so, with the exploding growth of virtual machine sprawl, setting these controls properly such that co-located virtualized applications get enough resources to meet their respective service level objectives (SLOs) becomes a nearly insoluble task. These challenges present unique opportunities in leveraging the rich telemetry collected from applications and systems in the cloud, and in applying statistical learning, optimization, and control based techniques to developing model-based, automated application performance management frameworks. There has been a large body of research in this area in the last several years, but many problems remain. In this talk, I'll highlight some of the automated and data-driven performance management techniques we have developed, along with related technical challenges. I'll then discuss open research problems, in hope to attract more innovative ideas and solutions from a larger community of researchers and practitioners.

Categories and Subject Descriptors

D.2.9 [**Software Engineering**]: Management

Keywords: performance, learning, control, optimization

ICPE'14, March 22–26, 2014, Dublin, Ireland.
ACM 978-1-4503-2733-6/14/03.
http://dx.doi.org/10.1145/2568088.2576098

Software Contention Aware Queueing Network Model of Three-Tier Web Systems (Work-In-Progress)

Shadi Ghaith, Miao Wang, Philip Perry and Liam Murphy
School of Computer Science and Informatics
University College Dublin, Ireland
shadi.ghaith@ucdconnect.ie

ABSTRACT

Using modelling to predict the performance characteristics of software applications typically uses Queueing Network Models representing the various system hardware resources. Leaving out the software resources, such as the limited number of threads, in such models leads to a reduced prediction accuracy. Accounting for Software Contention is a challenging task as existing techniques to model software components are complex and require deep knowledge of the software architecture. Furthermore, they also require complex measurement processes to obtain the model's service demands. In addition, solving the resultant model usually require simulation solvers which are often time consuming.

In this work, we aim to provide a simpler model for three-tier web software systems which accounts for Software Contention that can be solved by time efficient analytical solvers. We achieve this by expanding the existing "Two-Level Iterative Queuing Modelling of Software Contention" method to handle the number of threads at the Application Server tier and the number of Data Sources at the Database Server tier. This is done in a generic manner to allow for extending the solution to other software components like memory and critical sections. Initial results show that our technique clearly outperforms existing techniques.

Keywords

performance models, performance prediction, web applications, software contention

1. INTRODUCTION

Using modelling to predict application performance under various possible hardware (and software) configurations is becoming widely used in capacity management processes [1] [2]. It saves time and also removes the need to physically build and evaluate a number of possible alternative systems. A Queueing Network Model (QNM) which represents the various hardware and software resources of the system can be solved by either analytical techniques (which are fast but

are limited to simple QNMs) or by simulation solvers (which can be applied to more complex QNMs but require a much longer time to run the model).

The work done by Kounev et al [2] shows that building QNMs to represent hardware resources only (such as CPU) is relatively simple and fast. Yet, they show that the calculated response times are much lower (more than 30%) than the real ones measured by conventional load testing. This large error is due to the absence of modelling contentions caused by software resources such as the limited number of threads [2]. This deviation can be offset by increasing the suggested hardware requirements which can result in wasted hardware resources. Some techniques were introduced to account for Software Contention (SC) [3] [4] [5] but suffer from increased complexity in the QNM and additional effort to measure the service demands as well as the increased time required to use simulation solvers. The time factor of performance prediction is important as simulation solvers may take hours for a medium size software system which is needed to be repeated many times varying hardware and software configuration options [6].

In his work [7] Menasce introduced a two layered iterative technique to model SC. The technique is simple and time efficient, but it is difficult to apply it to complex systems models. In addition it requires some specific instrumentation of the application code to measure various service demands required by the software modules on each hardware resource. In this paper, we aim to extend the technique proposed in [7] to model a general three-tier web system such as the one introduced in [2]. We also aim to reduce the collection difficulties encountered when measuring the service demands of the QNM. In doing so we expect to achieve the following objectives:

1. Generate a generic model for three-tier web systems which can account for contention caused by software resources. In particular, in this paper we consider the number of threads of the Application Server (AS) and the number of database Data Sources (DS).

2. The model is simple enough to be solved using time efficient analytical solvers.

3. The model is extendable to handle contention caused by memory management and critical sections.

Our work can improve the capacity planning and management process by enhancing its accuracy and significantly reducing the time required to solve the model. It will also be useful in other processes that rely on multiple solutions of

QNMs such as the performance regression testing technique [8] [9].

2. OVERVIEW

2.1 QNM of a Three-Tier Web System

A typical three-tier web system consists of the following three components [10]. First, the client component which usually contains client software such as the web browser that takes the user input and communicates with the server side over the network. After the server side performs the necessary functions, the client will then present the response to the user transaction and the user will launch the next transaction after thinking for a period of time known as Think Time (TT). Given that the client software is usually run on individual user machines, its hardware (and even software) service demands are very low and hence it is usually just represented by a delay station denoted TT. The second component is the AS which is usually composed of an application platform, such as the JEE container, over which the application is deployed. The platform usually assigns each request to a thread to allow for serving multiple clients at the same time. The number of available threads is limited [10] and so it is a key factor that affects the application performance. The third component is the Database Server (DBS) on which a relational database software (such as Oracle) is deployed and contains the application specific data. Before the AS communicates with the DBS (to store and read data) it requests a DS from the DBS to handle this communication. The number of DS's available from the DBS is also limited [10] and is another key factor for the performance of such systems. The three-tier web system is usually represented by a hardware QNM such as the one shown at the bottom of Figure 1.

2.2 Two-Level Iterative Queueing Modelling of Software Contentions

The work in [7] by Menasce is one of the simplest approximations to handle SC. Yet, it provides very good results, as shown in the paper and as we found in our experiments. This approach requires an iterative solution of two QNMs: One is the Hardware Queueing Network (HQN) and the other is the Software Queueing Network (SQN).

The HQN is a typical QNM such as the one shown at the bottom of Figure 1, where hardware resources such as CPU and hard disk are modelled as load independent queueing stations and the user TT node is modelled by a delay station. The SQN also contains the TT station as well as a set of nodes each of which represents a certain software module. Each software module either causes no queueing in which case it is represented by a delay station, or it can cause queueing (such as a critical section) in which case it is represented as a load independent queue station. For example, the critical section is represented by a station that has one processing unit and a queue. A simple SQN is shown at the top of Figure 1.

Each software module in the SQN has a service demand on each hardware node in the HQN. These are measured using a single user test by instrumenting the software code. The total service demand on each module in the SQN is calculated by the summation of all service demands for that module on each station in the HQN. While, the total service demands for each hardware station in the HQN is the summation of all service demands for that station caused by each software module in the SQN.

The SQN is first solved with the initial (single user) modules' total service demands using the total number of users accessing the system. Then the number of blocked users is calculated by finding out the number of users in each queue station within the SQN. The HQN is then solved with the total number of users excluding the users in the queues of the SQN and the total service demands of the hardware stations. After solving the HQN, the service demand of each module in the SQN is set to the sum of the fraction of the residence time (queueing and serving time) of each station in the HQN proportional to this module contribution to the original total service demands of each HQN station. Then the above is repeated again by solving the SQN with the new service demands and solving the HQN with the total number of users excluding the blocked users. This continues until the number of blocked users is reasonably stable.

The approximation above has the following drawbacks:

1. Finding the service demands per software module for each hardware resource is complicated. It requires instrumentation at the code level on the border of each software module and on each access to hardware resources within each module. This requires a detailed investigation of the code which will not be always possible, especially in industrial environments. On the contrary, the hardware service demands used for modelling the hardware resources, ignoring the SC, can be easily measured with a single user test [5].

2. The current approach has a single level (depth) of SC modules. But, in practice, and taking the example of the critical section in the AS where its code may access the database and such a call will suffer from another SC, i.e. the DS. Hence, a new level of SC is possible and needs to be modelled.

3. METHODOLOGY

In this section, we will extend and apply the core idea of the Two-Level Iterative Queueing Modelling of Software Contention to the three-tier web system (both introduced in the previous section). We start by modelling the number of threads in the AS in a way that simplifies the service demands measurement step. Then we show how we can work around the nesting of the software resources by converting the HQN and SQN to product form QNMs.

3.1 Applying Two-Level Iterative Queueing Modelling to Number of AS Threads

As discussed in Section 2.1, the AS dispatches each new job to a new thread which executes the required server module. During its execution, the thread accesses the hardware resources (CPU and hard disk) on both the AS and the DBS (we describe the DS contention in the next section). Given that we approximate that most of the AS code is executed within the thread (except the ignorable demands of the dispatching module), the SQN will only have one module. This module can be represented by a single-queue multi-server station, where the number of servers equals the number of available threads in the AS. Figure 1 shows both the HQN and the SQN in this case. Hence, the service demand for that single software module equals the sum of service demands over all the hardware resources both at the AS and the DBS. This simplification allows us to use the service demands measured by a single user test [5] on all system hardware resources.

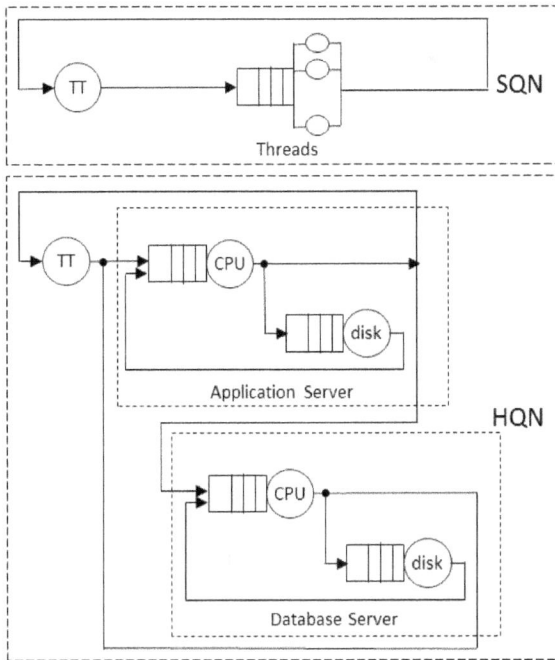

Figure 1: SQN-HQN of a Simple Three-Tier Web System with Application Server Threads.

The SQN can be solved analytically by modelling the single-queue multi-server station in the SQN as a load dependent station as detailed in [11]. Analytically solving the HQN with the non-blocked users is also straightforward. The performance of this solution is much better than the simulation techniques used to model the number of threads such as the Finite Capacity Region (FCR) of the Java Modelling Tool (JMT) [4] described in the Related Work section. The number of iteration was found to be small for such systems (i.e. less than 15 in the case study below).

If we omit the handling of the number of AS threads, the same technique can be used to model the DS, except that the service demands of the module in the SQN is the sum of the DBS CPU and hard disk. While the AS hardware stations, CPU and hard disk, will appear in the SQN and handled in a similar way to the TT station, i.e. they will not contribute to the DS module service demands in the SQN.

Trying to model both the AS threads and the number of DS's in the DBS results in a nested SQN modules, making the entire technique not viable in its current form.

3.2 Tiered Two-Level Iterative Queueing Modelling of Software Contention

The HQN in Figure 1 shows that the AS makes multiple calls to the DBS. The DBS returns the execution to the AS after each call and finally the AS returns back to the user (TT station). Given that the number of DS's on the DBS is also limited, the SC effect happens at both tiers of the system resulting in a complex nested SQN. To rectify this, we consider the approximation used in [2] by Kounev et al which approximates the QNM of a system similar to the

HQN of our work with a model in which each station is visited only once. This makes the HQN simpler as the AS will make one call to the DBS which will serve the job and return back to the TT station. This simplification is validated also with their results. We provided the theory behind this approximation based on the BCMP approximation [12] in our previous work [8].

In the same manner as explained for the HQN, and by applying the same theoretical background [8], we believe that the same approximation is valid on the SQN level. This means that we assume the job visits each software module (the AS threads and the DBS DS's) only once. The SQN contains two single-queue multi-server stations each of them is visited once as shown in Figure 2. Each software module only relies on the hardware service demands within the same tier i.e. the threads module only relies on the CPU and hard disk service demands of the AS and the DS module only relies on the CPU and hard disk service demands of the DBS. The blocked users are calculated to include users waiting in the queues of both single-queue multi-server stations representing the threads and DS modules. The SQN and HQN are iteratively solved in the same manner as explained above. This approximation can be generalized to n-tier systems and has been validated against the three-tier web system described in this paper.

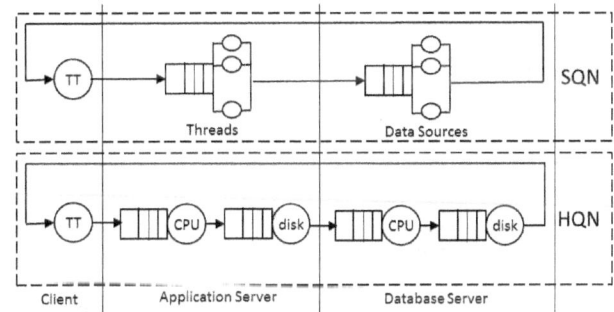

Figure 2: SQN-HQN of a General Three-Tier Web System with Tiered Software Modules (Threads and Data Sources).

4. VALIDATION

We verified the method developed in this paper on the TPC-W workbench application deployed on the IBM WebSphere Application Server and IBM DB2 Database Server with 500 users and three transaction types, as follows:

- Performed a load run using a load generator and measured each transaction response time and the resources utilization (CPU and hard disk on AS and DBS).

- Measured the various transactions service demands on all hardware resources by a single-user test.

- Predicted the response time of each transaction and resources utilization (CPU and hard disk on AS and DBS) by solving the QNM without taking the SC into account (i.e. similar to [2]).

- Used the technique presented in this paper to predict the same values.

- Solved the HQN model shown in Figure 2 using the FCR feature of the JMT.

We had the following observations for the transaction type with the highest response time:

1. The response time calculated using the normal QNM (i.e. not taking the SC into account) is 18% lower than that measured with the load test. While the resource utilizations are within 4% range. This confirms the results achieved by Kounev et al [2].

2. The response time calculated using the presented tiered HQN-SQN (i.e. taking the SC into account) is 6.5% lower than that measured with the load test. While the resource utilizations are within 3% range. That is, we had an improvement of about 300% for the accuracy of response time prediction compared to [2].

3. The presented technique converged within 2 seconds and needed 13 iterations, while the FCR approach required just over 2 minutes. That is, the presented tiered SQN-HQN technique takes around 10% of the time required by simulation.

5. RELATED WORK

Modelling three-tier web systems has been explored previously, particularly by Liu et al [10]. They built a QNM based on the architecture of typical three-tier web applications. The model incorporates the threads at all three tiers and then a solution is approximated by using the MVA technique. The solution augments the hardware and software components within the same elements of the QNM, which makes it hard to use such a model in capacity management where it is always required to modify hardware and software parameters separately to achieve the optimum configuration.

Layered Queueing Networks (LQN) were introduced to handle the SC issue [3]. LQN is based on software resources representing various software operations as the main nodes of the QNM, and hardware resources (such as CPU) as leaf nodes. Software resources call each other forming a multi-layered QNM. It is assumed that the service demands for each software resource on each hardware resource are known (i.e. either estimated by developers or measured by instrumenting the code). This assumption makes the approach difficult to adopt in capacity management processes where access to the code is usually not available. Even if code access is available, instrumenting the code to measure various service demands requires deep knowledge of all parts of the code, such knowledge is rarely available in large applications which are usually developed by multiple teams each responsible for just one software module. In addition, for any LQN with moderate complexity, the expansive simulation techniques are the only possible way to solve them.

Existing tools, such as the JMT, introduced some capabilities to model SC such as the FCR feature of the JSIMgraph part of the JMT [4]. The FCR is used to specify the number of jobs within a certain block of the QNM which allows modelling of constraints such as the number of threads and DS's. The performance of JSIMgraph (simulation), specifically when introducing FCRs prevent it from being used in real capacity management projects.

6. CONCLUSIONS AND FUTURE WORK

Current modelling techniques to account for SC require complex models, hard to obtain service demands for and are expensive to solve. Hence, capacity management projects typically rely on hardware models and apply some assumptions and rules of thumbs to account for SC. In this paper we reduced some of the difficulties of the "Two-Level Iterative Queuing Modelling of Software Contention" method by Menasce and applied it to the common three-tier web systems. We achieved a simplification of the model where it is easier to obtain service demands and can be solved quickly utilizing basic analytical solvers. We showed that our technique provides three times more accurate results in 10% of the time compared to other solvers with SC capabilities.

In this short paper, we explained the technique to account for the number of threads and the DS's; in the future we plan to account for other factors, mainly the memory and critical sections. Also, the technique will be verified on more complex systems, like those with clustered servers. In addition, we plan to show the improvement on actual capacity management projects and on other fields utilizing QNMs, such as the regression testing data analysis.

7. ACKNOWLEDGMENTS

Supported, in part, by Science Foundation Ireland grant 10/CE/I1855.

8. REFERENCES

[1] L. Grinshpan. *Solving Enterprise Applications Performance Puzzles*, pages 5–57. John Wiley and Sons, Inc., Hoboken, New Jersey, 2012.

[2] S. Kounev and A. P. Buchmann. Performance modeling and evaluation of large-scale j2ee applications. In *Int. CMG Conference*, pages 273–283, 2003.

[3] J.A. Rolia and K.C. Sevcik. The method of layers. *Software Engineering, IEEE Transactions on*, 21(8):689–700, 1995.

[4] M.Bertoli, G.Casale, and G.Serazzi. Jmt - performance engineering tools for system modeling. *ACM SIGMETRICS Performance Evaluation Review*, 36(4):10–15, March 2009.

[5] Samuel Kounev. J2ee performance and scalability-from measuring to predicting. In *Spec Benchmark Workshop*, page 12, 2006.

[6] CU Smith. *Performance Engineering of Software Systems*. Addison-Wesley, 1990.

[7] D. Menasce. Two-level iterative queuing modeling of software contention. In *Modeling, Analysis and Simulation of Computer and Telecommunications Systems, 2002. MASCOTS 2002. Proceedings. 10th IEEE International Symposium on*, pages 267–276, 2002.

[8] S. Ghaith, M. Wang, P. Perry, and J. Murphy. Automatic, load-independent detection of performance regressions by transaction profiles. In *Proceedings of the 2013 International Workshop on Joining AcadeMiA and Industry Contributions to testing Automation*, JAMAICA 2013, pages 59–64, New York, NY, USA, 2013. ACM.

[9] S. Ghaith, M. Wang, P. Perry, and J. Murphy. Profile-based, load-independent anomaly detection and analysis in performance regression testing of software systems. In *17th European Conference on Software Maintenance and Reengineering (CSMR'13)*, Genova, Italy, 2013.

[10] Xue Liu, J. Heo, and Lui Sha. Modeling 3-tiered web applications. In *Modeling, Analysis, and Simulation of Computer and Telecommunication Systems, 2005. 13th IEEE International Symposium on*, pages 307–310, 2005.

[11] G. Bolch, S. Greiner, H. de Meer, and K.S. Trivedi. *Queueing Networks and Markov Chains: Modeling and Performance Evaluation with Computer Science Applications*. Wiley, 2006.

[12] F. Baskett, K.M. Chandy, R.R. Muntz, and F.G. Palacios. Open, closed, and mixed networks of queues with different classes of customers. *Journal of the ACM, 22(2)*, pages 248–260, 1975.

Efficient and Accurate Stack Trace Sampling in the Java Hotspot Virtual Machine (Work in Progress Paper)

Peter Hofer
Christian Doppler Laboratory on Monitoring and
Evolution of Very-Large-Scale Software Systems
Johannes Kepler University Linz, Austria
peter.hofer@jku.at

Hanspeter Mössenböck
Institute for System Software
Johannes Kepler University Linz, Austria
hanspeter.moessenboeck@jku.at

ABSTRACT

Sampling is a popular approach to collecting data for profiling and monitoring, because it has a small impact on performance and does not modify the observed application. When sampling stack traces, they can be merged into a calling context tree that shows where the application spends its time and where performance problems lie. However, Java VM implementations usually rely on *safepoints* for sampling stack traces. Safepoints can cause inaccuracies and have a considerable performance impact.

We present a new approach that does not use safepoints, but instead relies on the operating system to take snapshots of the stack at arbitrary points. These snapshots are then asynchronously decoded to call traces, which are merged into a calling context tree. We show that we are able to decode over 90% of the snapshots, and that our approach has very small impact on performance even at high sampling rates.

1. INTRODUCTION

Software profiling measures the execution frequency or the run time of methods during program execution. It is useful for finding bottlenecks, identifying dead code, or determining test coverage. Typically, the profiling data is not captured per method, but rather by *calling context* (or *stack trace*), which is a chain of calls from the root method to an executing method. Calling contexts are commonly merged into a calling-context tree (CCT) [1]. In contrast to a call tree, a CCT merges identical children (callees) of a node.

In general, there are two approaches for collecting calling contexts. *Instrumenting profilers* insert code snippets in methods to record calls in the CCT. This approach yields a complete CCT, but the instrumentation can introduce significant overhead and can distort other observations such as method execution times. *Sampling profilers,* on the other hand, periodically interrupt the application to take snapshots of the entire chain of calls and to merge them into the CCT. This approach requires no instrumentation and typically causes less overhead, but it can miss method invocations and

thus results in an approximate CCT with only statistically significant information. Our research focuses on the sampling approach, because we strive for minimal overhead.

The Java Virtual Machine Tool Interface (JVMTI) [7] offers functions for both sampling calling contexts and instrumenting code and is supported by all common Java VM implementations. Because of its lower overhead, many monitoring tools prefer sampling over exhaustive instrumentation. However, implementations of JVMTI rely on *safepoints* for sampling, which are special locations in code where it is safe to pause the application, for example to perform garbage collection. Whenever JVMTI takes a sample, it requires all threads to run to the next safepoint, which introduces considerable overhead and makes sampling intervals irregular.

Some JIT compiler optimizations add to these problems. For example, a compiler may omit certain safepoint checks to increase performance, which can considerably increase the time to reach a safepoint. When safepoints in an inlined method are omitted, the invocation of that method never shows up in the samples. On the other hand, safepoints in tiny methods such as getters or setters can cause these methods to be overrepresented in the samples.

As a faster and more accurate alternative to JVMTI sampling, Oracle's Hotspot Java VM [8] offers an undocumented sampling mechanism that does not use safepoints. Instead, it uses a POSIX signal that is sent to Java threads to interrupt them. The signal handler can then walk the thread's stack and build a call trace. Because threads can be interrupted individually and at any point (not just at safepoints), this mechanism has a much lower performance impact.

In this paper, we present yet another approach that relies on the operating system and hardware timers to sample fixed-size fragments of Java stacks and to copy them into a buffer. An agent asynchronously reads this buffer, creates call traces from the stack fragments and adds them to a CCT. The agent uses a modified version of the OpenJDK 8 Hotspot VM to decode the stack frames. Our approach achieves very low overhead because analysis happens asynchronously and threads are interrupted only for copying the stack fragments, which can be done quite efficiently.

The main contributions of this paper are:

1. We describe a new technique for collecting call traces of Java applications. It is more efficient than JVMTI sampling and allows for higher sampling rates. Our technique also provides more accurate call traces than JVMTI and thus gives a better picture of where an application spends its time.

2. We describe new heuristics for analyzing stack contents at arbitrary sampling points.

3. We demonstrate the efficiency of our approach with the DaCapo benchmark suite, and the accuracy of our approach by comparing the generated calling context trees to those produced with JVMTI.

2. APPROACH

2.1 Taking Stack Samples

For sampling the stacks, we rely on the operating system to set up a timer to interrupt the application at regular intervals, and when these interrupts trigger, to copy a 16 KByte fragment of the executing thread's current stack. We chose to use the *perf* subsystem of the Linux kernel which already offers this functionality [5, 11]. Sampling a running thread with perf is enabled through a system call that takes a wealth of parameters including the sampling interval, the kinds of data to sample, and the size of the stack fragments. Once perf is enabled, it makes a buffer of collected data available via a file descriptor. This file can be mapped into user-space memory and then acts as a ring buffer of events with the requested data.

The perf subsystem even provides functionality for building call traces by following frame pointers on the stack. However, Java stacks are too complex for this mechanism and even native compilers can omit these links to increase performance, so we perform the stack analysis in user space.

2.2 Retrieving the Samples

For retrieving and processing the samples, we implemented a native *agent* that runs within the Java VM and interfaces with it using JVMTI. The agent registers for a callback when the Java application's main thread is launched. In that callback, it calls perf to start sampling stack fragments as well as the instruction pointer, stack pointer and frame pointer on that thread. The agent also enables inheritance, so sampling automatically applies to all threads the Java application launches.

Next, the agent launches a separate *reader thread* that periodically reads the buffer supplied by perf. The reader thread waits until the buffer is filled to a "watermark" that can be set in the initial system call. It then retrieves samples from the buffer and first copies each stack snapshot to a local buffer where it can be modified. Next, it scans the snapshot for addresses that point into the live stack, and adjusts them to point into the snapshot itself. The reader thread then submits the adjusted snapshot as well as the frame pointer (adjusted to point into the snapshot) and the instruction pointer to the Java VM using a JVMTI extension method that we introduced. This method finally returns a call trace that the reader thread merges into a single CCT.

In some cases, it is necessary to process the collected samples before the buffer is filled to the watermark. One of these cases is when the VM decides to unload compiled methods. Snapshots in which the instruction pointer or return addresses refer to unloaded code could otherwise no longer be transformed to call traces. Similarly, when the VM decides to unload entire classes, it disposes metadata that can then no longer be used to decode snapshots. Hence, our agent registers callbacks for the corresponding JVMTI events to process all buffered samples when one of these

situations occurs. Callbacks for such events are invoked from application or VM threads, so they need to synchronize access to the buffer with the reader thread.

2.3 Analyzing the Samples

Decoding stack snapshots to call traces requires knowledge of the frame layout, the frame sizes and other VM-internal information. Because all this is readily available within the VM, we decided to implement the analysis of stack snapshots within the OpenJDK 8 Hotspot VM and to make it available to the agent via JVMTI extension methods. Using JVMTI's extension mechanism also has the advantage that agents can probe for this capability and can fall back to some other type of sampling when it is not available.

We based our implementation on that of `AsyncGetCall-Trace`, an undocumented function of the Hotspot VM for walking stacks from within a POSIX signal handler. This function already handles several of the intricacies of analyzing stacks in a state where the topmost Java frame cannot be clearly identified. However, unlike `AsyncGetCallTrace`, our approach analyzes stacks asynchronously and thus cannot access the VM state at the time the sample was taken.

One case where it is difficult to walk the stack is when the sample was taken while the thread was executing native code, which the VM has no knowledge about. This occurs frequently because Java relies heavily on native calls for I/O. If the native code does not establish a proper chain of frame pointers (e.g., due to a compiler optimization), its frames cannot be walked and the topmost Java frame, where the native call occurred, cannot be determined. In such cases, `AsyncGetCallTrace` can retrieve the location of this frame from a VM-internal structure where it was recorded at the time of the call, but since we are analyzing the samples asynchronously, we have no access to this information. Therefore, we resort to a heuristic: we leave a "breadcrumb" of two words with specific "magic" values on the stack when a Java-to-native call occurs. When the top of the Java stack cannot be found, we simply scan for a breadcrumb and perform additional checks when found.

Native code invoked from Java can again call Java code via the Java Native Interface (JNI). In such cases, the stack consists of alternating sequences of Java frames and native frames. The resulting stack trace should contain all Java frames on the stack and not just the top frames, which again requires detecting Java/native boundaries. In this case however, we need not rely on breadcrumbs: when native code calls Java methods, the call leaves an entry frame on the stack with a link to the last Java frame below the native caller. Using this link, the stack walk can reliably skip the native frames.

Another problem occurs when frames from stub code are on top of the stack. Stub code refers to snippets of machine code that the Hotspot VM dynamically generates as call wrappers, compiler intrinsics and other helper code. Stub frames have no common layout and some do not even have a known frame size. When a snapshot contains a stub frame with unknown size, we merely scan the words below the stack pointer for a word that looks like a return address into Java code. When such an address is found and additional checks reassure that it is at the boundary to a Java frame, the stub frame is ignored and the call trace is created starting from the Java frame.

Occasionally, samples are also taken in a method's prologue, which is the entry code that saves the caller's frame pointer on the stack, makes the current stack pointer the new frame pointer and moves the stack pointer to the end of the new frame. These samples then have an incomplete frame on top, but this can be detected because Hotspot records where in each compiled method the prologue ends. Instead of discarding these snapshots, we use simple heuristics to find the frame below: we compare the word on top of the stack to the stack pointer and frame pointer to test if the caller's frame pointer has been pushed on the stack yet. The word below, or if the frame pointer has not be pushed, the word on top, should be a return address to Java code and the boundary to the frame below. We then start the stack walk from that frame, ignoring the incomplete frame.

Every sample contains only a fixed-size fragment of the stack. Thus, the stack walk can arrive at the end of the fragment before reaching the end of the stack. The end of the Java stack is denoted by a special entry frame. When this entry frame is not reached, we set a flag that signals to the agent that the stack trace is incomplete.

Our heuristics considerably increase the percentage of stack snapshots that can be turned into stack traces. However, there are still situations in which the topmost Java frame cannot be determined conclusively. The analysis method then simply returns an error and the agent ignores the sample.

3. EVALUATION

We evaluated our approach using the DaCapo 9.12 benchmark suite [3], which consists of open source, real-world applications with pre-defined, non-trivial workloads[1]. To compensate for the warm-up phase of the VM, we chose to run ten successive iterations of each benchmark and to use only metrics collected in the last iteration. We used a stack fragment size of 16 KB and intervals of 10ms, 1ms and 0.1ms between samples. These translate to sampling rates of at most 100, 1000 and 10000 samples per thread per second, which we refer to below. We executed 50 runs of each benchmark at each of these three sampling rates.

3.1 Success Rate

First, we measured how many collected samples could be successfully decoded to a stack trace. Table 1 shows the percentages for each benchmark at 10000 samples per second in the row labeled *Res*. On average over all benchmarks, 90.7% of all stack snapshots could be successfully processed. The *avrora* benchmark shows the lowest rate at 84.3%, while nearly all samples could be used in the *sunflow* benchmark at 96.8%. In almost all cases where the stack walk fails, the problem was in identifying the top Java frame or its caller frame. Hence, additional or better heuristics could improve this rate further and are part of our ongoing research.

3.2 Completeness of Traces

We measured how often the Java stack was larger than the fragment size, leading to incomplete stack traces. The *Inc.* row in Table 1 shows the resulting percentages by benchmark at 10000 samples per second. For ten out of the twelve benchmarks, less than 0.06% of stack traces were incomplete.

[1]We did not use the DaCapo suite's *batik* and *eclipse* benchmarks because they do not run on OpenJDK 8.

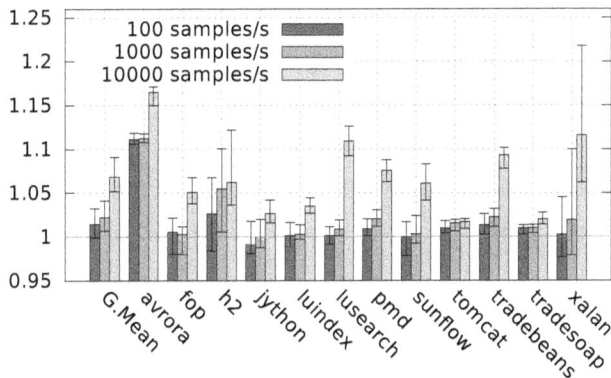

Figure 1: Sampling and analysis overhead for the DaCapo benchmarks

This shows that stack fragments with a size of 16 KB are typically sufficient to produce full stack traces.

With 4.09% incomplete stack traces, the *tomcat* benchmark seems to be an exception to this rule. However, increasing the fragment size had no substantial effect. We noticed that most of the incomplete stack traces are related to class loading and exception handling, and will examine these cases more closely to increase the completeness of our traces.

3.3 Performance Impact

Figure 1 shows the median execution time for each benchmark at the sampling rates of 100, 1000 and 10000 samples per second, normalized to the benchmark's median execution time without sampling. The error bars indicate the first and third quartiles. The *G.Mean* bars on the left show the geometric means over all benchmarks, which are 1.45%, 2.21% and 6.83% overhead at 100, 1000 and 10000 samples per second, respectively. Only the *avrora* benchmark shows consistently above 10% overhead.

For comparison, we implemented an additional agent that collects samples using JVMTI and builds a CCT from them as well. With OpenJDK 8, we determined a geometric mean overhead over all benchmarks of 5.4% at 100 samples per second, 45.2% at 1000 samples per second and 73.0% overhead at 10000 samples per second. Hence, our approach is clearly superior to JVMTI sampling, particularly at high sampling rates.

3.4 Accuracy

For assessing the accuracy of our approach, we compared the CCTs produced by our agent to those from the JVMTI agent. Our tests confirm that JVMTI frequently misrepresents how an application spends its time. An extreme example is SciMark 2.0 [9], a scientific computing benchmark that spends roughly equal times in five different computational kernels. The CCT with data from JVMTI, however, suggests that the program spends over 40% of its time in `kernel.measureLU()`, which represents just one of the five kernels, and in fact calls another method `LU.factor()` that performs the actual work. This suggests that the safepoints are placed unfavorably in SciMark so that the distribution of samples is distorted. The CCT produced with our approach distributes the execution time more evenly and attributes it to the computationally intensive methods.

	Mean	avrora	fop	h2	jython	luindex	lusearch	pmd	sunflow	tomcat	tradebeans	tradesoap	xalan
Res.	**90.7%**	84.3%	91.6%	88.7%	91.9%	96.0%	95.7%	85.8%	96.8%	87.8%	87.7%	88.3%	93.6%
Inc.	**0.41%**	0.00%	0.48%	0.01%	0.05%	0.04%	0.01%	0.06%	0.00%	4.09%	0.01%	0.03%	0.11%

Table 1: Fraction of resolved and incomplete stack traces by benchmark

3.5 Achievable Sampling Rates

Our approach allows for high sampling rates because of its low impact on performance and because taking samples is triggered by a hardware timer and is not delayed by any software mechanism. We were able to achieve sampling rates of more than 30000 samples per second. In comparison, the quickly increasing overhead of JVMTI sampling sets a much lower practical limit. Using POSIX signals with `AsyncGetCallTrace` has a practical limit as well, because rapidly successive signals are either coalesced into one signal or are all handled at once without the application running in between, producing samples of an identical state.

3.6 Redundancy of Samples

With both JVMTI sampling and `AsyncGetCallTrace`, it is not possible to determine whether a thread has been active before taking a sample. As a result, samples are often taken of unchanged states, such as when a thread is waiting. With our approach, the operating system only takes samples while a monitored thread is executing, or when a context switch occurs, which allows us to capture a thread's calling context before it enters a waiting state. This reduces the amount of collected data that needs to be processed.

4. RELATED WORK

Problems with Java stack sampling have been analyzed before. Mytkowicz et al. [6] demonstrate that four commonly used Java profilers often produce incorrect profiles due to safepoints and optimizations. They propose a profiler that pauses threads at arbitrary locations, but they choose to implement it entirely outside the VM, which restricts its use in the presence of optimizations. Binder [2] confirms the high overhead of sampling with JVMTI and presents a pure Java profiler that rewrites bytecode to maintain a shadow stack and periodically capture samples, which he claims is more accurate than JVMTI at comparable overhead.

To our knowledge, copying stack fragments for fast Java profiling has not been attempted before. Whaley [12] describes an in-VM Java profiler that samples threads at arbitrary points and avoids full stack walks by marking visited stack frames, claiming a low overhead of 2-4% at 1000 samples per second. However, the used VM performs thread scheduling itself ("green threads"), which permits certain assumptions and direct access to thread states. Green threads are uncommon in modern Java VMs because of their disadvantages in multi-processor systems. Inoue and Nakatani [4] describe a Java profiler that uses hardware events to take samples of only the executing method and the stack depth. It builds a CCT based on matching stack depths and caller information, and is reported to achieve an overhead of 2.2% at 16000 samples per second. Serrano et al. [10] present a Java profiler that uses hardware branch tracing to create partial call traces and attempt to merge them optimally into approximate CCTs, claiming to produce highly accurate CCTs at negligible overhead. Unlike our approach, both of these techniques require specific hardware and their accuracy can suffer from ambiguous callers.

5. CONCLUSIONS AND FUTURE WORK

We described an approach for Java stack trace sampling that relies on the operating system to capture stack fragments which are then asynchronously retrieved and analyzed. We further described a set of heuristics for identifying the topmost Java frame in these fragments for building stack traces from them. Our preliminary results show that these heuristics work for over 90% of the collected fragments, and that a fragment size of 16 KB is sufficient to obtain complete stack traces from more than 99.5% of samples. We further showed that the accuracy of our approach is high while its performance impact is very low even at high sampling rates, particularly when compared to JVMTI sampling.

As next steps, we plan to experiment with smaller fragments and to determine how well incomplete stack traces can be correctly matched to a CCT. We also consider using hardware performance counters instead of taking samples at fixed time intervals, which could further reduce overhead.

6. ACKNOWLEDGEMENTS

This work was supported by the Christian Doppler Forschungsgesellschaft, and by Compuware Austria GmbH.

7. REFERENCES

[1] G. Ammons, T. Ball, and J. R. Larus. Exploiting hardware performance counters with flow and context sensitive profiling. PLDI '97, pages 85–96, 1997.

[2] W. Binder. Portable and accurate sampling profiling for Java. *Software: Practice and Experience*, 36(6):615–650, 2006.

[3] S. M. Blackburn et al. The DaCapo benchmarks: Java benchmarking development and analysis. OOPSLA '06, pages 169–190, Oct. 2006.

[4] H. Inoue and T. Nakatani. How a Java VM can get more from a hardware performance monitor. OOPSLA '09, pages 137–154, 2009.

[5] kernel.org. perf: Linux profiling with performance counters. https://perf.wiki.kernel.org/.

[6] T. Mytkowicz, A. Diwan, M. Hauswirth, and P. F. Sweeney. Evaluating the accuracy of Java profilers. PLDI '10, pages 187–197, 2010.

[7] Oracle. JVM™Tool Interface version 1.2.1. http://docs.oracle.com/javase/7/docs/platform/jvmti/jvmti.html.

[8] Oracle. OpenJDK HotSpot group. http://openjdk.java.net/groups/hotspot/.

[9] R. Pozo and B. Miller. SciMark 2.0. http://math.nist.gov/scimark2/.

[10] M. Serrano and X. Zhuang. Building approximate calling context from partial call traces. CGO '09, pages 221–230, 2009.

[11] V. Weaver. The unofficial Linux perf events web-page. http://web.eece.maine.edu/~vweaver/projects/perf_events/.

[12] J. Whaley. A portable sampling-based profiler for Java virtual machines. Java Grande '00, pages 78–87, 2000.

PowerPerfCenter: A Power and Performance Prediction Tool For Multi-Tier Applications*

Varsha Apte, Bhavin Doshi†
Department of Computer Science and Engineering, IIT Bombay, Mumbai 76, India
{varsha,bhavin}@cse.iitb.ac.in

ABSTRACT

The performance analysis of a server application and the sizing of the hardware required to host it in a data center continue to be pressing issues today. With most server-grade computers now built with "frequency-scaled CPUs" and other such devices, it has become important to answer performance and sizing questions in the presence of such hardware. *PowerPerfCenter* is an application performance modeling tool that allows specification of devices whose operating speeds can change dynamically. It also estimates *power usage* by the machines in presence of such devices. Furthermore, it allows specification of a *dynamic workload* which is required to understand the impact of power management. We validated the performance metrics predicted by PowerPerfCenter against measured ones of an application deployed on a test-bed consisting of frequency-scaled CPUs, and found the match to be good. We also used PowerPerfCenter to show that power savings may not be significant if a device does not have different *idle* power consumption when configured with different operating speeds.

Categories and Subject Descriptors

C.4 [**Performance of Systems**]: Modeling Techniques

Keywords

Power, Performance Prediction, Frequency Scaled CPU

1. INTRODUCTION

Performance analysis continues to be a critical step in the life cycle of a server application. Typically, performance analysis starts when the functionality of the application is ready and it is deployed in a testbed. At this stage, comprehensive performance tests are undertaken, in which metrics

---

*Work-In-Progress Paper

†This research is partially supported by a grant from Tata Consultancy Services, Mumbai, India

ICPE'14, March 22–26, 2014, Dublin, Ireland.
Copyright 2014 ACM 978-1-4503-2733-6/14/03 ...$15.00.
http://dx.doi.org/10.1145/2568088.2576758.

such as throughput and response time of requests are plotted against load intensity (which is often in terms of "number of simultaneous users" of the application). However, since the production environment and workload of the application is most often different from the test environment, we need performance *models* which can help *estimate* application performance metrics, using mathematical or simulation methods.

The complexity of modern multi-tier networked server applications is such that performance modeling cannot be done manually. Hence several *modeling tools* have been developed, which accept a high-level description of an application and its hardware environment, and produce estimates of the application's performance metrics.

PerfCenter [1] is one such tool, which takes as input the description of the hardware, software and network architecture of a server application and its deployment, and produces estimates based on queuing analysis or discrete event simulation. PerfCenter offers an intuitive specification framework from the point of view of a "data center" operator who needs to host this application in an efficient manner. PerfCenter capabilities, along with examples of how it can be used for modeling the performance of an application, were described in detail in a previous paper [5]. In that paper, the authors show how PerfCenter is used for making configuration decisions such as the number of CPUs in a host, the number of hosts allocated to a server, or to determine the optimal number of threads that a server should be configured with.

In the recent years, *energy* has emerged as a valuable resource that is consumed by a data center. Studies have shown that power costs dominate data center operating costs [4]; hence several power optimization technologies have emerged and are being used in data center hardware. The impact of these technologies can be understood, and design choices analyzed, only if we have modeling tools that can predict energy usage by applications deployed in such a data center.

Energy optimization in server computing has been mainly done by using devices whose power usage can be regulated by manipulating their speeds. "Frequency-scaled CPUs" [6] are an example of a device whose operating frequency (and thus power drawn) can be changed dynamically. Frequency scaled CPUs have become standard in server-grade computers; thus performance modeling tools need to be capable of predicting performance in the presence of such CPUs and other power-managed devices.

In this paper, we present *PowerPerfCenter* - an enhanced and extended version of PerfCenter which allows for specification of *power managed devices* in host machines. It also

```
host h1[1]              server web              device    lan
corei5 count 1          thread count 150        corei5    lan1
corei5 buffer 99999     thread buffer 0         core2duo  end
corei5 schedP fcfs      thread schedP fcfs      disk
corei5 power_managed    task send_to_db         end
  governor conservative task to_html_login
disk count 1            ...                     deploy h1[1] lan1
disk ...                end                     deploy h2[1] lan1
end                                             deploy web h1[1]
                        server db               deploy db h2[1]
host h2[1]              thread count 150
  ...                   thread buffer 0          modelparams
end                     thread schedP fcfs        method
task send_to_db         task get_creds          simulation
  corei5 servt 0.05     ...                        type closed
end                     end                        confint true
task to_html_login                                 simendtime 6000
  corei5 servt 0.236    loadparams                 replicationno 5
end                       thinktime exp(6)       end
task get_creds          end
  core2duo servt 0.003   scenario Login prob 0.18846
end                        send_to_db get_creds 200 SYNC
                           get_creds to_html_login 100
                         end
```

Figure 1: PerfCenter Input File Snippets

allows specification of a *dynamic workload*, which highlights the impact of power management. It estimates performance metrics in such a scenario, and additionally estimates various *power consumption metrics* that can help analyze the "power-performance trade-off". To our knowledge, *PowerPerfCenter* is the only "software performance modeling" tool that is capable of modeling power-managed devices.

The rest of the paper is as follows: in Section 2 we recap the basic PerfCenter model, and present the details of the power-related enhancements in PowerPerfCenter. In Section 3 we present validation results and an analysis of the power-performance trade-off for the "WebCalendar" application. We conclude the paper in Section 4.

2. POWERPERFCENTER

The PerfCenter system model captures the essential components of a multi-tier application deployed in a data center that are required to analyze its performance. It consists of a set of machines, or Hosts, which are an aggregation of Devices (such as CPU, disk, RAM etc); a set of Servers (e.g. Web server, database server) which are described by attributes such as number of threads, and the set of Tasks that they perform. These servers together constitute a multi-tier application that can be used to fulfill various user requests, which we call Scenarios. A scenario is described by a probabilistic call graph of Tasks that are carried out by various servers to fulfill a request. The calls can be described as "synchronous" or "asynchronous", and are specified with the size of data that is exchanged when the call is made. Tasks are specified with service time requirements on various devices. Servers are "deployed" on Hosts and Hosts can be deployed on a LAN. Finally, two LANs can be connected via a point-to-point WAN Link, which is described by its bandwidth and propagation delay.

The workload model is as follows: scenarios are specified with arrival probabilities, and the load is specified with either an open arrival rate, or a number of users and think time, which implies a closed system. Figure 1 shows snippets of a very basic PerfCenter input file.

With this specification, PerfCenter generates the underlying queuing network model and solves it using discrete event simulation. PerfCenter can report various performance metrics such as response time, throughput, utilization etc. at the device, scenario, server and system level. We refer the reader to the earlier paper on PerfCenter[5] for further details on the existing capabilities of PerfCenter.

2.1 Power Managed Devices in PerfCenter

Many devices in a computer today are able to dynamically reduce power usage, when peak power is not required. This is especially applicable to two of the most commonly used devices, namely, CPU and disk. In case of modern CPUs, power saving is achieved by clocking the CPU at a lower rate (through Dynamic Voltage and Frequency Scaling (DVFS) [6]), resulting in effectively *slowing* it down. Hard Disk Drives save power by slowing the spin rate, i.e. spinning down its platters [4]. The power consumed is a function of the operating speeds of these devices.

There are several models that relate the CPU operating frequency, to the power consumed by a machine. A widely accepted model is where power is assumed to have a *static* and a *dynamic* component [6]. The static power component represents the power that is consumed by the powered-on but idle device. The dynamic component is a function of the instantaneous utilization of the device. Also, both static, i.e. idle, and dynamic power depend on the instantaneous operating speed of the device. PowerPerfCenter's power model assumes that when the operating speed of a device is s, and its utilization is ρ, the power consumed is given by $\gamma_i(s) + \rho \times \gamma_d(s)$, where $\gamma_i(s)$ is the idle power, and $\gamma_d(s)$ is the maximum additional power consumed by the device while operating at speed s and at full utilization ($\rho = 1$).

Every device in PowerPerfCenter can optionally be declared as a power-managed device. For a power-managed device, PowerPerfCenter expects the specification of operating speeds (s), idle power consumptions $\gamma_i(s)$, and the maximum dynamic power consumptions $\gamma_d(s)$.

Power-managed devices are controlled by a "governor" which decides when it should change the operating speed and by how much. Currently, PowerPerfCenter's power-managed device abstraction is modeled after frequency-scaled CPUs, and hence it offers four basic governors that are found in a typical Linux implementation [2]: powersave, performance, ondemand and conservative. Of these powersave represents a static governor which fixes the operating speed to the lowest. performance fixes the operating speed to the highest. ondemand and conservative change the frequencies dynamically. Each of these governors probes the CPU after a fixed duration of time, called probeinterval. At each probe, the utilization of CPU in the previous interval is seen. If it is above (below) a threshold, called up (down) threshold, then the governor decides to increase (decrease) the frequency. The ondemand governor increases the frequency to the highest, and decreases to the next lower step, when thresholds are crossed. The conservative governor changes frequency in steps when thresholds are crossed.

Power-managed devices in PowerPerfCenter are specified as follows:

```
powermanagement corei5
speed_levels 1.2 2.26 2.39 2.53 2.66 2.79 2.93
        3.06 3.19 3.19 end
power_consumed 90 122 127  135  140  150  159
```

```
        168    176    176  end
idlepower 56 56 56 56 56 56 56 56 56 56 end
probe_interval 0.080
governor_up_threshold 80
governor_down_threshold 20 end
```

Note that since there are multiple operating speeds of the device, the specified service demands of the `tasks` that require such a device are now assumed to be corresponding to the lowest speed of the device.

2.2 Energy Metrics in PerfCenter

A performance analysis of an application running on power-managed devices would be incomplete without estimation of the power consumed by these devices. Thus, PowerPerfCenter offers the following additional metrics to be evaluated when power-managed devices are used: the *average power* consumed by each instance of a power-managed device, the *energy consumed per request*, and the *power efficiency*, which is defined as requests served per unit of energy. Using these metrics, and the existing performance metrics, the power-performance trade off can be effectively analyzed for different scenarios.

2.3 Dynamic Workload in PowerPerfCenter

Devices that can dynamically change their operating speeds and thus power consumed, are useful primarily in a scenario where the *workload* itself is dynamic. Thus, this modeling capability is useful only if we can specify a time-varying workload pattern.

PowerPerfCenter allows the specification of a dynamic workload profile, which is then implicitly *repeated* if the simulation time is longer than the duration of the workload profile. The workload is defined as a set of tuples - each tuple corresponds to a load level and the duration of this load level. The exact specification is as follows:

```
workload cyclic
noofusers 25   35   45   35   30   15   20   end
interval  300  300  300  300  300  300  300  end end
```

When dynamic workload is specified, the performance metrics are produced separately for each load level.

3. RESULTS AND VALIDATION

For illustrating the use of PowerPerfCenter and validating its prediction, we used the "Webcalendar" application deployed on a testbed. Webcalendar is a standard two-tiered calendaring application, provided using a Web server and a database server. It supports various use cases such as Login, ViewDay, ViewWeek, ViewMonth, ViewEvent, etc. The Web server was hosted on a machine with the Intel Core i5 650 processor, 4 GB RAM and 1 TB HDD. The database server was hosted on a machine with the Intel Core2 Duo E4500 2.2 GHz processor, 2 GB RAM and 160 GB HDD. We used the Web server machine to experiment with performance in presence of CPU frequency scaling. The Intel Core i5 in this machine supports frequency settings in the range of 1.2 GHz to 3.19 GHz. The idle power consumption (γ_i) of this CPU as reported in [8] is the same (56W) at all frequencies. The dynamic component (γ_d) of the overall power does depend on the operating frequency and is given in the results in [8].

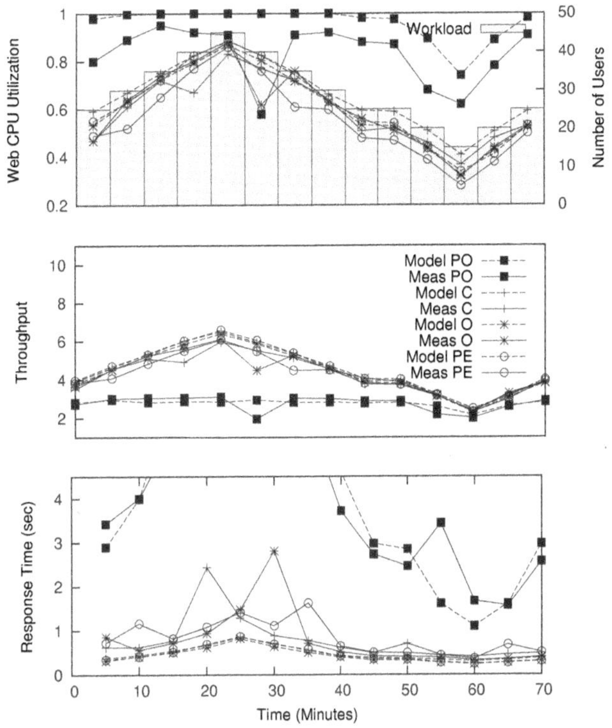

Figure 2: Measured (solid lines) vs model (dotted lines) metrics for the Webcalendar application for the four governors. Abbreviations: PO: Powersave, C: Conservative, O: Ondemand, PE: Performance. The legend shown is common to all graphs.

This testbed was populated with a dataset of 5000 distinct users with their own calendars. Each user's calendar was populated with 100 random events over the year 2013.

We carried out load tests on this deployment and generated graphs of average scenario response times, throughputs and server CPU utilizations as a function of the number of users. We used a load generator (*AutoPerf* [7]) which is capable of generating requests probabilistically, and also reports server statistics at each load level. The load generator machine had the Intel Xeon E5405 2 GHz processor, 8 GB RAM and 1 TB HDD. All the machines were connected via a single 100 Mbps switch.

This application and its deployment was then specified in PowerPerfCenter. Most of the architectural details are readily available. For obtaining the service times of the tasks, we used *AutoPerf*'s server profiling capability. This gives the service demand of each type of request on the Web server and database server CPUs and other resource usage data such as disk and network bytes read and written per request by each host. This completes the system specification.

We tested and modeled this application for a dynamic workload of varying number of users, each with an exponentially distributed think time of 6 seconds, and a pre-specified scenario generation probability. Measured vs model predicted values of the *performance* metrics were compared for various settings of power governors at the Web server. Figure 2 shows the comparison results.

The results show that the performance, ondemand and conservative governors are able to support the load, while the powersave governor runs out of capacity at just 15 users. Furthermore the performance metrics of the ondemand and conservative governors are almost indistinguishable from those of the performance governor. This might be because as the load increases, the dynamic governors speed up the CPU quickly to reach the level of the performance governor. After the CPU is at its highest frequency, it can be seen from Figure 2 that load does not become low enough for the CPU utilization to cross the low threshold of 0.2, so the dynamic governors do not reduce the CPU frequency, and continue to operate at the level of the performance governor.

PowerPerfCenter is able to predict the throughput and utilization metrics quite accurately. For these metrics, more than 80% of the values had relative error of less than 20%. In case of response time, the match is good for the powersave governor (higher values are not shown in the graph). In case of the other governors, the measured values of the response times were highly variable. Nonetheless, the overall trend is predicted well by PowerPerfCenter.

3.1 Power Performance Trade-Off

The conservative, ondemand and performance governors have fairly comparable performance. Figure 3(a) shows the average response time and the average power consumed with the Core i5 in the Web server host for the four governors. Note that in this graph, the values are as predicted by PowerPerfCenter - we do not have measurement results for power consumption. Workload-1 (w1) is as shown earlier in Figure 2. To study the effect of a more "skewed" workload with a short-lived peak and long-lived low load period, we also analyzed the power-performance trade-off for another workload (Workload-2 (w2): 75 users for 60 seconds, and 3 users for 600 seconds) on the same setup.

In case of both these workloads, we see (from Figure 3(a)) that the powersave governor achieves power savings at the cost of a high response time. But the performance governor consumes only slightly more energy than the ondemand and conservative governors. This happens because for Core i5, the idle power consumption is the same at all operating speeds [8]. The performance governor, because of its high frequency setting, results in low average CPU utilization (especially for Workload-2) and thus the CPU is idle most of the time. Consequently, the difference between average power consumption by the performance governor and the ondemand or conservative governors is not significant.

To understand this further, we carried out a "what-if" analysis by specifying a different CPU in the Web server host model, whose power consumption figures were based on experiments reported in [3] on the Intel Core i7 processor. This processor has markedly different idle power consumption at different operating frequencies. Figure 3(b) shows the response time and power consumption values as predicted by PowerPerfCenter in this case. We can now see the advantage of using the dynamic governors - the ondemand and conservative governors use 17% less power and 40% less power than the performance governor in case of Workload-1 and Workload-2 respectively, with a negligible increase in response time.

4. CONCLUSIONS AND FUTURE WORK

Energy usage by data centers has become a matter of concern in today's world, and has thus resulted in usage of devices that intelligently optimize power by tuning their operating speeds. In this paper, we presented a tool *PowerPerfCenter* which can predict application performance metrics

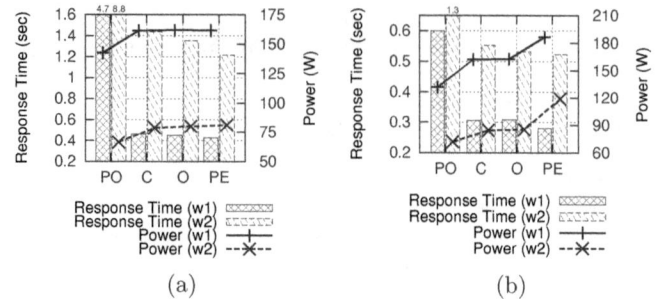

Figure 3: Power-Performance Trade-off for (a) Core i5 and (b) Core i7

in presence of such devices, and which can further estimate power consumption of such devices, for *dynamic* workloads. Comparison of performance metrics predicted by this tool against those obtained from measurements showed a good match. The estimated power usage metrics showed how savings in power usage are significant when the *idle power consumption* of a device is lower at a lower speed. If idle power consumption is the same for all speeds, there may not be much gain in running dynamic speed governors on a device. PowerPerfCenter can provide such critical insights into the power-performance trade-off.

5. REFERENCES

[1] PerfCenter: A Datacenter Application Performance Modeling Tool.
http://www.cse.iitb.ac.in/panda/perfcenter.

[2] Power governors, documentation of linux kernel 2.6.32.
http://www.mjmwired.net/kernel/Documentation/cpu-freq/governors.txt.

[3] Power governors, documentation of linux kernel 2.6.32.
http://www.xbitlabs.com/articles/cpu/display/power-consumption-overclocking_13.html#sect0.

[4] L. A. Barroso and U. Holzle. The case for energy-proportional computing. *IEEE Computer*, 40, 2007.

[5] A. Deshpande, V. Apte, and S. Marathe. Perfcenter: a performance modeling tool for application hosting centers. In *Proceedings of WOSP 2008*, pages 79–90, New York, NY, USA, 2008.

[6] A. Miyoshi, C. Lefurgy, E. Van Hensbergen, R. Rajamony, and R. Rajkumar. Critical power slope: understanding the runtime effects of frequency scaling. In *Proceedings of the 16th ACM International Conference on Supercomputing*, pages 35–44, 2002.

[7] S. S. Shirodkar and V. Apte. Autoperf: An automated load generator and performance measurement tool for multi-tier software systems. In *Proc. of the ACM WWW 2007*, pages 1291–1292, New York, NY, USA, 2007.

[8] S. P. Srinivasan and U. Bellur. A novel power model and completion time model for virtualized environments. Technical Report TR-CSE-2014-58, Department of CSE, IIT Bombay, Mumbai, India, January 2014.

Acknowledgements

The authors wish to thank Yogesh Bagul and Rakesh Mallick for their contribution to PowerPerfCenter development.

Modelling Database Lock-Contention in Architecture-level Performance Simulation

Philipp Merkle
Chair for Software Design and Quality
Karlsruhe Institute of Technology (KIT)
76131 Karlsruhe, Germany
merkle@kit.edu

Christian Stier
Chair for Software Design and Quality
Karlsruhe Institute of Technology (KIT)
76131 Karlsruhe, Germany
christian.stier2@student.kit.edu

ABSTRACT

Databases are the origin of many performance problems found in transactional information systems. Performance suffers especially when databases employ locking to isolate concurrent transactions. Software performance models therefore need to reflect lock contention in order to be a credible source for guiding design decisions. We propose a hybrid simulation approach that integrates a novel locking model into the Palladio software architecture performance simulator. Our model operates on a row level and is tailored to be used with architecture-level performance models. An experimental evaluation leads to promising results close to the measured performance.

Categories and Subject Descriptors

C.4 [**Performance of Systems**]: Modelling techniques

Keywords

Database; Lock Contention; Performance Prediction; Simulation; Palladio Component Model

1. INTRODUCTION

Relational database management systems (DBMS) are an integral part of many business information systems. They encapsulate established practices from decades of research, thereby hiding functional complexity from developers. Their complex performance behaviour, however, can neither be hidden from clients, nor be easily understood by developers. This dilemma gave rise to model-based approaches that seek to explain different aspects of database performance (cf. [10]). Database performance models can help software engineers to proactively evaluate the performance impact of design alternatives before they are translated into database schemas, queries, or source code in general. Ideally, the underlying methodology encapsulates knowledge of DBMS performance behaviour, thus relieving software developers

from understanding performance-influencing subtleties of a database, its configuration or its workload.

In contrast to database performance models, architecture-centric performance models (e.g. [1]) provide decision support on a higher level of granularity, such as component composition and deployment. If database performance, however, dominates the overall system performance, architecture models must also capture database-related performance factors to achieve a sufficient accuracy. This is especially true for software systems that employ locking-based databases. Locking ensures proper isolation of concurrent transactions, so that inconsistencies due to conflicting data accesses (e.g. reading and writing at the same time) are prevented. Contention for locks on database items can severely impact system performance. This is why we address lock contention as a first step toward a performance modelling method for database-intensive software systems as motivated in our earlier work [5].

The contribution of this work-in-progress paper is an approach to modelling and simulation of database lock contention within architecture-level software performance simulation. First, we suggest a hybrid simulation model of row-level two-phase locking (2PL) tailored to architecture-level simulation. Second, we integrate our locking model into the Palladio software architecture simulator [1]. Third, we present an experimental evaluation that compares simulation results to measurements from a MySQL database.

2. SIMULATING LOCK CONTENTION

The transaction manager (TM) is responsible for lock management in a DBMS. It decides for arriving transactions if requested locks may be granted or must be denied to preserve the demanded isolation level. In the following, we propose a performance model of a TM. It utilises a model we establish for determining conflicts between transactions. This model is referred to as *conflict model* throughout this paper and will be introduced stepwise. Initially, we ignore shared locking to establish the fundamentals of the conflict model. On this basis, Sec. 2.3 outlines our extensions to shared locking.

2.1 Model Assumptions

In our model, a table is characterised solely by the number of contained rows. Rows neither have an identity nor any other distinguishing feature—all appear the same. Transactions are sequences of data access operations and end either with a commit or an abort. An access operation refers to a single table and is characterised by the number of accessed

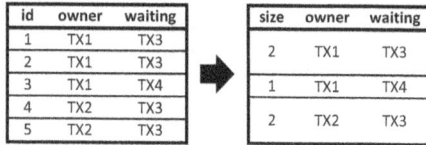

id	owner	waiting
1	TX1	TX3
2	TX1	TX3
3	TX1	TX4
4	TX2	TX3
5	TX2	TX3

size	owner	waiting
2	TX1	TX3
1	TX1	TX4
2	TX2	TX3

Figure 1: Row-level lock information (left) translated to conflict objects without row identities (right)

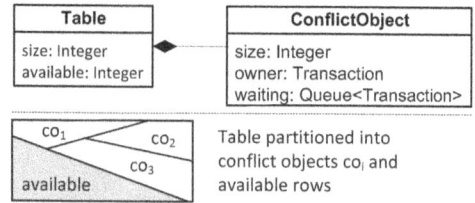

Figure 2: Bookkeeping of lock ownership and conflicts

tuples and by the access type (read or write). A transaction submitting an access operation claims all rows at once. In case a lock request has to be denied due to conflicts, the transaction must wait for the lock to become available. Locks acquired by a transaction are only released once the transaction has been committed or aborted. This resembles rigorous 2PL. Table accesses are uniformly distributed, meaning every row is equally likely to be locked. Note that access hot-spots can still be modelled as is discussed in [12]. Finally, tables do not change in size over the course of an analysis.

2.2 Conflict Model (Exclusive Locks)

Our conflict model is inspired by the work of Morris and Wong [7], namely by their use of hypergeometric distributions to determine the probability of lock conflicts under 2PL. In general, a hypergeometric distribution yields the probability to select i balls of one type from an urn containing two types of balls. For simplicity, balls of one type are often referred to as *successes*, and one is then interested in the probability for selecting i successes out of the population. The hypergeometric distribution as applied in [7] takes as parameters the table size, the number of rows already locked, and the number of requested rows. These parameters provide a good level of abstraction for architectural modelling of database conflicts where knowledge of query-specific data distributions and access patterns should not be taken for granted.

Morris and Wong abstract from individual tables and assume that a database consists of a single table. Every transaction accesses the same number of tuples. The number of accessed tuples needs to be known at the time a transaction starts. Shared and exclusive accesses aren't distinguished. More importantly, however, the model of Morris and Wong does not take into account lock dependencies between conflicting transactions. This means once a transaction ends, every waiting transaction is equally likely to be continued, regardless of its arrival time or its actual conflicts.

Especially the last assumption hampers the applicability of their conflict model in software performance simulators such as Palladio. At simulation runtime, system requests have an identity that they inherit to their transactions. Throughout simulation, each individual request is tracked in order to collect corresponding performance measures. This can reveal, for example, a system design where two components mutually degrade their performance by frequently locking the same data items. By contrast, if conflict dependencies are neglected, requests may regularly continue their operation before their lock requests have actually been granted. We therefore extend Morris and Wong's stochastic conflict model by bookkeeping of conflicts.

The conflict bookkeeping keeps track of lock ownership and blocked transactions. This is similar to lock tables known from ordinary TMs. A lock table maps database elements (e.g. rows) to lock information about this element, including the current lock owner and waiting transactions organised as a queue [4]. While lock tables usually maintain an entry for each locked row, this fine-grained bookkeeping of locks does not fit well in our case, where rows do not have identities. We therefore abstract from individual rows using *conflict objects*. A conflict object subsumes a set of locked rows that share the same owner and the same waiting transactions (cf. Fig. 1). It is characterised by the number of rows it represents, by its owning transaction, and by the queue of transactions waiting for the conflict object—or more precisely, the represented rows—to be released. Note that conflict objects never overlap; they partition the locked rows of a table into disjoint subsets (cf. Fig. 2). Despite its name, a conflict object must not be involved in a lock conflict; the waiting queue remains empty until a conflict occurs.

Once a transaction requests access to one or more rows, the TM must determine conflicts with other active transactions. Only if the conflict size is zero, the transaction may proceed. Otherwise, it is blocked. The procedure we use for this is shown in Alg. 1. Depending on the access size, the table size, and the number of locked rows, we draw a series of samples from hypergeometric distributions. Each draw determines the overlap either with an existing conflict object or with the set of available (unlocked) rows. Step 1 calculates the overlap between requested and available rows. Access to these rows can be granted immediately. All remaining requested rows must be involved in a lock conflict. Step 2 provides the cause of each lock conflict by calculating the overlap of denied lock requests with existing conflict objects. If the overlap is larger than zero (i.e. there is a conflict), the requesting transaction needs to be enqueued as a waiting transaction—but only for a subset of the conflict object if the overlap does not involve the entire conflict object. In such a case, we *split* the conflict object into two conflict objects with the same owner and waiting transactions. Their size sums up to the size of the original conflict object. The requesting transaction can then be enqueued with the newly created conflict object representing the discovered conflict. Step 2 is repeated until all denied lock requests have been attributed to an existing conflict object. If the algorithm was able to grant all lock requests, the transaction may proceed. Otherwise, it is blocked and must wait.

Once a transaction commits or aborts, all held locks are released. If no transaction waits for the released conflict object, it is destroyed and the number of available rows is increased accordingly. Otherwise, the simulator selects the new owner from the queue of waiting transactions.

2.3 Conflict Model (Shared Locks)

So far we assumed exclusive access to data items. To support shared locks, we distinguish between shared and exclusive conflict objects. Shared conflict objects may have multiple owners. For each transaction, we record its demanded access type (shared vs. exclusive) in relation to a

Algorithm 1: access operation of transaction tx on a table t with k rows to be accessed

Input : t : *Table*, tx : *Transaction*, k : *Integer*
Output: blocked : *Boolean*

```
    // Step 1:  Determine overlap with available rows
1   grantedLocks : Integer ← draw sample from
      hypergeometric distribution with population ← t.size,
      successes ← t.available, sample ← k
2   tx.ownedLocks.add(new ConflictObject of size
      grantedLocks))
3   t.available ← t.available − grantedLocks

    // Step 2:  Determine overlap with conflict objects
4   remainingConflicts : Integer ← k − grantedLocks
5   conflictCandidates : Integer ← t.size − t.available
6   foreach co ∈ t.conflictObjects do
7   │   conflictSize ← draw sample from hypergeometric
    │     distribution with population ← conflictCandidates,
    │     successes ← co.size, sample ← remainingConflicts
8   │   if conflictSize = 0 then continue
9   │   if co.owner ≠ tx then
10  │   │   if conflictSize = co.size then
11  │   │   │   co.waiting.enqueue(tx)
12  │   │   else
13  │   │   │   split ← clone co
14  │   │   │   split.size ← conflictSize
15  │   │   │   co.size ← co.size − conflictSize
    │   │   │   split.waiting.enqueue(tx)
16  │   else
17  │   │   grantedLocks ← grantedLocks + conflictSize
18  │   conflictCandidates ← conflictCandidates − co.size
19  │   remainingConflicts ← remainingConflicts − conflictSize
20  return grantedLocks ≠ k
```

conflict object. This applies to transactions that own a conflict object, as well as to transactions waiting in the queue of a conflict object. A lock is only granted if the access type is compatible to the conflict object's type. This is referred to as lock compatibility (cf. [4]). A modified access algorithm that respects lock compatibility is discussed in detail in [11].

3. INTEGRATION INTO PALLADIO

In order to enable system-level QoS-analysis of transactional software systems, we integrate our work into the Palladio approach [1]. Palladio provides modelling and simulation capabilities for QoS-analysis of component-based software systems. Such a system can be modelled using the Palladio Component Model (PCM), a domain-specific language based on EMF[1]. A PCM instance includes the specification of components in terms of their performance-related behaviour, their assembly, and their deployment. Typical use cases of the modelled system are described in usage profiles. A PCM instance serves not only documentation purposes, but can especially be used for software quality simulation. Our integration encompasses metamodel extensions to the PCM, as well as extensions to EventSim [6], a discrete-event simulator for PCM instances.

Our metamodel can be seen in Fig. 3. All shown superclasses are imported from PCM. Component behaviour in the PCM is modelled by means of resource-demanding service-effect specifications (RDSEFFs). Similar to UML activity diagrams, an RDSEFF comprises linked actions. Unlike UML, however, the actions in an RDSEFF form a

chain. Control flow constructs, such as branches, are modelled with nested RDSEFFs (ResourceDemandingBehaviour), one for each branch transition in our example. Similarly, we model a transaction (TransactionAction) as a nested RDSEFF (TransactionActionBehaviour). It encapsulates operations to be performed in the transaction's scope. Besides regular actions, transactions may contain DataAccessActions, which represent READ or WRITE access to one or more entities (e.g. tables). The accessSize attribute refers to the number of accessed data items (e.g. rows). It is characterised as a PCMRandomVariable, which can be a constant, a variable, a random variable, or a combination thereof.

DataEntities (e.g. customers or invoices) are declared in the repository model. Their characterisation is outsourced to the entitymapping model. This separation is mainly motivated by the separation of developer roles in PCM. Component developers that maintain the repository should not be forced to characterise entities in terms of their table size (cardinality) or their row size (bytesPerInstance). Furthermore, speaking of entities leaves open the decision in favour of or against a relational data persistence technology.

Instances of the extended PCM can be fed into EventSim, which maps actions of the type TransactionAction and DataAccessAction to calls to the coupled TM simulator. The coupling ensures that requests in EventSim are blocked until acquired locks are actually granted, thereby reflecting the effects of concurrency control.

4. EXPERIMENTAL EVALUATION

We evaluated our approach by comparing simulation results to measurements from a database. We chose MySQL 5.6.14 in combination with the InnoDB storage engine. The isolation level has been set to *serializable* so that InnoDB uses 2PL. All experiments and measurements were conducted through OLTP-Bench [3]—a benchmark suite for OLTP database workloads. We used a modified subset of the *Resource Stresser* benchmark that models a lock contention scenario. It comprises a single table updated by multiple transactions in parallel. Each transaction first updates a set of m rows within a single query. Affected rows are drawn from a discrete uniform distribution without replacement. Then, the transaction sleeps for a second before it commits. Multiple instances of this transaction are executed in a closed workload of size k.

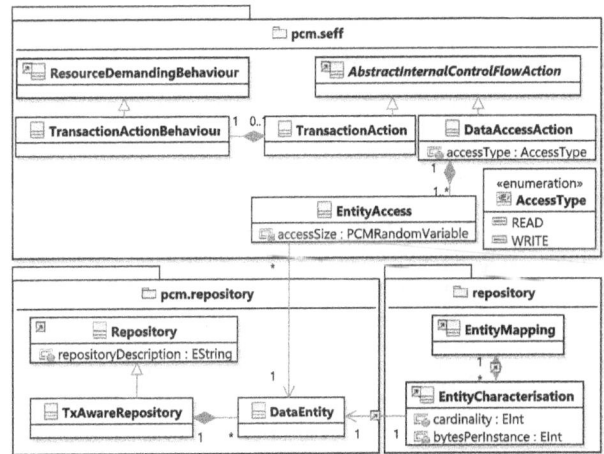

Figure 3: PCM metamodel extensions

---
[1]http://www.eclipse.org/modeling/emf/

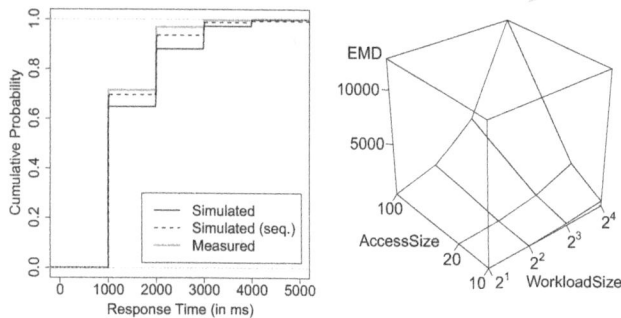

(a) ECDF for workload size $k = 8$, access size $m = 10$ (b) Earth mover's distance predicted vs. measured results

Figure 4: Measurements compared to simulation results

In our setting, the table holds 1024 entries. The workload size k takes the values (2, 4, 8, 16); the access size m takes the values (10, 20, 100). For each combination of k and m, we measured the response time of approximately 1000 transactions. In addition, each experiment has been modelled and simulated with our Palladio extension. The earth mover's distance (Fig. 4b) between simulation results and measurements indicates that simulation accuracy suffers from highly contended tables. Results for low to moderate contention, however, appear promising. Results for a moderate contention scenario ($k = 8$, $m = 10$) are therefore compared in Fig. 4a (ignore for the moment the sequential simulation). The observed differences lead us to further analyses of InnoDB's locking behaviour. From the INNODB_LOCKS information schema, it becomes apparent that locks for a query are not requested all at once. Rather, a transaction in InnoDB blocks upon the first conflict and does not request remaining locks before this conflict is resolved. This sequential locking policy leads to lower lock contention compared with our conflict model. To emulate sequential locking in PCM, we split the DataAccessAction representing the update of m rows into a sequence of m sequential DataAccessActions, each with $m = 1$. The results in Fig. 4a for the sequential simulation are now close to the measurements. Remaining differences can mostly be explained by the increased deadlock risk caused by the model adjustments. Being prone to deadlocks and due to its increased modelling and computational complexity, the sequential modelling is impractical. Still, the measurements suggest that our simulated conflict model is a valid performance model of 2PL.

5. RELATED WORK

A multitude of approaches has been developed to evaluate database performance. A recent survey by Osman and Knottenbelt [10] provides an extensive comparison of queuing network (QN) based approaches. While QNs are well-suited for modelling database-induced hardware contention, they lack expressiveness to capture lock-contention sufficiently. Coulden et al. [2] therefore propose to use queueing Petri nets (QPN) for modelling table-level 2PL. QPNs combine the strengths of Petri nets and QNs, thus allowing for representing both software and hardware contention. Based on [2], Osman et al. [9] present their efforts toward row-level 2PL. The QPNs in [2] and [9] reflect the database schema but abstract from the system architecture. Recently, Mozafari et al. [8] introduced DBSeer, a holistic approach to database performance evaluation based on statistical models. DBSeer

aims at supporting database administrators while our work targets software engineers from early development stages on.

6. CONCLUSION

This paper presented our work towards performance simulation of database-intensive software systems. We proposed a novel locking model that resembles the performance behaviour of 2PL sufficiently. Its integration with Palladio's software architecture simulation enables software engineers to evaluate transaction-related design decisions on a model basis. So far high contention scenarios cannot be sufficiently simulated: First, conflict objects might degenerate due to continuous split operations until their size reaches one, leading to a computationally expensive access algorithm. Second, simulation accuracy suffers from high contention. Reducing these limitations is subject to future work. Our next goal is to reflect different isolation levels in the simulation.

7. REFERENCES

[1] S. Becker, H. Koziolek, and R. Reussner. The Palladio component model for model-driven performance prediction. *The Journal of Systems and Software*, 82:3–22, 2009.

[2] D. Coulden, R. Osman, and W. J. Knottenbelt. Performance modelling of database contention using queueing Petri nets. In *Proceedings of the International Conference on Performance Engineering*, 2013.

[3] D. E. Difallah, A. Pavlo, C. Curino, and P. Cudre-Mauroux. OLTP-Bench: An extensible testbed for benchmarking relational databases. *Proceedings of the VLDB Endowment*, 7(4), 2013.

[4] H. Garcia-Molina, J. D. Ullman, and J. Widom. *Database system implementation*. Prentice Hall, 2000.

[5] P. Merkle. Predicting transaction quality for balanced data consistency and performance. In *Proceedings of the International Doctoral Symposium on Components and Architecture*, 2013.

[6] P. Merkle and J. Henss. EventSim – an event-driven Palladio software architecture simulator. Karlsruhe Reports in Informatics 32, KIT, 2011.

[7] R. Morris and W. Wong. Performance analysis of locking and optimistic concurrency control algorithms. *Performance Evaluation*, 5:105–118, 1985.

[8] B. Mozafari, C. Curino, A. Jindal, and S. Madden. Performance and resource modeling in highly-concurrent OLTP workloads. In *Proceedings of the SIGMOD International Conference on Management of Data*, 2013.

[9] R. Osman, D. Coulden, and W. J. Knottenbelt. Performance modelling of concurrency control schemes for relational databases. In *Analytical and Stochastic Modeling Techniques and Applications*. Springer, 2013.

[10] R. Osman and W. J. Knottenbelt. Database system performance evaluation models: A survey. *Performance Evaluation*, 69(10):471 – 493, 2012.

[11] C. Stier. Transaction-aware software performance prediction. Master's thesis, KIT, 2014.

[12] Y. C. Tay, R. Suri, and N. Goodman. A mean value performance model for locking in databases: The no-waiting case. *Journal of the ACM*, 32:618–651, 1985.

Benchmarking Graph-Processing Platforms: A Vision

Yong Guo
TU Delft
The Netherlands
Yong.Guo@tudelft.nl

Ana Lucia Varbanescu
University of Amsterdam
The Netherlands
A.L.Varbanescu@uva.nl

Alexandru Iosup
TU Delft
The Netherlands
A.Iosup@tudelft.nl

Claudio Martella
VU University Amsterdam
The Netherlands
claudio.martella@vu.nl

Theodore L. Willke
Systems Architecture Lab
Intel Corporation, USA
theodore.l.willke@intel.com

ABSTRACT

Processing graphs, especially at large scale, is an increasingly useful activity in a variety of business, engineering, and scientific domains. Already, there are tens of graph-processing platforms, such as Hadoop, Giraph, GraphLab, etc., each with a different design and functionality. For graph-processing to continue to evolve, users have to find it easy to select a graph-processing platform, and developers and system integrators have to find it easy to quantify the performance and other non-functional aspects of interest. However, the state of performance analysis of graph-processing platforms is still immature: there are few studies and, for the few that exist, there are few similarities, and relatively little understanding of the impact of dataset and algorithm diversity on performance. Our vision is to develop, with the help of the performance-savvy community, a comprehensive benchmarking suite for graph-processing platforms. In this work, we take a step in this direction, by proposing a set of seven challenges, summarizing our previous work on performance evaluation of distributed graph-processing platforms, and introducing our on-going work within the SPEC Research Group's Cloud Working Group.

Categories and Subject Descriptors

C.4 [**PERFORMANCE OF SYSTEMS**]: Measurement techniques

Keywords

Graph processing; Benchmarking; Performance; Experimentation

1. INTRODUCTION

Graph processing is of increasing interest for many revenue-generating applications and scientific areas, such as social networking, bioinformatics, and online retail and online gaming. To answer to the growing diversity of graph datasets and graph-processing algorithms, developers and system integrators have created a large variety of graph-processing *platforms*—which we define as the combined hardware, software, and programming system that is being

used to complete a graph processing task [17]. Although these platforms are already much used, it is currently difficult to decide on deploying a new platform and to tune existing deployments, due to a lack of comprehensive understanding of the performance of these platforms. To gain more and more in-depth knowledge about graph-processing platforms, and to enable their comparison, we envision a comprehensive benchmarking suite, which is the focus of this work.

At least three dimensions of diversity complicate gaining knowledge about the performance of graph-processing platforms [17]: dataset, algorithm, and platform diversity. *Dataset diversity* derives from the data deluge we are experiencing—graphs from hundreds of areas, from genomics to consumer profiles, from social gaming networks to business decision support, with periodic updates and different data structures. *Algorithm diversity* is a consequence of the many different goals of processing graphs, with a variety of graph algorithms for calculating basic graph metrics [22], for traversing graphs [24, 27, 30], and for predicting graph evolution [20], etc. *Platform diversity* is the result of the uncoordinated effort of a multitude of developers, to answer their community of users, sometimes additionally influenced by the wide diversity of infrastructure (compute and storage systems); this has led, for example, to graph processing with generic platforms such as Hadoop [29] and YARN [5], with distributed graph-processing platforms such as Giraph [2] and GraphLab [21], etc.

Not understanding the performance of the graph-processing platform can lead to significant time- and revenue-loss, and may eventually even limit the growth, for the entire community. For example, it took many tries, but by now the community agrees that using Hadoop as a graph-processing platform generally leads to poor performance [17,23,25]. For specific datasets and algorithms, platforms may experience crashes, due to inefficient data structures [17, 25], network-stack overloads [13, 17], etc. For different datasets and algorithms, platforms may exhibit very different relative execution-profiles [17]; tuning for one input workload may be lead to sub-optimal results for another.

Although sorely needed, relatively few studies focus on the performance of graph-processing platforms; the few that do use few datasets, few algorithms, and few metrics to characterize the platform. The de-facto state-of-the-art in benchmarking, Graph500 [15] and its energy-aware relative Green Graph500, is based on a single dataset type, on a single algorithm, and on just a few metrics. Most empirical comparisons of graph-processing platforms occur in articles focusing on new designs, and thus may lack depth and objectivity. For example, a recent study of Trinity [25] focuses on novel techniques for in-memory graph processing, but the experiments, although commendable, only compares Trinity with Giraph and PBGL [16], only uses three algorithms, and only reports average response time and memory usage.

We formulate in this work our vision for benchmarking graph-processing platforms that considers *all three* sources of diversity. Our work consists of defining a comprehensive evaluation process, of selecting important performance metrics, representative datasets, and typical algorithms, of conducting and executing the experiments, and of analyzing and reporting the results. This vision extends our own recent work [17] and other recent experience reports [6, 11, 12] with a set of methodological and practical challenges, a survey of graph-processing use, and a call to combine efforts within the SPEC Research Group's Cloud Working Group. It also extends traditional benchmarking with graph-specific elements and with aspects related to new infrastructures (e.g., clouds). Our main contribution is three-fold:

1. We discuss seven methodological and practical challenges in benchmarking graph-processing platforms (Section 2).
2. We summarize our work towards evaluating and benchmarking graph-processing platforms, including understanding the workloads of graph processing, and our previous work [17] about proposing a method for benchmarking graph-processing platforms and a first comprehensive performance comparison of six popular graph-processing platforms (Section 3).
3. We call for the entire community to participate in the creation of a benchmark and give examples of on-going work (Section 4).

2. OUR VISION FOR BENCHMARKING GRAPH-PROCESSING PLATFORMS

Benchmarking is a traditional approach to evaluate the performance of systems, with many well-known challenges: simplicity, cost- and time-effectiveness, verifiability, etc. However, benchmarking systems under different application can lead to specific challenges. In this section, we discuss seven challenges in benchmarking graph-processing platforms. Although there are more challenges to resolve, we argue that these would lead to a good benchmarking process, similar to what has been achieved by the TPC and SPEC communities for benchmarking databases, CPU power and energy, etc.

2.1 Methodological Challenges

Challenge 1. Evaluation process: Traditionally, it is a challenge to define an evaluation process that would define an equivalent benchmarking process for each platform (for example, not controlling the amount of tuning can lead to a war-of-wizards). For graph-processing platforms, the evaluation process needs to fairly define at least the data format, realistic processing workflows, and the multi-tenancy rules—although these concepts have been considered in the past, they need revisiting for graph processing. Although the mathematical notion of a graph allows for only a few varieties, in graph-processing applications we have seen various data structures, input formats, and number of dimensions for the dataset. Similarly to the idea that a single query may expand in several data operations, in graph-processing it is likely that processing workflows comprised of several atomic operations (single algorithms) is representative of the typical analysis task; the evaluation process should also include such workflows. Because graph-processing platforms are typically serving multiple users, much like modern databases and distributed batch-processing systems, the evaluation process should also consider how the workloads of multiple system tenants influence each other.

Challenge 2. Selection and design of performance metrics: To serve more users, one important issue for benchmarking graph-

processing platforms is to provide performance metrics for a variety of platform characteristics. Typical performance metrics such as execution time, resource utilization, scalability, system overhead, power consumption, cost, etc., may be included. To compare platforms on top of various types and amounts of hardware resources (e.g. number of cores or size of memory), new normalized metrics may need to be defined and adopted. For example, Graph500 introduces the graph-specific metric *traversed edges per second* (TEPS). We argue that there is much room for metric definition. As another example, as the field spans database, parallel, and distributed systems, normalized metrics for weak and strong scaling of possibly heterogeneous platforms need to be devised. Moreover, there is a need to adapt traditional metrics to an elastic infrastructure, for example because the local infrastructure may be complemented with nodes leased temporarily from Infrastructure-as-a-Service clouds [14].

Challenge 3. Dataset selection: Selecting a representative dataset is a traditional problem in benchmarking, which requires revisiting for each new domain. As we present in section 1, graphs may differ significantly in size, structure, directivity, connectivity, etc. The main goal of the dataset selection is to choose relevant graphs with different characteristics; to make the benchmark time- and cost-effective, they should also be *few*, easy to generate at different scales (see Challenge 5), and stored in a similar format (see Challenge 1). Additionally, this challenge also requires that the selected graphs should be able to stress bottlenecks of graph-processing platforms.

Challenge 4. Algorithm coverage: Similar to Challenge 3, we find challenging the selection of a representative, reduced set of graph-processing algorithms, which may stress diverse components of the graph-processing platform. To reduce the number of algorithms, it should be possible to divide them into classes, based on their functionality and to select representative algorithms from each class. This solution also has some limitations: how to define the classes? how to select a representative algorithm from a class? how to allow future algorithms to participate in the benchmark? etc.

2.2 Practical Challenges

Challenge 5. Scalability of evaluation and selection processes: It is challenging to allow the users of a benchmark—developers and integrators of platforms, graph analysts, etc.—to cope with the scale of either the evaluation or the selection processes.

For the evaluation process, we aim at benchmarking platforms deployed on both large-scale infrastructure (e.g., wide-area multicluster systems, large data centers, supercomputers, etc.) and small-business infrastructure (e.g., clusters of only a few nodes, a single albeit powerful machine). Thus, the benchmarking suite, and in particular the input datasets, should match various operational scales—for datasets, from megabytes to petabytes. Currently, few real-world graphs of petabyte scale are available for bechmarking activities, and even datasets of hundreds of gigabytes are rare. Graph generators could produce graphs for testing of the required scale, for example the Kronecker generator used in Graph500, but pose important parallel/distributed computing challenges and may not have the characteristics of real-world graphs.

For the selection process, a community-oriented benchmarking process should also be able to match the possibly hundreds of metrics with the interests of the users. For graph analysts, a specific application may need to be matched against an entire database of benchmarking results, and a few most-promising systems should be selected. For system integrators, it would be helpful to identify which algorithms and graphs can stress the system for each selected metric. We believe that designing a community database of open results would be beneficial in addressing this challenge, but its design should be able to accommodate a wide variety of settings and thus remains an open challenge.

Challenge 6. Portability: As we discussed in the methodological challenges, the benchmarking suite includes a number of performance metrics, algorithms, and graphs. When benchmarking a platform, the graph-processing algorithms need to be re-implemented based on the platform's programming language and model and, possibly, also based on infrastructure characteristics. Re-implementing algorithms correctly and re-configuring reasonably of a platform need a solid experience of programming and a detailed understanding of the platform. The challenge is, thus, to design a benchmarking suite that balances the portability requirements with all the desired features.

Challenge 7. Result reporting: Another non-trivial practical aspect is to report benchmarking results, which should be done according to a precisely defined format. Comprehensive and standardized reports traditionally facilitate the understanding and the comparison of the performance of platforms. When users consider several performance metrics when comparing graph-processing platforms, a mechanism to combine the results from different performance metrics and report a single result may not be straightforward—in our experience [17], none of the distributed graph-processing platforms can deliver the best performance across all datasets and algorithms, even for the same metric. Other communities have faced this challenge in the past and were able to solve it. For example, SPEC benchmark results can include a full disclosure of the system configuration parameters; SPEC users can report both baseline (not tuned) and peak (tuned) performance results of systems. However, it took years of development and effort to achieve this by SPEC benchmarks.

3. TOWARDS ACHIEVING OUR VISION

In this section we summarize our work on benchmarking and evaluating graph-processing platforms. We emphasize on two aspects: understanding graph-processing requirements, and proposing a method for benchmarking and performance evaluation of graph-processing platforms.

3.1 Understanding Graph-Processing Workloads

We believe that a variety of workloads—in this work, defined as combinations of datasets and algorithms, inter-dependencies between inputs of an algorithm and outputs of another (effectively, a workflow structure), and a general process for submission for execution to the platform—have appeared in the context of graph processing, with variety due to application domain, independent communities developing their own workload policies, and perhaps even due to the availability of different processing platforms. However, there is no common repository of algorithms, datasets, workflows, etc., which makes Challenges 1–4 difficult to address.

To address Challenges 2–4, we have conducted comprehensive literature surveys of metrics, datasets, and algorithms used in practice (not reported in our previous work [17]). We have specifically targeted articles about graph processing published in top research conferences in the fields of databases, distributed systems, and information retrieval, such as SIGMOD, (P)VLDB, HPDC, etc.; our assumption is that these prestigious conferences have attracted a knowledgeable audience, and represent a meaningful sample of industry and scientific efforts in graph processing. We have searched for articles including the words "graph processing", "social network", etc. In total, we have extracted information from 124 ar-

Table 1: Survey of graph algorithms.

Class	Typical algorithms	Number	Percentage [%]
General Statistics	Triangulation [28], Diameter [19], BC [26]	24	16.1
Graph Traversal	BFS, DFS, Shortest Path Search	69	46.3
Connected Components	MIS [8], BiCC [10], Reachability [9]	20	13.4
Community Detection	Clustering, Nearest Neighbor Search	8	5.4
Graph Evolution	Forest Fire Model [20], Preferential Attachment Model [7]	6	4.0
Other	Sampling, Partitioning	22	14.8
Total		149	100

ticles published in 10 representative conferences over the period 2009–2013.

Challenge 2: Few performance metrics are tested and reported in these articles; most of the performance evaluation focuses only on the job execution time, and, seldomly, they report on metrics such as scalability and throughput, and on memory consumption.

Challenge 3: We have observed that a large number of datasets, from various areas, are processed in previous research. In general, these graphs can be divided into two categories, real-world and synthetic. Real-world graphs are collected by researchers from their own applications or from public graph archives, for example, from the Stanford Network Analysis Project (SNAP) [4] and from the Game Trace Archive (GTA) [18]. Synthetic graphs with different structures are generated from several graph generators, such as Kronecker, Erdős-Rényi, and R-MAT. Notably, the maximum size reported in these articles for real graphs (1.7 billion vertices and 7.9 billion edges) is significantly *smaller* than that of synthetic graphs (274.9 billion vertices and 4.4 trillion edges).

Challenge 4: We have found that a large variety of graph-processing algorithms are reported in practice. Table 1 summarizes the algorithms identified in our survey—149 in 124 articles. We categorize these algorithms into several groups by functionality, consumption of resources, etc. Almost half of the articles we survey (46.3%) use some form of graph traversal in their experimental work. The next most-represented classes of algorithms compute general graph statistics (16.1%), and extract or use connected components (13.4%). A variety of algorithms are present in less than 3% of the articles we have surveyed; together, they account for over a seventh (14.8%) of the articles.

3.2 Method for and Performance Evaluation of Graph-Processing Platforms

In our previous work [17], we have taken first steps to defining an empirical method for benchmarking graph-processing platforms (Challenge 1), applied it in practice by porting the benchmarks to six different platforms (Challenge 6), and reported on the experience (Challenge 7). We summarize here our main achievements, towards addressing the challenges.

Challenge 1: We have used both synthetic (Kronecker) and real datasets (SNAP and GTA): both directed and undirected graphs, with unweighted edges, and vertices represented by numeric identifiers. We have employed a vertex-based data storage; only atomic operations (single algorithms, so no workflows); and a single user (no multi-tenancy). We intend to extend our experiments towards workflows and multi-tenancy. From our survey (see Section 3.1), we have selected one exemplary algorithm for each of the most-represented five algorithmic classes.

Challenge 6: We have ported the five graph-processing algorithms on six popular graph-processing platforms: Hadoop, YARN, Stratosphere, Giraph, GraphLab, and Neo4j [3]. The first five platforms are distributed systems. We select the single-node platform Neo4j as a reference for comparison. We have also analyzed the time taken to port the codes to each platform; in total, between days and weeks. We have further deployed all these platforms in a cluster of up to 50 computing nodes from the DAS4 cluster. [1].

Challenge 7: We have reported metrics on four typical performance aspects: *raw processing power*, defined as the ability of a platform to process (large-scale) graphs; *resource utilization*, defined as the ability of a platform to efficiently utilize the resources it has; *scalability*, defined as the ability of a platform to maintain its performance behavior when resources are added to its infrastructure; and *overhead*, defined as the part of wall-clock time the platform does not spend on true data processing. The metrics include traditional system parameters (e.g., job execution time, the CPU and network load, and the OS memory consumption); normalized graph-specific metrics, such as TEPS; etc.

4. A CALL TO ARMS

Graph processing is rapidly expanding in volume and diversity of datasets, algorithms, and overall usage. To prevent that the domain becomes too fragmented, and to allow graph analysts and system integrators to compare existing platforms, we envision the creation of a benchmarking suite for graph-processing platforms.

We have identified seven main challenges, and conducted work in understanding graph-processing workloads and in the comprehensive performance evaluation of six popular platforms, but much remains to be done. We urge the community to join forces and conduct peer work in the SPEC Research Group's Cloud Working Group. The SPEC Research Group (RG) is a new group within the Standard Performance Evaluation Corporation (SPEC). The Cloud Working Group[1] (CWG) is a branch of the SPEC RG that aims to develop the methodological aspects of cloud benchmarking—among its activities, we have included Graph Processing as a Service, which relies on quantifiable service performance and thus benchmarking. Within the Cloud Working Group, we are currently addressing all the challenges introduced in Section 2, but in particular:

1. *Challenge 1:* Defining workloads that include processing workflows and multi-tenancy aspects.
2. *Challenges 2–4:* Through a survey of relevant graph analysts and system integrators[2], understanding the metrics, datasets, and algorithms used in practice.
3. *Challenge 1, 2, and 7:* Evaluating and reporting on the platform–storage engine relationship.

5. REFERENCES

[1] DAS4. http://www.cs.vu.nl/das4/.
[2] Giraph. http://giraph.apache.org/.
[3] Neo4j. http://www.neo4j.org/.
[4] SNAP. http://snap.stanford.edu/index.html.
[5] YARN. http://hadoop.apache.org/docs/current/hadoop-yarn/hadoop-yarn-site/YARN.html.
[6] D. D. Abreu, A. Flores, G. Palma, V. Pestana, J. Piñero, J. Queipo, J. Sánchez, and M.-E. Vidal. Choosing between graph databases and rdf engines for consuming and mining linked data. In *COLD*, 2013.
[7] A.-L. Barabási and R. Albert. Emergence of scaling in random networks. 1999.
[8] A. Buluç, E. Duriakova, A. Fox, J. R. Gilbert, S. Kamil, A. Lugowski, L. Oliker, and S. Williams. High-Productivity and High-Performance Analysis of Filtered Semantic Graphs. In *IPDPS*, 2013.
[9] J. Cai and C. K. Poon. Path-hop: efficiently indexing large graphs for reachability queries. In *CIKM*, 2010.
[10] G. Cong and K. Makarychev. Optimizing Large-scale Graph Analysis on Multithreaded, Multicore Platforms. In *IPDPS*, 2012.
[11] M. Dayarathna and T. Suzumura. Xgdbench: A benchmarking platform for graph stores in exascale clouds. In *CloudCom*, pages 363–370, 2012.
[12] B. Elser and A. Montresor. An evaluation study of bigdata frameworks for graph processing. In *IEEE BigData*, 2013.
[13] S. Ewen, K. Tzoumas, M. Kaufmann, and V. Markl. Spinning fast iterative data flows. *PVLDB*, 5(11):1268–1279, 2012.
[14] B. Ghit, N. Yigitbasi, and D. Epema. Resource Management for Dynamic MapReduce Clusters in Multicluster Systems. In *SC|12 MTAGS*, 2012. Best paper award.
[15] Graph500. http://www.graph500.org/.
[16] D. Gregor and A. Lumsdaine. The Parallel BGL: A Generic Library for Distributed Graph Computations. *POOSC*, 2005.
[17] Y. Guo, M. Biczak, A. L. Varbanescu, A. Iosup, C. Martella, and T. L. Willke. How well do graph-processing platforms perform? an empirical performance evaluation and analysis. In *IPDPS*, 2013. http://www.pds.ewi.tudelft.nl/~iosup/perf-eval-graph-proc14ipdps.pdf.
[18] Y. Guo and A. Iosup. The Game Trace Archive. In *NetGames*, 2012.
[19] W. Jiang and G. Agrawal. Ex-MATE: Data Intensive Computing with Large Reduction Objects and Its Application to Graph Mining. In *CCGRID*, 2011.
[20] J. Leskovec, J. Kleinberg, and C. Faloutsos. Graphs over Time: Densification Laws, Shrinking Diameters and Possible Explanations. In *SIGKDD*, 2005.
[21] Y. Low, D. Bickson, J. Gonzalez, C. Guestrin, A. Kyrola, and J. M. Hellerstein. Distributed GraphLab: A Framework for Machine Learning and Data Mining in the Cloud. In *VLDB*, pages 716–727, 2012.
[22] A. Lugowski, D. M. Alber, A. Buluç, J. R. Gilbert, S. Reinhardt, Y. Teng, and A. Waranis. A Flexible Open-Source Toolbox for Scalable Complex Graph Analysis. In *SDM*, 2012.
[23] G. Malewicz, M. H. Austern, A. J. Bik, J. C. Dehnert, I. Horn, N. Leiser, and G. Czajkowski. Pregel: A System for Large-scale Graph Processing. In *SIGMOD*, pages 135–146, 2010.
[24] D. Merrill, M. Garland, and A. S. Grimshaw. Scalable GPU graph traversal. In *PPOPP*, 2012.
[25] B. Shao, H. Wang, and Y. Li. Trinity: A distributed graph engine on a memory cloud. In *SIGMOD*, 2013.
[26] J. Shun and G. E. Blelloch. Ligra: a lightweight graph processing framework for shared memory. In *PPOPP*, 2013.
[27] E. Solomonik, A. Buluç, and J. Demmel. Minimizing Communication in All-Pairs Shortest Paths. In *IPDPS*, 2013.
[28] N. Wang, J. Zhang, K.-L. Tan, and A. K. H. Tung. On Triangulation-based Dense Neighborhood Graphs Discovery. *VLDB*, 2010.
[29] T. White. *Hadoop: The definitive guide*. O'Reilly Media, Inc., 2012.
[30] B. Wu and Y. Du. Cloud-Based Connected Component Algorithm. In *ICAICI*, pages 122–126, 2010.

---

[1] http://research.spec.org/working-groups/rg-cloud-working-group.html

[2] You are invited to participate, http://goo.gl/TJwkTg.

Real-Time Multi-Cloud Management Needs Application Awareness

John Chinneck
Carleton University
Ottawa, Canada
+1-613-520-5733
chinneck@sce.carleton.ca

Marin Litoiu
York University
Toronto ,Canada
1-416-485-4003
mlitoiu@yorku.ca

Murray Woodside
Carleton University
Ottawa, Canada
1-613-520-5721
cmw@sce.carleton.ca

ABSTRACT
Current cloud management systems have limited awareness of the user application, and application managers have no awareness of the state of the cloud. For applications with strong real-time requirements, distributed across new multi-cloud environments, this lack of awareness hampers response-time assurance, efficient deployment and rapid adaptation to changing workloads. This paper considers what forms this awareness may take, how it can be exploited in managing the applications and the clouds, and how it can influence cloud architecture.

Categories and Subject Descriptors
D.4.8 [**Performance**]: Measurements, Modeling and Prediction, Queuing Theory

Keywords
Cloud management; optimization; performance models; layered queueing.

1. INTRODUCTION
Multi-clouds comprise several geographically dispersed clusters with possibly separate management. An example is the SAVI multi-tier cloud [14], developed by a group of universities and companies in Canada. It consists of a core cloud filling a role similar to current clouds, with substantial resources, and small edge clouds, distributed geographically and integrated with the network elements such as routers. By minimizing the distance between the end user and the computing elements, low latency and high bandwidth applications such as real time or multimedia can achieve their minimum levels of quality of service. At the same time, the core cloud supports other requirements of the application, such as a high volume of computations and storage. Similar concerns apply to other multi-cloud architectures, such as hybrid clouds.

The common approach to resource management in IaaS clouds is for each application manager to determine its needs in terms of VMs and request them from the cloud, while the cloud manager

ICPE'14, March 22 - 26 2014, Dublin, Ireland
Copyright 2014 ACM 978-1-4503-2733-6/14/03 ...$15.00.
http://dx.doi.org/10.1145/2568088.2576763

determines their placement. However, to take advantage of the multi-cloud architecture, an application should be aware of cloud topology and resources. On the other hand, to fulfill applications requirements and to achieve its own objectives, a cloud infrastructure should be aware of the application objectives and the time-relationships of its components.

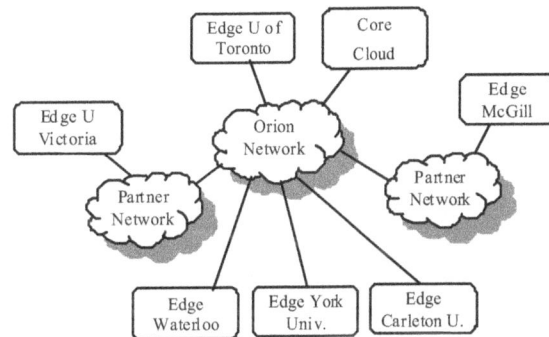

Figure 1: SAVI Edge and Core Clouds

We are motivated by mobile interactive applications in the cloud with a strong requirement for fast and time coordinated user responses, and heavy data streams in both directions. Examples include multiplayer games on mobile devices, image- handling interactive applications, flash crowds, etc. . The edge cloud can make these applications more responsive, while the core cloud to handles globally shared data and carries out data-intensive computations.

Awareness is Essential: For these applications running on multi-clouds, application awareness is not optional. It is essential for obtaining adequate responsiveness and efficient adaptation. Fundamentally, balancing the deployment of parts of the application over two sub-clouds may introduce unacceptable delays due to communications between the parts; the manager that decides the deployment must be aware of the communication delays, which are a combination of application properties (internal communications patterns) and cloud properties (such as the communication delay between sub-clouds).

2. MANAGEMENT ARCHITECTURES AND AWARENESS
This "application-awareness" applies in both directions, and can take several forms as discussed in Section 3 below. Consider a set of applications deployed over a set of clouds or sub-clouds, with representative members illustrated in Figure 2.

Figure 2(A) shows collaboration between separate managers for If each application and each cloud. Awareness data can flow between them as indicated by

- AiAD to represent "Application i Awareness Data"

- CjAD to represents "Cloud j Awareness Data".

Figure 2(B) shows a management architecture in which the application manager determines it awareness data but delegates the immediate adaptive decision-making to the cloud.

Figure 2(C) shows an all-knowing global manager which makes decisions for all applications over all clouds. It is generally true that the availability of more information allows better management of any system.

There are three potential gains from application awareness:

- More efficient deployment.
- QoS-based decisions.
- Adaptive deployment across multiple clouds, in order to provide lower user-to-cloud latency.

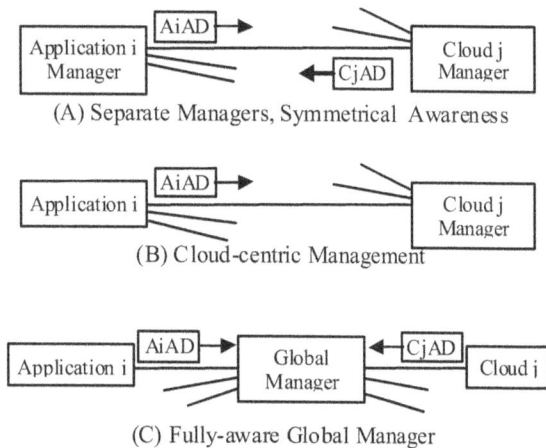

(A) Separate Managers, Symmetrical Awareness

(B) Cloud-centric Management

(C) Fully-aware Global Manager

Figure 2 Management Architectures to exploit Awareness

Actual clouds use separate managers as in (A), with minimal mutual awareness. The cloud publishes its available resources, and the application tells it which ones it wishes to reserve. To adapt, the application tracks its status and changes its resource reservations over time, and the cloud executes these changes and also may redeploy VMs to consolidate workloads.

The simultaneous optimization of multiple applications is an ideal problem for large-scale techniques such as mixed-integer programming. The optimization may reflect the goals of the application and cloud managers by minimizing the number of hosts, their operating costs or energy costs, or some combination of these balanced against the cost of poor application response times. The constraints on the deployment can include the CPU and memory of each host (required for deployed VMs), the QoS guarantees or (more indirectly) the resource utilizations that result from the deployment, the number of replicas of certain tasks (due to license availability or cost), and the number of VMs per host.

Global decisions and large-scale optimization methods can provide a benchmark for simpler, more practical techniques. Taking advantage of full awareness, they can determine the best possible decisions. They can also be used to study the impact on the applications and the cloud of different optimization goals, for example does an energy-efficiency goal impact the applications compared to a total cost-saving goal?

2.1 Effectiveness of Different management Architectures

Separate Managers

This is the prevalent approach.

Most studies do not use an exchange of awareness data, but some of them at least use performance awareness within the application level management. Cardellini et al [1] considered formal optimization by the application manager of its requests for VM reservations. Wang et al. use a performance model within the application manager to determine what VMs to request and for what period.

Wu et al [11] propose a cloud manager with complex heuristics based on credit levels and future plans communicated from the application manager, which is a form of partial awareness.

Separate Managers and exchange of awareness data seems to be a future research topic, as discussed below.

Global Manager

The authors have experimented with a global manager for multiple applications running on a single cloud, with large-scale optimization techniques. Application awareness was provided by a detailed performance model which adapts to the application status [5][6][7][8]. Global optimization was compared to optimization of each application separately, and to using a simple rule that corresponds to separate management with low awareness.

Some challenges to using global optimization were evaluated: the model had to be extended to accommodate different kinds of constraints, such as license limits, and a two-stage approach combining bin-packing heuristics and mixed-integer programming (MIP)was needed for scalability. Scalability was still limited by the MIP solvers.

Other authors have also considered versions of full application awareness with different models For example, Ghanbari et al [4] optimize a utility function combining an application-level SLAs and resource costs with tunable parameters for the administrator to specify trade-offs between the two.

Cloud-centric Management

Van et al [9] describe experience with Cloud-centric architecture, for a single cloud. They maximized a global utility function combining the utility of each application with that of the cloud provider. Applications provided the cloud manager with a function to evaluate the effects of a deployment, or an adaptive change, on utility, so the cloud manager can evaluate trade-offs between applications.

Zhang et al [10] define a multi-cloud manager with minimal application awareness, and consider game-theoretic strategies to resolve resource conflicts between applications. They do not consider responsiveness in deriving the deployments.

For practical management the most promising way forward seems to be to improve the separate managers (architecture A) with greater awareness, particularly to ensure that response times can be guaranteed for a multi-cloud deployment. Awareness can take many forms.

3. FORMS OF AWARENESS

We use the term *awareness* for the information exported about an application or a cloud, to describe itself and its current state. It can take different forms, which impact how useful it is for management.

Awareness of the Application

Some examples of the awareness exported by an application to a cloud, in increasing order of complexity, are:

1. **VMs:** the number and the type of VMs required for the application (minimal awareness)
2. **Aggregate host demand:** The total CPU demand of the application, in CPU-sec/sec, that are to be provided (this is essentially the number of cores required, without providing any margin), plus the total network traffic generated say in MB/second (low application awareness).
3. **VM demands:** The list of VMs to be deployed (possibly in multiple replicas), with the CPU demand of each, and the network traffic between pairs of VMs. This determines the total cores required for each VM, and indicates the traffic pattern between them. It can be used to make decisions about the "size" of VMs. (partial application awareness).
4. **App-Opt Properties:** optimization-related properties indicating the value to the application users and application manager of additional resources, derived from a local optimization, combined with willingness to pay for them. Application details are not revealed. (partial application awareness).
5. **Predictive Awareness:** An performance model which predicts the response time as a function of the deployment(full application awareness).

Awareness can be regarded as a kind of *model* of the application. The first model above corresponds to what is provided by current cloud users in their requests for services. The second would allow the cloud manager to determine the number and size of the VMs. The third conveys additional but partial information that could be used by the cloud provider to determine the VM size and host to which each task should be deployed, taking into account the internal cloud communications structure for inter-VM capacity. At present the application manager deploys tasks to VMs without knowledge of the host location. The fourth model could relate to a decentralized optimization strategy where the awareness coordinates the separate decision-making optimizers. The fifth is essentially a performance model (more or less detailed) that could be used by the cloud manager to find deployments that satisfy application QoS requirements such as user-perceived latencies. Detailed predictive awareness is provided in our research by a Layered Queueing Network (LQN) model, which is illustrated in Figure 3. The blocks represent application deployable units (tasks), with sub-rectangles representing the operations performed by the tasks, with their CPU demands. Calls (service requests) between operations are indicated by arrows annotated by the number of calls per operation and the mean data transfer size for the request and the reply together. This model is fitted by a statistical model-tracking procedure [13]. There is a large literature on LQN models and their use to model distributed systems [1]. Other performance models could also be used for application awareness; but for reasons of space we do not address them here.

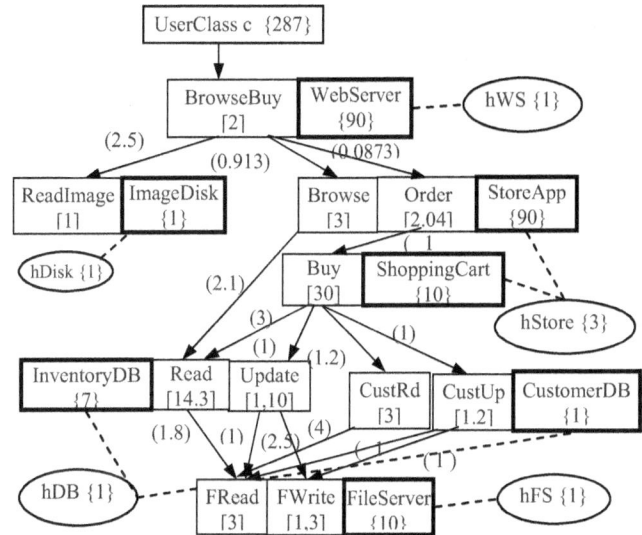

Figure 3 LQN model of a three-tier service system, deploying one replica per task

In [9] an empirical fitted linear response-time model was conveyed from the application manager to the cloud manager, based on total VM capacity provided by a single cloud.

Awareness of the Cloud

To guide an application manager which does not delegate its decisions, each cloud can provide awareness of its state. Some options, in increasing order of complexity and completeness, are:

1. **Available resources:** the cloud publishes the availability of VMs of different capacities (minimal awareness)
2. **Cloud-Opt Properties:** optimization-related properties of the cloud provider, such as the cost and availability of different resources (partial cloud awareness)
3. **Predictive Awareness:** A performance model for the total cloud infrastructure which can predict the delay effect of a deployment (full cloud awareness).

Again, awareness can be considered to comprise a model of the cloud resources, including communications delays. For a hierarchical cloud like SAVI, or a multi-cloud, it should include communications delays between the sub-clouds as well.

Awareness of cloud state is of more use to a global manager than an application manager, simply because the application manager does not make detailed deployment decisions. However it needs awareness of cloud delays to determine how to distribute the application across multiple clouds, to achieve response time goals.

4. EXPLOITING PARTIAL APPLICATION AWARENESS

Our vision is a flexible architecture combining a manager for each cloud and each application. Cloud managers would determine detailed deployment of VMs, and might make additional decisions (such as tuning the capacity allocated to a VM, or even moving a VM to another cloud). Application managers would request resources from the separate clouds. The managers would exchange a variety of forms of information according to their own capabilities and policies about revealing their critical information. The separate managers therefore should be capable of interpreting as many kinds of awareness data as possible, in reaching their own decisions.

Partial application awareness has not been much addressed as yet. It may however be more realistic in the near term. Interesting research questions include:

1. What is the impact on deployment of optimization using different degrees of awareness?
2. What is the value of application awareness? That is, what is the improvement in various optimization cost functions such as monetary cost of operation of the cloud, energy cost of the cloud, aggregate penalty cost (of some kind) related to the provided QoS to all applications together?
3. Following from 2, what is the most useful form of application awareness?
4. Using App-Opt Properties, some kind of collaborative optimization may adequately coordinate two separate managers for the application and the cloud, without revealing to each other their inner workings. A decomposed optimization strategy might be considered, exchanging marginal resource pricing, and the value of additional capacity to the application users, expressed in suitable units.

5. IMPACT ON CLOUD ARCHITECTURE

A defining characteristic of cloud computing is that there is little concern for *where* in the cloud a computing task takes place. However, when communication latencies are vital to meeting response time requirements for modern cloud-based applications, where the task is allocated relative to the entities it communicates with becomes vital. This has a direct impact on cloud architecture.

For example, the SAVI concept envisions small clouds that are located close to the users (both physically and in the sense of latency). Given some awareness of the application (such as an LQN model), the cloud manager can then make sure to co-locate tasks that communicate heavily and are highly latency-sensitive. For example, if building a real-time 3-dimensional view from multiple cell phone camera inputs, then low latencies to the users, is critical, implying that tasks handling the video streams should be co-located on the edge cloud.

Providing full application awareness, as in the LQN model, allows the cloud manager to decide where to allocate tasks so that it can meet response time requirements. Given the LQN, it can identify tasks that are best handled on the edge cloud while other latency-insensitive tasks can be handled centrally in the main cloud, or even a much more physically remote but lightly loaded cloud.

Some of the cloud architecture issues that arise include: How much computing power should be available in an edge cloud? How many edge clouds should there be (e.g. several per city?)? Should there be a hierarchy of clouds, e.g. several small edge clouds in a city linked to an intermediate size city cloud, which is itself linked to the main cloud center?

6. CONCLUSIONS

Greater levels of awareness of the cloud by an application manager, or of its applications by a cloud manager, is a largely unexplored approach which appears to be necessary for managing real-time dynamically changing applications over multi-clouds. We are pursuing this approach in the context of the SAVI cloud.

ACKNOWLEDGMENTS
This research was supported by the SAVI Strategic Research Network (Smart Applications on Virtual Infrastructure, funded by NSERC (the Natural Sciences and Engineering Research Council of Canada).

REFERENCES

[1] V. Cardellini, E. Casalicchio, F. Lo Presti, L. Silvestri, "SLA-Aware resource management for application service providers in the cloud", Proc 1st Int. Symp on Network Cloud Computing and Applications (NCCA), pp 20 - 27, Toulouse, Nov 2011

[2] S. Costache, N. Parlavantzas, C. Morin, S. Kortas, "An Economic Approach for Application QoS Management in Clouds", Euro-Par 2011 Workshops Part II, LNCS 7156, Springer, pp. 426–435, 2012.

[3] Franks, G., T. Al-Omari, et al. (2009). "Enhanced modeling and solution of layered queueing networks." IEEE Transactions on Software Engineering 35(2): 148-161.

[4] H. Ghanbari, B. Simmons, M. Litoiu, and G. Iszlai, "Feedback-based optimization of a private cloud," Future Generation Computer Systems , 2011.

[5] J. Li, J. Chinneck, C.M. Woodside, M. Litoiu, G. Iszlai, "Performance Model Driven QoS Guarantees and Optimization in Clouds", in Proc Workshop on Software Engineering Challenges in Cloud Computing @ ICSE 2009, Vancouver, May 2009.

[6] Li, J., Chinneck, J., Woodside, M., Litoiu, M, "Fast Scalable Optimization to Configure Service Systems having Cost and Quality of Service Constraints", Proc 6th Int Conf on Autonomic Computing (ICAC.09), Barcelona, June 2009.

[7] Li, J., Chinneck, J., Woodside, M., Litoiu, M, "Deployment of Services in a Cloud Subject to Memory and License Constraints", in Proc 2nd IEEE Intl Conf on Cloud Computing , Bangalore, India, September 21-25, 2009.

[8] Li, J., Chinneck, J., Woodside, M., Litoiu, M., "CloudOpt: Multi-Goal Optimization of Application Deployments across a Cloud", 7th Int. Conf. on Network and Service Management (CNSM 2011), October 24-28 2011, Paris, France

[9] H.N. Van, F. D. Tran, J.-M. Menaud, "SLA-aware virtual resource management for cloud infrastructures", 9th IEEE Int. Conf. on Computer and Information Technology (CIT'09), Xiamen, China (2009)

[10] X. Wang, Y. Xue, L. Fan, R. Wang, Z. Du , "Research on adaptive QoS-aware resource reservation management in cloud environments", Proc. 2011 IEEE Asia-Pacific Services Computing Conference (APSCC), pp.147 - 152, Dec. 2011.

[11] L. Wu, . S. K. Garg, S. Versteeg, and R. Buyya. "SLA-based Resource Provisioning for Software as a Service Applications in Cloud Computing Environments", IEEE Transactions on Services Computing preprint, 21 Nov. 2013

[12] Q. Zhang, Q. Zhu, M. F. Zhani, and R. Boutaba, "Dynamic service placement in geographically distributed clouds," in Distributed Computing Systems (ICDCS), 32nd International Conference on . IEEE, 2012, pp. 526–535.

[13] T. Zheng, C.M.,Woodside, M. Litoiu, "Performance Model Estimation And Tracking Using Optimal Filters", IEEE Trans on Software Engineering, Vol. 34 , No. 3, pp. 391-406, 2008.

[14] SAVI Strategic Network, http://savinetwork.ca, Jan 2013

Author Index